Market-driven Management

MARKET-DRIVEN MANAGEMENT

Strategic and Operational Marketing

Second edition

Jean-Jacques Lambin
in association with
Ruben Chumpitaz and Isabelle Schuiling

Tome 2

First published in 2007 by
PALGRAVE MACMILLAN
Houndmills, Basingstoke, Hampshire RG21 6XS and
175 Fifth Avenue, New York, N.Y. 10010
Companies and representatives throughout the world.

PALGRAVE MACMILLAN is the global academic imprint of the Palgrave
Macmillan division of St. Martin's Press, LLC and of Palgrave Macmillan Ltd.
Macmillan® is a registered trademark in the United States, United Kingdom
and other countries. Palgrave is a registered trademark in the European
Union and other countries.

ISBN-13: 978–1–4039–9853–8 (hardback)
ISBN-10: 1–4039–9853–1 (hardback)
ISBN-13: 978–1–4039–9852–1 (paperback)
ISBN-10: 1–4039–9852–3 (paperback)

This book is printed on paper suitable for recycling and made from fully
managed and sustained forest sources. Logging, pulping and manufacturing
processes are expected to conform to the environmental regulations of
the country of origin.

A catalogue record for this book is available from the British Library.

Library of Congress Cataloging-in-Publication Data

Lambin, Jean-Jacques, 1933–
    Market-driven management : strategic and operational
  marketing / by Jean-Jacques Lambin, Ruben Chumpitaz and
  Isabelle Schuiling. – 2nd ed.
        p. cm.
      Includes bibliographical references and index.
      ISBN-13: 978–1–4039–9853–8 (cloth)
      ISBN-10: 1–4039–9853–1 (cloth)
      ISBN-13: 978–1–4039–9852–1 (paper)
      ISBN-10: 1–4039–9852–3 (paper)
        1. Marketing – Europe. 2. Marketing – Europe – Management.
    I. Chumpitaz Caceres, Rubén. II. Schuiling, Isabelle, 1962– III. Title.

HF5415.12.E8L36 2007
658.80094—dc22   2006047166

10 9 8 7 6 5 4 3 2 1
16 15 14 13 12 11 10 09 08 07
Printed in China

Short contents

Contents

Part 1   the changing role of marketing

Part 4   implementing operational marketing

Part 5   implementation of market-driven management

List of figures

List of tables

List of boxes

List of exhibits

Preface

Based on positive feedbacks from students, professors and marketing practitioners, and in view of the success of the other editions of the book in French, Spanish, Italian, Portuguese, Polish and Russian, we were encouraged to propose a new English edition of *Market-driven Management*.

The distinctive feature of the book remains its focus on the concept of *market orientation* as a substitute to the traditional *marketing concept* of the 4Ps popularised by the US Business Schools. This is more than just a semantic issue. The traditional marketing orientation concept tends to be more short-term oriented and mainly concerned with the functional role of marketing in co-ordinating and managing the four Ps to promote the firm's offerings. The market orientation concept, by contrast, (a) de-emphasises the functional roles of marketing departments; (b) enlarges the market definition not only to the key market actors, direct and indirect customers but also online market actors, distributors, competitors, influencers and other stakeholders; (c) states that developing market relations and enhancing customer value is the responsibility of everyone in the organisation; (d) claims that creating customer value is the only way for a firm to achieve its objective of profit and growth, thereby, creating shareholder value. These necessary changes of emphasis are motivated by the increased complexity of the competitive environment which becomes global, deregulated and deeply modified by the information technology revolution.

This second edition builds and reinforces on these themes in several ways. Special effort was made to include more coverage on (a) the *'solution-to-a-problem'* approach as the best way to create customer value; (b) on *E-marketing* by making a distinction between two types of markets, Global Traditional Markets (GTM) and Global Electronic Markets (GEM) and by introducing the concept of virtual or meta markets in demand analysis; (c) on *Customer Relationship Management* (CRM) thanks to the potential provided today by IT to manage one-to-one relationships with customers; (d) on the *management of brands* which are now present everywhere in B2C and B2B markets and are viewed as real assets providing a strong competitive advantage for firms owing them; (e) on the *emergence of new values* promoting a market economy model aiming at a sustainable development; (f) finally, on presenting a *European perspective* with the vast majority of examples and short case histories being drawn from the European scene. It is also well illustrated with up-to-date European data and statistics.

An Instructor's Resource Manual is available on line and in hard-copy format. For each chapter of the book, a PowerPoint slide presentation is available with the more representative tables and figures that cover the major concepts of the chapter. The instructor manual presents a teaching note for each case as well as the solutions of the problems presented at each chapter's end.

A Student Resource Centre Website is also available for students or instructors who would like to communicate with the author. The Palgrave Student Website will list complementary readings related to both strategic and operational marketing. Throughout the text, you will find icons like this *(i)* indicating that linked information is available on the book's companion website, www.palgrave.com/business/lambin. At the end of each chapter in which these icons appear, you will find a box giving more detailed information on the material to be found on the website.

Structure of the book

The overall structure of the book is summarised in Figure I. It comprises five parts and fifteen chapters in all.

Part 1 is devoted to the analysis of *the changing role of marketing* in the European market. In Chapter 1, we introduce a distinction between operational marketing (the action dimension) and strategic marketing (the analytic and philosophy dimension). In the new European macro-marketing environment (Chapter 2), marketing is confronted with new challenging roles and priorities which require a reinforcement of strategic marketing and the adoption of a market orientation within the entire organisation. The proactive firm must evolve from marketing management to market-driven management. This chapter is central in the book and provides a full development of the market orientation concept and also a measurement instrument.

The objective of *Part 2* is to analyse *the customer's purchase and response behaviour*, be it an individual or an organisation. Strategic marketing is, to begin with the analysis of customers' needs and purchase behaviour (Chapter 3). From a marketing point of view, the customer's choice behaviour is not after a product as such, but after a solution to his

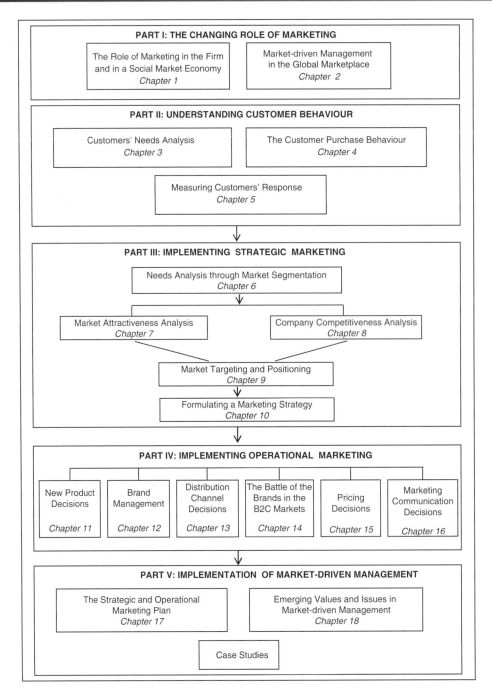

Structure of the book

or her problem (Chapter 3). The role of market information system (Chapter 4) is essential to gain certified knowledge to understand and predict customers' behaviour and response.

Part 3 analyses the specific tasks to be performed by *strategic marketing*. The role of strategic marketing is to follow the evolution of the firm's *reference market* and to identify various potential product-markets or segments on the basis of an analysis of the needs which must be met (Chapter 6). Once the potential product-markets are identified, the *attractiveness* of the economic opportunities must be evaluated. The appeal of a product-market is quantitatively measured by the notion of market potential and dynamically measured by its economic life or its life cycle (Chapter 7). For any given firm, the appeal of a product-market depends on its *competitiveness*, in other words, on its capacity to meet buyers' needs better than its rivals can. This competitiveness will exist as long as the firm holds a competitive advantage, either because it can differentiate itself from its rivals due to sustainable distinctive qualities, or because of higher productivity putting it at a cost advantage (Chapter 8). On the basis of this strategic audit, the market-driven firm can formulate an appropriate *marketing strategy* for each business unit included in its product portfolio (Chapter 9). The strategic *marketing plan* describes objectives, positioning, tactics and budgets for each business unit of the company's portfolio in a given period and geographical zone (Chapter 10).

Part 4 is devoted to *operational marketing* and to the implementation issues of strategic marketing decisions. In this perspective, the five new product decisions (Chapter 11), distribution channel decisions (Chapter 12), pricing decisions (Chapter13), marketing communication decisions (Chapter 14) and media advertising decisions are discussed.

Finally, *Part 5* presents ten cases studies to be used to illustrate strategic and operational marketing decisions. The cases are very short and lend themselves to class discussion without extensive advanced preparation.

Distinctive features

This text offers full coverage of both strategic marketing and of operational. In addition, it has the following distinctive characteristics:

- It discusses the ideological foundations of marketing and its role in the turbulent environment of today's market economy;
- it introduces the concept of market orientation as a substitute to the traditional marketing concept;
- it analyses the structure of needs of both the individual consumer and
- of the business-to-business customer;
- it examines the different roles of a customer as buyer, payer and user;
- it integrates important theoretical concepts such as, customer behaviour theory, attitude models, information theory ..., and stresses the application of this conceptual material to the realities of marketing;
- it provides an integrated treatment of consumer and business-to-business marketing underlining practical differences and conceptual similarities;
- it offers thorough coverage of macro- and micro-segmentation analyses illustrated by numerous examples taken from the European scene;
- it provides an overview of marketing research methods and particularly of survey research;
- it gives a general overview of the most popular market response measures provided by marketing research, void of all technical development;
- it integrates international and global marketing throughout the text rather than relegating it to a single chapter;
- it contains a section devoted to the distributor's strategic marketing, a topic often neglected in marketing textbooks;
- it raises the issues of responsible marketing;
- it devotes several sections on e-commerce and introduces the concept of meta-market and of the customer chain of activities;
- it is illustrated with numerous real-life examples and up-to-date European data and statistics.

Why a European perspective ?

Another claim of this book is to propose to the reader a *'European Perspective'* in Strategic Marketing. The question that comes readily to mind is then: *Is European marketing really different from, let's say, American or Japanese ways of conducting marketing ?* We strongly believe that significant differences do exist, not so much in terms of concepts or methods, but rather in terms of priorities, complexity and business philosophy. Three factors explain these differences:

- the challenge of European market integration;
- European cultural diversity and pluralism;
- the social accountability of European society.

European countries are confronted with a formidable challenge, the idea of unifying the European market by removing all non-tariff barriers that have existed in some countries for centuries. At a business level, European companies are analysing the impact of this market transformation, redefining their reference market, reassessing their competitiveness and determining appropriate strategies and organisational structure. The successful launching of the euro has created an entirely new European context, where sound strategic thinking and analysis is becoming more than ever a priority preoccupation, not only for multinational firms, but for small and medium-sized companies as well.

The European market is highly fragmented both in terms of culture and of consumer habits. The elimination of all barriers among European countries will create a borderless single market but not, however, a homogeneous single market. Cultural differences and variations in consumer attitudes across Europe will remain, even if European firms will have the possibility of executing a common marketing programme throughout Europe. Thus European firms have to cope with this cultural complexity and find adapted solutions. A level of standardisation of consumer behaviour similar to the one observed in the US market will never be reached in Europe. The capacity to respect this diversity and to discover supranational segments will be a key factor to success.

European public authorities are more concerned than American authorities by the protection and the integration of individual, family and social values in economic life and public policy. The European firm has to cope with more severe societal constraints than the American firm. The slogan, largely accepted until recently by the business community – *'the business of business is business'* – is no longer true and the European firm cannot remain immune from societal interference and accountability. These societal constraints are the expressions of new needs in society and come from public policy regulations, EU directives, green consumerists or environmentalists. They induce companies to widen the traditional marketing concept and to develop an increased consciousness of fallout generated by their marketing activity. In today European socio-economic context, this greater societal sensitivity makes the concept of *accountable market-driven management* particularly relevant.

Finally, this book offers a European perspective with the vast majority of examples and case histories being drawn from the European scene. It is also well illustrated with up-to-date European data and statistics.

Ancillary material

An Instructor's Resource Manual will be available on line and in hard-copy format. For each chapter of the book, a PowerPoint slide presentation is available with the more representative tables and figures that cover the major concepts of the chapter. The instructor manual presents a teaching note for each case as well as the solutions of the quantitative problems presented at each chapter's end.

A Student Resource Centre Website is also available for students or instructors who would like to communicate with the author. The Student Website will list new articles related to new developments in both strategic and operational marketing and will also publish fact and figures (taking the form of exhibits) illustrating euro and global marketing strategies.

Acknowledgements

Several people have directly or indirectly contributed at various stages of this new edition and, in particular, my colleagues from ISTEI at the Università degli studi di Milano-Bicocca (Italy) and from the marketing unit at my former University, IAG School of Management (Université catholique de Louvain (Louvain-la-Neuve, Belgium).

A word of gratitude for the feedback received from the users of the first edition of the book in their teaching: Silvio Brondoni, Margherita Corniani and Emanuela Tesser from Milano-Bicocca, Chantal de Moerloose and Isabelle Schuiling both from IAG Louvain School of Management, Carlo Gallucci from ESADE, Ruben Chumpitaz (IESG, Lille) and Sergey Koutsch from the State University of Saint Petersburg.

I am also grateful to my students of International Executive MBAs – in particular at ESADE, at the Baltic Management Institute (Lithuania), at the Saint Pertersburg School of Management (SOM) and at the Institut de la Francophonie pour l'Entrepreneuriat (IFE, Mauritius) – who, captive but challenging customers, have helped me to improve this text over the years.

Last but not least, many thanks to Ruben Chumpitaz and to Isabelle Schuiling, my co-authors, for their intellectual and editorial input, without which this second English edition would not have been possible.

Bousval,
Jean-Jacques Lambin

To Daisy, Sophie and Lara

About the Authors

Jean-Jacques Lambin

Jean-Jacques Lambin is Professore Ordinario at the Università degli Studi di Milano-Bicocca (Italy) and Professor Emeritus at the Institut d'Administration et de Gestion (IAG) of the Université Catholique de Louvain (UCL), at Louvain-la-Neuve (Belgium). Lambin is the past joint editor-in-chief of the review *European Business Forum* (EBF), a quarterly review jointly published by the *Community of European Management Schools* (CEMS) and by *PricewaterhouseCoopers* (London).

Past President of IAG Louvain School of Management and past Dean of Lovanium International Management Centre (LIMC), Lambin is the author of several articles published in major academic and professional journals, including *Harvard Business Review, Journal of Marketing Research, Journal of Business*, etc. His most important book, *Strategic and Operational Marketing* has been translated in eight languages (English, Italian German, Japanese, Spanish, Polish, Portuguese and Russian). The sixth French edition has been published by Dunod (France) early 2005.

A specialist of strategic marketing, Lambin works as a market analyst on restructuring and redeployment issues triggered by the internationalisation of the European and of the World market and on methods to develop and implement market-driven management strategies within the firm. In 1995–99, Lambin has been the head of a European co-operation programme between the European Union and the countries of South-east Asia (ASEAN).

Lambin is Doctor of Applied Economics from UCL and has participated in the MBA programme of the University of California (Berkeley) as a CRB Graduate Fellow. In 1996, he has been nominated *Economist of the Year* (section Management) by the French magazine, *Le Nouvel Economiste*, and in 1998 he has received a *Doctor Honoris Causa* degree from the Université Laval (Québec).

lambin@mark.ucl.ac.be

Ruben Chumpitaz Cáceres

Ruben Chumpitaz is Associate Professor and Head of the Department of Marketing at the IESEG School of Management in the Catholic University of Lille. He earned his MBA in 1995 and PhD in 1998, both from the Louvain School of Management at the Catholic University of Louvain in Belgium.

Dr Chumpitaz currently is a professor of marketing and has taught such courses as Strategic Marketing and Company Observation, Marketing Research Seminar, Multivariate Data Analysis and Forecasting Methods for Marketing. His teaching experience include executive and MBA programs in Argentina, Belgium, France, Paraguay, Peru, Spain and Uruguay.

Prior to entering academia, Dr Chumpitaz worked several years in management in the telecommunication industrial sector and for almost fifteen years he has served as an analytical consultant for marketing research projects and agencies. Chumpitaz research focuses on customer satisfaction, brand loyalty, market orientation and service recovery. His research has been published in academic and professional journals such as the *Managing Service Quality*, *International Review of Retail, Distribution and Consumer Research, European Business Forum, European Journal of Marketing, Recherche et Application en Marketing*.

r.chumpitaz@ieseg.fr

Isabelle Schuiling

Isabelle Schuiling is Associate Professor at the IAG Louvain School of Management at the Université Catholique de Louvain (Belgium, Louvain-la-Neuve). She holds a PhD in Management from Louvain (2002) and an MBA from the University of Chicago (1985). Prior to her academic career, she has worked for more than 12 years as Marketing Director Europe at Procter & Gamble where she was Member of the P&G Management Committee.

Dr Schuiling is a Professor of Marketing. She teaches 'Strategic Marketing' 'International Marketing' and 'Brand Management'. She is also very active in international Executive MBA programmes in different countries such as in Russia (State University of Saint Petersburg), in Lithuania (Vilnius) or in Italy (Milan). She also teaches in HEC Paris in the CEMS programme.

Her research interests focus on branding and international marketing, more specifically on the development of local and global brands. She has published several articles in international marketing journals and has received the 2004 Cavusgil Best Paper Award from the American Marketing Association for an article published in the *International Marketing Review*. Her course in International Marketing at the CEMS programme was selected as the 'CEMS Course of the year 2006'.

schuiling@mark.ucl.ac.be

Part 1

the changing role of marketing

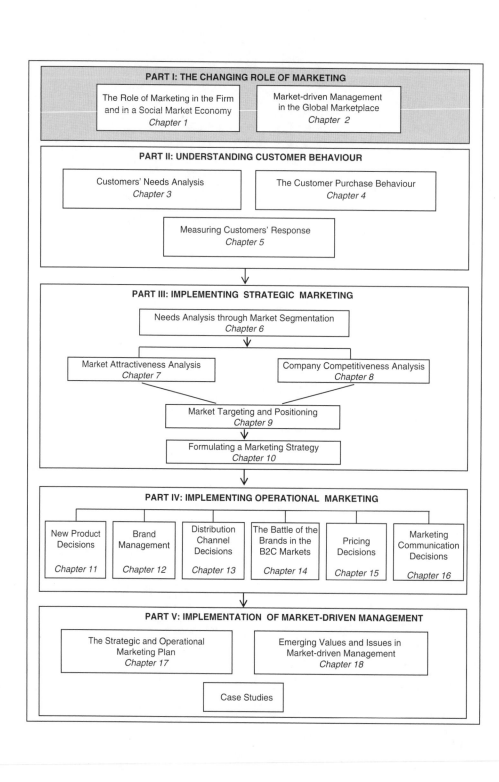

PART I: THE CHANGING ROLE OF MARKETING

The Role of Marketing in the Firm
and in a Social Market Economy
Chapter 1

Market-driven Management
in the Global Marketplace
Chapter 2

PART II: UNDERSTANDING CUSTOMER BEHAVIOUR

Customers' Needs Analysis
Chapter 3

The Customer Purchase Behaviour
Chapter 4

Measuring Customers' Response
Chapter 5

PART III: IMPLEMENTING STRATEGIC MARKETING

Needs Analysis through Market Segmentation
Chapter 6

Market Attractiveness Analysis
Chapter 7

Company Competitiveness Analysis
Chapter 8

Market Targeting and Positioning
Chapter 9

Formulating a Marketing Strategy
Chapter 10

PART IV: IMPLEMENTING OPERATIONAL MARKETING

New Product
Decisions

Chapter 11

Brand
Management

Chapter 12

Distribution
Channel
Decisions

Chapter 13

The Battle of the
Brands in the
B2C Markets

Chapter 14

Pricing
Decisions

Chapter 15

Marketing
Communication
Decisions

Chapter 16

PART V: IMPLEMENTATION OF MARKET-DRIVEN MANAGEMENT

The Strategic and Operational
Marketing Plan
Chapter 17

Emerging Values and Issues in
Market-driven Management
Chapter 18

Case Studies

the role of marketing in the firm and in a social market economy

Chapter contents

Chapter learning objectives

When you have read this chapter, you should be able to understand

- the theoretical and ideological foundations of the marketing process;
- the difference between 'strategic' and 'operational' marketing;
- the differences between 'response' and 'creative' strategic marketing;
- the tasks performed by marketing in a social market economy;
- the different organisational structures of the marketing function;
- the limitations of the traditional marketing concept;
- the distinctive characteristics of the market orientation concept.

Chapter introduction

Marketing is both a business philosophy and an action-oriented process. Chapter 1 aims to describe the system of thought, to clarify the ideological foundations of marketing and their main implications regarding the firm's operations and organisation. As an active process, marketing fulfils a number of tasks necessary for the smooth functioning of a market economy. A second objective of this chapter is to describe these tasks – the importance and complexity of which have evolved with changes in technology, economics, competitiveness and the international environment. Within this framework, we shall examine the implications of these environmental changes, for the management of the firm, and particularly for the marketing function.

1.1. The ideological foundations of the marketing process

The term marketing, which has even entered the non-English vocabulary, is a word heavily loaded, debased and often misunderstood, not only by its detractors, but also by its proponents. Three popular meanings recur regularly.

1. Marketing is advertising, promotion and hard selling, in other words a set of particularly aggressive selling instruments, used to penetrate existing markets. In this first, very mercantile sense of the word, marketing is viewed as mainly applicable to mass consumer markets and much less to more sophisticated sectors, such as high technology, financial services, public administration, social and cultural services.
2. Marketing is a set of market analysis tools, such as sales forecasting methods, simulation models and market research studies, used to develop a prospective and more scientific approach to needs and demand analysis. Such methods, often complex and costly, are often considered to be only available to large enterprises, and not to small and medium-sized ones. The image projected is often that of unnecessarily sophisticated tools, entailing high costs and little practical value.
3. Marketing is the hype, the architect of the consumer society; that is, a market system where individuals are commercially exploited by sellers. It is necessary to create new needs continuously, in order to sell more and more. Consumers become alienated from the seller, just as workers have become alienated from the employer.

Implicit in this vision of the role of marketing is the idea that marketing and advertising are omnipotent, that they are capable of making the market accept anything through powerful methods of communication. Such hard-selling methods would often be devised independently of any desire to satisfy the real needs of buyers. The focus is on the needs of the seller, that is to achieve a sale.

The myth of the power of marketing is a persistent theme, despite the fact that there exists abundant proof to the contrary. For example, the high proportion of new products and brands that fail (more than 40 per cent according to Ernst & Young and Nielsen 1999) bears witness to the capacity of the market's resistance to the allegedly seductive powers of marketers.

Behind these somewhat oversimplified views, there are three characteristic dimensions to the market orientation concept (see Table 1.1): a *culture* dimension (a business philosophy), an *analysis* dimension (the strategic brain) and an *action* dimension (the commercial arm). More often than not, the tendency is to reduce marketing to its action dimension – that is, to a series of sales techniques (operational marketing) – and to underestimate its analytic dimension (strategic marketing). The whole process is market-oriented management. In what follows, we use the terms 'marketing process' and/or 'market-driven management' to refer to these three dimensions (Table 1.1).

1.1.1. The principle of customer sovereignty

Although this misunderstanding goes very deep, the theory or ideology that is the basis of marketing is totally different. The philosophy at the root of marketing – what may be called the market orientation concept – rests, in fact, on a theory of individual choice through the principle of consumer sovereignty. An idea that by no means is new since already expressed by the Roman emperor Marcus-Aurelius in his *Meditations on Stoic*

Table 1.1   The three dimensions of the market orientation concept

Components	Activities	Organisational position
Culture	A business philosophy	Managing Director
Analysis	The strategic brain	Corporate Marketing Officer and brand managers
Action	The commercial arm	Brand and sales management

Source: Authors.

Philosophy (AD 160): 'if you serve others you serve yourself.' In this framework, the marketing process is no more than the social expression of the principles advocated by classical economists, at the turn of the eighteenth century, and translated into operational rules of management. These principles, which were set forth by Adam Smith (1776), form the basis of the market economy and can be summarised as follows:

Society's well being is the outcome, not so much of altruistic behaviour, but rather of the matching, through voluntary and competitive exchange, of the buyer and seller's self-interest.

Starting from the principle that the pursuit of personal interest is an unfailing tendency in most human beings – which might be morally regrettable but remains a fact – Adam Smith suggested accepting people as they are, but developing a system that would make egocentric individuals contribute to the common good despite themselves. This is then the system of voluntary and competitive exchange, administered by the invisible hand, or the selfish pursuit of personal interests that in the end serves the interests of all. Those ideas have been developed and implemented in management by authors such as Chamberlin (1933), Drucker (1954), Abbott (1955), Alderson (1957), McKitterick (1957), Felton (1959), Howard and Sheth (1969) and Kotler (1967/2005), the main founding fathers of today's marketing.

Although in modern economics this basic principle has been amended with regard to social (solidarity) and societal (external effects, collective goods, government regulations) issues, it nevertheless remains the main principle driving the economic activity of a successful firm operating in a free – but regulated – competitive market. Furthermore, it is now clearer than ever before that those countries that rejected Adam Smith's ideas have discovered that they have regressed economically. The turmoil in Eastern Europe and the growth of emerging economies (such as India and China) having adopted the market economy system (through deregulation and privatisation) give a clear illustration of this.

At the root of the market economy, we find four central ideas. These ideas seem simple, but have major implications regarding the philosophical approach to the market:

1. Individuals strive for *rewarding experiences*; it is the pursuit of one's self-interest that drives individuals to produce and to work. This search is the engine of growth, of individual development, and eventually determines the overall well-being.
2. *Individual choice* determines what is rewarding. This varies according to tastes, culture, values, and so on. Apart from respecting the ethical, moral and social rules imposed by society, no other judgement is implied as to the value or the triviality of this choice, or what might be regarded as 'true' or 'false' needs. The system is pluralistic and respects the diversity of tastes and preferences.
3. It is through *free and competitive exchange* that individuals and the organisations they deal with will best realise their objectives. When exchange is free, it only takes place if its terms generate utility for both parties; when it is competitive, the risk of producers abusing their market power is limited (Friedman and Friedman, 1980).
4. The mechanisms of the market economy are based on the principle of individual freedom, and more particularly on the *principle of consumer sovereignty*. The moral foundation of the system rests on the recognition of the fact that individuals are responsible for their own actions and can decide what is or is not good for them.

Such is the ideology on which marketing is based. One can imagine that there may be a large gap between what marketing claims to be and what it is in reality. Flaws come readily to mind. Nevertheless, the successful firm must pursue the ideal of market-driven management (Figure 1.1). It may be a myth (like democracy), but it is a *driving myth*, which must continuously guide the activities of the firm.

1.1.2. The fields of marketing

Marketing is rooted in these four principles. This gives rise to a philosophy of action valid for any organisation serving

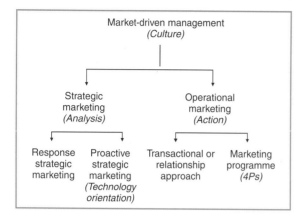

Figure 1.1 Structure of market-driven management

Source: Authors.

the needs of a group of buyers. The areas of marketing can be subdivided into three main fields:

1. *Consumer marketing* (B2C), where transactions are between companies and end-consumers, individuals or households.
2. *Business marketing* (B2B or business-to-business marketing), where the two parties in the exchange process are organisations.
3. *Social marketing*, which covers the field of activity of non-profit organisations such as museums, universities, and so on.

This approach implies that all activity within the organisation must have the satisfaction of its customers' needs as its main objective, given that this is the best way of achieving its own goals of growth and profitability. It is not altruism, but the organisation's self-interest that dictates this course of action. As discussed later in this chapter, implementation of the market orientation concept implies ways and means that vary with the complexity of the economic and competitive environment.

1.1.3. The two faces of the marketing process

The application of this philosophy of action assumes a twofold approach on the part of the firm, as shown in Figure 1.2:

1. The objectives of *strategic marketing* typically include: a systematic and continuous analysis of the needs and requirements of key customer groups and the design and production of a product or service package that will enable the company to serve selected groups or segments more effectively than its competition. In

serving these objectives, a firm is ensured a sustainable competitive advantage.
2. The role of *operational marketing* involves the organisation of distribution, sales and communication policies in order to inform potential buyers and to promote the distinctive qualities of the product while reducing the information costs.

These objectives, which are quite complementary, are implemented by the firm's branding policy, a key instrument for the application of the market orientation concept in a market economy. We therefore propose the following definition of the marketing process:

> In a market economy, the role of market-driven management is to design and promote, at a profit for the firm, added value solutions to people and/or organisations problems.

The term 'design' refers to strategic marketing and the term 'promote' to operational marketing; by 'added value solutions' one means products or services satisfying customers' needs (articulated or unarticulated) better than competitors' offerings.

1.1.4. Polysemy: the chronic disease of the marketing discipline

The linguistic definition of polysemy refers to 'a word that has multiple but related meanings' (*Oxford Concise Dictionary*). Unlike finance people, marketing people are still divided by their understanding about the meaning of the word 'marketing'. One symptom of the lack of consensus on language among managers – and in particular among CEOs – is evidenced by the type of answer received to the following first interview question to a sample of CEOs: 'How has marketing been changing in your company in the past three years?' with a comment along the lines of '… that depends upon what you mean by marketing' (quoted by Webster *et al*., 2005, p. 36).

This level of confusion remains high among marketing practitioners and scholars as well. For example, while we call 'market-driven management' what the whole firm is doing (strategic and operational marketing) to secure customer preference and thereby achieve higher returns, Ambler (2000, p. 61) uses the term 'Pan-company marketing' and Kotler and Keller (2006, p. 17) use the term 'holistic marketing'. In many sectors, companies tend to equate marketing with sales; others with brand management and sales; others with advertising, merchandising and sales; and still others with sales and communication, and so on. We believe that our terminology, as defined in Table 1.1 and in Figure 1.1, has the merit of simplicity and clarity: it is also gaining acceptance in the academic community, as evidenced by

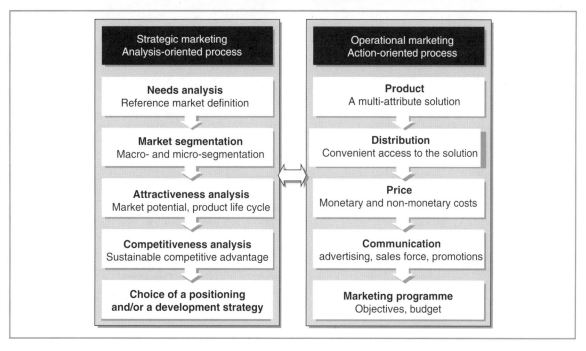

Figure 1.2   The two faces of the marketing process
Source: Authors.

the growing number of publications referring to market-driven management.

1.2. Implementation of the marketing process

The term 'marketing' – literally the process of delivering to the market – does not express the inherent duality of this process very well and emphasises the 'active' side of marketing more than the 'analytic' side. As an aside, we may point out that to avoid the ambiguity – and the use of an English word in the common vocabulary – the French Academy (l'Académie Française) coined the terms *'la mercatique'* and *'le marchéage'* to illustrate these two facets of marketing. In practice, however, the French business community does not use these terms.

1.2.1. Strategic marketing

Strategic marketing is, to begin with, the analysis of the needs of individuals and organisations. From the marketing viewpoint, the buyer is not seeking a product as such, but is after the solution to a problem, which the product or the service might provide. This solution may be obtained via

different technologies, which are themselves continually changing. The role of strategic marketing is to follow the evolution of the reference market and to identify various existing or potential product markets or segments on the basis of an analysis of the diversity of needs to be met.

Once the product markets are identified, they represent economic opportunities whose attractiveness needs to be evaluated. The appeal of a product market is quantitatively measured by the notion of the potential market, and dynamically measured by its economic life, or its life cycle. For a given firm, the appeal of a product market depends on its own competitiveness, in other words, on its capacity to meet buyers' needs better than its rivals. This competitiveness will exist as long as the firm holds a competitive advantage, either because it can differentiate itself from its rivals owing to sustainable distinctive qualities, or because of higher productivity, putting it at a cost advantage.

Figure 1.3 shows the various stages of strategic marketing in relation to the firm's other major functions. Irrespective of whether a product is market-pull or company-push (or technology-push), it has to undergo the process of strategic marketing to evaluate its economic and financial viability. The interface between research and development, operations and strategic marketing plays a decisive role in this respect. The choice of the product market that results from this confrontation is of crucial

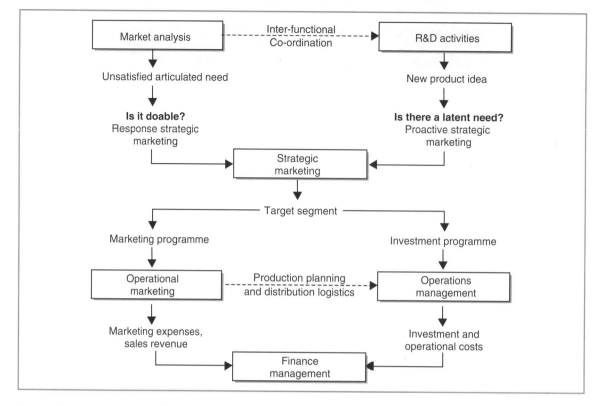

Figure 1.3   The two roles of strategic marketing in the firm
Source: Authors.

importance in determining production capacity and investment decisions, and hence is vital to the equilibrium of the firm's overall financial structure. The role of strategic marketing is therefore (a) to lead the firm towards existing opportunities or (b) to create attractive opportunities, that is, opportunities which are adapted to its resources and know-how and which offer a potential for growth and profitability. The process of strategic marketing has a medium- to long-term horizon; its task is to specify the firm's mission, define objectives, elaborate a development strategy and ensure a balanced structure of the product portfolio. The tasks of strategic marketing are summarised in the left column of Figure 1.2.

1.2.2. Operational marketing

Operational marketing is an action-oriented process that is extended over a short- to medium-term planning horizon and targets existing markets or segments. It is the classical commercial process of achieving a target market share through the use of tactical means related to the product, distribution (place), price and communication (promotion) decisions, the 'four Ps', or the 'marketing mix', as they are

called in the professional jargon (McCarthy, 1960/2005). The operational marketing plan describes objectives, positioning, tactics and budgets for each brand of the company's portfolio in a given period and geographical zone.

The economic role that marketing plays in the operation of the firm is shown in Figure 1.3. The main relationships between the four major managerial functions (research and development, operations, marketing and finance) are illustrated. The main task of operational marketing is to generate sales revenues that are the target turnover. This means to 'sell' and to obtain purchase orders by using the most efficient sales methods while at the same time minimising costs. The objective of realising a particular sales volume translates into a manufacturing programme as far as the operations department is concerned, and a programme of storage and physical distribution for the sales department. Operational marketing is therefore a determining factor that directly influences the short-term profitability of the firm.

The vigour of operational marketing is a decisive factor in the performance of the firm, especially in those markets where competition is fierce. Every product, even those of superior quality, must have a price acceptable to the market, be available in the network of distribution adapted to the purchasing habits of the targeted customers, and be supported by some form of communication which promotes the product and enhances its distinctive qualities. It is rare to find market situations where demand exceeds supply or where the firm is well known by potential users or where competition is non-existent.

There are many examples of promising products that have failed to prevail in the market due to insufficient commercial support. This is particularly the case in firms where the 'engineering' spirit predominates, whereby it is believed that a good quality product can gain recognition by itself, and the firm lacks the humility to adapt to the needs of customers.

> Latin culture is especially susceptible to this attitude. Mercury was the god of merchants as well as of thieves and Christ expelled the tradesmen from the Temple; as a result, selling and advertising are still often viewed as shameful diseases.

Operational marketing is the most dramatic and the most visible aspect of the discipline of marketing, particularly because of the important role played by advertising and promotional activities. Some firms have embarked on marketing through advertising. In contrast, some other firms – such as many producers of industrial goods – have for a long time tended to believe that marketing does not apply to their business, thus implicitly linking marketing to advertising.

Operational marketing is therefore the firm's commercial arm without which even the best strategic plan cannot lead to satisfactory results. However, it is also clear that without solid strategic options, there can be no ultimately profitable operational marketing. Dynamism without thought is merely unnecessary risk. No matter how powerful an operational marketing plan, it cannot create demand where there is no need, just as it cannot keep alive activities doomed to disappear. Hence, in order to be profitable, operational marketing must be founded upon a strategic design, which is itself based on the needs of the market and its expected evolution. The tasks of operational marketing are summarised in the right column of Figure 1.2.

1.2.3. The marketing programme

This job of reflection and strategic planning is very different from operational marketing and requires different talents in the individuals who exercise it. Nevertheless, the two roles are closely complementary, as illustrated by Table 1.2, in the sense that the design of a strategic plan must be carried out in close relation to operational marketing. Operational marketing emphasises non-product variables (distribution, pricing, advertising and promotion),

whereas strategic marketing tends to emphasise the ability to provide a product with superior value at a competitive cost. Strategic marketing leads to the choice of product markets to be exploited in order of priority and the forecast of primary demand in each of these product markets. Operational marketing, on the other hand, sets out market share objectives to reach in the target product market, as well as the marketing budgets necessary for their realisation.

As shown in Figure 1.4, the comparison of the market share objective and primary demand forecast in each product market makes it possible to develop a sales objective first in volume and then in terms of turnover, given the chosen pricing policy. The expected gross profit is obtained after deducting direct manufacturing costs, possible fixed costs for specific structures, marketing expenditure attributed to the sales force, and advertising and promotion as allowed for in the marketing budget. This gross profit is the contribution of the product market to the firm: it must cover overhead and leave a gross profit. The content and structure of the marketing plan are described in detail in Chapter 16.

1.2.4. Response versus proactive strategic marketing

As illustrated in Figure 1.3, innovations or new product ideas can have two very distinct origins: the market or the firm. If the new product idea comes from the market as a result, for example, of a market research study having identified unfilled (or poorly filled) needs or wants, the market observation is communicated to R&D people who will try to find an appropriate response to this unfilled need. The question is: 'is it feasible?' The innovation is *market-pull*. The role of operational marketing will then be to promote the new solution proposed to the identified target segment.

Table 1.2   Contrasting operational and strategic marketing

Operational marketing	Strategic marketing
Action oriented	Analysis oriented
Existing opportunities	New opportunities
Non-product variables	Product-market variables
Stable environment	Dynamic environment
Reactive behaviour	Proactive behaviour
Day-to-day management	Longer range management
Marketing function	Cross-functional organisation

Source: Authors.

Another origin of an innovation may be the laboratory or R&D people who, as a result of fundamental or applied research, discover or develop a new product, a new process or a new organisational system to meet better existing or latent needs. Many companies gain competitive advantage and roar past rivals by creating breakthrough innovations. These companies are *technology-driven* rather than customer-oriented (See Box 1.1.). Such innovations come from the creativity and insight of scientists and engineers who make technological discoveries and then work them into radically new products. The innovation is *technology-push*.

In this case, the role of strategic marketing is more complex. The question is: 'Is there a need and a potentially profitable market segment?' Strategic marketing will then

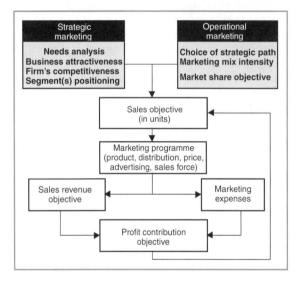

Figure 1.4   The integrated marketing process
Source: Authors.

have to assess the size of the target segment and the success factors of the innovation. The role of operational marketing may be more complex and challenging because its role is to create the market for a product or service which is not explicitly demanded or expected by the market and which may require from potential customers a change in their consuming or using habits.

Thus, in strategic marketing, a distinction must be made between two distinct but complementary approaches: response strategic marketing and creative (or technology-driven) strategic marketing.

1. In *response strategic marketing*, the objective is to meet expressed needs or wants and to fill them. The goal of operational marketing is to develop an existing demand or potential market. Innovations are market-pull.
2. In *supply-driven or proactive strategic marketing*, the objective is to identify latent or unarticulated needs or to find new ways to fill existing needs or wants. The objective is to create new markets through technology and/or organisational creativity. Innovations are technology-push (See Box 1.2.).

In affluent economies, where most needs and wants are well met and where the majority of existing markets are stagnant, proactive strategic marketing has an important role to play to create new market opportunities in the future. As Akio Morita, Sony's leader, puts it:

> Our plan is to lead the public with new products rather than ask them what kind of products they want. The public does not know what is possible, but we do. So instead of doing a lot of market research, we refine our thinking on a product and its use and try to create a market for it by educating and communicating with the public. (Quoted by Schendler, 1992)

BOX 1.1

IMPLEMENTATION PROBLEM: IS A TECHNOLOGY-DRIVEN STRATEGY A REAL ALTERNATIVE TO A MARKET-DRIVEN STRATEGY?

Some marketing scholars (Hayes and Abernathy, 1980; Bennett and Cooper, 1981) have argued that the market orientation concept hurts rather than helps the competitive performance of firms because of its over-reliance on market-pull innovations (i.e. response strategic marketing). Many companies, indeed, gain competitive advantage by being primarily technology-driven and not customer-driven. Imagine – say these scholars – consumers trying to tell a market researcher about their need for a mobile phone or a digital camera before those products were introduced.

This criticism is based on a truncated view of the market orientation concept by ignoring the proactive approach of strategic marketing. Scientists and engineers, rather than consumers, may well be the source of new product ideas in technology-driven companies, but the products that arise from those ideas must satisfy customers' needs, even if latent or unarticulated, or they will end up serving no market at all. Thus, technology-driven companies must ultimately apply the market orientation concept if they are to be successful. There are enough examples, in industrial history, of technological monsters developed in ivory towers by engineers that have never found a market.

BOX 1.2

IMPLEMENTATION PROBLEM: HOW TO PROMOTE A PROACTIVE STRATEGIC MARKETING?

- Helping customers anticipate developments in their markets.
- Continuously trying to discover additional needs of customers of which they are unaware.
- Incorporating solutions to unarticulated customer needs in new products or services.
- Brainstorming on how customers use our products and services.
- Innovating even at the risk of making our own products obsolete.

- Searching for opportunities in areas where customers have a difficult time expressing their needs.
- Working closely with lead users who try to recognise customer needs months or even years before the majority of the market recognise them.
- Extrapolating key trends to gain insight into what users in a current market will need in the future.

Source: Narver *et al.* (2004).

Kotler and Kellis, in their apology of excellent 'holistic marketing' practice make a distinction between 'market-driven' and 'market-driving' management (Kotler and Kellis, 2005, p. 724). We agree with G.S. Day (1999, p. 37) who says that, *this is a distinction without a difference*. Market-driven firms are not only reactive through response strategic marketing, but they are also driving changes by breaking the rules of the game through proactive strategic marketing. Good examples of proactive strategic marketing are given by firms, such as Swatch, Dell Computers or Ikea.

In short, the objective of strategic marketing is not only (a) to listen to customers and then to respond to their articulated needs, but also (b) to lead customers where they want to go, even if they do not know it yet. Thus, the importance of the distinction between expressed (or *articulated*) and latent (or *unarticulated*) needs. What a customer wants is an appropriate solution to his or her problem. Merely satisfying expressed needs may be insufficient for a firm to attract or to retain customers.

1.3. Role of the marketing process in a social market economy

In a market economy, the role of marketing is to organise free and competitive exchange so as to ensure efficient matching of supply and demand of goods and services. This matching is not spontaneous and requires liaison activities at two levels:

1. Organisation of *exchange*, in other words the physical flow of goods between the manufacturing and the consumption sites.
2. Organisation of *communication*, in other words the flow of information to precede, accompany and follow

exchange in order to ensure efficient meeting of supply and demand.

The role of marketing in society is therefore to organise exchange and communication between sellers and buyers. This definition emphasises the tasks and functions of marketing, irrespective of the purpose of the process of exchange. As such, it applies to both commercial and to non-profit-making activities, and in general to any situation where free exchange takes place between an organisation and the users of the products and services it offers.

1.3.1. Organisation of exchange transactions

The organisation of the exchange of goods and services is the responsibility of the distribution process, whose task is to move goods from a state of production to a state of consumption. This flow of products to the consumption state creates three types of utility generating the added value of distribution.

1. *State utility.* The set of all material transformations putting goods in a consumable state: these are operations such as fragmenting, packaging, sorting, and so on.
2. *Place utility.* Spatial transformations, such as transport, geographical allocation, and so on, which contribute to putting goods at the disposal of users at places of utilisation, transformation or consumption.
3. *Time utility.* Temporal transformations, such as storage, which make goods available at the time chosen by the user.

It is these various functions that make manufactured goods accessible and available to the targeted customers, and thus allow the actual matching of supply and demand.

Historically, autonomous intermediaries, such as sales agents, wholesalers, retailers and industrial distributors, have mainly performed these tasks of distribution, in other words, by what is called the distribution sector. Some functions of the distribution process have been integrated, for instance on the manufacturing side (direct marketing), on the consumption side (consumers' co-operatives) and on the distribution side (supermarkets, chain stores, and so on).

Furthermore, some vertical marketing systems have been developed which group together independent firms involved at various stages of the production and/or distribution process. This is done in order to co-ordinate their commercial activities, to realise economies in operating costs and thus to reinforce their impact on the market. Examples include voluntary chains, retailer co-operatives and franchise organisations. In many sectors, vertical marketing systems tend to supplant the very fragmented traditional distribution channels. They form one of the most significant developments in the tertiary sector, which has helped to intensify the competitive struggle between various forms of distribution and to improve the productivity of distribution significantly.

The added value of distribution is measured by the distribution margin, which is the difference between the price paid to the producer by the first buyer and the price paid by the ultimate user or consumer of the product. The distribution margin may therefore include the margins of one or many distributors; for example, those of the wholesalers and the retailers. Therefore, the distributive margin remunerates the functions performed by the intermediaries. In the consumer goods sector, it is estimated that the cost of exchange, covering the whole range of tasks performed by distribution, is about 40 per cent of the retail price. The cost of distribution represents a significant part of the price paid by the buyer in all sectors of activity.

1.3.2. Organisation of communication flows

The merging of the various practical conditions for exchange is not sufficient to ensure efficient adjustment of demand and supply. For exchange of goods to take place, potential buyers must be equally aware and informed of the existence of goods or of the combination of alternative attributes likely to meet their needs. Communication activities are aimed at accumulating knowledge for manufacturers, distributors and buyers. As shown in Figure 1.5, it is possible to distinguish seven different flows of communication in a typical market.

1. Before investing, the collection of information is initiated by the producer in order to identify the buyers' needs and wants which constitute an attractive opportunity for him or her. This is typically the role of market research prior to an investment decision.

2. Similarly, the potential buyer (mostly industrial) initiates a study of the possibilities offered by suppliers and invitations to tender (sourcing research).

3. After production, the manufacturer's communication programme is oriented towards distribution – a push strategy – with the objective of obtaining product referencing and the co-operation of distributors with regard to selling space, promotion and price.

4. The manufacturer initiates collection of information on all forms of brand advertising or direct selling activities aimed at making end-buyers aware of the existence of the brand's distinctive qualities: a pull strategy.

5. Activities of promotion and communication prompted by distributors is aimed at creating store loyalty, building traffic through promotional activities, supporting proprietary brands, informing about sales terms, and so on.

6. After utilisation or consumption of goods, the measurement of satisfaction or dissatisfaction, through surveys or consumer panels, is carried out by the marketer so as to enable the firm to adjust supply to buyers' reactions.

7. After utilisation or consumption of goods, claims and evaluations through comparative testing is transmitted spontaneously by buyers, acting alone or in organised groups (consumerism).

In small markets, communication takes place spontaneously between the various parties of the exchange process. In large markets, there is a significant physical and psychological gap between the parties, and communication needs to be specifically organised.

1.3.3. Other business models

The traditional role of the marketing process is described in Figure 1.5. In this conception of the marketing process, the three key actors – manufacturers, distributors and customers – are distinct entities playing different roles independently of each other.

■ Production and value creation through the firm's offerings occur inside the firm at the initiative of manufacturers.

■ Distributors organise the value exchange process in the market place.

■ Targeted segments of customers extract value from the firm's offerings.

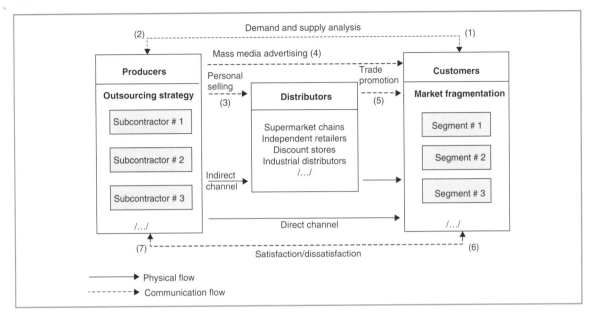

Figure 1.5   Role of the marketing process in a market economy
Source: Authors.

This traditional view of the marketing process is *company-centric* and manufacturers largely control the flows of communication to potential customers. As the balance of power among these market players evolves, the nature of their relationships is also changing. Two other distinct business models can be identified: the 'manufacturer-dominated' and, the 'retailer-dominated' models.

The manufacturer-dominated model

In this market configuration depicted in Figure 1.6, the manufacturer reinforces its domination of the marketing process (1) by bypassing distributors and/or by controlling the exchange of value process and/or (2) by creating customers preference, exclusivity and loyalty through a powerful branding policy. Here are three typical European examples of this strategy.

Other examples of successful direct marketing are given by the Swedish firm Ikea in the furniture market and by the American company Dell Computer in the PC market. In the manufacturer-dominated model, the firm always assumes the R&D activities, even if the manufacturing activities are sometimes subcontracted to another party through contract manufacturing or assumed by a virtual organisation (Exhibit 1.1).

The retailer-dominated model

In this model represented in Figure 1.7, the distributor is the key market player. This situation prevails mainly in the fast moving consumer goods (FMCG) sector in Europe and in the United States, where, from passive intermediaries, retailers have become active marketers developing new stores concepts, launching their own store brands competing directly with manufacturers' brands. Three typical examples of this strategy are presented in Exhibit 1.2. Many of the private label products sold by these large retailers are made by well-known brand manufacturers and shipped in different packaging. The hard discounters like Aldi and Wal-Mart still make a profit on the low-cost sale because they buy in large quantity.

1.3.4. Marketing as a factor of business democracy

Marketing, and specifically strategic marketing, has an important role to play in a market economy, not only because it contributes to an efficient matching between demand and supply, but also because it triggers a virtuous circle of economic development, as illustrated in

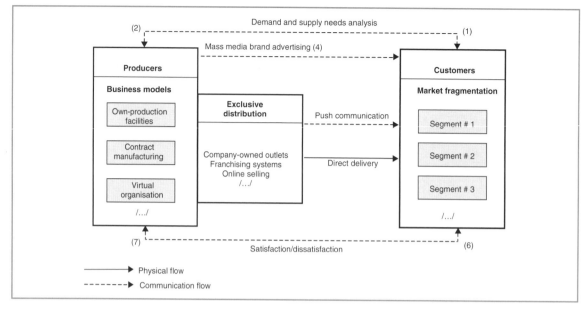

Figure 1.6   The manufacturer-dominated business model
Source: Authors.

EXAMPLES OF SUCCESSFUL MANUFACTURER-DOMINATED BUSINESS MODELS

- The Swiss firm *Nespresso System* has teamed with appliance makers including Saeco International and Miele to produce expresso makers displayed in an exclusive network of Nespresso boutiques that display espresso makers and where customers can buy packages of capsules of coffee from Moscow to New York. Nespresso sales rose to $362 million in 2002.
- The Italian shoemaker *Geox Group* is Italy's first and world's fourth-ranking foot wear brand. The success of Geox is based on a revolutionary idea: 'the shoe that breathes'. It is sold in over 68 countries worldwide through a widespread

tailored distribution network of 278 exclusive stores and of 900 independent multibrand point of sale.
- The Spanish firm *Zara Inditex* is selling design-led fashion clothing through 2,240 stores in 56 countries. Zara has challenged many of the traditional ways of operating in the clothing industry. Zara studies the demands of the customers in its stores and then tries to deliver an appropriate design at lightning speed and can get clothes from the design studio onto racks in as little as 2 weeks.

Source: Authors and published sources.

Figure 1.8. The steps of this development process are the following:

1. Strategic marketing helps identify poorly satisfied or unmet market needs (articulated or latent) and stimulates the development of new or improved products.
2. Operational marketing designs a dynamic marketing programme to create and/or develop market demand for these new products.

3. This increased demand generates cost decreases that make possible price reductions, thereby opening the market to new groups of customers.
4. The resulting enlargement of the market requires new investments in production capacity that generates economies of scale and stimulates further efforts in R&D to create new generations of products.

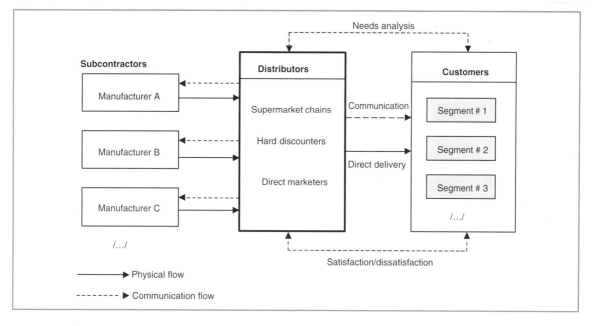

Figure 1.7   The retailer-dominated business model

Source: Authors.

EXHIBIT 1.2

EXAMPLES OF SUCCESSFUL RETAILER-DOMINATED BUSINESS MODELS

- *The British Tesco*, the leading retailer in the United Kingdom with small grocery stores under the Tesco Metro brand name, big supermarkets outside cities (Tesco Extra) and 24-hour stores (Tesco Express), is the king of supermarkets in Britain. Tesco has adapted to rapid technological changes. It makes an astonishng profit from its online sales site Tesco.com. Tesco also owns petrol stations and provides financial sevices, a joint venture with the Royal Bank of Scotland. Tesco is a global player well established in Ireland, Central Europe and Asia.
- The *German retailer Aldi* (short for Albrech Discount) has become one of the largest grocery chain, running more than 7,000 stores worldwide by offering deeply discounted prices on about 7,000 popular food items. Aldi buys cheap sites mostly on city outskirts, keeps a tiny staff and carries mostly private label items displaying them on pallets rather than shelves.

- With $256 billion in sales revenue in 2004, the *American Wal-Mart* is the world's largest company. Every week 138 million shoppers visit Wal-Mart's 4,750 stores in the United States. At Wal-Mart 'every day low price' is more than a slogan. Economists estimate that Wal-Mart saved its customers $100 billion last year alone. They refer to a 'Wal-Mart Effect' that has suppressed inflation and rippled productivity gains through the economy. The 12 million worth of Chinese goods that Wal-Mart bought in 2002 represented 10 per cent of all US imports from China. Wal-Mart operates in ten countries including the United Kingdom (Asda) and Germany.

Source: Authors and published sources.

Strategic marketing contributes to the development of a business democracy because (a) it starts with the analysis of citizen-consumers' expectations, (b) it guides investment and production decisions on the basis of anticipated market needs, (c) it is respectful of the diversity of tastes and preferences by segmenting markets and developing adapted products and (d) it stimulates innovation and entrepreneurship (see Exhibit 1.1).

As already underlined, reality is not always in line with theory. The market orientation business philosophy has been progressively accepted and implemented by firms in Western economies (see Exhibit 1.3).

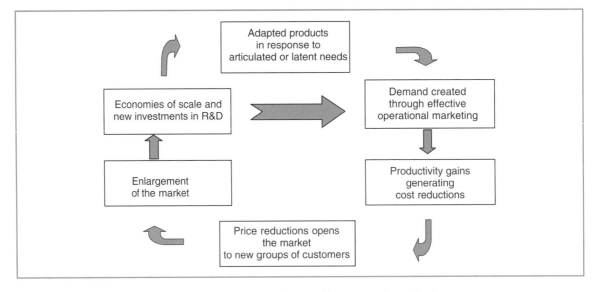

Figure 1.8   The virtuous circle of development triggered by strategic marketing

Source: Authors.

EXHIBIT 1.3

THE PRAISING OF MERCANTILISM

Once again I am reminded of the wretchedness of my solitude. Where I am concerned, to sow and reap is good: the evil sets in when I grind and knead and bake, for then I am working only for myself. The American colonist need have no misgivings about making bread; he will sell the bread, and the money he stores in his chest represents the saving of time and work. But I in my solitude am deprived of the benefits of money, although I have no lack of it.

Today I can measure the folly and malice of those who affect to despise money, that divine institution. Money spiritualises all that it touches by endowing it with a quality that is both rational (measurable) and universal, since property reckoned in terms of money is accessible to all men. Venality is one of the cardinal virtues. The venal man suppresses his murderous and anti-social instincts – honour, self pride, patriotism, political ambition, religion, fanaticism, and racialism – in favour of his need to co-operate with others, his love of fruitful exchange, his sense of human solidarity. The term Golden Age

should be taken literally, and I see now that mankind would swiftly achieve it were its affairs wholly in the hands of venal men. Alas, it is nearly always high-minded men who make history, and so the flames destroy everything and blood flows in torrents; The plump merchants of Venice afford us an example of the luxurious happiness possible in a state governed solely by the law of lucre, whereas the emaciated wolves of the Spanish Inquisition show us the infamies of which men are capable when they have lost the love of material well-being. The Huns would soon have checked their advance if they had known how to profit by the riches they have acquired. Encumbered with their gains, they would have stayed to enjoy them, and life would have resumed its course. But they were disinterested savages. They despised gold. They rushed onward, burning as they went.

Source: Tournier (1969, pp. 61–2).

1.4. The changing priority role of the marketing process

Viewed from the standpoint of the organisation of communication and exchange in a market economy, it is clear that, in spite of its current prominence, marketing is not a new activity, given that it covers tasks which have always existed and have always been taken care of one way or another in any system based on free exchange.

Even in an autarky, founded on the most elementary form of exchange – barter – there are flows of exchange and communication, but their manifestation is spontaneous and neither requires the allocation of specific resources, nor any form of organisation to ensure their functioning.

It is the complexity of the technological, economic and competitive environment that has gradually led firms first to create and then to reinforce the marketing function. Hence it is interesting to follow the history of this

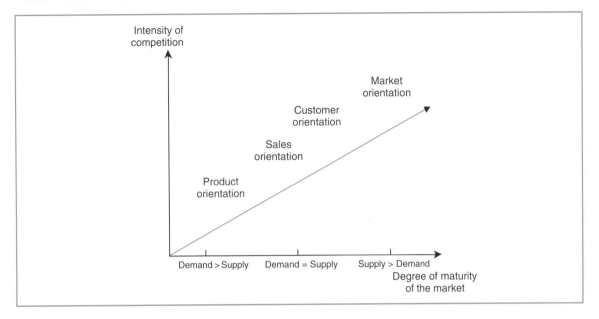

Figure 1.9 Evolution of the business philosophy
Source: Authors.

evolution in order to understand better the present role of marketing (Figure 1.9). One can distinguish three stages, each characterised by different priority marketing objectives: passive marketing, operational marketing and strategic marketing.

1.4.1. Product orientation: passive marketing

Passive marketing is a form of organisation prevalent in an economic environment characterised by the existence of a potentially important market, but where supply is scarce, with insufficient available production capacity to meet the market's needs. Demand is therefore higher than supply. Passive marketing, to work, also implies that needs are known and stable and that technological innovation in the reference market proceeds at a slow pace.

> This type of economic situation was observed, for instance, at the beginning of the century during the industrial revolution, and more recently in the period immediately after the Second World War. This environment continues to prevail in many developing countries at present and particularly in Eastern Europe.

It is clear that in a situation characterised by scarce supply, marketing has a limited and passive role. Given that needs are known, strategic marketing is performed naturally, operational marketing is reduced to organising the flow of manufactured goods, and promotional activity

is rendered superfluous, given that the firm cannot supply the market as it would have liked.

Contacts with the market are often limited to the first echelon, which is the first buyer of the product, who is usually an intermediary, wholesaler or industrial distributor. There is therefore little contact with final demand and market research is infrequent. This state of affairs is also reflected in the organisation of the firm, which is dominated by the operations function, with the development of production capacity and improvement of productivity as the main priorities. Marketing is there to sell what has already been produced.

When a firm adopts the 'product concept' it is, in general, structurally organised with the following characteristics (see Figure 1.10).

- A functional disequilibrium in the sense that, in the organisational chart, marketing does not occupy the same hierarchical level as the other functions, such as operations, finance or personnel.
- The first level of marketing is commercial service, in charge of sales administration and in contact with the first buyer in the distributive chain, not necessarily with the end-user.
- Operations management makes the product decisions; selling prices and sales forecasts are the responsibility of the financial department.

There is typically a dispersion of responsibilities as far as the marketing instruments are concerned (the *four Ps*).

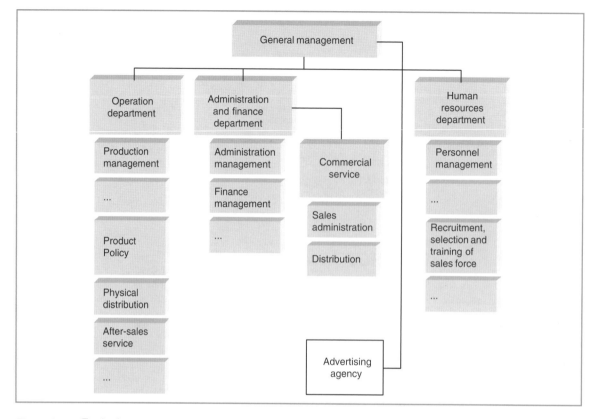

Figure 1.10   Typical organisation of a product-oriented company
Source: Authors.

The product concept

This kind of organisation fosters the development of the product concept based on the implicit assumption that the firm knows what is good for the buyer and the latter shares this conviction. Moreover, the managers of such firms are often convinced that they are producing a superior good and tend to take it for granted that buyers will continue to want their products. They tend to have an inside-in perspective, where the emphasis is placed on internal constraints and preoccupations and not on the customer's requirements or expectations. Such a viewpoint – typical of a bureaucratic organisation – is therefore completely opposed to the idea of the buyer who views a product as a solution to a problem.

This state of mind is conceivable in an environment where demand exceeds supply, where buyers are prepared to buy any kind of product if they can find it. In reality, such market conditions are exceptional, and when they prevail they are temporary. The danger of the product concept is that it makes the firm myopic in its outlook and does not encourage a proactive behaviour, that is, one that will anticipate a change in the environment and prepare itself accordingly.

Limitations of the product concept

Passive marketing is a form of marketing organisation that is no longer suitable for the environment facing the majority of firms in industrialised countries today. The product concept nevertheless persists in some firms, mainly among firms selling standardised products or commodities or high-tech companies confronted with a fast growing demand. The lack of market orientation is a major cause of many bankruptcies, as illustrated in 2001 by the collapse of the start-ups in e-commerce. It is also the dominant state of mind observed among Eastern European firms, which have found themselves suddenly confronted with the formidable challenge of the market and of competition. Thus, in a product-oriented company, the dominant business philosophy can be summarised in the following terms:

■ The key to business success is producing quality goods and services at a reasonable cost.
■ Good products and services sell themselves.
■ If possible, products and services should be standardised to keep costs down.

Until recently, the product concept also dominated in developing countries, mainly among experts of economic development having little concern for creating favourable conditions for an endogenous development using local resources to meet the needs of local people. But even there strategic marketing can play an active role and contribute towards economic development, to the extent however that such methods are now adapted to situations which are totally different from industrialised countries.

1.4.2. Sales orientation: operational marketing

Operational marketing puts the emphasis on the action dimension of the market orientation concept. In Western European countries, firms in the consumer goods industry progressively adopted this approach to management during the 1950s, when demand was expanding rapidly and production capacity was available. On the other hand, although these markets were in full growth, the distributive system was often deficient and unproductive.

The following changes in the economy are the cause of this new approach to marketing management:

1. The appearance of new forms of distribution, mainly self-service, has helped to modify the productivity of conventional distribution networks that were not adapted to the requirements of mass distribution.
2. The geographical widening of markets, and the resulting physical and psychological gap between producers and consumers, have made it increasingly necessary to resort to means of communication such as mass media advertising.
3. The development of branding policies, a requirement for self-service selling and a way for the firm to control its final demands.

The priority objective of the marketing process at this stage is to create an efficient commercial organisation. The role of marketing becomes less passive. Now the task is to find and organise markets for the products made. At this stage, most firms concentrate on the needs of the central core of the market, with products that satisfy the needs of the majority of buyers. Markets are therefore weakly segmented, and strategic decisions regarding product policy remain the responsibility of the operations department. The main function of marketing is to organise the efficient distribution of products and to manage all tasks that fall under this process of commercialisation.

As far as the organisational structure is concerned, these changes in priorities translate into the creation of a sales or a commercial department, and one can observe a readjustment of functions (see Figure 1.11). These sales departments are given the task of setting up a sales network, organising physical distribution, advertising and promotion. They also manage market research programmes, which are beginning to manifest their

importance, for example, in analysing buying habits, the effectiveness of advertising and the impact of branding and packaging policies, and so on.

The selling concept

The selling concept is a characteristic often present in organisational marketing. Its implicit assumptions are as follows:

■ Consumers naturally tend to resist buying 'unsought products'.
■ Consumers can be pushed to buy more by using different means of sales stimulation.
■ The firm must create a powerful sales department and use substantial promotional means to attract and keep customers.

Thus, within the firm, marketing people tend to have an *in*side-out perspective, and to give priority to the company's objectives over the customer's post-purchase satisfaction. The underlying assumption is that good selling is always 'salesperson-driven'.

Some industries which make products not naturally sought by buyers, such as life insurance or control instruments, have developed hard-selling techniques, which have become popularised through various writings on the '*Art of Selling*'. Furthermore, when there is extra capacity in a sector, it is not unusual to see firms wanting to liquidate their stocks employing these methods by aggressively using television commercials, direct mail, newspaper advertisements, and so on. It is therefore not surprising to see that the public at large, as well as some firms, tends to equate marketing with hard selling or even forced selling.

Thus, in a sales-oriented company, the dominant business philosophy can be summarised in the following terms:

> The key to business success lies in persuading potential customers to buy your goods and services through advertising, personal selling or other means. Potential customers must be informed and convinced of the benefits of the products.

The risk of manipulative or wild marketing

Operational marketing has encouraged the development of the selling concept, which implies a high degree of commercial aggressiveness, with the implicit assumption that the market can absorb everything, if enough pressure is applied. Judging by the high growth rate of private consumption and the level of household equipment purchased during the immediate post-war period, this selling policy did prove to be efficient.

However, the efficiency of the selling concept must be evaluated by keeping in mind the situation at the time,

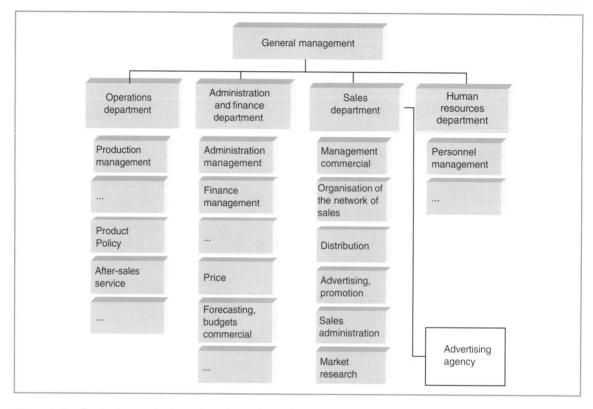

Figure 1.11   Typical organisation of a sales-oriented company
Source: Authors.

that is, a fundamentally expanding market, weakly differentiated products and consumers who were less experienced as buyers. The risk run by the selling concept is to consider this commercial approach as being valid in any situation and to confuse it with the marketing concept. Levitt (1960, p. 48) compares the two concepts as follows:

> Selling focuses on the needs of the seller, marketing on the needs of the buyer. Selling is preoccupied with the seller's need to convert his product into cash; marketing with the idea of satisfying the needs of the customer by means of the product and the whole cluster of things associated with creating, delivering and finally consuming it.

An over-enthusiastic use of advertising and selling can lead to manipulative marketing or wild marketing, which tries to mould demand to the requirements of supply rather than adapt supply to the expectations of demand. Exhibit 1.4 gives some examples of commercial practices that can be classified as wild marketing.

The excesses of wild marketing have led to the birth of a countervailing power in the form of consumers' organisations, initiated by consumers, and in the form of legislation that increasingly reinforces the protection of

consumers' legal rights prompted by public authorities. Self-discipline by companies and the adoption of rules of ethics has also contributed to the development of ethical behaviour. It is clear today that 'wild marketing' is self-destructive for a company or for a brand and goes against its best long-term interest.

1.4.3. Customer orientation: strategic marketing

The temptation is great to confine the market orientation concept to operational marketing particularly when markets are fast growing and when the size of the untapped market potential is large. The necessity to integrate the strategic dimension of the market orientation concept is perceived when markets reach maturity, segmentation and positioning strategies become key issues, competition intensifies and the pace of technological innovation accelerates. In this environment, the role of marketing is not simply to exploit an existing market through mass marketing techniques. The priority objectives are to detect new segments or niches having a growth potential, to develop new product concepts, to diversify the firm's product portfolio, to find a

EXHIBIT 1.4

SOME EXAMPLES OF WILD MARKETING PRACTICES

- Sales of defective or dangerous products.
- Exaggeration of the product's content through the use of flashy packaging design.
- Resorting to fraudulent practices with regard to price and delivery policies.
- Resorting to promotional techniques that exploit impulsive buyer behaviour.
- Advertisements that exaggerate the product's attributes and the promises that these attributes represent.

- Advertisements that exploit the agonies and anxieties of individuals.
- Enticing people to over-consume using hard-selling methods.

/ ... /

In the long run, wild marketing is self-destructive for a company or for a brand and goes against its best interests.

Source: Authors.

---

sustainable competitive advantage and to design a marketing strategy for each business unit. The analysis dimension of the market orientation concept becomes the critical management skill. Its role is to select solid strategic options on which more efficient operational marketing programmes will be based. At this stage, a market-oriented firm has an *outside-in perspective*.

The integration of the marketing concept has taken place at different periods according to sectors depending on the development stage reached by the market. The firms operating in the FMCG sectors were among the first to adopt the strategic dimension of the market orientation concept. Other sectors, such as the computer and the petroleum industries, suddenly exposed in the 2000s to a structural slowing down of demand, have discovered the necessity to become more market-driven.

The phase of reinforcement of the market orientation is characterised by the development and/or the reinforcement of the role of strategic marketing and by the adoption of a customer orientation within the firm. Two factors are at the root of this evolution:

- The maturity of markets and the progressive saturation of the needs of the core market.
- The acceleration in the rate at which technological progress diffuses and penetrates.

We will examine these two factors of change successively, as well as their implications for the marketing function in the firm.

Saturation of the core market

The rapid expansion of the economy during the last millennium led to a saturation of demand for products corresponding to the basic needs of the market, and this evolution is a second significant change that has contributed once again to the modification of the role of marketing in the firm. This change manifested itself with

the appearance of a potential demand for products adapted more specifically to the needs of distinct groups of customers. This evolution, which appeared at different times in different sectors, leads to market fragmentation and strategies of segmentation. As an example, let us examine the following fictitious case.

A firm is contemplating the launching of a new aperitif in the market and is wondering about the preference of potential customers as to the degree of bitterness of the aperitif. Various tests are organised showing that the majority of potential customers prefer a medium level of bitterness, as shown in the preference distribution of Figure 1.12.

The tests also show that some consumers, fewer in number, prefer a higher degree of bitterness and others a lower degree of bitterness. A situation of diffused preferences is typical of a latent market and the firm must decide how to position its product with respect to this dominant feature.

The natural tendency is to follow *the majority rule* and develop a product at a medium level (say level 4) of a significant product characteristic, so as to correspond to the preferences of the core of the market and thus minimise total dissatisfaction and fulfil the expectations of the greatest number. The pioneering firm thus finds access to the most important potential market and also benefits from economies of scale in production and distribution. At this stage, the firm will be exercising operational marketing to penetrate the market as rapidly as possible.

Market choices will therefore crystallise over products designed to meet the expectations of the majority. Peripheral preferences will not be met and these groups of consumers will have to accept compromises. If successful, the pioneer will soon be followed by many imitators and the situation will progressively lead towards the 'majority fallacy' (Kuehn and Day, 1962), whereby all competing

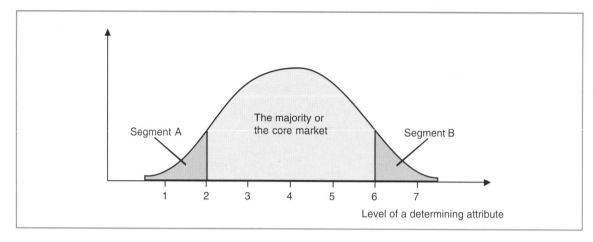

Figure 1.12   The majority rule fallacy
Source: Kuehn and Day (1962).

brands are clustered at the same medium level of the relevant product characteristic.

The strategic marketing stage appears when the needs of the core market are saturated as a result of this situation, where a large number of competitors are making similar offers. At this stage it becomes worthwhile to rediscover the neglected differences in preferences and pay attention to the peripheral segments by launching products specially conceived to meet their needs.

> In the fictitious example above, the latecomer on the market, analysing consumers' preferences makes the same observations as before. However, by launching one very smooth (level 2) and simultaneously one very bitter aperitif (level 6), the alert firm can hope to gain a total market share well over what it would gain if it launched a similar product (a 'me too') to the existing ones at level 4, where all the competing brands are clustered.

These segments are certainly smaller, but nevertheless they constitute an unexploited potential, given that these consumers have never found a product in the market corresponding to their real preferences. The firm will adopt a segmentation strategy (based here on taste) and the market will subdivide into segments that correspond to the differentiated products. This stage, called the 'segmentation stage', requires a finer understanding from the firm of the market and of the benefits sought by different groups of potential customers.

At this maturity stage of the market, product policy must therefore be increasingly based on the analysis of needs and the services expected from products. In industrialised economies, most markets adequately meet

basic needs. Finding growing segments is not an easy task, but requires a deep understanding of markets, needs, users and usages of products. This knowledge can only be achieved by strengthening the 'analytic' aspect of marketing, that is, by using strategic marketing and by adopting a customer orientation.

Technological progress

One of the significant features of the last hundred years is the extraordinary diffusion of technological progress, which penetrated and influenced most industrial sectors within a few years. As a result, we saw a continuous growth, a real explosion of new products and new industries, both quantitatively and qualitatively. A large number of products that we use daily today did not exist a short while ago.

> According to the Nielsen Company, 100 new products are launched every day on the sole French food market that is about 37,000 new products per year. (Boisdevésy, 1996, p. 61)

The diffusion of technological progress results from acceleration, generalisation and systematic approach in scientific research.

1. The diffusion of technological progress is *accelerated*: we mean that we observe an increasing rate of innovation and a shorter time frame required to pass from development to commercial exploitation on a large scale.

This evolution implies a shorter technological life of products and hence the time available for recovering

Table 1.3 The shortening of the product life cycle (an example: the computer market)				
	Average duration (months)			
Development phases	1981	1984	1988	1991
R&D	24	20	18	8
Market research	9	7	4	2
Expected life	88	48	24	12

Source: Dataquest, April ,1992, SVM 25.

R&D costs. Table 1.3 illustrates this point in the computer market sector.

2. The spread of technological progress is *generalised* throughout sectors, firms and countries. Few sectors have been sheltered from technological innovations, some of which are, as Schumpeter (1949) put it, 'destructive', that is, they menace or eliminate existing industries.

Basic sectors, such as steel, leather, textiles, paper, have always been threatened by substitutes coming from industries that are technologically very distant. This evolution calls for a closer scrutiny of the technological and competitive environment.

3. The spread of technological progress is *systematic*, in the sense that, unlike the days when more or less isolated individuals carried out scientific research, it has now become institutionalised in firms, universities and private or public specialised centres. Governments play a significant role in this domain, by allocating important resources to help scientific and industrial research.

Technological innovation no longer depends on the chance of inventions. An innovation is the outcome of a concerted and planned effort, which itself is directed by some theoretical representations. There is continuity in the elaboration of theoretical tools, which is the job of fundamental research, and the implementation of methods that can be directly used in the production of goods and services. Research itself is planned according to tested methods and in terms of objectives laid out in advance.

This technological evolution has a direct bearing on product policy and forces the firm, for example, to review the structure of its product portfolio at a much faster rate than before. Among successful firms it is frequent to observe that 40–60 per cent of their turnover is achieved with products non-existing 5 years ago.

At Hewlett-Packard, for instance, more than 50 per cent of the turnover is generated by products launched into the market during the last three years and more than 500 projects of new product are currently in the process of development. (House and Price, 1991)

This increased dependence on the technological environment calls for a reinforcement of the market monitoring system within the organisation.

Organisation of the marketing function

The three groups of changes we have just examined all imply a consolidation of strategic marketing in the firm. As far as the organisation of the firm with an 'active marketing' orientation is concerned, the significant change will be with regard to product decisions, which will henceforth be the responsibility of the marketing department in close liaison with the R&D department and the manufacturing department. This means that in actual practice, strategic marketing regulates product policy and decides whether products are economically viable. The idea for new products may come from anywhere: manufacturing, R&D or any other source, but it must first pass through the test of strategic marketing before adoption and manufacturing.

Firms, which have integrated the strategic marketing concept, will have a marketing department (see Figure 1.13) whose responsibilities will comprise all the tasks that flow from operational marketing and strategic marketing, including the choice of product markets. At this stage, the market-oriented firm has an *outside-in perspective* and places priority emphasis on customers' expectations as a starting point for its product policy.

In a customer-oriented firm, the role of the seller has changed and is very different from the one observed in sales-oriented companies. The customer orientation concept has replaced and reversed the logic of the selling concept. As stated by the General Electric Company shortly after the Second World War,

> Rather than making what you have always made, then trying to sell it, find out what will sell, and then try to make it.

In this framework, the role of the seller becomes less one of 'trying to sell' as one of 'helping to buy'. The process of selling initially bases itself on the needs of the customer. This kind of commercial attitude can only be practical in an organisation where the customer orientation dominates. To quote Drucker (1973)

> There will always, one can assume, be need for some selling. But the aim of marketing is to make selling superfluous. The aim of marketing is to know and understand the customer so well that the product or service fits him and sells itself. Ideally, marketing should result in a customer who is ready to buy. All that should be needed then is to make the product or service available.

This ideal situation will only rarely be achieved, but it is important to remember that such is the objective of the

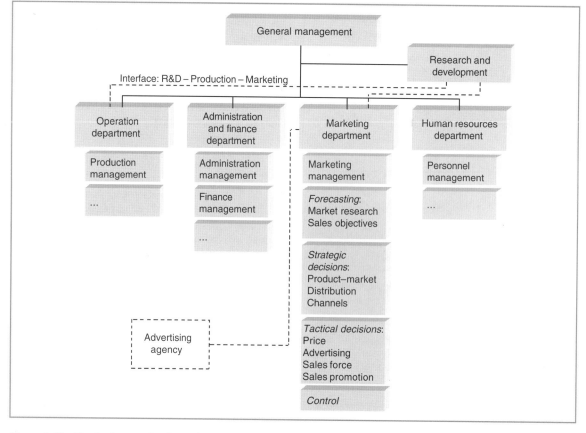

Figure 1.13   Typical organisation of a customer-oriented company

market orientation theory discussed earlier. In a customer-oriented company, the dominant business philosophy can be summarised in the following terms:

The key to business success is to integrate all company activities and personnel towards satisfying customers, while providing satisfactory profits to the firm. The firm should find out what benefits customers want and then provide these benefits through goods and services.

To achieve this objective, the marketing department has an important role to play.

Limitations of the traditional customer orientation concept

The implicit assumption at the root of the market orientation concept is that satisfying customers' needs is the prime objective of the firm, not because of altruism, but because it is the best way for the firm to achieve its own profit and/or growth objectives. This is, what we call the *traditional marketing concept*.

In practice, the market orientation concept is integrated differently in the firms – as illustrated in Table 2.5 – even if most claim to be inspired by it. In fact, as we mentioned earlier, the concept is an ideal to be reached, rarely fully realised, but one that should nevertheless guide all the activities of the firm.

As in the case of the product concept and the selling concept, the customer orientation concept has its own limitations, of which one should be aware. Three major limitations or questions are usually raised against the traditional marketing concept.

1. When referring to needs satisfaction, does the customer orientation concept refer to short-term or to long-term satisfaction? Should marketing management be concerned with the well-being of customers?

We are confronted here with a basic issue that is raised more and more frequently in industrialised economies, where social aspirations have shifted from quantity to 'quality' of life. In this end of century's social environment, the firm is expected to behave as a good citizen and to assume social accountability as well as to maintain affluence. Thus, the traditional marketing concept must evolve towards the accountable or societal marketing concept (Kotler, 1967/2005).

2. Is the objective of individual needs' satisfaction made at the expense of social needs? Is the social cost of consumption a cost neglected by traditional marketing?

This second question is the result of the public's awareness of the scarcity of non-renewable resources and of the impact of consumption on the environment, which until recently was viewed as a free public good. In advanced economies, the socio-ecological view of consumption 'from cradle to grave' is a largely accepted vision that induces firms to redesign their product concepts in a green perspective. Thus, the traditional marketing orientation must evolve towards the green marketing concept.

3. Does an over-enthusiastic adoption of the customer orientation concept lead the firm to put too much emphasis on products in high demand, or market-pull, at the expense of products yet unknown but pushed by technology?

A marketing strategy exclusively guided by market wishes inevitably tends to favour minor and less revolutionary innovations than those proposed by the laboratory. Such innovations, which correspond to needs felt and expressed by the market, are by this token less risky and are therefore seen as more attractive to the firm. On the other hand, a strategy based on technological advance is more likely to lead to a breakthrough innovation and hence ensure that the firm has a long-term competitive advantage that is more difficult to catch up with. Many breakthrough innovations in fact originate from the laboratory (or from the firm) and not from the market. It is therefore important to maintain a balance between these two strategies of product development: 'technology or company-push' and

'market-pull', that is, between response and proactive strategic marketing.

1.4.4. Market orientation: market-driven management

Market orientation and market-driven management are the tentative responses to the three challenging questions listed above. This new evolution in the business philosophy is the outgrowth of three ongoing changes in the macro-marketing environment: (1) the globalisation of the world economy, (2) the revolution in the new technologies of information and communication (TICS) with the resulting development of electronic commerce and (3) the emergence of new values promoting a market social economy aimed at sustainable development.

These three evolutionary changes which will be reviewed in the next chapter call for a new evolution of the role and organisation of the marketing function within the firm. At the beginning of the new millennium, the ongoing change in alert companies is the move from a customer orientation towards a broad orientation, where the market is viewed as complex ecosystem and where the culture dimension of the market orientation concept is disseminated in the entire organisation.

Is the market orientation concept really different?

Many authors and managers do not make a careful distinction among *customer-oriented*, *marketing-oriented* and *market-driven* concepts. They lean towards the traditional marketing concept presented in the last section to describe the orientation of a firm that stays close to its customers. For over 50 years, managers have been exhorted 'to put the customer at the top of the organisational chart' and to use the paradigm of the four *Ps* to implement such customer-oriented strategy. Today, the analysis of the world market as an interconnected global economy has the merit to evidence the complexity of today's global markets and the shortcomings of the traditional marketing concept that provides *an incomplete view of a business*. Focusing mostly on consumers and ignoring the effects of other key market actors can indeed be misleading. Knowing what customers want is not too helpful (a) if the new product idea is too revolutionary, (b) if powerful competitors are already providing the same product or service, (c) if powerful distributors prevent the firm from reaching the targeted customers, (d) if powerful influencers do not certify and shortlist the product or (e) if other stakeholders decide to boycott the brand.

One can identify four elements of differentiation between the traditional marketing concept and the market orientation concept presented in more detail in Chapter 2.

The marketing process in practice	The marketing process in theory		
	Action	Analysis	Culture
Passive marketing	—	—	—
Operational marketing	Yes	—	—
Strategic marketing	Yes	Yes	—
Market-driven management	Yes	Yes	Yes

Table 1.4   The changing role of the marketing process

Source: Authors.

1. The traditional marketing concept is basically customer-oriented, while market orientation is oriented towards the key market actors (customers, competitors, distributors, influencers and other stakeholders).
2. The traditional marketing concept is based on commonsensical 'market-pull' model (response strategic marketing), while the market orientation concept is based, of course, on the 'market-pull' and *also* on the 'technology-push' (proactive strategic marketing) innovation models.
3. The traditional marketing concept is basically 'action-oriented' using the four Ps paradigm, while the market orientation concept is based on the 'culture–analysis–action' paradigm.
4. The traditional marketing concept is generally confined to the marketing function, while the market orientation concept is viewed as a culture disseminated at all levels and in every function of the firm.

In Chapter 2, we shall analyse in more depth the managerial and organisational implications of this new business philosophy.

CHAPTER SUMMARY

Marketing is both a business philosophy and an action-oriented process. One can identify three dimensions in the marketing concept: culture, analysis and action. The ideological foundations of marketing are deeply rooted in the principles that govern the functioning of a social market economy. Within the firm, marketing's function is twofold: (a) to create opportunities or to lead the firm towards market opportunities adapted to its resources and know-how and which offer a potential for profit and growth (strategic marketing); (b) to be the firm's commercial arm for achieving a targeted market share through the use of tactical means related to product, distribution, price and communication decisions (operational marketing). The role of marketing in a social market economy is to organise exchange and communication between sellers and potential customers, thereby assuming an efficient matching of supply and demand. This role is of an increased complexity in the global economy and determines the productivity of the entire market system. The priority role of the marketing process in the firm has evolved with the complexity of the economic, technological and competitive environment. In current marketing practice, one can identify four business philosophies: product orientation and passive marketing, sales orientation with operational marketing, customer orientation with strategic and operational marketing, market orientation with the emergence of market-driven management. Each of these business philosophies has its own limitations.

Review and Application Questions

1. Marketing is both a business philosophy and an action-oriented process which is valid for every organisation in contact with its constituency of users. Select a non-profit organisation (university, hospital, museum, etc.) and discuss this proposition by reference to Figures 1.2 and 1.4. As a support for your analysis, read Sheth (1993).
2. Is marketing applicable in a firm operating in a developing country? How would you describe the priority objectives of strategic marketing in this type of environment? What would be the relative importance of each marketing instrument (the four Ps)?
3. Compare and contrast product orientation, sales orientation and customer orientation. What are the organisational implications for each of these three business philosophies?
4. Referring to your personal experience as a consumer, give examples of wild marketing practices. Which remedies would you suggest to deter companies from using these practices?
5. You have to audit the marketing function of a firm operating in a high-tech industrial market. To assess the degree of customer orientation of this firm, prepare a set of questions to be discussed with the general management of the firm.
6. How would you proceed to introduce strategic marketing in a small- or medium-sized company which has limited financial and human resources?
7. Companies that are not market-driven are inclined to focus primarily on operational marketing. What are the risks of such strategic option?

Bibliography

Abbott, L. (1955), *Quality and Competition*, New York, John Wiley & Sons.

Alderson, W. (1957), *Marketing Behavior and Executive Action*, Homewood, IL, R.D. Irwin.

Ambler, T. (2000), Marketing Metrics, *Business Strategy Review*, 11, 2, pp. 59–66.

Bennett, R. and Cooper, R. (1981), The Misuse of the Marketing Concept: An American Tragedy, *Business Horizons*, 24, 6, November–December, pp. 51–60.

Boisdevésy, J.C. (1996), *Le marketing relationnel*, Paris, Les Éditions d'Organisation.

Chamberlin, E.W. (1933/1962), *The Theory of Monopolistic Competition*, Cambridge, MA, Harvard University Press.

Day, G.S. (1999), *The Market Driven Organization*, New York, The Free Press.

Drucker, P. (1954), *The Practice of Management*, New York, Harper & Row.

Drucker, P. (1973), *Management: Tasks, Responsibilities, Practices*, New York, Harper & Row.

Ernst & Young and AC Nielsen (1999), *New Product Introduction Successful Innovation/Failure: A Fragile Boundary*.

Felton, A.P. (1959), Making the Marketing Concept Work, *Harvard Business Review*, 37, July–August, pp. 55–65.

Friedman, R. and Friedman, M. (1980), *Free to Choose*, New York, Avon Brooks Science Institute.

Hayes, R. and Abernathy, W. (1980), Managing our Way to Economic Decline, *Harvard Business Review*, 58, 4, July–August, pp. 67–78.

House, C.H. and Price, R.L. (1991), The Return Map; Tracking Product Teams, *Harvard Business Review*, 69, January–February, pp. 92–100.

Howard, J. and Sheth, J.N. (1969), *The Theory of Buyer Behaviour*, New York, John Wiley & Sons.

Kotler, P. (1967/2005) *Marketing Management*, Englewood Cliffs, NJ, Prentice Hall. See also the 12th edition published in 2005 with Keller K.L.

Kotler, P. (1977), From Sales Obsession to Marketing Effectiveness, *Harvard Business Review*, 55, November–December, pp. 67–75.

Kotler, P. and Kellis, K.L. (2005), *Marketing Management*, Upper Saddle River, NJ, Pearson Education, 12th edition.

Kuehn, A.A. and Day, R.L. (1962) Strategy of Product Quality, *Harvard Business Review*, 40, November–December, pp. 100–10.

Levitt, T.H. (1960), Marketing Myopia, *Harvard Business Review*, 38, July–August, pp. 24–47.

McCarthy, J. (1960/2005), *Basic Marketing: A Managerial Approach*, Homewood, IL, R.D. Irwin, 1st edition.

McKitterick, J.B. (1957), What is the Marketing Management Concept, in *The Frontiers of Marketing Thought and Science*, Bass, F. (ed.), Chicago, IL, American Marketing Association.

Narver, J.C., Slater, S.F. and MacLachlan, D.L. (2004), Responsive and Proactive Market Orientation and New-Product Success, *Journal of Product Innovation Management*, 21, pp. 334–47.

Schendler, B.R. (1992), How Sony Keeps the Magic Going, *Fortune*, February.

Schumpeter, J.A. (1949), *The Theory of Economic Development*, Cambridge, MA, Harvard University Press.

Smith, A. (1776), *The Wealth of Nations*, London, Methuen.

Tournier, M. (1969), *Friday*, Baltimore, MD, The Johns Hopkins University Press.

Webster, F.E., Malter, A.J. and Ganesan, S. (2005), The Decline and Dispersion of Marketing Competence, *MIT Sloan Management Review*, Summer, 45, pp. 35–43.

COMPANION WEBSITE FOR CHAPTER 1

Visit the *Market-driven Management* companion website at www.palgrave.com/business/lambin to find:

A Questionnaire to Measure the Level of Market Orientation of a Firm

market-driven management in the global marketplace

2

Chapter contents

Chapter learning objectives

When you have read this chapter, you should be able to understand

- the industry globalisation drivers;
- the benefits and drawbacks of globalisation;
- the new complexity of market viewed as an ecosystem;
- the role performed by the different market players;
- the market orientation concept;
- the characteristics of a market-driven organisation.

Chapter introduction

We have seen in the previous chapter that, during the last decade, the macro-marketing environment of the firm has changed dramatically. Powerful drivers of market orientation are at work with privatisation and deregulation policies, economic integration and globalisation of the world economy. The first question examined in this chapter is to review the benefits and the drawbacks of globalisation and its impact on market-driven management. Seond, the development of the Internet technology is shaping two types of markets: global traditional markets (GTM) and global electronic markets (GEM). In the context of these dual trading areas, market participants have different roles and expectations that we shall review in this chapter.

2.1. The impact of globalisation

In the last two decades, global marketing was adopted by a majority of international companies. Globalisation was the name of the game and all business sectors were concerned. By virtually any measure – development of international trade, growing interdependence and interconnectivity of markets, transnational terrorism, cross-border mergers and acquisitions, and strength of the alter-globalisation debate – globalisation is becoming increasingly pervasive. For empirical evidence, see the A.T. Kearny Globalisation Index (A.T. Kearney, 2002). Globalisation is no longer confined to enterprises in few industries, such as electronics, pharmaceuticals, automobiles or branded consumer goods. In the last decade, globalisation has become a reality even for companies that used to own and manage local service firms, for example supermarkets (Carrefour, Ahold, Ikea), neighbourhood cafés (Starbucks cafés), banks (Citybank, Amro, etc.), corner photography shops (Fnac, Kodak kiosks, etc.) and fast food restaurants (McDonalds, Quick, Haagen Daz, etc.).

In this context, firms concentrated their efforts on the development of global brands that could ideally attract a maximum number of people on a global basis with the same standardised marketing approach. These global brands became powerful tools to penetrate international markets: they are real assets for companies and, by way of consequence, are highly valued by financial markets. For example, according to Kiley (2006), the top five brands in the world in terms of financial valuation (in $ billions) are: Coca-Cola ($67), Microsoft ($61), IBM ($54), GE ($44) and Intel ($33). These are all American brands.

2.1.1. Typology of international environments

The necessity for the firm to adopt a global approach in international marketing is dependent upon the characteristics of its market environment. Goshal and Nohria (1993) suggest analysing the international environment by reference to two dimensions.

1. *Local forces*, such as local customers, tastes, purchasing habits, governments and regulatory agencies, which create strong needs for *local responsiveness and adaptation*.
2. *Global forces*, such as economies of scale, uniform customer demands, worldwide competition and product uniformity that are powerful incentives for *global integration and standardisation*.

For each of these two dimensions, one can identify two levels (weak and strong) and broadly distinguish among four environmental conditions faced by multinational companies as illustrated in Figure 2.1.

- The environment is *global* when forces for global integration are strong and local responsiveness weak. In such markets, structural uniformity in the organisation is best suited to these conditions. It is the situation observed in many high-technology markets where local forces are non-existent and inoperative. The trend is towards standardisation and centralisation of responsibilities.
- In the *multinational (or multidomestic)* environment, on the contrary, the forces for national responsiveness are strong and the forces for global integration weak. In this type of market, adaptation to local conditions is a key success factor and companies tend to adopt different governance modes to fit to each local context. Many food companies fall into this category, where taste and culinary habits are important determinants of preferences and of purchase behaviour.
- In the *placid international environment* both forces are weak. The business of producing cement is an example.

Cement products are highly standardised and distribution systems are similar across countries. Thus demands for local responsiveness are weak. However, the trade-offs between the economics of cement production and transport costs are such that global integration is not attractive. (Goshal and Nohria, 1993, p. 26)

■ In the *transnational* environment both forces, local and global, are strong. It is the most complex situation where some degree of standardisation and centralisation is necessary. In addition, maintaining the capacity to respond to local situations is also required.

It is the case, for example, of a brand like Carlsberg, which has all the characteristics of a global brand. Distributed in 130 countries throughout the world, its taste, logo and bottle design are identical. Nevertheless, the 'beer culture' is very different from one country to the other, even within Europe. Thus a transnational organisation combining centralisation and local (or regional) adaptation is better suited to this brand.

Another example is the case of Volvo Truck (Lambin and Hiller, 1990). Trucks are designed upfront for the world market and are identical with few minor adaptations. But a key success factor in any market remains the role played by the local dealer who is in charge of after-sales service and of the warranty. A highly centralised organisation would not suite this market environment.

2.1.2. Benefits of marketing globalisation

The benefits generated by a globalisation strategy are well known, and several authors (Buzzell, 1968; Levitt, 1983; Boddewyn *et al.*, 1986; Quelch and Hoff, 1986; Jain, 1989, Lambin, 2001) have highlighted the potential advantages that marketing globalisation can bring (see Exhibit 2.1).

The most important benefit is certainly the possibility of generating important *economies of scale*. Having a scale superiority effect reduces costs and this is a key competitive advantage that all companies want to achieve. Economies of scale can be found in many areas of the business system; in R&D by concentrating research in a few geographic locations and on a limited number of product ranges; in manufacturing by concentrating production on a limited number of plants in a few countries worldwide; in logistics by the development of standardised products to be marketed all over the world; in selling and distribution by standardising operational marketing and in particular packaging and communication. Most international companies have already restructured their operations to benefit from these economies of scale.

The second major benefit is the *speed to market*. Globalised firms are much more centralised. This enables them to centrally plan and organise new product introductions worldwide within less than 1 year. This is not possible with a multi-domestic international organisation, where every local subsidiary has a decision power in product or branding policies. The centralisation of all R&D efforts on a limited number of innovations also has an impact on quality and costs.

A third key benefit is the advantage of creating a *unique worldwide brand name* and a brand identity for the global company. This leads to substantial savings in communication by targeting the same segments of customers worldwide with the same product concept. This is particularly important for luxury and fashion goods, for global food products but also for hi-tech products (computers, phones Hi-fi, etc.) targeting transnational segments of customers.

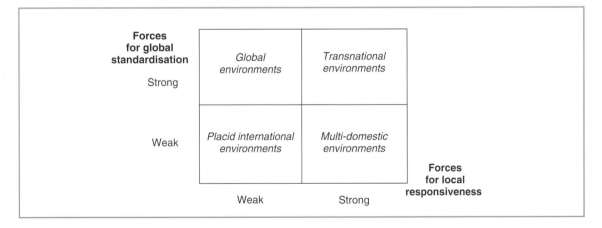

Figure 2.1   Typology of international environments
Source: Adapted from Goshal and Nohria (1993).

EXHIBIT 2.1

MCDONALD: A SUCCESSFUL GLOBALISATION?

The folks at McDonald's like to tell the story about the young Japanese girl who arrived in Los Angeles, looked around and said to her mother: 'look, Mom, they have McDonald's here too'. You could excuse her for being surprised that this was an American company. With 2,000 restaurants in Japan, McDonald's Japan is the biggest McDonald's franchise outside the United States. 'You don't have 2,000 stores in Japan by being seen as an American company', said James Cantalupo, head of McDonald's International.

The way McDonald has packaged itself is to be a 'multi-local' company. By insisting on a high degree of local owner-ship, and by tailoring its products just enough for local cultures, it has avoided the worst cultural backlashes that some other US companies have encountered. Not only do the localities now feel a stake in McDonald's success but also, more important, do the countries. Poland, for instance, has emerged as one of the largest regional suppliers of meat, potatoes and bread for McDonald's in Central Europe. That is real power. McDonald is gradually moving from local sourcing of its raw materials to regional sourcing and to global sourcing. One day soon, all McDonald's meat in Asia would come from Australia, and all its potatoes would come from China. Already, every sesame seed on every McDonald's bun in the world comes from Mexico. That is as good as a country discovering oil.

Source: Friedman (1996).

2.1.3. Drawbacks of marketing globalisation

It is clear that the benefits of standardisation are mostly supply-driven and not market-driven. Several drawbacks also exist and cannot be underestimated.

The first possible drawback is the negative effect of centralisation. Centralisation can accelerate the speed of major product launches on a worldwide basis but it can also *slow down other marketing decisions*. Too slow reactions to local competitor's actions or to specific local consumer problems can be dangerous. The reason is that too many layers often exist in a centralised organisation between the local brand managers and the marketing directors based in the company headquarters.

The second potential drawback is the insensitivity to local market conditions and a resulting *lower responsiveness*. Since most marketing initiatives and strategies are developed in the company headquarters, marketing managers have fewer contacts with local markets. They do not perceive well local consumer problems or insights. Their objective is to build on similarities among markets and not on what differentiate them. At the end, there is a loss of knowledge of local consumers.

The third potential drawback is the danger of developing products that are not in line with consumer needs. The objective of product standardisation is to develop products that meet the needs of a majority of people on a global basis. Products are therefore developed on the *lowest common denominator*. There is the risk that at the end, consumers are not satisfied with the standardised product.

A last pitfall that is not often underlined is related to *risk management*. A portfolio of brands constituted of a majority of global brands is *more vulnerable*. As the world becomes more linked and interconnected by global media such as CNN and the Internet, a problem arising in a local country on a global brand is rapidly made public and can be communicated to the whole world within a few hours or even minutes. It is therefore much more financially risky for the bottom line of the firm. If we take the example of a large multinational firm in the food or the pharmaceutical industries, a quality problem arising on one of its global brands might have a devastating impact on the results of the total company (see Exhibits 2.2 and 2.3).

2.1.4. Traditional industry globalisation drivers

A global strategy is mainly supply-driven and developed at the expense of a more market- or customer-driven strategy in order to achieve the benefits of globalisation described above. Management has to recognise when industry conditions are favourable: as suggested by Yip (1989), four industrialisation drivers should be analysed. They are summarised in Table 2.1.

2.1.5. Emerging market globalisation drivers

In the last two or three years, several signals suggest that globalisation has reached a critical turning point. A first signal is given by several global firms, among the most prestigious, having realised that going too far on the globalisation track was detrimental to their success. Companies such as Coca-Cola and Procter and Gamble (see Exhibits 2.2 and 2.3), for example, have dramatically

---

EXHIBIT 2.2

A GLOBAL MARKETPLACE MEANS GLOBAL VULNERABILITY

Coca-Cola Co., one of the world's most powerful corporations, discovered last week (14–19 June 1999), what it feels like to be on the losing end of globalisation. The soft-drink giant was rocked by a health scare in Europe that spread faster than a computer virus. Regulators in Belgium, France, Luxembourg and the Netherlands pulled the company's soft drinks from shelves after reports of contaminated Coke. And Coca-Cola spokesmen, after curtly insisting there wasn't any danger, began scrambling to offer assurance and apologies.

The Coca-Cola flap shows that just as capital and technology move instantaneously in the global economy, so does bad news. Consumer problems that start in Belgium can race around the globe tarnishing the world's most powerful brand name and even affecting its stock price on Wall Street. For America's hard-charging corporate executives, this is the flip side of globalisation. For even as the technology revolution is empowering corporations, it is also giving new leverage to regulators and consumer groups. There are no such things as a 'local problem' anymore, as the Coca-Cola experience shows. 'Global brand name recognition has an Achilles heel of vulnerability', says the consumer advocate Ralph Nader. [...]. The vents last week show that the value of Coca-Cola's brand, built up over more than a century, can be shaken as suddenly and capriciously as the Thai baht or the Indonesian ringgit.

Source: International Herald Tribune, 22 June 1999.

---

changed their international strategy in the last two years. A second signal comes directly from the market. Socio-economic and cultural changes are modifying the balance of power between international firms and their customer base. These two evolutionary changes will have a fundamental impact on the level of globalisation that companies will adopt in the future. The main changes coming from the market are linked to social and political factors. They are summarised in Table 2.2.

A first change is the anti-globalisation movement and the popular success of the *alter-globalisation* movement. Consumers are looking today for more diversity in their brand choices. Also, they are less attracted by low prices but are rather looking for better value for money. They are not satisfied anymore with a limited number of global brands present in every store they visit and in different countries when they travel. Consumers are not necessarily attracted by the same global names in every product category. As a consequence, a multiplicity of supranational segments have emerged reflecting this diversity of needs and behaviours.

A growing number of consumers feel that they have lost their identity in the current globalised world and develop *nostalgia* vis-à-vis traditional brand names in several markets. People are happy to find traditional brand names that they are familiar with since so many years. Old brand names are even re-launched to capitalise on this trend. Interestingly, in Eastern European countries, there is also a return to old brand names. The US brands do not necessarily attract consumers as strongly as before.

In Hungary, for example, consumers are attracted by names from the old Soviet time. They prefer 'Tizsa' shoes instead of Nike and they drink 'Traubisoda' drink instead of Coca-Cola.

A recent study (Schuiling and Kapferer, 2004) has indicated that local brands generate more trust than their global counterparts.

Negative reactions against the economic and political power of the United States and against the power of global brands (mostly American) are voiced, as illustrated by the successful plea of Naomi Klein (1999) in her book *No-Logo*.

2.2. The new complexity of the global market

As already underlined, markets become more interdependent and complex to manage, not only because today's customer is more connected, informed and discerning than ever in the past, but also because of the growing power of new market actors – indirect customers, partners, online market places – who are joining the market. The development of Internet technologies in the global economy is shaping two types of markets: Global Traditional Markets (GTM) and Global Electronic Markets (GEM) (Guo and Sun, 2004). The market forces of GEM come from the demand and supply of global services generated by global market participants in both traditional markets and electronic markets. In this dual-trading context, market players have different roles and motivation that we review in the following subsections.

EXHIBIT 2.3

THE VIOXX CASE

An example of global brand vulnerability is given by the Vioxx case in the pharmaceutical industry. In September 2004, the company Merck announced that they would immediately withdraw from the world market their 'block buster' Vioxx brand. They have discovered that the brand – launched in 1999 – was causing cardiovascular problems. The brand is estimated to have caused 150,000 heart attacks and 27,785 deaths since its launch. This is a major scandal from the patients' point of view. It also represents, not only a financial loss of an estimated $50 billion value for the stockholders, but a substantial damage to the firm's corporate image as a result of the extensive media coverage.

Table 2.1   Industry globalisation drivers

To achieve the benefits of globalisation, managers have to recognise when industry conditions are favourable. Four industry globalisation drivers should be analysed: market, costs, governmental and competitive drivers.

1. Market drivers
   - Homogeneous customer needs: customers in different countries want essentially the same type of product or service.
   - Global customers: global customers buy on a centralised or co-ordinated basis for decentralised use.
   - Global channels of distribution: channels of distribution may buy on a global or at least on a regional basis.
   - Transferable operational marketing: operational marketing elements, such as brand names and advertising, require little local adaptation.

2. Cost drivers
   - Economies of scale and scope: a single country market may not be large enough for the local business to achieve all economies of scale or scope.
   - Learning and experience: expanded market participation and activity concentration can accelerate the accumulation of learning and experience.
   - Sourcing efficiencies: centralised purchasing of new materials can significantly contribute to lower costs.
   - Favourable logistics: a favourable ratio of sales value to transportation cost enhances the company's ability to concentrate production.
   - Differences in country costs and skills: factor costs generally vary across countries as well as the availability of particular skills.
   - Product development costs: developing few global or regional products rather than several national products can reduce these costs (see Exhibit 2.4).

3. Governmental drivers
   - Favourable trade policies: import tariffs and quotas, non tariff barriers, export subsidies, local content requirements, currency and capital flow restrictions, and requirements on technology transfer directly affect the globalisation potential.
   - Compatible technical standards: differences in technical standards limit the extent to which products can be standardised.
   - Common operational marketing regulations: the marketing and advertising environment of individual countries affect the extent to which uniform global operational marketing approaches can be used.

4. Competitive drivers
   - Interdependence of countries: when activities such as production are shared among countries, a competitor's market share in one country affects its scale and overall cost position in the shared activity.
   - Globalised competitors: matching or pre-empting individual competitor moves may be necessary.

Source: Yip (1989).

2.2.1. The market as a customer ecosystem

In nature, an ecosystem is a complex grouping of mutually dependent living elements (flora, fauna, insects and micro-organisms) and still elements (soil, water, and climate) that continuously interact and benefit from one other, within a well-defined spatial territory (Krebs, 1988).

In a market economy, an ecosystem is a complex grouping of companies and customers, suppliers, competitors, distributors, prescribers and partners that gain mutual benefit from one another (Manning and Thorne, 2003). In a *customer ecosystem*, market activities – such as investment, joint product development, market communications, logistics and transactions – are undertaken and controlled by the customer rather than by the supplier. The different participants are functionally connected through flows of information, influence and economic impact to create demand (directly and indirectly)

EXHIBIT 2.4

EVEN LITTLE COMPANIES ARE NOW GOING GLOBAL

Philip Chigos and Mary Domenico are busy building a children's pyjama business. They are refining patterns, picking fabrics and turning the basement of their two-bedroom apartment into office. Then there is a critical step of finding the seamstresses in China: [.] A growing number of tiny mom-and-pop operations, industry experts say, are turning to places like Sri Lanka, China, Mexico and Eastern Europe to make clothes, jewellery, trinkets and even software programs [...] The ability of Chigos, 26, and Domenico, 25, to reach across borders has as much to do with technology as it does with globalisation. Computers, the Internet and modern telecommunications,

of course, make it possible for start-ups to market their goods to customers anywhere.

That infrastructure also enables even the smallest employers to find workers far away in countries they will never visit and in factories they will never inspect. They can communicate with those workers cheaply via e-mail messages and telephone, transmit images and design specifications and track inventory. Off shoring for small entrepreneurs can be rough, however.

Source: Ritchell (2005).

Table 2.2   The emerging globalisation market drivers

Traditional market drivers	Emerging market drivers
Isolated individual consumers	Powerful consumerist movements
Passive and docile consumers	Educated and smart shoppers
Interest for low price	Search for more value for money
Homogeneous customer needs	Multiplicity of supranational segments
Attractiveness of global culture	Search for local identity
Prestige of global brands	Nostalgia for local brands
Undisputed power of global brands	Development of private labels
Politically uncommitted consumption	'Politically correct' consumption
Low sensitivity for ethical issues	Growing sensitivity to ethical issues
Low interest for product greenness	Eco-conscious consumers
No concern for product origin	International traceability

Source: Schuiling and Lambin (2003).

---

for products and services. They create a complex network of co-operation and competition. A customer ecosystem exists within a well-defined macro-marketing environment and can be completely modified by the emergence of a disruptive technological innovation like, for example, the digital technology revolution in photography.

Driven by cut-throat competition, digital photography is transforming the global photography industry with new ways of capturing, storing and developing pictures and with new competitors coming from the electronics and entertainment market (like Sony) and from the computer industry (like Hewlett-Packard).

As illustrated in Figure 2.2, in the general case (highly simplified here), several market players participate in the customer ecosystem being part of an industrial supply chain regrouping all the stages of production, from raw material acquisition to transformation, incorporation, assembling and distribution to the end-customer. These activities are performed in the two global markets: GTM

and GEM. There is a hierarchy of companies, which are either clients or suppliers of a given firm according to whether they are upstream or downstream.

2.2.2. The market actors in the customer ecosystem

Thus, in the general case, we define the market by reference to five market actors: customers, partners, distributors, competitors, prescribers and other market stakeholders. To these traditional market participants, new actors coming from GEM are playing an increasingly important role.

Direct and end-customers

Customer satisfaction is at the core of the traditional marketing concept. It implies the commitment to understand customer needs, to create value for the

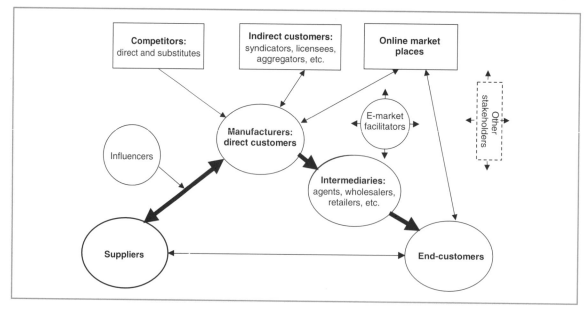

Figure 2.2   The key market actors in the global market
Source: Authors.

customer and to anticipate new customers' problems. Customers may be close to, or remote from, the firm depending on the type of organisation: B2C or B2B markets. B2B firms generally operate within an industrial chain and are confronted with several customers: its direct customer and the customers of its customer, the end-customer being situated at the end of the chain. Being customer-oriented involves taking actions based on market intelligence, not only on direct customers, but on end-customers as well. Increasingly B2C and B2B customers have access to the GEM and are ordering across country borders. They expect broader selections, cheaper prices and customised services.

Partners and indirect demand

Direct and end-customers belong to the traditional or core market of the firm and express a 'direct demand' for the goods or services and the firm knows who these customers are and how to satisfy them. In many sectors, however, there are additional customer groups representing a potential demand often ignored because firms are not able to reach these customers directly. This 'indirect demand' exists because the value of certain products is realised when they are used with other products.

At first sight there is no reason why Nestlé a manufacturer of chocolate confections should have any dealing with Baxter international; a medical device conglomerate and distribution company. In fact, the two companies have formed an alliance for jointly offering

liquid nutritional supplements to be used intravenously with hospital patients who therefore are indirect customers of Nestlé.

To become fully demand-driven by satisfying indirect demand as well, many companies have adopted a 'solution-selling' approach. For the company aiming at becoming a solution provider, it is unlikely that it will have the resources to supply all the required solutions components (e.g. products, service, financing). Therefore, the challenge is to find the right partners to take advantage of indirect demand. To target direct demand, wholesalers and retailers are the traditional business partners. For targeting indirect demand, many more functions than simply location and assortment must be provided. The types of partners found in various customer ecosystems are integrators, syndicators, aggregators, educators and underwriters (see Box 2.1; Manning and Thorne, 2003).

Distributors and resellers in GTM

The struggle for the control of the end-market has always been a major issue both for manufacturers and distributors. In the food sector, for many years, manufacturers have succeeded in restricting the role of distributors to the physical tasks of distribution. Their relationship was more of partners having common interests, even if conflicting interests were inevitably also present. The retailer looks for maximum return on space and contribution to overall retailer image. The supplier seeks maximum shelf space, trial for new (unproved) products and preference over

BOX 2.1

IMPLEMENTATION PROBLEM: WHO ARE THE POTENTIAL PARTNERS TO TARGET INDIRECT DEMAND?

1. *Integrators.* Integrators incorporate your product or service within another service or product, thereby improving the value of the product.

2. *Syndicators.* Syndicators package, bundle and resell your product or service and thus distribute it to a broader market.

3. *Aggregators.* Aggregators provide a broad access to indirect demand by collecting different products or services that together give value because of their proximity with one another.

4. *Corporate licensing.* Renting a corporate trademark or logo made famous in one category and using it in a related or unrelated product category.

5. *Underwriters.* They provide credit and facilitate demand development from a financial perspective through deferred payments or credit cards.

6. *Educators.* They provide a curriculum for the public and for other partners to learn about a product, service or category. With increasing complexity of products and services, technical education helps to support demand.

Source: Adapted from Manning and Thorne (2003).

Concentration rate among distributors	Concentration rate among manufacturers	
	Low	High
High	Distributors' domination (1)	Mutual interdependence (2)
Low	Relative independence (3)	Manufacturers' domination (4)

Table 2.3   Market structure and manufacturers–distributors relationships

Source: Authors.

competitors. It is easy to see where the potential for conflicts lie.

The shift of power from suppliers to mass retailers in the fast moving consumer goods (FMCG) sector requires the adoption of a much more proactive strategy vis-à-vis distributors. Today, as emphasised above, key changes in the environment include increasing retailer concentration, the growth of internationally based retail buying groups and the growing use of information technology by European food retailers. Although suppliers would like to see retailers as partners, it is clear that retailers tend to see their relationships with manufacturers more in terms of competition than co-operation.

As shown in Table 2.3, the level of competition or co-operation is influenced by the market structure that determines the power of prospective partners in a market. With the exception of the situation where both levels of concentration are weak (see cell 3), manufacturers have to explicitly define appropriate relationship of marketing strategy vis-à-vis distributors.

In the food sector, the level of concentration of mass retailers is very high in several countries of Western Europe and the situation is clearly that described in cell 1 (see Table 2.3). Thus, in the current market situation many brand manufacturers tend to become more retailer-driven

to avoid the risk of being delisted and design retailer-driven marketing programmes by raising questions like: how can we reduce the costs of our distributors? Can we eliminate their inventory costs, improve their cash flow, and support their store positioning strategy? and so on.

Thus, being distributor-driven is simply the application of the market orientation concept to distributors, who are no longer viewed as partners but as customers in their own right. In order to manage this relationship with retailers, manufacturers will have to develop an in-depth understanding of their generic needs (see Box 2.2), their desired store image and the perceived importance of a particular product category for the chain store's positioning.

Online market facilitators

Market facilitators are a special group of service providers in both GTM and GEM. They are motivated to provide infrastructure of markets and secure the operations of markets. In GTM, banks, warehouse, shipping companies, customs and taxation offices are market facilitators. In GEM, providers of Internet services, online financial services, logistics, security and legal services are the new market facilitators.

BOX 2.2

IMPLEMENTATION PROBLEM: HOW TO DESIGN A DISTRIBUTOR-DRIVEN STRATEGY?

The strategy should meet the generic needs of distributors, which are the following:

- Freedom to price their merchandise in line with their own goal and interests.
- Freedom from pressure to implement supplier-designed promotions.
- Adequate trade margins when selling at the manufacturer's suggested price trade to cover costs operation and to generate a profit.
- Protection from undue competition, like selling to too many other resellers; selling the merchandise to off-price resellers; engaging itself in direct selling to end-users.

- Support from manufacturers in training, advertising, promotion, merchandising and information on new developments on the market.
- Support given to the store positioning strategy of the distributor by providing an appropriate assortment of products.
- Efficient order fulfilment to minimise inventory-carrying costs and to avoid stock outs through joint management of inventory flows.

Source: Sheth *et al.* (1999, pp. 663–8).

Where dis-intermediation takes place, the absence of physical contact between the seller and the buyer creates a new need among consumers, the need for assistance in collecting and processing information. In traditional markets, and in particular in B2C markets, the seller has more information than the buyer: information on costs, levels of quality, product availability and prices of competing or substitute products. Different levels of middlemen (wholesalers, retailers, agents) were there to disseminate this information along the distribution chain. The elimination of these filters transfer the responsibility of the search and of the selection costs directly to the consumer who is confronted with a problem of information overload. For an analysis of the motives for e-marketplace participation, see Rask and Kragh (2004).

In markets driven by EC, a new breed of intermediaries – the *infomediaries* – is emerging and assumes the management of information on behalf of the customer. Websites regrouping buyers and organising auctions are a case in point. As a result, market transparency increases and the negotiation advantage switches to the buyer (see Exhibit 2.5). In contrast with traditional intermediaries who typically relay the manufacturer's message and share its profit margin, these new networks of middlemen reverse the communication flow through systematic use of tenders.

The success factor for the *infomediary* is customer trust. This new type of middleman can solve four problems for the consumer: (a) to reduce the costs of collecting information, (b) to provide relevant and unbiased information, (c) to certify the reliability and quality of the suppliers and (d) to facilitate transactions.

Direct and substitute competitors

The traditional marketing concept focuses solely on customer's needs and ignores the effects of competition thereby providing an incomplete view of a market. Competitors, be they direct and/or substitute competitors, are key market participants and the attitude to be adopted towards competition is central in any strategy formulation, since it will serve as the basis for defining competitive advantage. As noted by Trout (1985):

> Knowing what the customer wants isn't too helpful if a dozen other companies are already serving the customer's wants.

The objective is to set out a strategy based on a realistic assessment of the forces at work and to determine the most appropriate means of achieving defined objectives. Competitors' orientation includes all the activities involved in acquiring and disseminating information about competitors in the target market.

The firm's autonomy is influenced by two kinds of factors: the sector's competitive structure and the importance of the product's perceived value for customers. Table 2.4 presents these two factors, each at two levels of intensity. With the exception of the situation of perfect competition depicted in cell (4), an explicit account of competitors' position and behaviour is required in the most frequently observed common market situations.

In saturated or stagnant markets, the aggressiveness of the competitive struggle tends to increase and a key objective is to counter rivals' actions. In this competitive climate, the destruction of the adversary often becomes the primary preoccupation. The risk of a strategy based only on warfare marketing, however, is that too much energy is devoted to driving rivals away at the risk of losing sight of the objective of satisfying buyers' needs. A proper balance between customers' and competitors' orientations is therefore essential and a market orientation, as described in this chapter, tends to facilitate the implementation of this objective.

EXHIBIT 2.5

NETCHISING: THE NEXT GLOBAL WAVE

Companies have long taken 'going global' to mean having a physical presence at locations everywhere. It has meant executives in transit and bricks-and-mortars facilities on the ground. Today an increasing number of companies are succeeding overseas without massive foreign investments by adopting the global business model called 'netchising' (Morrison *et al.*, 2004). This new business model relies on the Internet for procurement, sales and maintaining customer relationships, and non-equity partnership arrangements to provide direct customer interfaces and local adaptation and delivery of products and services. Netchising offers potentially huge benefits over traditional exporting or foreign direct investment approaches to globalisation.

Source: Adapted from Morrison *et al.* (2004).

Table 2.4 Competitive environments and autonomy in strategy formulation

Market power: perceived value of the product	Number of competitors	
	Low	High
High	Monopoly or differentiated oligopoly (1)	Monopolistic competition (2)
Low	Undifferentiated oligopoly (3)	Perfect competition (4)

Source: Authors.

Online marketplaces

A growing number of firms are experimenting with buying and selling goods through e-marketplaces, which become increasingly important in B2B markets to the organisation for procurement and sales activities. An e-marketplace may be defined as an inter-organisational information system which allows the participating buyers and suppliers to exchange information about prices and product offerings, thereby eliminating inefficiencies of traditional supply chain.

> A dirty little secret of B2B supply chain is that they are rife with inefficiencies. Engineers or purchasing agents can take days, sometimes weeks to find the right product and they often must settle for second best because of the time or cost of searching. Orders are often entered manually and with frequent re-keying, order-entry errors rates of 15%, 20% or even 25% are common. Poor manufacturer forecasts result in long lead times, partial shipment or costly returned purchases. (R.L. Segal, 2000)

Frustrated by these inefficiencies, e-entrepreneurs have launched marketplaces like www.Netbuy.com with a virtual inventory four times larger than the biggest distributor in the electronic components market. The result? Product searches that took a week of catalogue sifting and phone calls now take seconds. Companies such as Paper Exchange, Chemdex, Plastic Net, alibaba.com among many others, are doing the same thing.

Prescribers and influencers

In many markets, in addition to the traditional market actors – customers, distributors and competitors – other individuals or organisations can play important roles in advising, recommending or prescribing brands, companies, products or services to customers or to distributors. The most obvious example is the pharmaceutical market where doctors exert a key influence on the success of a drug and are viewed by pharmaceutical companies as the most important market player or intermediate customer, even if they are not actually users, buyers or payers.

> A similar role is assumed in the home building market by architects, who are important influencers for many construction pieces of equipment, such as window frames, glass, heating systems, and so on. Independent designers in the furniture market or in the 'haute couture' or fashion markets are also playing an important role as influencers.

In B2B markets, engineering companies, experts or consulting firms that recommend certain equipment and publish shortlists of products meeting the required specifications, often take the role of prescribers. To be considered by potential buyers, you have to be on the 'shortlist'. This is the current practice in official public tenders.

A prescriber orientation implies that the firm identifies the key influencers or opinion leaders, assesses the nature of their role and needs in the purchase decision process and develops a specific communication programme to inform them, to motivate them and to obtain their support.

Other stakeholders

In a social market economy, many other actors can have a powerful influence in the market. Who are these other stakeholders? A popular definition is that 'stakeholders' are any group or individual who can affect or are affected by the firm's objectives. Thus, in addition to the above key market players, other stakeholders could be employees, unions, non-governmental organisations (NGOs), local community, consumerists and, last but not least, the environment. The role of these other stakeholders will be reviewed in the last chapter of this book (see Chapter 17) devoted to the future of market-driven management.

2.2.3. Degrees of market orientation

In the general case, that is when the four key market participants are active, the firm must be fully market-oriented and should integrate the four orientations in its business practice.

Thus, in the general case, the firm must be fully market-oriented and should integrate the four orientations in its business practice. In several markets, less complex

market configurations can exist, however. As shown in Table 2.5, in some markets, manufacturers are dealing directly with end-customers bypassing distributors or are creating their own exclusive distribution network. Also, prescribers are not always significant market players. Still in other markets – such as public services – there is no competition, a situation that becomes exceptional.

2.2.4. A new managerial model: the customer solution approach

As the market-driven business philosophy is gaining acceptance in industry, many product companies have tried to partner with their customers and other market players to become a *solution provider* by selling solutions, that is, 'a unique combination of products and services components' – rather than mere products – that could solve a customer's problem. On the solution-to-a-problem approach, see: Roegner *et al.* (2001), Foote *et al.* (2001), Sheridan and Bullinger (2001) and Johansson *et al.* (2003).

The decision to sell solutions is usually based on two objectives: to obtain higher profit margins than sales of products and to generate longer customer contracts. Solutions are proving lucrative for many companies, even as the profitability and growth of their products have come under pressure. In the case of IBM, $38 billion of its revenue – 43 per cent of the total – now comes from the solution-related businesses it has developed since the early 1990s (Foote *et al.*, 2001, p. 84).

Before adopting the solution approach, firms must have a good understanding of what a solution is and how it differs from products or bundles of products and services as illustrated in Figure 2.3. In the broadest sense, a solution is a combination of products and services that *create value beyond the sum of its parts*.

Table 2.5   The different degrees of market orientation

Company examples	Degree of market orientation				
	Customers (K)	Competitors (C)	Distributors (D)	Prescribers (P)	Other stakeholders (S)
Pfizer/SKG/etc.	Yes	Yes	Yes	Yes	Yes
P&G/Unilever/etc.	Yes	Yes	Yes	—	Yes
Ryan Air/ Dell/etc.	Yes	Yes	—	—	Yes
Recticel/Intel/etc.	Yes	Yes	—	Yes	Yes
BR/ Eurostar /etc.	Yes	—	Yes	—	Yes
RATP / EDF / GDF	Yes	—	—	—	Yes

Source: Authors.

Many companies are failing for one of the three following reasons.

1. Some companies believe that they are selling solutions by merely bundling products and/or services that create little value when offered together and then have difficulty of obtaining a premium price.
2. Second they underestimate the difficulty of selling solutions which costs more to develop, have longer sales cycle and demand a deep understanding of the customer problems.
3. Third, many companies sell solutions (intangible services) much as they sell products and do not adopt a relationship selling strategy instead of the traditional transactional selling.

Thus, a solution is not simply the bundling together of related components. It is the level of customisation and of integration that sets solutions above products or services or bundles of products and services and that justifies a price premium (see Box 2.3).

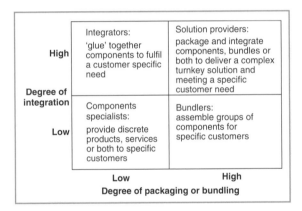

Figure 2.3   Solutions providers versus integrators and bundlers

Source: Roegner *et al.* (2001).

Take the fast food example. Customers can buy a hamburger, fries and a soft drink separately, or they can get a 'meal deal' that groups all three together. In both cases, the solution 'assuage the hunger' is achieved. But the extra value they get from the deal is a discount the restaurant grants. The meal deal is simply a bundling achieving commercial integration but not the customisation needed to justify a premium price. On the contrary, the restaurant must provide a discount.

What makes a solution valuable and distinctive is that it focuses on results by applying some level of expertise and at times a proprietary method that justifies a premium price. In contrast, look at the following case of paint manufacturer (Johansson *et al.*, 2003).

A manufacturer that had long supplied paints to carmakers used its knowledge of them and of its industry, as well as proprietary knowledge, to become a solutions provider. Recognising that customers would place a higher value on a delivered service – painted cars – than on paint alone, it offered to take over their paint shop operations and very quickly helped a carmaker use 20 per cent less paint per automobile. This distinctive offering enabled the paint manufacturer to become the leading provider of paint solutions to automakers around the world, with 70 per cent of the market. In so doing, the company created value for its customers and changed its value metric from the product-oriented dollars per gallon of paint to the customer-oriented dollars per painted car.

2.3. Market orientation and business performance

As stated above, the market orientation theory suggests that there is a relationship between market orientation (MO)

BOX 2.3

IMPLEMENTATION PROBLEM: HOW TO BECOME A SUCCESSFUL SOLUTION PROVIDER?

Five success factors can be identified.

■ Solution design must reflect a *deep understanding of customers' needs* and of the pattern of their business issues. The firm must move closer to its customers.
■ The firm must augment its internal capabilities by *finding partners* who can help provide a complete solution by providing all the required components.
■ Effective solutions demand the company's best thinking and the establishing of a *cross-functional solution team* comprising people from multiple product units and having the authority to define the value proposition.

■ The sales approach is *relationship selling* and should reflect the differences between selling products and selling solutions where the solution provider is a business partner that helps customer at every stage.
■ The firm must create a *solution-based organisation* that requires a new more flexible set of competencies, because the sales process is less predictable than the sales of a product.

Source: Sheridan and Bullinger (2001).

intensity and economic performance (EP). Thus, the hypothesis is: 'A firm that becomes more market-oriented will, in the long term, improve its economic and competitive performance'. Several theoretical and empirical observations support this proposition:

1. Satisfied customers in general are more exclusive and loyal (Lash, 1990; Anderson and Sullivan, 1993; Reichheld, 1996; Goderis, 1998), more receptive to the supplier firm's innovations (Cooper, 1993); more willing to communicate their satisfaction through informal word of mouth communication (Swan and Oliver, 1989); less price sensitive and more susceptible to accept a price higher than the one charged by direct competitors (Chamberlin, 1933/1962; Nagle and Holden, 1994; Homburg et al., 2005).
2. Companies having developed a competitors' monitoring system are better aware of the strengths and weaknesses of their competitors and of their action and reaction capabilities and therefore better positioned to gain a sustainable competitive advantage (Alderson, 1957; Porter, 1980; Schnaars, 1998).
3. Companies having established a partnership with their distributors (Narus and Anderson, 1986; Buzzell and Ortmeyer, 1995) are able to substantially reduce transaction costs and improve the co-operation of their distributors.
4. Similarly, companies working closely with influencers and experts are well placed to develop innovative product concepts that are better adapted to customers needs and to receive in addition the support (certification, signature, recommendation) from influential key institutions or reference groups (Bearden and Etzel, 1982).

These conditions, when met, directly or indirectly, contribute to the firm's long-term business performance. Various indicators of business performance can be used: returns on capital, sales or market share growth, success

rate of new products, Tobin index, and so on (see Exhibit 2.6). For a comprehensive review of the literature on this subject, see Gotteland (2005). See in particular: Narver and Slater (1990); Kohli and Jaworski (1990); Lambin and Chumpitaz (2000); Narver et al. (2004); Kirca et al. (2005).

2.3.1. Complexity of the MO–performance relationship

The relationship between the firm's market orientation (MO) and its economic performance (EP) is not simple. To measure this relationship, two other variables or groups of variables have to be identified: the moderating effect of the macro-marketing environment and the mediating effect of the firm's internal organisation (Kohli and Jaworski, 1990).

2.3.2. The moderating effect of the macro-marketing environment

Within any reference market, macro-environmental trends – demographic, economic, political/legal, technology and socio-cultural – bear on the market's future development (see Exhibit 2.7). These external factors can provide productive opportunities or severe limitations for the company's products. The market-oriented firm must develop an environment monitoring system to help it to anticipate these changes or to facilitate and accelerate the adoption of corrective actions (see Box 2.4).

It is fashionable to downplay the usefulness of planning systems. Experiences with such largely unforeseen upheavals such as the stock market crash of 2001, the rise of the euro and the fall of the US dollar, the 9/11 terrorists attack, the Ukrainian soft revolution, and so on have

---

EXHIBIT 2.6

CUSTOMER SATISFACTION AND SHAREHOLDER VALUE

Employing the American Customer Satisfaction Index (ACSI) database of nearly 200 publicly traded *Fortune 500* firms from 1994 to 1997, Anderson, Fornell and Mazvancheryl (2004) observed a positive association between customer satisfaction and shareholder value as measured by the Tobin q index, a capital market based measure of the value of the firm. Given the overall estimate of the association between ACSI and Tobin's q of 1.62, a 1% change in customer satisfaction (as measured by the ACSI) is associated with an expected 1.0162% change in shareholder value (as measured by *Tobin's q*). The average level of Tobin's q for the overall set of data

($n = 456$) is 1.73, which translates into an increase in q of approximately 0.027 for a 1% increase in satisfaction. For a *Business Week* 1,000 firms with average assets of approximately $10 billion, a 1% improvement in satisfaction implies an increase in the firm's value of approximately $275 million. This effect would be much greater for larger firms and for firms with a stronger association between satisfaction and shareholder value.

Source: Anderson et al. (2004).

EXHIBIT 2.7

COMPONENTS OF THE MACRO-MARKETING ENVIRONMENT

Socio-cultural

Population, demography, income distribution, social mobility, changes in life styles, attitude vis-à-vis labour and leisure, consumerism, education level, social organisation, inguistic development.

Technology

Government support for R&D, specialisation of industrial research efforts, innovation intensity, speed of technology transfer, rate of obsolescence.

Economy

Business fluctuations, GDP growth, interest rates, monetary, inflation, unemployment, disposable income, savings, energy cost and availability, economic integration, deregulations.

Ecology

Ecology movement, green marketing development, life cycle inventory, strength of the political support, eco-taxes and eco-fees, waste management.

Political/legal

Anti-trust legislation, environmental protection laws, fiscal legislation, foreign trade regulations, employment support, economic and trading blocs, deregulation and privatisation laws, government stability, etc.

Source: Authors.

---

revealed the shortcomings and the limitations of planning systems which are too rigid. Just because a strategy must be developed and implemented under turbulent and uncertain conditions is not a sufficient reason for abandoning the discipline of structured planning. Planning is necessary for the functioning of the firm. What is important in a turbulent environment, however, is to keep enough flexibility in the system and to systematically explore worst or extreme cases through the scenario method, risk and contingency planning and crisis recovery plans. Thus, the macro-marketing environment is typically a moderating variable.

2.3.3. The mediating effect of interfunctional co-ordination

The key idea here is to consider that market orientation is the business of everyone and not just of marketing people. Masiello (1988) gives four reasons why many companies are not spontaneously market-oriented:

1. Functional areas do not understand the concept of being market-driven.
2. Most employees do not know how to translate their classical functional responsibilities into market/customer responsive actions.
3. Most functions do not understand the role of other functions.
4. Employees in each functional area do not give meaningful input to the market orientation of the company (Masiello, 1988).

In addition to these organisational problems, Webster (1997) suggests two other factors. *First*, managers in other functions

have other constituencies than customers (shareholders, suppliers, personnel, scientists) that must be served and satisfied and the trade-offs between these potentially conflicting interests must be co-ordinated and managed. *Second*, managers in other functions may honestly believe that they are putting the customer's interest first when they look at things from their own internal company perspective and it is easy for them to refuse to be guided by the information provided by the marketing department alone.

Thus, dissemination of market information, formally and informally, interfunctionally prepared decisions, co-ordination of activities and regular contacts with customers are the key remedies to use in order to instil a sense of market orientation regardless of functional boundaries. The indicators used to measure the extent of interfunctional co-ordination are presented in the "Market Orientation Measurement Questionnaire" available in the Web site companion of this book.

Interfunctional co-ordination is viewed here as an organisational factor, which will facilitate the involvement of all levels in the firm's organisation and will create the market orientation culture. Interfunctional co-ordination allows for communication and exchange between the different departments that are dealing or confronted with some or all of the four market stakeholders. Without interfunctional co-ordination, the market orientation process could be dominated by a single preoccupation (competitors or distributors) that would reduce the potential business performance. Thus, interfunctional co-ordination is viewed as a mediating variable, to the extent that it accounts for the relationship between market orientation and business performance.

BOX 2.4

IMPLEMENTATION PROBLEM: HOW TO MONITOR THE MACRO-MARKETING ENVIRONMENT?

- Development of a business intelligence system.
- Involvement of the firm in professional and/or political lobbies.
- Knowledge of the vulnerability factors for the business.

- Early warning indicators on the vulnerability factors.
- Crisis recovery plan to handle strategic surprises.
- Use of the scenario method and of contingency planning.

Table 2.6   Main responsibilities of brand managers: a survey

To co-ordinate all activities related to the product	To order marketing research studies
To prepare the marketing plan	To brief market research companies
To fix the sales price	To design and decide on packaging
To estimate the unit cost	To choose the advertising platform
To prepare the marketing budget	To monitor laws and regulations
To compare actual and expected sales	To train the sales force
To propose promotional actions	To prepare the contracts and agreements
To assist the sales force	

Source: Kueviakoe (1996, p. 81).

By way of conclusion of the last two sections, it appears that the market orientation concept covers a field, which is much broader than the traditional domain of marketing management, since it includes the organisational culture and the climate that most effectively encourages the behaviours that are necessary for the successful implementation of a market orientation.

2.4. Reinventing the marketing organisation

The analysis of today's markets reveals an explosion of customers segments, products, media vehicles and distribution channels that has made market-driven management more complex, more costly and less effective. With the growing fragmentation of markets, products and services options available have doubled or even tripled. As subbrands and line extensions multiply, so do the messages and the media required to sell them. The increasing number of distribution channels such as the Internet, product resellers, large retailers and online market places has become important players that sell to consumers and businesses alike. All these factors taken together have dramatically pushed up the complexity and the cost of designing and managing a marketing programme, just when boards and CEOs have been pushing their chief marketing officers (CMOs) to improve the return on marketing expenditures. To meet this new challenge, a new model of marketing management must be developed.

2.4.1. Traditional organisation of the marketing function

From an organisational viewpoint, the implementation of the traditional marketing concept has been achieved by the creation of powerful marketing departments (see Figure 1.10) in charge of both strategic and operational marketing. Brand and product management play a key role in these organisational structures. A brand manager is concerned with strategic issues such as R&D and product innovation, branding policies and communication, business analysis and forecasting. His or her task is also to organise a dialogue with the other functions within the firm and to co-ordinate and control all the operations or activities related to the brand. A separate sales department is responsible for the sales tasks and for getting products on to retailers' shelves. This system, adopted by most consumer goods companies and also by many industrial firms, contributed to establishing manufacturers' brand dominance in the market.

The brand management system

According to a survey conducted in France (Kueviakoe, 1996), the responsibilities of a typical brand or product manager would be the ones presented in Table 2.6, in their order of importance. Inspection of Table 2.6 suggests that most of these responsibilities pertain more to operational than to strategic marketing. In principle, the product manager is supposed to be responsible for the medium- to long-term development of the product, whereas sales people are responsible for the implementation of the marketing plan in the short term, under the leadership of the marketing manager. The product management organisation introduces several *advantages*:

1. The presence of a brand manager creates dynamism and emulation in the organisation by designating individuals in charge of the development of the different brands. He behaves more like an entrepreneur responsible for his own product development (a mini-president).
2. Smaller brands are less neglected, because they have a product advocate.
3. The product manager is well placed to harmonise and co-ordinate all the activities related to his own brand or product, thereby increasing efficiency.
4. The product manager can react more quickly to problems in the marketplace than a committee of functional specialists.
5. The product manager is a single point of contact for all the other functions and therefore internal communication is greatly facilitated.
6. By being responsible or by the preparation of the annual marketing plan, the product manager can concentrate on developing a cost-effective marketing mix for the product to ensure its profitability.
7. By being in charge of the medium- to long-term development of the product, the product manager can initiate product improvements in co-operation with R&D people to take advantage of new market opportunities.

However, a price has to be paid for these advantages. Among the *problems and difficulties* generated by a product management organisation (see Figure 2.4), let us consider the following points:

1. The product management system is based on the principle of decentralisation and delegation, and this implies a clear political accord between the managing director and the marketing manager.
2. The product manager has a staff position and as such does not necessarily have enough authority to carry out his responsibilities effectively. He or she has to rely on persuasion to get the co-operation of advertising, sales, manufacturing and other departments. The function is demanding and requires diplomatic skills.
3. The product management system is costly and implies a duplication of contacts between the sales force, the functional specialists and the product managers.
4. Product managers are generally junior people who normally manage their brand for only a short time. This short-term involvement induces them to give priority to short-term operational marketing activities, at the expense of longer-term strategic thinking.

In this structure, it is up to the marketing manager to deal with potential conflicts between the product managers, the sales force and other functional departments and to delineate clearly the limits of the product managers' role and responsibility. Brand managers report directly to the marketing manager who can, therefore, devote time and effort to strategic issues in close liaison with the managing director.

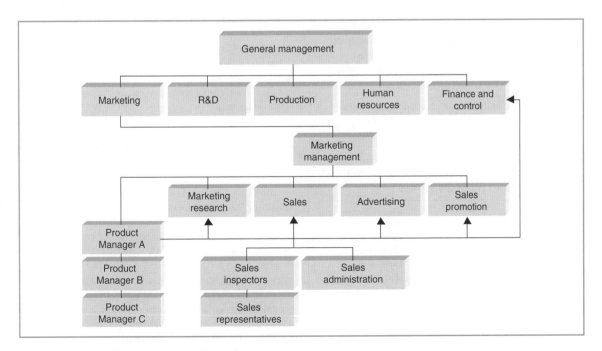

Figure 2.4   The traditional marketing department
Source: Authors.

Strategic marketing in small business firms

The product or brand management organisation is a costly structure, unaffordable by a small or medium-sized business firm. An alternative, which works well, is the cross-functional team in charge of strategic marketing issues. It is composed of the key functional managers (operations, finances, human resources, operational marketing) and is chaired by the firm's CEO. Two different structures can be considered:

- The *temporary ad hoc team* – or task force – in charge of a specific problem during a limited period of time, typically the launching of a new product.
- The *permanent cross-functional team* reviewing regularly (twice a month) strategic marketing problems, typically the management of the firm's product portfolio, a task which does not necessarily require a full-time job.

One of the benefits of this organisation structure, in addition to its low cost, is the dissemination of the market orientation culture in the entire organisation.

2.4.2. A credibility gap for marketers

As put in a recent McKinsey report (Cassidy *et al.*, 2005), 'marketers have a credibility problem because the creativity that is their lifeblood often runs counter to the discipline required to excel in other parts of the organisation'. Today's marketers must tailor and integrate their strategies with a more complex set of approaches to product development, supply chains, manufacturing and relationship selling, and so on. These approaches imply close co-operation with the other functions. In the McKinsey survey (see Table 2.7), most CEOs expressed some variation on the concern that

> [m]arketers in spite of their creative strengths don't think like businessmen and display behaviour that is more akin to a recalcitrant child than an adult.

Table 2.7   Attributes of marketers that are most frequently cited by CEOs/CMOs

Positive attributes	Negative attributes
Committed	Inconsistent
Creative	Undisciplined
Energetic	Expensive
Essential	Narrow
Hard working	Self-important
Inspiring	Uncommercial
Passionate	Not accountable
Talented	Faddish

Quoted by: Cassidy *et al.* (2005).

Many CEOs, for instance, expressed frustration at being asked for funds in absence of – or even in contradiction to – data regarding the proposed initiatives.

In recent years, several studies published in the United States (Rust *et al.*, 2004; Cassidy *et al.*, 2005; Webster *et al.*, 2005) and in Europe (Lambin and Chumpitaz, 2006) have evidenced a growing dissatisfaction from CEOs and from board directors with the performance of traditional marketing and, in particular, with its lack of financial accountability and with the low productivity of traditional functional organisations, similar to the one presented in Figure 1.10. The main reproaches or criticisms about traditional marketing's performance are the following:

- To have confined market orientation to the marketing department, thereby preventing the development of a market culture within the organisation.
- To be a big spender and to have failed to put in place metrics and processes to track the impact of marketing initiatives.
- To have privileged tactical marketing instruments over strategic ones, by giving precedence to advertising and promotions over product innovations.
- To be risk-adverse by placing more emphasis on minor market-pull innovations over more revolutionary (but more risky) technology-push innovations.
- To have responded to environmentalism by green advertising unsupported by prior product redesign, thereby undermining the credibility of green marketing.
- To have neglected in B2C markets the 'fewer frills, low price' segments, thereby opening the door to the development of private labels.
- To have created confrontational rather than collaborative relationships with large retailers and to lose the battle of the brand in several product categories.
- To lose contact with the new consumer and to have failed to develop a long-term relationship with the customer base.

Marketers need a more rigorous approach, one that jettisons mentalities and behaviour from advertising's golden age and treats operational marketing not as 'spend' but as the investment it really is (Court, 2004).

Today, an increasing number of firms believe that the marketing function must reinvent itself in a way that reinforces the overall market orientation of the firm. Thus the problem is not with marketing, but rather with the marketing function (see Christensen *et al.*, 2005; Webster *et al.*, 2005). In the new competitive environment, market-driven management has become too important to be left to the marketing function alone. In the new world economy, the marketing directors' jobs have never been so difficult or so potentially rewarding. Today's marketers need to be skilled and well trained to analyse international markets, understand the cultural differences and get insights from consumers from all over the world.

2.4.3. The cost of a weak market orientation

The absence of a strong market orientation culture may have significant impact on the competitiveness of the firm. Several potential problems may arise:

1. *Environment monitoring*. If the marketing function is the only one in charge of managing the interface between the firm and its environment, is there not a risk to see the announced changes underestimated by the other functions within the organisation? Does the marketing staff have enough credibility and enough weight to induce major changes within the firm? For example, it is surprising to see how the chemical industry was caught unprepared, when new legislation suddenly imposed severe restrictions on non-recyclable plastic bottles, while this environmentalist issue had been a much-debated question for more than 20 years.

2. *The links between R&D and innovations*. If the market orientation is confined within the marketing department, the dialogue between R&D and strategic marketing will be more difficult and the link between inventions and innovations weaker. As a consequence, R&D activities will give rise to fewer successful implementations of inventions. According to a recent European study, it seems that fundamental research in Western Europe is indeed less productive than in the United States and Japan.

3. *New product development process*. Developing a new product is typically a cross-functional effort which involves not only the marketing department, but all other functions as well (see Exhibit 2.8). In companies where the dominant culture is not the market orientation, new product development processes are generally sequential and the project is passed from one specialist to another. This process ends up with a desirable 'target price' reflecting the successive internal costs and which becomes the

---

EXHIBIT 2.8

THE TOP PRIORITY OF INNOVATIONS

More than two-thirds of the 100 global companies surveyed in 2004 by the Conference Board indicated that innovation is a top priority (Conference Board, 30 June 2004). Separate research on the manufacturing sector confirms the expected pace: By 2007, notes Deloitte, sales of new products introduced in the three preceding years are expected to generate 34% of total revenue – up from 21% only seven years ago (Deloitte Research, March 2004). Yet CEOs are often disappointed by the level of innovation in their businesses, a situation for which they hold marketing at least partially accountable.

Quoted by: Webster *et al.* (2005, p. 41).

---

market price suggested to (or imposed upon) sales personnel. In a market-driven company, on the other hand, it is the 'acceptable market price' which is identified upfront and which becomes the constraint to be met by R&D and production people. The success rate of new products is much higher in this second case.

4. *Competitive advantage and the value chain*. The definition of a sustainable competitive advantage is a major responsibility of strategic marketing. As shown by Porter (1980), the value chain is a basic tool for diagnosing competitive advantage and finding ways to create and sustain it. Thus, a firm must define its competitive advantage by reference to the different value activities – primary and support – that are performed. Each of these value activities, and not only the marketing activities, can contribute to a firm's relative cost position and create a basis for differentiation. If the firm is not market-oriented, it is not easy to induce the non-marketing activities to participate in the search for a sustainable competitive advantage. The risk is then to base competitive positioning on minor points of differentiation of low added value to the customer.

5. *Financial implication of sales promotions*. A good indicator of performance for the marketing department is an increase in sales revenue that, in non-expandable markets, implies a market share increase. In B2C markets, an easy but short-sighted way to achieve this objective is to embark on trade promotions and coupon offers which is in fact a disguised form of price-cutting. These promotional actions, because of their effectiveness, generate strong retaliatory actions from competition who respond by more promotions or coupon offers. This escalation leads to a situation of almost permanent promotions that eventually undermine brand loyalty and profitability. As a result of this 'marketing myopia', marketing activities are under increasing challenge and control from the finance department that questions the wisdom of this type of action.

6. *Transactional versus relationship selling*. Finding new customers is traditionally an important objective of transactional marketing that is mostly interested in immediate sales results. In mature markets, this objective loses relevance, and cultivating the existing customer base becomes the priority goal. In B2B marketing, the repeat purchase rate of satisfied customers is around 90–95 per cent (Goderis, 1998) and therefore, attracting new customers is viewed as an intermediate objective. Relationship selling tries to create and maintain a long-term mutually profitable relationship with customers. This customer satisfaction objective, however, is not just the responsibility of the marketing function, but again of all other functions participating in the process of value creation for the customer. Thus, everyone within the organisation must share the customer satisfaction objective.

Thus, it appears that the lack of market orientation of a given firm may seriously undermine its capacity to meet the challenges of the new macro-marketing environment.

2.4.4. Characteristics of a market-driven organisation

In the professional literature and in business quarters as well, the terms 'market orientation' and 'marketing orientation' are often used interchangeably (Shapiro, 1988).

■ The *marketing orientation concept* tends to be concerned more with the American view of the marketing concept (McCarthy, 1960/2005; Kotler 1967/2005), especially marketing's functional role in co-ordinating and managing the four Ps to make a firm more responsive to meeting customers' needs.

■ The *market orientation concept* in contrast (Lambin, 1986/2005; McGee and Shapiro, 1988; Webster, 1988; Day, 1990, 1999; Shapiro, 1992) de-emphasises the functional roles of marketing departments, enlarges the market definition to the key market actors (and not only to the customer) and states that developing customer relations and enhancing customer value is the responsibility of everyone in the organisation.

In this book, we promote the term 'market orientation' to emphasise the importance of the 'culture' and 'analysis' dimensions of the concept (see Table 1.1, p. 5) in contrast with the single 'action' dimension.

The developments in the macro-marketing environment and the wide adoption of a market orientation at all levels of the firm have had several implications for the marketing function.

First, the brand management system so successfully adopted by many companies (see Table 1.4, p. 25) during the last 40 years seems, today, unable to face the complex challenges of the new environment. As put by George *et al.* (1994) from McKinsey, brand managers today are

■ too junior, too inexperienced and too narrowly centred on operational marketing;
■ too removed from added value activities (which is not just advertising);
■ too overwhelmed with day-to-day tasks (like developing trade promotions);
■ too focused on implementing quick fix solutions that will get them promoted in 18 months.

They are not the 'mini general managers' they were supposed to be and are not able to provide the cross-functional leadership required in complex markets.

Second, as the market orientation concept becomes more and more accepted and increasingly implemented across all functions within the firm – in particular as a result of the adoption of the solution-to-a-problem approach described above – the specific role of marketing as a separate function is coming under questioning and has to be reassessed.

As suggested by Day (1999), the main characteristics of a market-driven company can be summarised as follows.

1. An externally oriented *culture* with dominant beliefs, values and behaviours emphasising superior customer value and the continual quest for new sources of advantages.
2. Distinctive *capabilities in market sensing*, market relating and anticipatory strategic thinking. This means market-driven firms are better educated about their markets and better able to form close relationships with valued customers.
3. A *configuration* that enables the entire organisation continually to anticipate and respond to customer requirements and market conditions.

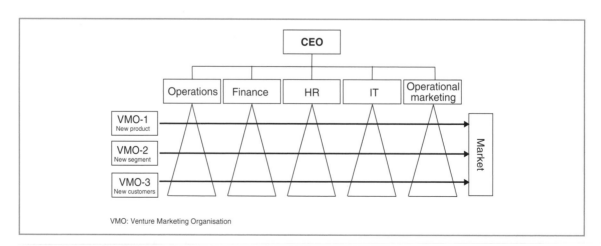

Figure 2.5   Typical organisation of a market-oriented company
Source: Authors.

Supporting these three elements is a shared knowledge base in which the organisation collects and disseminates its market insights. This knowledge builds relationships with customers, informs the company strategy and increases the focus of employees on the needs of the market.

The challenge for a market-driven organisation is to devise a structure that combines the depth of knowledge found in a vertical hierarchy with responsiveness of horizontal process teams as illustrated in the matrix organisation form presented in Figure 2.5.

2.4.5. Towards cross-functional forms of organisations

The matrix form is a grid-like organisational structure that allows a company to address multiple business dimensions using multiple command structure (Sy and D'Annunzio, 2000). As illustrated in Figure 2.5, basic matrix structures have two dimensions: a function and a specific project, such as a new product launching, category management or customer relationship management assumed by a cross-functional team, also called Venture Marketing Organisation (VMO). The matrix allows companies to leverage resources while staying small and task-oriented and to focus employees on market orientation. This matrix structure also facilitates the dissemination of the market culture throughout the entire organisation and encourages innovation and fast action.

This cross-functional team approach extends the idea of venture teams as a way of responding to high priority opportunities faster than conventional organisational approaches allow. The VMO adopts the principles of venture capitalism. They have a number of defining characteristics (Aufreiter *et al.*, 2000):

- Fluidity to keep pace with the market – the VMO continually reconfigures, with little formal structure or fixed membership in opportunity teams.
- People are allocated roles, not jobs – the issue is managing talent within the organisation.
- Fast decision-making is made from the top – opportunity identification is everyone's job.
- Resources are focused on the highest payback opportunity and losers are quickly pruned.

According to McKinsey, today's marketing organisations are organised around two roles, integrators and specialists, linked together through teams and processes rather than functional or business unit structures:

1. *Integrators (or process managers).* They are marketers with broad skills who will play the critical role of guiding activities across the firm's entire value chain; identifying which market segments to compete in and which levers to pull to maximise long-term profitability. They will be charged with tearing down the walls that divide function from function and with leading cross-functional teams to execute these strategies. Typically, they will be responsible for marketing strategy development. Integrators can be responsible for a distinct end-user segment (consumer integrators) or specific group of business customers like giant retailers (customer integrator) or be responsible for a process, like new product development (process integrators).

2. *Specialists.* They provide the technical and specialised skills required to successfully implement the marketing strategy in the different disciplines such as marketing research, business intelligence, pricing strategy, advertising, promotion, direct marketing, and so on. The trend is also towards subcontracting to outside specialists marketing activities such as market research and analysis, database management, and even the execution of some operational marketing tasks.

In the new organisational context, interfunctional co-ordination is particularly important because it implies the involvement of all levels in the firm's organisation. The key idea here is to consider that market orientation is the business of everyone and not only of the marketing people. But marketers have a key role to play in disseminating the market orientation culture within the organisation. They have to take the lead in turning the organisation in this direction.

One major issue faced by many companies is where and how to position Internet-based channels in the marketing organisation. Early organisation systems isolated Internet channels from the rest of the business, thereby creating conflicts between GTM and GEM. The real challenge is to integrate the Internet in the core business by adopting bricks and clicks marketing systems (see Chapter 13).

The evolution of the changing priority role of marketing is summarised in Table 2.8. The environmental changes mentioned above all imply a reinforcement of the market orientation for companies operating in highly industrialised markets. Companies need to review their strategic options in order to face the new challenges presented by the economic, competitive and socio-cultural environment and by the internationalisation of the world economy.

Table 2.8 Evolution of the priority role of marketing	
Product orientation	The firm is product-oriented and has an *inside-in* perspective
Sales orientation	The firm is sales-oriented and has an *inside-out* perspective
Customer orientation	The firm is customer-oriented and has an *outside-in* perspective
Market orientation	The firm is market-oriented and has a *global* perspective
Source: Authors.	

CHAPTER SUMMARY

The globalisation of the world economy combined with the development of the new technologies of information and communication (TICS) has considerably increased the complexity of markets. To remain competitive in the environment of the twenty-first century, excellent companies are going one step further today and are moving from a customer-oriented to a market-oriented culture. In today's turbulent environment, market orientation is too important to be left to the marketing department alone. The market culture should be diffused at all levels within the organisation through interfunctional co-ordination. In this new context, market-driven management is more important than ever but the marketing department as a separate function is being critically questioned and should reinvent itself. Market-driven management should be viewed as a process integrating the different functions and not a separate entity within the organisation. In the current macro-marketing environment new priorities emerge for the firm.

Review and Application Questions

1. Which factors explain the development of global marketing?
2. What are the major risks, for a firm, of pushing too far the globalisation strategy? Take the Procter & Gamble and the Coca-Cola companies as examples.
3. What are the strategies and/or policies to be adopted by firms operating exclusively on their domestic market, to reinforce their competitiveness within the enlarged European market?
4. Select a company you know well and measure its level of market orientation, using the indicators presented in Table 2.8. Construct an aggregate score of market orientation and a separate score for the 'analysis', 'action' and 'interfunctional co-ordination' components. Interpret the results and formulate recommendations on how to reinforce the firm's market orientation.
5. What difference do you see for a firm to be customer-oriented or market-oriented?
6. Select a market you know well and identify the main market actors and their inter-relationships that form the market ecosystem.
7. To what extent is a global marketing strategy a market-oriented strategy?

Bibliography

A.T. Kearney Inc. (2002), *Globalization's Last Hurrah?* A.T. Kearney/Foreign Policy Magazine Globalization Index, January–February.

Alderson, W. (1957), *Marketing Behaviour and Executive Action*, Homewood, IL, R.D. Irwin, Inc.

Anderson, E.W., Fornell, C. and Mazvancheryl, S.K. (2004), Customer Satisfaction and Shareholder Value, *Journal of Marketing*, 68, October, pp. 172–85.

Anderson, M. and Sullivan, M. (1993), The Antecedents and Consequences of Customer Satisfaction for Firms, *Marketing Science*, 12, pp. 125–42.

Aufreiter, N.A., Lawver, T.L. and Lum, C.D. (2000), A New Way to Market, *McKinsey Quarterly*, 2, pp. 43–61.

Bearden, W.O. and Etzel, M.J. (1982), Reference Group Influence on Product and Brand Purchase Decision, *Journal of Consumer Research*, 9, 2, pp. 183–94.

Boddewyn, J.J., Soel, R. and Picard, J. (1986), Standardisation in International Marketing: Is Ted Levitt in Fact Right? *Business Horizons*, November–December, pp. 68–75.

Buzzell, R.D. (1968), Can you Standardize Multinational Marketing?, *Harvard Business Review*, 46, 6, pp. 106–13.

Buzzell, R.D. and Ortmeyer, G. (1995), Channel Partnership Streamline Distribution, *Sloan Management Review*, Spring, pp. 85–96.

Cassidy, F., Freeling, A. and Kiewell, D. (2005), A Credibility Gap for Marketers, *McKinsey Quarterly*, 2, pp. 9–10.

Chamberlin, E.H. (1933/1962), *The Theory of Monopolistic Competition*, Cambridge, MA, Harvard University Press.

Christensen, C.M., Cook, S. and Hall, T. (2005), Marketing Malpractice: The Cause and the Cure, *Harvard Business Review*, December, pp. 76–83.

Conference Board (2004), *Innovation Becoming Higher Priority in Global Companies*, 30 June.

Cooper, R.G. (1993), *Winning at New Products*, Reading MA, Addison Wesley.

Court, D.C. (2004), A New Model for Marketing, *McKinsey Quarterly*, 4, pp. 4–6.

Day, G.S. (1990), *Market-driven Strategy*, New York, The Free Press.

Day, G.S. (1997), Aligning the Organisation to the Market, in *Reflections on the Future of Marketing*, Lehmann and Jocz, C. (eds), Cambridge, MA, Marketing Science Institute.

Day, G.S. (1999), *The Market-driven Organisation*, New York, The Free Press.

Deloitte Research (2004), *Mastering Innovation: Exploiting Ideas for Profitable Growth*, Part 3 of the Global Benchmark Study, March.

Foote, N.W., Galbraith, J., Hope, Q. and Miller, D. (2001), Making Solutions the Answer, *McKinsey Quarterly*, 3, p. 84.

Friedman, T.L. (1996), McDonald: A Successful Globalization?, *International Herald Tribune*, 12 December.

George, M., Freeling, A. and Court, D. (1994), Reinventing the Marketing Organisation, *McKinsey Quarterly*, 4, pp. 43–62.

Goderis, J.P. (1998), Barrier Marketing: From Customer Satisfaction to Customer Loyalty, *CEMS Business Review*, 2, 4, pp. 285–94.

Goshal, S. and Nohria, N. (1993), Horses for Courses: Organizational Forms for Multinational Corporations, *Sloan Management Review*, 34, 2, pp. 23–35.

Gotteland, D. (2005), *L'orientation marché: nouvelles méthods, nouveaux outils*, Paris, Editions d' Organisation.

Guo, J. and Sun, C. (2004), Global Electronic Markets and Global Traditional Markets, *Electonic Markets*, 14, 1, pp. 4–12.

Homburg, C., Koschate, N. and Hoyer, W.D., (2005), Do Satisfied Customers Really Pay More? A Study of the Relationship Between Customer Satisfaction and Willingness to Pay, *Journal of Marketing*, 69, 1, pp. 84–96.

Jain, S.C. (1989), Standardisation of International Marketing Strategy: Some Research Hypotheses, *Journal of Marketing*, 53, 1, pp. 70–9.

Johansson, J.E., Krishnamurthy, C. and Schlissberg, H.E. (2003), Solving the Solutions Problem, *McKinsey Quarterly*, 3, pp. 16–25.

Kiley, D. (2006), Best Global Brands, *Business Week*, 7 August, pp. 54–5.

Kirca, A.H., Jayachandran, S. and Bearden, W.O. (2005), Market Orientation: A Meta-analytic Review and Assessment of its Antecedents and Impact on Performance, *Journal of Marketing*, 69, 2, pp. 24–41.

Klein, N. (1999), *No Logo*, Knopf Canada.

Kohli, A.K. and Jaworski, B.J. (1990), Market Orientation: The Construct, Research Propositions and Managerial Implications, *Journal of Marketing*, 54, 2, pp. 1–18.

Kotler, P. (1967/2005), *Marketing Management*, Englewood Cliffs, NJ, Prentice-Hall Inc. 1st and 9th edition.

Krebs, C.J. (1988), *The Message of Ecology*, New York, Harper Collins.

Kueviakoe, D. (1996), Entre grande stabilité et faible autorité: la position du chef de produit dans les entreprises, *Revue Française du Marketing*, 156, 1, pp. 79–91.

Lambin, J.J. (1986/2005), Le marketing stratégique, Paris, Ediscience International.

Lambin, J.J. (1994), *Problèmes de marketing*, Paris, Ediscience International. Also in Quelch J.A., Buzzell, R.D. and Salama, E.R. (eds) (1991), *The Marketing Challenge of Europe 1992*, Boston, Addison–Wesley.

Lambin, J.J. (2001), The Benefits of Globalisation, *European Business Forum*, 6, Summer, pp. 67–70.

Lambin, J.J. and Chumpitaz, R. (2000), Being Customer-driven is Not Enough, *European Business Forum*, 2, pp. 2–8.

Lambin, J.J. and Chumpitaz, R. (2006), L'orientation-marché est.elle unse stratègie rentable pour l'entreprise? *Recherche et Applications en Marketing*, 21, 2, June.

Lambin, J.J. and Hiller, T.B. (1990), Volvo Trucks Europe, in *Strategic Marketing Problems*, Kerin, R.A. and Peterson, R.A. (eds) (1993), Boston, MA, Allyn & Bacon.

Lash, M.L. (1990), *The Complete Guide to Customer Service*, New York, John Wiley & Sons.

Levitt, T. (1983), The Globalization of Markets, *Harvard Business Review*, 61, 3, pp. 92–102.

Manning, B. and Thorne, C. (2003), *Demand Driven*, New York, McGraw-Hill.

Masiello, T. (1988), Developing Market Responsiveness Throughout Your Company, *Industrial Marketing Management*, 17, 2, pp. 85–93.

McCarthy, J. (1960/2005), *Basic Marketing: A Managerial Approach*, Homewood, IL, R.D. Irwin, 1st edition.

McGee, L.W. and Shapiro, R.L. (1988), The Marketing Concept in Perspective, *Business Horizons*, 31, 3, pp. 40–5.

Morrison, A., Bouquet, C. and Beck, J. (2004), Netchising: The Next Global Wave? *Long Range Planning*, 37, 1, p. 7.

Nagle, T.T. and Holden, R.K. (1994), *The Strategy and Tactics of Pricing*, Englewood Cliffs, NJ, Prentice-Hall, 2nd edition.

Narus, J.A. and Anderson, J.C. (1986), Turn Your Industrial Distributors into Partners, *Harvard Business Review*, 64, 2, pp. 66–71.

Narver, J.C. and Slater, S.F. (1990), The Effect of a Market Orientation on Business Profitability, *Journal of Marketing*, 54, 4, pp. 20–35.

Narver, J.C. Slater, S.F. and MacLachlan, D.L. (2004), Responsive and Proactive Market Orientation and New Product Success, *Journal of Product Innovation Management*, 21, pp. 334–47.

Porter, M.E. (1980), *Competitive Strategy*, New York, The Free Press.

Quelch, J.A. and Hoff, E.J. (1986), Customizing Global Marketing, *Harvard Business Review*, 64, 3, pp. 59–68.

Rask, M. and Kragh, H. (2004), Motives for E-market Participation: Differences and Similarities Between Buyers and Suppliers, *Electronic Markets*, 14, 4, pp. 270–83.

Reichheld, F. (1996), *L'effet loyauté*, Paris, Dunod.

Ritchell, M. (2005), Even Little Companies are Now Going Global, *International Herald Tribune*, June 19.

Roegner, E.V., Seifert, T. and Swinford, D.D. (2001), Putting a Price on Solutions, *McKinsey Quarterly*, 3, pp. 93–7.

Rust, R.T., Ambler, T., Carpenter, G.S., Kumar, V. and Srivastava, R.K. (2004), Measuring Marketing Productivity, Current Knowledge and Future Directions, *Journal of Marketing*, 68, 4, pp. 76–89.

Schnaars, S.P. (1988), *Marketing Strategy: Customers and Competitors*, New York, The Free Press, 2nd edition.

Schuiling, I. (2002) *La force des marques locales et ses déterminants spécifiques par rapport aux marques internationales*, Louvain La Neuve, Presses Universitaires de Louvain, Belgium.

Schuiling, I. and Kapferer, J.N. (2004), Real Differences Between Local and International Brands: Strategic Implications for International Marketers, *Journal of International Marketing*, 12, 4, pp. 97–112.

Schuiling, I. and Lambin, J.J. (2003), Do Global Brands Benefit from a Unique Worldwide Image? *Symphonya: Emerging Issues in Management*, 2. Also in: *The ICFAI Journal of Brand Management*, 2, 2, June 2005.

Segal, R.L. (2000), Online Marketplaces: A New Strategic Option, *Journal of Business Strategy*, 21, 2, pp. 26–90.

Shapiro, B.P. (1988), What the Hell is Market Oriented? *Harvard Business Review*, 66, 6, pp. 119–25.

Sheridan, S. and Bullinger, N. (2001), Building a Solution-based Organisation, *Journal of Business Strategy*, 22, 1, pp. 36–40.

Sheth, J., Mittal, B. and Newman, B.I. (1999), *Customer Behavior, Consumer Behavior and Beyond*, Forth Worth, The Dryden Press.

Swan, J.E. and Oliver, R.L. (1989), Postpurchase Communications by consumers, *Journal of Retailing*, 65, 4, pp. 516–33.

Sy, T. and D'Annunzio, L.S. (2000), Challenges and Strategies of Matrix Organizations, *Human Resources Planning*, 28, 1.

Trout, J. (1985), Forget Satisfying the Consumer – Just Outfox the Competition, *Business Week*, 7 October, 2915, pp. 55–8.

Webster, F.E. (1988), *The Rediscovery of the Marketing Concept, Business Horizons*, 31, 3, pp. 29–39.

Webster, F.E. (1992), The Changing Role of Marketing in the Corporation, *Journal of Marketing*, 56, 4, pp. 1–17.

Webster, F.E. (1997), The Future Role of Marketing in the Organization in *Reflections on the Futures of Marketing*, Lehman, D.R. and Jocz, K.E. (eds), Cambridge, MA, Marketing Science Institute.

Webster, F.E., Malter, A.J. and Ganesan, S. (2005), The Decline and Dispersion of Marketing Competence, *MIT Sloan Management Review*, 46, 4, pp. 35–43.

Yip, G.S. (1989), Global Strategy in a World of Nations, *MIT Sloan Management Review*, Fall. Also in Gupta, A.K. and Westney, D.E. (eds) (2003), *Smart Globalization*, San Francisco, Jossey Bass.

COMPANION WEBSITE FOR CHAPTER 2

Visit the *Market-driven Management* companion website at www.palgrave.com/business/lambin to find:

A Questionnaire to Measure the Level of Market Orientation of a Firm

Part 2

understanding customer behaviour

PART I: THE CHANGING ROLE OF MARKETING

The Role of Marketing in the Firm
and in a Social Market Economy
Chapter 1

Market-driven Management
in the Global Marketplace
Chapter 2

PART II: UNDERSTANDING CUSTOMER BEHAVIOUR

Customers' Needs Analysis
Chapter 3

The Customer Purchase Behaviour
Chapter 4

Measuring Customers' Response
Chapter 5

PART III: IMPLEMENTING STRATEGIC MARKETING

Needs Analysis through Market Segmentation
Chapter 6

Market Attractiveness Analysis
Chapter 7

Company Competitiveness Analysis
Chapter 8

Market Targeting and Positioning
Chapter 9

Formulating a Marketing Strategy
Chapter 10

PART IV: IMPLEMENTING OPERATIONAL MARKETING

New Product
Decisions

Chapter 11

Brand
Management

Chapter 12

Distribution
Channel
Decisions

Chapter 13

The Battle of the
Brands in the
B2C Markets

Chapter 14

Pricing
Decisions

Chapter 15

Marketing
Communication
Decisions

Chapter 16

PART V: IMPLEMENTATION OF MARKET-DRIVEN MANAGEMENT

The Strategic and Operational
Marketing Plan
Chapter 17

Emerging Values and Issues in
Market-driven Management
Chapter 18

Case Studies

customers' needs analysis 3

Chapter contents

Chapter learning objectives

When you have read this chapter, you should be able to understand

- the difference between generic and derived needs;
- the importance of unarticulated or latent needs;
- the determinants of well-being;
- the multidimensional structure of customers' needs;
- the motivation of the B2B customer;
- the concept of industrial decision centre.

Chapter introduction

The objective of this chapter is to present a general conceptual framework describing the way market-driven management decodes customer purchasing motivation in consumer (B2C) and organisational (B2B) markets. The satisfaction of customers' needs is at the heart of a market economy and of market-driven management. This chapter aims to make clear such basic conceptions of the needs theory as generic absolute versus relative needs, generic versus derived needs and needs hierarchy. In the first step, we shall examine the main positions of economics and marketing theoreticians concerning the role that strategic marketing plays in adapting firms to the constant development in needs satisfaction. Then we shall turn to psychology and in particular to the contributions that experimental psychology has made in the study of human motivation. In B2B markets, we introduce the concept of the customer as a decision centre and we analyse the motivation of the B2B customer.

3.1. The notion of generic need

The notion of need is a term that creates endless polemic because it contains elements of subjective judgement based sometimes on morality or ideology. Beyond the vital minimum that everyone accepts – but which no one tries to define – is it really necessary to vary one's food to satisfy taste, to travel out of curiosity or to have different hobbies? We must admit that, at least as far as consumer markets are concerned, these questions are not irrelevant, especially in view of the following facts: (a) the uninterrupted arrival of new products and brands on the market; (b) the continuous and spectacular presence of advertising in increasingly varied forms and (c) the relative stability of the level of consumer satisfaction, despite the undisputed improvement in standard of living. These facts then raise the following questions:

1. Do all these new products and brands really correspond to pre-existing needs?
2. Would producers accept such high advertising expenditures if consumers were not allowing themselves to be influenced?
3. Is the growth and economic development that marketing claims to encourage useful in the long term?

Economic theory does not help to answer these questions. Economists believe it is not part of their discipline to worry about what motivates an action, or to enter into an introspection, which is always difficult, or especially to formulate a value judgement. It is useless to say that man strives for pleasure and avoids pain; it suffices to see that this indeed is the essence of the 'want to use' to justify its utility. The driving force, economic or otherwise, that makes an individual take an economic action, is outside the scope of economics; only the results are important. The wish to be satisfied is the only acknowledged cause of

behaviour. A need must be felt before a choice is made, which means that the scale of preferences logically precedes effective choices. If an individual is intellectually adult and reasonable, it should be possible to predict the person's behaviour, which results from rational calculation.

The economic theory of consumer behaviour is therefore limited to the analysis of the logical implications of the hypothesis of man's rationality. The problem of motivation is totally avoided, since economists believe that the real behaviour of the consumer reflects his or her preferences and inversely that the consumer's preferences are revealed by his or her behaviour.

The weakness of the basic assumptions in economics has been underlined on many occasions. In economic theory, the concept of rationality is defined as equivalent to the concept of coherence. However, the predictive value of coherence conditions depends mainly on the existence of well-known and stable preferences in the mind of the decider. But this is far from being satisfied if the original motivations are ignored, poorly known or simplified to the extreme, as is the case in economic models. How can we then be surprised by the observed difference between the 'economic person' and the 'real person'? We should nevertheless mention that, over the last 50 years, many serious efforts have been made to enrich the abstract psychology of the economic person and to come closer to the real person. Some examples of this approach are given by the works of Katona (1951), Abbott (1955), Becker (1965), Lancaster (1966), Ratchford (1975) and Sheth *et al.* (1991).

3.1.1. The stability of generic needs

According to the dictionary, a generic need is a *requirement of nature or of social life*. This definition distinguishes two kinds of needs: innate or *absolute needs*, which are natural, inherent in nature or in the human organism, and *relative needs*, which are cultural and social and depend on experience, environmental conditions and the evolution of society.

In the frame of market-driven management analysis, it is practical to view *generic needs* – both absolute and relative – as *problems* of potential customers who try to solve them by acquiring different products or services. If we take this view, then, following Abbott (1955) we can define a *derived need* as a particular technological response (the product or the service) to the generic need, as well as being the object of desire.

> For example, the car is a derived need with respect to the absolute generic need of individual mobility. Similarly, the ownership of a costly and prestigious car can be a response to the relative generic need of social recognition.

Thus, the popular view is that the firm's marketing activity that creates needs has to be revised. Marketing cannot create generic needs that pre-exist and are inherent to human nature, but it can only create demand for the derived need, that is, the demand addressed to a specific technological response.

Generic needs are stable and cannot become obsolete. Obsolescence relates only to derived needs, in other words to the dominant technological response at the time. At a given point, one may detect a tendency towards the saturation of the derived need, because of increased consumption of the good at a particular stage in its life cycle. The marginal utility of the derived need tends to diminish. But the generic problems (personal mobility, social recognition, protection, and so on) do not disappear, which means that generic needs remain unaffected. Thanks to the impulse given by technological progress, the generic need simply evolves towards higher levels due to the arrival of improved products and, therefore, new derived needs.

The production of goods for the satisfaction of generic needs will therefore be incessantly subject to the stimulus of its own evolution. The latter will encourage the arrival of new products on the market, which are more suitable to satisfying the new level of needs. These derived needs will become obsolete in their turn and be replaced by new, more developed, products.

The phenomenon of relative obsolescence (decline) brought about by technological progress, which is the basis of the product life cycle (PLC) model discussed later on in this book, is observed for most goods and at two levels: *first*, in the improvement of technological performance of products themselves (more economical cars, more powerful computers, and so on); and *second*, in the pure and simple substitution of a particular technological answer by another with higher performance (compact disc replacing vinyl records, fax replacing telex, and so on). The latter form of innovation, or destructive innovation, is becoming ever more important due to the generalisation of technological progress in all sectors, as mentioned before.

Furthermore, it seems that the move to a product that is hierarchically superior tends to increase the marginal utility yet again. The decline of the marginal utility is thus interspersed with sudden peaks. Goods are often desired for their novelty features and the privilege of owning them, even if little is added to their performance.

Therefore, the distinction between generic and derived needs makes it clear that, although there can be no general satiation, it is perfectly possible to detect sectoral technological decline. An important role for strategic marketing is thus to encourage the firm to adapt to this observed development in needs satisfaction. In this framework, it is better for the firm to define its mission by reference to generic rather than derived needs, given that the latter are changing and continually influenced by technology while the former are not. These are the basics of the market orientation concept described in the previous chapter.

3.1.2. The satiation impossibility of relative generic needs

Going further in the analysis of generic needs, Keynes (1936) underlined the fact that satiation is possible only for a certain part of them, for the absolute needs.

> needs which are absolute in the sense that we feel them whatever the situation of our fellow human beings may be, and those which are relative in the sense that we feel them only if their satisfaction lifts us above, make us feel superior to our fellows. (Keynes 1936, p. 365)

Absolute needs are satiable, whereas relative needs are not. Relative needs are insatiable, because the higher the general level, the more these needs tend to surpass that level. This is how individuals, even when they have in absolute terms enjoyed net improvements in their standard of living, often tend to think that their situation has deteriorated if those who normally serve as the yardstick have improved more relative to them. Cotta (1980, p. 17) writes, 'others' luxury becomes one's own necessity'. The distance between reality and the level of aspiration tends to move continuously with growing dissatisfaction.

In these conditions, producing to satisfy relative needs is tantamount to developing them, that is, to trigger a process of escalation and of higher bids in the process of relative needs satisfaction. As pointed out by Rochefort (1995, p. 13), the relative disenchantment of consumers in affluent societies can be explained by three factors.

1. First of all, affluent consumers are becoming less aware of the improvements in their living conditions as these

become less spectacular in view of the progress already achieved in their standard of living.

2. Second, well-being and comfort induce people to forget what a choice implies in demanding at the same time the butter and the money for the butter, more free time and more money, more social protection and higher salaries, and so on.

3. Finally, the loss of the time perspective and of the resulting patience: consumers today want everything and everything right now.

The distinction between absolute and relative needs is not always clear cut as one might at first think. One could say, for example, that anything essential to survival is infinitely more important that any other consumption. This idea is inexact.

> To live is certainly an important objective for each of us, but suicide exists. Heroic acts too. More generally, every consumer, in his day-to-day search for satisfaction of various needs, takes risks that put his life in danger either immediately or in the long run. Smoking, overeating, driving, working too hard or not looking after one's health properly, travelling: these are all activities that one should avoid if survival is placed above all else. (Rosa, 1977, p. 161)

Needs of a psycho-sociological origin may be felt just as strongly as the most elementary needs. For example, being deprived of intimacy and attention may provoke death or serious deficiencies in psychic and social functioning in the more extreme cases.

Despite this lack of clear-cut clarity, the distinction between absolute and relative needs remains interesting in two respects. On the one hand, it shows that relative needs can be just as demanding as absolute needs. On the other, it brings to the fore the existence of a dialectic of relative needs which leads to the observation of the general impossibility of satiation. Even the tendency towards material comfort cannot objectively define a state of satisfaction. When an individual reaches a predefined level, he or she can then catch a glimpse of a new stage of possible improvement.

3.1.3. Latent versus expressed needs

Understanding customer needs and wants is not always a simple task and it is useful to establish a distinction between latent and expressed needs. Latent needs or latent solutions are defined as needs and solutions of which the potential customer is unaware. Latent needs are no less 'real' than expressed needs. But they are not in the consciousness of the customer.

For example, at the outset of the development of personal computers, mobile or digital photography, the

need for the benefits of these new product categories was a latent need.

Latent needs are universal. They exist in every customer and the role of proactive strategic marketing is to discover them and to analyse their profit potential through an inter-functional dialogue between R&D, market analysts and operations people as discussed in Chapter 1 (see Figure 1.2). The following distinction is useful.

■ Articulated needs
  stated needs (what the customer says);
  unstated needs (what the customer expects);
  imaginary needs (what the customer dreams of).

■ Unarticulated needs
  real needs (the well-being of the customer);
  unconscious needs (what unconsciously motivates the customer).

As illustrated in Figure 3.1, responding only to the customer's articulated needs may be misleading, leaving interesting opportunities unexploited. The objective of strategic marketing is to provide customers with an appropriate solution based on a good understanding of their real needs, be they articulated or not. The success story of Geox (see Exhibit 3.1) is interesting in this respect.

3.1.4. False needs versus true needs

The criticism frequently levelled at modern marketing is that it has changed the market into a mechanism that creates needs rather than satisfies them. We have seen above that this argument can have some validity for derived needs but not for generic needs.

One of the extreme views was put forward by Attali and Guillaume (1974). They believe that producers exploit the

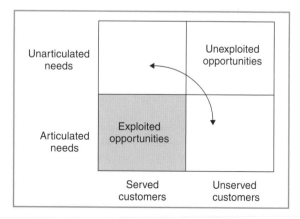

Figure 3.1   Beyond articulated needs
Source: Hamel and Prahalad (1994).

EXHIBIT 3.1

EXAMPLE OF LATENT NEED: THE SWEATY FEET PROBLEM

The problem

Our feet produce up to 100 litres of sweat a year. Rubber soles cause condensation on the sole of the foot giving you that classic feeling of wet feet. Rubber soles create a plastic-bag effect around the foot.

The solution

Geox's CEO Mario Moretti Polegato has developed a revolutionary technology consisting of covering a perforated rubber sole with a special membrane lining (the same material used by NASA for astronauts' suits) that lets perspiration through but not water, achieving the first rubber sole in the world that keeps water out and the feet dry. The benefit of this technology is that the feet are always dry, eliminating once and for all the problems of perspiration, overheating and unpleasant odours.

Interview of the Geox's Chairman

'The footwear market is saturated today and everyone is competing according to an overworked common denominator: design. Geox stands out from the crowd with this new technology [...]. Today's consumers are much more attentive to health. It is important to know how to interpret consumers' needs when they are clear and *to foresee them when latent and unexpressed*. We have to anticipate rather than follow, innovate rather than copy, ride the wave of change immediately and not when it is so high that we risk being overpowered by its explosive force.'

Source: Interview of Mario Moretti Polegato, Chairman of Geox.

---

dynamics of wants to find markets allowing them to preserve their economic power. Rosa (1977) notes that this analysis makes the implicit assumption that there are 'real' needs and 'false' needs and that the false needs are created by society and by the producer.

> In this school of thought, there is a fundamentally unequal exchange relationship between a dominated consumer and a dominant producer; society corrupts the individual by creating artificial wants in order to better subjugate and alienate him. The conclusion that follows is simple; it suffices to make the 'good' political choice to get 'good' structures which will necessarily develop the flourishing and expression of 'real' needs. (Rosa 1977, p. 176)

This analysis, which is still widespread among so-called *left intellectuals* in Europe at one stage (see, for example, Henochsberg, 2001) has one important weakness, in that it never indicates how to distinguish true needs from false needs. Given that the vast majority of our present wants are indeed of a cultural origin, where should we draw the line, and especially who will be the enlightened dictator of consumption? Clearly it is very difficult to answer these questions objectively.

> To substitute the disputed sovereignty of the consumer for the questionable sovereignty of a bureaucrat or of an intellectual can only create more problems that it can ever hope to resolve. (Rosa 1977, p. 159)

It should also be added that the hypothesis of individual consumer impotence is daily rejected by facts such as the figures available on the rates of failure of new products; more than one in two products fails to enter the market successfully. The discretionary power of the consumer is a

reality and firms know it well. We must therefore recognise that the debate of 'true' versus 'false' needs is in the first place an ideological debate.

3.2. Motivation of the individual customer

Economists, as we saw, make no distinction between what consumers choose and what suits them, and never consider the process of needs formation. What do individuals seek in their quest for well-being and how does this state of well-being come about? These two questions are never tackled by economic theory. Yet it is clear that a more thorough analysis of consumer behaviour and the structure of their motivation would make it easier to understand the links that both economists and marketing try to establish between supply and demand. Experimental psychology has made enlightening contributions in this field and helps us discover a whole range of general motivational orientations that determine various individual behaviours. This section is based on the works of Hebb (1955), Duffy (1957), Berlyne (1960), Scitovsky (1976) and Nuttin (1980).

3.2.1. The 'stimulus–response' theory

A central preoccupation of the theory of motivation has been to study why the organism moves into a state of activity. Motivation here becomes energy mobilisation. Originally, experimental psychology was mostly interested in needs and drives of a purely physiological nature, such as hunger, thirst, sex, and so on. In this scheme, called the 'stimulus–response theory' (or S–R theory) the stimulus is considered as the active starting point of the organism's reaction. One then speaks of *homeostasis*, which is a mechanism whereby a disorder creates an urge, giving rise to activity that restores equilibrium and thus removes the urge. In this framework, the organism is basically assumed to be reactive: in other words, it responds in specific ways to stimuli. This more or less repudiates the problem of motivation. Inactivity is supposedly the natural state of the individual.

We observe, however, that the human organism does not always react to the stimulus presented by its surroundings. Furthermore, it is a common occurrence to find individuals embarking on activities that disrupt equilibrium and setting up states of tension which would be hard to explain if one believed the S–R theory. This theory reduces the mechanism of motivation to a process of reducing tension and practically ignores the ascending phase of motivation, that is, the process by which new tensions or conflicts are worked out. However, this type of behaviour is frequently observed, especially in affluent societies, where basic needs are mostly met. A need, seen as a homeostatic need, cannot totally explain individual behaviour.

> More mysterious than the process of discharge is the process that can be called recharging; and more central than the reduction of tension is the act by which man seeks increased responsibilities, takes bigger risks and finds himself new challenges. (Nuttin, 1980, p. 201)

Today, experimental psychology emphasises more and more the spontaneous activity of the nervous system and considers behavioural activity to be tied to the organism's being, just as much as physiological activity is.

3.2.2. The concept of arousal

Motivation theorists nowadays tend to explain behaviour in a new way, particularly because of the fact that neuro-physiologists have considerably improved their knowledge of the way the brain functions and now have a completely different viewpoint. Hebb (1955, p. 246), for instance, formulates a hypothesis that is based, not on reactivity, but on the natural activity of the nervous system. Contrary to the beliefs held until then, the brain does not have to be excited from outside in order to be active and to discharge. It is not physiologically inert and its natural activity constitutes a system of self-motivation. Hebb, and also Duffy (1957, p. 267), put forth the idea that the general state of motivation can be equated with arousal, or the activity emanating from the reticular formation of the brain stem. Activity level depends on the degree of organic energy mobilised, which is on the variation in the level of arousal and vigilance. The level of arousal is measured by the variations in electric current controlled with an electroencephalogram (EEG); these variations show up as waves in the EEG; the faster the electric discharge of neurones, the higher the level of arousal and the higher the frequency of oscillations in the EEG, measured in periods per second.

Scitovsky (1976) underlines the importance of the concept of arousal in understanding the reasons for a given behaviour.

> A high arousal is associated with vigilance and quick response; it makes the senses more sensitive to stimuli, increases the brain's capacity to process information, readies the muscles for action, and so shortens the total reaction time that elapses between an incoming sensation and the response through action. It makes you feel excited, emotional, anxious and tense. On the other hand, when you feel slow, less than vigilant, lax and drowsy, you are in a state of low arousal. (Scitovsky, 1976, p. 19)

The increased level of arousal increases the organism's state of vigilance, thus providing favourable ground for the cerebral mechanism of stimulus–response to function rapidly and directly. The psychological measures of the level of arousal therefore provide a direct measure of the motivational and emotional (drive) force of a given situation for the individual (Duffy, 1957, p. 267). Also, this description of the concept of arousal suggests the existence of a continuum in the individual's level of activation.

3.2.3. Well-being and the optimal level of arousal

It is clear that the level of arousal has a great influence on the feeling of well-being or discomfort felt in general by people, and consequently bears on the determination of their behaviour. Excessive stimulation provokes tension, anxiety, nervousness, worry, frenzy, even panic; on the other hand, stimulation which is too weak, or non-existent, brings about boredom, or a certain degree of displeasure, and creates the desire for a bigger stimulation. A job, which is too simple or too monotonous, can become painful if one is forced to pursue it without interruption over a long time. In fact, psychologists (Hebb, 1955, p. 250) accept that there is an optimal level of arousal and stimulation, optimal in the sense that it creates a feeling of comfort and well-being. Deviations below the optimum provoke a feeling of weariness, and deviations above the optimum provoke a sensation of fatigue and anxiety. Experimental observations show that, on the whole, individuals try to maintain an intermediary level of activation (Berlyne, 1960, p. 194).

We can identify here an aspect of the general direction of motivation in individuals: ensure comfort and prevent discomfort. This motivation implies, on the one hand, the reduction of tensions, which satisfies various corporal and mental needs and reduces the level of arousal, which may be too high; on the other hand, it implies a battle against boredom, a behaviour which looks for stimulation and thus increases the level of arousal, which might be too low. These two types of behaviour have one thing in common; both try to fill up a gap and to ensure a 'negative good', that is to stop pain, inconvenience and discomfort (Scitovsky, 1976, p. 69).

For economists, the reduction of arousal and tension is particularly important because as far as they are concerned almost all human activity, including consumption, is based on this process. We find here the notion of need defined by economists as simply a state of deficiency. However, economists ignore the other type of behaviour that is the raising of a level of arousal that is too low. This is commonly observed in more affluent economies, where prosperity has largely eliminated discomfort due to tension, but where the search for stimulation, novelty and change is becoming ever more important.

> The consumer is also a dreamer. She (or he) buys a product, certainly to use it, but even more for the magic it offers him as premium. (Séguéla, 1982, p. 50)

In some situations, finding sufficient stimulation to combat boredom can be a matter of life or death. This is true for old people, for example. It is also well known that longevity is strongly related to having been able to keep a satisfying job late in life.

3.2.4. The need for stimulation

Berlyne's work in this area is interesting, especially because it is based on solid experimental ground. Berlyne (1960) shows that novelty (meaning anything surprising, different from past events and from what one expected) attracts attention and has a stimulating effect.

> Novelty stimulates and pleases especially when it creates surprising-ness, change, ambiguity, incongruity, blurredness and power to induce uncertainty. (Berlyne, 1960, p. 290)

It is as if the incongruence of the new event produces a dynamic effect which sets in motion exploratory actions. It must, however, be made clear that the new and surprising is attractive only up to a limited degree, beyond which it becomes disturbing and frightening. Attractiveness first increases, then diminishes with the degree of newness and 'surprising-ness'. This relationship takes the shape of an inverted U-curve, known as the Wundt curve (Berlyne, 1960), shown in Figure 3.2. What is not new or surprising enough is boring, and what is too new is bewildering. An intermediate degree of newness seems to be the most pleasing.

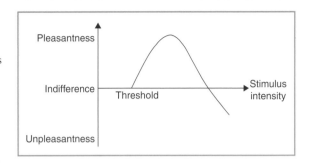

Figure 3.2 The Wundt curve
Source: Berlyne (1960).

The stimulation provoked by the collative properties of goods forms an important source of satisfaction for individuals. Much of the activity of marketers, such as new product policies, segmentation and positioning, communication and promotion, focuses on meeting this expectation. For better or for worse, goods act as stimuli over the nervous system, a little bit like toys for children. The intelligence of a child can become stagnant with lack of adequate toys. In the same manner, an adult deprived of all the stimuli, provided notably by the consumer society, can be overcome with boredom, depression and alienation.

> Many people feel younger when they purchase a brand new car and associate the age of their car with that of their own body. Thus buying a new car takes on symbolic proportions by representing physical rejuvenation. (Valaskakis *et al.*, 1978, p. 167)

Therefore, the organism needs a continuous stream of stimuli and different experiences, just as it needs air and food. Human beings need to need. This basic motivation, as well as the more obvious motivation of reducing tensions, explains a large variety of individual behaviour that can only elude the deductions made by economists. The theory of 'novelty seeking' provides an explanation for consumers' actions, which introduce change, variety and novelty into their lifestyle.

3.2.5. The need for pleasure

The sensation of comfort or discomfort is related to the level of arousal and depends on the latter's situation with respect to the optimum. Experimental psychologists have now proven that pleasure exists as a phenomenon different from absence of suffering or presence of comfort. The sensation of pleasure begins with variations in the level of arousal, in particular when a level of arousal, which is too low or too high, is approaching its optimum (Berlyne, 1960, p. 187).

Two sources of pleasure can be identified: one results from the satisfaction of a need and the resulting reduction in tension; the other comes from the stimulation itself. Satisfaction of a need is pleasant in itself and drives the organism to pursue its activity to the point of satiation and even beyond.

> In very poor communities, families often plunge into debt for the sake of a funeral feast or a wedding celebration. Such behaviour horrifies economists of the not-so-poor countries … Yet the very universality of the custom of feasting among the poor people of so many different cultures is evidence that the pleasures of a good meal for those who seldom taste one are very great and weigh heavily against the biological needs of survival. (Scitovsky, 1976, p. 66)

The economic theory of the rational behaviour of consumers implies a judicious balance between different needs and does not take into account pleasure, which can lead the individual to an allocation different from that predicted by economic theory. It is, in fact, frequently observed that people behave so as to have full satisfaction from time to time, and they properly space out the moments or periods during which they completely fulfil their wants. This type of behaviour is frequently observed in industrialised countries, in the leisure sector, for example, and in particular in holiday expenditure.

Note that the pleasure inherent in the satisfaction of a need implies that discomfort must precede pleasure. This common-sense rule is a very old one; the ancient Greeks debated it. Psychiatrists call it the *law of hedonic contrast*. It follows from the rule that too much comfort may preclude pleasure (a child who is nibbling all day long cannot appreciate a good meal). This fact can explain the malaise observed at times in affluent societies, when satisfaction of needs does not bring about any pleasure. By eliminating simple joys, excessive comfort forces us to seek strong sensations.

At this stage, the second source of pleasure, the one resulting from the stimulation itself, comes into its own. Here the object of the need is not to make up for a shortage, but to contribute to the development of the individual. To quote Nuttin (1980), this is the ascending phase of motivation; a phase in which new tensions and discordance are established, giving individuals the will to progress and surpass themselves. This is Maslow's self-actualisation need. People take pleasure in excitement. They get more satisfaction out of the struggle of reaching an objective than they get when they actually reach it. Once individuals have passed the moment of triumph, they almost regret having reached their goal. Most people then give themselves an even more distant objective, probably because they prefer to act and fight rather than passively observe their success (Nuttin, 1980, p. 201). In this way, individuals force their environment to stimulate them or to continue to stimulate them.

The pleasure of this type of stimulation results from the temporary tension it creates. Such pleasure is more constant than the pleasure of comfort and outlasts it, because this stimulation leaves more room for imagination and creativity to the individual.

> [T]he object of this stimulation is almost unlimited. By meeting them, tension goes up rather than down. Thus the tendency persists beyond the point where the objective is reached. (Nuttin, 1980, p. 202)

Here, we are now talking about insatiable needs. It is in the nature of self-development needs to know neither the saturation nor the periodicity of homeostatic needs.

> We see here what pleasure is and its relation to comfort: the former is the variation of the latter. If happiness is simply comfort, then it depends on the intensity of satisfied wants. Pleasure is complete when the want is a little or much more satisfied than it was. If happiness is not comfort but pleasure, then it is condemned to only live some privileged moments, prolonged with the help of memory. (Cotta, 1980, pp. 11–12)

From the psychologist's point of view, seeking pleasure is an important factor in human behaviour, and it is a fundamental motivational force that must be taken into account in any analysis of individual buying behaviour.

3.2.6. Determinants of the individual's well-being

An overview of the major contributions of experimental psychology to the study of human motivation finally arrives at a much wider understanding of the notion of need. We started from the point of view of economists, for whom need is essentially a 'state of shortage' revealed by the buying behaviour, without any explanation of the origin or the nature of motivations at the root of this state of deficiency. The absence of theory about motivations leads economists to make normative recommendations which have as much value as their starting assumptions, but which have little to do with actual observed behaviour. An interesting analysis of the notion of well-being in relation with marketing is made by Gibbs (2004).

Research by psychologists makes it possible to retain three general motivational directions, which can explain a large variety of behaviours and which appear to be factors that explain the individual's general well-being. These determinants can be regrouped as comfort, pleasure and stimulation. Figure 3.3 explains diagrammatically the relations between these three determinants on the one hand, and their relation to individual well-being on the other.

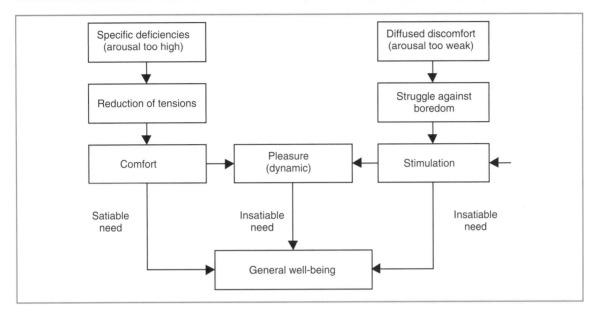

Figure 3.3   The determinants of well-being
Source: Author.

The *three motivational forces*, determining individual well-being, can be briefly described as follows:

- The search for *comfort*, which results from two kinds of behaviour: one that reduces tensions by satisfying homeostatic needs; and one that struggles against boredom with the help of stimuli such as novelty, change, incongruity, uncertainty, risk, and so on.
- The search for *pleasure*, which also results from two sources: pleasure inherent in the reduction of tensions and pleasure obtained from stimuli.
- The search for *stimulation*, not only as a means to combat boredom, but as a goal in itself, without any other objective in mind but the tension it arouses, generating pleasure and creating the opportunity of development and actualisation for the individual.

The search for comfort aims to make up for a deficiency and thus to ensure a defensive good; pleasure and stimulation aim to ensure a creative good.

By relying on this description of the major motivational forces, we are in a better position to answer the questions facing marketing mentioned at the beginning of this chapter. The increased use of marketing – which takes the form of products being continually renewed, more and more subtle differentiation, sophisticated perceptual positioning, advertising suggesting elaborate lifestyles, and so on – in reality only responds to the rise in needs of pleasure and stimulation observed in richer societies, where basic needs are well met, but where, on the other hand, needs such as novelty, surprise, complexity and risk have become vital necessities.

The need to try varied experiences, to live different lifestyles, and the possibility to try new products and to have new sources of satisfaction form an important subject matter in this type of society. This search is endless, because there is no possible saturation in this type of need.

Some philosophers advocate rising above all wants in order to escape this endless escalation, which, far from bringing internal peace, causes worry and creates an internal cycle. The wise Hindu Sarna Lakshman writes:

> Desire tells us: get this and then you will be happy. We believe it and we try to acquire the relevant object. If we don't get it, or if we don't get enough, we suffer. If we get it, then desire immediately suggests another objective, and we don't even see that we have been fooled. (Quoted by Boirel, 1977)

These philosophers are advocating the ideal of ataraxy, that is, the absence of turmoil as a result of the extinction of desire. The alternative to this extreme solution is *creative consumption*, that is, consumption that encourages ascending motivations of progress, self-actualisation and excellence. If it is true that 'man prefers hunting to the catch', as Pascal said, then want, as being the driving force of activity, can be the first cause of satisfaction brought about by creative consumption.

3.3. The multidimensional structure of the individual customer's needs

The contributions of motivation theory help us to identify more general motivational orientations in human beings. These orientations govern a large variety of individual behaviour. These disciplinary contributions, however, provide only a general description of the needs structure, with little attempt at operationalisation and no explicit reference to buying behaviour. Moreover, they tend to focus on one dimension of behaviour (economic, social, psychological, and so on) and do not propose a comprehensive framework that integrates the concepts used in each contributing discipline. The question is to know what are the values sought by the buyer and how to translate these values in products and services adapted to the buyers' expectations. Several attempts have been made to develop a comprehensive list of the needs sought.

Well-being means having a product or service to satisfy each need, so a natural approach is to develop a list of needs and to compare it with available goods. The word 'goods' here has a special meaning. They are not only physical entities or services, but may be abstract, social or psychological entities, such as love, prestige, and so on. The seminal works of Murray (1938), Maslow (1943), Rokeach (1973) and Sheth *et al*. (1991) are representative of this approach.

3.3.1. Murray's inventory of human needs

Murray calls a need a hypothetical construct because it is of a physiochemical nature that is unknown. It resides in the brain and is thus in a position to control all significant behaviour. In Murray's words:

> A need is a hypothetical construct that stands for a force in the brain region that organises and directs mind and body behaviour so as to maintain the organism in its most desirable state. (Murray, 1938, p. 123)

Murray gives a rather systematic inventory, classifying individuals' needs into four dimensions: *primary (viscerogenic) and secondary (psychogenic)* needs, according to whether they are of physiological origin or not; *positive and negative needs*, depending on whether the individual is attracted by the object or not; *manifest or latent needs*, according to whether the need drives to a real or imaginary behaviour; and *conscious or unconscious needs*, according to whether or not they drive the individual to take introspective steps. Murray lists 37 needs covering these categories.

Murray believes that all people possess the same needs, but he recognised that the expression of them differs from one person to another because of differences in personality and environmental factors. Needs could be provoked by either internal or external stimuli, and they could be weak or strong at any particular time. Needs exist in three different states: (1) refractory, in which no incentive arouses it; (2) inducible, in which a need is inactive but susceptible to excitation; and (3) active, in which the need is determining the behaviour of the organism (Murray, 1938, pp. 85–6). Thus, marketing activities could have a direct impact on inducible needs.

3.3.2. Maslow's need hierarchy

Maslow (1943) adopts a similar approach, grouping fundamental needs into five categories: physiological, safety, social, esteem and self-actualisation needs. Exhibit 3.2 describes these needs. Maslow's analysis,

---

EXHIBIT 3.2

MASLOW'S HIERARCHY OF NEEDS

Primary needs

- Physiological needs – these are fundamental; once satisfied, they cease to be determinant factors of motivation and no longer influence behaviour.
- Safety needs – physical safety, preservation of the physical structure of the organism, psychological safety, conservation of the psychic structure of personality. Need for own identity, to feel in charge of one's destiny.

Secondary needs

- Social needs – people are social animals and feel the need to fit into a group, to associate with their fellows, they feel the need to love and be loved. Mutual help, belonging and sense of community are also social needs.

- Self-esteem needs – self-esteem, personal dignity, confidence in oneself and one's own competence. The feel that one's objectives are valid. The esteem that others feel for us. The need for recognition, to be respected, to have a social status.

Tertiary needs

- Self-actualisation needs – those needs are at the top of the scale of human needs, and include self-realisation and development; the need of people to surpass themselves; to use all their capacities and push their limits; and to give a meaning to things and find their 'raison d'être'.

Source: Adapted from Maslow (1943).

however, goes further and is not limited to a simple classification. Maslow postulates the existence of a hierarchy of needs, which depends on the individual's state of development.

According to Maslow, there is an order of priorities in needs, in the sense that we begin to try to satisfy dominant needs before going on to the next category. Once the needs of a lower order have been satisfied, they allow needs of the higher order to become motivators and influence our behaviour. There is a progressive abatement in the intensity of needs already met and an increasing intensity of needs of a higher order not yet satisfied. As illustrated in Figure 3.4, we observe an evolution of the structure of needs depending on the individual's development as he or she goes from an overall objective of survival or living standard towards more qualitative objectives regarding lifestyle or quality of life.

Maslow's analysis is interesting because it puts forth not only the multidimensional structure of needs, but also the fact that needs have different degrees of intensity in different individuals. In reality, there is always some coexistence of these categories of needs, with one category or another becoming more important according to the individual, or according to the circumstances of one particular individual.

Products to be developed for satisfying needs must therefore be planned accordingly. A good or product may have more than one role or function beyond just the basic one. Individuals use goods not only for practical reasons, but also to communicate with their environment, to show who they are, to demonstrate their feelings, and so on.

For example, the food products available on the market today provide at the same time (a) physiological solutions to consumers due to their nutritional structure, (b) safety guaranteed through the certified quality control and labelling, (c) belonging and sense of

community through the signals as local or regional products, and (d) self-esteem created by the prestige or reputation of the brand (see Table 3.1).

It is important for marketing to be aware of the role played by goods and brands, not simply for their functional value, but also for their emotional or symbolic values. We shall see later in this chapter that the multidimensional structure of needs also exists with the organisational customer.

3.3.3. Rokeach's list of values

Research on human values stresses the important goals that most people seek. Values are closely linked to human needs, but exist at a more realistic level. They are the mental representations of underlying needs, not only of individual needs but also of societal and institutional needs. In other words, values are our ideas about what is desirable.

> A value is an enduring belief that a specific mode of conduct or end-state of existence is personally or socially preferable to an opposite or converse mode of conduct or end-state of existence. A value-system is an enduring organisation of beliefs concerning preferable modes of conduct or end-states of existence along a continuum of relative importance. (Rokeach, 1973, p. 5)

There are two types of values: (1) terminal and (2) instrumental. Terminal (or end-state) values are beliefs we have about the goals or end-states for which we strive (e.g. happiness, wisdom, and so on). Instrumental (or means) values refer to beliefs about desirable ways of behaving to help us attain the terminal values (e.g. behaving honestly or accepting responsibility).

Since values are transmitted through cultures, most people in a given society will possess the same values, but to different degrees. The relative importance of each value

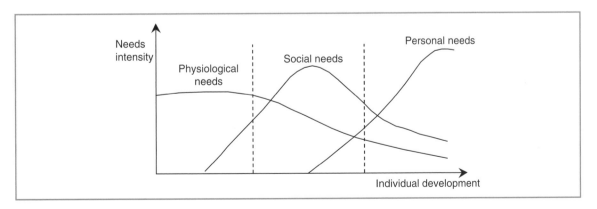

Figure 3.4 Maslow's hierarchy of needs
Source: Adapted from Maslow (1943).

Table 3.1 Organic food interpreted by Maslow's hierarchy

Needs hierarchy	Interpretation
Self-actualisation needs	It helps save the planet
	It is better for the environment
Esteem needs	It is trendy
	It is healthier
Social needs	I support local farmers
	I am doing the right thing
Safety needs	It is better for my children
	It is safer
Physiological needs	It tastes better

will therefore be different from one individual to another and these differences can be used as market segmentation criteria, as shown in Chapter 6 of this book. The prominence of different values can also change over time. Rokeach postulates that the total number of values that a person possesses is relatively small. In his empirical work, Rokeach identifies 18 terminal and instrumental values (Rokeach, 1973, p. 28).

In recent years, researchers have been working to develop a shortlist of values that can be measured in a reliable manner. Kahle (1983) has identified eight summary terminal values

- self-respect,
- security–Warm relationships,
- sense of accomplishment,
- self-fulfilment,
- being well-respected,
- sense of belonging,
- fun/enjoyment/excitement.

Several researchers have found that these values relate well to various aspects of consumer behaviour or to social change.

> For example, people who value fun and enjoyment may desire a cup of coffee for its rich taste, whereas people who value a sense of accomplishment may wish to use coffee as a mild stimulant to increase productivity; and people who value warm relationships with others may want to share a cup of coffee as an aspect of a social ritual. (Kahle *et al.*, 1988)

The logic of this methodology can be summarised as follows: to understand individuals' motivation, one place to start is to try to understand their values, particularly with products that involve consumer value. Also, an understanding of the way values are changing in a given society will facilitate the development of effective strategies for dealing with the dynamics of societal change.

3.3.4. The means–end chain model

The works of Maslow (1943) and Rokeach (1973) have shown values to be a powerful force in governing the behaviour of individuals in all aspects of their lives. Their use in marketing research is interesting, both from an analytical and predictive point of view, to relate consumers' behaviour to their values. Such is the objective of the means–end chain (MEC) concept developed by Gutman (1982) and by Reynolds and Gutman (1988).

> For example, knowing that consumers want to look well dressed doesn't tell us much about their values level consideration, unless we know why they want to look that way, that is their 'desired end-state'. Is it a purely functional objective, a desire to seduce a partner, the search for novelty and stimulation, a concern for integration in a social or professional group, or simply a personal accomplishment objective?

The MEC model attempts to explain how consumers select products that will be instrumental in helping them achieve their desired consequences, which in turn move consumers towards their valued end-states. The means are the purchased products or services, while the ends are the desired terminal values proposed by Rokeach and viewed as desirable end-states of existence sought by individuals through their consumption behaviour. As illustrated in Figure 3.5, a conceptual representation of the chain is divided into three parts: (a) the product attributes (tangibles and intangibles); (b) the consequences (physiological or psycho-sociological) resulting from the consumption behaviour accruing directly or indirectly to the consumer, and (c) the terminal or instrumental values.

For uncovering means and ends hierarchies as described above, Reynolds and Gutman (1988) have developed an in-depth interviewing and analysis methodology, called the laddering technique, which involves a tailored individual interviewing format with the goal of determining the links between the key perceptual elements across the range of attributes, consequences and values. Interpretation of this type of information permits an understanding of consumers' underlying personal motivation with respect to a given product class. This is more the field of qualitative or in-depth research. To go further on this topic, see Reynolds and Gutman (1988), Valette-Florence (1994) and Pellemans (1998).

3.3.5. The Sheth–Newman–Gross theory of consumption values

Applying the concept of 'value' to buying behaviour, Sheth, Newman and Gross (1991, pp. 18–25) describe market choice as a multidimensional phenomenon

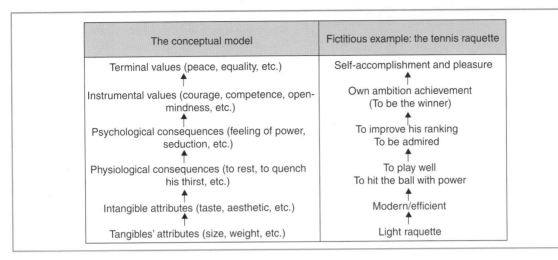

The conceptual model	Fictitious example: the tennis raquette
Terminal values (peace, equality, etc.)	Self-accomplishment and pleasure
↑	↑
Instrumental values (courage, competence, open-mindness, etc.)	Own ambition achievement (To be the winner)
↑	↑
Psychological consequences (feeling of power, seduction, etc.)	To improve his ranking To be admired
↑	↑
Physiological consequences (to rest, to quench his thirst, etc.)	To play well To hit the ball with power
↑	↑
Intangible attributes (taste, aesthetic, etc.)	Modern/efficient
↑	↑
Tangibles' attributes (size, weight, etc.)	Light raquette

Figure 3.5   The means–end chain model
Source: Adapted from an example proposed by Derbaix (1997).

involving multiples values: functional, social, emotional, epistemic and conditional. They define these values as follows:

1. *Functional value*. The perceived utility acquired by an alternative as the result of its ability to perform its functional, utilitarian or physical purposes. Alternatives acquire functional value through the possession of salient functional, utilitarian or physical attributes.

2. *Social value*. The perceived utility acquired by an alternative as a result of its association with one or more social groups. Alternatives acquire social value through association with positively or negatively stereotyped demographic, socio-economic and cultural ethnic groups.

3. *Emotional value*. The perceived utility acquired by an alternative as a result of its ability to arouse feelings or affective states. Alternatives acquire emotional value when associated with specific feelings or when they facilitate or perpetuate feelings.

4. *Epistemic value*. The perceived utility acquired by an alternative as a result of its ability to arouse curiosity provides novelty and/or satisfies a desire for knowledge. Alternatives acquire epistemic value through the capacity to provide something new or different.

5. *Conditional value*. The perceived utility acquired by an alternative as a result of the specific situation or the context faced by the choice-maker. Alternatives acquire conditional value in the presence of antecedent physical or social contingencies that enhance their functional or social value, but do not otherwise possess this value.

These five values make differential contributions to specific market choices in the sense that some values can contribute more than others. Those values are also independent. They relate additively and contribute incrementally to choice. Although it is desirable to maximise all five values, users are often willing to accept less of one value to obtain more of another. That is why buyers are willing to trade off less salient values in order to maximise those that are most salient (Sheth *et al.*, 1991, p. 12).

Considerable overlaps are observed, when comparing these summary values with the different need categories proposed by diverse disciplines. The functional value corresponds to the general motivation for comfort in Murray's viscerogenic needs and in Maslow's safety and physiological needs. The social and emotional functions correspond with Maslow's social needs of belongingness and love, with Rokeach's values of 'social recognition' and 'true friendship' and with the more general motivation for stimulation. The epistemic value is similar to Maslow's need for 'self-actualisation', to Rokeach's values of 'exciting life' and 'pleasure' and also to the general need for stimulation and pleasure. Previous contributions did not include the conditional value construct, which is particularly well adapted to the situation of buying behaviour. In addition, Sheth *et al.* (1991; see Chapter 5) have operationalised their theory by developing a generic questionnaire and a standardised procedure for adapting the analysis to any specific market situation.

The 'value' approach provides the market analyst with a simple but comprehensive framework for analysing the need structure of the individual buyer and for segmenting markets. The five summary values proposed by Sheth–Newman–Gross theory will be used in the following section to define the concept of the multi-attribute product.

3.4. The Motivation of the B2B Customer

So far, our analysis has concerned only the needs and motivations of the individual as a customer. But a large part of commercial activity, in any economy, is made up of transactions between organisations, or business-to-business. This includes firms selling equipment, goods, intermediary products, raw materials, and so on to other firms which use these products in their own manufacturing process. Although the principles governing marketing are just as pertinent for firms selling industrial goods as for firms selling consumer goods, the concrete manner in which these principles are implemented may appear very different.

3.4.1. Specificities of business-to-business markets

The main differences between consumer and business-to-business marketing can be regrouped into three categories according to whether they relate to demand, to the profile of the organisational customer and to the characteristics of the industrial products or services (Bingham and Gomes, 2001).

The demand for industrial goods

The industrial or organisational demand is a derived demand, that is, a demand expressed by an organisation which uses the products purchased in its own manufacturing process, in order to meet either the demand of other organisations or the demand of the end-user. Thus, industrial demand is part of a chain – a supply chain – which depends on a downstream demand and is ultimately 'derived' from the demand of consumer goods. Industrial demand, and particularly capital equipment demand, is highly fluctuating and reacts strongly to small variations in final demand (the acceleration principle). Industrial demand is often price inelastic, in so far as the product represents a small fraction of its costs or constitutes a key component, perhaps made to exact specifications, which has no substitute.

The organisational customer

The industrial firm faces several customers: its direct customers and the customers of its direct customers also participating in the supply chain. At each level of the supply chain, the organisational customer has a collegiate structure: a group of individuals, the buying centre, who exercise different functions and roles and have distinct competencies and motivations. The organisational customer is a professional buyer,

technically competent; the purchase decision involves a degree of normalisation not found in consumer purchasing. Thus, the problem-solving approach in business-to-business markets is in general extensive.

Industrial product characteristics

The products sought are generally well defined by the customer who knows what is wanted; specifications are clearly defined and the supplier has little room for manoeuvring. Industrial products enter into the manufacturing process of the industrial customer and thus have a strategic, if not vital, importance. Industrial products often have a very large number of different uses, unlike consumer goods that are almost inevitably for a specific use.

3.4.2. The B2B customer as a decision centre

In an industrial firm, buying decisions, and especially the more important ones, are mostly taken by a group of people called the buying group or the buying centre.

> The buying centre is defined as consisting of those individuals who interact for the specific purpose of accomplishing the buying task … These persons interact on the basis of their particular roles in the buying process. The buying group is characterised by both a pattern of communication (interaction) and a set of shared values (norms) that direct and constrain the behaviour of the individual within it. (Webster and Wind, 1972, p. 35)

There are several distinct roles in the buying centre: users, influencers, purchasers, deciders and gatekeepers. These individuals are either involved in the purchase itself or are concerned about its possible consequences on the firm's activity, and thus participate in the purchase decision-making process one way or another. Understanding those roles will help one understand the nature of interpersonal influence in the buying decision process. The buying

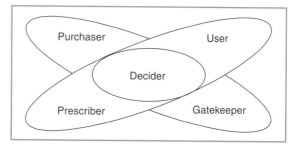

Figure 3.6 Typical composition of the B2B customer's decision centre

Source: Adapted from Webster and Wind (1972).

centre comprises individuals with different functions and therefore with different goals, motivations and behaviours. Hence many purchase decisions are conflicting, and they follow a complex process of internal negotiation. The composition of the buying centre varies with the importance of the decisions to be made. In general, the buying decision centre includes the following five roles (Figure 3.6), which can be occupied by one or several individuals:

1. *Purchasers* have formal authority and responsibility for selecting alternative brands and suppliers and for determining the terms of purchase and negotiating contracts. The purchasing manager usually does this.
2. *Users* are the persons who use the product: the production engineer or the workers. The users can formulate specific purchase requirements or refuse to work with some materials. Generally speaking, users are better placed for evaluating the performance of purchased goods and services.
3. *Influencers* do not necessarily have buying authority but can influence the outcome of a decision by defining criteria that constrain the choices that can be considered. R&D personnel, designers, engineers and consultants, and so on typically belong to this category.
4. *Deciders* have formal authority and responsibility to determine the final selection of brands or vendors. There is generally an upper limit on the financial commitment that they can make, reserving larger decisions for other members of the organisation, for instance the board of directors.
5. *Gatekeepers* are group members who control the flow of information into the group and who can exercise indirect influence on the buying process.

The composition of the buying centre will vary with the complexity and the degree of uncertainty of decisions in the firm. One can distinguish three kinds of situation:

1. *New task*: the purchase of a new product in a new class of products for the client organisation.

2. *Modified rebuy*: problem and product are known, but some elements of the buyers' specifications are modified.
3. *Straight rebuy*: purchase of a known product, not modified and with which the firm has extensive experience.

In the first two cases the buying centre intervenes totally. One can see that it is vital for the supplier to identify all those involved in the purchasing process, because it must identify the targets of its communication policy. It is equally important to understand how these participants interact among themselves and what their dominant motivation is.

3.4.3. Generic needs of the B2B customer

The industrial customer is therefore identified with the 'buying centre' that comprises persons from different functions in the organisation, who thus have distinct personal and organisational motivations. The notion of need in industry goes beyond the conventional idea of rational choice based only on the quality–price criterion. Choices are rational, as in the case of the individual consumer, in so far as all motivations and constraints with a bearing on purchase decisions are taken into account: personal motivations, interpersonal relations, economic and organisational constraints, environmental pressures, and so on. As in the case of the individual consumer, need therefore has a multidimensional structure. The generic needs of an industrial customer can be described with reference to at least five values:

1. *Technology*: product specifications, state-of-the-art technology, up-to-date and constant quality, just-in-time delivery, and so on.
2. *Finance*: price competitiveness, transfer costs, installation and maintenance costs, payment terms, delivery reliability, and so on.

EXHIBIT 3.3

THE NEEDS OF AN INDUSTRIAL CUSTOMER: AN EXAMPLE

The statement from the purchase manager: 'No, we won't work with this supplier any more, they are not reliable', may have different meanings:

- The quality of their products is not constant (technical value).
- Their prices are whimsical (financial value).
- They were supposed to have repaired a machine two months ago (assistance value).

- They have promised to send one of their engineers to tell us about new products being developed; we have called many times and they still have not done it (information value).
- They treat us as insignificant (psycho-sociological value).

Source: Valla, (1980, p. 25).

3. *Assistance*: after-sales service helps with installation and operation, technical assistance and servicing, and so on.
4. *Information*: communication, qualified sales personnel, priority access to new products, training, business intelligence, and so on.
5. *Strategy*: reciprocal relations, compatibility of organisational forms, brand or company reputation, and so on.

The examples presented in Exhibit 3.3 illustrate the multidimensional nature of the industrial customer's need.

We note that the determinants of well-being for the industrial client are of a very different nature from those governing the well-being of the individual consumer.

The structure of motivations of the industrial customer is both more complex and simpler. It is more complex because it involves an organisation and different individuals operating in the organisation; it is simpler because the main motivations are more objective and thus easier to identify. However, despite the real differences that exist between the two areas, the basic ideas of the market orientation concept have the same relevance in the industrial market as they have in the consumer market: to adjust supply to the overall need of the customer.

If this principle is not implemented, the penalty in the industrial market is probably paid more rapidly because of the buyer's professionalism and the fact that needs are more clearly defined.

CHAPTER SUMMARY

The satisfaction of customers' needs is at the heart of a market economy, yet it is popular in some quarters to claim that marketing creates needs. The notion of need generates controversy because it contains value judgement based on morality or ideology. Apart from the ethical or social rules imposed by society, marketing is pluralist and respects the diversity of tastes and preferences. The distinction between absolute and relative generic needs brings to the fore the existence of a dialectic of relative needs which leads to the general impossibility of saturation. Similarly, the distinction between generic and derived needs shows that saturation does not relate to generic needs but only to derived needs, that is, the dominant technological response at the time. Experimental psychology has proposed a range of motivational orientations. Particularly useful are the conceptual frameworks proposed by the stimulus–response theory, Maslow's need hierarchy and the Sheth–Gross–Newman theory of consumption values. If the principles governing organisational or business-to-business marketing are the same as for consumer marketing, a major difference exists. The industrial customer is represented by a group of individuals, called the buying centre, who exercise different functions and have distinct motivations.

Review and Application Questions

1. What are the implications of Galbraith's criticism of marketing as the creator of artificial needs?
2. How do generic needs differ from derived needs? Give two examples.
3. Is the Maslow's hierarchy of needs still valid today more than 50 years after its publication?
4. By reference to the typology as proposed by either Maslow or Sheth, Newman and Gross, explain the success of products such as Coca-Cola, Club Med, Swatch. Choose a product to illustrate your answer.
5. Describe and compare the structure of the needs of an individual customer and those of an industrial customer. Identify the main similarities and differences.
6. Describe the needs of each member of a buying decision centre in a company which produces high-tech goods.
7. Is it possible to imagine a point of complete saturation of consumption?

Bibliography

Abbott, L. (1955), *Quality and Competition*, New York, John Wiley & Sons.

Attali, J. and Guillaume, M. (1974), *L'anti-èconomique*, Paris, Presses Universitaires de France.

Becker, G.S. (1965), A Theory of the Allocation of Time, *The Economic Journal*, September, pp. 494–517.

Berlyne, D.E. (1960), *Conflict, Arousal and Curiosity*, New York, McGraw-Hill.

Bingham, F.G. and Gomes, R. (2001), *Business Marketing*, Chicago, IL, NTC Contemporary Publishing Inc. Second Edition.

Boirel, M. (1977), *Comment vivre sans tension?* Brussels, Marabout.

Cotta, A. (1980), *La société ludique*, Paris, Grasset.

Derbaix, C. (1997), *Analyse du comportement du consommateur*, Notes de cours, FUCAM.

Duffy, E. (1957), The Psychological Significance of the Concept of Arousal and Activation, *The Psychological Review*, 64, September, pp. 265–75.

Gibbs, P. (2004), Marketing and the Notion of Well-being, *Business Ethics: A European Review*, 13, 1, January, pp. 5–14.

Gutman, J. (1982), A Mean-end Chain Model on Consumer Categorization Processes, *Journal of Marketing*, 46, Spring, pp. 60–72.

Hamel, G. and Prahalad, C.K. (1994), *Competing for the Future*, Boston, MA, Harvard University Press.

Hebb, D.O. (1955), Drives and the C.N.S. (Conceptual Nervous System), *The Psychological Review*, 62, July, pp. 243–54.

Henochsberg, M. (2001), *La place du marché*, Paris Denoel.

Kahle, L.R. (1983), *Social Values and Social Change, Adaptation to Life in America*, New York, Praeger.

Kahle, L.R., Poulos, B. and Sukhdial, A. (1988), Changes in Social Values in the United States During the Past Decade, *Journal of Advertising Research*, February–March, pp. 35–41.

Katona, G. (1951), *Psychological Analysis of Economic Behavior*, New York, McGraw-Hill.

Keynes, J.M. (1936), *Essays in Persuasion – Economic Possibilities for our Grandchildren* [The Collected Writings of J.M. Keynes], Vol. 9, London, Macmillan.

Lancaster, K.J. (1966), A New Approach to Consumer Theory, *The Journal of Political Economy*, 74, April, pp. 132–57.

Maslow, H. (1943), A Theory of Human Motivation, *The Psychological Review*, 50, pp. 370–96.

Murray, H.A. (1938), *Explorations in Personality*, New York, Oxford University Press.

Nuttin, J. (1980) *Théorie de la motivation humaine*, Paris, Presses Universitaires de France.

Pellemans, P. (1998) *Le marketing qualitatif*, Brussels, De Boeck Université.

Ratchford, B.T. (1975), The New Economic Theory of Consumer Behaviour. An Interpretive Essay, *Journal of Consumer Research*, 2, September, pp. 65–78.

Reynolds, T.J. and Gutman, J. (1988), Laddering Theory, Method, Analysis and Interpretation, *Journal of Advertising Research*, February–March, pp. 11–31.

Rochefort, R. (1995), *La société des consommateurs*, Paris, Odile Jacobs.

Rokeach, M.O. (1973), *The Nature of Human Values*, New York, The Free Press.

Rosa, J.J. (1977), Vrais et faux besoins, in *L'économique retrouvé*, Rosa, J.J. and Aftalion, F. (eds), Paris, Economica.

Scitovsky, T. (1976), *The Joyless Economy*, Oxford, Oxford University Press.

Séguéla, J. (1982), *Hollywood lave plus blanc*, Paris, Flammarion.

Sheth, J.N., Newman, B.I. and Gross, B.L. (1991), *Consumption Values and Market Choices: Theory and Applications*, Cincinnati, OH, South Western Publishing Company.

Valaskakis, K., Sindell, P. and Smith, J. G. (1978), *La société de conservation*, Montreal, Les éditions Quinze.

Valette-Florence, P. (1994), Introduction à l'analyse des chaînages cognitifs, *Recherche et Applications en Marketing*, 9, 1, pp. 93–117.

Valla, J.P. (1980), Le comportement des groupes d'achat, in *L'action marketing des entreprises industrielles*, Paris, Collection Adetem, pp. 22–38.

Webster, F.E. and Wind, Y. (1972), *Organizational Buying Behavior*, Englewood Cliffs, NJ, Prentice Hall.

the customer purchase behaviour 4

Chapter contents

Chapter learning objectives

When you have read this chapter, you should be able to understand

- the different customer roles in B2C markets;
- the customer problem-solving approach in B2C and B2B markets;
- the concept of industrial supply chain;
- the product viewed as a bundle of attributes;
- the concept of Customer Relationship Management;
- the customer behaviour after usage or consumption;
- the measures of satisfaction/dissatisfaction.

Chapter introduction

The objective of this chapter is to describe the way customers make purchasing decisions. We shall first describe the different customer roles in B2C markets and then the customer purchasing behaviour successively in the B2C and in the B2B environments. In the B2B section, we will introduce the concept of the industrial supply chain, a key notion in B2B market-driven management. We will also present the concept of a product viewed by the customer as a bundle of values. Finally, after a brief discussion of the customer response behaviour, we shall analyse the customer after usage behaviour.

4.1. The different customer roles

Any marketplace transaction requires at least three customer roles: (1) buying (i.e. selecting) a product or service; (2) paying for it and (3) using or consuming it. Thus, a customer can be a buyer, a payer or a user/consumer (Sheth *et al.*, 1999):

1. The user is the person who actually consumes or uses the product or receives the benefits of the service.
2. The payer is the person who finances the purchase.
3. Finally, the buyer is the person who participates in the procurement of the product from the marketplace.

Each of these roles may be carried out by the same person (e.g. the housewife) or an organisational unit (e.g. the purchase department) or by different persons or departments (see Figure 4.1). As underlined by Sheth *et al.* (1999, p. 6), the person who pays for the product or service is not always the one who is going to use it. Nor is the person who uses it always the person who purchases it. Any of the three customer roles (user, payer or buyer) makes a person a customer. Table 4.1 illustrates the cross-classification of customer roles and values.

It is therefore important in any market situation to know the possible ways in which customers divide their roles among themselves in order to adapt the marketing efforts to the type of role specialisation. Four types of role specialisation can be identified.

1. *User is buyer and payer.* Most consumer products purchased for personal use fall into this category, like clothing, watches, sporting goods, haircuts, and so on. A single person combines all three roles. This is the traditional domain of consumer analysis, even if the same concentration of roles can also be observed in business markets for small business owners.

2. *User is neither payer nor buyer.* Here the user is different from both the payer and the buyer, a situation met in consumer markets for a whole range of products purchased by the housewife for her household or children's use (Exhibit 4.1). Similarly, in business-to-business markets, the purchasing department is buying and paying for many products like office furniture and equipment, consumable products for employees who are using the goods, while not associated in the buying decision. As we shall see in the next section, in business-to-business markets, for high perceived risks buying decisions, the purchasing process is more complex and the role specialisation less clearly defined.

3. *User is buyer but not payer.* In some situations, the user may be the buyer but not the payer for the product or service. All purchasing decisions made on expense accounts fall into this category. Also the user, who is nevertheless the buyer, does not pay the services offered within the framework of insurance coverage or social security programmes. For example, in many companies, a large variety of health plans are offered from which employees choose. Although the employee will be the buyer and the user, he is not paying. The risk of over-consumption is often observed in this type of situations.

4. *User is payer but not buyer.* In some cases, the user is payer but not the buyer. For example, in business-to-business markets, an external agent may be retained to purchase equipment, raw materials or supplies for a

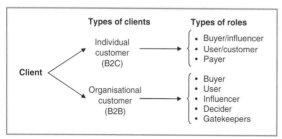

Figure 4.1 The different customer roles in B2C and B2B markets

Source: Authors.

Table 4.1   Cross-classification of customer roles and values

Values	Buyer	Payer	User
Universal	Service value	Price value	Performance value
Group-specific	Convenience value	Credit value	Social value
Individual-specific	Personalisation value	Financing value	Emotional value

Source: Sheth *et al.* (1999, p. 61).

EXHIBIT 4.1

FAMILY AS A PURCHASE DECISION CENTRE

As discussed in more detail below, the question of the *buying centre* and its structure is fundamental in B2B markets. It is also important in B2C markets, since buying decisions are hardly ever made by isolated individuals and mostly made within the family, which, in fact, constitutes a buying centre comparable to the one observed in an organisation.

Knowledge of purchasing habits implies identification of the respective roles (buyer, user, payer) of the mother, the father and the children, and this by-product category and at different stages of the buying process. These questions are important to marketers, who must adapt their product, price and communication policies to their real client, especially since the distribution of the roles and influence of spouses tends to change, due in particular to the rapidly changing role of women in society. One of the first proposed typologies suggests four allocations of roles (Herbst, 1952):

- autonomous decision by the husband or the wife,
- dominant influence of husband,
- dominant influence of wife,
- synchretic decision, that is, taken together.

The role of children is still to be taken into account. Comparison of the results of studies on the allocation of roles for various product categories shows that the influence of spouses varies greatly according to the type of product (Davis and Rigaux, 1974).

Pras and Tarondeau (1981, p. 214) emphasise that the aim of this kind of research is to define the strategies to be adopted due to a better understanding of the behaviour of the target group. Their relevance can be summarised as follows:

- Properly choose the persons to be questioned.
- Determine the content of advertising messages.
- Choose the best adapted support material.
- Adapt product conception to the needs of the person with greatest influence.
- Choose the most appropriate distribution network.

Mastering this set of information about buying habits will contribute to a significant improvement in the firm's marketing practice and thus increase the impact of behavioural response.

---

company which uses and pays for them. In the financial markets, stockbrokers act as agents for clients.

When a single customer embodies all the roles, the firm will use a different strategy than when different people are user, payer and buyer.

4.2. The purchasing process in B2C markets

From the marketing point of view, buying behaviour covers all activity preceding, accompanying and following the purchase decisions. The individual actively takes part in the decisions in order to make choices in a systematic way, as opposed to random or stochastic selections. The purchasing behaviour can be seen as a process of problem solving. The field of customer behaviour analysis is described in Figure 4.2. below.

4.2.1. Steps in the purchasing process

All possible steps that may have something to do with the resolution of the problem are therefore part of the buying process. They can be grouped into five stages:

1. Problem recognition.
2. Information search.
3. Evaluation of alternatives.
4. Purchase decision.
5. Post-purchase behaviour.

This view of an active buyer is in total contrast with that of the passive buyer who is dominated by the unconscious and is defenceless against the selling activities of the firm and advertisers. The complexity of the decision process varies, however, with the type of buying decisions and with the risk implied by the choice.

4.2.2. The principle of limited rationality

In this framework, purchasing behaviour is neither erratic nor conditioned by the environment. It is rational in the sense of the principle of limited rationality, which means within the bounds of individuals' cognitive and learning capacities. The implicit assumptions are the following:

- Consumers make choices after deliberation, the extent of which depends on the importance of the perceived risk.
- Choices are based on anticipation of future data and not only on short-term observations.
- Choices are also guided by the principle of generalised scarcity according to which any human acts. Any decision has an opportunity cost.

We live in an environment where everything is scarce: not only money and goods, but also information and especially time, our scarcest resource because it is perfectly inextensible (Becker, 1965).

This approach is called a *rational approach to problem solving*. The use of the term 'rational' is not in contrast with the term 'emotional', which implies a value judgement on the quality of the choice. The steps undertaken are considered to be rational as long as they are 'consistent' with the set objectives, whatever these objectives may be.

For example, an individual, for whom the social value or status effect is important, is prepared to pay more for a product with the same quality. Such action is considered to be rational because the behaviour is consistent.

In other words, as long as information about the objective is sought, critically analysed and processed, behaviour is rational within the limits of the gathered information and the cognitive capability of the individual. This, however, does not exclude the existence of another 'better' choice.

We are using here the notion of 'consistency' that is so dear to economists, with a fundamental difference. The consumer is consistent with respect to his or her own set of axioms, and not with respect to a set of axioms defined with no reference to a specific situational context or preference structure. Rational behaviour does not exclude impulsive behaviour. As long as the latter is adopted deliberately, either for the simple pleasure of acting impulsively, or for the excitement of being confronted with unexpected consequences, the behaviour is said to be rational.

Rationality here implies no more than the adoption of a kind of systematic choice procedure. This could be defined as the coherent use of a set of principles forming the basis of choice. When choice is made at random, behaviour is unpredictable and erratic, and analysis is impossible. Marketing accepts the existence of the latter type of behaviour, but believes that it is not representative of actual behaviour observed in most real-life situations.

This concept of consistency of behaviour makes it possible to reconcile different disciplinary approaches (economic, psychological and sociological) in the study of buying behaviour. Market-driven management is interested in the real person, the individual with all his or her diversity, as illustrated by the list of values described in the previous chapter. Actual choices are influenced by several values, but the individual or the organisation may very well accept a sub-optimal level of functional value, for example, in order to maximise social or epistemic value. This type of choice will be termed 'rational' because it is consistent with the personal set of values prevailing in the specific choice situation (conditional value).

4.2.3. The different problem-solving approaches

Three types of approach to problem solving can be distinguished, routine response behaviour, and limited and extensive problem-solving behaviours (Howard and Sheth, 1969):

1. *Extensive problem solving* is adopted when the value of information and/or the perceived risk are high. For example, this happens in situations where the buyer is confronted with an unfamiliar brand in an unfamiliar product class. The choice criteria by which alternatives are assessed will be weak or non-existent and an intensive information search will be necessary to identify the relevant criteria.

2. *Limited problem solving* applies to the situation of a buyer confronted with a new, unfamiliar brand in a familiar product class, usually where existing brands do not provide an adequate level of satisfaction. Choice criteria already exist, but there will still be a certain amount of search and evaluation prior to purchase.

3. *Routine response behaviour* is observed in the case where the consumer has accumulated enough experience and knowledge and has definite preferences about one or more familiar brands within a familiar product category. Here the process of choice is simplified and repetitive, with little or no prior information search. Under this situation of low involvement, considerable consumer inertia and/or brand loyalty would be expected.

4.2.4. Importance of the perceived risk

Not every purchase decision requires a systematic information search. The complexity of the approach to problem solving depends on the importance of the perceived risk associated with the purchase, in other words, on the uncertainty about the scope of the consequences of a particular choice. There are six kinds of risk or unfavourable consequences normally perceived by the buyer (Jacoby and Kaplan, 1972):

1. A *functional risk*, if the product characteristics or attributes are not in conformance with prior expectations.
2. A *financial loss*, when the product is faulty and needs replacement or repair at one's own expense.
3. A *loss of time*, due to hours of making complaints, returning to distributors, repairs, and so on.
4. A *physical risk*, due to the consumption or use of products potentially harmful to one's health or the environment.
5. A *social risk*, if the brand purchased conveys a social image which does not correspond to the true personality of the customer.
6. A *psychological risk*, when a bad purchase leads to loss of self-esteem or creates general dissatisfaction.

Market research shows that buyers develop strategies and ways of reducing risk that enable them to act with relative confidence and ease in situations where their information is inadequate and the consequences of their actions are incalculable (Bauer, 1960, p. 120).

To reduce the perceived risk before the purchase decision, the buyer can use various forms of information, such as personal sources (family, neighbours, friends), commercial sources (advertising, salespersons, catalogues), public sources (comparative tests, official publications) and experimental sources (product trials, inspection). The higher the perceived risk, the more extensive the information search will be.

The concept of *consumer involvement* has received considerable attention in the marketing literature. Involvement can be defined as:

> a state of energy (arousal) that a person experiences in regard to a consumption-related activity. (Wilkie, 1994, p. 164)

Thus involvement implies attention to something because it is somehow relevant or perceived as risky. High involvement requires high levels of prior deliberation and strong feelings, whereas low involvement will occur when consumers invest less energy in their thoughts and feelings. The concept of involvement, which overlaps somewhat with Howard and Sheth's classification of problem-solving situations above, is useful for analysing consumer behaviour

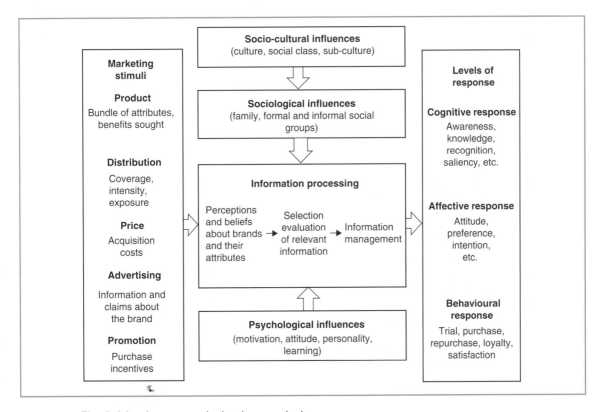

Figure 4.2   The fields of customer behaviour analysis

Source: Authors.

at different levels of involvement and for deciding on the type of communication strategy to adopt in each situation.

4.2.5. The costs of information

An individual facing a problem of choice undertakes the search for information mainly to reduce uncertainty about available alternatives, their relative values and the terms and conditions of purchase. We can classify the various costs incurred by this information search into three categories:

- *Inspection costs*, implied by studying different markets and defining the range of possibilities (including substitutes) that the buyer could include in the set being contemplated.
- *Perception costs*, borne in view of identifying the relevant characteristics of goods included in the choice set, as well as the terms of exchange (places of purchase, price, guarantee, and so on).
- *Evaluation costs*, resulting from the evaluation of how much the sought attributes are present and how authentic the market signals are about the quality of goods.

These costs are mainly in the form of time spent. But the cost of time – measured by its opportunity cost – varies from individual to individual; it also varies with factors of circumstance. For example, the cost of time is not the same during holidays as it is during a period of work. Therefore, it is not always in the consumer's interest to prolong the information search beyond a certain level. The extent of searching efforts will also vary with the degree of perceived risk in the buying decision under consideration.

4.2.6. The sources of information

The cost of perceiving attributes varies with the observable nature of the products' attributes and benefits. Nelson (1970, p. 214) establishes a distinction between *search goods* (having observable external qualities), *experience goods* (having verifiable internal qualities) and *credence goods* (having unverifiable internal qualities). For the first category of goods, the product attributes can easily be checked before purchase by simple inspection; these are products such as clothing, furniture and toys for which the choice criteria can easily be verified with little cost. For experience goods, however, the most important characteristics are only revealed with use, after purchase. Examples of this type of products are books, medicines, cars and computers. For this type of product, perception

costs can be very high for a single individual, and even higher for credence goods (like professional services). But the efficiency of surveying can be improved by using different sources of information, which have various degrees of reliability:

Information sources dominated by the producer: in other words advertising, opinions and advice given by sellers and distributors, displays and brochures. The advantage of this kind of information is that it is free and easily accessible. The information is, however, incomplete and biased, in the sense that it emphasises the positive qualities of the product and tends to overshadow others (Abernathy and Frank, 1996).

Personal information sources: dominated by consumers; this is information communicated by friends, neighbours, opinion leaders or what is better known as 'word of mouth'. This kind of information is often well adapted to the needs of the future buyer. Its reliability obviously depends on that of the person transmitting the information.

Information sources which are neutral: such as articles published in newspapers and reviews specialising in housing, furnishing, hunting, audio-visual products and automobiles. Such publications often provide a lot of information at a relatively low cost. This category also includes publications such as official reports or reports of specialised agencies, laboratory tests and comparative tests initiated by consumer associations. The advantage of this source of information is its objectivity, its factual nature and the competence of the opinions reported.

It is worth underlining here the specific role played by consumer associations. In a situation where the perception of the attributes of a product is particularly costly, it is in the interest of the individual consumer to regroup with other consumers in order to proceed with a thorough analysis that would be impossible for an individual alone. This is a form of unionisation of consumers, which constitutes a countervailing force vis-à-vis the firm, and has the reduction of the cost of information to the consumer as its main objective.

4.3. The purchasing process in B2B markets

The analysis of the buying process basically consists of identifying the specific roles played by each member of the buying centre at different stages of the decision-making process, their choice criteria, their perceptions of the performance of products or firms in the market and the weight given to each point of view, and so on.

Table 4.2   Decision stages and roles of the buying decision centre

Stages in the buying process	Composition of the buying centre				
	User	Influencer	Buyer	Decider	Gatekeeper
Identification of needs	*				*
Establishing specifications	*	*			*
Identifying alternatives			*		*
Evaluating alternatives	*	*	*	*	*
Selecting the supplier			*	*	*
Evaluation of performances	*				

Source: Webster and Wind (1972).

IMPLEMENTATION PROBLEM: HOW TO ANALYSE THE DECISION PROCESS IN A B2B MARKET?

The analysis of the purchasing process must answer the following questions:

- Who is a major participant in the decision-making process of buying a given industrial product?
- Who are the key influencers intervening in the process?
- What is the level of their influence?
- What evaluation criteria does each decision participant use?
- What is the weight given to each criterion?

4.3.1 Steps in the buying process

As in the case of the buying decision of the individual consumer, the industrial buying process can be divided into several stages. As illustrated in Table 4.2, Webster and Wind (1972, p. 80) suggest six phases in the process:

1. Anticipation and identification of need.
2. Determination of specifications and scheduling the purchase.
3. Search for buying alternatives.
4. Evaluation of alternative buying actions.
5. Selection of suppliers.
6. Performance control and appraisal.

This is typically the same sequence as that observed in the case of an *extensive problem-solving approach*.

Clearly, the decision of an industrial client does not always follow this process. The complexity of the decision and its degree of risk or novelty determine how formal the buying process will be. Furthermore, the decision-making and organisational processes can also vary according to the firm, both in terms of its size and its fields of activity. One can imagine that the roles of the members of the buying centre are different at each stage of the decision-making process.

The type of information required to understand the decision process in a B2B company is summarised in Box 4.1. This information is usually collected by survey. It helps to clarify the issue, particularly when it comes to training salespeople by helping them to understand the mechanism of the industrial buying process better.

Valla (1980, p. 27) underlines the fact that training salespeople to understand this type of analysis particularly helps them to

- understand better the buyer's role as well as the system of motivations and constraints within which the buyer operates;
- go beyond mere contact with the purchaser by identifying other possible communication targets within the industrial client's organisation;
- determine better when is the best moment to directly intervene vis-à-vis appropriate targets in order to increase efficiency of contacts;
- be in a better position to take advantage of opportunities when they present themselves, due to broader relations with all members of the buying centre.

We shall see in the following chapter that the way the buying centre functions is an important segmentation criterion in industrial markets.

4.3.2. The industrial supply chain

A central concept in B2B markets is the industrial supply chain. The notion of an industrial chain goes beyond a list of names by branch or by sector and makes the conventional division of the economy into primary, secondary and tertiary sectors out of date. An industrial chain consists of

all the stages of production, from raw materials to satisfying the final need of the consumer, irrespective of whether this final need concerns a product or a service.

There is a hierarchy of industries that are either clients or suppliers of a given firm according to whether they are upstream or downstream. The strategic force of an industrial client depends, among other things, on his ability to anticipate and control the end-market of the chain in which it participates.

4.3.3. Typical structure of an industrial chain

The following list describes the structure of a typical industrial demand (see Figure 4.3). Clearly the chain of demands may be much longer and more complex in some

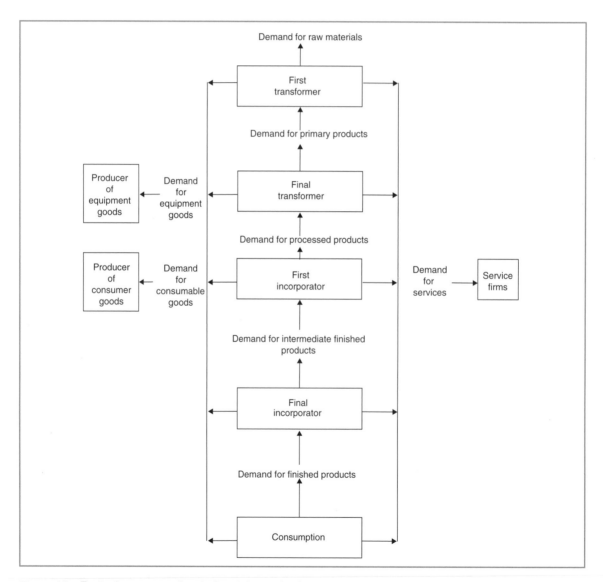

Figure 4.3   Typical structure of an industrial supply chain
Source: Authors.

cases. Without claiming this to be an exhaustive list, the following distinctions can be established:

First transformation. Demand is for processed materials that are transformed into semi-finished goods, for instance, steel bars, sheets, chemicals, leather, and so on.

Final transformation. Demand is for primary products that will be transformed into more elaborate processed products. For example, transformation of raw sheet metal into rustproof sheet metal either plated or pre-painted. Bekaert transforms raw steel into wires of different diameters.

First incorporation. Demand is for finished goods used to manufacture more complex products which are themselves components of other products. For example, pre-painted sheet metal is used to manufacture radiators; wires are used to manufacture radial tyres.

Final incorporation. Demand is for finished products incorporated in manufacturing finished products for final demand, for example, tyres and batteries, spark plugs, TV tubes, automobile windscreens, and so on.

Assemblers. Demand is for a large variety of products that will be put together to form systems or large compounds. For example, radiators are placed with other products to form a heating system. Similarly, a system of public transport, such as an underground rail system, brings together a tremendous variety of different products.

In addition to these successive demands that follow one another in a chain, there are also lateral demands of capital equipment goods, consumable items (fuel, wrapping materials, office supplies, and so on) and services (maintenance and repair, manufacturing and business services, professional services).

Therefore, the industrial firm in the position of the beginning of the production chain is faced with a sequence of independent demands that finally determine its own demand. It faces two categories of clients: its direct customers and the customers of its customers. In order to apply active marketing, the firm must take into account the specific demands of its direct customers, of the intermediary customers and of those who express final demand at the end of the chain. Figure 4.4 gives an example of the successive customers, direct and indirect, facing a manufacturer of heat pumps.

4.4. The product as a bundle of benefits

We have seen that, from a customer's point of view, a product can be defined as a 'bundle of attributes' which provides the customer with the functional value or 'core service' specific to that class of product, as well as a set of secondary values or utilities (called benefits or services) which may be necessary or added (see Figure 4.5). These additional services differentiate the brands and may have a determining influence on customers' preferences.

4.4.1. The core service or benefit

The core service provided by a brand corresponds to the functional value of its class of product; it is the basic and

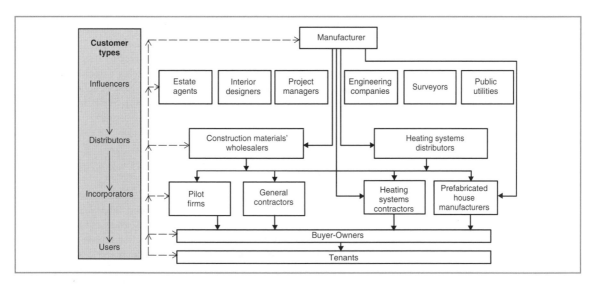

Figure 4.4 Vertical structure of the domestic heat pump market
Source: Authors.

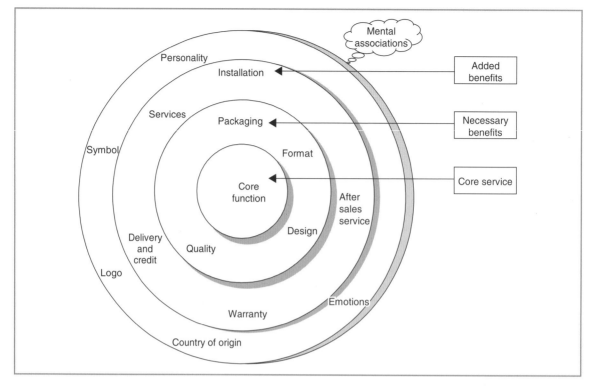

Figure 4.5   The branded product as a package of benefits

Source: Authors.

generic benefit provided by each of the brands in a given product category.

> For an air compressor, the core service is the production of compressed air; for a toothpaste, dental hygiene; for a watch, it will be time measurement; for an airline company, the transportation from Paris to New York; for wallpaper, home decoration, and so on.

As underlined earlier, the core service defines the reference market in generic terms by providing an answer to the question: 'What business are we in?' The rationale is the following:

- The customer is not looking for a product as such, but for the core service it provides.
- The customer can get the same core service from technologically different products.
- Technologies are moving and changing rapidly and profoundly, whereas the needs, to which the core service responds, remain stable.

Levitt (1980) states that in order to avoid the risk of myopia, it is in the firm's best interest to define its *reference market* with respect to the core service provided, rather than to a particular technology. This allows potential customers to identify the alternative solutions likely to be

considered when they are confronted with a choice problem.

All brands in the same reference market provide the customer with the same core service in a way that tends to become uniform, given that competition and the diffusion of technological progress balance out technological performance. Consequently, in a significant number of markets, the core service by itself is no longer a determining factor in the customer's decisions. The way in which the core service is provided or delivered becomes more of a deciding factor. See Exhibit 4.2 and Table 4.3.

4.4.2. The peripheral services

In addition to the basic functional utility, a brand provides a series of other utilities or peripheral services, which are secondary compared to the core service, but which may prove to be decisive when competing brands tend to have even performances. These peripheral services may be of two kinds: 'necessary' services and 'added' services.

Necessary peripheral services identify with the mode of production of the core service (fuel efficiency, roominess, noise, and so on) and all that normally accompanies the core service (packaging, delivery, payment terms, after-sales service, and so on).

For example, Atlas-Copco 'oil-free' compressors produce compressed air which is totally free of oil particles; Epson printers are particularly quiet; Japanese cars are well-known for their reliability; Apple microcomputers are very user-friendly; Bang and Olufsen products have an outstanding design; Swatch has a large variety of designs, and so on.

Added peripheral services are utilities unrelated to the core service, which the brand provides as extras. Hence they constitute an important source of differentiation.

For instance, Singapore Airlines offers a frequent flyers programme 'Privileged Passenger Service' (PPS) that is especially attractive; some makes of cars include radio equipment in their basic price; some credit cards give the right to preferential conditions in five star hotels; and so on.

These peripheral services themselves, whether necessary or added, form attributes which generate satisfaction for the customer. These attributes may differ greatly according to the brand and can thus be used as choice criteria (for an example see Table 4.4). Furthermore, one can imagine that different buyers attach different degrees of importance to the presence of some attributes. Thus, a brand can be defined as a bundle of attributes that produces the core service plus the peripheral services, necessary or added, whose importance and performance potential customers can differently perceive.

Note that any brand has at least one unique feature (generally more than one), which is simply its brand name

---

EXHIBIT 4.2

CONTRASTING PRODUCT CHARACTERISTICS. BENEFITS AND VALUES

- Characteristic: The physical or technical features of the product
  (A fry pan coated with Teflon)

- Benefit: The advantage brought to the customer by the characteristic
  (A non-sticky cooking)

- Value: The mental representation of the need met; thanks to the benefit
  (The pleasure of a trouble-free culinary experience)

Table 4.3   The bundle of attributes: the brand Hagen Daz

Objective characteristics	Brand attributes	Values
Patronymic brand name from the Polish founder based in the US	A suggestive Danish name, a country known for the quality of its dairy products	Healthy product
Percentage of air in the cream: 10% against 50% in competing brands	Full mouth – high density of the cream; unctuousness	Gourmet pleasure
Four noble ingredients: milk cream instead of butter; sugar cane; egg yolk instead of sweetening; farm milk instead of powder milk	Good and powerful taste; fully natural product	Reassurance
Vanilla from Madagascar; pecan nuts, strawberries from Oregon	Large variety of flavours	Diversity
Box of 500 ml designed by HD; easy to store	Exclusive package stored in refrigerated	Convenience
Price twice that of competing brands but affordable by everybody	Image of craft product – mass deluxe concept	A treat
Identical concept, brand name, packaging and communication worldwide	A global brand	Guarantee

Source: Authors.

and also mental associations (emotion, symbolic value, personality, and so on), which form the brand identity, a concept reviewed in Chapter 12. The customer's global perception of a brand is commonly referred to as the brand image.

4.5. Customer Relationship Management

The customer's satisfaction is at the heart of the marketing process and yet it is only in the 1980s (Berry, 1983) that companies have begun to systematically measure the degree of satisfaction felt by customers and to follow-up

---

EXHIBIT 4.3

EXAMPLES OF PACKAGE OF BENEFITS

- Small electrical motors: power, reliability, consumption, resistance, response speed, safety, size, weight.
- Industrial equipment: performance, reliability, ease of use, versatility, installation, maintenance, repair parts, delivery time, information, resell value.
- Automobiles: power, consumption, comfort safety, design, maintenance, resell value, prestige.
- Toothpaste: whitens teeth, fresh breath, cavity protection, gums protection, taste, pleasant texture.

---

their attitude and satisfaction after use or consumption. Previously, analysis was restricted to internal measures of quality such as ISO-9000. The most obvious level of satisfaction would seem to be the level of sales or market share, just as the number of complaints would be the sign of dissatisfaction.

In fact, things are much more complicated. There can be a big difference between what the company thinks customers want and what the customer is really looking for. In other words, the gap between the designed and the expected quality may be very large, even if the customer never formally expresses his or her dissatisfaction. This is why it is necessary to directly interview customers to assess scientifically their level of satisfaction/dissatisfaction. The value of this type of study is also to permit international comparisons for the same brand from country to country and to allow longitudinal analyses to keep track of the changes in satisfaction over a certain period.

4.5.1. Defining Customer Relationship Management

Although the term Customer Relationship Management, or CRM, is relatively new, the principles behind it are not: firms have long practiced some form of CRM generally assumed by the sales administration service. As explained by Payne and Frow (2006), what sets present-day CRM

Table 4.4   Evaluation of a supplier in an industrial market: viewed as a bundle of attributes

Macro-attributes (and weight)		Key sub-attributes	Internal metrics
Equipment	(30)	Reliability Easy to use Features/functions	% Repair call % Calls for help Function performance test
Sales	(30)	Knowledge Response Follow-up	Supervisor observations % Proposals made on time % Follow-up made
Installation	(10)	Delivery interval Does not break Installed when promised	Average order interval % Repair reports % Installed on due date
Repair	(15)	No repeat trouble Fixed fast Kept informed	% Repeat reports Average speed of repair % Customers informed
Billing	(15)	Accuracy: no surprises Resolve on first call Easy to understand	% Billing inquiries % Resolved on first call % Billing inquiries
Total	(100)	—	—

Source: Adapted from Kordupleski *et al.* (1993).

apart is that organisations now have an increased potential to utilise technology and manage *one-to-one relationships* (Pepper and Rogers, 1993) with potentially huge number of customers in a context of the global market. The purpose of Customer Relationship Management or CRM, is

> to efficiently and effectively increase the acquisition and retention of profitable customers by selectively initiating, building and maintaining appropriate relationships with them. (Payne and Frow, 2006, p. 136)

The objective of *relationship marketing* is to develop long-term and mutually profitable relationships not only with valued customers but with multiple stakeholders, although the focus of *customer relationship management* should be primarily on the customer.

The starting point is to identify in the target segment the *suspects*, that is, those potential customers who could have a strong potential interest in the product or service, *prospects* are those potential customers having a strong interest in the product and the ability to pay for it and *disqualified prospects* are those whom the company rejects because they have poor credit or would be unprofitable to serve. The firm will then try to convert qualified prospects in to *first-time customers*, and if satisfied in to *repeat customers or clients*. The next challenge is to *turn clients in to advocates, that is*, customers who praise the company and encourage others to buy from it (Griffin, 1995). See Figure 4.6.

Advances in information technology can help in building these selective relationships. Companies have at their disposal a range of database, data mart, and data warehouse technologies, as well as a growing number of CRM software programs. Such developments make it possible to gather vast amounts of customer data and to analyse, interpret and utilise it constructively. Furthermore, the advantages presented by increasingly powerful hardware, software and e-services are augmented by decreasing costs of running them. By using a wide range of CRM tools, companies can potentially target their most promising client opportunities more effectively (Payne and Frow, 2006).

This does not mean that such benefits will automatically be achieved by the purchase of CRM software solutions, as illustrated by many examples of CRM failure (Fournier *et al.*, 1998). Research has shown that successful CRM demands that members of different functions such as operational marketing, information technology and human resources management work to gather in cross-functional teams. It also implies that the market or the customer orientation culture is well disseminated at all levels within the firm. CRM is *customer-centric* and this business philosophy is prerequisite for successful application of CRM. In the 8th Bain & Company Annual Management Tools Survey, of the 25 tools rated by respondents, CRM ranked fourth from last for use satisfaction with a 35% global usage rate (Siddle and Rigby, 2001).

4.5.2. The B2B customer–supplier relationship management

In B2B markets, customers are more or less willing and able to control the customer–supplier relationship or to be actively involved in their relationship with their suppliers, as implied by CRM. In B2B markets, one can identify three major categories of customers, each varying in their

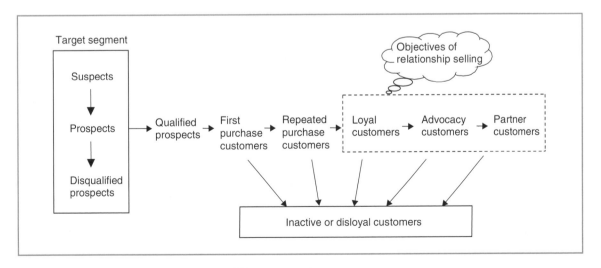

Figure 4.6   Typology of customers in a CRM perspective
Source: Griffin (1995).

degree of control and willingness to co-operate over their customer experience (Manning and Thorne, 2003).

The collaborative customer. These customers are able and willing to share in the control of the relationship with their suppliers. Shared control involves an exchange of information on the wants and desires of the customer along with the basic offerings by the supplier. This is the ideal type of customer orientation for one-to-one marketing to work. In the automotive sector, for example, parts suppliers are increasingly expected to provide expertise in the development and engineering of products.

The activist customer. In some circumstances, customers seek a high level of control of the business customer experience. In many industrial markets, this is the most common relationship. Manufacturers that act as customers set the specifications, delivery requirements and costs parameters, and their suppliers meet these terms.

The passive customer. A passive customer is primarily one who has a low level of involvement with his customer experience. Passive customers do not tend to be particularly loyal and they show low willingness to become more knowledgeable or to participate in the development of new products or solutions.

This typology of customers is important to adapt customer management relationships (CRM).

4.6. Customer post-purchase behaviour

The objective of CRM is to build long-term and mutually profitable relationships with valued customers. To achieve this objective (a) monitoring customer satisfaction, (b) handling properly complaints of dissatisfied customers, (c) designing appropriate solutions to their problems and (d) rewarding loyal customers are the key ingredients for success. The relationship selling approach and its pitfalls will be described in more details in Chapter 14.

4.6.1. The behaviour of dissatisfied customers

In a meta-analysis of customer satisfaction studies based on 500 surveys conducted in Europe in B2B business sectors, with an average of 300 interviews per survey, Goderis (1998, p. 285) obtained the following data:

- Only 2.9 per cent of sales transactions result in complaints made directly to the company.
- On average, 28.6 per cent of transactions result in indirect complaints to the sales representatives, neighbours, friends, and so on.
- In addition, 9.2 per cent of the complaints are never communicated.

There are two different explanations for this last group. Buyers have either minimised the problem or they were pessimistic about the outcome of a complaint, given the dominant position of the supplier or because, in previous instances, a complaint has remained unanswered. Thus, in total, 40.7 per cent of the transactions of an average firm may cause problems to customers, a level of dissatisfaction that is not well reflected by the tip of the iceberg, which is 3 per cent of formal complaints.

In so far as a complaint is efficiently handled by after-sales service, the negative consequences for the firm can be limited (see example given in Exhibit 4.4). On the other hand, a real problem remains with the 30 per cent group of dissatisfied customers who do not communicate with the supplier but who could really affect market share in the long run. This is why the adoption of a proactive attitude here is important by measuring regularly the level of satisfaction/dissatisfaction of different customer groups and identifying their causes. Remember that, in sectors where primary demand is non-expansible, 80–90 per cent of the turnover is due to existing customers. It is easy to understand why it is important to maintain satisfaction for this portfolio of existing customers

An additional argument is provided by analysis of the behaviour of dissatisfied customers whose complaints were

EXHIBIT 4.4

AIRLINE DELIGHT: AN EXAMPLE

If you dropped your cash-filled wallet in an airline seat, your natural expectation is that it is gone forever. You would be *satisfied* if the ground staff handled your report promptly with a promise, even without guarantees, that they would try their best to recover your wallet. You would be *annoyed* if you encounter red tape and indifference when you filed the report. You would be *delighted* if the airline found your wallet in no time and notified you that you may get your wallet with all the cash intact at the airline counter in your next destination. You would be *surprised* if an airline staff carries your wallet to your home. As a delighted and a surprised customer, you would write an unsolicited letter of compliment to the airline management; you would also become a loyal frequent flyer and tell the whole world about your wonderful experience with the airline.

Source: Domingo (1997, p. 282).

well handled by the firm. The findings reported in the Goderis study (1998, p. 286) have shown the following results:

■ For satisfied customers, the average repeat purchase rate is 91 per cent.
■ Among customers who had made a complaint but had received a poor response from the firm, the repeat purchase rate drops to 54 per cent.
■ Of dissatisfied customers who had complained and had received an appropriate response from the firm, the repeat purchase rate was 96 per cent, a rate higher than that observed for satisfied customers.

Problem customers are (a) those dissatisfied but who do not complain and (b) those that complain but are not happy with the way their complaint has been treated by the company (see Figure 4.7 for an example). The loss of customers comes from these two groups which constitute a form of negative advertising by word of mouth, costly for the firm and very difficult to control. Research findings (Rhoades, 1988) show that 'dissatisfied customers will tell ten other people about their bad experience with a company or a brand'.

Three important conclusions can be drawn from these various studies on dissatisfied customers' behaviours.

■ The level of satisfaction/dissatisfaction is key input data in the market information system of any company.
■ A complaint is not necessarily negative because the customer will accept a problem to the extent the company finds a good solution to the problem.
■ Complaints are important sources of information, allowing a company to better understand customer needs and their perception of the product quality.

Current complaint management is only one aspect, necessary but insufficient, of a total quality programme aiming at complete customer satisfaction.

4.6.2. Methods of measuring satisfaction/ dissatisfaction

The conceptual model underlying satisfaction/ dissatisfaction research is simply the attitude that the multi-attribute model discussed earlier in this chapter. The questions concern the importance of each attribute and the degree of perceived presence of the attribute (performance) in the evaluated product or service.

The interviewing procedure is in three steps. First, the overall level of satisfaction is obtained from the respondent; then importance and performance scores are requested for each attribute on a 10 points rating scale. Finally, repeat purchase intentions are measured.

4.6.3. Analysis of customer satisfaction

The first step is to calculate the average performance score for each attribute as well as its standard deviation. These scores are then compared to the average scores observed in the sector or to the scores obtained by priority competitors. This comparison will result in a good picture of how the market perceives the quality of the product, viewed as a package of benefits.

The performance scores obtained on the attributes are situated along two axes: on the horizontal axis are placed

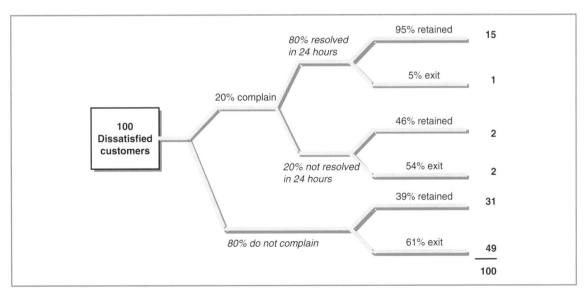

Figure 4.7   Customer base analysis
Source: Best (2003).

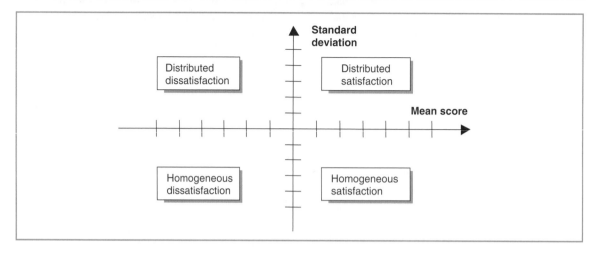

Figure 4.8 The 'satisfaction/dissatisfaction' matrix
Source: Goderis (1998).

the average performance scores and on the vertical axis the standard deviations for these scores. A high standard deviation means that few respondents have the same opinion and a low standard deviation will, on the contrary, show that most customers share the same opinion.

The choice of a cut-off point for these two axes is always a sensitive problem. It is common practice to use the average score observed in the sector or the score of the priority competitor. We then have a two-by-two matrix defining four quadrants as shown in Figure 4.8.

In the lower right-hand quadrant, the attributes of brand or company X have an average score superior to the sector's average and also a lower than average standard deviation. This means that customers are generally satisfied and agree to say so. We have here a case of 'homogeneous satisfaction'.

In the top right-hand quadrant, the brand's attributes also have an above average score, but the standard deviation this time is high which means that customers have varying opinions. We thus have a situation of 'distributed satisfaction', which can be caused, for example, by a lack of consistency in the quality of the services provided. Identification of the dissatisfied customers and of the causes of their dissatisfaction is a priority objective to adopt the individualised remedial actions before customers switch to competition.

In the upper left quadrant, the average is below the sectoral average and the standard deviation is high. This is a case of 'distributed dissatisfaction'; most of the customers are dissatisfied, but some are less dissatisfied than others are. This state of affairs can be explained by a product or service ill adapted to some customer group(s).

In the last quadrant, the lower left-hand one, customers are dissatisfied and agree to say so. This is the most unfavourable situation of 'homogeneous dissatisfaction'.

4.6.4. Satisfaction–dissatisfaction response styles

Customers can and do engage in multiple responses to satisfaction or dissatisfaction. The typology proposed by Jones and Sasser (1995) is particularly useful. Six types of loyalty behaviour are proposed.

- The *apostle*: a very satisfied customer who tells it to other prospects.
- The *loyalist*: a satisfied customer but who does not tell it to other people.
- The *defector*: a dissatisfied customer who keeps quiet.
- The *terrorist*: a very dissatisfied customer who talks too much.
- The *mercenary*: a customer who is mostly satisfied but who would do anything for obtaining a better deal.
- The *hostage*: a customer, satisfied or not, who has no option or no other choice.

Each company should analyse its customer base using this typology in order to adapt its response behaviour. An example of such an analysis is presented in Exhibit 4.5.

4.7. The satisfaction–loyalty relationship

As already underlined, a high level of satisfaction leads to increased customer loyalty, and increased customer loyalty is the single most important driver of long-term financial performance. The relationship between satisfaction and loyalty has been empirically established, namely by Jones and Sasser (1995), as shown in Figure 4.9.

EXHIBIT 4.5

COMPLAINT BEHAVIOUR IN THE PROFESSIONAL SERVICE SECTOR: AN EXAMPLE

Dart and Freeman (1994) have developed a typology of response styles among professional service clients. Three factors or types of complaint behaviour were identified.

- *Voice*: responses directed toward the firm.
- *Private*: word of mouth communication and/or discontinuance of the relationship with the firm.
- *Third party*: complaining to external agencies.

In a cluster analysis conducted on a sample of 224 respondents among business users of professional services (accounting), four segments were identified.

- *Passives (42 per cent)*: customers whose intentions to complain are below average on the three factors, especially for voicing complaints directly to the firm.

- *Voicers (34 per cent)*: dissatisfied customers who are more likely to complain to the firm and to engage in negative word-of-mouth behaviour.
- *Irates (5 per cent)*: customer who demonstrate above average private response such as negative word-of-mouth or switching firms.
- *Activist (19 per cent)*: customers who are likely to engage in above average behaviour in all three types of complaint behaviour.

Source: Dart and Freeman (1994).

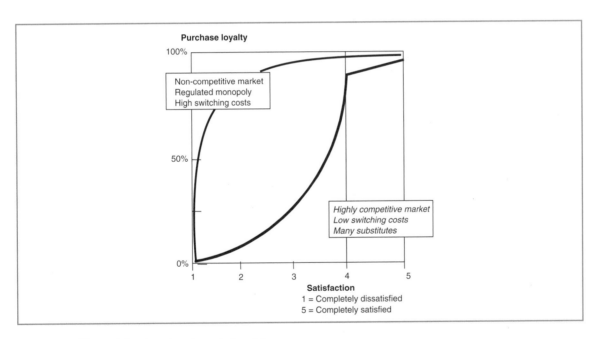

Figure 4.9   The satisfaction–loyalty relationship
Source: Adapted from Jones and Sasser (1995).

4.7.1. The brand loyalty concept

There are several approaches for operationally defining brand loyalty and for long the most popular one was based on the observation of purchase sequence. For example, a 12-trial purchase sequence of: AABAACAADAAE would qualify a consumer as being loyal to Brand A according to a per cent-of-purchase definition, but not according to most sequence definitions which require three or four consecutive purchases of the same brand as the criterion of loyalty. This purely behavioural view of loyalty has clear limitations, because attention is focused entirely on the *outcome of*, rather than the *reasons for*, behaviour.

For example, is the woman who always buys brand A because it is the cheapest, 'loyal' in the same sense as the woman who buys brand A because she prefers it? And what of the woman who buys brand A because it has the most favourable shelf space or because it is the only nationally advertised and distributed brand carried by the store in which she shops? (Day, 1969)

It is clear that, underlying the loyalty behaviour, there is an *evaluative process or an attitudinal component* linked to the purchaser's degree of satisfaction that must be identified. The repeat purchase behaviour is a necessary but not sufficient condition for defining brand loyalty. Jacoby and Kyner (1973) have presented six criteria considered necessary and collectively sufficient for defining brand loyalty.

Brand loyalty is (1) the biased (i.e. non-random), (2) behavioural response (i.e. purchase), (3) expressed over time, (4) by some decision-making unit, (5) with respect to one or more alternative brands out of a set of such brands, and (6) is a function of psychological (decision-making, evaluative) processes. (Jacoby and Kyner, 1973)

The term 'decision-making unit' implies that the decision-maker need not be (a) the user or even the purchaser of the product; but can also be the prescriber. Similarly, the decision-making unit can be an individual or a collection of individuals (family or organisation). The fifth condition is important because it introduces the concept of *multibrand loyalty, or brand repertoire*: Individuals can be, and frequently are, multibrand loyal. A brand switch can occur within a set of brands to which the buyer remains loyal. This behaviour is revealing of a loyal behaviour to a reduced set of brands, a construct close to the consideration set concept (see Howard and Sheth, 1969).

The brand (or company) loyalty concept is important in several respects, and in particular, in view of the relationship existing between loyalty and satisfaction – as discussed in the next section – and also because of the impact of customer loyalty on corporate profitability, as illustrated in Figure 4.10. (See also Exhibit 4.6.)

4.7.2. The satisfaction–loyalty relationship

According to conventional wisdom, the relationship between satisfaction and loyalty should be a simple linear relationship: as satisfaction increases, so does loyalty. A research conducted at Rank Xerox and replicated by Jones and Sasser (1995) showed a much more complex relationship. The two extreme curves of

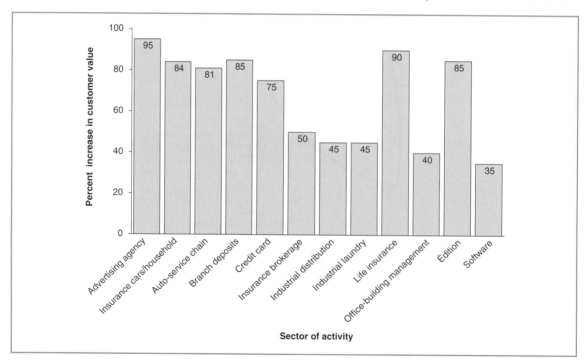

Figure 4.10 Impact of a 5 per cent increase of the loyalty rate on the net present value of a customer
Source: Reichfeld (1996, p. 48).

Figure 4.9 are representative of two different competitive situations:

1. *In non-competitive markets* – the upper-left zone – satisfaction has little impact on loyalty. These markets are typically regulated monopolies such as telecommunication, electrical or transportation utilities; or market situations where switching costs are very high. Customers in fact have no choice; they are captive customers. This situation can change rapidly, however, if the source of monopoly disappears, because of deregulation or the emergence of alternative technology.

2. *In competitive markets* – the lower-right zone – where competition is intense with many substitutes and low switching costs, a very large difference is observed between the loyalty of 'satisfied' (score of 4) and 'completely satisfied' (score between 4 and 5) customers.

This was namely the discovery made at the Xerox Corporation:

> its totally satisfied customers were six times more likely to repurchase Xerox products over the next 18 months than its satisfied customers. (Jones and Sasser, 1995, p. 91)

The implications are profound. Merely satisfying customers who have the freedom to make choices is not enough to keep them loyal. The only truly loyal customers are totally satisfied customers.

EXHIBIT 4.6

CUSTOMER LONGEVITY IS PROFITABLE

The more a customer is loyal, the more he contributes to the profitability, since the costs to find a new customer are supported only once. If every year, 5 per cent of the customer base quit and must be replaced, it means that a customer has an average life of 20 years. If the loyalty rate can be increased from 95 to 96 per cent thanks to a higher customer satisfaction level, only 4 per cent of customers have to be replaced and the average customer life jumps to 25 per cent, with a resulting strong improvement of the firm's profitability.

CHAPTER SUMMARY

A customer can be a buyer, a payer or a user/consumer. It is therefore important to know the possible ways in which customers divide their roles among themselves in order to adapt the marketing efforts to the type of role specialisation. In B2C markets, these three roles are often played by the same individual. In B2B markets, on the contrary, these roles are assumed by different persons.

Customer purchasing behaviour is neither erratic nor conditioned by the environment. It is rational in the sense of the principle of limited rationality, which means within the bounds of individuals' cognitive and learning capacities.

An industrial chain consists of all the stages of production, from raw materials to satisfying the final need of the consumer, irrespective of whether this final need concerns a product or a service.

From a customer's point of view, a product can be defined as a 'bundle of attributes' which provides the customer with the functional value or 'core service' specific to that class of product, as well as a set of secondary values or utilities (called benefits or services) which may be necessary or added. These additional services differentiate the brands and may have a determining influence on customers' preferences.

What sets present day Customer Relationship Management (or CRM) apart is that organisations now have an increased potential to utilise technology and manage one-to-one relationships with potentially huge number of customers in a context of the global market. The purpose is to efficiently and effectively increase the acquisition and retention of profitable customers by selectively initiating, building and maintaining appropriate relationships with them.

Customers' response means all mental or physical activity caused by a marketing stimulus. The various response forms of the buyer can be classified in three categories: cognitive response, which relates to retained information and knowledge, affective response, which concerns attitude and evaluation, behavioural response, which describes the actions taken, not only at the moment of purchase but also after the purchase. Post-behaviour is based mainly on the degree of satisfaction–dissatisfaction of customers. A good indicator of customer satisfaction is its loyalty rate.

Review and Application Questions

1. Give an example of each of the following from product categories of your choice: (a) when the user is neither a buyer nor a payer; (b) when the user is a buyer but not a payer; (c) when the user is also the buyer and the payer.
2. What is impulse buying? Can one consider that impulse buying is compatible with the theory of limited rationality purchase behaviour?
3. How do consumers differ from customers? Why is the distinction important?
4. Select a consumer product category you know well and prepare a questionnaire to measure unaided, aided and qualified awareness of the main competing brands within the category. How would you proceed to analyse the results?
5. Brand A has a 30 per cent occupation rate and a 60 per cent exclusivity rate. Buyers of this brand usually consume the same quantity of the product, as do buyers of the competing brands; what is brand A's market share? If the exclusivity rate drops to 50 per cent, what will be brand A's market share?
6. What are the benefits for a bank to adopt Customer Relationship Management (CRM)? What are the prerequisites for successful implementation of CRM?
7. Why are satisfied customers not necessarily loyal customers?
8. Why do companies insist on keeping existing customers instead of searching for new customers?

Bibliography

Abernathy, A.M. and Frank, G.R. (1996), The Information Content of Advertising: A Meta-analysis, *Journal of Advertising*, 25, 2, pp. 1–17.

Bauer, R.A. (1960), Consumer Behaviour as Risk Taking, in *Proceedings, Fall Conference of the American Marketing Association*, Hancock, A.S. (ed.), Chicago, IL, June, pp. 389–98.

Becker, G.S. (1965), A Theory of the Allocation of Time, *The Economic Journal*, September, pp. 494–517.

Berry, L.L. (1983), Relationship Marketing, in *Emerging Perspectives on Services Marketing*, Berry, L.L., Shostack, G.L. and Upah, G. (eds), Chicago, IL, American Marketing Association, pp. 25–8.

Davis, H.L. and Rigaux, B.P. (1974), Perceptions of Marital Roles in Decision Processes, *Journal of Consumer Research*, 1, 1, pp. 51–62.

Dart, J. and Freeman, K. (1994), Dissatisfaction Response Styles Among Clients of Professional Accounting Firms, *Journal of Business Research*, 29, 1, pp. 75–81.

Day, G.S. (1969), A Two-dimensional Concept of Brand Loyalty, *Journal of Advertising Research*, 9, 3, pp. 29–35.

Domingo, R.T. (1997), *Quality Means Survival*, Singapore, Prentice-Hall.

Festinger, L. (1957), *A Theory of Cognitive Dissonance*, New York, Harper and Row.

Fournier, S., Dobscha, S. and Mick, D.G. (1998), Preventing the Premature Death of Relationship Marketing, *Harvard Business Review*, 76, 1, pp. 42–51.

Goderis, J.P. (1998), Barrier Marketing: From Customer Satisfaction to Customer Loyalty, *CEMS Business Review*, 2, 4.

Griffin, J. (1995), *Customer Loyalty: How to Earn It? How to Keep It?* New York, Lexington Books.

Herbst, P.G. (1952), The Measurement of Family Relationships, *Human and Relations*, 5, pp. 3–34.

Howard, J.A. and Sheth, J.N. (1969), *The Theory of Buyer Behaviour*, New York, John Wiley & Sons.

Jacoby, J. and Kaplan, L.B. (1972), The Components of Perceived Risk, in *Proceedings, 3rd Annual Conference*, Venkatesan, V. (ed.), College Park, MD, Association for Consumer Research.

Jacoby, J. and Kyner, D.B. (1973), Brand Loyalty versus Repeat Purchasing Behavior, *Journal of Marketing Research*, 10, 1, pp. 1–19.

Jones, T.O. and Sasser, W.E. (1995), Why Satisfied Customer Defect?, *Harvard Business Review*, 73, 6, pp. 88–99.

Kapferer, J.N. and Laurent, G. (1983), *La sensibilité aux marques*, Paris, Fondation Jours de France.

Kordupleski, R.E., Rust, R.T. and Zahorik, A.J. (1993), Why Improve Quality Doesn't Improve Quality (or Whatever Happened to Marketing?), *California Management Review*, 35, 3, pp. 82–95.

Levitt, T. (1980), Marketing Success through Differentiation – of Anything, *Harvard Business Review*, 58, 1, pp. 83–91.

Manning, B. and Throne, C. (2003), *Demand Driven*, New York, McGraw-Hill.

Nelson, D. (1970), Information and Consumer Behaviour, *Journal of Political Economic*, 78, March–April, pp. 311–29.

Payne, A. and Frow, P. (2006), Customer Relationship Management: From Strategy to Implementation, *Journal of Marketing Management*, 22, pp. 135–68.

Pepper, D. and Rogers, M. (1993), *The One-to-One Future*, New York, Doubleday/Currency.

Pras, B. and Tarondeau, J.-C. (1981), *Comportement de l'acheteur*, Paris, Editions Sirey.

Reichfeld, F.F. (1996), *L'effet loyauté*, Paris, Dunod.

Rhoades, K. (1988), The Importance of Consumer Complaints, *Protect Yourself*, January, pp. 115–18.

Rogers, E.M. (1962), *Diffusion of Innovations*, New York, The Free Press.

Sheth, J., Mittal, B. and Newman, B.I. (1999), *Customer Behaviour, Consumer Behaviour and Beyond*, Fort Worth, TX, Dryden Press.

Siddle, R. and Rigby, D. (2001), What's the Matter with CRM?, *European Business Forum*, 7, Autumn, pp. 48–50.

Economist (2005), A Survey of Consumer Power, 2 April, pp. 3–16.

Valla, J.D. (1980), Le comportement des groupes d'achat, in *L'action marketing des entreprises*, Paris, Collection Adetem, pp. 22–38.

Webster, F.E. and Wind, Y. (1972), *Organizational Buying Behaviour*, Englewood Cliffs, NJ, Prentice-Hall.

Wilkie, W.L. (1994), *Consumer Behaviour*, New York, John Wiley & Sons, 3rd edition.

COMPANION WEBSITE FOR CHAPTER 4

Visit the *Market-driven Management* companion website at www.palgrave.com/business/ lambin to find information on:

The Importance–Performance Matrix
Brand Switching Analysis

measuring customers' response 5

Chapter contents

Chapter learning objectives

After reading this chapter, you should be able to understand

- the importance of market information in a market-driven company;
- the structure of a market information system;
- why marketing research must be scientifically conducted;
- the differences between exploratory, descriptive and causal research;
- the characteristics of the main primary data collection methods;
- the potential of the new methods of causal research.

Chapter introduction

The central problem confronting a market-oriented organisation is how to monitor the needs of customers and the evolution of the macro-marketing environment in order to anticipate the future. In response to this need for information, the concept of a formalised market information system (MIS) has emerged to acquire and to distribute market data within the organisation, thereby facilitating market-oriented decisions. The objective of an MIS is to integrate market and customers' data into a continuous information flow for decision-making in marketing. Within an MIS, marketing research has mainly an *ad hoc* data-gathering and analysis function to perform. Marketing research can supply information regarding many aspects of customers' behaviours. In this chapter, we shall review the main components of an MIS, in placing more emphasis on the tasks and methods of marketing research.

5.1. Structure of a market information system

Few managers are happy with the type of market information they receive. The usual complaints are the following:

- Available information is very often not relevant to decision needs.
- There is too much information to be used effectively.
- Information is spread throughout the firm and difficult to locate.
- Key information arrives too late to be useful or is destroyed.
- Some managers may withhold information from other functions.
- The reliability and accuracy of information are difficult to verify.

The role of a market information system (MIS) is to study information needs carefully, to design an information system to meet these needs, to centralise the information available and to organise its dissemination throughout the organisation. An MIS has been defined as follows:

> A marketing information system is a continuing and interacting structure of people, equipment and procedures to gather, sort, analyse, evaluate and distribute pertinent, timely and accurate information for use by marketing decision makers to improve their marketing planning, implementation and control. (Kotler, 1967/2006)

The best performing companies have developed an 'information orientation' comprising not only good IT practices but also information management practices and information behaviour and values (Marchand, 2002). The

structure of an MIS is described in Figure 5.1. The figure shows the macro-marketing environment to be monitored by management. These flows of information are captured and analysed through three subsystems of data collection: the internal accounting system, the business intelligence system and the marketing research system. A fourth subsystem – the analytical market system, which is in charge of the data processing and transfer of information to management, as aids to understanding, decision and control – will be discussed in the following chapter.

Thus, viewed in this perspective, marketing research appears as only one component of an MIS. The role of marketing research is clear and confined to a specific decision problem, whereas the role of an MIS is much broader and is organised on a permanent basis. Let us briefly examine the tasks and content of the three subsystems.

5.1.1. The internal accounting system

All organisations collect internal data as part of their normal operations. These data, which are collected for purposes other than research, are called internal secondary data. Sales data are recorded within the 'order–shipping–billing' cycle. Cost data are recorded, sales representatives and dealers submit sales reports, advertising and promotion activities are recorded, R&D and manufacturing reports are made. These are but a few of the data sources available for research in a modern organisation. Sales records should allow for classification by type of customer, payment procedure, product line, sales territory, time period, and so forth. By way of

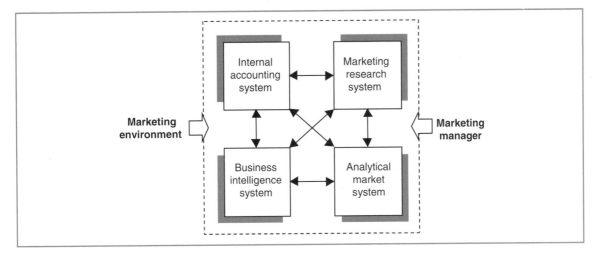

Figure 5.1   Structure of an MIS

Source: Adapted from Kotler (1967/2006).

illustration, a monthly sales statement classified by product, customer group, and sales territory will permit the following analyses:

- Comparison of year-to-date sales in volume and value.
- Analysis of the product mix structure of the total turnover.
- Analysis of the concentration rate of the turnover per customer.
- Evaluation of the sales efficiency by comparing territory sales, number of sales calls, average revenue per sales call, and so forth.
- Analysis of the market penetration per territory by reference to buying power indices.

Many companies do not collect and maintain sales and cost data in sufficient detail to be used for research purposes. These data, stored and processed by the market analytical subsystem, should constitute a database of time series useful, namely, for forecasting purposes. The types of analyses to be conducted are, for example:

- Graphic analyses to identify trends, seasonality patterns and growth rates.
- Short-term sales forecasts based on endogenous sales forecasting techniques, such as exponential smoothing.
- Correlation analyses between sales and key explanatory factors such as distribution rates, advertising share of voice, relative price.
- Multivariables or multi-equation econometric models.

The generalised use of computers has greatly facilitated the development of internal accounting systems. A certain

number of attributes should be met in designing a reporting system:

Timeliness: the information must be available when needed and not reported too late.

Flexibility: the information must be available in varied formats and detail such that the specific information needs of alternative decision situations can be served.

Inclusiveness: the reporting system must cover the entire range of information needs, while avoiding the risk of information overload.

Accuracy: the level of accuracy should fit the needs of the decision situation, and the information should not be presented in too much detail.

Convenience: the information must be easily accessible to the decision-maker and presented in a clear and usable manner.

Data from the internal accounting system originate within the organisation and are available at minimal cost. They constitute the backbone of the MIS. As illustrated by Figure 5.2, the sources of information used by firms are multiple and varied. It is interesting to note in this particular example that the most important source of information are the customers themselves.

5.1.2. The business intelligence system

The data provided by the internal accounting system must be complemented by information about the macro-marketing environment and about competition. It is the role of the business intelligence subsystem to gather

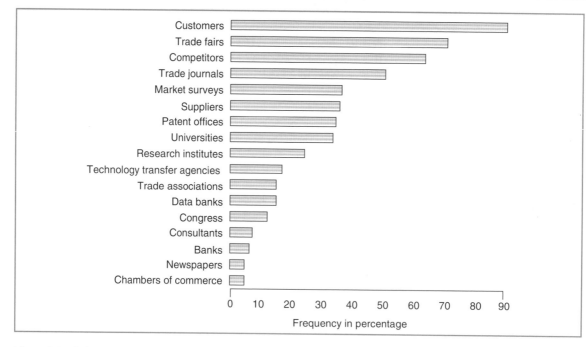

Figure 5.2   Information sources of hidden champions
Source: Simon (1996).

information about developments in the environment, to enable management to monitor the strengths and weaknesses of the firm's competitive position. A detailed description of the type of information to collect is presented in Chapter 11.

Several methods can be used to collect business intelligence information: the casual method, the use of the sales force, the establishment of information centres or the purchase of data from syndicated services.

1. The *casual method* is the informal search for information carried on by managers on their own through reading newspapers and trade publications, talking to suppliers, distributors, customers, or by participating in professional meetings, trade shows, and so on.
2. The *sales force* is often in good position to provide data regarding many aspects of the market situation and to spot new market developments or new competitive actions. Sales representatives should be trained and motivated to report market information.
3. The staff may systematically scan and analyse major trade, industrial or professional publications. For example, much can be learned about competition through reading competitors' published reports. Newsletters or bulletins are then published and disseminated within the company.

4. Most companies also purchase *syndicated data* from outside firms, which collect and sell standardised data about market shares, retail prices, advertising expenditures, promotions, and so on.

Besides internal accounting information and market intelligence, marketing management also requires studies on specific problems or opportunities, such as a product concept test, a brand image study or a sales forecast for a particular country or region. It is the role of marketing research to conduct these types of focused studies.

5.1.3. The marketing research system

The role of marketing research is to provide market information data that will help management to adopt and implement a market orientation. Its role can be defined in the following terms:

Marketing research involves the diagnosis of information needs and the selection of relevant interrelated variables about which valid and reliable information is gathered, recorded and analysed. (Zaltman and Burger, 1975, p. 3)

According to this definition, marketing research has four distinctive functions to perform:

1. The *diagnosis of an information need*, which supposes a good interactive relationship between the decider and the market analyst.
2. The *selection of the variables* to be measured, which implies the capacity to translate a decision problem into empirically testable research questions.
3. The *responsibility of the internal and external validity* of the collected information, which implies a good command of the research methodology.
4. The *transfer of information* to management as an aid to understanding, decision and control.

The role of the market analyst is not confined, therefore, to the technical aspects linked to the execution of a research project. He or she has to participate actively in the research problem definition, the design of the research plan and the interpretation and exploitation of the research results.

Managerial usefulness of marketing research

Marketing research has its usefulness for strategic and operational marketing decisions. Three types of objectives can be identified:

Understanding aid: to discover, describe, analyse, measure and forecast market factors and demand.

Decision aid: to identify the most appropriate marketing instruments and strategies and determine their optimal level of intervention.

Control aid: to assess the performance of the marketing programmes and evaluate results.

The first objective is more directly linked to strategic marketing decisions and has an important creative component: to discover new opportunities and/or untapped market potential. The other two objectives are felt more directly by operational marketing people.

Marketing research often has important implications for functions other than marketing. For example, research results on the changing mood of the market vis-à-vis ecology may induce R&D and production staff to develop environmentally sound products. Similarly, sales forecasting is a key input for financial analysis and for distribution planning and logistics.

Timing of market research

A key question for a manager faced with a decision problem is to decide whether or not a specific marketing research study should be conducted. Several factors must be considered in examining this question:

1. *Time constraint*. Marketing research takes time, and in many instances decisions have to be taken rapidly even if the information is incomplete. The time factor is crucial and the urgency of the situation often precludes the use of research. This factor reinforces the importance of the MIS, which is a permanent information system.

2. *Availability of data*. In many instances, management already possesses enough information and a sound decision may be made without further research. This type of situation will occur when the firm has a well-managed permanent MIS. Sometimes, marketing research is nevertheless undertaken to prevent the criticism of ill-prepared decisions. Marketing research here takes the form of an insurance that will be useful if the decision taken happens to be the wrong one.

3. *Value to the firm*. The value of marketing research will depend on the nature of the managerial decision to be made. For many routine decisions, the cost of a wrong decision is minimal and substantial marketing research expenditures are difficult to justify. Thus, before conducting a research, managers should ask themselves: 'Will the information gained by marketing research improve the quality of the marketing decision to an extent large enough to warrant the expenditure?' In many cases even a modest marketing research study may substantially improve the quality of managerial decisions. Figure 5.3 illustrates the marketing research expenditures in European markets.

Frequently, marketing research projects are not directly linked to a particular decision, but are purely exploratory. The objective is then to improve the understanding of a market or to search for opportunities in a new unknown market. This type of research is likely to improve the choice of strategic options by the firm.

5.2. Marketing research and the scientific method

If nobody questions today that management is much more of an art than a science, it is important to state clearly that marketing research must be scientific. It is important because marketing research has to deal with accredited (or certified) knowledge, and without accredited knowledge good management decisions cannot be made (Zaltman and Burger, 1975, p. 7). The implication of this statement is that the scientist attempts to uncover objective 'truths'. Because management is primarily interested in making decisions based on accurate and unbiased data, it is clear that the market researcher must follow a scientific procedure in order for data to be collected and analysed properly.

The rules of the scientific method are designed to provide, among others, two types of validity, internal and external:

- *Internal validity* is concerned with the question of whether the observed effects of a marketing stimulus (price, advertising message, promotion, and so on) could have been caused by variables other than the factor under study. Is the relationship established without ambiguity? Without internal validity, the experiment is confounded and the causal structure is not established.

■ *External validity* is concerned with the generalisability of experimental results. To what populations, geographic areas and treatment variables can the measured effects be projected?

This problem of scientific reliability is fundamental because, on the basis of marketing research results, management will make highly risky decisions, such as the launch of a new product, modification of a price or adoption of a specific advertising theme.

5.2.1. Characteristics of scientific knowledge

The understanding of the main features of science is essential to performing marketing research scientifically, and therefore we shall now briefly review the main scientific knowledge that is factual. Science starts by establishing facts and seeks to describe and explain them. Established facts are empirical data obtained with the aid of theories and, in turn, help to clarify theories.

1. *Science goes beyond facts.* The market analyst should not confine his or her work to facts that are easily observed and already in existence. Thus qualitative research is an integrated part of the research process. The market analyst may want to find new facts, but new facts should be authentic and lend themselves to empirical verification or falsification.

2. *Scientific knowledge is verifiable (or falsifiable).* Scientific knowledge must be testable empirically through observational or experimental experiences. This is one of the basic rules of a science. It must be possible to demonstrate that a given proposition or theory is false. The scientist can only say: 'I have a theory which I have objectively tested with data and the data are consistent with my theory.'

3. *Science is analytic.* The market researcher tries to decompose the buying decision process into its basic parts to determine the mechanisms that account for the way the process functions. After analysing the component parts separately and also in their interrelationships, the market researcher is then able to determine how the whole decision process emerges. An illustration of this analytic process is given in the Chapter 6 in the discussion of concept of attitude.

4. *Scientific knowledge is clear and precise.* Scientific knowledge strives for precision, accuracy and reduction of error although it is almost impossible to achieve these completely. The researcher attempts to reach these objectives by stating questions with maximal clarity, giving unambiguous definitions to concepts and measures and recording observations as completely and in as much detail as possible.

5. *Scientific knowledge is communicable.* Research must be in principle communicable – that is, it must be sufficiently complete in its reporting of methodologies used and sufficiently precise in the presentation of its results to enable another researcher to duplicate the study for independent verification or to determine if replication is desirable.

6. *Scientific knowledge is general.* The market researcher should place individual facts into general patterns, which should be applicable to a wide variety of phenomena. This provides generalisations that can guide marketing decisions. The market analyst is concerned with learning not just what an individual buyer does, but rather what that buyer does that others are also likely to do in the same situation.

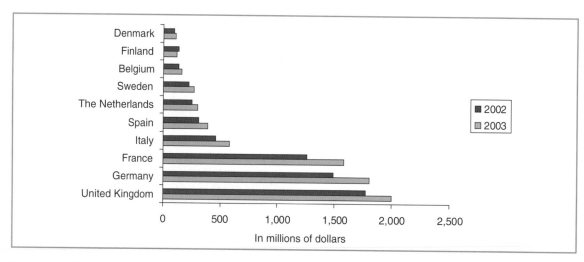

Figure 5.3   Top ten European markets by marketing research expenditures
Source: ESOMAR, Amsterdam, Netherlands.

5.2.2. The manager–researcher interface

The managerial value of marketing research is largely determined by the quality of the interface between the market analyst responsible for the research project and the decision-maker who has to use the research results. In many instances, market researchers are not sufficiently management-oriented and many managers are not sufficiently research-oriented. To overcome this difficulty of communication, the manager and the researcher's responsibilities should be clearly defined and accepted by both parties.

The user of the research should keep the market researcher informed on

- the precise problem faced by the firm and the way that a decision is going to be made;
- the background of the problem and its environment;
- all limitations on costs and time for doing the study and on the courses of action that the company can realistically consider;
- what data will be provided by the firm and where to obtain it;
- any changes in the situation that arises as the study is under way.

Similarly, the *responsibilities of the researcher* are

- being honest and clear regarding the meaning and any limitations of the expected findings;
- being of maximum help in presenting and explaining the conclusions and aiding the decision-maker's application;
- demanding that the decision-maker provide the information needed to plan and conduct the study;
- insisting that valid and full reporting be made of the findings;

- refusing to distort or abridge them on behalf of the user's biases and prejudices.

In reporting research findings some researchers fail to recognise that their role is *advisory*; they are not being asked to make the decision for management. Similarly, some managers operate as if the researcher is clairvoyant regarding the nature of the decision situation and the information needed to reduce the decision uncertainty. Consequently, many research projects are not decision-oriented because of the manager's poor communication skills.

5.2.3. Stages in the research process

Systematic inquiry requires careful planning in an orderly investigation. Marketing research, like other forms of scientific research, is a sequence of interrelated activities. The five stages of the research process are presented in Figure 5.4.

1. *Problem definition.* The first step in research calls for the manager (the user of the research result) and the market analyst (the researcher) to define the problem carefully and to agree on the research objective. In marketing research, the old adage, 'a problem well defined is a problem half solved' is worth remembering. Another way to express the same idea would be: 'if you don't know what you are looking for, you won't find it'. Thus, at this stage a working interface 'decider–analyst' is essential and the research objective should state, in terms as precise as possible, the information needed to improve the decision to be made.

2. *Research design.* The research design is a master plan specifying the methods and procedures for collecting

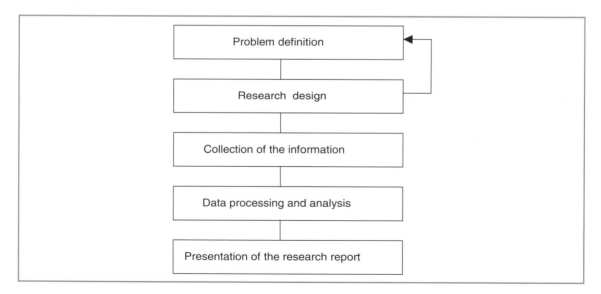

Figure 5.4 Stages in the research process
Source: Lambin (1990).

and analysing the needed information. It is a framework for the research plan of action. This is typically the responsibility of the market analyst. The research plan should be designed professionally and specify the hypotheses and the research questions, the sources of information, the research instrument (focus groups, survey or experimentation), the sampling methodology, the schedule and the cost of the research. The decider should approve the research plan to ensure that the information collected is appropriate for solving his or her decision problem.

3. *Collection of the information.* Once the research design is approved, the process of gathering the information from respondents may begin. In many cases, the data collection phase is subcontracted to a specialised market research company. Data collection methods are rapidly changing under the impact of telecommunications and computers. Telephone interviews combined with data-entry terminals, computer-assisted interviews, interactive terminals in shopping malls, fax interviews, electronic cash registers using the Universal Product Code (UPC) are new techniques, which accelerate the data-gathering process and also eliminate the risks of errors. There are generally two phases in data collection: pre-testing and the main study. The pre-test phase, based on a small subsample, is used to determine whether the data-gathering plan for the main study is appropriate.

4. *Data processing and analysis.* Once the data have been collected, they must be converted into a format that will answer the manager's questions. This stage implies editing the data, coding, tabulating and developing one-way or two-way frequency distributions. These tasks are also generally subcontracted to specialised agencies and strict controls should be made on the rules and procedures adopted. Statistical analysis techniques will be used to summarise the data, to present them in a more meaningful way, to facilitate the interpretation or to help discover new findings or relationships. Advanced multivariate statistical analyses should be used only if they are relevant for the purpose of the study.

5. *Presentation of the research report.* The final stage in the research process is that of interpreting the information and making conclusions for managerial

decisions. The research report should communicate the research findings effectively, that is, in a way which is meaningful to a managerial audience. The risk here is to place too much emphasis on the study's technical aspects, even if any responsible manager will want to be convinced of the reliability of the results, otherwise he or she will not use them. Thus again a close interaction between the manager and the researcher is a key success factor.

This research process is of general application even if the stages of the process overlap continuously. The relative importance of each phase also varies with the nature of the market research.

5.2.4. Types of marketing research

Marketing research studies can be classified on the basis of techniques or of the nature of the research problem. Surveys, experimentation or observational studies are the most common techniques. The nature of the problem will determine whether the research is exploratory, descriptive or causal. Examples are provided in Table 5.1.

Exploratory research. It is conducted to clarify the nature of a problem, to gain better understanding of a market situation, to discover ideas and insights and to provide directions for any further research needed. It is not intended to provide conclusive evidence from which to determine a particular course of action. The methods used are desk research and qualitative studies.

Descriptive research. It seeks to determine answers to 'who', 'what', 'when', 'where' and 'how' questions. Descriptive research is concerned with determining frequency with which something occurs or the relationship between two variables. Unlike exploratory research, descriptive studies are based on some previous understanding of the nature of the research problem. Descriptive information is often all that is needed to solve a marketing problem. The methods used are typically secondary data, observation and communication. Most marketing research studies are of this type.

Table 5.1 Types of marketing research problems		
Exploratory research	Descriptive research	Causal research
Sales of brand A are declining and we don't know why?	What kind of people buy our brand? Who buys the brand of our direct competitor?	Do buyers prefer our product in an 'eco-design' package?
Would the market be interested by our new product idea?	What should be the target segment for our new product?	Which of the two advertising themes is more effective?

Source: Adapted from Churchill and Iacobucci (2005).

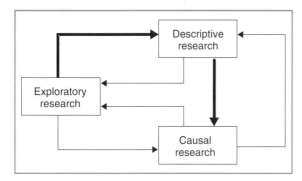

Figure 5.5   The different sequences of research
Source: Churchill and Iacobucci (2005).

Causal research. It is the most ambitious form of research and is concerned with determining cause-and-effect relationships. In causal studies, it is typical to have an expectation of the relationship, which is to be explained, such as predicting the influence of price, packaging and advertising. Causal studies usually take the form of controlled experiments.

In principle, exploratory and descriptive research precedes cause-and-effect relationship studies and is often seen as preliminary steps, as illustrated in Figure 5.5. But other sequences may also exist. For example, if a causal hypothesis is discovered, the analyst might need another exploratory or descriptive study. In the following sections, we shall analyse in more detail the objectives and the methods used in these three types of market research studies.

5.3. Exploratory research studies

Marketing research is of an exploratory type when the emphasis is placed on gaining insights and ideas rather than on formally testing hypotheses derived from theory or from previous research studies. This type of study is very popular among firms because of its low cost, speed, flexibility and emphasis on creativity, and on the generation of ideas.

5.3.1. Objectives of exploratory research

The need for exploratory research typically arises when the firm is confronted with ill-defined problems such as: 'sales of brand X are declining and we do not know why' or 'would people be interested in our idea for a new product?' In these two examples, the analyst could guess a large number of possible answers. Since it is impractical to test them all, exploratory research will be used to find the most likely explanation(s) that will then be tested empirically.

Thus, the main objectives of exploratory research are the following:

- To give a rapid examination of the threats of a problem or the potential of an opportunity.
- To formulate a poorly defined problem for more precise investigation.
- To generate hypotheses or conjectural statements about the problem.
- To collect and analyse readily available information.
- To establish priorities for further research.
- To increase the analyst's familiarity with a problem or with a market.
- To clarify a concept.

In general, exploratory research is appropriate to any problem about which little is known.

5.3.2. Hypothesis development

Exploratory research is particularly useful at the first stage of the research process at the problem formulation phase, to translate the research problem into specific research objectives. The objective is to develop testable hypotheses. Hypotheses state what we are looking for; they anticipate the possible answers to the research problem and add a considerable degree of specificity. Normally there will be several competing hypotheses, either specified or implied.

How does the analyst generate hypotheses? The process of hypothesis development is illustrated in Figure 5.6. Four main sources of information can be identified, namely

1. theory from such disciplines as economics, psychology, sociology or marketing,
2. management experience with related problems,
3. the use of secondary data (see section 5.3.3) or
4. exploratory research when both theory and experience are lacking.

After an exploratory research, the market analyst should know which type of data to collect in order to verify or falsify the competing explanations. An example is presented in Table 5.2, concerning the low level of market penetration of cable TV in some regions. The exploratory study has identified seven possible explanations (or hypotheses). The derived research objectives clearly indicate the type of data required to verify these tentative explanations.

Since the objective of exploratory studies is to find new ideas, no formal design is required. Flexibility and ingenuity characterise the investigation. The imagination of the researcher is the key factor. The techniques used are the study of secondary data, key informant survey, analysis of related cases and qualitative research through focus groups.

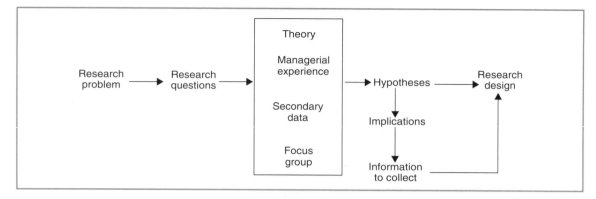

Figure 5.6   The process of hypothesis development
Source: Authors.

Table 5.2 From a research problem to research questions	
Hypotheses	**Research questions**
Research problem: Why is the penetration rate of TV cable in private homes far below average in several geographic areas?	
1. Good TV reception is available without cable.	How is the quality of TV reception without cable?
2. Residents are illegally connecting their sets to the cable network.	Is it technically possible to be illegally connected?
3. There is a very transient population in these regions.	What is the mobility rate in these regions?
4. Residents have had poor experience with cable services.	What is the corporate image of the cable company in the regions?
5. The price is too high given the level of income in the region.	How different are income statistics among regions?
6. The sales force coverage has been inadequate.	How active was the sales force in the regions?
7. Large part of the residents is in age or social class groups that watch little TV.	Analyse demographic and social class statistics per region.
Source: Adapted from Kotler (1967/2005).	

5.3.3. Use of secondary data

Secondary data are previously published data collected for purposes other than the specific research needs at hand. Primary data, on the other hand, are collected specifically for purposes of the investigation. The main sources of secondary data, internal and external, are presented in Figure 5.7.

Secondary data can be classified as coming from internal or external sources, the former being available within the organisation and the latter originating from outside. Internal data are centralised in the internal accounting system described in the first section of this chapter. External data come from an array of sources such as government publications, trade association data, books, bulletins, reports and periodicals. Data from these sources are available at minimal cost or free in libraries (Table 5.3 gives selected government data sources). External sources not available in a library are usually standardised marketing data, which are expensive to acquire. These syndicated data sources are consumer panels, wholesale data, media and audience data, and so on.

To start with, secondary data are the most logical thing to work on and their usefulness should not be underestimated. The primary advantage of secondary data is that it is always faster and it is less expensive to obtain them than to acquire primary data. Also, they may include information not otherwise available to the researcher.

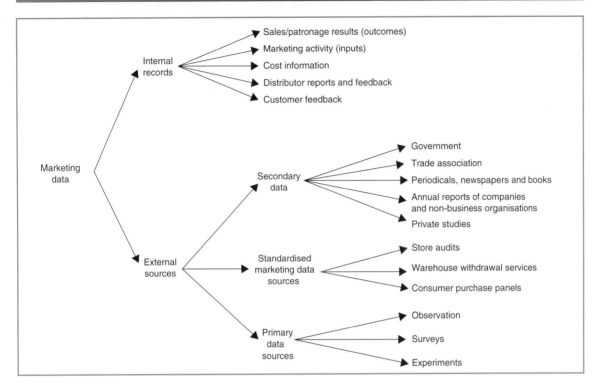

Figure 5.7 Sources of marketing data

Source: Aaker and Day (1980).

For example, truck and car registrations are secondary data published by the car registration administration. A competent market analyst should be familiar with the basic sources pertaining to the market studied.

Secondary data, however, present a certain number of disadvantages and the market analyst should examine their relevance thoroughly. The most common problems associated with secondary data are as follows: (1) outdated information, (2) variation in definition of terms, (3) different units of measurement. Another shortcoming is that the user has no control over the accuracy of secondary data. Research conducted by other persons may be biased to support the vested interest of the source. Also, the user of secondary data must critically assess the data and the research design to determine if the research methodology was correctly implemented. The following rules should be followed in the use of secondary data:

- Always use the primary source of secondary data and not secondary sources that secured the data from the original source.
- Assess the accuracy of secondary data by carefully identifying the purpose of the publication.
- Examine the overall quality of the methodology; a primary source should provide a detailed description of

how the data were collected, including definitions, collection forms, sampling, and so forth.

The above points are not to say that the analyst cannot use such data. Rather, it is simply to suggest that such data should be viewed more critically.

5.3.4. Key informants' survey

After having explored secondary sources, additional insights and ideas can be gained by talking with individuals having special knowledge and experience regarding the problem under investigation. These knowledgeable persons may be 'players' or 'experts'. By 'players' we mean anyone participating in the market situation, such as the personnel within the firm, wholesalers, retailers, suppliers or consumers. By 'experts' we mean anyone having privileged information due to their function, such as civil servants, economists, sociologists, R&D personnel, members of a professional organisation, and so forth.

For example, a publisher of children's books [who is] investigating a sales decrease gained valuable insights

Table 5.3   Selected government data sources

Source	Website	Type of information
European Union	www.europa.eu.int	Statistical information on members countries
Euromonitor International	www.euromonitor.com	Information on the EU and other countries, and companies
University of Strathclyde, UK	www.strath.ac.uk	Company profiles, country information, economic export data and company directories
OECD	www.oecd.org	Statistics, economic indicators and other information on member countries
Eurostat	www.europa.eu.int/comm/ eurostat/	Statistics at European level that enable comparison between countries and regions
Europe Direct	www.europa.eu.int/ europedirect/	Information on the EU
Department of Trade and Industry	www.dti.gov.uk	Information on UK companies and trade
Financial Times	www.ft.com	Several data banks, for example, on mergers and acquisitions
Business Week	www.businessweek.com	Information on companies, for example, top 500 firms
World Bank	www.worldbank.org	Economic, social and national/regional information on more than 200 countries
International Trade Administration, USA	www.ita.doc.gov	ITA helps US firms to compete in foreign markets
Center for International Business Education and Research (MSU-CIBER). A centre at Michigan State University, USA	www.ciber.bus.msu.edu	A website presenting different market information in the world
Trade Compass	www.tradecompas.com	Business-related information on different markets and companies

Source: Authors.

by talking with librarians and schoolteachers. These discussions indicated that an increased use of library facilities, both public and school, coincided with the product's decline in sales. These increases were, in turn, attributed to a very sizeable increase in library holdings of children's books resulting from federal legislation that provided money for this purpose. (Churchill and Iacobucci, 2004, p. 78)

No attempt should be made to have a probability sample in this type of survey, but it is important to include people with different points of view. The interviews are informal and do not use structured questions, such as those on a questionnaire. Rather, very flexible and free-flowing situations are created in order to stimulate the search for

ideas and to uncover the unexpected. Various hypotheses may be presented to these individuals to test their reaction and see whether reformulation is necessary.

5.3.5. Analysis of selected cases

A third method currently used in exploratory research is the detailed analysis of cases that are similar to the phenomenon under investigation in order to seek explanations or to gain ideas for actions. For example, in many situations, the United States are ahead of Europe and it is interesting to analyse the US situation to understand the problems that might occur in the European market.

For example, convenience stores in petrol stations have been in operation in the United States for many years. Petroleum companies in Western Europe have recently adopted the same concept. A detailed study of selected stores in the United States proved to be very useful when determining the types of assortment, the opening hours and the layout of these convenience stores.

Some situations are particularly productive of hypotheses – namely, cases reflecting abrupt changes or cases reflecting extreme behaviour.

5.3.6. Focus group discussions

The focus group interview is a more elaborate exploratory study. A focus group interview is an unstructured, free-flowing interview with a small group of 8–12 people. It is not a rigidly constructed question-and-answer session but a flexible format discussion of a brand, an advertisement or a new product concept. A focus group functions as follows: the group meets at a location at a pre-designated time; it consists of an interviewer or moderator and 8–12 participants; the moderator introduces the topic and encourages group members to discuss the subjects among themselves. Focus groups allow people to discuss their true feelings, anxieties and frustrations as well as the depth of their conviction.

The primary advantages of focus group interviews are that they are relatively rapid, easy to execute and inexpensive. In an emergency situation three or four group sessions can be conducted, organised and reported on in less than a week. From the first discussion the analyst invariably learns a great deal. The second interview produces more, but less is new. Usually, in the third and fourth sessions, much of what is said has been heard before and there is little to be gained from continuing. By way of illustration, the result of a group discussion about coffee consumption is presented in Exhibit 5.1.

In addition to the advantage of time, the following *advantages* for group interviews also exist:

■ The group interview is a superb mechanism for generating hypotheses when little is known about the problem under study.
■ The group method drastically reduces the distance between the respondent who produces research information and the client who uses it.
■ Another advantage of the group interview technique is its flexibility, in contrast with survey interviewers who work from a rigid question schedule.
■ The group interview has the ability to handle contingencies of consumer behaviour of the type: 'if … otherwise', an answer unlikely to emerge in a survey.
■ In a group discussion respondents stimulate one another and more information is spontaneously obtained than in individual interviews.
■ Finally in a group interview study, the findings emerge in a form that most people fully understand.

The *limitations* of focus group interviews are important and should not be underestimated:

■ The respondents are not representative of the target population given their number and the recruiting procedure. Thus, the external validity of the results is necessarily limited.
■ The interpretation of the results is typically judgemental and highly dependent on the personality of the analyst. Given the absence of a structured questionnaire and the wealth of disparate comments usually obtained, the analyst can always find something which agrees with his

EXHIBIT 5.1

THE RESULTS OF A GROUP DISCUSSION: MOTIVATIONS FOR COFFEE CONSUMPTION IN BELGIUM

1. *Time and space structure.* Coffee gives a certain rhythm to your day; it is a ritual, which punctuates the different parts of a day: morning, morning break, mealtime, after a meal, evening, weekend, afternoon break, etc. Each moment has its own identity, typical to its environment and conditions for the expected satisfaction for consumption.

2. *Social function.* Offering a cup of coffee is a typical sign of hospitality. A cup of coffee relaxes and welcomes, develops a feeling of harmony, a certain atmosphere. Coffee brings people together, is the excuse for bringing people together.

3. *Sensorial function.* Coffee is satisfying to the individual himself or herself, catering as much to the emotions as to the senses. The sense of smell, taste, the appearance and the warmth of coffee are all involved.

4. *Function as a stimulant.* Coffee supposedly acts as both a physical and psychological stimulant. Even a restorative, curative function is attributed to coffee; it picks you up; it is an affective, emotional comforting tonic.

Source: MDA Consulting Group, Brussels.

or her view of the problem. The importance of this bias is difficult to measure, however.

■ The risk always exists to see one participant dominating the session and to provoke negative reactions from the other members of the group.

■ Evaluations by means of group interviews tend to be conservative. It favours ideas that are easy to explain and understand and, therefore, not very new.

■ Very disturbing is the unethical practice of some market research firms specialising in focus groups to recruit 'professional respondents' to make the session go well.

Despite these limitations, focus group interviews are very popular, particularly among advertising agencies. A more recent development in the field of qualitative research is the use of interpretation models, such as the Freudian or the Jungian models (Pellemans, 1999). The risk here is to privilege one scheme of interpretation. To avoid this trap, several interpretation models should be used simultaneously and their results confronted.

5.3.7. Projective techniques

Respondents are often reluctant or embarrassed to discuss their feelings but may be more likely to give a true answer (consciously or unconsciously) if the question is disguised. A projective technique is an indirect means of questioning that enables respondents to 'project' their beliefs or feelings into a third person when exposed to an unstructured stimulus. Projective techniques are currently used in clinical and personality tests. The theory behind such a technique is that when a person is asked to structure or organise an essentially unstructured or ambiguous situation he can do so only by calling upon and revealing his own personality or attitudinal structure.

> The more unstructured and ambiguous a stimulus, the more a subject can and will project his emotions, needs, motives, attitudes and values. (Kerlinger, 1973, p. 515)

The most common projective techniques in marketing research are picture–story association, sentence completion, word association, and role-playing.

5.3.8. Limitations of exploratory research

Exploratory research cannot take the place of quantitative, conclusive research. Nevertheless, there is great temptation among many managers to accept small sample exploratory results as sufficient for their purpose because they are so compelling in their reality. The dangers of uncritical acceptance of the unstructured output from a focus group or a brief series of informal interviews are twofold.

■ First, the results are *not representative* of what would be found in the population and, hence, cannot be projected.

■ Second, there is typically a great deal of *ambiguity* owing to the moderator's interpretation of the results.

In fact, the greatest danger of using exploratory research to evaluate an alternative advertising copy strategy, a new product concept, and so on is not that a poor idea will be marketed, because successive steps of research will prevent that; the real danger is that a good idea with promise may be rejected because of findings at the exploratory stage. In other situations, where everything looks positive in the exploratory stage, there is the temptation to market the product without further research (Adler, 1979).

In view of these pitfalls, these methods should be used strictly for insights into the reality of the customer's perspective and to suggest hypotheses for further research.

5.4. Descriptive research studies

Descriptive studies, as their name suggests, are designed to describe the characteristics of a given situation or of a given population. Descriptive studies differ from exploratory studies in the rigour with which they are designed. Exploratory studies are characterised by flexibility. Descriptive studies attempt to obtain a complete and accurate description of a situation. Formal design is required to ensure that the description covers all phases desired and that the information collected is reliable. The most popular technique used in descriptive research is the survey.

5.4.1. Objectives of descriptive studies

Descriptive research encompasses a vast array of research objectives. The purpose is to provide a graph of some aspect of the market at a point of time or to monitor an activity over time. The objectives of descriptive studies are the following:

■ To describe the organisation, the distribution channels or the competitive structure of a specific market or segment.

■ To estimate the proportion and the socio-demographic profile of a specified population which behaves in a certain way.

■ To predict the level of primary demand over the next 5 years in a given market using heuristic or extrapolating sales forecasting methods.

■ To describe the buying behaviour of certain groups of consumers.

- To describe the way buyers perceive and evaluate the attributes of given brands against competing brands.
- To describe the evolution of lifestyles among specific segments of the population.

Descriptive research should be based on some previous understanding and knowledge of the problem in order to determine with precision the data collection procedure. As illustrated in the previous section, it should rest on one or more specific hypotheses. Three conditions must be met before beginning a descriptive research:

1. One or several hypotheses or conjectural statements derived from the research questions to guide the data collection.
2. A clear specification of the 'who', 'what', 'when', 'where', 'why' and 'how' of the research.
3. A specification of the method used to collect the information: communication or observation.

A specification of the information to collect is presented in Exhibit 5.2.

Two types of descriptive studies can be identified; longitudinal and cross-sectional.

1. *Cross-sectional studies* involve a sample from the population of interest and a number of characteristics of the sample members are measured once at a single point of time.
2. *Longitudinal studies* involve panels; they provide repeated measurement over time, either on the same variables (panels) or on different variables (omnibus panels).

The sample members in a panel are measured repeatedly, as contrasted to the one-time measurement in a cross-sectional study. The most common form of cross-sectional study is the sample survey.

5.4.2. Primary data collection methods

In Figure 5.6 a distinction was made between three methods of primary data collection: observation, communication and experimentation. Experimentation differs from the other methods in terms of degree of control over the research situation. Experimentation is the method typically used in causal research and its characteristics will be discussed in the next section. The observation and the communication methods are used for cross-sectional and longitudinal studies.

Observation methods

Scientific observation is the systematic process of recording the behavioural pattern of people, objects and occurrences without questioning or communicating with them. The market analyst using the observation method of data collection witnesses and records information as events occur or compile evidence from records of past events. At least five kinds of phenomena can be observed:

1. Physical actions and evidence, such as purchases, store locations and layout, posted prices, shelf space and display, promotions.
2. Temporal patterns, such as shopping or driving time.
3. Spatial relations and locations, such as traffic counts or shopping patterns.
4. Expressive behaviour, such as eye movement or levels of emotional arousal.
5. Published records, such as analysis of advertisements or newspaper articles.

The most important advantage of the observational method is its unobtrusive nature since communication with the respondent is not necessary. The 'observer' may be a person or the data may be gathered using some mechanical device such as a traffic counter, TV audiometers placed in

---

EXHIBIT 5.2

SPECIFICATION OF THE INFORMATION TO COLLECT

A firm is considering the launching of new food product to be purchased by medium–high income family housewives. The questions which must be examined before the beginning of the field work are the following:

1. *Who?* Who is the target person? The buyer, the user, the prescriber?
2. *What?* Which characteristics to measure: the socio-demographic profile, the attitude, preferences, purchasing habits, and so on?
3. *When?* When to ask? Before or at the purchasing time, after the use of the product, how long after, and so on?

4. *Where?* At the purchasing place, at home, at the working place, and so on?
5. *Why?* What is the purpose of the study, what use will be made of the results?
6. *How?* How to proceed? Face-to-face interview, telephones, mail, and so on.

The answers to these questions are not obvious. The results of the exploratory study should be useful to reduce the sources of uncertainty.

homes to record and observe behaviour, or optical scanners in supermarkets to record sales and purchase behaviour. Observational data are typically more objective and accurate than communication data.

Technological systems such as the Universal Product Code (UPC) have had a major impact on mechanical observations, and UPC consumer panels now provide companies with quick, accurate and dynamic data about how their products are selling, who is buying them and the factors that affect purchase.

Despite their advantages, observation methods have one crucial limitation; they cannot observe motives, attitudes, preferences and intentions. Thus, they can be used only to secure primary behavioural data.

Communication methods

Communication involves questioning respondents to secure the desired information, using a data collection instrument called a questionnaire. The questions may be oral or in writing and the responses may also be given in either form. There are four methods of collecting survey data: personal interviewing, telephone interviewing, mail or self-administered questionnaires and online surveys.

1. *Personal interviewing.* This method is well suited for complex product concepts requiring extensive explanations or for new products. Information is sought in face-to-face question-and-answer sessions between an interviewer and a respondent. The interviewer usually has a questionnaire as a guide, although it is possible to use visual aids. Answers are generally recorded during the interview. Personal interviews get a high response rate, but are also more costly to administer than the other forms. The presence of an interviewer may also influence the subjects' responses.

2. *Telephone interviewing.* This is best suited for well-defined basic product concepts or specific product features. Questioning is done over the telephone. The information sought is well defined, non-confidential in nature and limited in amount. The method has the advantage of speed in data collection and lower costs per interview. However, some telephone numbers are not listed in directories, and this causes problems in obtaining a representative sample. Absence of face-to-face contact and inability to use visual materials are other limitations.

3. *Mail questionnaires.* These are used to broaden the base of an investigation. They are most effective when well-defined concepts are involved and specific limited answers are required. They are generally less expensive than telephone and personal interviews, but they also have a much lower response rate. Several methods can be used

to encourage a higher response rate. Questionnaires by mail must be more structured than others.

4. *Online surveys.* A comparison of the advantages and disadvantages of these four methods is made in Table 5.4. Each method of data collection has its own merits. Often these methods can be used in combination; for example, the telephone can be used to introduce the topic and to secure co-operation from the respondent. If the attitude is positive, the questionnaire is then sent by mail with a covering letter. Through this procedure, reasons for refusal can be obtained and follow-up calls can be made to secure the needed response.

5.4.3. Questionnaire design

Good questionnaire design is the key to obtaining good survey results. A questionnaire is simply a set of questions selected to generate the data necessary for accomplishing a research project's objective. Developing questionnaires may appear to be simple, especially to those who have never designed one.

> A good questionnaire appears as easy to compose, as does a good poem. The end product should look as if effortlessly written by an inspired child, but it is usually the result of long, painstaking work. (Erdos, 1970)

The function of the questionnaire is that of measurement. The questionnaire is the main channel through which data are obtained from respondents and transferred to researchers, who in turn will transfer this certified knowledge to managers for decision-making. This channel has a dual communication role: (a) it must communicate to the respondent what the researcher is asking for and (b) it must communicate to the researcher what the respondent has to say (see Figure 5.8). The accuracy of data gathered through questionnaires will be greatly influenced by the amount of distortion or 'noise' that occurs in the two types of communication. A sloppy questionnaire can lead to a great deal of distortion in the communication from researcher to respondents, and vice versa.

> To assume that people will understand the questions is a common error. People simply may not know what is being asked. They may be unaware of the product or topic of interest; they may confuse the subject with something else, or the question may not mean the same thing to everyone interviewed. Respondents may refuse to answer personal questions. Most of these problems may be minimised if a skilled researcher composes the questionnaire. (Zikmund,1986/1994, p. 371)

Table 5.4 Comparison of survey methods

Type	Advantages	Disadvantages
Personal interview	1. Allows interviewer to gain additional information from his own observation. 2. Better control over the sequence of questions. 3. Allows more detailed information to be gathered. 4. Usually gets a higher percentage of completed answers, since interviewer is there to explain exactly what is wanted. 5. Can use visual aids (e.g. tables, charts, samples and prototypes) to demonstrate concepts. 6. Allows in-depth exploration of product attributes and how to solve problems. 7. Is flexible to allow interviewer to adjust questions to respondent's greatest interests. 8. Personal contact often stimulates greater co-operation and interest by respondents.	1. Can be costly when compared to other methods, especially when wide geographic areas must be covered. 2. Interviewer bias can seriously cause misleading responses and misrecording of answers. 3. Requires detailed supervision of data-collection process. 4. Time consuming to train interviewers and to obtain data. 5. May distract respondents if interviewer is talking and writing answers at the same time. 6. Different approaches by different interviewers make it difficult to standardise conduct of survey.
Telephone survey	1. Fast (e.g. quicker than personal interview or mail). 2. Inexpensive (e.g. cost of an equal number of personal interviews would be substantially greater). 3. Easier to call back again if respondent is busy at the time. 4. Usually has only a small response bias because of closed-end questions. 5. Has wide geographical reach.	1. Limited to number published in telephone directory. 2. Can usually obtain only a small amount of information. 3. Can usually provide only limited classification of data. 4. Difficult to obtain motivational and attitudinal information. 5. Difficult for highly technical products or capital goods. 6. Can become expensive if long distance calls are involved.
Mail survey	1. Can get wide distribution at a relatively low cost per completed interview. 2. Helps avoid possible interviewer bias; absence of interviewer may lead to a more candid reply. 3. Can reach remote places (e.g. drilling engineer on site in Saudi Arabia). 4. Unless his name is requested, the respondent remains anonymous and, therefore, may give confidential information that otherwise would be withheld. 5. Respondent may be more inclined to answer since he can do so at his leisure.	1. Accurate, up-to-date mailing lists are not always available to ensure successful distribution. 2. As many as 80–90% may not return questionnaires. Respondents generally have stronger feelings about the subject than non-respondents do. 3. Questionnaire length is limited. 4. Inability to insure those questions is understood fully and answers are properly recorded. 5. It is difficult to lead respondents through questions one at a time since the respondent can read the entire questionnaire before answering. 6. Time consuming. 7. Troublesome with certain highly technical products.
Online survey	1. The fastest and least expensive method. 2. Possibility of world coverage. 3. Good control on the order of questions. 4. Automatic control of material errors (recall of non-respondents, possibility of multiple answers). 5. Immediate encoding. 6. Possibility to use visual aid. 7. No bias due to the interviewer.	1. Bad representation: limited to the population having Internet access and having good control. 2. Non-random sampling. 3. Poor control and identification of the respondent. 4. Impersonal contact. 5. Fear of private life invasion (lack of confidentiality).

Source: Authors.

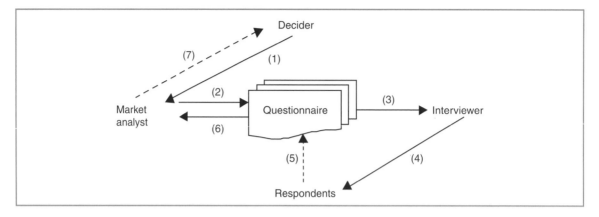

Figure 5.8   The key role of the questionnaire in a survey
Source: Lambin (1990).

Figure 5.8 shows that the questionnaire is at the interface of the four participants in any survey:

1. The decider, who needs specific information to solve a decision problem.
2. The market analyst, whose role is to translate the research problem into research questions.
3. The interviewer, who has to collect reliable information from respondents.
4. The respondents, who have to agree to communicate the information sought.

One important characteristic of a good questionnaire is its degree of standardisation – a condition required ensuring that the answers obtained from different respondents and through different interviewers are indeed comparable and therefore lend themselves to statistical analysis.

5.4.4. Sampling methods

Once the market analyst has developed and tested the questionnaire, the next question is the selection of the respondents from whom the information will be collected. One way to do this would be to collect information from each member of the target population through a census. Another way would be to select a fraction of the population by taking a sample of respondents. The census approach is frequently adopted in industrial market research studies when the target population has a total size of 100–300 units. In most situations, however, the population sizes are large and the cost and time required to contact each member of the population would be prohibitively high. Thus, sampling can be defined as follows:

> Sampling is the selection of a fraction of the target population for the ultimate purpose of being able to

draw general conclusions about the entire target population.

Sampling techniques can be divided into two broad categories of probability and non-probability samples:

- In a *probability sample*, an objective selection procedure is used and each member of the population has a known, non-zero chance of being included in the sample.
- In a *non-probability sample*, the selection procedure used is subjective and the probability of selection for each population unit is unknown.

These two sample selection procedures have their own merits. The main superiority of probability sampling is that there are appropriate statistical techniques for measuring random sampling error, while in non-probability samples the tools of statistical inference cannot be legitimately employed. If, as a general rule, a probability sample should be preferred, there are situations where non-probability samples are useful, namely because they are less costly and easier to organise.

Probability samples

The different types of probability samples are simple random samples, stratified samples (proportionate or disproportionate), cluster samples and multistage area samples:

1. A *simple random sample* is a sampling procedure that assures that each element of the population will have not only a known but also an equal chance of being included in the sample. Different drawing procedures exist (random number or systematic sampling), which all presuppose the existence of a list of the population members.

2. In a *stratified sample* the target population is subdivided into mutually exclusive groups – based on criteria such as size, income or age – and random samples are drawn from each group, called a 'stratum'. In a proportionate stratified sample, the total sample is allocated among the strata in proportion to the size of each stratum, while in a disproportionate stratified sample, the total sample is allocated on the basis of relative variability observed in each stratum.

3. In a *cluster sample*, the target population is divided into mutually exclusive subgroups called clusters instead of strata, and a random sample of the subgroups is then selected. Thus, each subgroup must be a small-scale model (or a miniature population) of the total population.

4. *Multistage area sampling* involves two or more steps that combine some of the probability techniques of cluster sampling. Instead of picking all the units from the randomly chosen clusters (or area), only a sample of units is randomly picked from each of them; the selected subclusters themselves can be subsampled. The main advantage of multistage area sampling is to permit probability samples to be drawn even when a current list of population is unavailable.

In general, probability sampling methods will be more time consuming and expensive than non-probability sampling methods because (1) they require an accurate specification of the population and an enumeration of the units of the population and (2) because the selection procedure of the sample units must be precisely followed.

Non-probability samples

Three types of non-probability sampling can be identified: convenience, judgemental and quota.

■ *Convenience sampling* refers to a sampling procedure of obtaining the respondents who are most conveniently available for the market analyst.

■ *Judgemental sampling* is a procedure in which the market analyst exerts some effort in selecting a sample of respondents that he or she feels most appropriate for the research objectives.

■ *Quota sampling* resembles stratified random sampling and convenience sampling. The interviewer finds and interviews a prescribed number of people in each of several categories. The sample units are selected on a subjective rather than a probabilistic basis.

In general, the choice between probability and non-probability sampling involves a trade-off between the capability to generalise the sample results to the target population with a known degree of accuracy and lower time/cost requirements.

5.4.5. Errors in survey research

One of the main responsibilities of the market analyst in charge of a survey is to estimate the overall accuracy and reliability of the survey results. The total error associated with a survey can be subdivided into two broad categories: sampling error and non-sampling error, also called systematic bias. The different sources of error, sampling and non-sampling, are described in Figure 5.9.

The size of the sampling error can be reduced by increasing the sample size or by improving the design of the sampling procedure. More difficult to control are the non-sampling errors, which arise from a multitude of factors, such as poor questionnaire construction, ill-trained interviewers, errors from respondents or errors in coding responses. The best way to minimise non-sampling errors is to have a strict control over the entire process of primary data gathering, coding and analysis. If the survey research is subcontracted to a market research company, the market analyst should give precise instructions and closely supervise the fieldwork.

5.4.6. From data collection to knowledge

Once data have been collected, emphasis in the research process turns to analysis. The raw data collected in the field must be transformed into information that will help to answer the questions raised by the decider. The transformation of raw data into information and to knowledge is achieved in several steps: data conversion, descriptive analysis and inferential analysis.

■ *Data conversion* implies data editing, coding, storing and tabulating, in order to obtain an organised collection of data records (called a data set or data bank) which lends itself to analysis.

■ *Descriptive analysis* gives an initial idea about the nature of the data; it involves obtaining appropriate measures of central tendency and of dispersion of the data for all variables, frequency distribution, cross-tabulations, graphic representations, and so forth. Multivariate techniques such as factorial analysis can also be used to summarise data.

■ *Inferential analysis* aims at exploring the extent and nature of possible associations between pairs of variables, to test hypotheses about the target population or to examine the statistical significance of differences.

Attitude and brand (or corporate) image measurement is an important application of surveys. Several multivariate data analysis methods are based on survey data. These methods are used to extract meaningful information from primary data. The most popular ones are: simple and regression analysis, discriminant analysis, factorial analysis, multidimensional scaling and cluster analysis.

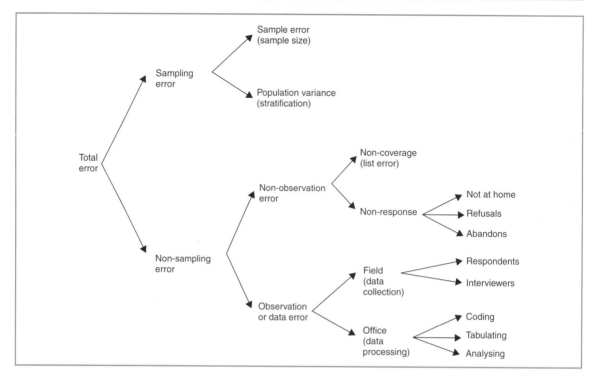

Figure 5.9   Total error in survey research

Source: Churchill and Iacobucci (2005).

For an overview of applications and problems of these techniques, see Hair *et al*. (1992).

5.5. Causal research studies

The use of a two-way table to uncover a relationship between two variables is common practice in descriptive research. A frequent temptation when a two-way table shows evidence of a statistically significant relationship, especially if one variable is presumed to influence the other (as in regression analysis) is to view this result as conclusive evidence of a causal relationship. This temptation should be resisted unless the empirical evidence stems from an experiment in which the other variables that may influence the response variable were controlled. A causal research design is required to establish the existence of a causal link. A descriptive study can only suggest the existence of a causal link. The basic tool used in causal studies is the controlled experiment.

5.5.1. Objectives of causal studies

In descriptive studies it is impossible to separate entirely the effect of a given variable from the effect of other variables.

Causal studies overcome this difficulty by organising the data-gathering procedure in such way as to permit unambiguous interpretation. Causal studies have three distinct, although very complementary, research objectives.

- To establish the direction and the intensity of a causal link between one or several action variables and one response variable.
- To measure in quantitative terms the rate of influence of an action variable on a response variable.
- To generate predictions of a response variable for different levels of the action variables.

These three objectives can be dissociated and several causal studies have the sole objective of establishing a cause-and-effect relationship in order to gain a better understanding of the phenomenon under study. In these cases, no quantitative estimates of the influence rate are sought.

Three rather intuitive types of evidence are relevant for evaluating causal relationships:

- Evidence that the action variable precedes the response variable.
- Evidence that a strong association exists between an action and an observed outcome.
- Evidence that the influence of other possible causal factors has been eliminated or controlled.

This last condition is particularly demanding and requires that all extraneous variables be controlled in order to ensure that the experiment has not been confused. The most important threats to internal validity in an experiment are briefly described here:

History: event external to the experiment that affects the responses of the people involved in the experiment.

Maturation: changes in the respondents that are a consequence of time, such as ageing, getting hungry or getting tired.

Testing effect: awareness of being in a test, which can sensitise and bias respondents.

Before-measure effect: the before-measure effect can also sensitise and bias respondents, therefore influencing both the after-observation and the respondent's reaction to the experiment treatment.

Instrumentation: the measuring instrument may change, for example, when there are many observers or interviewers.

Mortality: respondents may drop out of the experiment.

Selection bias: an experimental group may be systematically different in some relevant way from the target population.

The market analyst has to ensure that these extraneous factors are eliminated or controlled specifically to construct an experimental design.

5.5.2. Experimentation defined

Experimentation is a scientific investigation in which the researcher manipulates and controls one or more action variables and observes the response variable(s) for variation concomitant to the manipulation of the action variable. Treatments are the action variables that are manipulated and whose effects are measured. The test units are the entities, respondents or physical units to whom the treatments are presented and whose response is measured.

An experimental design involves the specification of (a) the treatments that are to be manipulated, (b) the test units to be used, (c) the response variable to be measured and (d) the procedure for dealing with extraneous variables.

Two types of experimentation can be distinguished:

- In a *laboratory experiment* in which the researcher creates a situation with the desired conditions (a trailer set up as a store or a survey situation) and then manipulates some variables while controlling others.
- A *field experiment* is organised in a realistic or natural situation (in-store test), although it too involves the manipulation of one or more action variables under carefully controlled conditions.

In general, field experiments are superior to laboratory experiments in terms of external validity.

5.5.3. Types of experimental design

In a typical experiment, two groups of respondents (or stores) are selected in such a way that the groups have similar characteristics as far as the purpose of the study is concerned. The causal factor or the treatment (e.g. advertising A) is introduced into one of the two groups, called the experimental group. No such factor is introduced in the other group, called the control group. If sales increase within the experimental group but not in the control group, it is inferred that the hypothesis is tenable, that is, that advertising caused the sales increase. If no sales increase occurs in the experimental group, or if sales increase to the same extent in the control group, it is inferred that the hypothesis is not tenable (Boyd and Westfall, 1956, p. 82).

Within this general pattern, experimental designs vary in the manner in which experimental and control groups are selected, and the degree of control that is exercised over the extraneous factors that affect the results. To illustrate this, two pre-experimental designs and two true experimental designs will be discussed briefly.

1. *The 'one shot' case study*. A single group of test units is exposed to treatment (X) and then an 'after' measurement (O) is then taken on the response variable. Thus we have

$$X \, O$$

This is not a true experimental design and it is clearly impossible to draw any meaningful conclusions from it. The observed level of O may be the result of many uncontrollable factors and in the absence of pretreatment observation, it is impossible to conclude.

2. *The one group 'before–after' design*. In this design a 'before' measurement is made in addition to the 'after' measurement. Thus, we have

$$O_1 \, X \, O_2$$

The difference between the 'after' and 'before' measurements ($X_2 - X_1$) would be assumed to be the effect of the treatment (X). This assumption is questionable, however, because the difference between the 'after' and the 'before' measurements could very well be a measure of the treatment plus the changes caused by all the uncontrolled factors, such as history, maturation, testing effect, and so on.

3. *The 'before–after' design with control group*. A true experiment is one where the researcher is able to eliminate all extraneous factors as competitive hypotheses to the treatment. An experimental and a control group are selected in such a way that they are interchangeable for purposes of the experiment. The control group is measured

at the same time as the experimental group, but no treatment is introduced. Thus, we have

$$\text{Experimental group: } O_1 \, X \, O_2$$
$$\text{Control group : } O_3 \quad O_4$$

Thus, the difference between the 'after' and the 'before' measurements of the control group ($O_4 - O_3$) is the result of uncontrolled variables. The difference between the 'after' and 'before' measurements of the experimental group ($O_2 - O_1$) is the result of the treatment plus the result of the same uncontrollable events affecting the control group. The effect of the treatment alone is obtained by subtracting the difference in the two measurements of the control group from the two measurements of the experimental group.

$$\text{True treatment effect} = [O_1 - O_2] - [O_4 - O_3]$$

All potential destroyers of internal validity are controlled by this design, except the testing effect in the experimental group, which is not eliminated.

Thus, when the 'before' measurement is made in an undisguised way – for example, by interviewing respondents – the interactive testing effect is likely to be present and cannot be separated from the treatment effect. If the collection of the data is made without the knowledge of the individuals involved, this design is appropriate. In the other cases, a way to escape the problem of the testing effect is the 'after-only with control group' design.

4. *'After-only with control group' design.* In this design, the experimental and the control groups are selected in such a way as to be equivalent. No 'before' measurement is made in both group and the treatment is introduced in one of the groups selected as the experimental group.

$$X \quad O_1$$
$$O_2$$

The effect of the treatment is determined by computing the difference between the two 'after' measurements ($O_2 - O_1$). In this design, uncontrollable factors influence both the control and the experimental groups and there is no testing effect because no pre-measurements are made. The only weakness of this design is its static nature, which does not permit an analysis of the process of change as in the 'before–after' design. A classic example of application of this design is the 'Instant Nescafe study' summarised in Table 5.5.

> The objective of the study was to determine the image of the housewife who uses instant coffee. Two comparable groups of housewives were shown similar shopping lists and asked to describe the housewife who prepared the list. On the list shown to the control group, one item was Maxwell House Coffee, a well-known drip grinds coffee brand. On the list shown to the experimental group, Nescafé Instant Coffee, a relatively new concept at the time, replaced the item. The results measured were the percentages of the respondents who described the shopping list author as having various characteristics. The effect of the treatment (Nescafé Instant Coffee user) was the difference in the percentage ascribing each characteristic to the 'instant coffee woman' from the percentage ascribing the same characteristics to the 'drip grind' woman. (Boyd and Westfall, 1956/1972, p. 96)

The results of this experiment, a replication of a study conducted by Mason Haire in 1950 – are summarised in Table 5.5. A chi-square test shows that there are no significant differences between characteristics ascribed to the Maxwell shopper and those for the Nescafé shopper (Webster and von Pechmann, 1970, pp. 61–3).

A fundamental principle is implicitly assumed to be applicable in experimental design: the market analyst does not care what extraneous factors are operative as long as they operate equally on all experimental and control groups. Thus, random selection of the test units and of the groups and random allocation of the treatments among the groups are key conditions of validity.

With the development of scanner systems in supermarkets, the organisation of marketing experiments is greatly facilitated today.

Table 5.5 Results of the instant coffee experiment		
Measurements	Experimental group	Control group
Before measurement	No	No
Treatment variable	Instant coffee (Nescafé)	Drip grind coffee (Maxwell)
After measurements	Lazy 18%	Lazy 10%
	Thrifty 36%	Thrifty 55%
	Spendthrift 23%	Spendthrift 5%
	Bad wife 18%	Bad wife 5%

Source: Webster and von Pechmann (1970, p. 62).

5.5.4. Conjoint analysis

Conjoint analysis is a multivariate technique used specifically to understand how consumers develop preferences for products or services and to formulate predictions about market attitude vis-à-vis new product concepts. The method is based on the multi-attribute product concept (see Chapter 3) that is on the premise that consumers evaluate the value or utility of a product/service idea, by combining the separate amounts of utility provided by each attribute. The power of the method is to provide an explanatory model of consumers' preferences, which can then be used to define the product concept constituting the optimum combination of attribute levels. In a more precise way, a conjoint analysis brings answers to the following questions (see Table 5.6):

- For the respondent, what is the *partial utility* (or value) of each level of each attribute used to define the product/service?
- What is the *relative importance* (weight) of each attribute in the overall evaluation of the product concept?
- How do you compare the *total utilities of several concepts* representing different bundles of attributes?
- What kind of *trade-off or arbitrage* are potential consumers willing to make between levels of attributes?
- What is the *share of preferences* of potential buyers for the different product concepts investigated?

A more detailed description of conjoint analysis is available in the website, www.macmillanbusiness/lambin.

5.5.5. Structural equations modelling

Data analysis methods have made considerable progress during the last decade and these techniques, called second generation data analysis methods, or structural equation modelling (SEM), have the capacity to examine a series of dependence relationships simultaneously, while standard multivariate techniques can examine only a single relationship at a time. In reality, the market analyst is often faced with a set of interrelated questions. For example, in a study aiming at measuring the performance of a store, the following interrelated questions have to be examined:

- What variables determine a store's image?
- How does that image combined with other variables (proximity, assortment) affect purchase decisions and satisfaction at the store?
- How does satisfaction with the store result in long-term loyalty to the store?
- How does loyalty to the store affect visit frequency and exclusivity?
- How does visit frequency and exclusivity determine the store profitability?

We have here a series of dependence relationships where one dependent variable (store image) becomes an independent variable (among others) in subsequent dependence relationship (satisfaction), which in turn 'explains' another dependent variable (loyalty), and so on. Until the 1980s, none of the multivariate techniques allowed us to address these questions with a single comprehensive method. For a review of these methods, see Hair *et al.* (1992) and Croutsche (1997).

5.5.6. The neural network technology

Neural network technology belongs to the field of artificial intelligence and gets its name because it performs many of the kinds of task that humans do. These include making distinctions between items (classification), dividing similar things into groups (clustering), associating two or more things (associative memory), learning to predict outcomes based on examples (modelling), being able to predict into the future (time series forecasting), and finally juggling multiple goals and coming up with a good-enough solution (constraint satisfaction) (Gibus, 1966, p. 41).

Neural network is a computing model grounded on the ability to recognise patterns in data. In contrast with SEM described in the preceding section, it is a model-building approach that *does not require prior definition of the causal structure*. Neural networks learn from examples. They take complex, noisy data and make educated guesses based on what they have learned from the past. It is a heuristic process. The user specifies a type of pattern and the so-called intelligent agent searches the data, looking for the particular pattern. Neural networks are said to be 'intelligent', because they learn from examples, just like children learn to recognise dogs from examples of dogs, and because they exhibit some structural capability for generalisations and memorisation.

The field of artificial intelligence is vast and clearly beyond the scope of this book, but its potential for market research is considerable. To go further on this topic and for a description of how neural networks can be applied to business problems, see the excellent book by Gibus (1996).

Marketing applications of the neural network technology

At present, the most commonly used applications of neural networks are the areas of micro-marketing, risk management and fraud detection. An example of micro-marketing is given by the US giant retail chain Wal-Mart, a frequent user of market basket analysis through this technology to find associations between products.

Table 5.6   Statistical tools used in marketing decision system

Objectives of statistical tools	Marketing application
Multiple regression A statistical technique that can be used to analyse the relationship between a single dependent variable and several independent variables. The objective is to use the independent variable whose values are known to predict the single dependent value.	The marketing manager is interested for estimate on how the company sales are influenced by changes in the level of advertising expenditures, sales force size, price and competition intensity.
Discriminant analysis The objective is to identify the variables that discriminate 'best' between two or more groups. Using the identified variables for developing an index that will parsimoniously represent the differences between the groups and develop a rule to classify future observations into one of the groups.	The marketing manager is interested in determining the salient characteristics that successfully differentiate between brand loyal and non-loyal customers, and employing this information to predict purchase intentions of potential customers.
Logistic regression A statistical technique similar to discriminant analyses but the logistic regression does not make any assumptions about the distribution of the independent variables.	The marketing manager is interested in determining the probability that a household would subscribe to a package of premium channels given the occupant's income, education, occupation, age, marital status and number of children.
Canonical correlation The objective is to correlate simultaneously several metric dependant variables and several metric independent variables. The underlying principle is to develop a linear combination of each set of variables in a manner that maximises the correlation between the two sets.	The marketing manager of a consumer goods firm is interested in determining if there is a relationship between type of products purchased and consumers' lifestyles and personality.
Factor analysis The objective is to represent a set of observed variables in terms of a smaller number of hypothetical, underlying and unknown dimensions, which are called factors.	The marketing manager of an apparel firm wants to determine whether or not a relationship exists between patriotism and consumers' attitudes about domestic and foreign products.
Cluster analysis The objective is to separate objects into groups such that each object is more like other objects in its group than like objects outside the group.	A marketing manager is interested in identifying groups of consumers who have similar behaviour and attitudes.
Multidimensional scaling The objective is to determine what dimensions respondents use when evaluating objects, how many dimensions they may use and the relative importance of each dimension.	A marketing manager wants to see where his brand is positioned in relation to the national and international competitive brands.

Source: Authors.

This information is then used to determine product affinities and suggest promotion that can maximise profits.

In trawling through some historical data and analysing it, the manager of a large US retailer noticed a distinct correlation between the sales of nappies and beer, just after work hours, which was particularly marked on a Friday. Further research confirmed the explanation: the man of the family was stopping off on his way home to pick up nappies for the baby – and a six-pack for himself. The retailer responded by merchandising nappies closer to the beer section and was rewarded by an increase in sales of both items. (Gooding, 1995, p. 25)

Other applications of the neural network technology are found in *micro-segmentation and in risk management*, particularly in the personal credit and the private insurance sectors.

In insurance, for example, it has long been recognised that female drivers are a lower risk than their male counterparts and can be offered cheaper car insurance premiums. Data mining is used to find further subsegments of female drivers with different price and risk profiles; instead of providing a standard premium to women in the same age category, insurers can now price differently in order to retain their most profitable customers or encourage customers who are likely to be unprofitable to go elsewhere.

A third popular domain of application is *fraud detection* as used by the credit card company Visa International. In concept, neural networks are extremely simple. People tend to have patterns of buying. They tend to spend within certain limits, buy certain types of goods, and acquire new things at a fairly predictable rate. Neural networks are designed to identify behaviours that do not fit these patterns. The expert system uses 30–35 different parameters and routinely analyses millions of transactions every day from around the world to detect patterns that

appear fraudulent and send the scores to the card-issuing banks several times a day. It is then up to the local bank to decide whether or not to contact customers.

An example of an established fraud pattern is as follows: a credit card is used to pay for petrol at a service station and that transaction is followed by the purchase in rapid succession of a series of large price-tag consumer electronics. The purchasing pattern would alert the neural network to possible fraud, immediately signalling the likelihood of a credit card theft by a criminal intent on using up all remaining credit as quickly as possible.

The field of information technology is changing fast with the increasing use of microcomputers, the proliferation of mobile phones and the explosion of the Internet. Information technology really does have the potential to make marketing management more effective because it enables organisations to build powerful personal relationships with their customers, to understand better their needs and to respond faster to their expectations. For an introduction to the subject, see O'Connor and Galvin (1997).

CHAPTER SUMMARY

A market-oriented firm has to develop a market information system to monitor changes in the macro-marketing environment. The role of marketing research is to provide market information data that will help management to implement a market-oriented strategy. Marketing research has to provide management with accredited (or certified) knowledge and, for this reason, has strictly to follow the rules of scientific method. The development of a research project implies a sequence of interrelated activities, which ensures a systematic and orderly investigation process. Three types of marketing research can be identified: exploratory, descriptive and causal studies. The objective of exploratory research is to generate hypotheses and to translate the research problem into research objectives. The techniques of exploratory research are: use of secondary data, key informant surveys, analysis of selected cases and focus group discussions. Group discussions, also called qualitative research, are particularly useful, but they should be used strictly to suggest hypotheses for further research and not as conclusive evidence. Descriptive studies attempt to obtain a complete, quantitative and accurate description of a situation and must follow a precise methodology. The techniques used are observation and communication. The most popular communication method is by far the survey method through personal, telephone or mail interviewing. Good questionnaire design is the key to obtaining good survey results and a seven-step procedure is proposed to help in designing a questionnaire. Sampling techniques can be divided into two categories: probability and non-probability samples. These two sampling techniques have their own merits. The two sources of error in survey research are sampling and non-sampling errors. To minimise non-sampling error the market analyst should have strict control over the entire data-gathering process. Causal research is used to establish the existence of a causal link between an action and a response variable. An experimentation is a scientific investigation in which the researcher manipulates and controls one or more action variables and observes the response variable for variation concomitant to the manipulation of the action variable. Different types of experimental designs exist which vary in the way the analyst controls extraneous factors.

Review and Application Questions

1. State (a) the complaints that managers typically have against marketing researchers and (b) the complaints that marketing researchers typically have against managers.
2. What is the difference between external and internal validity and which research procedure(s) will contribute towards an improvement in the validity of both?
3. Why is it important to determine research hypotheses before undertaking survey research?
4. What is the basic difference between exploratory and conclusive research?
5. Compare and contrast quantitative and qualitative research in terms of the following: (a) the purpose of the research, (b) the data collection methods used, (c) the analysis procedure and (d) how the findings can be used by marketing managers.
6. What are the general advantages and disadvantages associated with obtaining information by questioning or by observation?
7. What distinguishes a probability sample from a non-probability sample? Compare the merits and weaknesses of these two sampling procedures.

Bibliography

Aaker, D.A. and Day, J.S. (1980), *Marketing Research*, New York, John Wiley & Sons, 2nd edition.

Adler, L. (1979), To Learn What's on the Consumers' Mind, Try Focus Group Interviews, *Sales and Marketing Management*, pp. 76–80.

Boyd, H.W. and Westfall, R. (1956/1972), *Marketing Research: Text and Cases*, Homewood, IL, R.D. Irwin Inc.

Churchill, G.A. and Iacobucci, D. (2005), *Marketing Research, Methodological Foundations*, Orlando, FL, Thompson, South Western, 9th edition.

Croutsche, J.J. (1997), *Pratique de l'analyse des données*, Paris, Editions ESKA.

Erdos, P.L. (1970), *Professional Mail Surveys*, New York, McGraw-Hill.

Gibus, J.J. (1996), *Data Mining with Neural Networks: Solving Business Problems from Application Development to Decision Support*, New York, McGraw-Hill Book Company.

Gooding, C. (1995), Boosting Sales with the Information Warehouse, *Financial Times*, March 1.

Hair, J., Anderson, R.E., Tatham, R.L. and Black, W.C. (1992), *Multivariate Data Analysis*, New York, Macmillan Publishing Company, 3rd edition.

Kerlinger, F.N. (1973), *Foundations of Behavioural Research*, London, Holt Rinehart and Winston Inc.

Kotler, P. (1967/2005), *Marketing Management*, Englewood Cliffs, NJ, Prentice-Hall, Inc., 10th edition with Keller.

Lambin, J.J.L. (1990), *La recherché marketing*, Paris, McGraw-Hill.

Marchand, D. (2002), Is Your Company Effective at Using Information? *European Business Forum*, 8, Winter, pp. 54–7.

O'Connor, J. and Galvin, E. (1997), *Marketing and Information Technology*, London, Pitman Publishing.

Pellemans, P. (1995), *Jungian Analysis as a Tool for New Qualitative Research Methods in Marketing*, Unpublished Working Paper, IAG, Louvain-la-Neuve, Belgium.

Pellemans, P. (1999), *Recherche qualitative en marketing: une perspective psychologique*, Brussels, De Boeck Université.

Simon, H. (1996), *The Hidden Champions*, Boston, MA, Harvard Business School Press.

Webster, F.E. and von Pechmann (1970), A Replication of the Shopping List Study, *Journal of Marketing*, 34, April, pp. 61–77.

Zaltman, G. and Burger, P.C. (1975), *Marketing Research: Fundamentals and Dynamics*, Hinsdale, IL, The Dryden Press.

Zikmund, W.G. (1986/1994), *Exploring Marketing Research*, Chicago, IL, The Dryden Press, 2nd and 5th editions.

COMPANION WEBSITE FOR CHAPTER 5

Visit the *Market-driven Management* companion website at www.palgrave.com/business/lambin to find information on:

Questionnaire Design Procedure
Conjoint Analysis
Examples of Questions Used in Survey Research
Selected Reviews and Journals Useful in Marketing Research

Part 3

implementing strategic marketing

PART I: THE CHANGING ROLE OF MARKETING

The Role of Marketing in the Firm
and in a Social Market Economy
Chapter 1

Market-driven Management
in the Global Marketplace
Chapter 2

PART II: UNDERSTANDING CUSTOMER BEHAVIOUR

Customers' Needs Analysis
Chapter 3

The Customer Purchase Behaviour
Chapter 4

Measuring Customers' Response
Chapter 5

PART III: IMPLEMENTING STRATEGIC MARKETING

Needs Analysis through Market Segmentation
Chapter 6

Market Attractiveness Analysis
Chapter 7

Company Competitiveness Analysis
Chapter 8

Market Targeting and Positioning
Chapter 9

Formulating a Marketing Strategy
Chapter 10

PART IV: IMPLEMENTING OPERATIONAL MARKETING

New Product
Decisions

Chapter 11

Brand
Management

Chapter 12

Distribution
Channel
Decisions

Chapter 13

The Battle of the
Brands in the
B2C Markets

Chapter 14

Pricing
Decisions

Chapter 15

Marketing
Communication
Decisions

Chapter 16

PART V: IMPLEMENTATION OF MARKET-DRIVEN MANAGEMENT

The Strategic and Operational
Marketing Plan
Chapter 17

Emerging Values and Issues in
Market-driven Management
Chapter 18

Case Studies

market segmentation analysis **6**

Chapter contents

Chapter learning objectives

When you have read this chapter, you should know and understand

- the concept of reference market;
- the objectives of market segmentation;
- the advantages and disadvantages of different segmentation methods;
- the requirements for effective segmentation.

Chapter introduction

One of the first strategic decisions a firm has to make is to define its reference market and to choose the customer segment(s) to target (Smith, 1956). This choice implies the splitting of the total market into groups of customers with similar needs and behavioural or motivational characteristics, and which constitute distinct market opportunities. A firm can elect to serve all possible customers or to focus on one or several specific segments within the reference market. The typical output of a segmentation analysis is a segmentation grid, describing the qualitative and quantitative profile of the most important segments (generally four or five). Using this mapping of the reference market, the firm will then evaluate the attractiveness of each segment (see Chapter 7) and assess its own competitiveness (see Chapter 8) before making decisions regarding which segment(s) to target and which positioning to adopt within each chosen segment (see Chapter 9).

6.1. Steps in the strategic segmentation process

The implementation of the strategic segmentation process consists of four basic steps (see Figure 6.1).

1. *Segmentation analysis*, or subdividing product markets into distinct groups of potential buyers having the same expectations or requirements (homogeneity condition), and being different from customers who are in other segments (heterogeneity condition).
2. *Market targeting*, or selecting particular segment(s) to target, given the firm's strategic ambition and distinctive capabilities, a decision based on the results of the attractiveness (Chapter 7) and competitiveness (Chapter 8) analyses.
3. *Market positioning*, or deciding how the firm wants to be perceived in the minds of potential customers, given the distinctive quality of the product and the positions already occupied by competitors.
4. *Marketing programming* aimed at target segments. This last step involves the development and deployment of specific marketing programme(s) specially designed to achieve the desired positioning in the target segment(s) (Chapter 10).

The first step, segmentation analysis of the reference market is generally done in two steps, corresponding to different levels of total market desegregation. The first step, called *macro-segmentation*, has the objective of identifying 'product markets', while in the second, called *micro-segmentation*, the goal is to uncover customers' 'segments' within each product market previously identified. Micro-segmentation can be implemented in four different ways.

- *Descriptive segmentation*, which is based on socio-demographic characteristics of the customer irrespective of the product category.
- *Benefit segmentation*, which considers explicitly the product category and the person's system of values.
- *Lifestyle segmentation*, which is based on socio-cultural characteristics of the customer, irrespective of the product category.
- *Behavioural segmentation*, which classifies customers on the basis of their actual purchasing behaviour in the marketplace.

Each of these segmentation methods has its own merits and weaknesses, which will be discussed in the following sections.

6.2. Macro-segmentation analysis

In the majority of markets, it is almost impossible to satisfy all customers with a single product or service. Different consumers have varying desires and interests. This variety stems from diverse buying practices and basic variations of customers' needs and the benefits they seek from products. Increasingly, therefore, companies have found it essential to move away from mass marketing towards target marketing strategy, where the focus is on a particular group of customers. This identification of target customer groups is market segmentation, where the total market is desegregated into subgroups, with similar requirements and buying characteristics. Knowing how to segment a market is one of the most important skills a firm must possess. Segmentation defines what business the firm is in, guides strategy development and determines the capabilities needed in the business unit.

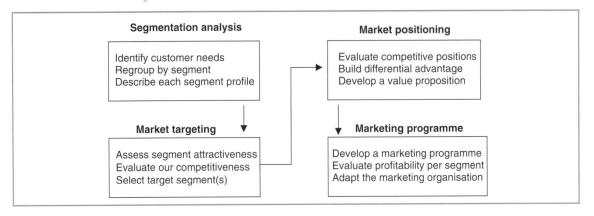

Figure 6.1   Steps in the strategic marketing process
Source: Authors.

6.2.1. Defining the reference market in terms of solution

Implementing a market segment strategy should begin with a business definition statement that reveals the true function or purpose of the firm in a customer-oriented perspective. Three fundamental questions should be addressed:

- What business(es) are we in?
- What business(es) should we be in?
- What business(es) should we not be in?

To answer these questions in a customer-oriented perspective, the business definition should be made in a generic term, which is in terms of the 'solution' sought by the customer and not in technical terms, to avoid the risk of myopia.

The rationale behind the solution approach has been explained in Chapter 3. It can be summarised as follows:

- To the buyer, the product is what it does.
- No one buys a product per se. What is sought is a solution to a problem.
- Different technologies can produce the same function.
- Technologies are fast changing, while generic needs are stable.

It is therefore important for the market-oriented firm to define its reference market in terms of a generic need, rather than in terms of a product. Examples of market reference definitions: are presented in Box 6.1.

Ideally, the business definition should be stated in terms narrow enough to provide practical guidance, yet broad enough to stimulate imaginative thinking, such as openings for product line extensions or for diversification into adjacent product areas. At the Grumman Corporation, the guidelines for the mission statement advise:

> We should be careful not to confine the market boundaries by our existing or traditional product participation. The market definition analysis is purposely meant to create an outward awareness of the total surrounding market, and of its needs and trends that may offer opportunity for, or on the other hand challenges to, our current or contemplated position. (Hopkins, 1982, p. 119)

The business definition is the starting point for strategy development. It helps identify the customers to be served, the competitors to surpass the key success factors to master and the alternative technologies available for producing the service or the function sought.

The adoption of the solution approach in defining the reference market substantially changes the nature of the firm's business, since the firm is transforming itself into a service provider.

6.2.2. Conceptualisation of the reference market

The objective is to define the reference market in the buyer perspective and not from the producer's point of view, as is too often the case. As suggested by Abell (1980), a reference market can be defined in three dimensions:

> Customer group or who is being satisfied; customer functions or needs. What is being satisfied; and the technologies used to meet the needs. How customer needs are being satisfied.

BOX 6.1

IMPLEMENTATION PROBLEM: EXAMPLES OF REFERENCE MARKET DEFINITION IN TERMS OF GENERIC NEEDS

- *Lego*, the Danish toy company has a worldwide market share in the construction-toy market of 72 per cent. The company has redefined its market as the 'edutainement' (education–entertainment) market, '*having fun and exercising the mind*'.
- *Colgate-Palmolive* defines its reference market as the *oral care* market and proposes a full range of toothpastes, mouthwash, toothbrushes and cleanup tools.
- *Derbit Belgium* is operating in the European roofing market and manufactures membranes of APP-modified bitumen. The company defines its market as follows: 'We are selling guaranteed waterproof solutions to flat roofing problems in partnership with exclusive distributors and highly qualified roofing applicators.'
- *Sedal*, a small French company manufacturing metallic ventilation grids, defined its business as the 'air and temperature control' business and expanded its offerings to air ventilation and air conditioning systems (see Figure 6.2).
- *Automatic Systems* manufactures gates and doors, but defines its business as the sales of 'access control solutions' and offers its customers the hardware and the software (security systems) as well.
- *IBM* defines its mission in the following terms: 'we are in the business of helping customers solve problems through the use of advanced information technology. We are creating value by offering the solutions, products and services that help customers succeed.'

Source: Authors.

We thus have a three-dimensional framework, as shown in Figure 6.3. To segment the market, the first step is to identify the relevant criteria for describing each of these three dimensions.

Needs or functions

We refer here to the need to be fulfilled by the product or the service. Examples of functions would be:

> Home interior decoration; international transportation of goods; waterproof roof protection; rust prevention; teeth cleaning; deep versus shallow drilling; diagnostic imaging; and so on.

Functions have to be conceptually separated from the way the function is performed (that is the technology). The dividing line between 'functions' and 'benefits' is not always clear, as functions are narrowly subdivided or as assortments of functions are considered, for example, teeth cleaning plus decay prevention, shampoo with anti-dandruff treatment. Thus, functions can also be defined as a package of benefits sought by different customer groups.

Customers

We describe the different customer groups that might buy the product. The most common criteria used are:

> households versus industrial buyers, socio-economic class, geographic location, type of activity, company size, original equipment manufacturer versus user, decision-making unit, and so on.

At this level of macro-segmentation, only broad customer characteristics are retained. For consumer goods, more detailed criteria are often necessary, such as age group, benefits sought, lifestyle, purchase behaviour, and so on. This is the object of micro-segmentation.

Technologies

These describe the alternative ways in which a particular function can be performed for a customer.

> For example, paint or wallpaper for the function of home interior decoration; road, air, rail or sea for international transportation of goods; bitumen or plastic for roof protection; toothpaste or mouthwash

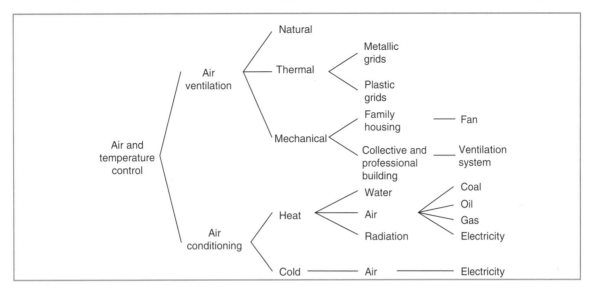

Figure 6.2 Example of a reference market definition
Source: Adapted from Lyon, E.M. (1976).

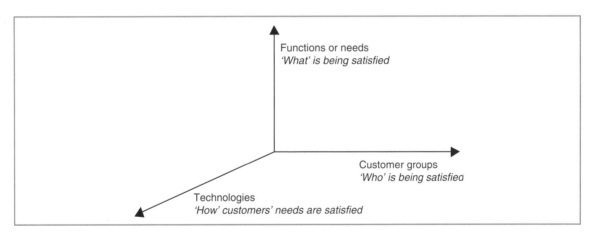

Figure 6.3 The three-dimensional framework of a reference market
Source: Adapted from Abell (1980).

for teeth cleaning; X-ray, ultrasound or computerised tomography for diagnostic imaging, and so on.

As underlined above, the technology dimension is dynamic, in the sense that one technology can displace another over time. For example, ultrasound, nuclear medicine and CT scanning as alternative imaging diagnostic techniques are displacing X-rays. Similarly, electronic mail is tending to displace printed materials in the field of written communication.

6.2.3. Market boundary definitions

Using this framework, we may distinguish between a 'product market', a 'solution market' and an 'industry' (Figure 6.4):

- A specific customer group, seeking a specific function or assortment of functions based on a single technology defines a *product market*.
- A *solution market* is defined by the performance of given functions in given customer groups, but including all the substitute technologies to perform those functions. It corresponds to the concept of 'category'.
- An *industry* is based on a single technology, but covers several businesses, that is, several functions or assortments of functions and several customer groups.

These alternative boundary definitions correspond to different market coverage strategies, each having their own merits and weaknesses.

The *industry definition* is the most traditional one, but also the least satisfactory because it is supply-oriented and not market-oriented. From a marketing point of view, this definition of the reference market is much too general, since it includes a large variety of functions and customer groups. In the household appliances industry, for example, this would include microwave ovens and laundry irons, two very different products in terms of growth potential and customers' behaviour characteristics. However, most industrial and foreign trade statistics are industry-based and it is therefore difficult to avoid industry definitions completely.

The *solution market definition* is very close to the generic need concept and has the merit of emphasising the existence of substitute products or technologies for performing the same function. A technological innovation can dramatically change existing market boundaries. The monitoring of substitute technologies is enhanced by this reference market definition. The major difficulty stems from the fact that the technology domains involved may be very different.

Customers with a need for a 6 mm hole will normally use a metal twist drill, but some segments are finding lasers or high-pressure water jets to be a better solution. Also, Companies that refine cane sugar wrestle with this question often. Their product is a sweetener, but the needs of soft drink and candy manufacturers for sweetening can be satisfied with sugar made from corn (fructose) or sugar beets. Depending on market conditions, these alternatives may be cheaper. Should they offer all sweetening materials? (Day, 1990, p. 27)

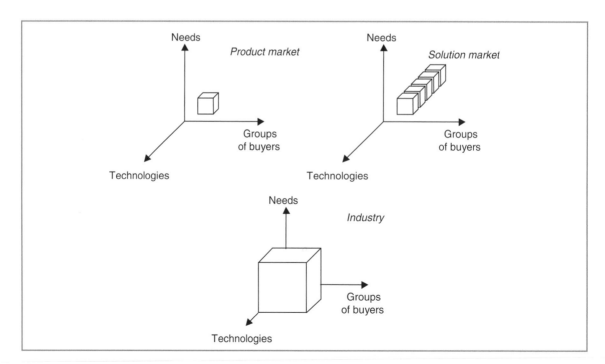

Figure 6.4   Reference market boundaries

Source: Adapted from Abell (1981).

EXHIBIT 6.1

THE MARKETING MIX AND THE 'SOLUTION-TO-A-PROBLEM' APPROACH

- *Product*: a solution to a problem and the package of benefits that the product represents.
- *Category*: the set of products giving a solution to the customers' problem.
- *Place*: a convenient access to the solution sought by the buyer.
- *Price*: all the costs, including price, supported by the buyer to acquire the solution sought.

- *Advertising*: the messages and signals communicated about the solutions available and about their distinctive qualities.
- *Selling*: the negotiation process or the dialogue organised with the potential buyer in his search for the appropriate solution to his (or her) problem.

Source: Authors.

The solution market definition is very useful for giving directions to R&D and for suggesting diversification strategies and also for organising markets. Category management is based on this concept, which also modifies substantially the marketing mix concept (see Exhibits 6.1 and 6.2).

The *product market definition* is the most market-oriented definition. It corresponds to the notion of 'strategic business unit' (SBU) and is very close to the real-world market. This market definition automatically dictates six key elements of the firm's strategic thrust, namely

- the customers to be served;
- the package of benefits to be provided;
- the direct competitors to surpass;
- the substitute technologies and competitors to monitor;
- the key capabilities to acquire;
- the main market actors to deal with.

This partitioning of the total reference market into product markets will guide market coverage decisions and will determine the type of organisational structure to adopt. One shortcoming of this market definition is the difficulty of finding appropriate market measurements, most government statistics being industry-based and not market-based.

6.3. Development of a macro-segmentation grid

Once the relevant segmentation variables are identified, the next task is to combine them to develop a segmentation grid. To illustrate this process, let us consider the market of heavy-duty trucks. The identified segmentation variables are the following:

- Needs: regional, national and international transport of goods.
- Technologies: air, rail, water and road.

- Customers: types of activity – own account, professional transporters and renting companies; size of fleet – small (1–4 trucks), medium (5–10 trucks) and large (>10 trucks).

If we consider all possible combinations, we have here a total of 108 (3 × 4 × 3 × 3) possible segments. To refine the analysis, let us adopt the following rules:

- Ignore transportation modes other than road transportation.
- Establish a distinction between trucks below and above 16 tonnes.
- Forget about truck renting companies.
- Subdivide regional transport into three categories: distribution, construction and others.

We now obtain 60 (5 × 2 × 2 × 3) segments as shown in Table 6.1, which is still much too high. The size of these segments varies widely, however, as the figures of Table 6.1 show. Those numbers represent the percentage of registered license plates for trucks within each segment. Each segment does not necessarily have to be considered, as the pertinence analysis should demonstrate.

6.3.1. Pertinence analysis

In developing a realistic segmentation grid, the following rules should be adopted:

- The analyst should start with the longest list of segmentation variables to avoid overlooking meaningful criteria.
- Only those variables with a truly significant strategic impact should be isolated.
- Collapsing together variables that are correlated can reduce the number of variables.
- Some cells are generally unfeasible combinations of segmentation variables and therefore can be eliminated.

EXHIBIT 6.2

IMPLICATIONS OF THE SOLUTION APPROACH: FROM SELLING WIDGETS TO PROVIDING SERVICES

From General Electric Co. to Wang Laboratories Inc., from Xerox Corp. to Hewlett-Packard Co., American companies that a few years ago got almost all their profits from selling widgets are rapidly transforming themselves into service providers. Computer companies such as Unisys Corp., and IBM Corp. are designing, installing and running other companies' computer operations. Document processors such as Xerox and Pitney Bowes Inc. now run mailrooms and copy centres and distribute documents electronically. Honeywell redesigns refineries. Hewlett-Packard not only designs and operates data systems, but also pays for the whole package and then leases it out. 'Customers want to finance a solution, not a little piece of it', says Ann Livermore, vice-president of Hewlett-Packard's service operations. The move to services is one of the hottest strategies in US business, and it is driven by changes at the very foundations of manufacturing. [...] 'Services generate huge cash flows and today's business are run for cash flow', said Nicholas Heymann an analyst with NatWest securities.

Source: Deutsch C.H., International Herald Tribune.

Table 6.1 Macro-segmentation of the truck market (percentage of total truck population)

	Fleet size and weight						
	Small (1–4)		Medium (4–10)		Large (>10)		
Activity/Functions	<16t	>16t	<16t	>16t	<16t	>16t	Total
Own account transporters	Segment 1: 19.3%				Segment 2: 11.1%		
Distribution	7.3	4.5	1.1	1.8	0.4	2.1	16.2
Construction	0.1	1.1	0.9	1.4	1.7	1.6	6.8
National	4.7	1.6	1.4	3.8	1.7	3.6	16.8
International	1.3	0.9	0.2	1.3	—	1.4	5.1
Others	—	0.6	0.3	—	2.5	—	3.4
Professional transporters	Segment 3: 13.9%				Segment 4: 26.1%		
Distribution	1.1	0.8	0.9	1.6	—	1.6	6.0
Construction	0.2	1.6	—	0.4	—	1.2	3.4
National	1.4	1.5	1.4	3.0	2.5	8.5	18.3
International	0.2	0.7	0.5	6.1	0.4	14.7	22.6
Others	—	0.4	—	—	—	—	0.4
Total	16.3	13.7	6.7	19.4	9.2	34.7	100.0%

Source: (Lambin and Hiller, 1990).

- Some segments can be regrouped if the differences among them are not really significant or their size is too small.
- The segmentation grid should include potential segments as well and not only segments that are currently occupied.

In the case of Volvo Trucks Company, re-examination of the segmentation grid suggested the regrouping of the most similar segments that must be served together, to retain eventually four major segments, which altogether represent 70.5 per cent of the total truck population in the Belgian market.

This phase is the most difficult one. The task is to conciliate realism and efficiency, two often-contradictory objectives. When eliminating segments, one must eliminate only the unfeasible combinations of segmentation variables but keep the empty cells, which, while currently unoccupied, could become potential segments in the future.

6.3.2. Testing the macro-segmentation grid

To verify the usefulness of the grid, the company's customers and direct competitors should be located in the different segments. The objective is to evaluate the potential of each segment in terms of size and growth, and to measure the market share held by the firm within each segment. The questions to examine are the following:

- Which segment(s) display the highest growth rate?
- What is our present market coverage?
- Where are our key customers located?
- Where are our direct competitors located?
- What are the requirements of each segment in terms of service, product quality, and so on?

The answers to these questions will also help the firm to define its market coverage strategy and to regroup segments having the same requirements and/or the same competitors.

6.3.3. Searching for new segments

Some segmentation variables are readily apparent as a result of industry convention or established norms for dividing buyers. Macro-segmentation analysis goes beyond conventional wisdom and accepted classification schemes and gives the opportunity for discovering new ways of segmenting the market (Box 6.2). Finding new ways to segment the market can give the firm a major competitive advantage over rivals.

In a given sector of activity, business definitions may differ from one competitor to another. A firm specialising in a particular function can be confronted by a rival specialising in a particular customer group interested in the same function. The first competitor will probably have a cost advantage over the second, who will be probably more efficient in terms of distribution or customer service. The competitor analysis system should help identify the distinctive qualities of direct competitors (Box 6.3).

6.3.4. Changes in market boundaries

Under the pressure of technological progress and changing consumption habits, definitions of market boundaries keep on changing along any one of three dimensions: functions, technologies or customers.

- Extension to new customer groups through a process of adoption and diffusion, for example, adoption of microcomputers in the classroom.
- Extension to new functions through a process of systematisation and through the creation of products to serve a combination of functions, for example, telephone sets combined with a fax and with an automatic answering device.
- Extension to new technologies through a process of technological substitution, for example, digital photography replacing chemical-based photography.

These changing forces explain the changing profiles of product life cycles (PLCs), a key criterion for assessing the attractiveness of product markets. The PLC model will be analysed in the next chapter.

6.4. Micro-segmentation analysis in B2C markets

The objective of micro-segmentation is to analyse the diversity of customers' requirements in a more detailed way within each of the product markets (or macro-segments) identified at the stage of macro-segmentation analysis. Within a particular product market, customers seek the same core service, for instance, time measurement in the watch market. However, keeping in mind the multi-attribute product concept, the way the core service is provided and the secondary services that go with the core service can be very different. The goal of micro-segmentation analysis is to identify customer groups searching for the same package of benefits in the product. This can lead to a

---

BOX 6.2

IMPLEMENTATION PROBLEM: HOW TO DISCOVER NEW POTENTIAL SEGMENTS?

In searching for potential new segments, the following questions should be considered:

- Are there other technologies to perform the required functions?
- Could an enhanced product perform additional functions?
- Could the needs of some buyers be better served by reducing the number of functions and possibly by lowering the price?
- Are there other groups of buyers requiring the same service or function?
- Are there new channels of distribution that could be used?
- Are there different bundles of products and services that could possibly be sold as a package?

BOX 6.3

IMPLEMENTATION PROBLEM: HOW TO VERIFY THE HETEROGENEITY CONDITION BETWEEN SEGMENTS?

The following questions can also help decide whether or not two products belong to the same strategic segment:

■ Are the main competitors the same?
■ Are their customers or groups of customers the same?

■ Are the key success factors the same?
■ Does divesting in one affect the other?

Positive answers to these four questions would tend to show that both products belong to the same product market.

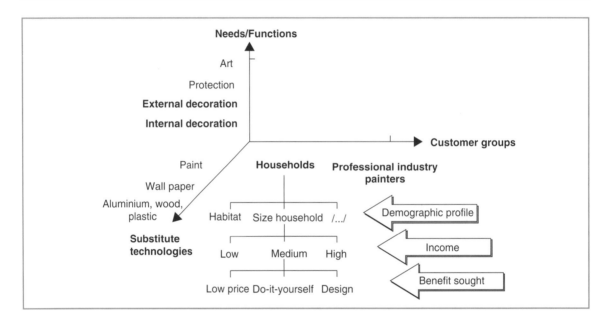

Figure 6.5　From macro- to micro-segmentation: an example
Source: Authors.

differentiation strategy to obtain a competitive advantage over rivals by doing a better job of satisfying customer requirements. Figure 6.5 illustrates the relationship between macro- and micro-segmentation.

6.4.1. Descriptive or socio-demographic segmentation

Socio-demographic segmentation is an indirect segmentation method. The basic assumption embedded in this buyer's classification is the following:

> People having different socio-demographic profiles also have different needs and expectations regarding products and services.

This is obvious in many fields. Women and men have different needs for products such as clothes, hats, cosmetics, jewellery, and so on, and similarly for teenagers or senior citizens, for low- and high-income households, for rural versus urban households, and so on. Thus, socio-demographic variables are used as proxies for direct need analysis.

The most commonly used variables are: sex, age, income, geographic location, education, occupation, family size and social class, all variables which reflect the easily measurable vital statistics of a society. Frequently, a socio-demographic segmentation combines several variables, as shown in Figure 6.6. The case analysed here is that of a recently launched new brand in the food sector. The market response is described by reference to two dependent variables: the proportion of households having purchased the brand (market occupation rate) and the average quantity purchased per household (market penetration rate). The national average is at the intersection of the two lines; the other points describe the behaviour of different socio-economic subgroups.

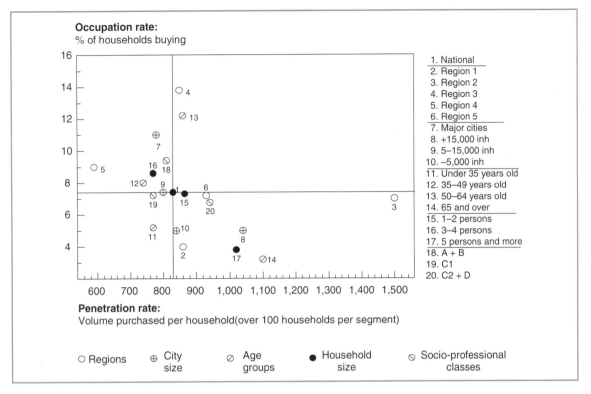

Figure 6.6   Socio-demographic segmentation: the case of a new food product
Source: Industry.

For instance, one observes that the highest occupation rates are within the subgroups denoted respectively 5/13/7/18: (region 3), (age group 50–65), (large cities), (classes A+B). Similarly, the market penetration rate is higher within the following subgroups: 3/15/8/17: (region 2), (age group 65 and higher), (middle size cities), (household composition: 5 persons and higher).

This information is essential to verify whether the target group has been reached and, if not, to adjust the marketing programme accordingly.

Usefulness of socio-demographic data

The merits of socio-demographic segmentation are its low cost and ease of application. In most markets, information on socio-demographic variables is readily available in published sources. In addition, consumer panels use these criteria in their monthly or bimonthly reports on a similar base across the main European countries.

Also, in recent years, significant socio-demographic changes have been observed in industrialised countries. Among these changes are

- declining birth rate,
- increase in life expectancy,
- increasing number of working women,

- postponement of the age of marriage,
- increasing divorce rate,
- increasing numbers of single-parent families.

These changes all have direct implications on the demand structure and on consumer purchase behaviour. They create new market segments and new requirements in existing segments. Examples are

- the senior citizen (over 65) segment for banking services, recreational activities, medical care, and so on;
- the segment of single-adult households, that is, the unmarried, divorced, widowed or single-parent families;
- the dual-income households having higher discretionary income, also called the 'DINKS' (double income no kids);
- the segment of working women for all time-saving goods and services, such as microwave ovens, catalogue shopping, easy-to-prepare foods, fast-food restaurants, and so on.

Several uses are currently made of socio-demographic data, namely

- to describe and better understand present customers,
- to have the ID profile of a target segment,
- to select media having a higher probability of reaching a target group,
- to identify prospective buyers of a new product.

Table 6.2 Changing society: implications for organic food	
Changing features in society	**Organic food implications**
Smaller households; more singles	Desire for smaller portions and more eating out habits.
Children at older age	Mature purchase decision-making.
	Purchasing higher quality food.
More women in the work force	Less time available – guilt, convenience food.
Rich getting richer	Non-price sensitive food purchasing.
Healthy living	Increased concern for diet (salt, fat, additives etc.)
Vegetarianism	Much greater awareness of food and food ingredients.
Multiculturalism	Increased variation in diet, and new food types.
Globalisation	Expectation of consistent year-round supply; loss of seasonal food consumption.

Source: Coriolis Research.

The application problem presented in Table 6.2 provides an illustration of the usefulness of socio-demographic data.

Limitations of descriptive segmentation

Socio-demographic segmentation (as well as behavioural segmentation) is ex post analysis of the kind of people who make up specific segments. The emphasis is on describing the characteristics of segments rather than on learning what causes these segments to develop. This is why it is called 'descriptive segmentation'.

Another major weakness is the declining predictive value of socio-demographic segmentation in industrialised countries as, increasingly, different persons adopt the same consumer behaviour with the growing standardisation of consumption modes across social classes. In other words, the fact of belonging to the upper class no longer necessarily implies the existence of purchase behaviour different from that of a middle-class person. Today, two consumers of the same age, same family structure and same income may have extremely different behaviours and attitudes, reflected in different buying habits, product preferences and sometimes completely opposite reactions to advertising. Socio-demographic segmentation must be complemented by other methods to understand and predict a buyer's behaviour.

6.4.2. Benefit segmentation

In benefit segmentation, the emphasis is placed on differences in peoples' values and not on differences in socio-demographic profiles. Two persons identical in terms of socio-demographic profiles may have very different value systems. Moreover, the same person having different experiences with products can hold different values towards each product that is purchased.

For example, a person who buys a refrigerator because it is the cheapest available may want to buy the most expensive TV set simply because of its superior design. Or, the individual who pays a high price for a bottle of wine may own a very cheap watch.

Thus, as discussed in Chapter 3, the value or the benefit sought in purchasing a particular product is the critical motivational factor to identify. The objective of benefit segmentation is to explain differences in preferences and not simply to give ex post descriptions of purchase behaviour.

In the watch market, for instance, one can identify four distinct benefit segments, each representing different values attributed to watches by different groups of consumers:

Economy segment. This group sees a watch mainly as a time-measurement device and purchases it mainly on the basis of price for any watch that works reasonably well. Brands such as Seiko, Pulsar and Citizen are typically in this segment.

Prestige and quality segment. This group wants a watch with a long life, good workmanship, good material and good styling. They are willing to pay for these product qualities. Omega and Rolex are in this segment.

Fashion segment. This group wants useful product features but also meaningful emotional qualities. The watch is viewed as a fashion accessory and is issued in many different faces and colours. It appeals as a fashion item to young active and trendy people. The leading brand in this segment is clearly Swatch, who created the 'funwear' concept.

Symbolic segment. Here, a well-known brand name, fine styling, a gold or diamond case and a jeweller's recommendation are important. The symbolic segment has become more sophisticated with new benefits emerging, such as elegance and fashion (Gucci and Armani), sport (Tag Heuer, Breitling), luxury and refinement (Patek Philippe).

Without such an understanding, the demographic characteristics of customers were most confusing. It turns out, for example, that people with both the highest and the lowest incomes buy the most expensive watches. On the other hand, some upper-income consumers are no longer buying costly watches, but are buying cheap, well-styled watches to throw away when they require servicing. Other upper-income consumers, however, continue to buy fine, expensive watches for suitable occasions.

At one time, most watch companies were oriented almost exclusively towards the prestige and quality segment, thus leaving the major portion of the market open to attack and exploitation. The US Time Company, with the Timex brand, took advantage of this opening and established a very strong position among buyers in the economy segment and later Swatch in the fashion segment.

Required market data

Benefit segmentation requires obtaining detailed information on consumer value systems. Each segment is identified by the benefits it is seeking. It is the total package of benefits sought, which differentiates one segment from another, rather than the fact that one segment is seeking one particular benefit and another a quite different benefit. Individual benefits are likely to have appeal for several segments. In fact, most people would like as many benefits as possible. However, the relative importance they attach to individual benefits when forced to make trade-offs can differ a great deal and, accordingly, can be used as an effective criterion in segmenting markets. Thus, opportunities for segmentation arise from trade-offs consumers are willing to make among the benefits possible and the prices paid to obtain them.

Thus, the multi-attribute product concept is the implied behavioural model in benefit segmentation. Its implementation requires the following information from a representative sample of target consumers:

- The list of attributes or benefits associated with a product category.
- An evaluation of the relative importance attached to each benefit.
- A regrouping procedure of consumers with similar rating patterns.
- An evaluation of the size and profile of each identified segment.

Thus, in the oral care market for instance, the attributes identified through consumer research were the following: whiteness, freshness, good taste, product appearance, decay prevention, gum protection and economy. Four segments can be identified as shown in Table 6.3. Supplementary information should also be collected about the people's profile in each of these segments:

1. *The cosmetic segment*: comprises people who mainly show concern for fresh breath and the brightness of their teeth. It includes a relatively large group of young married couples. They smoke more than average and their lifestyle is very active. New offerings have emerged in this group with the launching of the whitening and the herbal toothpastes. The tooth-whitening subsegment is fast growing in this toothpaste category.

2. *The therapeutic segment*: contains a large number of families with children. They are seriously concerned about the possibilities of cavities and gum protection. They show a definite preference for paramedical brands sold

---

Table 6.3   Benefit segmentation of the toothpaste market

Benefits sought	Benefits segments			
	Cosmetic	Therapeutic	Sensory	Economy
White and Freshness Whitening Night-time breath	Colgate, White Glo Signal, Arm&Hammer P.M.			
Cavity, tartar and gum protection Sensitive teeth		Crest, Parogencyl, Parodontax Sensodyne		
Taste, Flavor, Colour, Fun			Colgate Barbie, Crest Kids	
Core function Low price All-in-one				Private labels

Note: Reprentative brands only. Toothpaste companies have a multisegment strategy.
Source: Authors.

mainly in pharmacies, at a price three times the price of a regular cosmetic brand. A new offering in this segment is the brand Sensodyne designed for people having very sensitive teeth.

3. *The sensory segment*: is particularly concerned with the flavour and the appearance of the product. In this segment, large portions of the brand users are children, the kids' subsegment. Their use of spearmint toothpaste is well above average. Toothpaste manufacturers are licensing cartoon characters, like Colgate Barbie. A new arrival in this toothpaste category is the night-time toothpaste to fight night-time's breath, with the Arm & Hammer's P.M. brand.

4. *The economy segment*: is price-oriented and shows a dominance of men. It tends to be above average in terms of toothpaste usage. People in this segment see very few meaningful differences between brands and are attracted by all-in-one brands like Aquafresh and by private labels.

Benefit segmentation has important implications for the product policy of the firm. Once marketing understands the expectations of a particular consumer group, new or modified products can be developed and aimed at people seeking a specific combination of benefits (Exhibit 6.3).

Limitations of benefit segmentation

The greatest difficulty in applying this approach lies in the selection of the benefits to emphasise, mainly, in the consumer goods markets. When market analysts ask consumers what benefit they want in a product, they are not likely to provide very new information about product benefits, since they are not highly introspective. If direct market analysis is supplemented with information about consumers' problems, however, new insights can be obtained.

For example, in the toothpaste market, protection of sensitive teeth is a new benefit promoted by brands having adopted a paramedical positioning. This is the outcome of dental hygiene analysis conducted with the dental profession.

Another difficulty of benefit segmentation stems from this fact: if we are gaining in understanding of consumer preferences, we are losing in terms of knowledge of the socio-demographic profiles of different customer groups. How do we reach, selectively, the 'worriers'? Thus, additional information must be collected to be able to describe these segments in socio-demographic terms.

Benefit segmentation analysis requires the collection of primary data, always a costly exercise. In addition, sophisticated multivariate measurement techniques (cluster analysis) must be used to identify the different customer groups. In some cases, however, interesting insights on benefits sought can be obtained through qualitative research, as illustrated in Table 6.4 with an example from the hi-fi chains market.

Segmenting markets with conjoint analysis

The method of conjoint analysis has been described and illustrated in Chapter 5. As explained, the focus of conjoint analysis is on the measurement of buyer preferences for product attribute levels and of the buyer benefits generated by the product attributes. Since measurements are made at the individual level, if preference heterogeneity exists, the market analyst can detect it and regroup individuals displaying the same utilities.

An empirical example will clarify the methodology. The application involves a bimonthly book magazine that publishes new book reviews, book guidance and advice, book digests and short articles. The editor is

---

EXHIBIT 6.3

THE CREST BRAND SUCCESS STORY

Crest, a brand made by Procter & Gamble, was first introduced in 1955 as the first toothpaste clinically proven to help prevent cavities and tooth decay. A new formula was released in 1981. Crest is endorsed by the American Dental Association (ADA) as an 'effective decay-preventive dentifrice that can be of significant value'. Crest became the leader in the US market. The Crest brand now covers over 20 brands of toothpaste, toothbrushes, mouthwash and dental floss. Crest also has a teeth-whitening product called Crest Whitestrips. In 1955, most toothpaste companies, and the market leader Colgate-Palmolive in particular, were mostly concentrated in the cosmetic segment. Crest was the first offering to the latent therapeutic segment. Since then Crest has lost its exclusive therapeutic positioning as most brands today offer a combination of the cosmetic and therapeutic benefits (see Table 12.7). Also the strong therapeutic positioning of Crest has made its forays in cosmetic dentistry less credible. Similarly, for the foray of the cosmetic Colgate into the therapeutic segment.

Source: Published sources.

> **Table 6.4   Hi-fi chains market: benefit segments and principal benefits sought**
>
> 1. The technicians
>   - Mean to enjoy high-fidelity sound in its technical aspects.
>   - Look for the quality and purity of the sound.
>   - Mostly interested by the technical features without being necessarily qualified.
> 2. The musicians
>   - Mean to enjoy music.
>   - Look for the spirit of the music, its musical space and colour.
>   - Mostly interested by the musical interpretation without having necessarily a great musical culture.
> 3. The snobs
>   - Mean to show their resources, taste and aesthetic sense.
>   - Look for prestige, demonstration effects and social integration.
>   - Often poorly informed, tend to buy what is known and safe.
> 4. The others
>
> *Source*: Francois, J.

considering three alternative modifications of the editorial content:

1. Concentrating on book reviews and analyses and dropping all the other editorial sections (book review).
2. Concentrating on guidance and advice on a larger number of books using standardised evaluation grids (reader's guide).
3. Limiting the number of book reviews, but adding a section on literary news with interviews of authors and special topical sections (literary news).

A do nothing alternative is also considered, that is, to keep the present editorial content unchanged. As to the selling price, three levels are considered: the present price of BF152, an increased price of BF200 and a decreased price of BF100, with the number of pages remaining unchanged (30 pages). A questionnaire was mailed to 500 respondents selected among a group of readers and 171 valid questionnaires were used to estimate the utility functions. A cluster analysis programme was then used to regroup the respondents having the same utilities.

As shown in Table 6.5, four different segments were identified:

- In segment 1, the respondents seem to be happy with the present editorial content. They react very negatively to the first two alternatives, and positively, but without enthusiasm, to the 'literary news' concept.
- In segment 2, there is a clear preference for the 'book reviews' concept and a negative attitude towards the other two editorial concepts.
- In segment 3, it is the 'reader's guide' concept which is preferred, the other two being clearly rejected.
- In segment 4, the present editorial content is the best alternative, but the range of utilities is also the smallest.

Thus in terms of benefits sought, the four segments are very different. As to the prices, the largest price sensitivity is observed in segment 4, as evidenced by the range, while segments 1 and 2 react in a very similar way, segment 3 being the least price sensitive. Analysis of the composition of these four segments showed that segment 4 was largely composed of librarians, while high-school teachers were an important group in segment 3.

For a comprehensive review of the contributions of conjoint analysis in market segmentation, see Green and Krieger (1991). See also Box 6.4 describing ways to exploit different price sensitivities per segment.

6.4.3. Behavioural segmentation

Usage segmentation attempts to classify consumers on the basis of their actual purchase behaviour in the marketplace. As such, it is also a descriptive and ex post segmentation method. The criteria most commonly used are product usage, volume purchased and loyalty status.

1. *Product-user segmentation.* A distinction can be made between users, non-users, first users, ex-users, potential users and occasional versus regular users. A different selling and communication approach must be adopted for each of these user categories.

2. *Volume segmentation.* In many markets, a small proportion of customers represents a high percentage of total sales. Often, about 20 per cent of the users account for 80 per cent of total consumption. A distinction between heavy, light and non-users is often very useful. Heavy users, or key accounts, deserve special treatment.

3. *Loyalty segmentation.* Among existing customers a distinction can be made between hard-core loyal, soft-core

Table 6.5   Benefit segmentation through conjoint analysis: book review example

Attributes	Segment 1 (35.5%)	Segment 2 (21.0%)	Segment 3 (11.3%)	Segment 4 (32.2%)
Content				
Book review	−6.1	1.2	−6.2	−1.8
Book guide	−6.4	−6.9	2.9	−3.1
Present content	0	0	0	0
Literary news	0.3	−2.1	−6.8	−3.3
Range	6.7	9.1	9.7	3.3
Price				
BF100	0.5	0.6	0.3	1.1
BF152	0	0	0	0
BF200	−0.7	−0.6	−0.4	−1.0
Range	1.2	1.2	0.7	2.1

Source: Adapted from Roisin (1988).

BOX 6.4

IMPLEMENTATION PROBLEM: HOW TO EXPLOIT DIFFERENT PRICE SENSITIVITIES PER SEGMENT?

■ Consider a firm having the following target prices: $50 at 20K units and $35 at 50K units. The additional cost of producing a superior version of the same product is $10. Two segments of about the same size exist (20K each) but have different price sensitivity. The luxury segment is not price sensitive and potential customers are ready to pay $50 for the superior version. The other segment is price sensitive and will not pay more than $30. What market coverage strategy should be adopted? In what version and at what price should the firm sell the product?

■ Costs and profit constraints seem to exceed prices if the firm decides to sell to only one segment at only one price. If the firm targets the low price segment, the market potential is limited to 20K customers and the maximum acceptable price is $30, while the target price at this level of production is $50.

Similarly, if the firm targets the high price segment, the market potential is 20K customers willing to pay $50, but the target price is now $60 ($50 + $10). This strategy is also unfeasible.

■ A premium price strategy can solve the problem. The firm should produce 50K units and sell 20K units of the standard product for $30 and 20K units of the superior version for $50, for an average target price of $50. The target prices are respectively $35 and $55, but the market prices will be $30 and $50. Thus, the firm takes a premium on its higher priced version and a loss on its lower priced version, but can profitably produce and sell the product to both segments.

Source: Adapted from Tellis (1986).

---

loyal and switchers. Markets such as cigarettes, beers and toothpaste are generally brand-loyal markets. Keeping loyal customers is the objective of relationship marketing. Appropriate marketing strategies can be developed to attract competitors' customers or to increase the loyalty of switchers.

Note that behavioural segmentation – like socio-demographic segmentation – is an ex post segmentation method based on the internal information system of the firm and on the customer data banks. This method is extensively used in *Customer Relationship Management* (CRM) also called relationship selling (see Chapter 14).

6.4.4. Socio-cultural or lifestyle segmentation

As mentioned above, socio-demographic criteria are losing predictive value in affluent societies as consumption patterns become more and more personalised. Individuals from the same socio-demographic groups can have very different preferences and buying behaviour, and vice versa.

Socio-cultural segmentation, also called lifestyle or psychographic segmentation, seeks to supplement demographics by adding such elements as activities, attitudes, interests, opinions, perceptions and preferences to obtain a more complete consumer profile. It attempts to draw human portraits of consumers adding detail at the less obvious levels of motivation and personality. Wells and Tigert make the following point:

> Demographics have been and continue to be extremely useful, but they are unsatisfying. They lack colour. They lack texture. They lack dimensionality. They need to be supplemented by something that puts flesh on bare statistical backbone. (Wells and Tigert, 1971, published in Wells, 1975, p. 37)

The basic objective is to relate personality-type variables to consumer behaviour. Lifestyle descriptors are used as proxies for personality traits. 'Lifestyle' refers to the overall manner in which people live and spend time and money. A person's lifestyle (or psychographic profile) can be measured and described in a number of ways:

- At the most stable and persistent level is the person's valuing system and personality traits, which are, of course, more difficult to measure.
- At an intermediate level, a person's activities, interests and opinions reveal her or his value system.
- At a superficial level, but directly observable, consumers' lifestyles are reflected by the products and services purchased and by the way in which buyers are using or consuming them.

Valette-Florence (1986) suggests defining a person's lifestyle as the interaction of these three levels: the group of persons having a similar behaviour at each of these levels is homogeneous in terms of lifestyle. Thus a lifestyle is the outgrowth of a person's value system, attitudes, interests and opinions (AIO) and of the individual's consumption mode. It describes the sort of person she (or he) is and at the same time it differentiates her (or him) from other persons. Lifestyle studies can be conducted at one of these three levels. The closer we are to actual purchase decisions, the easier the measurements, but also the more volatile the conclusions. The largest majority of

empirical lifestyle studies have been conducted at the AIO level, where research measures

- people's activities in terms of how they spend their time;
- their interests, what they place importance on in their immediate surroundings;
- their opinions in terms of views of themselves and the world around them;
- some basic demographic characteristics such as their stage in the life cycle, income, education and where they live.

Table 6.6 lists the elements included in each major dimension of lifestyle.

Lifestyle studies provide a broad everyday view of consumers, a living portrait that goes beyond flat socio-demographic descriptions and helps understand actual consumer behaviour.

Limitations of lifestyle segmentation

The results of lifestyle studies are stocked and regularly updated. Factorial analyses are used to uncover principal components or macro-characteristics and meaningful clusters of answers, which correspond to stereotypes or socio-styles observed in society or within the specific group under study. Two kinds of lifestyle studies can be made: general lifestyle or product-specific lifestyle studies.

General lifestyle studies classify the total population into groups based on general lifestyle characteristics, such as 'receptivity to innovation', 'family centred', 'ecological sensitivity', and so on. Each subgroup represents a different pattern of values and motivations and the analyst can discern which types of consumers are strong prospects for their products, what other things appeal to these prospects and how to communicate with them in the most effective way.

Table 6.6 Lifestyle dimensions

Activities	Interests	Opinions	Demographics
Work	Family	Themselves	Age
Hobbies	Home	Social issue	Education
Social events	Job	Politics	Income
Vacation	Community	Business	Occupation
Entertainment	Recreation	Economics	Family size
Club membership	Fashion	Education	Dwelling
Community	Food	Products	Geography
Shopping	Media	Future	City size
Sports	Achievements	Culture	Life cycle

Source: Plummer (1975).

EXHIBIT 6.4

FORCES OF SOCIAL CHANGE

- *Self-development*. Affirming oneself as an individual.
- *Hedonism*. Giving priority to pleasure.
- *Plasticity*. Adapting to circumstances.
- *Vitality*. Exploiting one's energy.
- *Connectivity*. Relating to others: clicking in and out, mixing cultures.
- *Ethics*. Searching for authenticity and meaning in life.

- *Belongings*. Defining social links and cultural identities.
- *Inertia*. Actively, or more often passively, resisting change.

Source: Hasson (1995).

The researchers of the International Research Institute on Social Change (RISC) have identified eight socio-cultural forces that shape our society and in particular European society. They are presented in Exhibit 6.4.

The updating of lifestyle data keeps track of the changing emphasis of the different socio-styles and keeps up with the changes in motivation and behaviour of different social subgroups. The usefulness of lifestyle analyses is twofold, namely

1. to identify emerging trends and sensitivities within society and to assess the opportunities and threats associated with these changes; it is the dynamic aspect;
2. to determine whether a particular subgroup is ahead of or lagging in a socio-cultural trend; it is the more static aspect of the analysis.

In product-specific lifestyle studies, the objective is to understand consumer behaviour related to a particular product or service. The AIO statements are then more product-specific. To illustrate, here are examples of AIO statements adapted to the credit cards market:

- I like to pay cash for everything I buy.
- I buy many things with a credit card or a charge card.
- In the past year, we have borrowed money from a bank or finance company.
- To buy anything other than a house or a car on credit is unwise.

Lifestyle research methodology also has some important advantages over motivation research and in-depth interviews: (a) samples are large; (b) conclusions do not rely heavily on interviewer's interpretation of relatively unstructured responses; (c) data are easily analysed by a variety of well-understood statistical methods and (d) less highly trained interviewers can be employed. Exhibit 6.5 gives the examples of general lifestyle statements.

6.5. Micro-segmentation analysis in B2B markets

Conceptually, there is no difference between business-to-business (or industrial) and consumer market segmentation, but the criteria used to segment the market vary greatly. The same distinction between macro- and micro-segmentation can be made. The method of macro-segmentation described earlier in this chapter is of direct application. The micro-segmentation criteria tend to be different, however.

6.5.1. Descriptive segmentation

The simplest way to segment industrial markets is to use broad firmographic characteristics describing the profile of the B2B customer, such as industrial sectors (NACE or SIC category), company size, geographic location, shareholder composition or end-market served. This information is easily accessible since this type of data is readily available through government agencies, which publish detailed industrial classifications. For an example see Figure 6.8. Many companies choose to have separate sales service for large and small customers. The company directly services large customers while distributors will deal with small customers.

An example of segmentation from the corporate banking market is presented in Figure 6.7. One key finding of this research was to discover that a rather large number of non-profit organisations (social and philanthropic) had in fact substantial financial funds – therefore representing an attractive segment for banks – while the majority of banking services offered were designed for profit organisations and poorly adapted to the specific needs of non-profit organisations.

EXHIBIT 6.5

EXAMPLES OF GENERAL LIFESTYLE STATEMENTS

- I find myself checking the prices in the grocery stores even for small items (price conscious).
- An important part of my life and activities is dressing smartly (fashion conscious).
- I would rather spend a quiet evening at home than go out to a party (homebody).

- I like to work on community projects (community minded).
- I try to arrange my home for my children's convenience (child oriented).
- / ... /

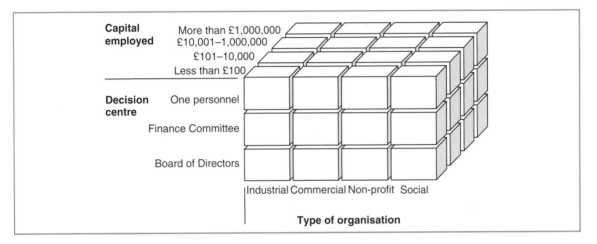

Figure 6.7 Example of descriptive segmentation in the service sector: the corporate banking market
Source: Yorke (1982).

6.5.2. Benefit segmentation

As for consumer goods, benefit segmentation is the most natural method. It is based on the specific needs, in general well defined, of the business-to-business customer. In industrial markets, this means classifying the customers by type of industry or by end-use. End-users are generally looking for different benefits, performance or functions in a product. Industrial products often have a wide range of possible uses, for instance in electric motors, ball bearings, steel sheets, and so on. The classification by industry type points out the priority needs and their relative importance.

By way of illustration, let us consider the case of a company specialising in the manufacture of small electric motors, a product that has a very large number of possible uses. For each end-use, beyond the core function, one or several product characteristics may be particularly important. This is the case for the following three

industrial applications:

- Motors incorporated in petrol pumps: security norms (spark-free) are essential.
- Motors incorporated into computers or in medical instruments used in hospitals: the response time must be instantaneous.
- Motors incorporated in industrial sewing machines; resistance to frequent stopping and starting is important and fast reaction is secondary.

The functions of an industrial good and their importance in the customer's industrial process vary according to whether it is a major equipment good (turnkey factory, steel mill, alternator) or secondary equipment good (radiator, light trucks, typewriter); semi-finished intermediate products (coated steel sheets); parts to be incorporated (electric motors, gear shifts); finished goods (tools, oil); raw materials (coal, grease, polyurethane foam); services (engineering, industrial cleaning, maintenance) (see Figure 4.3). In each case, the perceived economic value of the product by the customer will be very different. (See Figure 6.8 for a comparative analysis of segment profiles.)

It is important to recall that in many business-to-business sectors, sales are based on orders with detailed specifications. In this type of market situation, the product is naturally adjusted to the particular needs of the customer.

6.5.3. Behavioural segmentation

Behavioural segmentation is important for industrial markets. Its purpose is to develop a strategy for approaching business-to-business customers according to their structures and the way their buying decision centre operates. The way a buying decision centre works was discussed in Chapter 4 of this book, where we also saw that the buying process can be more or less formalised

according to the complexity of decisions and organisational structures.

In some companies, buying is centralised and precise rules govern the purchase decisions. In other companies, in contrast, decentralised buying is undertaken and the approach to such a company will be similar to that used for a smaller firm. Other characteristics of the buying centre are also important: motivations of different members of the buying team, the different forces at play between the representatives of different functions, the degree of formalism and the length of time necessary for a decision. These behavioural characteristics are not usually directly observable and thus are often hard to identify. However, as seen above, these are important things for salespeople to be aware of.

Because of the complexity and variety of possible bases for segmentation industrial markets, Shapiro and Bonona (1983) have expanded the use of macro- and micro-segmentation into what is called a *nested approach*.

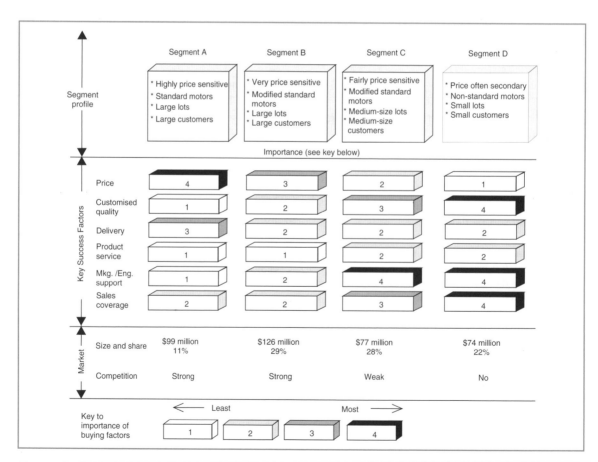

Figure 6.8   Typical segmentation grid: comparative analysis of the segment profiles
Source: Adapted from Day (1984, p. 90).

This method assumes a hierarchical structure of segmentation bases that move from very broad or general bases to very organisation-specific bases. Rather than a two-step process, the nested approach allows three, four or five steps. The list of segmentation criteria is presented in Table 6.7.

Benefit segmentation is also easier in industrial markets than in consumer markets, because users are professional people who have less difficulty in expressing their needs and in qualifying the relative importance of different product attributes (see Figure 6.9).

In practice, several segmentation methods are used simultaneously as illustrated in Figure 6.10 presenting a segmentation analysis of the aluminium market.

6.6. Requirements for effective segmentation

Before examining the targeting and positioning decisions, a preliminary question must be raised, however, to verify to what extent the requirements for effective segmentation are met. To be effective and useful a segmentation analysis should identify segments that meet five criteria: differential response, adequate size, measurability, accessibility and actionability (Kotler, 1967/2006).

6.6.1. Differential response

This is the most important criterion to consider when choosing a segmentation strategy. The segments must be

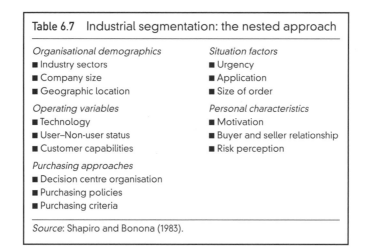

Table 6.7   Industrial segmentation: the nested approach

Organisational demographics
■ Industry sectors
■ Company size
■ Geographic location

Operating variables
■ Technology
■ User–Non-user status
■ Customer capabilities

Purchasing approaches
■ Decision centre organisation
■ Purchasing policies
■ Purchasing criteria

Situation factors
■ Urgency
■ Application
■ Size of order

Personal characteristics
■ Motivation
■ Buyer and seller relationship
■ Risk perception

Source: Shapiro and Bonona (1983).

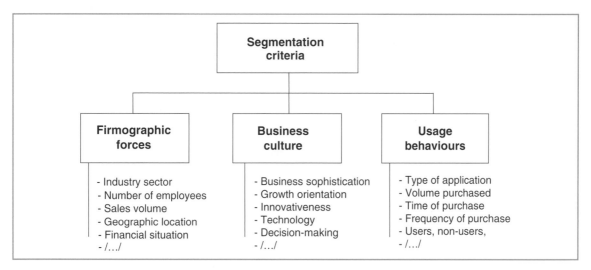

Figure 6.9   Segmentation criteria in B2B markets
Source: Best (2000/2003).

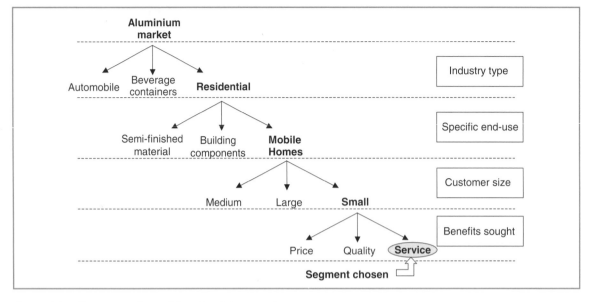

Figure 6.10 Segmentation of the aluminium market
Source: Industry.

different in terms of their sensitivity to one or several marketing variables under the control of the firm. The segmentation variable should maximise the behavioural difference between segments (heterogeneity condition) while minimising the differences among customers within a segment (homogeneity condition).

A key requirement is to avoid segment overlapping, the risk being the possibility of cannibalism among products of the same company but targeted to different segments. The more a product has distinctive and observable characteristics, the more homogeneous the segment will be.

We must, however, remember that segment homogeneity does not necessarily imply that all categories of buyers are mutually exclusive. An individual may of course belong to more than one segment. Products from different segments may be bought by the same person for different people within the household, for different types of use or just for the sake of variety. Observation of shopping trolleys outside a supermarket often shows that brands from both the high and the low end of the range have been purchased at the same time. One segment does not necessarily cover the buyers, but rather the products purchased by the buyers.

6.6.2. Adequate size

Segments should be defined so that they represent enough potential customers to provide sufficient sales revenue to justify the development of different products and marketing programmes. See Table 6.8 for a comparison of two segments profile.

Identified segments must represent a market potential large enough to justify developing a specific marketing strategy. This condition affects not only the size of the segment in volume and frequency of buying but also its life cycle. All markets are affected by fashion. It is essential to verify that the targeted niche is not temporary and that the product's lifespan be economically long. Finally, the size requirement also implies that the added value of the product, because of its specificity, will be financially worthwhile, in the sense that the market price acceptable by the target segment is sufficiently rewarding for the firm.

Meeting this requirement often implies a trade-off between two logics: the logic of marketing management, which tries to meet the needs of the market through a narrow definition of segments in order to adapt the firm's offering to the diversity of market needs as best as possible, and the logic of operations management, which emphasises the benefits of economies of scale through standardisation and long production runs.

6.6.3. Measurability

Before target segments can be selected, the size, purchasing power and major behavioural characteristics of the identified segments must be measured. If the segmentation criteria used are very abstract, such information is hard to find. For example, if the prospects were companies of a certain size, it would be easy to find information about their number, location, turnover, and so on. But a segmentation criterion like 'innovativeness of companies' does not lend itself to easy measurement and the firm would probably have to conduct its own market survey. Abstract criteria are often used in benefit and lifestyle segmentations, while descriptive segmentation is based on more concrete and observable criteria (Figure 6.6).

6.6.4. Accessibility

Accessibility refers to the degree to which a market segment can be reached through a unique marketing programme. There are two ways to reach prospects:

1. *Customer self-selection* involves reaching a more general target while relying on the product and appeal of advertising to the intended target group. These consumers select themselves by their attention to the advertisements.
2. *Controlled coverage* is very efficient because the firm reaches target customers with little wasted coverage of individuals or firms who are not potential buyers.

Controlled coverage is more efficient from the firm's point of view. This communication strategy implies a good knowledge of the socio-demographic profile of the target group, which is not always the case when using benefit or lifestyle segmentation.

6.6.5. Actionability

Specific marketing programme can be formulated to reach the segments.

6.7. Emergence of transnational market segments

In the Triad countries, one observes the existence of *transnational segments*, that is, groups of consumers present in each country and having the same needs and expectations. Thus globalisation need not mean standardisation of lifestyles across countries. In the world today, in parallel with the globalisation of the economy, there has been an explosion of identity crises among nations, regions, religions, ethnic and linguistic groups having the desire to maintain and to claim their cultural difference. So globalisation does not mean uniformity.

> The fact that one dominant country tends today, consciously or not, to impose its culture, its language, its lifestyles can create the illusion of uniformity. But behind a superficial layer of uniformity created by a few popular brands (always the same: Disney, Hollywood, McDonald, Coca-Cola, Marlboro, CNN, etc.) are hidden important cultural, religious, racial and linguistic differences.

We are confronted with a paradox. The interdependence of markets referred to above, combined with this cultural fragmentation, results in a cultural convergence, thereby creating transnational market segments, that is, groups of consumers present in each country and having the same needs and expectations. Thus globalisation need not mean standardisation of lifestyles across countries. It simply means that, across countries, there are groups of consumers with the same profiles that can be approached with the same brands and communication campaigns.

Table 6.8	Profitability analysis per segment: an example		
Segments profile	Core segment	Alternate care segment	Total market
Value driver	Cost of service	Value-added service	
Primary benefit	Low price	Training and support	
Price sensitivity	High	Low	
Firmographics	Hospitals	Health care offices	
Waste expertise	Above average	Poor	
Number of clients	10,000	630,000	640,000
Revenue per client	$35,000	$530	$1,075
Margin per client	$2,345	$250	$284
Per cent margin	6.7%	47.3%	26.4%
Waste volume (tons)	490,000	145,000	635,000
Volume per client	98,000 lb	460 lb	1,984 lb
Price per pound	$0.41/lb	$2.06/lb	$0.79/lb
Margin per pound	$0.03/lb	$0.87/lb	$0.45/lb

Source: Best (2000/2003, p. 303).

It is still difficult today to refer to a European consumer, even if one observes a growing convergence in lifestyles and in consuming habits within the European Union. By contrast, there are numerous transnational segments such as executives of international companies, students in management, sports professionals, high-fashion conscious women, and so forth.

The affirmation of the individual and the identity crisis forces companies to adopt a *mass-customisation strategy* whereby goods and services are individually customised in high volumes but at relatively low cost. Flexible manufacturing and electronic commerce make possible today this mass customisation approach.

With the globalisation of the world economy, opportunities are growing to create demand for universal products. International segmentation is a way in which a global approach can be adopted to sell a physically similar product worldwide. The objective is to discover in different countries and/or regions groups of buyers having the same expectations and requirements vis-à-vis products, despite cultural and national differences. Those segments, even if they are small in size within each country, may represent in total a very attractive opportunity for the international firm. To adjust to local differences, the physical product can be customised through services, accessories or inexpensive product modifications. The potential for globalisation is not the same for each product category and different approaches can be adopted. For a review of the literature on this topic, see Gupta and Westney (2003).

CHAPTER SUMMARY

In a market-oriented company, the target market is identified in the buyer's perspective, that is, by reference to the 'solution' sought by the customer and not in technical terms. Given the diversity of buyers' expectations, the choice of a target market implies the partitioning of the total market into subgroups of potential customers with similar needs and behavioural characteristics. A first level of market segmentation, called macro-segmentation, splits the market by reference to three criteria: (a) solutions or functions performed, (b) groups of buyers and (c) technologies. A key output of this exercise is a segmentation grid, which can help to decide on the market coverage strategy, and which can also be used as an instrument to discover new potential segments. The objective of micro-segmentation is to analyse the diversity of potential customer profiles in a more detailed way within each previously identified macro-segment. Four micro-segmentation methods exist which each have their own merits and weaknesses: socio-demographic, benefit, lifestyle and behavioural segmentation. Different market coverage strategies can be considered: undifferentiated or standardised marketing, differentiated or focused marketing. To be effective, a segmentation strategy must meet four criteria: differential response, adequate size, measurability and accessibility. International segmentation is a key issue in global marketing. The objective is to identify supranational or universal segments that can be reached with a standardised marketing programme.

Review and Application Questions

1. Use the macro-segmentation method based on the three criteria 'function/buyers/technologies' in one of the following industrial sectors: paint, fax, banking services or medical imaging. In each case, define the product-markets, the market and the industry.
2. A European importer of Japanese digital cameras wishes to have a benefit segmentation analysis of the European market. Construct a segmentation grid that seems appropriate and propose a procedure to collect the required market data to verify the value of the proposed segmentation scheme.
3. In a survey conducted in the photo developing market, the following data have been collected from a representative sample of amateur photographers:

Segment	Quality	Price	Convenience	Speed	Return	Diverse
1	6.80	5.83	5.83	5.50	5.66	3.96
2	6.71	5.76	3.38	5.00	5.66	3.80
3	5.60	6.60	6.20	5.80	3.50	2.60
4	6.57	6.28	5.52	3.66	2.80	2.57
5	6.90	3.55	5.63	5.55	3.55	3.36

Note: Scores are mean values on a 7-point scale where 1 meant 'not important' and 7 meant 'extremely important'.
Source: Sheth et al. (1999, p. 552).

Analyse these data and describe the type of benefit package sought by different groups of buyers.

4. What are the difficulties of benefit and lifestyle segmentation methods?

5. In affluent societies, consumers are increasingly seeking solutions adapted to their specific problems. For the firm the question is to know how far to go in segmenting a market. Analyse the factors in favour of a fine market segmentation strategy (hyper-segmentation) and the arguments, which, in contrast, suggest a standardised strategy (counter-segmentation).

6. In affluent societies, one observes a growing fragmentation of markets, buyers requesting more and more products adapted to their specific needs. How can we reconcile this fact with the objectives of global marketing that emphasises a strategy of standardisation of products and brands across the entire world?

7. In the car market, companies are used to subdivide the market into so-called segments: small, medium and large cars based on the cubic capacity of the car. Is this way of segmenting the car market appropriate? What would you propose as an alternative?

Bibliography

Abell, D.F. (1980), *Defining the Business: The Starting Point of Strategic Planning*, Englewood Cliffs, NJ, Prentice-Hall.

Best, R.J. (2000/2003), *Market-based Management*, Upper Saddle River, NJ, Prentice-Hall, 2nd and 3rd editions.

Coriolis Research (2000), *Organics in the United Kingdom: A Market Overview*, Research Report, November.

Day, G.S. (1984), *Strategic Market Planning*, St Paul, MN, West Publishing.

Day, G.S. (1990), *Strategic Market Planning*, St Paul, MN, West Publishing.

Deutsch, C.H. (1997), A New High-Tech Code: From Widgets to Service, *International Herald Tribune*.

Ecole de Management de Lyon (1976), *Marketing industriel appliqué*, Le Cas Sedal.

Green, P.E. and Krieger, A.M. (1991), Segmenting Markets with Conjoint Analysis, *Journal of Marketing*, 55, 4, pp. 20–31.

Gupta, A.K. and Westney, D.E. (eds) (2003), *Smart Globalization*, Boston, MA, Jossey-Bass, A Wiley Reprint.

Hasson, L. (1995), Monitoring Social Change, *Journal of the Market Research Society*, 37, pp. 69–80.

Hopkins, D.S. (1982), *The Marketing Plan*, New York, The Conference Board.

Kotler, P. (1967/2006), *Marketing Management*, Upper Saddle River, NJ, Prentice-Hall, 12th edition.

Lambin, J.J. and Hiller, T.B. (1993), Volvo Trucks Europe, in *Strategic Marketing Problems*, Kerin, R.A. and Peterson, R.A. (eds), Boston, MA, Allyn & Bacon.

Plummer, J.T. (1974), The Concept and Application of Life Style Segmentation, *Journal of Marketing*, 38, 1, pp. 33–7.

Roisin, J. (1988), *Etude du concept d'une revue littéraire: une application de l'analyse conjointe*, Louvain-la-Neuve, IAG.

Shapiro, B.P. and Bonona, T.V. (1983), *Segmenting Industrial Markets*, Lexington, MA, Lexington Books.

Smith, W. (1956), Product Differentiation and Market Segmentation as Alternative Marketing Strategies, *Journal of Marketing*, 21, 1, pp. 3–8.

Tellis, G.C. (1986), Beyond the Many Faces of Price: An Integration of Pricing Strategies, *Journal of Marketing*, 50, 4, pp. 146–60.

Valette-Florence, P. (1986), Les démarches de style de vie: concepts, champs d'investigation et problèmes actuels, *Recherches et Applications en Marketing*, 1, pp. 1–2.

Wells, W.D. and Tigert, D.J. (1971), Activities, Interests and Opinions, *Journal of Advertising Research*, 11, 4, pp. 27–35.

Yorke, D.A. (1982), The Definition of Market Segments for Banking Services, *European Journal of Marketing*, 16, 3, pp. 14–22.

market attractiveness analysis 7

Chapter contents

Chapter learning objectives

When you have read this chapter, you should be able to

- describe the major concepts of demand analysis;
- understand the concepts of virtual and meta-markets;
- explain the structure of demand for consumer and industrial goods, for durable and non-durable goods and for services;
- explain how to detect growth opportunities in a given market through gap analysis;
- describe the product life cycle (PLC) model and its strategic implications;
- understand the financial implications of the PLC.

Chapter introduction

The output of a segmentation analysis takes the form of a segmentation grid displaying the different segments or product markets, which belong to the reference market. The next task is to assess the business opportunity of each of these segments in order to decide which segment(s) to target. Attractiveness analysis has the objective of measuring and forecasting the size, life cycle and profit potential of each segment or product market. Measuring the sales potential of a market is the responsibility of strategic marketing. These market projections will then be used by general management to calibrate investments and production capacity. Market potential forecasting and measurement is a key input for these decisions. The objective of this chapter is to review the major concepts of demand analysis and in particular the concept of virtual market.

7.1. Basic concepts in demand analysis

At its simplest level, the demand for a product or service is the quantity sold. At the outset it is important to distinguish clearly between two levels of demand: primary demand or total market demand, and company demand (also called selective demand).

> The primary demand for a particular product is the total sales volume bought by a defined customer group, in a defined geographic area, time period, economic and macro-marketing environment.

The term product category need, or category need, is also commonly used. Thus, primary demand measurement implies prior definition of the segment or product market. Also, it is a function of both environmental and total industry marketing efforts.

> Company demand is the company or brand's share of primary demand in the product category in a specific product-market or segment.

Any diagnostic of a given firm or brand performance makes implicit reference to these two notions. Let us examine the following three fictitious cases.

1. Brand A sales in volume have a yearly growth of 15 per cent, a result which seems very satisfactory. Given that primary demand in the reference market is also growing by 15 per cent the brand performance is modest having simply succeeded to keep its market share unchanged.
2. With the same growth rate of 15 per cent for brand A, if primary demand has increased instead by 20 per cent, the performance is very mediocre since brand A has a decreasing market share in a fast growing market. By contrast, if primary demand's growth is only 10 per cent, brand A performance is excellent.

3. Finally, if brand A sales are declining in volume by 5 per cent, while primary demand is declining by 10 per cent, brand A performance is also very good with a growing market share in a declining market.

Thus, any interpretation of brand A performance is dependent on the selected benchmark that will be determined by the segmentation of the reference market.

7.1.1. Expansible versus non-expansible primary demand

Two well-differentiated market situations can be observed: markets where primary demand is expansible and markets where demand is stagnant and non-expansible.

> Primary demand is said to be expansible, when it is influenced by the macro-marketing environment and by the size and intensity of total marketing efforts.

This situation will prevail in the introduction and growth phases of the product life cycle (PLC) of a product new to the world (see below), when the market occupation rate (horizontal coverage) and the penetration rates (vertical coverage) are weak (say below 20 per cent).

> Primary demand is said to be non-expansible when the level of total sales is not affected by the macro-marketing environment and by the marketing efforts of the competing firms. Markets are stagnant.

This situation is observed in the markets having reached maturity, where market occupation and penetration rates are very high and where replacement demand for durable goods is the largest part of market sales. In this type of market situations, the firm knows that any major increase of its sales will come only through an increase of its market share.

7.1.2. Primary demand as response function

Primary demand is not a fixed number but a function, which relates the level of sales to its causes, termed demand determinants. The causes of sales are twofold: external or uncontrollable factors linked to the macro-marketing environment and controllable factors represented by the total marketing efforts made by the competing firms in the market.

The impact of marketing factors

The relationship between primary demand and total industry marketing efforts is depicted in Figure 7.1. The response function is S-shaped with total demand on the vertical axis and total marketing intensity on the horizontal axis. The curve of Figure 7.1 is defined assuming a constant macro-marketing environment.

Typically, the relationship is not linear. Some minimum level of demand (Q_0) will occur at zero marketing intensity; as the total marketing pressure on the market increases, sales also increase, but at a decreasing rate. Beyond a certain level of marketing intensity, primary demand reaches an upper limit (Q_m) called the saturation level or the *current market potential*.

The impact of the macro-marketing environment

The level of primary demand is influenced not only by the total marketing efforts made by the firms operating in the segment, but also by environmental factors. A change in the socio-economic environment will move the response curve vertically, as illustrated in Figure 7.2. A distinction must be made, therefore, between a movement along the response curve and a shift of the response curve itself.

Two scenarios are represented in Figure 7.1: a scenario of prosperity and a scenario of recession. Under the prosperity scenario, the forecast or expected level of total sales is $E(Q)$, assuming the level M for total industry marketing effort. Now, if the recession scenario prevails, to achieve the same sales volume, total marketing effort should be at the level M' and not M.

Firms cannot do much about the prevailing market scenario, except to try to anticipate future environmental conditions as best as possible. In the turbulent and disruptive environment of the 2000s, this is a particularly difficult task and many firms are systematically developing alternative scenarios (such as a worst-case scenario) to increase their capacity to react quickly to a disruptive change in the environment.

7.1.3. Absolute versus current market potential

One can establish a distinction between current market potential as defined above and absolute market potential (AMP). As illustrated in Figure 7.1, the current market potential is the limit approached by primary demand as total industry marketing efforts tend towards infinity, in a given environment and in a given time period.

The AMP defines the upper limit of the market size under the somewhat artificial assumption of optimum market coverage. Thus, AMP corresponds to the total sales level (in volume or value) that would be observed under the following three assumptions:

- Everyone who could reasonably be expected to use the product is using it.
- Everyone who is using it is using it on every use occasion.
- Every time the product is used, it is used to the fullest extent possible (i.e. full dosage, full serving, and so on).

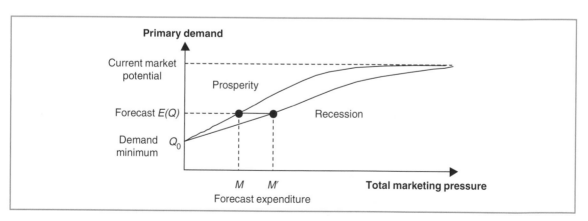

Figure 7.1 Primary demand as function of total marketing efforts

Source: Adapted from Kotler (1967/2005).

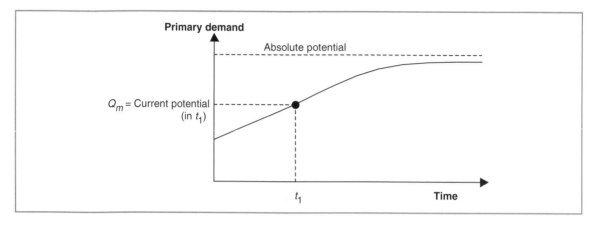

Figure 7.2   AMP is time dependent
Source: Authors.

The concept is useful for assessing the size of a business opportunity and for estimating the growth opportunity in a particular market given the present level of primary demand. Examples of estimation of AMP are presented in Exhibits 7.3–7.5.

The AMP is time dependent, as illustrated in Figure 7.2. Its evolution over time under the influence of diffusion and contagion effects or caused by external factors such as change in level of prices, government regulations, and so on. The firm has no direct control over these factors, yet they have a decisive influence on the development of the market. Occasionally, firms are indirectly able to influence these external causes (through lobbying, for instance), but their power is limited. Most of the firm's efforts, therefore, are directed towards the anticipation of changes in the environment.

7.2. Business opportunity analysis in the virtual market

The development of the Internet technology and of electronic commerce has enlarged considerably the size of the potential market by making virtual markets accessible by the firm. Virtual markets lead to an offering or to an assortment of offerings defined by reference to all the activities undertaken and all the services sought by the customer to achieve a specific generic result. While, in general, markets are organised around the supply of products and services, the customer purchasing process is structured by reference to activities that are linked in his (or her) cognitive space.

7.2.1. The cognitive space of the customer

To achieve the generic result sought, customers engage in different activities directly or indirectly related to the desired outcome. Thus, a virtual market represents an end-to-end temporal sequence of logically related activities in the cognitive space of customers.

> For example, as illustrated in Figure 7.3, to achieve the 'home ownership' generic need, customers might engage with contractors, realtors, insurance companies, mortgage firms, removal companies, telecom, interior designers, etc.

Similarly, in the personal mobility virtual market, in addition to car purchasing, related activities cover car maintenance, car insurance, roadside assistance, emergency services dispatch, route support, stolen vehicle location, etc.

In a virtual market, the activities undertaken by potential customers generally cut across traditional industry and product-market boundaries and are not necessarily in the traditional core business of the firm. As a result, virtual markets absorb a much higher proportion of customer spending than a specific product-market and represent a higher market potential. Thus to confine the market to the product-market may be misleading, as illustrated by the case of Lego, the Danish toy company presented in Exhibit 7.1.

The challenge for the firm is to move from the rather abstract concept of virtual market to the *meta-market* (Sawhney *et al.*, 2004) that consists in an offering or in an assortment of offerings defined by reference to all the elements (activities and services), which comprise the cognitive space of the client. In other words, a meta-market

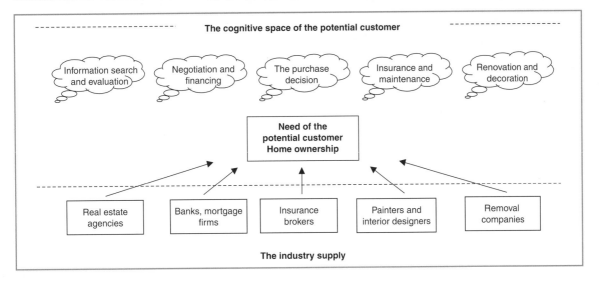

Figure 7.3   The home ownership virtual and meta-markets
Source: Authors.

EXHIBIT 7.1

THE VIRTUAL MARKET OF THE LEGO COMPANY

In 1995, the Lego company had a worldwide market share of 72 per cent in the construction toy market. But children were spending more spare time with computers, video games and television than with traditional toys. So while Lego had been gaining market shares in its traditional product-market, toys in general and construction toys in particular, had been losing their share of children's spare time activities. In fact, the generic need addressed by Lego is family 'edutainement'

(education–entertainment) and not simply construction toy. The generic need can be defined as 'having fun and exercising the mind'. The Lego virtual market is a convergence of toys, education, interactive technology, software, computers and consumer electronics.

Source: Sawhney *et al.* (2004).

---

is created when the cognitive association between different logically related activities are reproduced in the physical market place, thereby streamlining customer activities and providing them with seamless experience.

7.2.2. How to build a meta-market?

The virtual market concept is at the foundation of the 'solution-to-a-problem' approach discussed in Chapter 3. Increasingly, market-oriented companies aim at partnering with their customers and to becoming a 'solution provider' by assembling a unique combination of products and services that could solve a customer's problem. The implications for a solution-based organisation are

summarised in Box 7.1. Internet technology makes this solution approach more achievable.

The *benefits* of the meta-market concept are important.

- The concept is perfectly aligned on the customer views and thereby facilitating communication.
- The revenue potential of a meta-market is always larger than the discrete product-market.
- It enables the firm to offer a total solution to customers, thereby building exclusivity, loyalty and trust.
- It helps identifying growth opportunities in activities directly or indirectly related to the core service.
- It helps identifying who are the indirect or potential competitors.

An example of meta-market is presented in Figure 7.4. Kodak is the leader in helping people take, share, print and

---

BOX 7.1

IMPLEMENTATION PROBLEM: HOW TO BUILD A META-MARKET?

- Do not define your reference market in terms of product categories (cars, metallic grids, construction toys, etc.).
- Refer to the result or the generic outcome customers want to achieve (personal mobility, access control, edutainment, etc.).
- Identify all the activities, which, from the customer point of view, are part of the virtual market.

- Create the reference meta-market by reproducing in the physical marketplace the mental associations made by the customers.
- If necessary, augment the internal capabilities of the company by finding the right solution partners.
- Present to customers the total solution they seek.

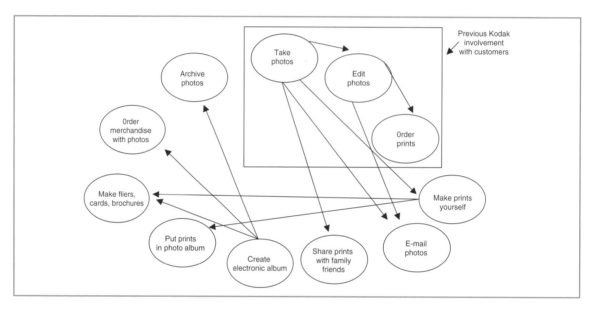

Figure 7.4 The meta-market of Kodak in the digital photography market

Source: Sawhney *et al.* (2004).

---

view images for information or for entertainment. Today, Kodak has created new services designed to provide to consumers a total solution to help consumers 'manage and share memories' using digital photography. Until the advent of digital photography, Kodak's involvement with customers ended with when they ordered prints. The company has since found ways to add significantly to its interaction with consumers, namely through the acquisition of a start-up called Ofoto (Sawhney *et al.*, 2004).

7.2.3. The customer activity chain concept

In seeking a particular outcome, customers engage in activities. These activities can be mapped along a

customer activity chain (Figure 7.5; Vandermerwe, 1993, 2000), which describes a sequence of directly or indirectly related activities undertaken by customers before, during or after the purchasing decision.

- Before, when customers are deciding what to do.
- During, when customers are doing what they decided upon.
- After, when customers are maintaining the results obtained (reviewing, renewing, extending, upgrading, updating, etc.).

This methodology can help managers to assess the opportunities for providing new kind of services in filling gaps in the activity chain that could give access to competitors. The case of IBM is interesting in this respect.

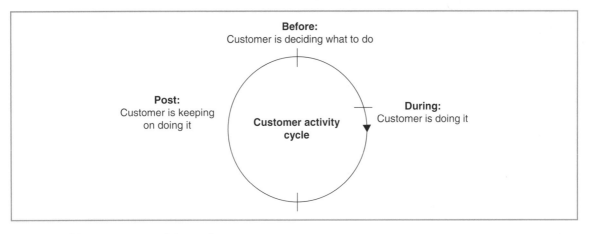

Figure 7.5   The customer activity cycle

Source: Vandermerwe (2000).

THE CASE OF THE DUTCH CONSTRUCTION GROUP HEIMANS N.V. – INTERVIEW OF ITS CEO

'Both individuals and organizations are now looking for construction companies that can provide a complete set of services: design, financing, construction maintenance and other services. This is why we have decided to increase our activity in the front end of the value chain – in particular activities giving us a greater grip on the development phases of a project – from its current level 25 per cent, to 35 per cent by 2008. We also want to increase our presence at the back end of the value chain – namely, more maintenance activities and take it from its current level of 5 per cent to 20 per cent in 2008.'

'We need to bolster our full-service offerings through partnership not only with our customers, but also with our suppliers and sub-contractors. This is the exciting part of a growing business like ours, because it marks a historical turn in the company's development: from a technologically driven entity to a market-driven service provider.'

Source: Bain and Company News Letter (2004).

In the late 1980, IBM was so fixated on PCs and mainframes (viewing itself as hardware provider) that it allowed consultants, software houses, procurements specialists and third-party maintenance providers to leap into IBM's value gaps and siphon-off both customers and potential wealth from the 'global-networking-capability' market space. (Vandermerwe, 2000, p. 32)

Having redefined its business in terms of a solution-provider of global-networking-capabilities, today IBM earns more money from value add-on services than from its hardware, software and middleware. For another example see the case of the group Heimans presented in Exhibit 7.2.

7.3. Structure of primary demand for consumer goods

Demand analysis, measurement and forecast are the primary responsibility of market research. The goal is to estimate in quantitative terms the size of the market potential and the current level of demand, and to formulate forecasts of its future development over a number of years. Aggregate estimates of total demand are rarely available and the role of the market analyst is to identify and estimate the key components of market potential. The structure of demand is different for consumer products (durable or non-durable goods), for industrial goods and for services.

7.3.1. Demand for consumer goods

Demand estimates are usually based on two factors: the number of potential consuming units (n) and the quantity purchased per unit (q). Thus, we have

$$Q = n \times q,$$

where 'Q' designates total demand in units. Similarly, total sales revenue will be given by

$$R = n \times Q \times P,$$

where 'R' denotes total sales revenue and 'P' the average price per unit. The empirical measurement of these basic concepts raises different issues depending on the type of product category. We will examine the demand structure for the main product categories.

7.3.2. Demand for non-durable consumer products

If the consumer good is *not linked to the use of a durable good*, total demand can be estimated in the following ways:

- Number of potential consuming units.
- Proportion of customers using the product (market occupation rate).
- Size or frequency of purchases (market penetration rate).

The distinction between *occupation rate* and *penetration rate* is important to identify the priority objectives in a market development strategy: increase the number of users or increase the average quantity used per user.

The AMP is determined by assuming a 100 per cent occupation rate and the optimum penetration per use occasion. (An example is given in Exhibit 7.3.) The current level of primary demand implies data on current purchasing behaviour. These data can sometimes be obtained from trade associations, from government publications or through primary market research. A major problem in measuring current demand is the degree to which purchase rates vary among different customer groups. Only primary sources of market research, such as consumer panels, can provide this type of data.

If the consumer good is *linked to the use of a durable good* (soap and washing machines, for instance), the equipment rate of the consuming units must be considered, in addition to the utilisation rate of the equipment. We thus have

- number of potential consuming units;
- rate of equipment of these consuming units;
- equipment utilisation rate;
- consumption rate per use occasion.

Here also, the AMP can be determined assuming a 100 per cent equipment rate, an average utilisation rate and an average consumption rate that is technically defined in most cases. As for the estimation of the level of current market demand, primary market research data are necessary (Exhibit 7.4).

7.3.3. Demand for durable consumer goods

In this case, a distinction must be made between first equipment demand and replacement demand. The components of *first equipment demand* are

- number of effective users and rate of increase of their equipment rate;
- number of new users and equipment rate of these new using units.

The diffusion rate is an important factor in the growth of first equipment demand within the target population.

EXHIBIT 7.3

ESTIMATION OF PRIMARY DEMAND FOR DIAPERS

N = Number of children below 3 years of age.
h = Per cent of children using disposable diapers (occupation rate or horizontal penetration).
q = Number of diapers used per child per year (penetration rate or vertical penetration).

Current level of primary demand,
N = 330,000 children below 3 years of age (110,000 births per year).

h = 90 per cent of children using diapers.
q = 6 diapers per day (7 per day up to 2.5 years old and 1 after) or 2,200 per year.
$Q = N \times h \times q$ = 653.4 million diapers per year, or 90 per cent of the AMP.

Source: Authors.

EXHIBIT 7.4

PRIMARY DEMAND FOR SOAP IN DISHWASHING MACHINES (HOUSEHOLDS SEGMENT)

Primary demand = $Q = N \times e \times f \times q$,

N = number of potential consuming units (number of households),

e = equipment rate (per cent of households with dishwasher),

f = use frequency of the equipment (number of use per week × 52),

q = quantity used per use occasion (quantity of soap per usage).

Example: Estimation of primary demand for soap for dishwashing machines

N = 420,000 households,

e = 37 per cent of households having the equipment,

f = 4 uses in average per week, or 200 per year,

q = 1 scoop or 20 g per use occasion.

$Q = N \times e \times f \times q = 6{,}216$ tons of diswasher soap per year.

The AMP can be calculated by taking maximum values for e, f and q.

Source: Authors.

The analysis of penetration curves for similar products is very useful in this respect.

Replacement demand is more complex to estimate. The following components of replacement demand must be identified and estimated:

- Size of the current population.
- Age distribution of the current population.
- Service life of the equipment (technical, economic or fashion obsolescence).
- Scrappage rate.
- Substitution effect (new technologies).
- Mortality rate of users.

Replacement demand is directly dependent on the rate at which owners scrap a product because of wearing out or obsolescence. Market analysts can estimate scrappage rates either by examining the technical service life of a product or the historical long-term rate of voluntary scrappage. See Exhibit 7.5.

If historical data on scrappage rates can be calculated from a sample of users, market analysts can use actuarial methods to estimate the replacement potential for products of different ages.

Replacement demand depends directly on the size of the current population and on the service life of the durable good. The replacement rate is not necessarily identical to the scrappage rate. Scrappage rate designates the fraction of the stock of existing durable goods, which is sent to breakage, or in other words which disappears. A durable good can be obsolete because its economic performance has become inferior or simply because it is out of fashion in the eyes of the users.

In general, one tends to consider that scrappage rates are proportional to the length of the physical life cycle of the products of a given product category. In other words, if the average duration is 12 years, the annual scrappage rate should in theory be equal to its reciprocal, that is, 8.3 per cent.

The predictions made about the technical service life of a durable good will have a direct impact on the expected level of primary demand in the years to come. Some of the data required to estimate the size of primary demand can be derived from times series sales data, namely the size of the population and its age distribution. The age distribution can also be estimated through sampling of car owners, for instance, when they decide to replace their old equipment. The estimated replacement rates do not permit us to identify, however, the type of obsolescence responsible for the replacement decision. A technically well-functioning product can be replaced for economic reasons; for instance, if the operating costs of newly developed products are sharply reduced. It can also be replaced for psychological reasons when the user is sensitive to the design of the new models. Finally, at the time of the replacement decision, the buyer can also decide to switch to another product category performing the same core function.

Significant technical progress has been made in the market of central heating systems, with low temperature boilers, which are much more economical in terms of fuel consumption. This innovation has accelerated the replacement rate of existing boilers. In parallel, other technologies have also improved their technical performance, like heat pumps that, for many applications, were substituted for traditional fuel heating systems.

In most Western economies' markets, household equipment rates are very high and close to the maximum and therefore the largest share of sales of durable goods correspond to a replacement decision.

7.4. The demand for consumer services

The demand structure for services can be estimated as described above for consumer goods. It depends on the number of potential consumers and on the frequency rate of use of the service. Services have, however, a certain number of characteristics that greatly impact their

EXHIBIT 7.5

ESTIMATION OF PRIMARY DEMAND FOR TELEVISION SETS

Q = First equipment demand + Replacement demand, that is,

$$Q = [(n \times \Delta e) + (\Delta n \times e)] + [t \times (s + 1/v)],$$

n = number of consuming units (number of households)

Δe = increase of the equipment rate (Δ of average number of TV/household)

Δn = net increase of new consuming units (number of new households – death)

e = Equipment rate of households (average number of TV/new household)

t = size of the TV population (number of TV sets)

v = average life (number of years of a TV set)

s = substitution rate (percentage of TV replaced by new models).

Example: Estimation of primary demand for TV sets

N = 4,200,000 households

Δe = 2 per cent of households having a TV and buying another each year

Δn = 35,000 new households per year

e = 1.2 TV per new household

t = 5,000,000 TV (4,200,000 × 1.2)

s = 5 per cent of replacement by a new model

v = life 10 years (or 10 per cent of replacement for technical deficiency).

$Q = [(n \times \Delta e) + (\Delta n \times e)] + [t \times (s + 1/v)],$

$Q = [(4,200,000 \times 0.02) + (35,000 \times 1.2)] + [5,000,000 \times (5\% + 10\%)],$

Q = 80,000 additional TV per households already equipped + 42,000 TV for new households + 25,000 TV of new models + 50,000 defective TV,

Q = 197,000 TV per year.

The AMP can be calculated by using maximum values for Δe, e, s and v.

Source: Authors.

---

marketing management. These characteristics are due to their intangible and perishable nature and to the fact that their production implies direct contact with the service person or organisation. The managerial implications of these characteristics are significant (Shostack, 1977; Berry, 1980; Eiglier and Langeard, 1987).

7.4.1. Classification of services

There are a large variety of services and several attempts have been made to classify them in a meaningful way. One classification system is based on the evolution of services in five categories:

1. *Unskilled personal services.* This category includes housekeeping, janitorial work, street cleaning, and so on, as observed in a traditional society.

2. *Skilled personal services.* These emerged as society became more industrialised, as it passed out of the subsistence stage and as needs arose for government services, repair businesses and retail/wholesale specialists.

3. *Professional services.* As products became more plentiful, highly skilled specialists appeared, such as lawyers, accountants, consultants and marketing researchers.

4. *Mass consumer services.* Discretionary income gave rise to any number of consumer service industries that flourished because of scale effects. These include national and international transport, lodging, fast food, car rental and entertainment companies.

5. *High-tech business services.* The growth in the use of sophisticated technologies has created a need for new

services as well as more efficient older ones. Thus, in recent years, we have seen a rapid growth in repair services relating to information processing, telecommunications and other electronic products.

Services can also be classified by whether they are equipment or people-based, by the extent of customer contact, by a public or private organisation.

7.4.2. Unique service characteristics

Intangibility of services

Services are immaterial. They exist only once produced and consumed. They cannot be inspected before purchase and the selling activity must necessarily precede the production activity. As the consumer goods firm, the service firm is selling a promise of satisfaction. But contrary to a consumer good, the service sold has no physical support, except the organisational system of the service firm when visible to the customer. The service cannot be seen, touched, smelled, heard or tasted prior to the purchase, except when service firms have tangible assets or physical structures (buildings, aircraft, hotel facilities, and so on) that are used to perform the service.

Thus, from the buyer's point of view the uncertainty is much larger and the communication role of the firm is to reduce that uncertainty by providing physical evidence, signs, symbols or indicators of quality. On this topic, see Levitt (1965) and Zeithmal *et al.* (1990).

Perishability of services

Since services are intangible, they cannot be stored. The service firm has a service production capacity, which can be used only when demand is expressed. Demand peaks cannot be accommodated and the potential business is lost.

For example, if an airliner takes off with 20 empty seats, the revenue that these 20 seats could have produced is lost forever. In contrast, if a pair of jeans does not sell today, a retailer can store it and sell it at a later time.

Perishability can cause the reverse to occur. Demand can be greater than supply. In this situation, for example, the airline does not have enough seats for everyone. Customers are left at the gate and the sale is lost.

Thus, a key challenge for service firms is to better synchronise supply and demand, not only by adjusting production capacity that is by reshaping supply, but also by reshaping demand through pricing incentives and promotions.

Inseparability of services

Services are produced and consumed at the same time, and the customer participates in the process of service production. The implication is twofold here. First, the service provider necessarily has a direct contact with the customer and is part of the service. There is a large human component involved in performing services. Thus, standardisation is difficult because of the personalised nature of services. Second, the client participates in the production process and the service provider–customer interaction can also affect the quality of the service.

An implication of these characteristics is the difficulty of maintaining a constant level of quality of the services. Total quality control of services is a major issue for the service firm. The components of service quality are described in Chapter 10.

Variability of service quality

A distinction is usually made between search quality goods or services that can be evaluated prior to purchase, *experience quality* goods that can be evaluated only after purchase and *credence quality* goods and services difficult to evaluate even after the purchase. Services tend to be high in experience and credence qualities. It is particularly the case for the services provided by consultant, lawyers, doctors, accountants, advertising agencies, and so on.

In discussing service quality, four characteristics of services should be kept in mind:

- Service quality is more difficult for the consumer to evaluate than the quality of goods, because services tend to be high in experience and credence qualities.
- Service quality is based on consumers' perception, not only of the outcome of the service, but also on their evaluation of the process by which the service is performed.
- Service quality perception results from a comparison of what the consumer expected prior to the service and the perceived level of the service received. Different individuals can have different perceptions and different prior expectations.
- A human factor is heavily involved in the process of service delivery and therefore a stable and fully standardised level of quality is more difficult to achieve. Different individuals will perform differently in delivering the same service and the same service provider can have a different performance level from one time to another.

To go further on the issue of service quality measurement see Zeithmal *et al.* (1990) and Berry (1999). For a good text on services marketing, see Kurtz and Clow (1998). The managerial implications of theses characteristic are summarised in Exhibit 7.6.

	Degree of interaction and customisation	
	Service factories	**Service shop**
High	Airlines	Hospitals
	Trucking	Car repair
	Hotels	Other repair services
Degree of labour intensity	**Mass service**	**Professional service**
	Retailing	Doctors
Low	Wholesaling	Lawyers
	Schools	Accountants
	Low	High

Figure 7.6   The service process matrix

Source: Schemenner (1986).

7.4.3. Implications for services management

These characteristics of the demand for services have direct implications on the management of services and firms must try to reconcile (a) productivity constraints leading to standardisation and to the maximum use of information technology, (b) quality control objectives, leading to the development of personal interaction with customers and finally (c) differentiation objectives. As illustrated in Figure 7.6, service delivery activities can be classified by reference to two main dimensions at two levels each: labour intensity of the service delivery activity and degree of interaction and customisation.

As shown in Figure 7.6, using these two dimensions, four types of service activities can be identified:

1. *Service factories.* Service businesses that have a relatively low labour intensity and a low degree of customer interaction, such as airlines, trucking, hotels and resorts.

2. *Service shops.* Here the degree of customer interaction or customisation increases. These service businesses still have a high degree of plant and equipment relative to labour, but they offer more interactions and customisation; hospitals, car repair garages and restaurants are examples of service shops.

3. *Mass service.* These businesses have a high degree of labour intensity but a rather low degree of interaction and customisation, such as retailing, schools, laundry, cleaning, and so on.

4. *Professional services.* When the degree of interaction with the customer increases and/or customisation of this service becomes the watchword, mass services give way to professional services: doctors, lawyers, accountants, architects are classic examples.

This classification of services is not necessarily fixed as service firms innovate or modify their service operations.

EXHIBIT 7.6

MARKETING MIX IMPLICATIONS OF SERVICE CHARACTERISTICS

Intangibility	Services cannot be seen, touched, tasted, felt, etc., making it difficult to communicate service features and quality; communication must 'tangibilise' the service by relating to familiar situations or experiences; also difficult to set prices.
Perishability	Difficult to balance capacity and demand because services cannot be inventoried; services cannot be returned for credit or exchange; need to manage demand in peak periods, utilise capacity in off-periods and have good service recovery.
Inseparability	Simultaneous production and consumption make customers and service providers part of the service process; sales precedes production; manage service interactions for customers' satisfaction; educate customers about the service process (and their role in it).
Variability	Lack of standardisation; inconsistent service delivery and quality from one encounter to the next due to human involvement in service; minimised by employee selection and training and clearly understood service performance standards.

Source: Authors.

For example, with the advent of fast food, interaction and customisation for the consumer have been lowered dramatically, as has labour intensity. Fast food restaurants are moving to the service factory quadrant.

Similarly, in the retailing sectors, the expansion of catalogue stores, electronic commerce and warehouse stores has shifted the emphasis of traditional retailing operations towards a lower degree of labour intensity. The opposite evolution is also observed in retailing with the proliferation of boutiques within stores, where interaction and customisation are stressed. In this last example, the evolution is from the lower left quadrant to the lower right quadrant.

7.5. The demand for industrial goods

We have seen in Chapter 3 that industrial demand is actually derived from the consumer marketplace. Thus, industrial marketers must be cognizant of conditions in their own markets, but must also be aware of developments in the markets served by their customers and by their customers' customers. Of course, many industrial products are far removed from the consumer and the linkage is difficult to see. This separation becomes more apparent as the number of intermediate customers increases between a given manufacturer and the end-user. In other cases, the linkage is quite clear, such as the impact of car sales on the steel industry.

> Thus, if consumers are not buying homes, autos, clothing, stereos, educational or medical services, there will be less need for lumber, steel, cotton, plastics, computer components and hospital forms. Consequently, industry will require less energy, fewer trucking services and not as many tools or machines. (Morris, 1988, p. 390)

The planning task can become quite complex when a manufacturer's output is used in a wide variety of applications.

The demand for industrial goods is structured differently according to whether they are consumable goods, industrial components or industrial equipment. The data needed for the evaluation of demand are practically identical to the data for consumer goods, with only few exceptions.

7.5.1. The demand for industrial consumable goods

We have here products that are used by the industrial firm but not incorporated in the fabricated product. The components of demand are the following:

- Number of potential industrial users (by size).
- Proportion of effective users (by size).
- Level of activity per effective user.
- Usage rate per use occasion.

The usage rate is a technical norm easy to identify. The number of companies classified by number of employees, payroll, value of shipments, and so on can be obtained in the Census of Manufacturers. An example is presented in Exhibit 7.7. The current proportion of effective users in this example is the major source of uncertainty.

7.5.2. The demand for industrial components

Industrial components are used in the product fabricated by the customer. Thus, their demand is directly related to the volume of production of the client company. The components of their demand are the following:

- Number of potential industrial users (by size).
- Proportion of effective users (by size).
- Quantity produced per effective user.
- Rate of usage per product.

Producers of car parts are a good example of a sector that responds to this type of demand (Exhibit 7.8). Fluctuation in consumer demand for cars will eventually result in a variation of the demand for their components. Thus a careful observation of the evolution of demand for the end-product is imperative for the producer of industrial components who wishes to predict his own demand (Figure 7.7).

EXHIBIT 7.7

ESTIMATING THE DEMAND FOR A CONSUMABLE INDUSTRIAL PRODUCT

The Cleanchem company has developed a water treatment chemical for paper manufacturers. Total paper shipments in the Northeast region represent a value of $700 million. Data found in trade reports and information received from local water utility show that paper mills use 0.01 gallons of water per dollar of shipment value. Cleanchem engineers recommend a minimum of 0.25 ounces of the water treatment chemical per gallon of water and 0.30 ounces per gallon of water to be optimal. The AMP is estimated to range between 1,750,000 ounces ($700 million times 0.01 times 0.25) and 2,100,000 ounces. These estimates must be adjusted for the activity level of paper mills.

Source: Morris (1988, p. 183).

7.5.3. The demand for industrial equipment

Here we have products such as industrial machines or computers that are necessary to the production activity. They are durable goods and thus the distinction between primary and replacement demand is important. Primary equipment demand is determined by the following factors:

- Number of companies equipped (by size).
- Increase of the production capacity.
- Number of new-user companies (by size).
- Production capacity.

Replacement demand is determined by the following factors:

- Size of the existing population.
- Age distribution and technology level of the population.
- Distribution of the product life spans.
- Rate of replacement.
- Effect of product substitution.
- Effect of reduction of production capacity.

EXHIBIT 7.8

ESTIMATING REPLACEMENT DEMAND: AN EXAMPLE

By way of an example let's look at the car market. Let us assume that the average technical service life is around 10–11 years. If the expectation is to have a service life of 12.5 years, the yearly scrappage rate will be around 8 per cent, which represents a level of replacement demand of 1.7 million cars, given the current size of the car population. If on the contrary, the expected service life were only 9 years, the scrappage rate would be 11.1 per cent with a level of replacement demand of 2.1 million.

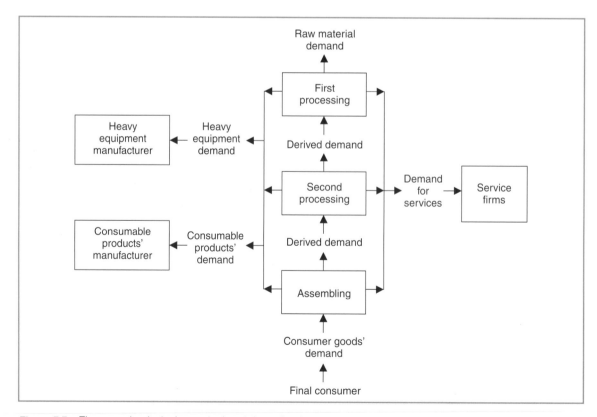

Figure 7.7 The supply chain for an industrial equipment
Source: Authors.

7.5.4. The acceleration effect

The demand for industrial equipment is directly related to the production capacity of the client companies, and thus even a small fluctuation in final demand can translate into a very large variation in the demand for industrial equipment. This phenomenon is known as the acceleration effect.

For example, suppose that the life span of a population of machines is ten years. If the demand for the consumer goods produced by these machines increases by 10 per cent, 10 per cent of the existing population will need to be replaced, and an additional 10 per cent production capacity will be needed to meet the increased demand. Thus the demand for the machines will double. If the demand for the consumer goods decreases by 10 per cent, the required production capacity will only be 90 per cent, and thus the 10 per cent that fail will not need to be replaced. Thus the demand for the machines falls to 0.

The volatility of the demand for industrial equipment means that for accurate demand forecasting, companies must analyse both their own demand and the final demand of the companies they supply. The data in Figure 7.8 show evidence of an 'acceleration effect' in two different markets.

7.5.5. Marketing implications of industrial derived demand

In addition to the difficulty of forecasting sales, derived demand also has implications for operational marketing.

The dynamic industrial firm may decide to target its selling efforts not only on the immediate customer but also towards indirect customers further down the production chain, as shown in Figure 7.9.

Thus Recticel has advertised the benefits of its polyurethane foam to armchair and sofa distributors and to the general public as well. Its goals are twofold here: first to encourage end-users and distributors to place demands upon various furniture manufacturers to begin using the Recticel foam as a component in their production process; and second, to provide promotional efforts for furniture manufacturers currently using Recticel's product.

By focusing efforts further down the industrial chain, the industrial firm is adopting a pull-strategy which complements more traditional selling efforts targeted at direct customers (push-strategy). To limit their dependence on direct customers, dynamic industrial firms have to adopt a proactive marketing behaviour and to play an active role in demand stimulation at each level of the industrial chain.

7.6. Growth opportunity analysis in the existing market

The gap between the current and the absolute level of primary demand is indicative of the rate of development or underdevelopment of a product market. The larger the gap, the greater the growth opportunity; conversely, the smaller the gap, the closer the market is to the saturation level.

Weber (1976) has developed a framework, called gap analysis, to analyse the gaps between AMP and current company sales. Four growth opportunities are identified as

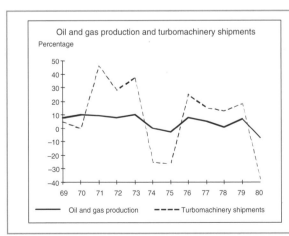

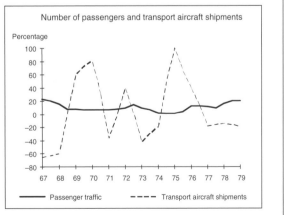

Figure 7.8   Examples of volatile equipment demands
Source: Bishop *et al.* (1984).

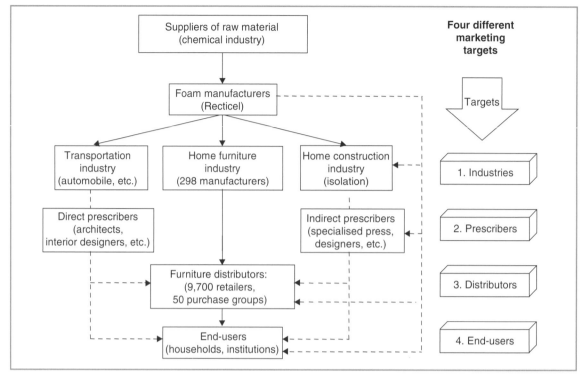

Figure 7.9   Example of derived demand: the market for polyurethane foam
Source: Authors.

shown in Figure 7.10: the usage gap, the distribution gap, the product line gap and the competitive gap. The competitive gap is due to sales of directly competitive brands within the product market and also to substitute products. The other gaps present growth opportunities that will be briefly reviewed below.

7.6.1. Distribution gaps

The distribution gap is due to absence or inadequate distribution within the product market. Three types of distribution gaps can be observed:

- The coverage gap exists when a firm does not distribute the relevant product line in all geographic regions desired.
- The intensity gap exists when a firm's product line is distributed in an inadequate number of outlets within a geographic region where the firm has distribution coverage.
- The exposure gap exists when a firm's product lines have poor or inadequate shelf space, location, displays,

and so on within outlets where the firm does have distribution for the product.

Sales of a particular product line can be adversely affected by any or all of these three different distribution gaps. Before adopting new product lines, the firm should try to close these distribution gaps.

7.6.2. Usage gaps

The usage gap is due to insufficient use of the product. Three types of usage gaps can be identified:

- The non-user gap, that is, the customer who could potentially use the product but are not using it.
- The light user gap, that is, the customer who uses the product but do not use it on every use occasion.
- The light usage gap, that is, the customers who use the product but by less than a full use on each use occasion.

A strategy aiming at closing these gaps will contribute to the development of primary demand and will therefore benefit all competing firms as well, and illustrated by Figure 7.10.

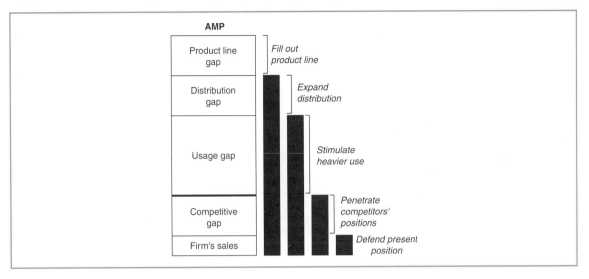

Figure 7.10 Analysis of growth opportunities
Source: Weber (1976).

7.6.3. Product line gaps

The product line gap is caused by the lack of a full product line. Seven types of product line gaps could exist:

1. *Size-related product line gaps.* Product 'size' can be defined along three dimensions: 'container size' for consumables such as soft drinks or detergents, 'capacity' for durables such as refrigerators or computers and 'power' for car engines or industrial machinery.

2. *Options-related product line gaps.* A firm desiring to cater to specific demands of individual customers can offer optional features. Cars serve as one good example. By offering a large number of options, car manufacturers can produce a large number of cars, each one in some way different from every other one.

3. *Style, colour, flavour and fragrance-related product line gaps.* Style and colour can be important for clothing, shoes, appliances, cars, and so on; flavours and fragrances can become important means of expanding product lines in food and drink products, tobaccos, toiletries, and so on.

4. *Form-related product line gaps.* One form of a product may be more attractive for customers than another. Possible dimensions of form include method or principle of operation (petrol versus electric mowers),

product format (antacids: chewable, swallowable liquid, effervescent powder or tablets); product composition (corn oil, vegetable oil, margarine) and product containers (resealable, returnable, throwaway bottles, easy-open cans).

5. *Quality-related product line gaps.* Price lining is a popular practice used by marketers to provide consumers with a choice of products differentiated by overall quality and prices. Sporting goods manufacturers market tennis rackets and golf clubs in a range from beginners' models (low price) up to professional models (high price).

6. *Distributor brand-related product line gaps.* Many manufacturers realise a significant proportion of their sales through selling to retailers who then put their own brand names on the products, like Saint Michael for Marks and Spencer in the United Kingdom. For manufacturers who recognise the private brand market as a separate segment, private brands can account for product line gaps.

7. *Segment-related product line gaps.* As discussed in Chapter 6, a firm can adopt different market coverage strategies. A firm has a product line gap for any segment for which it does not have a product.

Each of these identified product line gaps constitutes a growth opportunity for the firm through innovation or product differentiation.

The types of development strategies to be considered to close these gaps are briefly presented in Figure 7.10. Those strategies will be described in more detail in Chapter 9. In addition to these development strategies operated by the firms, one must add the natural changes in the size of the industry market potential, which is linked to the PLC. Growth opportunities can also be evaluated in qualitative terms using selected attractiveness indicators as shown in Figure 7.11. These qualitative indicators can then be quantified as shown in Table 7.1.

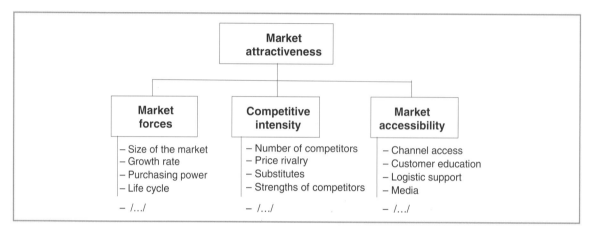

Figure 7.11   Selected indicators of market attractiveness

Source: Adapted from Best (2000/2003).

Table 7.1   Main indicators of market attractiveness: an example

Indicators of attractiveness	Weight (100)	Weak 1–2	Moderate 3–4	Strong 5
		Evaluation scale		
Market accessibility	—	Outside Europe and USA	Europe and USA	Europe
Market growth rate	—	≤5%	5–10%	≥10%
Length of the life cycle	—	≤2 years	2–5 years	≥5 years
Gross profit potential	—	≤15%	15–25%	≥25%
Strength of competition	—	Structured oligopoly	Unstructured competition	Weak competition
Potential for differentiation	—	Very weak	Moderate	Strong
Concentration of customers	—	Very dispersed	Moderately dispersed	Concentrated

Source: Authors.

7.7. The product life cycle model

In attractiveness analysis, market potential analysis is a first, and essentially quantitative, step. The analysis must be completed by a study of the product life cycle (PLC), or the evolution of the potential demand for a product or service over time.

An essentially dynamic concept borrowed from biology, the PLC model takes the form of an S-shaped graph comprising five phases (Day, 1981). The first phase is a take-off, or introductory phase, followed by an exponential growth phase, a shakeout phase, a maturity phase and a decline phase. Figure 7.12 presents an idealised representation of the PLC, while Figure 7.13

portrays the life cycle of audio products in France, and in particular long-playing records and the compact disc.

7.7.1. Determinants of the PLC model

Before moving to an explanation of the PLC, its stages and its marketing implications, it is important to explain what type of products should be dealt with in a life cycle analysis. Should it be a category of products (computers), a particular type of product within the category (microcomputers), a specific model (laptop computers or note books) or a specific brand (Compaq)?

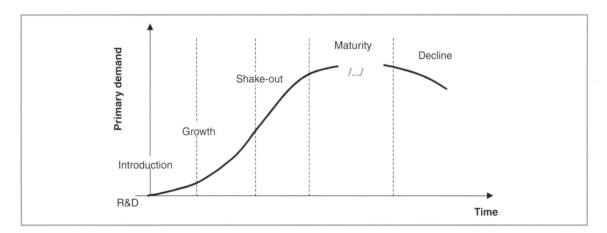

Figure 7.12   The idealised shape of the PLC model

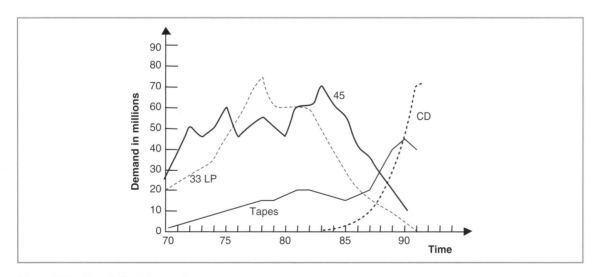

Figure 7.13   The PLC of the audio market
Source: Industry.

While a life cycle analysis at any level can have value if properly conducted, the most useful level of analysis is that of a *product market*, in the sense given in Chapter 4. A product market lends itself best to a life cycle analysis because it best describes buying behaviours within a particular product category and it most clearly defines the frame of reference: a product seen as a specific package of benefits, targeted to a specific group of buyers. The same product can very well have different life cycle profiles in different geographic markets or different segments within the same market. Every product market has its own life cycle which reflects not only the evolution of the product, largely determined by technology, but also the evolution of primary demand and of its determinants.

Thus, a clear distinction should be made between the product life cycle (PLC) and the brand life cycle (BLC).

7.7.2. The product-market life cycle (PLC) model

For a product market, primary demand is the principal driving force and its determining factors are both non-controllable environmental factors and industry's totally controllable marketing variables. One of the most important non-controllable factors is the evolution of technology, which pushes towards newer, higher performance products, and makes older products obsolete. A second factor is the evolution of production and consumption norms, which makes certain products no longer suitable for the market and calls for others. Thus, the PLC model portrays the sales history of a particular product technology, which constitutes one specific solution (among many others) for a specific group of buyers to a market need.

These factors exist in all business sectors, which do not however exclude the possibility that certain better-protected product markets have a much longer life cycle than others. The life cycle also remains largely influenced by industry marketing efforts, particularly when the market is expanding. Dynamic companies are the driving force in a market, guiding its evolution, development and eventual relaunch sparked by modifications to the product. The PLC is thus not fixed, and research in the field has identified a great variety of life cycle patterns (Cox, 1967; Swan and Rink, 1982).

7.7.3. Strategic implications of the PLC

As product markets grow, mature and decline over time, marketing strategy must evolve with the changing buyers' behaviour and competitive environment. To say that a product has a life cycle implies four things:

- The economic and competitive environment is different at each phase.
- The priority strategic objective must be redefined at each phase.
- Products' cost and profit structures are different at each phase.
- The marketing programme must be adapted in each stage of the PLC.

The shortening of the PLC is a major challenge for the innovative firm which has less and less time to achieve its objectives.

7.7.4. The introductory phase

In the introductory phase, the market is often (not always) characterised by a slow growth of sales because of various environmental factors:

1. The first of these is the *technology uncertainty*, which is often not yet entirely mastered by the innovating company that has to exploit its first-mover advantage (see Table 7.2). In addition, the technology may

---

Table 7.2   First-mover advantage: myth or reality?

First-mover advantages	Free-rider advantages
Image and reputation	Risk reduction in time and money
Brand loyalty	Lower R&D costs
Opportunity for the best market position	Lower education costs
Technological leadership	Entry through heavy promotion
Opportunity to set product standards	Technological leapfrog
Access to distribution	Imposing a new standard
Experience effects	Learning from a changing market
Patents as barrier to entry	Shared experience
Switching costs as barrier to entry	

Source: Adapted from Schnaars (1998, pp. 160–5).

still be developing or evolving in reaction to the first applications, and thus the producer cannot yet hope to produce at maximum efficiency.

2. *Distributors* are a second environmental force, and can be very reluctant at this stage to distribute a product that has not yet proven itself on the larger market. In addition, an industrial distributor will need to familiarise himself with the product, its technical characteristics and its principal functions, which will additionally slow the process.

3. *The potential customer* makes up a third environmental factor. They can often be slow to change their consumption or production habits because of switching costs and caution towards the innovation. Only the most innovative of consumers will be the first to adopt the new product. This group constitutes a rather small initial segment for a product in the introduction phase, and is thus another contributing factor to slow sales.

4. A final environmental force is the *competition*. Typically, the innovating company is without direct competition for a period of time, depending on the strength of the patent protection if any. Substitute product competition can still be very strong, however, excepting in the case of breakthrough innovation.

This phase is characterised by a high degree of uncertainty because, as technology is still developing, competitors are not yet identified, the reference market is blurred and there is little market information available. The more revolutionary the innovation, the larger is the uncertainty.

Internal company factors, which also characterise the introduction phase, include highly negative cash flows, large marketing expenses, high production costs, and often-large R&D costs to be amortised. All of these factors put the new product in a very risky financial position. For this reason, the shorter the introduction phase of the product, the better for the company's profitability.

The *length of the introductory phase* of the PLC is a function of the speed of adoption of the less innovative potential buyers, which is influenced by various factors such as

- importance to the buyer of the new product's benefits;
- presence or absence of adoption costs to be borne by the buyer;
- compatibility of the product with current modes of consumption or production;
- observable nature of the new product's benefits;
- possibility of trying the new product;
- competitive pressures inducing buyers to adopt the innovation.

Given these factors, the company's highest priority strategic objective is to create primary demand as rapidly as possible and thus to keep the introduction phase as short as possible.

This *priority objective* includes

- creating awareness of the product's existence;
- informing the market of the new product benefits;
- inducing potential customers to try the product;
- securing channels for current and future distribution.

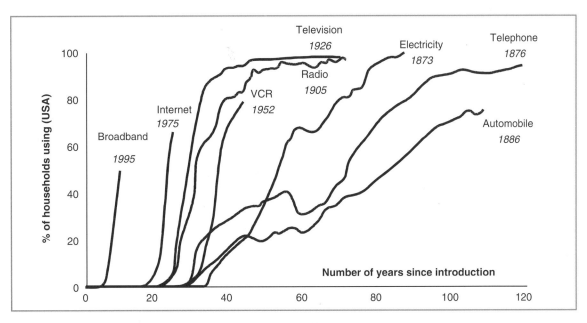

Figure 7.14 Examples of introductory phases of the PLC

Source: Industry.

Thus the marketing strategy in the early phase of the PLC typically stresses market education objectives. To respond to these priorities, the *marketing programme* in the introduction phase will tend to have the following characteristics:

- A basic, core version of the product.
- An exclusive or selective distribution system.
- A low price sensitivity situation.
- An informative communication programme.

Several alternatives exist as to the types of launching strategies, particularly in terms of pricing: the dilemma of 'skimming versus penetration' pricing will be discussed in more detail in Chapter 11. Examples of introductory phases of the PLC are presented in Figure 7.14.

7.7.5. The growth phase

If the product successfully passes the test of its introduction to the market, it enters into the growth phase. This phase is characterised by growth of sales at an accelerating rate. The causes of this growth are the following:

- The first satisfied users become repeat customers and influence other potential users by word of mouth; thus the rate of occupation of the market increases.
- The availability of the product due to wider distribution gives the product more visibility, which then further increases the product's diffusion in the market.
- The entrance of new competitors increases the total marketing pressure on demand at a moment when it is expansible and strongly elastic.

An important characteristic of this phase is the regular decrease of production costs due to the increase in the volume produced. The effect of experience also begins to be felt. Prices have a tendency to decrease, which allows progressive coverage of the entire potential market. Marketing expenses are thus spread over a strongly expanding sales base, and cash flows become positive.

The characteristics of the economic and *competitive environment* change markedly:

- Sales are growing at an accelerating rate.
- The target group is now the segment of early adopters.
- New competitors enter the market.
- The technology is well diffused in the market.

To meet these new market conditions, the strategic marketing objectives are changed as well. They now include:

- expanding the size of the total market;
- maximising the occupation rate in the market;
- building a strong brand image;
- creating brand loyalty.

To achieve these new objectives, *the marketing programme* will also be modified, as follows:

- Product improvements and features addition strategy.
- Intensive distribution and multiple channels strategy.
- Price reductions to penetrate the market.
- Image building and communication strategy.

This primary demand development strategy requires large financial resources, and, if the cash flows are positive and profits rising, the equilibrium break-even point is not necessarily reached yet.

At this time, there is no intensive competitive rivalry in the product market, since the marketing efforts of any firm contribute to the expansion of the total market and are therefore beneficial for other firms.

7.7.6. The shakeout phase

This is a transitory phase where the rate of sales growth is decelerating, even though it remains above that of the general economy. The target group is now the majority of the market. The weakest competitors start dropping out, as the result of successive decreases in the market price, and the market is becoming more concentrated. The competitive and economic environments once again have changed:

- Demand is increasing at a slower rate.
- The target is the majority group in the market.
- The weakest competitors are dropping out of the race because of the reduced market prices.
- The industrial sector is more concentrated.

The key message of the shakeout phase is that things will be more difficult in the market because of the slowing down of total demand. Competing firms are led to redefine their priority objectives in two new directions:

- First, the strategic emphasis must shift from developing primary demand to building up or maximising market share.
- Second, market segmentation must guide the product policy to differentiate the firm from the proliferation of 'me too' products and to move away from the core market. The majority rule has become the majority fallacy.

The new priority objectives are

- to segment the market and to identify priority target segments;
- to maximise market share in the target segments;
- to position the brand clearly in consumers' minds;
- to create and maintain brand loyalty.

To achieve these objectives, the marketing programme will stress the following strategic orientations:

- Product differentiation guided by market segmentation.
- Expansion of distribution to obtain maximum market exposure.
- Pricing based on the distinctive characteristics of the brands.
- Advertising to communicate the claimed positioning to the market.

The shakeout period can be very short. The competitive climate becomes more aggressive and the key indicator of performance is market share.

7.7.7. The maturity phase

Eventually, the increase of primary demand slows down and stabilises at the growth rate of the real GNP or the rhythm of demographic expansion. The product is in the phase of maturity. The majority of products can be found in this phase, which usually has the longest duration (see, for example, Exhibit 7.9). The causes of this stabilisation of global demand are the following:

- The rates of occupation and penetration of the product in the market are very high and very unlikely to increase further.
- The coverage of the market by distribution is intensive and cannot be increased further.
- The technology is stabilised and only minor modifications to the product can be expected.

At this stage, the market is very segmented as companies try to cover all the diversity of needs by offering a wide range of product variations. Over the course of this phase the probability of a technological innovation to relaunch the PLC is high, as everyone in the industry tries to extend the life of the product.

The emerging trends observed in the shakeout period have materialised and the characteristics of the economic and competitive environment are the following:

- Non-expansible primary demand growing at the rate of the economy.
- Durable goods demand is determined by replacement demand.
- Markets are highly segmented.
- A few powerful competitors dominate the market and the market structure is oligopolistic.
- The technology is standardised.

The firm's priority objective is to defend, and if possible to expand, market share and to gain a sustainable competitive advantage over direct competitors. The tools to be used for achieving this objective are basically of three types, namely

- to differentiate the products through quality, feature or style improvements.
- to enter new market segments or niches.
- to gain a competitive advantage through the non-product variables of the marketing mix.

The slowing of market growth certainly has an impact on the competitive climate. Production capacity surpluses appear and contribute to the intensification of the competitive situation. Price competition is more frequent, but has little or no impact on primary demand, which has become inelastic to price. It will only affect the market share of the existing competitors. Inasmuch as the industry succeeds in avoiding price wars, this is the phase where profitability is highest, as shown in Figure 7.15. In theory, this profitability will be as strong as the market share retained is high. As observed by Sheth and Sisodia (2002), in this type of market situation, the 'rule of three' applies in the sense that there is only room for three full-line generalists along with several product or market specialists.

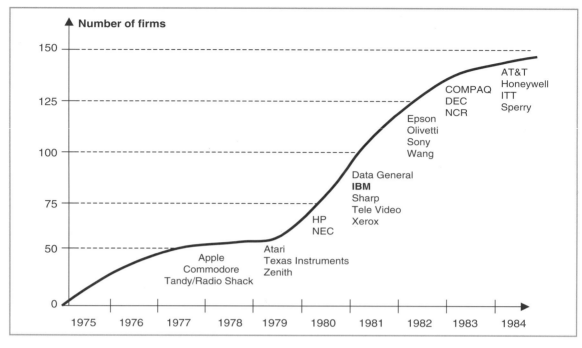

Figure 7.15   Entry of new competitors in the PC market in the United States of America

EXHIBIT 7.10

TRADITIONAL CHEMICAL-BASED CAMERAS WIPED OUT BY DIGITAL CAMERAS

Never in the history of leisure electronics, such a fast downturn of demand has been observed between two technologies. In France, digital cameras sales have started growing in 1999 and have more than doubled every year since then to reach 2.2 millions units in 2003 and 3.5 millions the following year, according to the last estimates of GFK. Distribution has of course followed the trend: if in 2001, 75 per cent of the space was dedicated to traditional cameras in the photographic equipment department of Fnac and 25 per cent to digital cameras, the proportion is exactly inversed today.

Source: Le Figaro Economie, 29 Octobre 2003

7.7.8. The decline phase

The decline phase is characterised by a structural decrease in demand for one of the following reasons:

- New, more technologically advanced products make their appearance and replace existing products with the same function (see Exhibit 7.10).
- Preferences, tastes or consumption habits change with time and render products outdated.
- Changes in the social, economic and political environment, such as modifications in environmental protection laws, make products obsolete or simply prohibited.

As sales and potential profits decrease, certain companies disinvest and leave the market, while others try to specialise in the residual market. This represents a valid option if the decline is progressive. Except in a turnaround of the market, which is sometimes observed, the abandonment of the technologically outdated product is inevitable.
In Table 7.3 a summary of the marketing strategies over the PLC is presented and in Table 7.4 the reader will find a PLC evaluation grid.

Table 7.3 Marketing programme over the PLC: a summary

Phase of the PLC	Macro-marketing environment	Priority strategic objectives	Marketing programme
Introduction	■ Slow growth of primary demand ■ Target: segment of innovators ■ Monopoly, or few rivals ■ Fast technological evolution	■ To create primary demand ■ To educate potential users ■ To induce trial purchase ■ To secure large distribution	■ Core product – basic model ■ Selective or exclusive distribution ■ Skimming or penetration pricing ■ Generic and informative communication
Growth	■ Growth at an accelerating pace ■ Target: segment of early adopters ■ Entry of new competitors ■ Diffused technology	■ To expand primary demand ■ To increase market occupation rate ■ To build brand or corporate image ■ To create brand or corporate loyalty	■ Improved product with new features ■ Intensive distribution and market coverage ■ Price reductions to enlarge the market ■ Image building communication
Shakeout	■ Growth at a declining pace ■ Target: majority of the market ■ Weakest rivals start dropping out ■ Second generation technology emerges	■ To target specific segments ■ To maximise market share ■ To position the brand clearly ■ To create and maintain brand loyalty	■ Differentiation based on segmentation ■ Intensive distribution ■ High price and value pricing strategy ■ Brand positioning communication
Maturity	■ Non-expandable primary demand ■ Highly fragmented market ■ Few powerful rivals dominate ■ Standardised technology	■ To differentiate products ■ To enter new segments or niches ■ To refine the positioning strategy ■ To add new product features	■ Differentiation based on segmentation ■ Return to selective distribution ■ Forms of non-price competition ■ Brand positioning communication
Decline	■ Zero growth or declining market ■ Target: segment of laggards ■ Competitors leave the market ■ Outdated technology	■ To divest quickly or selectively ■ To become the industry specialist ■ To slow down the decline of the market	■ Limited product line and assortment ■ Highly selective distribution ■ High prices due to low price sensitivity ■ Communication to hard core loyal

Source: Authors.

7.8. The PLC model as a conceptual framework

More than a planning tool, the life cycle model is a conceptual framework for analysing the forces which determine the attractiveness of a product market and which provoke its evolution. Markets evolve because certain forces change, provoking pressures or inciting changes. These changing forces are important to identify, and for that purpose the PLC model is useful (Levitt, 1965).

7.8.1. Diversity of actual PLC profiles

A difficulty in interpretating the PLC model comes from the fact that available experimental observations show that the PLC profile does not always follow an S-curve as

Table 7.4   PLC evaluation grid

Market characteristics	Introduction	Growth	Shakeout	Maturity	Decline
Primary demand					
Slow growth	——	——	——	——	——
Fast growth	——	——	——	——	——
Slowing down	——	——	——	——	——
Decreasing	——	——	——	——	——
New competitors					
Some	——	——	——	——	——
Many	——	——	——	——	——
Few	——	——	——	——	——
Even fewer	——	——	——	——	——
Real prices					
Stable	——	——	——	——	——
Decreasing	——	——	——	——	——
Erratic	——	——	——	——	——
Range of products					
Increasing	——	——	——	——	——
Few changes	——	——	——	——	——
Decreasing	——	——	——	——	——
Distribution					
Low growth	——	——	——	——	——
Fast growth	——	——	——	——	——
Few changes	——	——	——	——	——
Decreasing	——	——	——	——	——
Product modifications					
Few	——	——	——	——	——
Many	——	——	——	——	——
Very few	——	——	——	——	——
Communication content					
Core service	——	——	——	——	——
Main attributes	——	——	——	——	——
New uses	——	——	——	——	——
Secondary attributes	——	——	——	——	——

Phases of the PLC header spans Introduction, Growth, Shakeout, Maturity, Decline.

Source: Taylor (1986, p. 27).

suggested by the model. Rink and Swan (1979) identified as many as 12 different profiles. Sometimes products escape the introduction phase and enter directly into growth; others skip the maturity phase and pass directly from growth to decline; still others skip decline and find a new vigour after a brief slowdown, and so on (see Figure 7.16). Thus there is not only one type of evolution that will invariably intervene, and it is often difficult to determine in which phase a product is currently situated. This difficulty reduces the utility of the concept as a planning tool, and even more so as the duration of the phases varies from one product to another, not to mention from one country to another for the same product.

In 1960, most of the European producers of TV sets had planned their production capacity for colour TV (at that time in the introductory phase) by reference to the PLC of colour TV in the USA, which had a very long introductory phase. In Europe, however, the market penetration was very rapid, the European market and environment being very different.

The different profiles observed can be explained by the evolution of the following explanatory factors: technology, consumption habits and company dynamism. The PLC model does not exempt the market analyst from a systematic analysis of the driving forces at the origin of these changes. The obvious difficulty is to determine, before the facts, the type of evolution that will prevail.

7.8.2. Product rejuvenation strategies

Another explanation of the observed differences in the profiles comes from the fact that companies can act upon the pattern of the PLC profile by innovating, repositioning

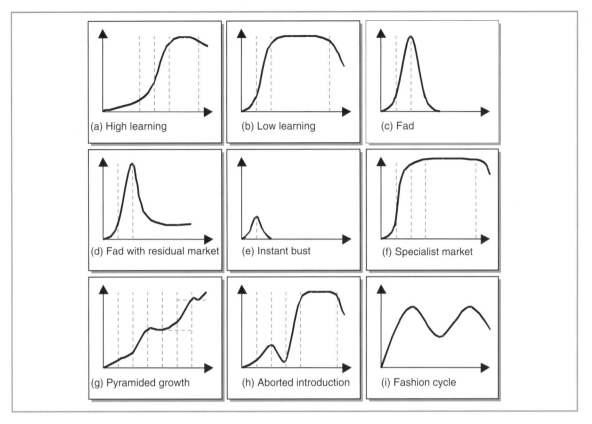

Figure 7.16   Diversity of PLC profiles

Source: Adapted from Wasson (1974).

the product, promoting its diffusion to other groups of consumers, or modifying it in various manners. Throughout the life cycle, the dynamic firm will try to pursue the following objectives:

- Shortening the introduction phase.
- Accelerating the growth process.
- Prolonging the maturity phase.
- Slowing the decline phase.

The ideal profile of a PLC is one where the development phase is short, the introduction brief, the growth phase rapid, the maturity phase long and the decline long and progressive. The initiatives taken by an innovating firm can thus modify the life cycle profile of a product market.

> A classic example of a life cycle with successive product relaunches is the nylon industry, where the growth phase was prolonged several times due to successive technological innovations. (Yale, 1964)

> It is clear that if all the competitors in a product market consider maturity or decline inevitable, the phases risk being realised sooner than expected. Some industrial sectors, once considered as declining or stagnant, have

suddenly experienced a new lease of life resulting from a rejuvenating supply-led innovation adopted by a manufacturer or by a distributor.

> Ikea, in the home furniture distribution, Swatch in the watches market, Benetton in the garment market and Kinepolis in the movie distribution market are good examples of placid or stagnant markets rejuvenated.

The relevant question to examine is to know whether the product market is really in decline or whether it is the strategy adopted by the competing firms within the product market which is obsolete or delivers only limited value to customers?

7.8.3. How to reconcile growth and profit objectives?

The structure of the financial flows which accompany the (idealised) evolution of primary demand over time is described in Figure 7.17. One observes that, in the general case considered here, the financial flows are very unevenly allocated among the different phases of the PLC.

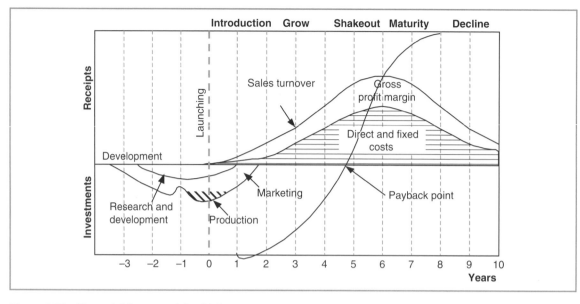

Figure 7.17   Financial flows and the PLC

Source: Authors.

In phases 1 and 2, past investments and marketing expenditures heavily undermine the profitability that can remain negative for a significant period of time, particularly in markets where the introductory phase is long. It is only in the shakeout or even in the maturity phase that the innovating firm reaches the profitability zone, having recouped previous losses and achieving higher gross profit margins and lower costs due to experience of economies of scale effects.

A golden managerial rule resulting from this cost and revenue allocation along the PLC is to maintain permanently a balanced structure of the firm's product portfolio in terms of profitability and growth.

It is clear, for example, that a firm having 85 per cent of its turnover achieved by products or activities situated in phases 1 or 2 of the PLC would have a high growth potential, but would certainly be confronted with severe liquidity or cash flow problems, being unable to generate enough cash to finance the firm's expansion. It is often the case for promising hi-tech companies having plenty of new product ideas, but not enough cash to finance them. Conversely, a firm achieving 85 per cent of its turnover through products or activities situated in phases 4 or 5, would have substantial financial means, but would be highly vulnerable in terms of growth potential, being completely dependent on a market turnaround or on a sudden decline of primary demand in its main reference markets.

A *balanced product portfolio* implies the presence of so-called cash cow products generating more cash than required for their development, and so-called problem children products or new products having a high growth potential but requiring substantial financial support to ensure their development. These objectives of balanced portfolio structure are at the basis of the portfolio analysis methods developed in Chapter 9 of this book.

CHAPTER SUMMARY

The key demand concepts are 'primary' versus 'company' demand, 'absolute' versus 'present' market potential, 'end' versus 'derived' demand, 'first equipment' versus 'replacement' demand for durable goods. The objective of demand analysis is to give an empirical content to these concepts through market research in order to objectively assess the attractiveness of each potential target segment and to identify the determinants of demand. *Virtual markets*: these concepts are useful for detecting growth opportunities in the reference market through gap analysis. The product life cycle (PLC) model is a conceptual framework which describes the evolution of primary demand in a dynamic perspective. A large variety of profiles exist for the PLC which can be explained by the evolution of technology and consumption habits and by the size of industry marketing efforts. The competitive situation and the financial structure (turnover and profits) are different at each stage of the PLC and the priority strategic objective and the marketing programme must be adapted accordingly.

Review and Application Questions

1. What is the relationship between current market potential and absolute market potential? Describe the factors which determine the level and the evolution of these market potential concepts.

2. You must estimate the size of the absolute market potential as well as the current level of equipment of households for home cinema in a given country. Describe the information as well as the methods needed to gather this information.

3. How does the price elasticity of primary demand develop during the various phases of its product life cycle (PLC)? What are the factors explaining this evolution and what are the managerial implications for the firm?

4. Is the PLC applicable in the service sector? Give examples to justify your answer.

5. In highly industrialised markets, the majority of consumer products have reached the maturity of their PLC. Does it mean that there is no more growth opportunities in these markets?

6. What are the main characteristics of consumer services and what are the implications of these differences for marketing management? Refer to airlines, restaurants, medical services or banks.

7. Describe the industrial supply chain of product categories such as computers, cars or digital photography.

Bibliography

Bain and Company News Letter (2004), *Interview of Guus Hoefloot, CEO of Heilmans*, September–October.

Berry, F.W. (1980), Services Marketing is Different, *Business Magazine*, May–June.

Berry, L. (1999), *Discovering the Soul of Service*, New York, The Free Press.

Best, R.J. (2000/2003), *Market-based Management*, Upper Saddle River, NJ, Prentice-Hall, NJ, 3rd edition.

Bishop, W.S., Graham, J.L. and Jones, M.H. (1984), Volatility of Derived Demand in Industrial Markets and its Management Implications, *Journal of Marketing*, 48, 4, pp. 95–103.

Cox, W.E. (1967), Product Life Cycle: Marketing Models, *Journal of Business*, 40, 4, pp. 375–84.

Day, G.S. (1981), The Product Life Cycle: Analysis and Application Issues, *Journal of Marketing*, 45, 4, pp. 60–7.

Eiglier, P. and Langeard, E. (1987), *Servuction*, Paris, Ediscience International.

Kotler, P. (1967/2005), *Marketing Management*, Upper Saddle River, NJ, Prentice-Hall.

Kurtz, D.L. and Clow, K.E. (1998) *Services Marketing*, New York, John Wiley & Sons.

Levitt, T. (1965), *L'imagination au service du marketing*, Paris, Econmica.

Morris, M.H. (1988), *Industrial and Organizational Marketing*, Columbus, OH, Merrill.

Rink, D.R. and Swan, J.E. (1979), Product Life Cycle Research: A Literature Review, *Journal of Business Research*, 7, 3, pp. 219–42.

Sawhney, M. (1999), Making New Markets, *Business 2.0*, May, pp.116–21.

Sawhney, M., Balasubramanian, S. and Krishnan, V.V. (2004), Creating Growth with Services, *MIT Sloan Management Review*, 45, 2, pp. 34–43.

Schemenner, R.W. (1986), How Can Service Business Survive and Prosper?, *Sloan Management Review*, Spring.

Schnaars, S.P. (1998), *Marketing Strategy*, New York, The Free Press.

Sheth, J. and Sisodia, R. (2002), The Rule of Three in Europe, *European Business Forum*, 10, Summer, pp. 53–7.

Shostack, G.L. (1977), Breaking Free from Product-marketing, *Journal of Marketing*, 41, 2, pp. 73–80.

Swan, J.E. and Rink, D.R. (1982), Fitting Market Strategy to Varying Product Life Cycles, *Business Horizons*, 25, 1, pp. 72–6.

Taylor, J.W. (1986), *Competitive Marketing Strategies*, Radnor, PA, Chilton Book Company.

Vandermerwe, S. (1993), Jumping in to the Customer Activity Cycle, *Columbia Journal of World Business*, 28, 2, pp. 46–65.

Vandermerwe, S. (2000), How Increasing Value to Customers Improves Business Results?, *MIT Sloan Management Review*, 42, 1, pp. 27–37.

Wasson, C.R. (1974), *Dynamic Competitive Strategy and the Product Life Cycle*, St Charles, IL, Challenge Books.

Weber, J.A. (1976), *Growth Opportunity Analysis*, Reston, VA, Reston Publishing.

Yale, J.P. (1964), The Strategy of Nylon's Growth: Create New Market, *Modern Textiles Magazine*, February.

Zeithmal, V.A., Parasuraman, A. and Berry, L.L. (1990), *Delivering Quality Service*, New York, The Free Press.

company competitiveness analysis

8

Chapter contents

Chapter learning objectives

When you have read this chapter, you should be able to

- define a competitive advantage that is sustainable in a target market;
- describe the nature and strengths of the competitive forces at play in an industry;
- assess the impact of the competitive situation on the strategic and operational marketing objectives;
- predict the type of competitive behaviour to expect given the competitive environment;
- explain the importance of differentiation as a source of competitive advantage;
- use the experience curve to measure the extent of a cost advantage or disadvantage over direct competitors;
- understand the concept of international competitive advantage.

Chapter introduction

Having evaluated the intrinsic appeal of the product markets and segments in the reference market, the next stage of strategic marketing is to analyse the climate or the competitive structure of each of the product markets, and then evaluate the nature and intensity of the competitive advantage held by the various competitors in each market. A product market may be very attractive in itself, but not so for a particular firm, given its strengths and weaknesses and compared to its most dangerous competitors. Therefore, the aim of measuring business competitiveness is to identify the kind of competitive advantage that a firm or a brand can enjoy and to evaluate to what extent this advantage is sustainable, given the competitive structure, the balance of existing forces and the positions held by the competitors.

8.1. A growing competitive interdependence

One of the most important effects of globalisation is the interdependence it creates between markets. National markets cannot be viewed as separate entities any more, but rather as belonging to a regional or world reference market. What happens in one market directly influences others. Here are two examples.

■ The relatively minor pollution problems of Coca-Cola in Belgium and in France in 1999 triggered a health scare that spread rapidly to other European nations, which hit the Coca-Cola share price on the New York stock market. Many commentators cited the crisis at the time as one of the contributory factors to the Coca-Cola CEO's surprise early retirement.

■ In few months, the SARS epidemic has contaminated 30 countries over the world and the bird flu is a global phenomenon.

An economy that is highly integrated in the world network becomes more vulnerable to external shocks such as devaluation, a sudden rise in the oil price, a financial crisis or a war threat. This evolution has several managerial implications.

1. The traditional multidomestic (or multinational) organisations become obsolete and are replaced by transnational organisations covering a region or the entire world. The problem is to develop a *global mind set* (Begley and Boyd, 2003) consisting in maintaining a good balance between

    ■ global formalisation and local flexibility of behavioural rules;
    ■ global standardisation or local customisation of products and brands and
    ■ global dictate versus local delegation of decisions.

What is clear today is that many firms are revisiting the full standardisation rule 'one size fits all'.

2. Mergers and acquisitions are necessary to reach the critical size required to compete in an enlarged market (Daimler–Chrysler, AOL–Time Warner, Carrefour–Promodès, ING–BBL), a strategic move which is far from being complete in Europe, in particular in view of the recent enlargement of the European Union to 25 countries.

3. Standardisation of brands and of communication strategies are motivated by the necessity to achieve economies of scale, to remain competitive in the enlarged market. This is the reason why, in 1999, the Unilever Company decided to concentrate its activities on 400 international brands and to eliminate 1200 brands or 75 per cent of its brand portfolio.

For an international firm, it is always difficult to maintain a good balance between the two conflicting objectives, standardisation – which is *supply-driven* – and adaptation – which is *market-driven* (Exhibit 8.1). The problem is to know how far to go in the standardisation track, the risk being to lose contact with the local market simply to reduce costs.

This issue is particularly topical in Europe since the launching of the euro, the new European currency, which by facilitating price comparisons between countries reveals substantial price disparities, which stimulate parallel imports with an alignment to the lowest current level of price.

This new competitive interdependence affects every company in their domestic market and in the international market and obliges them to re-evaluate their competitive advantage, taking as benchmark the strongest competitor in the enlarged reference market. Thus, in this new competitive environment, it is not enough to be customer-oriented. The firm must also become *competitor-oriented*. As discussed in Chapter 2, a competitors' orientation includes all activities involved in acquiring and disseminating information about competitors in the target market and requires an explicit account of competitors' position and behaviour in strategy definition.

EXHIBIT 8.1

EXAMPLES OF THE DILEMMA, 'ADAPTATION VERSUS STANDARDISATION'

- A recent study of 500 brands from the food sector covering four European countries (France, Italy, United Kingdom and Germany) has shown that local brands enjoyed a level of awareness higher than international brands and a stronger brand image on several attributes and in particular on the criterion of trust (Schuiling and Kapferer, 2004).
- The CEO of the Coca-Cola company, the undisputed leader of brand globalisation, has acknowledged that a too strong standardisation strategy damages the brand image. The CEO has invited the local country marketing teams to adapt locally the Coca-Cola brand strategy and even to introduce new local brands.
- In Belgium, Procter & Gamble, a strong supporter of global marketing, has unsuccessfully tried to weaken the local brand Dash, by stopping all advertising during more than 9 months, in order to push its international brand Ariel, only number 2 in the detergent market.

8.2. The notion of competitive advantage

Competitive advantage refers to those characteristics or attributes of a product or a brand that give the firm some superiority over its direct competitors. These characteristics or attributes may be of different types and may relate (a) to the product itself (the core service), (b) to the necessary or added services accompanying the core service or (c) to the modes of production, distribution or selling specific to the product or to the firm. When it exists, this superiority is relative and is defined with respect to the best-placed competitor in the product market or segment. We then speak of the most dangerous competitor, or the priority competitor. A competitor's relative superiority may result from various factors, and the value chain model is particularly useful to identify them. Generally speaking, these can be classified into three main categories, according to the nature of competitive advantage they provide.

8.2.1. The quality (or external) competitive advantage

A quality competitive advantage is based on some distinctive qualities of the product which give superior value to the customer, either by reducing its costs or by improving its performance, therefore giving the firm the capacity to charge a price higher than competition.

An external competitive advantage gives to the firm increased market power. It can force the market to accept a price above that of its priority competitor, which may not have the same distinctive quality. A strategy based on an external competitive advantage is a differentiation strategy, which calls into question the firm's marketing know-how, and its ability to better detect and meet those expectations of customers which are not yet satisfied by existing products.

To succeed with an external advantage strategy, the price premium that the customer is willing to pay must exceed the cost of providing that extra value.

8.2.2. The cost (or internal) competitive advantage

A cost competitive advantage is based on the firm's superiority in matters of cost control, administration and product management, which bring value to the producer by enabling it to have a lower unit cost than its priority competitor (Box 8.1). Internal competitive advantage results from better productivity, thus making the firm more profitable and more resistant to price cuts imposed by the market or by the competition.

A strategy based on internal competitive advantage is a cost domination strategy, which mainly calls into question the firm's organisational and technological know-how. To succeed, a cost strategy must offer acceptable value to customers, so that prices are close to the average of competitors. If too much quality is sacrificed to achieve a low-cost position, the price discount demanded by customers will more than offset the cost advantage.

8.2.3. The search for a sustainable competitive positioning

These two types of competitive advantage have distinct origins and natures, which are often incompatible because they imply different abilities and traditions. Figure 8.1 shows the two aspects of competitive advantage, which can be expressed as questions:

- *Market power*: to what extent are customers willing to pay a price higher than the price charged by our direct competitor?
- *Productivity*: is our unit cost higher or lower than the unit cost of our direct competitor?

The horizontal axis in Figure 8.1 refers to maximum acceptable price and the vertical axis to unit cost. Both are expressed in terms of percentages compared to the priority competitor:

- The productivity dimension enables a brand or firm to position itself in terms of cost advantage or disadvantage compared to its priority competitor. A positioning in the upper part of the axis reveals a cost disadvantage and in the lower part a cost advantage.
- The market power dimension describes the position of the brand by reference to its buyers' maximum acceptable price compared to that of its priority competitor. A positioning to the right indicates a high brand strength and the capacity to charge a premium price. A positioning to the left suggests, on the other hand, that the brand has a weak market power and that it

has to adopt a price lower than its priority competitors to be accepted by the market.

In Figure 8.1, the bisecting line separates the favourable and unfavourable positions. Four different competitive positioning can be identified:

1. The positioning in the upper-left quadrant is disastrous since the brand accumulates handicaps. The brand has a cost disadvantage over its priority competitor and has no market power to offset this cost handicap through a price premium. Sooner or later, a divestment or retreat strategy will have to be adopted.
2. The lower-right quadrant is the ideal situation where the brand would have the best of both worlds: low cost due to high productivity and high market-acceptable price due to high market power. Situations rarely observed in the real world, these two positionings imply two different corporate cultures.
3. The lower-left quadrant depicts the positioning of a brand having a cost advantage but a weak market power compared to its direct competitor. The strategy to adopt here is to target price sensitive market segments with a modest operational marketing budget or to subcontract operational marketing, for instance, to a large retail chain.
4. The upper-right quadrant describes a situation frequently observed in highly industrialised countries: the firm has a cost handicap but has a market power sufficiently strong to offset the cost handicap through a higher market-acceptable price. The strategy here is to search for higher added value and/or higher quality activities that will justify a price premium in the eyes of the buyer.

BOX 8.1

IMPLEMENTATION PROBLEM: HOW TO CREATE VALUE BY REDUCING CUSTOMER'S COSTS?

- Lower required rate of usage of the product.
- Lower delivery, installation or financing costs.
- Lower direct costs of using the product such as labour, fuel, maintenance, required space.
- Lower indirect costs of using the product.
- Lower customer's costs in activities unconnected with the product.
- Lower risk of failure and lower expected cost of failure.

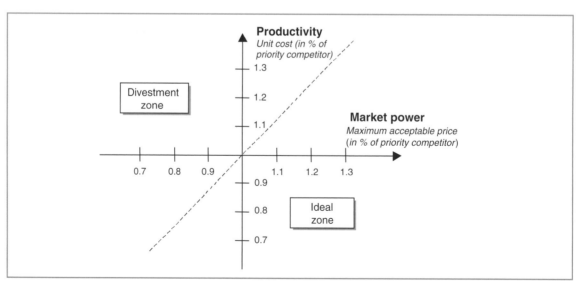

Figure 8.1   Competitive advantage analysis
Source: Authors.

BOX 8.2

IMPLEMENTATION PROBLEM: HOW TO MEASURE COMPETITIVE SUPERIORITY?

Customer metrics	Measured by
Relative satisfaction	Customer preference or satisfaction relative to average for market/competitors: the competitive benchmark should be stated.
Commitment	Index of switch ability (or some similar measure of retention, loyalty, purchase intent or bonding).
Relative perceived quality	Perceived quality satisfaction relative to average for market/competitors(s): the competitive benchmark should be stated.
Relative price	Market share (value) / market share volume.
Availability	Distribution for example, value-weighted percentage of retail outlets carrying the brand.

Source: Ambler (2000, p. 63).

The purpose of measuring business competitiveness is to allow the firm to find its own position on these axes and deduce its strategic priority objectives for each of the products of its portfolio.

To find its position along the market power axis, the firm will use information provided by brand image studies which, as seen in Chapter 4, help measure the brand's perceived value and estimate price elasticity. As for the productivity axis, the experience law can be used when applicable or else the firm can use information provided by the marketing intelligence unit which has, among other things, the task of monitoring competition. As illustrated in Box 8.2, for many market metrics, the question is not how satisfied the customer is, but how this compares with how satisfied the competitors' customers are.

8.2.4. Competitive advantage based on core competencies

A more general way to look at the type of competitive advantage refers to the core competency concept developed by Prahalad and Hamel (1990). A core competence is a special skill or technology that creates unique customer value (see Exhibit 8.2). A company's specialised capabilities are largely embodied in the collective knowledge of its people and the organised procedures that shape the way employees interact. These core competencies can be viewed as the roots of a firm's competitive advantage.

When appropriately applied, core competencies can create sustainable sources of competitive advantage over time that are implementable in other seemingly unrelated fields of business. To be sustainable, a core competency should:

- provide significant and appreciable value to customers relative to competitor offerings;
- be difficult for competitors to imitate or procure in the market, thereby creating competitive barriers to entry;
- enable a company to access a wide variety of seemingly unrelated markets by combining skills and technologies across traditional business units.

Identifying and developing core competencies involves isolating key abilities within the organisation and then honing them into a definition of the organisation's key strengths (Rigby, 1997). As reviewed in the following chapter, successful diversification strategies are often based on core competencies.

8.2.5. Operational versus strategic competitive advantage

The search for a sustainable competitive advantage is at the core of the strategy formulation process and is one of the main responsibilities of strategic marketing. A company can outperform rivals only if it can establish a difference that it can preserve. In this perspective a distinction can be made here between operational and strategic competitive advantages (Porter, 1996).

Gaining an operational competitive advantage (see Figure 8.2) in a given reference market means

EXHIBIT 8.2

FOUR EXAMPLES OF CORE COMPETENCIES

- 3M's competency was founded originally on sticky tape. Over time it has built from this unique bundle of skills in substrates, coatings, adhesives and various ways of combining them. These core competencies have allowed it to enter and excel in businesses as diverse as 'Post-it' notes, magnetic tape, photographic film, pressure-sensitive tapes and coated abrasives.
- Casio's core competencies are in miniaturisation, microprocessor design, material science and ultra-thin precision casings, it applies the same skills in its miniature card calculators, pocket TVs, musical instruments and digital watches.

- Canon (the number one in photography), thanks to its ability to combine and integrate optical and micro-electronic technologies and high precision mechanics, was able to move from photography to video, low price photocopiers, colour photocopiers, ink jet printers, laser printers and fax.
- Bic's core competence is the distribution of moulded plastic disposable mass consumer products (pens, lighters, razors).

Source: Authors.

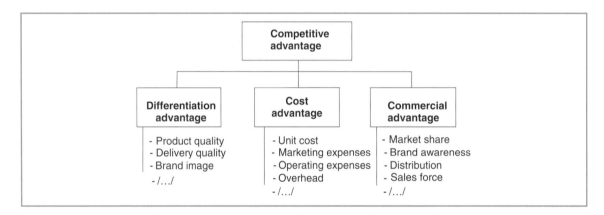

Figure 8.2   Sources of operational competitive advantage
Source: Adapted from Best 2003.

performing similar activities better than rivals perform them. It might mean:

- being better by offering a higher quality or same quality at a lower price;
- being better by offering a product reducing customers' costs;
- being better by offering lower cost and better quality at the same time;
- being faster in meeting customers' products or services;
- being closer to the customer and providing assistance in use.

Constant improvements in operational effectiveness are necessary to achieve superior profitability, but it is not usually sufficient. Every department within the firm has this responsibility. Staying ahead of rivals on the basis of operational effectiveness becomes harder every day because of the rapid diffusion of best practices. Competitors can quickly imitate management techniques, new technologies, input improvements and superior ways to meet customers' needs.

In contrast, gaining a strategic competitive advantage is about being different. It means (a) deliberately choosing a different set of activities from rivals or (b) performing similar activities but in a different way, to deliver a unique mix of values. Ikea, the global furniture retailer based in Sweden, has chosen to perform activities differently from rivals. Similarly, for Ryan-Air in the airline market.

In the search for a competitive advantage, it is important to make a clear distinction between these two types of competitive advantage, because a strategic positioning is likely to be more sustainable in the long term than an operational competitive advantage.

8.3. Forces driving industry competition

The notion of extended rivalry, due to Porter (1982), is based on the idea that a firm's ability to exploit a competitive advantage in its reference market depends not only on the direct competition it faces, but also on the role

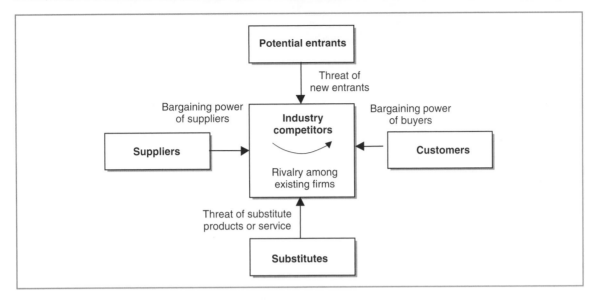

Figure 8.3   The forces driving industry competition
Source: Porter (1980).

played by rival forces, such as potential entrants, substitute products, customers and suppliers.

The first two forces constitute a direct threat; the other two an indirect threat, because of their bargaining power. It is the combined interplay of these five competitive forces, described in Figure 8.3, which determines the profit potential of a product market. Clearly, the dominant forces determining the competitive climate vary from one market to another. Using Porter's analysis, we will examine the role of these four external competitive forces successively. The analysis of rivalry between direct competitors will be left for later in this chapter.

8.3.1. Threat of new entrants

Potential competitors, likely to enter a market, constitute a threat that the firm must limit and protect itself against, by creating barriers to entry (See Box 8.3). Potential entrants can be identified as follows:

- Firms outside the product market which could easily surmount the barriers to entry.
- Firms for which entry would represent a clear synergy.
- Firms for which entry is the logical conclusion of their strategy.
- Clients or suppliers who can proceed to backward or forward integration (Porter, 1980, p. 55).

The importance of the threat depends on the barriers to entry and on the strength of reaction that the potential

entrant can expect. Possible barriers to entry are as follows:

- Economies of scale: these force the entrant to come in at large scale or else risk having to bear cost disadvantage.
- Legal protection obtained through patents, as we have seen in the case of the conflict between Kodak and Polaroid.
- Product differentiation and brand image, leading to a high degree of loyalty among existing customers who show little sensitivity to newcomers.
- Capital requirements, which can be considerable, not only for production facilities, but also for things like inventories, customer credit, advertising expenses, start-up losses, and so on.
- Switching costs, that is, one-time real or psychological costs that the buyer must bear to switch from an established supplier's product to that of a new entrant.
- Access to distribution channels: distributors might be reluctant to give shelf space to a new product; sometimes the new entrant is forced to create an entirely new distribution channel.
- Experience effects and the cost advantage held by the incumbent, which can be very substantial, especially in highly labour-intensive industries.

Other factors which may influence the entrant's degree of determination are the expectation of sharp reactions from existing firms and of the dissuasive nature of the

---

BOX 8.3

IMPLEMENTATION PROBLEM: HOW TO SPOT POTENTIAL COMPETITORS?

- Actively monitor notable market activities beyond your direct competitors.
- Take note of interesting mergers, acquisitions or alliances that may suggest threats or new business growth opportunities for your own company.
- Identify and track alliances and collaborations offering new products and services that change or shake up the industry.
- Ponder corporate alliances or mergers that are unexpected, surprising or combine firms from different industries.

- Look for pattern of alliances, mergers or acquisitions that combines apparently diverse product lines to create other value-added competences of offerings.
- Watch for newly emerging companies with proprietary new technologies, whose products or services may have broad applications.
- Form a cross-functional monitoring team or task force to search and evaluate alliances, mergers and acquisitions.

Source: Fox (2001).

---

retaliations they may organise. The following factors will in particular influence the degree of deterrence in the response:

- A history and reputation of aggressiveness vis-à-vis new entrants.
- Degree of commitment of established firms in the product market.
- Availability of substantial resources to fight back.
- Possibility of retaliation in the entrant's home market.

Put together, sustainable entry barriers and the ability to respond are the elements that determine the entry-deterring price.

8.3.2. Threats of substitute products

Substitute products are products that can perform the same function for the same customer groups, but are based on different technologies. Referring back to the distinctions made in Chapter 5, substitute products go hand in hand with the definition of a market which is the 'set of all technologies for a given function and a given customer group'. Such products are a permanent threat because a substitution is always possible. The threat can be intensified, for instance, as a result of a technological change that modifies the substitute's quality/price as compared to the reference product market.

The price decline in the microcomputer market has contributed to stimulate the development of electronic communication at the expense of traditional typographic equipment. Desktop publishing is taking over and many documents are now printed in-house and not subcontracted to outside printing companies.

Prices of substitute products impose a ceiling on the price firms in the product market can charge. The more attractive the price–performance alternative offered by

substitutes, the stronger the limit on the industry's ability to raise prices (Porter, 1982, p. 25).

This phenomenon is observable, for instance, in the market of primary energy sources. The successive increases of oil prices have stimulated the development of alternative energy resources like solar and nuclear energy.

Clearly, substitute products that deserve particular attention are those that are subject to trends improving their price–performance trade-off with the industry's product. Moreover, in such a comparison, special attention needs to be given to switching costs (real or psychological), which can be very high and, as far as the customer is concerned, offset the impact of the price differential.

Identifying substitute products is not always straightforward. The aim is to search systematically for products that meet the same generic need or perform the same function. This can sometimes lead to industries far removed from the main industry.

For example, in the home interior decoration market, the alternative technologies are: paint, wallpaper, textile, panels of wood, and so on. In the goods transportation market, the alternative technologies are: air, road, rail and water.

It would be insufficient simply to look at the common practices in the major customer groups, because the information risks appear too late. Therefore, it is necessary to have a permanent monitoring system of major technological developments in order to be able to adopt a proactive rather than a reactive behaviour. In this perspective, the concept of *solution-market* presented in Chapter 5 is useful because it induces the firm to define upfront its reference market in terms of the alternative technologies susceptible to perform the same core service to the buyer.

8.3.3. Bargaining power of customers

Customers have a bargaining power vis-à-vis their suppliers. They can influence an activity's potential profitability by forcing the firm to cut prices, demanding more extensive services, better credit facilities or even by playing one competitor against another. The degree of influence depends on a number of conditions (Porter, 1980, pp. 24–7):

- The customer group is concentrated and purchases large volumes relative to seller sales; this is so for large distributors, and, in France, for large shopping centres.
- The products that customers purchase from the industry represent a significant fraction of their own costs, which drives them to bargain hard.
- The products purchased are standard or undifferentiated. Customers are sure that they can always find alternative suppliers.
- The customers' switching costs, or costs of changing suppliers, are few.
- Customers pose a credible threat of backward integration, and are therefore dangerous potential entrants.
- The customers have full information about demand, actual market prices and even supplier costs.

These conditions apply equally to consumer goods as well as industrial goods; they also apply to retailers as against wholesalers, and to wholesalers as against manufacturers. Such a situation, where buyers' bargaining power is very high, is seen in Belgium and France in the food sector, where large-scale distribution is highly concentrated and can even dictate its terms to manufacturers.

These considerations underline the fact that the choice of buyer groups to target is a crucial strategic decision. A firm can improve its competitive position by a customer selection policy, whereby it has a well-balanced portfolio of customers and thus avoids any kind of dependence on the buyer group.

8.3.4. Bargaining power of suppliers

Suppliers can exert bargaining power because they can raise the prices of their deliveries, reduce product quality or limit quantities sold to a particular customer. Powerful suppliers can thereby squeeze profitability out of an industry unable to recover cost increases in its own prices.

> For instance, the increase in the price of basic steel products, imposed in Europe between 1980 and 1982 by the Davignon plan, contributed to profit erosion in the downstream steel transformation sector. Intense competition prevented firms in this sector from raising their prices.

The conditions making suppliers powerful are similar to those making customers powerful (Porter, 1980):

- The supplier is in a monopoly position.
- The supplier group is dominated by a few companies and is more concentrated than the industry it sells to.
- It is not facing other substitute products for sale to the industry.
- The firm is not an important customer of the supplier.
- The supplier's product is an important input to the buyer's business.
- The supplier group has differentiated its products or has built up switching costs to lock the buyers in.
- The supplier group poses a credible threat of forward integration.

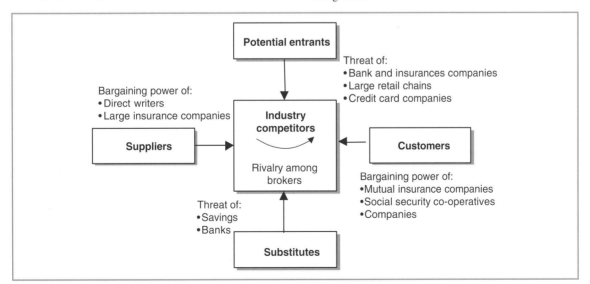

Figure 8.4   Competition analysis: the private insurance brokers market
Source: MDA Consulting Group, Brussels.

These four factors of external competition, together with rivalry among existing firms within the same product market, determine a firm's potential profitability and market power.

By way of illustration, the results of a competitive structure analysis in the private insurance brokerage market are presented in Figure 8.4.

8.3.5. Identification of Competitors

The five forces model is helpful for scanning the global competitive landscape of the reference market, but does not permit to identify the most dangerous competitors. There may be a temptation for management to pay attention only to competitors who display a product or technology overlap, because these competitors are salient. Note that the reference market definition in terms of solution sought and the macro-segmentation approach described in Chapter 6 should help avoid this myopic approach of competition definition. The diagram presented in Figure 8.5 can help management to maximise their awareness of competitive threats and to classify the types of competition they face or will face in a near future.

In Figure 8.4, the vertical axis measures the degree (low-high) to which a given competitor overlaps with the focal firm in terms of customers' needs served. This is consistent with the solution market definition used in Chapter 6 and recognises that competition may include firms that do not share the same technological platform (e.g. paint versus wall paper for home interior decoration).

The horizontal axis refers – also at two levels – to resource similarity as the extent to which a given competitor possesses strategic resources and capabilities

comparable to those of the focal firm. We can therefore identify four types of competitors.

1. The *direct competitors*, that is, the firms that score high in terms of both market needs and technological platform.
2. The *potential competitors* scoring high in terms of technological platform but that not presently serving the same market needs.
3. The *substitute competitors* that serve the same market needs than the focal firm but with different types of resources and/or technologies.
4. The *sleeping competitors* that constitute presently a low threat, having different market targets and technologies.

This framework can be useful not only for increasing the awareness of various dimensions of the competitive landscape, but it can be used to track the movements of potential competitors over time.

8.4. Competitive advantage based on market power

The intensity and form of the competitive struggle between direct rivals in a product market vary according to the nature of the actual competitive structure. This defines the degree of interdependence between rivals and the extent of market power held by each competitor. To analyse a particular market situation, it is convenient to refer to the various competitive structures proposed by economists, for which numerous theoretical and empirical studies exist. Four competitive structures are generally distinguished: pure (or perfect) competition, oligopoly, monopolistic

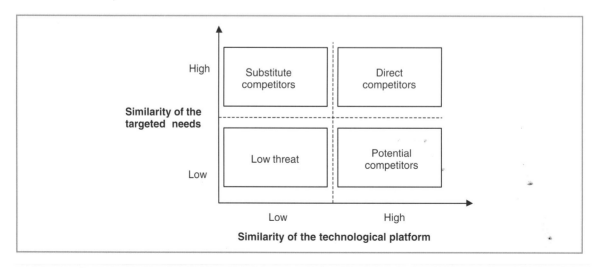

Figure 8.5   Competitors' identification matrix
Source: Adapted from Bergen and Peteraf (2002).

(or imperfect) competition and monopoly. We will examine each of these alternatives successively and describe the expected competitive behaviour in each case.

8.4.1. Pure or perfect competition

Perfect competition is characterised by the existence in the market of a large number of sellers facing a large number of buyers. Neither of the two groups is powerful enough to influence prices. Products have clearly defined technical characteristics, are perfect substitutes and sell at the market price, which is strictly determined by the interplay between supply and demand. In this kind of market, sellers have no market power whatsoever, and their behaviour is not affected by their respective actions. Key features are therefore the following:

- Large number of sellers and buyers.
- Undifferentiated and perfectly substitutable products.
- Complete absence of market power for each player.

This kind of situation can be seen in industrial markets for unbranded products, and in the commodity markets, such as soft commodities and the minerals and metals market. These are normally organised markets (terminal markets) such as the London Metal Exchange (LME) or the various commodity futures exchanges. In a perfectly competitive market, the interplay between supply and demand is the determining factor. As far as the firm is concerned, price is given (the dependent variable) and the quantity supplied is the action variable of interest.

To improve performance, the firm's only possible courses of action are either to modify its deliveries to the market, or to change its production capacity upward or downward, depending on the market price level. In the short term, it is essential for the firm to keep an eye on competitors' production levels and on new entrants in order to anticipate price movements.

In the long term, it is clearly in the firm's interest to release itself from the anonymity of perfect competition by differentiating its products to reduce substitutability, or by creating switching costs to the buyers in order to create some form of loyalty. One way of achieving this, for example, is to exercise strict quality control accompanied by a branding policy.

A number of countries exporting food products follow this kind of strategy to maintain their product's price and demand levels: Colombian coffee, Spanish oranges, Cape fruits and Chiquita bananas are attempts at this type of differentiation. Table 8.1 shows the price differentials observed for branded and non-branded vegetables.

Another way is to develop, downstream in the industrial chain, higher value-added activities incorporating the commodity, with the objectives of stabilising the level of demand and gaining protection from wild price fluctuations. It is for instance, the strategy followed by the steel industry which diversifies its activity by entering downstream in sectors of transformation of primary steel products such as steel shingles of steel storage equipment.

How to escape from the anonymity of price competition?

This question is relevant for all the basic products labelled 'commodities', that is, standard products sought by customers for their core function at the lowest possible price (Box 8.4). Such is the case for most agricultural products (wheat, corn, coffee, cocoa, sugar, and so on), non-ferrous products (copper, tin, aluminium, cobalt, and so on), chemical and petrochemical products, and also for products such as fruit, concentrated fruit juice, textiles, and so on. For the majority of these commodities, organised markets, or bourses, exist like the LME or the London Commodity Market, where it is the interplay of supply and demand that determines the market price, which is then used as a reference price by the buyers and imposed on the seller.

From the commodity firm's point of view, two steps are required to escape from this competitive stalemate: (a) a systematic search for differentiation opportunities and (b) a fine market segmentation to undercover segments of customers having more demanding purchase criteria.

A commodity is always a bundle of attributes

In approaching a commodity market, it is essential to analyse customers' needs in terms of a 'solution sought'

Table 8.1	Price differentials: branded products versus store brands		
Sun Maid Raisins	$4.47/lb	Store Brand raisins	$3.06/lb
Campbell's Chicken & Stars	$1.69/lb	Store Brand Chicken & Stars	$0.89/lb
Heinz Ketchup	$1.02/lb	Store brand Ketchup	$0.84/lb
Welch's Grape Juice	1.85/qt	Store Brand Grape Juice	$1.30/qt

Source: Stanton and Herbst (2005, p. 10).

BOX 8.4

IMPLEMENTATION PROBLEM: HOW TO ESCAPE FROM THE ANONYMITY OF PRICE COMPETITION?

- A commodity is always a bundle of characteristics or attributes.
- Differentiation opportunities always exist.
- A commodity market is never completely homogeneous.
- Three types of segments always exist: price conscious customers, service customers and commitment-focused customers.

Table 8.2   The search for differentiation opportunities

Value creation	Value delivery mode	
	Through product	Through service
Consistency	Quality control	Reliability
Customisation	Adaptation	Assistance
Convenience	Packaging	Just-in-time

Source: Hill *et al.* (1998).

and not just in terms of quantity to be sold. As explained above, to the customer a product is always a package of benefits or a bundle of attributes (see Figure 4.4 in Chapter 4) comprising, of course, the core service or function, but also peripheral services, necessary or added, which accompany the core service provided by the commodity. In a pure competition market, only the core service is identical from one rival to the other and cannot therefore justify a price premium. But the seller can still differentiate himself from competition through other services or attributes of the bundle, such as services, guarantee, assistance in use, technical support, and so on, and that, not only at the purchase phase, but also at each phase of the cycle 'acquisition–use–maintenance–destruction–recycling' of the commodity.

The problem is to discover what are the sensitive services to which the buyer is likely to respond and at what phase of the cycle. Hence, the importance of a fine market segmentation. As shown in Table 8.2, differentiation opportunities always exist, even in commodity markets, either through value creation or through delivery mode.

Segmentation of a commodity market

In commodity markets, it is common practice to segment their customers by product and consuming industry and not by reference to their purchasing behaviour. In reality, no market is completely homogeneous in terms of customers' needs or expectations and, as explained in Chapter 6, the objective of market behavioural segmentation is to uncover customer(s) group(s) having different purchase criteria, more specific or more demanding, and who would be ready to pay a price higher than the reference market price to obtain exactly what they need.

According to Booz, Allen and Hamilton (in Hill *et al.*, 1998) three types of customers always exist, even in commodity markets: the incorrigibles, the potentials and

the gold standard customers:

1. *The incorrigibles*: also called the price sensitive buyers, are the pure price buyers who treat suppliers as the enemy and focus exclusively on current delivered price. They are primarily concerned with the cost, as the product usually represents a major portion of their total product cost or because their needs are fairly standard. They will switch suppliers for even the slightest price differential. Unfortunately, they constitute half of the market or more. They are not attractive customers but are so prevalent, that no supplier can seriously think about refusing them.

2. *The potentials*: or the service customers, also place a high emphasis on pure price, but are occasionally willing to entertain the notion of selective relationships involving certain products or services. Customers in this segment, representing 30–45 per cent of the market, have some degree of interest in partnering in certain circumstances for reducing delivery costs, to avoid supply interruptions or for specific industrial applications. Once it is possible to move the dialogue beyond delivery price, the potential for differentiation exists.

3. *The gold standard customers*: also called the commitment-focused customers, value long-standing relationships through which superior product applications can be developed and employed in their own products and processes. They will pay a premium price for offerings that deliver true value in terms of process enhancement, cost reduction or benefits to end-user. They typically represent a small portion of the total market, anywhere from 5 to 25 per cent.

Booz, Allen and Hamilton (in Hill *et al.*, 1998) reports that one study in steel strapping found that 8 per cent of the customers fit into this last category, while another piece of research carried out by BAH found that segment ranging as high as 22 per cent in some chemical markets.

While most wheat buyers require wheat to meet only two or three specifications, demanding buyers such as the Japanese may have a list of 20 requirements. Using its computerised capacity to monitor the precise content

Table 8.3   How steel end-users choose suppliers

Purchase criteria used by buyers	Segments: buyers choose suppliers by		
	Price ($n = 113$)	Service ($n = 91$)	Commitment ($n = 96$)
Lowest price	3.4	2.3	2.5
Emergency response	3.4	3.7	3.2
On-time delivery	3.6	3.8	3.2
Responsive inside sales	2.9	3.5	2.8
Responsive after sales	2.3	2.3	2.3
Short lead time	3.1	3.3	2.5
Technical support	2.2	2.3	2.8
Industry commitment	2.9	2.2	2.7
Investment in mill	2.0	1.8	2.4
EDI links	1.4	1.4	1.9
Investment in R&D	1.4	1.9	2.4

Note: Criteria rated on a scale of 1 (not important) to 4 (very important).

Source: Schorsch (1994).

of the wheat in all 1500 of Australia's silos, the Australian Wheat Board track down the hard-to-find wheat the Japanese demand. Across all their customers, the Board earn a high price realisation of $2 a ton, a significant advantage in a low margin business. (Hill *et al*., 1998, p. 29)

This example (the steel industry) reveals differentiation opportunities for the seller who can propose offerings having superior value to the buyer. An interesting observation made in this steel survey reported by McKinsey (Schorsch, 1994) is that each industry segment contains price, service and commitment buyers (Table 8.3). Performance requirements simply do not correlate with industry segments (car customers, pipe and tube makers, construction, and so on).

8.4.2. Oligopoly

Oligopoly is a situation where the number of competitors is low or a few firms are dominant. As a result, rival firms are highly interdependent. In markets concentrated in this way, each firm knows well the forces at work and the actions of one firm are felt by the others, who are inclined to react. Therefore, the outcome of a strategic action depends largely on whether or not competing firms react.

The more undifferentiated the products of existing firms, the greater the dependence between them will be; in this case we talk about *undifferentiated oligopoly*, as opposed to *differentiated oligopoly*, where goods have significant distinctive qualities of value to the buyers.

Oligopolistic situations tend to prevail in product markets having reached the maturity phase of their life cycle, where primary demand is stagnant and non-expansible. As holds the 'rule of three' (Sheth and Sisodia, 2002), in this type of markets there is only room for three full generalists along several specialists.

The mechanisms of a price war

In undifferentiated oligopoly, products are perceived as 'commodities' and buyers' choices are mainly based on price and the service rendered. These conditions are therefore ripe for intense price competition, unless a dominant firm can impose a discipline and force a leading price. This situation is one of price leadership, in which the dominant firm's price is the reference price used by all competitors. On the other hand, if price competition does develop, it generally leads to reduced profitability for everyone, especially if primary demand is non-expansible. A price war then gets under way, as follows:

- A price cut initiated by one firm creates an important market share movement due to buyers attracted by the reduced price.
- The firm's market share increases. Other firms feel this immediately, given that their own shares drop. They begin to adopt the same price cut to overturn the movement.
- Price equality between rivals is restored, but at a lower level, which is less profitable for all.
- Since primary demand is non-expansible, the price cut has not contributed to increasing the market size.

Lack of co-operation or discipline causes everyone's situation to deteriorate. In a non-expansible market, competition becomes a zero-sum game. Firms seeking to increase sales can only achieve it at the expense of direct competitors. As a result, competition is more aggressive than when there is growth, where each firm has the possibility of increasing its sales by simply growing at the same pace as primary demand, which is keeping its market share constant.

Alternative competitive behaviours

In a stagnant oligopolistic market, explicit consideration of competitors' behaviour is an essential aspect of strategy development. Competitive behaviour refers to the attitude adopted by a firm in its decision-making process, with regard to its competitors' actions and reactions. The attitudes observed in practice can be classified into five typical categories:

1. *Independent behaviour*: is observed when competitors' actions and/or reactions are not taken into account, either implicitly or explicitly, in the firm's decisions. This attitude is observed in particular with regard to operational decisions, and is sometimes seen even in the case of strategic choices in firms with a dominant market position.

2. *Co-operative behaviour*: corresponds to a confident or complacent attitude which seeks, tacitly or explicitly, understanding or collusion rather than systematic confrontation. Tacit agreement is frequently seen between medium-sized firms; explicit or cartel agreement, on the other hand, takes place more between large firms in oligopolistic markets which are not subject to competition regulations or which are controlled very little in this respect. Anti-trust officials in the United States and the Competition Commission in the European Union are actively pursuing cartel agreements and can impose severe fines and prison sentences (see Exhibit 8.3).

3. *Follower behaviour*: is based on an explicit consideration of competitors' actions; it consists of adapting one's own decisions to the observed decisions of competitors, without, however, anticipating their subsequent reactions. If all existing competitors adopt this kind of behaviour, a succession of mutual adaptations is observed, until stability is achieved.

4. *Leader behaviour*: is a more sophisticated behaviour. It consists of anticipating competitors' reactions to the firm's own decisions, assuming they have the previous type of behaviour; here, the firm is assumed to know its rivals' reaction functions and to incorporate it when elaborating its strategy. As strategic marketing develops, it is seen ever more frequently in oligopolistic markets, where competition laws are strictly enforced.

5. *Aggressive or warfare behaviour*: also consists in anticipating competitors' reactions to the firm's decisions. But in this case, rivals' behaviour is assumed to be such that they always adopt the strategy most harmful to their adversaries. This type of behaviour is mainly observed in oligopolistic markets where primary demand is stagnant and any one firm's gains must be at the expense of the others. This kind of situation is analysed in game theory as a 'zero sum' game, with optimal strategy being the one with the lowest risk of loss.

The most frequent behaviour in undifferentiated oligopoly is of the follower or leader kind. It is, however, not rare to observe aggressive behaviour of the kind described in game theory, especially as regards price decisions, with the risk of leading to price wars that are generally harmful to all.

EXHIBIT 8.3

ANTI-TRUST LAWS IN ACTION

Two top European companies have been fined a record $725 million in the United States for their part in a 9-year conspiracy to control the market of vitamins. A former executive was jailed for 4 months and fined $100,000 for his role in the cartel. The cartel lasted almost a decade and involved a highly sophisticated and elaborate conspiracy to control everything about the sale of these products. The companies acted as if they were working for the same business, referred by executives as Vitamins Inc. Executives met once a year for a summit to fix their annual budget, setting prices, carving geographic markets and setting volumes of sales. The summit was followed by monitoring meetings, quarterly reviews and frequent correspondence. The European Commission was also investigating whether pharmaceutical companies had been involved in a vitamin price fixing cartel.

Source: Financial Times (1999).

Marketing warfare

In industrialised economies, oligopolistic situations are frequent. In many industrial sectors, firms face each other with weakly differentiated products, in stagnant and saturated markets, where one firm's gains are necessarily another's losses. A key factor in success is thwarting competitors' actions. This kind of competitive climate obviously breeds the adoption of marketing warfare, which puts the destruction of the adversary at the centre of preoccupations. Kotler and Singh (1981), Ries and Trout (1986), Durö and Sandström (1988) have taken the analogy with military strategy even further and proposed various typologies of competitive strategies directly inspired from von Clausewitz (1908). As put by Ries and Trout (1986, p. 7):

> The true nature of marketing is not serving the customer, it is outwitting, outflanking and outfighting your competitors.

This point of view is in conflict with the market-driven orientation presented in Chapter 2, which suggests that a balance should be maintained between customer and competitor orientations. What is the advantage, indeed, of beating competitors in products that the customer does not want?

The competitive reaction matrix

Firms compete with one another by emphasising different elements of the marketing mix and by insisting differently on each component of the mix. The competitive reaction matrix presented in Table 8.4 is a useful instrument for analysing alternative action–reaction patterns among two competing companies (Lambin, 1976, pp. 22–7). The matrix might include two brands, the studied brand and its priority competitor, and three or four components of the marketing mix, such as price, media advertising, promotion or product quality.

In Table 8.4 the horizontal rows designate the actions initiated by our brand A. The alternative actions might be to cut price, increase advertising or improve quality. The responses of brand B, the direct competitor, are represented by the vertical columns. The coefficients in the matrix are the reaction probabilities of brand B reacting to brand A's move.

On the diagonal we have the direct reaction probabilities, or the likelihood of brand B responding to a move of brand A with the same marketing instrument, that is, meeting a price cut with a price cut. Off-diagonal, we have the indirect reaction elasticity, or the probabilities of brand B responding to brand A with another marketing instrument, for example, meeting a price cut with increased advertising. These reaction elasticities can be estimated by reference to past behaviour or by seeking management's judgement concerning the strengths and weaknesses of competition. Once the matrix is developed, management can review each potential marketing action in the light of probable competitor reactions. The entries of the matrix are probabilities, as in Table 8.4, their horizontal sum must be equal to one.

> For example, if management considers that there is a 70 per cent chance that competition will meet our price cut, but only a 20 per cent chance that it will meet a quality increase, it might consider that a quality increase programme will help more to develop a unique marketing approach than the price cut, since it is less likely to be imitated.

The competitive matrix is useful in helping to develop a distinctive marketing approach to the market and to anticipate competitors' reactions. More columns can be added, representing other marketing instruments. Delayed responses can also be analysed. For an example of an application in the electric razor market, see Lambin et al. (1975).

Table 8.4   Competitive reaction matrix

Brand A's Actions	Competing brand B's reactions		
	Price (p)	Advertising (a)	Quality (x)
Price	Pp,p*	Pp,a	Pp,x
Advertising	Pa,p	Pa,a	Pa,x
Quality	Px,p	Px,a	Px,x

P = probability
* The first subscript is for the brand initiating the move; the second is for the rival's response.
Source: Lambin (1976, p. 24).

Competitors' analysis and monitoring system

The attitude to be adopted towards competitors is central to any strategy. This attitude must be based on a refined analysis of competitors. Porter (1980, p. 47) describes the purpose of analysing competitors as follows:

> The objective of a competitor analysis is to develop a profile of the nature and success of the likely strategy changes each competitor might make, each competitor's probable response to the range of feasible strategic moves other firms could initiate, and each competitor's probable reaction to the array of industry changes and broader environmental shifts that might occur.

There are several broad areas of interest that constitute the structure to guide the collection and analysis of information about competitors. The relevant questions are the following:

- What are the competitors' major objectives?
- What is the current strategy being employed to achieve the objectives?
- What are the capabilities of rivals to implement their strategies?
- What are their likely future strategies?

Together, these areas of information collection and analysis (see also Box 8.5) compose a fairly complete picture of the competitors' activities. Some companies have discovered the importance of competitor analysis. Some examples are given below:

- IBM has a commercial analysis department with thousands of branch office representatives responsible for reporting information about the competition.
- Texas Instruments has employees who analyse government contracts won by competitors to discern their technological strengths.
- Citicorp has an executive with the title 'manager of competitive intelligence'.
- McDonald's distributes a Burger King and Wendy's Competitive Action Package to its store managers.

Strong competitive interdependence in a product market is not very attractive, because it limits the firm's freedom of action. To escape it, the firm can either try to differentiate itself from rivals, or seek new product markets through creative market segmentation.

8.4.3. Imperfect or monopolistic competition

Monopolistic competition is halfway between competition and monopoly. There are many competitors whose market powers are evenly distributed. But their products are differentiated in the sense that, from the customer's point

---

BOX 8.5

IMPLEMENTATION PROBLEM: QUESTIONS TO BE ADDRESSED IN A COMPETITORS MONITORING SYSTEM

- Who are the priority competitors?
- What are competitor's mains strengths and weaknesses?
- What type of competitive advantage do we have over priority competitors?
- What is the current strategy of priority competitors?
- How are priority competitors performing financially?
- What proactive and reactive competitive actions can be expected?

---

of view, they possess significantly distinct characteristics and are perceived as such by the whole product market. Differentiation may take different forms. For example, the taste of a drink, a particular technical characteristic, an innovative combination of features which provides the possibility of a variety of different uses, quality and extent of customer services, a lower cost of utilisation, the distribution channel, power of brand image, and so on. According to Chamberlin (1933/1962, p. 56), a product is differentiated,

> If any significant basis exist for distinguishing the goods (or services) from one seller from those of another. Such a basis may be real or fancied, so long as it is of any importance whatsoever to buyers, and leads to a preference for one variety of the product over another?

Monopolistic competition is therefore founded on a *differentiation strategy* designed to generate on external competitive advantage.

Conditions for successful differentiation

For a differentiation strategy to be successful, a number of conditions need to be present:

- The differentiation should provide something that is *unique*, beyond simply offering a low price.
- The element of uniqueness must represent some *value to customers*.
- This value can either represent a *better performance* (higher satisfaction), or *reduced cost*.
- The value to buyers must be high enough for them to be prepared to pay a *price premium* to benefit from it.
- The element of differentiation must be *sustainable*; in other words, other rivals should not be able to imitate it immediately.

- The price premium paid by buyers must *exceed the cost supplement* borne by the firm to produce and maintain the element of differentiation.

Finally, in so far as the element of differentiation is not very apparent and is unknown by the market, the firm must produce *signals* to make it known.

Benefits of successful differentiation

The effect of differentiation is to give the firm some degree of *market power*, because it generates preferences, customer loyalty and lower price sensitivity. The result is a sort of 'mini-monopoly'. The customer's bargaining power is thus partially neutralised. Differentiation also protects the firm from rival attacks, given that as a result of the element of differentiation, substitution between products is reduced. The monopolistic firm is relatively independent in its actions vis-à-vis its rivals (Exhibit 8.4).

> Differentiation partially insulates sellers from ruinous cutthroat price competition. Tag Heuer, for example, the Swiss seller of upscale sports watches, does not tremble when Timex cuts prices on sport watches. Neither Nike, when faced with a price reduction in no-name, sell-them-out-of-bins sneakers. Differentiation exerts control over prices by reducing the direct substitutability of once-similar products. The true beauty of differentiation is that it allows consumers to elect to pay higher prices. (Schnaars, 1998, p. 35)

Finally, it also helps the firm to defend itself better against suppliers and substitute products. This is the typical competitive situation that strategic marketing seeks to create.

The importance/performance matrix presented in Figure 8.6 provides a good illustration of a successful differentiation strategy. The matrix is based on a survey conducted among the customers of three competing brands (brands A, B and C). Brand A is the leader with the highest market share and is perceived by customers as performing better than its competitors on four criteria out of five, despite the fact that brand A is the most expensive.

In monopolistic competition, the firm offers a differentiated product and thus holds an external competitive advantage. This 'market power' places it in a protected position, and allows the firm to earn profits above the market average. Its strategic aim is therefore to exploit this preferential demand, while keeping an eye on the value and duration of the element of differentiation.

8.4.4. Monopoly

This type of competitive structure is a limiting case, as for perfect competition. A single producer facing a large number of buyers dominates the market. Its product is therefore, for a limited period of time, without any direct competitor in its category. This kind of situation is observed in the introductory stage of a product's life cycle, namely in emerging industries characterised by high technology innovations.

If monopoly exists, the *innovative firm* has a market power that in principle is substantial. In reality, new entrants, who are attracted by the possibility of growth and profits, rapidly threaten this power. The *foreseeable duration of monopoly* then becomes an essential factor. It will depend on the innovation's power and the existence of

---

EXHIBIT 8.4

THE SEARCH FOR DIFFERENTIATION IDEAS

A differentiation strategy gives the firm the opportunity to claim its difference with its direct competitors. This strategy makes it possible, at a same price or at a higher price, to increase market share or to keep it unchanged. This strategy is feasible only if some distance exists on one or several important product attributes compared to competition. Chetochine (1997, p. 141) suggests four differentiation dimensions susceptible to create that distance vis-à-vis direct rivals.

A product or service can be different because it has one or several of the following innovative features: reformulating, simplifying, accelerating or improving.

- Reformulating: a product or service based on another technology or on another way to proceed, even if it produces similar results at the same price (phone banking).

- Simplifying: a product that saves efforts, steps or energy (the software Windows).
- Accelerating: a product that generates time savings compared to traditional products (the self-scanning system in supermarkets).
- Improving: a product providing to the user better service or a better performance (Pentium in microcomputers).

A product can distance itself from rivals on several dimensions. Phone banking, for example, is at the same time a new procedure, simplifying and accelerating, but not necessarily better in terms of service quality.

Source: Adapted from Chetochine (1997).

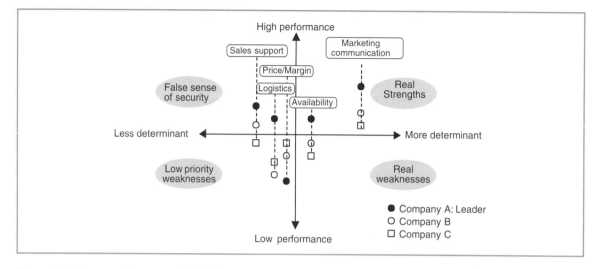

Figure 8.6   Impact of a successful differentiation strategy: the office equipment market

sustainable barriers to entry. A monopoly situation is always temporary, due to the rapid diffusion of technological innovations. We saw in the previous chapter the strategic options and the risks that characterise innovation monopoly. A monopolist is also subject to competition from substitute products.

The logic of *state or government monopolies* is different from that of private firms. It is no longer the logic of profit, but that of public good and public service. Fulfilling these objectives in public services is hard because there is no incentive to adopt a market orientation. On the contrary, the public or state organisation favours the adoption of a self-centred or bureaucratic orientation. This is one of the reasons in favour of the policy of deregulation adopted in many European countries. This problem is dealt with in the field of social marketing, or marketing of non-profit organisations, which has developed quite substantially over the last few years.

8.4.5. Dynamics of competition

Concluding the analysis of competitive forces, it is clear that market power and profit potential can vary widely from one market situation to another. We can thus put two limiting cases aside: one is the case where profit potential is almost zero; in the other case, it is very high. In the first case, which is the case of *perfect competition*, the following situation will be observed:

- Entry into the product market is free.
- Existing firms have no bargaining power as against their clients and suppliers.
- Competition is unrestrained because of the large number of rival firms.
- Products are all similar and there are many substitutes.

The other limiting case, which is close to the case of *monopoly* is where profit potential is extremely high:

- There are powerful barriers that block entry to new competitors.
- The firm has either no competitors or a few weak competitors.
- Customers cannot turn to substitute products.
- Customers do not have enough bargaining power to make prices go down.
- Suppliers do not have enough bargaining power to make increased costs acceptable.

This is the ideal situation for the firm that will have a very strong market power. Market reality is obviously somewhere in-between these two extreme cases. It is the interplay of competitive forces that favours one or other of these situations.

8.5. Competitive advantage based on cost domination

Gaining market power through successful product differentiation is one way to gain a competitive advantage. Another way is to achieve cost domination vis-à-vis competition through better productivity and cost controls. Cost reductions can be achieved in many ways, such as

- scales economies,
- experience effects,
- lower cost of inputs,
- more efficient use of the production capacity,
- More efficient manufacturing technology,
- better product design,
- more efficient organisation.

In many industries, where the value added to the product accounts for a large percentage of the total cost, it has been observed that there is an opportunity to lower costs as a firm gains experience in producing a product.

The observation that there is an *experience effects* was made by Wright (1936) and the Boston Consulting Group (1968), towards the end of the 1960s. They verified the existence of such an effect for more than 2,000 different products, and deduced a law known as the experience law (see Figure 8.7).

This law, which has had great influence on the strategies adopted by some firms, translates and formalises at the firm level what economists study at the aggregate level: improvements in productivity. We will first present the theoretical foundations of the experience law, and then discuss its strategic implications.

8.5.1. The experience law defined

The strategic importance of the experience law stems from the fact that it makes it possible not only to forecast one's own costs, but also to forecast competitors' costs. The law of experience stipulates that:

> The unit cost of value added to a standard product, measured in constant currency, declines by a constant percentage each time the accumulated production doubles.

A certain number of points in this definition deserve further comments:

- The word *'experience'* has a very precise meaning: it designates the cumulative number of units produced and not the number of years since the firm began making the product.

- Thus the *growth of production per period* must not be confused with the growth of experience. Experience grows even if production stagnates or declines.

- The experience law is a *statistical law* and not a natural one; it is an observation, which is statistically verified in some situations, but not always. Costs do not spontaneously go down; they go down if someone pushes them down through productivity improvements.

- Costs must be measured in *constant monetary units*, that is, they must be adjusted for inflation. Inflation can hide the experience effect.

- The experience effect is always stronger during the *launch and growth stages* of a new product's development cycle; later improvements are proportionally weaker and weaker as the product market reaches maturity.

- The experience law applies only to *value-added costs*, that is costs over which the firm has some control, such as costs of transformation, assembly, distribution and service. Recall that the value added is equal to selling price minus input costs: the cost of value added is given by unit cost minus input costs.

In practice, total unit cost is often used as the basis of observation of experience effects, especially because it is more easily accessible than value-added cost. The error introduced in this way is not too high when the cost of value added represents a large proportion of the total unit cost.

8.5.2. Causes of experience effects

Several factors contribute to drive unit costs down the experience curve. They are the improvements adopted by management in the production process as a result of

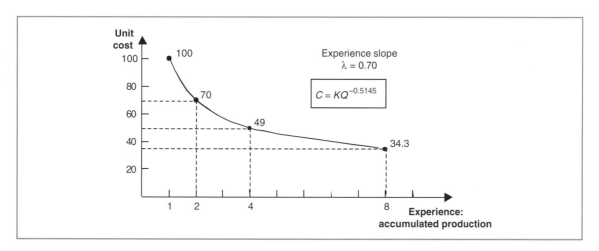

Figure 8.7   Example of an experience curve

learning from accumulated output. Abell and Hammond (1979) have identified seven sources of experience effects:

Labour efficiency. As workers repeat a particular task, they become more dexterous and learn improvements and short cuts that increase their efficiency.

Work specialisation and methods improvements. Specialisation increases worker proficiency at a given task.

New production processes. Process innovations and improvements can be an important source of cost reductions, such as the introduction of robotics or of computer-assisted systems.

Better performance from production equipment. When first designed, a piece of production equipment may have a conservatively rated output. Experience may reveal innovative ways of increasing its output.

Changes in the resource mix. As experience accumulates, a producer can often incorporate different or less expensive resources in the operation. For instance, less skilled workers can replace skilled workers, or automation can replace labour.

Product redesign. Once the firm has a clear understanding of the performance requirements, a product can be redesigned to incorporate less costly materials and resources.

These factors are all under the control of the firm. They are part of the general policy of the firm of productivity improvements aiming at making an equivalent product for less cost or at making a better product for the same cost or a combination of the two. Thus experience per se does not generate cost reductions, but rather provides opportunities for cost reductions. It is up to the management to exploit these opportunities.

8.5.3. Formulation of the experience law

The general expression of the experience curve is presented in Exhibit 8.5.

In Figure 8.7 we can see that the cost of the first unit is €100 and that of the second is €70. When the cumulative quantity has doubled from 1 to 2, unit cost has decreased by 30 per cent; the cost of the fourth unit will therefore be €49, the cost of the eighth unit €34.3, of the sixteenth €24, and so on. In this example, the rate of cost decline is 30 per cent per doubling, and the experience slope is 70 per cent. This corresponds to a cost elasticity of −0.515.

Often, the co-ordinates of an experience curve are expressed on a logarithmic scale, so as to represent it as a straight line. The larger the slope of the curve, the steeper the straight line. Experience slopes observed in practice lie between 0.70 (high degree of experience effect) and 1.00 (zero experience effect). The Boston Consulting Group observes that most experience curves have slopes between 70 and 80 per cent.

For a given firm, the impact of experience effects depends not only on its experience slope, but also on the speed at which experience accumulates. The possibility of reducing costs will be higher in sectors that have fast growing markets; similarly, for a given firm, the potential for cost reduction is high if its market share increases sharply, irrespective of whether or not the reference market is expanding.

EXHIBIT 8.5

THE MATHEMATICS OF EXPERIENCE CURVES

The mathematical expression for the experience curve is as follows,

$$C_p = C_b \cdot \left(\frac{Q_p}{Q_b}\right)^{-\varepsilon}$$

C_p = projected unit cost (p)
C_b = base unit cost (b)
Q_p = projected experience (cumulated volume)
Q_b = base experience (cumulated volume)
ε = constant: unit cost elasticity

Thus, we have,

$$\text{Projected cost} = \text{Base cost} \cdot \left(\frac{\text{Projected experience}}{\text{Base experience}}\right)^{-\varepsilon}$$

The cost elasticity (ε) can be estimated as follows:

$$\frac{C_p}{C_b} = \left(\frac{Q_p}{Q_b}\right)^{-\varepsilon}$$

and hence:

$$\varepsilon = -\frac{\log C_p - \log C_b}{\log Q_p - \log Q_b}.$$

In practice, it is convenient to refer to a doubling of experience. When the ratio of projected experience to base experience is equal to 2, we obtain,

$$\frac{C_p}{C_b} = 2^{-\varepsilon}$$

where, $2^{-\varepsilon}$ is defined as lambda (λ), the slope of the experience curve.

Source: Authors.

8.5.4. Strategic implications of the experience law

The experience law helps us understand how a competitive advantage can exist based on a disparity in unit costs between rival firms operating in the same market, and using the same means of production. The strategic implications of the experience law can be summarised as follows:

- The firm with the largest cumulated production will have the lowest costs, if the experience effect is properly exploited.
- The aggressive firm will try to drive down as rapidly as possible its experience curve, so as to build a cost advantage over its direct competitors.
- The goal is to grow faster than priority competitors, which implies increased relative market share.
- This growth objective is best achieved right at the start, when gains in experience are most significant.
- The most effective way of gaining market share is to adopt a price penetration strategy, whereby the firm fixes price at a level which anticipates future cost reductions.
- This strategy will give the firm above normal profit performance.

Thus, in an experience-based strategy, building market share and penetration pricing are the key success factors for achieving a competitive advantage based on cost domination. The left part of Figure 8.8 illustrates the mechanism of a price penetration policy.

The firm anticipates the movement of its unit cost in terms of cumulative production. It sets itself a target to reach, which implies a faster sales growth than in the reference market, and hence an increase in its relative market share. The selling price, when launching the product, is determined with respect to this anticipated volume. Once the level of experience has been reached, future cost decreases will be reflected in the price to maintain the advantage over priority competitors. The pricing strategy illustrated by the right-hand side figure in Figure 8.8 is more frequently observed because it is less risky: the price is reduced in parallel with the cost decline.

Assessing competitive costs disparities

If cumulative production does lead to the expected cost reduction, and if the dominant firm manages to protect the benefit of the experience it acquires, the experience effect creates an entry barrier to new entrants and a cost advantage for the leader. Firms with low market shares will inevitably have higher costs, and if they fix their prices at the same level as the dominant competitor they have to suffer heavy losses. Furthermore, the firm with the highest market share also enjoys larger cash flows. It can reinvest in new equipment or new processes and thus reinforce its leadership.

To illustrate, let us examine the data in Table 8.5. A comparison is made of movements in unit costs as a function of experience, for experience slopes equal to 70 per cent, 80 per cent and 90 per cent respectively.

Let us consider the case of two firms, A and B, using the same technology and having the same initial conditions; they both have an experience slope of 70 per cent. Firm A is at its first doubling of cumulative production, while firm B is at its fourth. Their costs are 70 and 24, respectively. One can imagine that it might be quite hard for firm A to close this gap, given that it needs to increase its market share quite considerably to achieve cost parity.

Now let us assume that the two firms A and B have the same experience; they are both at their fourth doubling. However, firm A has better exploited cost reduction opportunities and is on an experience curve of 70 per cent, whereas firm B's experience curve has a slope of only 90 per cent; their unit costs are 24 against 66. Here too, it would be difficult to close the gap. Experience effects can therefore create large disparities in costs of firms which are of equal size, but have failed to incorporate this potential equally in productivity improvements.

Experience curves as an early warning system

As mentioned above, the main usefulness of the experience curve is to assess the dynamics of cost competition between two or more firms operating in the same reference

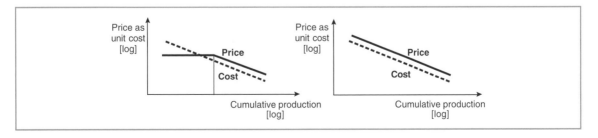

Figure 8.8   Price penetration strategies

Table 8.5   Evolution of unit cost as a function of experience effects

Cumulative production (× 1,000)	Number of doubling	Slope of the experience curve		
		70%	80%	90%
1	—	100	100	100
2	1	70	80	90
4	2	49	64	81
8	3	34	51	73
16	4	24	41	66
32	5	17	33	59
64	6	12	26	48

market and to alert management as to the necessity of making timely strategic changes. The short case presented in Figure 8.9 illustrates this last point.

The chart shows the cost and experience curves of a polyester fibre manufacturer. Prices and costs are expressed in constant $/kg. Prices declined on a 75 per cent experience curve while the slope of the cost curve was only 86 per cent. In this example, management of the plant could have predicted years before that it was too late that the cost and price curves were converging rapidly.

In 1980, the plant made no profit. Its management immediately embarked on a cost reduction programme, but at the same time demand slowed down. The plant was unable to operate at capacity level, which would have made the cost reduction programme effective. Unit costs remained unchanged. The plant closed down in 1983.

Had management read the early warning given by the experience curve analysis, it would have reacted early enough to decide between several possible remedial actions:

- Increase the capacity of the plant to accumulate faster and drive the unit cost down.
- Retool and/or improve the production process to operate on a 75 per cent cost slope that is a slope compatible with the price slope.
- Specialise in special purpose fibres and sell them at a higher price than the normal price for regular polyester fibre.
- Sell the plant while it was profitable or convert it to another production line.

Thus, the experience curves can be used to anticipate future developments and to simulate contemplated strategies. This type of simulation exercise can be very instructive, as the following example shows.

Consider a firm with 6 per cent of a market that is growing at an 8 per cent real growth rate and

whose leader has 24 per cent share. To catch up with the leader's share, our firm would have to grow at a 26 per cent growth rate in nine years, if the leader held its share by growing at the 8 per cent industry rate. That means expanding at over three times the industry rate for nine years, and that sales and capacity have to expand by 640 per cent. (Abell and Hammond, 1979, p. 118).

This is typically a 'mission impossible'. Before embarking on an experience-based strategy, it is essential to calculate the time and the investment required to achieve the objective. Some companies, such as Texas Instruments, use experience curve simulations systematically before pricing a new product.

8.5.5. Limits of the experience law

The experience law is not universally applicable; it holds mainly in sectors where large scale brings economic advantage and in which the process of learning is important (Abernathy and Wayne, 1974). To be more specific, situations in which the experience law is of little relevance are the following:

- Learning potential is low or the part of value-added cost in the total cost is not very significant.
- One competitor has access to a special source of supplies, thus having a cost advantage, which bears no relation to its relative market share.
- Technology changes rapidly and neutralises the experience-based cost advantage.
- The market is not price sensitive.
- There is large potential for product differentiation.

Thus, if a firm is dominated by a competitor having a major cost advantage, two basic strategies can be adopted

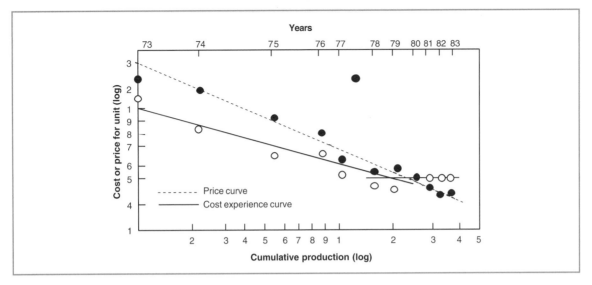

Figure 8.9   The experience curve as an early warning system
Source: Sallenave (1985).

to circumvent the experience advantage:

■ A differentiation strategy offering distinctive features valued by the buyer, who is ready to pay a premium price that would offset the cost handicap.
■ A technological innovation strategy that would place the firm on a new and steeper experience curve, thereby neutralising the cost advantage of the current market leader.

The experience curve gives the firm an operational competitive advantage. As already mentioned, this type of advantage is not always sustainable in the long term because of the rapid diffusion of best practices in a given sector, which enables competitors to easily imitate and neutralise the cost advantage.

8.6. The international competitive advantage

International trade theory has traditionally placed the emphasis on country comparative advantages. The focus was on a country's natural endowments, its labour force and its currency's values as main sources of competitiveness. Recently, economists have turned their attention to the question of how countries, governments and even private industry can alter the conditions within a country to create or reinforce the competitiveness of its firms. The leader in this area of research is Michael Porter (1990).

Industries globalise because shifts in technology, buyer needs and government policy or country infrastructure create major differences in competitive position among firms from different nations or make the advantage of global strategy more significant (Porter, 1990, p. 63).

According to Porter four broad attributes contribute to shape the environment in which local firms compete. These attributes promote or impede the creation of competitive advantage:

1. *Factor conditions.* The nation's position in factors of production, such as skilled labour or infrastructure, are necessary to compete in a given industry. Porter notes that although factor conditions are very important, more so is the ability of a nation to continually create, upgrade and deploy its factors and not just the initial endowment.

2. *Demand conditions.* The nature of home demand for the industry's product or service. The quality of home demand is more important than the quantity of home demand in determining competitive advantage. By quality, Porter means a highly competitive and demanding local market.

3. *Related and supporting industries.* The presence or absence in the nation of supplier industries and related industries that are internationally competitive. A firm that is operating within a mass of related firms and industries gains and maintains advantages through close working relationships, proximity to suppliers, and timeliness of product and information flows.

4. *Firm strategy, structure and rivalry.* The conditions in the nation governing how companies are

created, organised and managed and the nature of domestic rivalry. Porter notes that no one operational strategy is universally appropriate. It depends on the fit and flexibility of what works for that industry in that country at that time.

In the analysis of home demand composition, Porter identifies three home demand characteristics particularly significant in achieving a national competitive advantage:

1. *Large share of home demand.* A nation's firms are likely to gain competitive advantage in global segments that represent a large share of home demand but account for a less significant share in other nations. These relatively large segments receive the greatest and the earliest attention by the nation's firms, but tend to be perceived as less attractive by foreign competitors. The nation's firms may gain advantages in reaping economies of scale.

> A good example is Airbus Industries' entry into commercial airliners. Airbus identified a segment of the European market that had been ignored by Boeing: a relatively large capacity plane for short hauls. Such a need was quite significant in Europe with its numerous capital cities within short flying distances and served by few airlines, in sharp contrast with the US situation.

2. *Sophisticated and demanding buyers.* A nation's firms gain competitive advantage if domestic buyers are, or are among, the world's most sophisticated and demanding buyers for the product or service. Such buyers provide a window into the most advanced buyer needs. Demanding buyers pressurise local firms to meet high standards in terms of product quality and services.

> Japanese pay great attention to writing instruments, because nearly all documents have until recently been hand-written in Japan due to the impracticality of typewriters in reproducing Japanese characters. Penmanship is an important indication of education and culture. Japanese firms have been the innovators and have become world leaders in pens. (Porter, 1990, p. 91)

3. *Anticipatory buyer needs.* A nation's firms gain advantages if the needs of home buyers anticipate those of other nations. This means that home demand provides an early warning indicator of buyer needs that will become widespread.

> Scandinavian concern for social welfare and for the environment tends today to be ahead of that in the United States. Swedish and Danish firms have achieved success in a variety of industries where the heightened environmental concern anticipates foreign needs, such as in water pollution control equipment. (Porter, 1990, p. 92)

The composition of domestic demand is at the root of national advantage. The effect of demand conditions on competitive advantage also depends on other factors presented above. Without strong domestic rivalry, for example, rapid home market growth or a large home market may induce complacency rather than stimulate investment. Without the presence of appropriate supporting industries, firms may lack the ability to respond to demanding home buyers.

CHAPTER SUMMARY

Competitive advantage refers to a product superiority held by the firm over its direct competitor. Competitive advantages can be classified in two main categories: external advantages based on market power due to superior value to the buyer and internal advantages based on productivity generating a cost advantage. A firm's ability to exploit a competitive advantage depends on the strength, not only of direct competition, but also of other rival forces, such as potential entrants, substitute products, customers and suppliers. The intensity of direct competition varies according to the extent of market power held by each competitor. In an oligopoly, the degree of interdependence among rivals is high and explicit consideration of competitors' behaviour is an essential aspect of strategy development. In a monopolistic situation, products are differentiated in a way which represents a value to the buyer, either by reducing their cost or by improving their performance. The effect of product differentiation is to give the firm some degree of market power, customer loyalty and weaker price sensitivity. This is the typical competitive situation that strategic marketing seeks to create for the firm. Another way to gain a competitive advantage is cost domination through better productivity and cost controls. In many industries, there is an opportunity to lower costs as experience increases in producing a product. The strategic importance of the experience law stems from the fact that it is possible not only to forecast one's own costs, but also to forecast competitors' costs. Porter has identified four determinants of international competitive advantage which can be used by governments or management to create a favourable context in which a nation's firms compete.

Review and Application Questions

1. What differences do you see between a differentiated oligopoly and a situation of monopolistic competition? More specifically, what will be the expected competitive behaviour in each case?
2. What are the entry barriers that protect a firm like Coca-Cola?
3. Apply the five forces model of Porter to the case of Kodak in the digital photography market.
4. What are the reaction strategies to be contemplated by a firm leader in its market which is confronted with a price cutting strategy initiated by a competitor having a very low market share?
5. Give an example of a sustainable external competitive advantage for each of the following sectors: mineral waters, fire insurance, highly specialised machine tools.
6. What type of development strategy can be adopted by a small firm dominated in its reference market by an aggressive and powerful competitor having a strong cost advantage?
7. The Springer Manufacturing Corporation is considering producing and delivering 40 units of an industrial plating machine to a new customer. The customer has indicated that the maximum feasible price for each plating machine is €5,000. The average cost of building the first unit is estimated by research and development to be €8,000. In the past, the company has usually operated along an experience curve of 85 per cent. Several executives believe the potential price of €5,000 is too low. Prepare an analysis that answers their concern. In your analysis show the average and the total costs and the total revenue received for the following units: 1, 2, 3, 4, 8, 16, 32, 40.
8. Try to identify the threats of the competitive environment for one of the following industrial sectors: private insurance brokerage, typographic industry, television.

Bibliography

Abell, D.E. and Hammond, J.S. (1979), *Strategic Market Planning*, Englewood Cliffs, NJ, Prentice-Hall.

Abernathy, W. and Wayne, K. (1974), Limit of the Learning Curve, *Harvard Business Review*, 52, 5, pp. 109–19.

Ambler, T. (2000), Marketing Metrics, Business Strategy Review, 11, 2, pp. 59–66.

Begley, T.M. and Boyd, D.P. (2003), The Need for a Corporate Global Mind-Set, *MIT Sloan Management Review*, 44, 2, pp. 25–32.

Bergen, M. and Peteraf, M.A. (2002), Competitor Identification and Competitor Analysis: A Broad-Based Managerial Approach, *Managerial and Decision Economics*, 23, 4/5, pp. 157–69.

Best, R.J. (2000/2003), *Market-based Management*, Englewood Cliffs, NJ Prentice-Hall.

Boston Consulting Group (1968), *Perspectives on Experience*, Boston.

Chamberlin, E.H. (1933/1962), *The Theory of Monopolistic Competition*, Cambridge, MA, Harvard University Press.

Chetochine, G. (1997), *Stratégies d'entreprise face à la tourmente des prix*, Rueil Malmaison, Editions Liaisons.

Durö, R. and Sandström, B. (1988), *Le marketing de combat*, Paris, Les Editions d'Organisation.

Financial Times (1999), Anti-trust Laws in Action, May 21.

Fox, K.A. (2001), Invisible Competition: Some Lessons Learned, *Journal of Business Strategy*, 22, 4, pp.36–8.

Hax, A.C. and Majluf, N.S. (1984), *Strategic Management: An Integrative Perspective*, Englewood Cliffs, NJ, Prentice-Hall.

Hill, S.I., McGrath, J. and Dayal, S. (1998), How to Brand Sand?, *Strategy and Business*, Booz, Allen & Hamilton, 11, Second Quarter, pp. 22–34.

Kerin, R.A., Mahajan, V. and Varadjan, P.R. (1990), *Contemporary Perspectives on Strategic Market Planning*, Boston, MA, Allyn and Bacon.

Kotler, P. and Singh, R. (1981), Marketing Warfare in the 1980s, *Journal of Business Strategy*, 1,3, pp. 30–41.

Lambin, J.J. (1976), *Advertising, Competition and Market Conduct in Oligopoly over Time*, Amsterdam, North-Holland and Elsevier.

Lambin, J.J., Naert, P.A. and Bultez, A. (1975), Optimal Marketing Behavior in Oligopoly, *European Economic Review*, 6, 2, pp. 105–28.

Lochridge, R.K. (1981), *Strategies in the Eighties*, Boston, MA, The Boston Consulting Group Annual Perspective.

Porter, M.E. (1980), *Competitive Strategy*, New York, The Free Press.

Porter, M. (1990), *The Competitive Advantage of Nations*, London, Macmillan.

Porter, M.E. (1982), *Competitive Advantage*, New York, The Free Press.

Porter, M. (1996), What is Strategy?, *Harvard Business Review*, 74, 6, pp. 61–78.

Prahalad, C.K. and Hamel, G. (1990), The Core Competence of the Corporation, *Harvard Business Review*, 68, 3, pp. 79–91.

Ries, A. and Trout, J. (1986), *Marketing Warfare*, New York, McGraw-Hill.

Rigby, D.K. (1997), *Management Tools and Techniques: An Executive Guide*, Boston MA, Bain.

Sallenave, J.P. (1985), The Use and Abuse of Experience Curves, *Long Range Planning*, 18, 1, pp. 64–72.

Schorsch, L.L. (1994), You Can Market Steel, *The McKinsey Quarterly*, 1, pp. 111–20.

Schnaars, S.P. (1998), *Marketing Strategy, Customers & Competition*, New York, The Free Press, 2nd edition.

Schuiling, I. and Kapferer, J.N. (2004), Real Differences Between Local and International Brands: Strategic Implications for International Marketers, *Journal of International Marketing*, 12, 4, pp. 97–112.

Sheth, J. and Sisodia, R. (2002), The Rule of Three in Europe, *European Business Forum*, 10, Summer, pp. 53–7

Simon, H. (1996), *The Hidden Champions*, Boston MA, Harvard Business School Press.

Stanton, J.L. and Herbst, K.C. (2005), Commodities Must Begin to Act Like Branded Companies, *Journal of Marketing Management*, 21, 1/2, pp. 7–18.

Thomas, R. (1993), The Valuation of Brands, *Marketing and Research Today*, May, pp. 79–90.

Von Clausewitz, C. (1908), *On Wars*, London, Routledge & Kegan.

Wright, T.P. (1936), Factors Affecting the Cost of Airplanes, *Journal of Aeronautical Sciences*, 3, pp. 16–24.

 COMPANION WEBSITE FOR CHAPTER 8

Visit the *Market-driven Management* companion website at www.palgrave.com/business/lambin to find information on:

The Importance/Performance Matrix

Market Share Movements Analysis

market targeting and positioning decisions

9

Chapter contents

Chapter learning objectives

When you have read this chapter, you should know and understand

- the market targeting options to be considered;
- the objectives and tools of strategic positioning;
- the conditions for a successful differentiation strategy;
- the usefulness of the value chain in the search for differentiation;
- the different approaches in international market targeting.

Chapter introduction

Having completed the market segmentation and the 'attractiveness/competitiveness' analyses of the different product markets and segments, the next task is to decide on what type of market coverage and what positioning strategies to adopt within each targeted segment. Several market coverage strategies can be considered. Once the market coverage decisions are made, the choice of the positioning strategy will provide the unifying concept for the development of the marketing programme. This is one of the most important steps of the strategic marketing phase because it is the way the firm will identify how to best differentiate its brand versus all competitive brands. Several difficult questions have to be addressed. Do segments mesh with the company's long-run objectives? Will segments move the company towards its goals? Does the company possess skills and resources to succeed in the target segment? Can the firm develop some superior advantage over competition?

9.1. Reference market coverage strategies

The firm can consider different market coverage strategies. These are described in Figure 9.1, where the two extremes are the 'mass marketing' strategy and a 'mass customisation' strategy. Several intermediate options exist, however.

9.1.1. Focused strategy

The market boundaries are defined narrowly in terms of functions, technology and customer groups. This is the strategy of the *specialist* seeking a high market share in a narrow niche. The firm is concentrating its resources on the needs of a single segment or on a few segments, adopting a specialist strategy. The specialisation can be based on a function (functional specialist) or on a particular customer group (customer specialist).

Functional specialist. The firm serves a single or narrow set of functions but covers a broad range of customers. The market boundaries are defined narrowly by function, but broadly by customer group. Firms manufacturing intermediate components fall into this category.

Customer specialist. The market boundaries are defined broadly by function but narrowly by customer group. The focus is on the needs of a particular group of customers. Companies specialising in hospital or hotel equipment belong to this category. An example of a customer specialist is presented in Figure 9.1 as an example.

Through focused marketing, the company can expect to reap the benefits of specialisation and of improved efficiency in the use of the firm's resources. The feasibility

of a focused strategy depends on the size of the segment and on the strength of the competitive advantage gained through specialisation.

9.1.2. Full market coverage

Function and customer group defines the market boundaries broadly. The firm covers the whole market. A steel company is a good example of this kind of market. Two options are open to the firm adopting a full market coverage strategy: undifferentiated or differentiated marketing strategy.

1. By adopting an *undifferentiated marketing strategy or a mass marketing strategy*, the firm ignores market segment differences and decides to approach the entire market as a whole and not take advantage of segmentation analysis. It focuses on what is common in the needs of customers rather than on what is different. The rationale of this middle-of-the-road or standardisation strategy is cost savings, not only in manufacturing, but also in inventory, distribution and advertising. In affluent societies, this strategy is more and more difficult to defend, as it is rarely possible for a product or a brand to please everyone.

2. In a *differentiated marketing strategy or a mass customisation strategy*, the firm also adopts a full market coverage strategy but this time with tailor-made programmes for each segment. This was the slogan of General Motors, claiming 'to have a car for every "purse, purpose and personality" '. This strategy enables the firm to operate in several segments with a customised pricing, distribution and communication strategy. Selling prices will be set on the basis of each segment's price sensitivity. This strategy generally

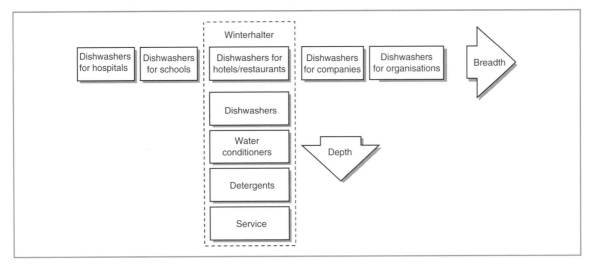

Figure 9.1   A focused market coverage strategy: the Winterhalter company
Source: Simon (1996).

implies higher costs, since the firm is losing the benefits of economies of scale. On the other hand, the firm can expect to hold a strong market share position within each segment.

Differentiated marketing does not necessarily imply full market coverage. The risk may be to oversegment the market, with the danger of cannibalism among the brands of the same company.

9.1.3. Mixed strategy

The firm is diversifying its activities in terms of functions and/or customer groups. This is one of the objectives of portfolio analysis (see Chapter 10), to ensure that the firm's portfolio is well balanced in terms of profit and growth potentials and well diversified in terms of risks.

The choice of any one of these market coverage strategies (see Figure 9.2) will be determined (a) by the number of identifiable and potentially profitable segments in the reference market and (b) by the resources of the firm. If a company has limited resources, a focused marketing strategy is probably the only option. In most cases, market coverage strategies are defined in only two dimensions: needs–functions and customer groups, because in general firms master only one technology, even if substitute technologies exist.

For example, (see Figure 9.3), fruit jam is in direct competition with melted cheese and chocolate pasta. Because the manufacturing requirements are so

different, none of the firms operating in the sector of fruit transformation has industrial operations in these adjacent sectors.

9.1.4. Hyper-segmentation versus counter-segmentation

A segmentation strategy can result in two extreme policies:

- A *hyper-segmentation* policy, which develops made-to-order products tailored to individual needs, offering many options and a variety of secondary functions along with the core function, and this at a high cost.
- A *counter-segmentation* policy, offering a basic product with no frills or extras, few options and at much lower cost.

This is the standardisation–adaptation dilemma mentioned in Chapter 2, which is faced by companies having to define a global or transnational strategy.

In the design of a segmentation strategy, two logics are often in conflict: the market-driven or the supply-driven logic:

- The *market-driven logic* calls for maximum adaptation to the diversity of needs and leads to the development of products customised by reference to client individual preferences.
- The *supply or manufacturing logic* tries to improve productivity as much as possible through product maximum standardisation.

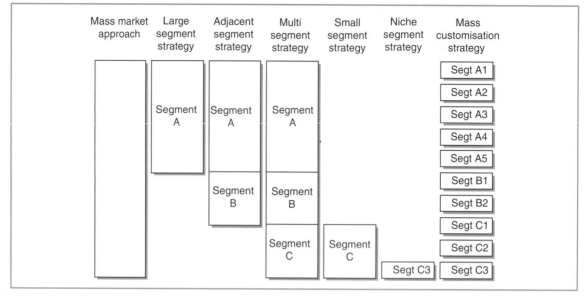

Figure 9.2   Alternative market coverage strategies
Source: Best (2003).

It is clear that increasing the number of formats, designs, sizes and colours of the same product in order to meet the diversity of needs can be counter-productive and undermine the productivity of the manufacturing process by reducing the potential gains due to economies of scale.

During periods of affluence of the last decade, companies operating in B2C markets tended to follow hyper-segmentation strategies by refining their segmentation strategies. The result was a proliferation of brands, an increase of production and marketing costs and eventually of retail prices.

The behaviour of the new consumers described in Chapter 4 gradually led them to become more aware of the 'price/satisfaction' ratio in their purchasing decision process.

More and more consumers behave like smart buyers and make trade-offs between price and product benefits. The success of generic brands and of private labels in Western economies is an example of this evolution.

In several sectors, and particularly in the fast moving consumer goods (FMCG) sector, there is a trend towards a return to voluntary simplicity that is towards less sophisticated products, providing the core function without frills, but sold at much lower prices – thanks to their high level of standardisation. This evolution explains the success of low-cost distributors like *Lidl* and *Aldi*. Thus, we have here a segmentation strategy based on the 'price/satisfaction' ratio, a segment too often neglected by manufacturers and very well covered today by large retailers.

9.1.5. Selection of priority segments

The segment targeting decision is compatible with broad market coverage and with the selection of one or several segments, where the firm will invest by priority. A golden rule is to target by priority customer group(s) for whom the product value is the highest and not – as it is tempting to do – the customer group(s) having the highest value for the firm. To illustrate this point in Figure 9.4, the customers' value is measured by his/her satisfaction score and the firm's value by the gross profit margin generated by the product. Each indicator is represented at two levels, low and high. Four different targets can be identified. The ideal target is, of course, in the upper-right quadrant which is a win-win situation and the least interesting is the lower-left quadrant. The firm having a product orientation (see Section 1.4.1) will be inclined to privilege the upper-left quadrant since this target is more profitable for the firm. On the contrary, the customer-oriented firm will concentrate its marketing efforts on the two right targets, while trying to improve the profitability of the lower-right offering.

9.2. The strategic positioning decision

Once the market coverage decisions are made, the next step is to decide on the positioning strategy to adopt within each targeted segment(s). Selection of the positioning

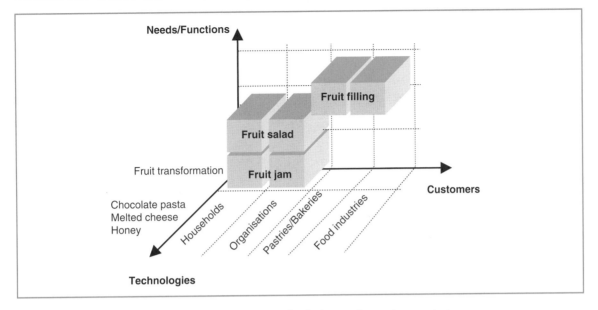

Figure 9.3   Example of limited market coverage: the fruit transformation market
Source: Industry.

strategy provides the unifying concept for the development of the marketing programme. This is one of the most critical steps in the implementation of strategic marketing, because the firm has to decide how to best differentiate its brand from competing brands.

9.2.1. Positioning defined

The word 'positioning' has been popularised by Ries and Trout (1981). They considered that positioning was the process of *positioning the product on the consumers' mind*. Our definition is slightly different. We define positioning as

> the decision of the company to choose the benefit(s) that the brand has to put forward to gain a distinctive place in the market.

The positioning can be summed up in four key questions:

- A brand for what? This refers to the brand promise and the customer benefit.
- A brand for whom? This refers to the target segment.
- A brand for when? This refers to the use or consumption situation.
- A brand against whom? This question refers to the direct competitor.

Positioning strategy is the operational way to implement a differentiation strategy based (a) on the internal analysis of the firm's strength and weaknesses, (b) on the competitive context and (c) on the type of distinctive and unique benefit the brand can provide to the customer.

The objective of the company will be then to communicate clearly this differentiation element to potential customers so that it is clearly registered in their minds. The perception of the brand in the mind of consumers is called brand image. The positioning will be the basis of the operational marketing programme, which should be consistent with the chosen brand positioning.

9.2.2. Conditions for positioning development

When selecting a positioning basis, a certain number of conditions must be carefully met:

- To have a good understanding of the present positioning of the brand or firm in the customers' minds. This knowledge can be acquired through brand image studies.
- To know the present positioning of competing brands, in particular those brands in direct competition.
- To select one positioning and to identify the most relevant and credible arguments which justify the chosen positioning.
- To evaluate the size and the potential profitability of the market involved by such a positioning.
- To verify whether the contemplated positioning is really specific and distinctive, while being suspicious of false market niches invented by advertising people or discovered through an invalidated qualitative study.

Figure 9.4   Identification of the priority segment(s)
Source: Authors.

- To verify whether the brand has the required personality potential to achieve the positioning in the minds of customers.
- To verify whether the contemplated positioning justify a price premium.
- To assess the vulnerability of the positioning. Do we have the resources required to occupy and defend this position? Do we have an alternative solution in case of failure?
- To ensure consistency in the positioning with the different marketing mix instruments: pricing, distribution, packaging, services, and so on.

Thus, not all brand or product differences are meaningful to customers. As already discussed in Chapter 8, the claim of differentiation should be 'unique', 'important' to the customer, 'sustainable', 'communicable' and 'affordable'.

Once the positioning strategy is adopted and clearly defined, it is much simpler for operational marketing people to translate this positioning in terms of an effective and consistent marketing programme.

9.2.3. Ways to position the brand versus competition

There are different ways to position the brand against competition. One can identify three types of differentiation strategies: product differentiation, price differentiation and image differentiation.

1. *Product differentiation*. The most classical way of positioning a brand is to leverage of the product benefits. Product characteristics, such as performance, durability,

reliability, design, novelty, etc., can be used to base a differentiation strategy. Bang and Olufsen is positioned on a superior design; Duracell on superior durability; Miele on superior reliability.

2. *Price differentiation*. Some companies can use price as a way to be different against competition. There might be different pricing strategy: the highest price in its category (Gucci in perfume, Cartier in jewellery); the best value for money (Ikea in the furniture industry; Nivea in the cosmetic sector), the lowest price in the category (Ryanair in the airline sector and Aldi in the food retail market).

3. *Image differentiation*. In many sectors, brands can not be differentiated on the basis of tangible characteristics. A certain image will differentiate a brand versus competition. In the perfume sector, each brand wants to own a certain image territory. This is similar in the cigarette (Marlboro) or alcohol (Absolut Vodka) sectors.

9.2.4. Credibility of the chosen positioning

Some companies are adopting a multiple benefit positioning strategy. It is the case, for instance, of the all-in-one product *Aquafresh*, the toothpaste brand launched by GlaxoSmithKline offering three benefits: anti-cavity protection, better breath and whiter teeth. The challenge is to convince people that the brand delivers all three benefits.

As the number of claims increases, the risk of a credibility gap also increases. As indicated by Kotler and Keller (2006), four major positioning errors should be avoided.

Under positioning. Potential customers have only a vague idea of the brand distinctive claim. They do not see anything special about it.

Over-positioning. Customers have a too narrow image of the brand, because it is perceived as too specialised or not affordable.

Confused positioning. Customers are confused because the firm makes too many claims or changes its positioning too often.

Doubtful positioning. Potential customers may find it hard to believe the brand claims in view of the past history of the brand, its price or its manufacturer.

This last error is probably the most frequent one observed, as illustrated by the case of the Bata company in India (see Exhibit 9.1).

9.3. Positioning response behaviour

One can identify different ways in which potential customers or customers respond to perceived information and producer stimuli. Here, 'response' means all mental or physical activity caused by a stimulus. A response is not necessarily manifested in external actions, but may be simply mental.

Economic theory is only interested in the act of purchase per se and not in the overall behavioural process, which leads to purchase. From the economist's point of view, as we saw earlier, preferences are revealed by behaviour and consumers' response is the same as the demand expressed by the market in terms of quantities sold.

In reality, market demand defined in this way is an ex-post or historical observation, often of little practical value to the decision-maker. Market analysts hope to retrace and understand the process followed by the buyer so as to intervene in that process in a better informed manner and to be able to measure the effectiveness of marketing actions. Therefore, response behaviour is a much broader notion to the marketer than it is to the economist.

9.3.1. The 'learn–feel–do' hierarchy

The various response levels of the buyer can be classified into three categories: (a) cognitive response, which relates to retained information and knowledge, (b) affective response, which concerns attitude and the evaluation system and (c) behavioural (or conative) response, which describes action – not only the act of purchasing, but also after-purchase behaviour. Table 9.1 describes the main measures currently used for each response level.

It has been postulated by practitioners in communication that these three response levels follow a sequence and that the individual, like the organisation, reaches the three stages successively and in this order: cognitive (learn)–affective (feel)–behavioural (do). We then have a learning process which is observed in practice when the buyer is heavily involved by his or her purchase decision, for example, when the perceived risk (Bauer, 1960) or the brand sensitivity (Kapferer and Laurent, 1983) is high.

The learning response model was originally developed to measure advertising effectiveness

---

EXHIBIT 9.1

THE BATA COMPANY IN INDIA: AN EXAMPLE OF DOUBTFUL POSITIONING

In the early 1990s, Bata decided to embrace the high-end segment of the Indian shoe market as a part of its target market. It launched quite a few brands for this segment with higher price tags. The move landed Bata in trouble. This segment was not meant for Bata. In the first place, this segment was not for a company like Bata. Second the segment did not gel with Bata's distinctive competence. The segment constituted a mere 5–10 per cent of the footwear market in India. It could not provide the volumes that Bata was used to at the mass-market end and high volume was essential for Bata having a healthy bottom-line. Worse still, adoption of the segment misdirected Bata's entire strategy. The top end of the market suddenly became the main focus of the company and it forgot its bread-and-butter shoes that had given the company its identity. Small regional players started nibbling away at Bata's mainstay.

Actually Bata was squeezed at both ends. At the lower end, smaller competitors attacked Bata's mass range of canvas shoes and school shoes slots, which the company had practically vacated on its own by ignoring them completely. At the high end, niche players, who were better prepared, were challenging Bata. From a market share of around 15 per cent in the mid-1980s, Bata found its share down to 10 per cent of the footwear market in the mid-1990s.

After learning the lessons the hard way, Bata did an about-turn from its adventure with high-end segment and returned to the mass segment. The new strategy was to get back to the original customers at the low end and keep that part of the market as its core focus. The company, of course, did not totally give up the new segment it had got to in the early 1990s. Brands such as Hush Puppies, for instance, continued to be sold by Bata, but in a selective way and through select stores only.

Source: Anil Chawla (2003).

Table 9.1   Key measures of market response

- Cognitive response
  Saliency; awareness; recall; recognition; knowledge; perceived similarity.
- Affective response
  Consideration set; importance; determinance; performance; attitude; preference; intention to buy.
- Behavioural response
  Fact-finding behaviour; trial purchase; repeat purchase; brand repertoire; share of category requirement (exclusivity); brand loyalty; satisfaction/dissatisfaction.

(Lavidge and Steiner, 1961) and later extended to include the process of adoption of new products (Rogers, 1962). Palda (1966) has shown that this model is not always applicable and that uncertainty remains as to the causal links and direction existing between the intervening variables. Moreover, the learning process hypothesis implies a well thought out buying process, observed only when the buyer is heavily involved in his purchase decision. Psycho-sociologists have also shown that other sequences exist and are observed, for example, when there is minimal involvement (Krugman, 1965), or when there is cognitive dissonance (Festinger, 1957).

Although the learning process hypothesis is not generally applicable, the 'learn–feel–do' model remains valuable in structuring the information collected on response behaviours, particularly when complemented with the concepts of 'perceived risk' and of 'buyer involvement', discussed in this chapter.

9.3.2. The Foote, Cone and Belding (FCB) involvement grid

The various paths of the response process may be viewed from a more general framework, which includes the degree of involvement and the perception of reality mode. Brain specialisation theory proposes that anatomical separation of the cerebral hemispheres of the brain leads to specialised perception of reality: the left side of the brain (or the intellectual mode) and the right side (or the affective or sensory mode):

- The left side, or intellectual mode, is relatively more capable of handling logic, factual information, language and analysis that is the cognitive 'thinking' function.
- The right side, or affective mode, which engages in synthesis, is more intuitive, visual and responsive to the non-verbal, which is the 'feeling' function.

In order to provide a conceptual framework which integrates the 'learn–feel–do' hierarchy with the consumer involvement and the brain specialisation theory, Vaughn (1986) presented a grid in which purchase decision processes can be classified along two basic dimensions: 'high–low' involvement and

	Intellectual mode *(think)*	**Affective mode** *(feel)*
High involvement	Learning *(learn–feel–do)*	Affective *(feel–learn–do)*
Low involvement	Routine *(do–learn–feel)*	Hedonism *(do–feel–learn)*

Figure 9.5   The involvement grid
Source: Vaughn (1986).

'think–feel' perception of reality. Crossing the degree of involvement with the mode of reality perception leads to the matrix in Figure 9.5 in which we can see four different paths of the response process:

Quadrant (1) corresponds to a buying situation where product involvement is high and the way we perceive reality is essentially intellectual. This situation implies a large need for information due to the importance of the product and mental issues related to it. Quadrant 1 illustrates the learning process described earlier, where the sequence followed was: '*learn–feel–do*'.

Major purchases with high prices and significant objective and functional characteristics, such as cars, electrical household goods and houses follow this process. Industrial goods also fall in this category. These factors suggest a need for informative advertising.

Quadrant (2) describes buying situations where product involvement is also high. Specific information is, however, less important than an attitude or an emotional arousal, since the product or brand choice reveals the buyer's system of values and personality and relates to the buyer's self-esteem. The sequence here is 'feel–learn–do'.

In this category we find all products that have important social and/or emotional value, such as perfumes, clothes, jewellery and motorcycles. These factors suggest a need for emotional advertising.

Quadrant (3) describes product decisions, which involve minimal thought and a tendency to form buying habits for convenience. As long as the product fulfils the expected core service, we find low product involvement and routine behaviour. Brand loyalty will be largely a function of habit. The hierarchy model is a 'do–learn–feel' pattern.

Most food and staple package goods belong in this category, which is somewhat like a commodity limbo. As products reach maturity, they are likely to descend into this quadrant. These factors suggest a need for advertising, which creates and maintains habits and stimulates a reminder of the product.

Quadrant (4) illustrates a situation where low product involvement coexists with the sensory mode. Products in this category cater to personal tastes involving imagery and quick satisfaction. The sequence is 'do–feel–learn'.

In this category, we find products such as beer, chocolates, cigarettes, jams and fast-food restaurants. For these

product categories, there is a need for advertising, which emphasises personal satisfaction. For an illustration of this matrix, see Ratchford (1987, p. 30).

An interesting observation emerging from consumer involvement analyses (see Kapferer and Laurent, 1983) is the large number of 'low risk–low involvement' product decisions. This fact constitutes a challenge for the firm and suggests that marketing and communication strategies must be adapted to deal with this situation where consumers just do not care very much about a large number of purchase decisions they make.

9.3.3. Attribute-based perceptual maps

The problem of *redundancy* remains as a final question about the relevance of attributes. Two attributes are said to be redundant when there is no difference in their significance.

> For example, in a study of the heavy trucks market in Belgium, two criteria of 'loading capacity' and 'engine capacity' were spontaneously evoked as important attributes. The two criteria are being used interchangeably, neither existing without the other.

If two determinant attributes are retained, but they both indicate the same characteristic, this situation is equivalent

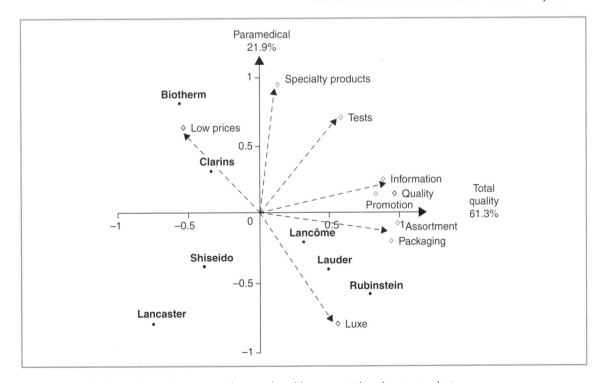

Figure 9.6   Attribute-based perceptual map: the skin-care and make-up market

Source: Van Ballenberghe (1993).

to selecting only one attribute. The analyst should establish a list of determinant but non-redundant attributes.

Brand image studies measure customers' perceptions and help in discovering market expectations. The perceptual map of Figure 9.6. illustrates this point. This map is based on the rating scores of 12 attributes obtained from a sample of regular users of skin-care and make-up brands. A Principal Components Analysis (Exhibit 9.2) of these scores identified two macro-attributes, which summarise 83 per cent of the total variance.

> In Figure 9.6, the first axis is total quality as perceived by the respondents and include the following micro-attributes: 'technical quality', 'extent of product line', 'quality of packaging', 'information's', 'attractive promotions'. These attributes are mentally opposed to 'attractive prices'. The second axis is strongly correlated with the attributes 'Medicare products', 'laboratory tests' and opposed to 'luxury design'. This axis reflects the paramedical nature of these products.

In the map of Figure 9.6, we can see that the brands Rubinstein, Lauder and Lancôme are well positioned along the total quality dimension, but poorly placed on the paramedical dimension. By opposition, the brands Biotherm and Clarins are perceived as paramedical brands while not having a high quality image. It is interesting to observe that the upper-right quadrant is unoccupied, a positioning probably difficult to defend.

9.3.4. Strategies for changing a positioning

Knowledge of the way consumers perceive competing products in a segment is important in determining the strategy to be adopted to modify an unfavourable positioning. Six different strategies may be considered (Boyd et al., 1972):

1. *Modifying the product.* If the brand is not up to market expectations of a particular characteristic, the product can be modified by reinforcing the given characteristic.

2. *Modifying attribute weights.* Convince the market that more importance ought to be attached to a particular characteristic that the brand exhibits well.

3. *Modifying beliefs about a brand.* The market may be badly informed and underestimate some real distinctive qualities of the brand. This entails perceptual repositioning.

4. *Modifying beliefs about competing brands.* This strategy is to be used if the market overestimates some characteristics of competitors. It implies the possibility of using comparative advertising.

5. *Attracting attention to neglected attributes.* This strategy usually involves the creation of a new benefit not yet considered by the target segment.

6. *Modifying the required attribute level.* It is possible that the market expects a quality level, which is not always necessary, at least as far as some applications are concerned. The firm can try to convince the segment that the quality offered for that particular dimension is adequate.

The major advantage of multi-attribute models over simple overall attitude measure is in gaining an understanding of the attitudinal structure of the segment under study, in order to identify the most appropriate strategies of positioning and communication.

9.4. The value chain in differentiation analysis

In the search for source uniqueness on which to base a differentiation strategy, two pitfalls should be avoided:

■ identify elements of uniqueness which customers value but that the firm is incapable of supplying;
■ identify elements of uniqueness which the firm is able to supply but which is not valued by customers.

For this purpose the value chain model (Porter, 1980) provides a particularly useful framework.

EXHIBIT 9.2

PRINCIPAL COMPONENTS ANALYSIS

The method used is factorial analysis, for example, Principal Components Analysis (PCA). This method is a statistical technique which organises and summarises a set of data (the N determinant attributes in this case) into a reduced set of factors called the principal components or *'macro-characteristics'*, which are independent of each other and which contrast best the objects under study (see Hair *et al.*, 1992). The output of a PCA is an attribute-based perceptual map. Each brand is positioned along the two or three retained components, which can be interpreted by the correlation observed between these principal components and each attribute. The interpretation of a perceptual map resulting from a PCA is as follows: two brands are close on the perceptual map if they are evaluated in the same way according to all retained attributes. Two attributes are close if they lead to the evaluation of brands in the same manner.

Every firm is a collection of activities that are performed to design, produce, market, deliver and support its products. As shown in Figure 9.7, these activities can be divided into two broad types, primary activities and support activities. A value chain is constructed for a particular firm on the basis of the importance and separateness of different activities and also on the basis of their capacity for creating differentiation.

9.4.1. The search for differentiation

By way of illustration, representative sources of differentiation for primary activities could be:

- Purchasing: quality and reliability of components and materials.
- Operations: fast manufacturing, defect-free manufacturing, ability to produce to customer specifications, and so on.
- Warehousing and distribution: fast delivery, efficient order processing, sufficient inventories to meet unexpected orders, and so on.
- Sales and marketing: high advertising level and quality, high sales force coverage and quality, extensive credit to buyers, and so on.
- Customer service: in-use assistance, training for customers, fast and reliable repairs, and so on.

Similarly, for support activities, potential sources of differentiation are:

- Human resources: superior training of personnel, commitment to customer service, stable workforce policies, and so on.

- R&D: unique product features, fast new product development, design for reliability, and so on.
- Infrastructure: corporate reputation, responsiveness to customers needs, and so on.

The objective is to identify the *drivers of uniqueness* in each activity, that is, the variables and the actions through which the firm can achieve uniqueness in relation to competitors' offerings and provide value to the buyer. The merit of the value chain model is to suggest that the search for a sustainable competitive advantage is the role of every function within the organisation and not only of the marketing function.

It is interesting in this respect to make reference to the work of Simon (1996), already quoted in this book, who has analysed the strategies adopted by a sample of 122 firms (a majority of German firms) which are (a) world or European leaders in their reference market, (b) of small or medium size and (c) unfamiliar to the general public. Inspection of Figure 9.8 shows that the type of competitive advantage held by those *Hidden champions* is largely based on product superiority.

9.4.2. Measuring market power

The degree of market power is measured by the firm's ability to dictate a price above that of its priority competitors. One measure of this sensitivity is the price elasticity of the firm for the differentiated product's demand. The lower this demand elasticity, the less volatile or sensitive will the market share be to a price increase.

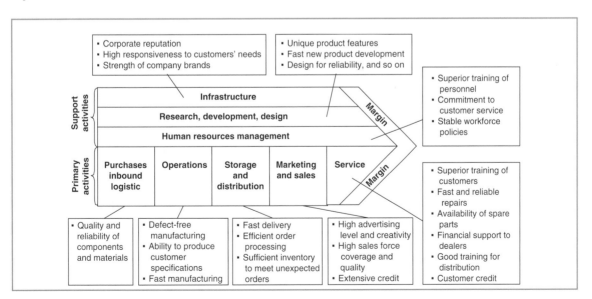

Figure 9.7 The generic value chain
Source: Porter (1980).

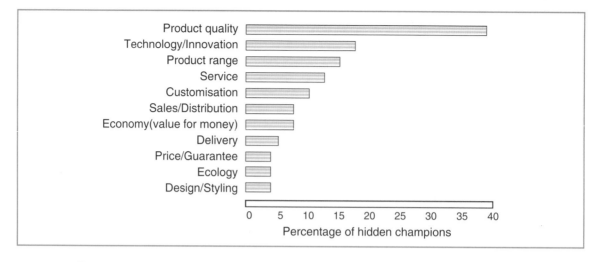

Figure 9.8   Frequency of hidden champions' competitive advantage
Source: Simon (1996, p. 151).

If brand A has price elasticity equal to -1.5 and brand B an elasticity of -3.0; the same price increase of 5 per cent will lower demand for A by 7.5 per cent and demand for B by 15 per cent.

Therefore, a firm or brand with market power has a less elastic demand than an undifferentiated product. As a result, the firm is in a position to make the group of customers, who are sensitive to the element of differentiation, *accept a higher price*.

The brand strength refers to the buyers' degree of attachment or loyalty to a brand or a company. Probably the best test of brand loyalty would be to know what a customer would do if she (or he) does not find her preferred brand in the visited store. Will she switch to another brand or will she visit another store to find her preferred brand? To measure brand power, one can identify at least five indicators of a brand's strength:

1. *Lower price sensitivity*. A strong brand displays a stronger resistance to a price increase than its competitors.

2. *Acceptable price premiums*. A brand is strong if people are prepared to pay more for it. Conversely, a weak brand has to propose a price lower than the price charged by its competitors.

3. *Exclusivity rate*. The more loyal customer is the one for whom the brand represents a higher share of category requirement.

4. *Dynamic loyalty rate*. An alternative to share of category requirement is to look at patterns of purchasing over time, and uses this to estimate the probability of a consumer buying the brand on the next purchase occasion.

5. *Positive attitudinal measures*. Indicators like familiarity, esteem, perceived quality, purchase intentions

(brand loyalty), and so on, are also good indicators of a brand's strength.

Examples of price premiums charged by powerful brands are presented in Table 9.2.

9.5. Targeting international market segments

Global market segmentation can be defined as the process of identifying specific segments, whether they are country groups or individual buyer groups, of potential customers with homogeneous attributes who are likely to exhibit similar buying behaviour. There are three different approaches for global segmentation: (a) identifying clusters of countries that demand similar products; (b) identifying segments present in many or most countries and (c) targeting different segments in different countries with the same product (Takeuchi and Porter, 1986, pp. 138–50).

9.5.1. Targeting country clusters

Traditionally, the world market has been segmented on geographic variables, that is, by grouping countries that are similar in terms of climate, language, religion, economic development, distribution channel, and so on. Products rarely require modification or tailoring for every single country, except for such things as labelling and the language used in the manuals and catalogues.

Table 9.2 Examples of price premium available to strong brands

Price premium available to Hertz and Avis compared with		Price premium available to IBM compared with		Price premium available to British Airways compared with	
Budget	20.4%	Apple	10.0%	Virgin	11.0%
Eurodollar	22.5%	Compaq	17.0%	Delta	41.0%
Europcar	24.0%	Amstrad	40.0%	Air India	45.0%
		Dell	46.0%		

Source: Thomas (1993).

On the European scene, natural clusters of countries would be, for example, the Nordic countries (Denmark, Norway, Sweden and maybe Finland); the Germanic countries (Germany, Austria, part of Switzerland), the Iberian countries, and so on. With this country segmentation strategy, products and communication would be adapted for each group of countries.

Within the European Community (EC), an argument in favour of this country approach lies in the high diversity of the different countries, as evidenced by the comparison of their socio-demographic profiles. See the social portrait of Europe published by the EC (Eurostat, 1996, 1999).

However, this approach presents three potential limitations: (a) it is based on country variables and not on consumer behavioural patterns, (b) it assumes total homogeneity within the country segment and (c) it overlooks the existence of homogeneous consumer segments that might exist across national boundaries. With the growth of regionalism within Europe, the second assumption becomes more and more a limiting factor. In fact, with the elimination of country borders more European firms are defining their geographic market zones by reference to regions and not to countries.

9.5.2. Selling to universal segments across countries

As discussed in Chapter 2, several trends are influencing consumption behaviour on a global scale and many consumer products are becoming more widely accepted globally, such as consumer electronics, automobiles, fashion, home appliances, food products, beverages and services. Many of these products respond to needs and wants that cut across national boundaries.

Thus, even if overall product needs vary among countries, there may be a segment of the market with identical needs in every country. The challenge facing international firms is to identify these 'universal' segments and reach them with marketing programmes that meet the common needs of these potential buyers. These universal segments are most likely to be high-end consumers, sports professionals, executives of multinational companies or, in general, sophisticated users. These groups tend to be the most mobile and therefore are most likely to be exposed to extensive international contacts and experiences.

A growing market segment on a global scale is composed of consumers aspiring to an 'élite lifestyle'. This élite, in Tokyo, New York, Paris, London, Hong Kong, Rio de Janeiro, and so on, is the target of brands that fit the image of exclusivity like Mercedes, Gucci, Hermès, American Express, Gold Card, Chivas, Godiva, and so on.

Such high-end brands can be targeted internationally to this universal segment in exactly the same way they are currently positioned in their respective home market. This international segmentation strategy is illustrated in Figure 9.9. The size of universal segments can be small in each country. What is attractive is the cumulative volume. For example, *Godiva* pralines are present in more than 20 different countries all over the world, sometimes with modest market shares. It is, nevertheless, the world's leading chocolate maker.

9.5.3. Targeting diverse segments across countries

Even if product needs vary among countries, the same product can sometimes be sold in each country but in different segments, by adopting different market positioning based on non-product variables such as distributive networks, advertising and pricing. This approach is illustrated in Figure 9.9.

The positioning adopted for the Canon AE-1 provides a good example of this international segmentation approach. The AE-1 was targeted towards young replacement buyers in Japan, upscale first-time buyers of 35-mm single-lens reflex cameras in the USA, and older and more technologically sophisticated replacement buyers in Germany. Three different marketing programmes were developed for Japan, the USA and Europe. (Takeuchi and Porter, 1986, p. 139)

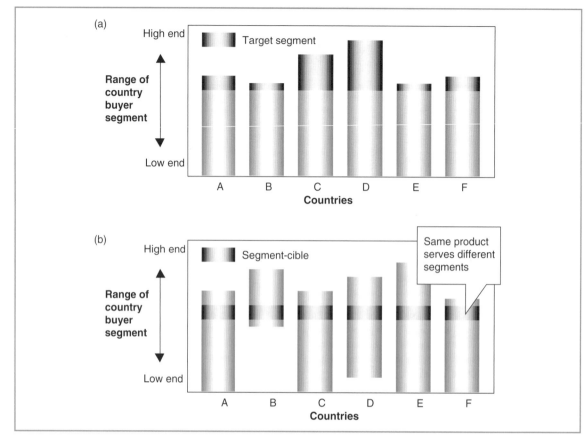

Figure 9.9   International segmentation: two different market positioning strategies – (a) universal and (b) diverse segment positioning across countries
Source: Takeuchi and Porter (1986).

This approach requires important adaptations of communication and selling strategies, which contribute to increasing costs, or at least to preventing cost decreases as a consequence of standardisation.

Of the three segmentation approaches, universal segmentation is the most innovative and also most likely to give the firm a significant competitive advantage, because product and communication can be standardised and transferred among countries. This gives the brand a reputation and coherence in image and positioning which is internationally reinforced. The diverse segmentation approach has the merit of taking into consideration differences in consumer behaviour among countries and of introducing adaptations to accommodate these differences (Exhibit 9.3). On the other hand, because of these country-to-country adaptations, the brand image in each country will probably be different.

9.5.4. The case of universal segments

The global approach in segmenting world markets looks for similarities between markets. The traditional international approach is multidomestic, which tends to ignore similarities. The global approach actively seeks homogeneity in product, image, marketing and advertising message, while the multidomestic approach maintains unnecessary differences from market to market. The goal, however, is not to have a uniform product line worldwide. Rather the goal is to have a product line that is as standardised as possible, while recognising that allowances for some local conditions are both necessary and desirable.

Trade-off between standardisation and customisation

In the great majority of market situations, some degree of adaptation will be necessary. The essence of international

EXHIBIT 9.3

THE CASE OF BLACK & DECKER

The case of Black & Decker provides a good illustration of the communication and selling strategy. Black & Decker are established in 50 countries and manufactures in 25 plants, 16 of which are outside the United States. It has a very high level of brand awareness worldwide, sometimes in the 80–90 per cent range. For Black & Decker the potential economies of scale and cost savings of globalisation were considerable. The challenges to be overcome were the following:

■ Different countries have different safety and industry standards that make complete standardisation impossible.

■ European and American consumers have very different responses to product design and even to colours.
■ Consumers use the products in different ways in different countries. For example, Europeans are more power-oriented in their electric tools than Americans.

Source: Farley (1986, p. 69).

Table 9.3   Strategies of international segmentation

	Expectations of segments				
	Homogeneous		Similar		
Global marketing strategies	Same culture	Different culture	Same culture	Different culture	Different
1. Unchanged product and operational marketing	1	—	—	—	—
2. Unchanged product and adapted operational marketing	—	2	2	2	—
3. Adapted product and operational marketing	—	—	—	3	3
4. New product and specific operational marketing	—	—	—	—	4

Source: Blanche (1987).

---

segmentation can be summarised as follows: think of global similarities and adapt to local differences. This perspective should help management to determine similarities across national boundaries while assessing within-country differences. The different strategies susceptible to adoption, depending on the diversity of expectations and cultural background, are presented in Table 9.3. Three types of product policy can be considered:

Universal product: the physical product sold in each country is identical except for labelling and for the language used in the manuals.

Modified product: the core product is the same, but some modifications are adopted, such as voltage, colour, size or accessories, to accommodate government regulations or to reflect local differences in taste, buying habits, climate, and so on.

Country-tailored product: the physical product is substantially tailored to each country or group of countries.

The financial and cost implications of these alternative product policies are, of course, particularly important.

Establishing a world brand

Every product does not have the same global potential, and some products may be easier than others to develop as world brands. Several brands on the market are recognised as world brands: Coca-Cola, Marlboro, Kodak, Honda, Mercedes, Heineken, Swatch, Canon, Gucci, British Airways, Perrier, Black & Decker, Hertz, Benetton, McDonald's, Godiva, and many others. It is worth noting that the popularity of these brands is independent of the attitude towards their country of origin.

In reality, the global potential of a product is closely linked to the universality of the benefit sought. To the extent that a product is a proven success in meeting the needs of a particular group of buyers in a given country, it is logical to expect a similar success with the same group of people in another country, provided, of course, that the product is adapted to local consuming habits or regulations. In other words, as suggested by Quelch and Hoff (1986), the driving factor in moving towards global marketing should be 'the efficient worldwide use of good marketing ideas rather than scale economies from standardisation'.

The closer the product to the high-tech/high-touch poles, the more universal it is. These two product categories have in common the fact of (a) being high-involvement products and (b) sharing a common language (Domzal and Unger, 1987, p. 28):

High-tech products: appeal to highly specialised buyers who share a common technical language and symbols. This is the case among computer users, tennis players and musicians, who all understand the technical aspects of the products. This is true for heavy machinery, computer hardware and financial services, but also for personal computers, video equipment, skiing equipment, and so on. The mere existence of a common 'shop talk' facilitates communication and increases the chance of success as global brands.

High-touch products: are more image-oriented than features-oriented products, but they respond to universal themes or needs, such as romance, wealth, heroism, play, and so on. Many products such as perfume, fashion, jewellery and watches are sold on these themes.

For these two product categories, customers all over the world are using and understanding the same language and the same symbols. Worldwide brand standardisation appears most feasible when products approach either end of the high-tech/high-touch spectrum (Domzal and Unger, 1987, p. 27).

CHAPTER SUMMARY

The firm can consider different market coverage strategies. There are described in Figure 9.1, where the two extremes are the 'mass marketing' strategy and a 'mass customisation' strategy. Several intermediate options exist, however. Selection of the positioning strategy provides the unifying concept for the development of the marketing programme. This is one of the most critical steps in the implementation of strategic marketing, because the firm has to decide how to best differentiate its brand from competing brands. There are different ways to position the brand against competition. One can identify three types of differentiation strategies: product differentiation, price differentiation and image differentiation. The effect of differentiation is to give the firm some degree of *market power*, because it generates preferences, customer loyalty and lower price sensitivity. In the search for a differentiation strategy, the value chain model (Porter, 1980) provides a particularly useful framework. There are three different approaches for global segmentation: (a) identifying clusters of countries that demand similar products; (b) identifying segments present in many or most countries; and (c) targeting different segments in different countries with the same product.

Review and Application Questions

1. Pick two magazines targeting a specific socio-demographic group (e.g. teenagers, seniors, housewives or an ethnic group). Select three or four advertisements and try to identify the positioning sought by the advertisers.

2. If a company was the first to identify a totally new segment, is it necessary to select a positioning in this segment?

3. How can you assess the efficiency of a chosen positioning? What are the criteria to be used?

4. Should the positioning decision be necessarily based on a long-term competitive advantage to be successful?

5. Explain why the positioning decision is so important for the design of the operational marketing programme?

6. In a brand image study, measures of perception of four brands (A, B, C and D) from the same product category were obtained from a sample of respondents. The importance scores of the four determining attributes are: 0.40/0.30/0.20/0.10. The performance scores for each brand are the following: A = 8/4/4/1; B = 8/3/5/3; C = 6/6/5/3; D = 5/9/6/5. Which brand will be preferred by the market if the buyers use (a) the compensatory model as decision rule, (b) the disjunctive model, (c) the conjunctive model with a minimum of 5 required for each attribute, (d) the lexicographic model?

Bibliography

Bauer, R.A. (1960), Consumer Behaviour as Risk Taking, in *Proceedings Fall Conference of the American Marketing Association*, Hancock, A.S. (ed.), Chicago, IL, pp. 389–98.

Best, R.J. (2000/2003), *Market-based Management*, Englewood Cliffs, NJ, Prentice-Hall, 3rd edition.

Blanche, B. (1987), Le marketing global: paradoxe, fantasme ou objectif pour demain?, *Revue Française du Marketing*, 115, p. 114.

Boyd, H.W., Ray, M.L. and Strong, E.C. (1972), An Attitudinal Framework for Advertising Strategy, *Journal of Marketing*, 36, 2, pp. 27–33.

Chawla, A. (2003), BATA, Wrong Target, in *Marketing Management, Workshop of Educational Institutes*, Bhopal, June.

Dalrymple, D.J. and Parsons, L.J. (1976), *Marketing Management: Text and Cases*, New York, John Wiley & Sons.

Day, G.S. (1990), *Market-driven Strategy*, New York, The Free Press.

Domzal, T. and Unger, L.S. (1987), Emerging Positioning Strategies in Global Marketing, *The Journal of Consumer Marketing*, 4, 4, pp. 23–50.

Eurostat (1991/1996), *A Social Portrait of Europe*, Brussels, European Commission.

Farley, L.J. (1986), Going Global: Choices and Challenges, *The Journal of Consumer Marketing*, 3, 1, pp. 67–70.

Festinger, L.(1957), *A Theory of Cognitive Dissonance*, New York, Harper and Row.

Gupta, A.K. and Westney, D.E. (2003), *Smart Globalization*, San Francisco, CA, John Wiley & Sons, Jossey Bass.

Hair, J.F., Anderson, R.E., Tatham, R.L. and Black, W.C. (1992), *Multivariate Data Analysis*, New York, Maxwell Macmillan.

Kapferer, J.N. (2004), *The New Strategic Brand Management*, London, Kogan Page.

Kapferer and Laurent (1983), *La sensibilité aux marques*, Paris, Fondation Jours de France.

Kotler, P. and Keller, K.L. (2006), *Marketing Management*, Upper Saddle River, NJ, Prentice-Hall, 12th edition.

Krugman, H.E. (1965), The Impact of Television Advertising: Learning without Involvement, *Public Opinion Quarterly*, 29, 3, pp. 349–55.

Lavidge, R.J. and Steiner, G.A. (1961), A Model for Predictions Measurement of Advertising Effectiveness, *Journal of Marketing*, 25, 6, pp. 59–62.

Palda, K.S. (1966), The Hypothesis of a Hierarchy of Effects, *Journal of Marketing Research*, 3, 1, pp. 13–24.

Porter, M.E. (1980), *Competitive Strategy*, New York, The Free Press.

Quelch, J. and Hoff, E.G. (1986), Customizing Global Marketing, *Harvard Business Review*, 64, 3, pp. 59–68.

Ratchford, B.T. (1987), New Insights about the FCB Grid, *Journal of Advertising Research*, 27, 4, pp. 24–38.

Ries, A. and Trout, J. (1981), *Positioning: The Battle for Your Mind*, New York, McGraw-Hill.

Rogers, E.M. (1962), *Diffusion of Innovations*, New York, The Free Press.

Simon, H. (1996), *Hidden Champions*, Boston, MA, Harvard Business School Press.

Takeuchi, H. and Porter, M.E. (1986), Three Roles of International Marketing in Global Industries, in *Competition in Global Industries*, Porter, M.E. (ed.), Boston, MA, Harvard Business School Press.

Thomas, R. (1993), The Valuation of Brands, *Marketing and Research Today*, May, pp. 79–80.

Valette-Florence, P. (1986), Les démarches de styles de vie: concepts, champs d'investigation et problèmes actuels, *Recherche et Applications en Marketing*, 1, 1, pp. 93–109.

Van Ballenberghe, A. (1993), Le comportement des consommateurs en période de promotion: analyse des perceptions des marques, Unpublished Working Paper, Louvain-la-Neuve, Louvain School of Management, Belgium.

Vaughn, R. (1986), How Advertising Works: A Planning Model Revisited, *Journal of Advertising Research*, 26, 1, pp. 57–65.

COMPANION WEBSITE FOR CHAPTER 9

Visit the *Market-driven Management* companion website at www.palgrave.com/business/lambin to find information on:

Measuring the Cognitive Response

Measuring the Affective Response

formulating a marketing strategy 10

Chapter contents

Chapter learning objectives

When you have read this chapter, you should be able to

- conduct a product portfolio analysis, using either the BCG growth-share matrix , the multifactor portfolio matrix or the SWOT analysis;
- discuss the merits and limitations of these two product portfolio analysis methods;
- understand the different views of strategy;
- describe the objectives and risks associated with the choice of a specific generic strategy;
- define the different strategic options a firm can contemplate in designing a development or growth strategy;
- describe the different competitive strategies a firm can consider vis-à-vis its rivals and their conditions of application;
- discuss the objectives and the various forms of international development.

Chapter introduction

The objective of this chapter is to examine how a market-driven firm can select the appropriate competitive strategy to achieve an above-average profit performance in the different business units included in its product portfolio. Two sets of factors determine the performance of a particular business unit: first, the overall attractiveness of the reference market where it operates, and second, the strength of its competitive position relative to direct competition. The reference market's attractiveness is largely determined by forces outside the firm's control (see Chapter 7), while the business unit's competitiveness can be shaped by the firm's strategic choices (see Chapter 8). Product portfolio analysis relates attractiveness and competitiveness indicators to help guide strategic thinking by suggesting specific marketing strategies to achieve a balanced mix of products that will ensure growth and profit performance in the long run. In this chapter, we shall first define the conceptual bases of portfolio analysis and then describe the types of mission or objectives the firm should assign to each of its business units given their differentiated positions along the attractiveness–competitiveness dimensions. Finally, we shall discuss the strategic alternatives open to the firm in the field of international development.

10.1. Product portfolio analyses

The purpose of a product portfolio analysis is to help a multi-business firm decide how to allocate scarce resources among the product markets they compete in. In the general case, the procedure consists in cross-classifying each activity with respect to two independent dimensions: the attractiveness of the reference market where the firm operates, and the firm's capacity to take advantage of opportunities within the market. Various portfolio models have been developed, using matrix representations where different indicators are used to measure attractiveness and competitiveness. Here we shall concentrate on the two most representative methods: the Boston Consulting Group's (BCG) method called the 'growth-share' matrix (Henderson, 1970; Boston Consulting Group, 1972) and the 'multifactor portfolio' matrix attributed to General Electric and McKinsey (Hussey, 1978; Abell and Hammond, 1979). Although the two methods have the same objectives, their implicit assumptions are different and the two approaches will likely yield different insights (Wind *et al.*, 1983).

10.1.1. The BCG growth-share matrix

The BCG matrix is built around two criteria: the reference market's growth rate (corrected for inflation), acting as an indicator of attractiveness, and market share relative to the firm's largest competitor, measuring competitiveness. As shown in Figure 10.1, we have a double entry table where

a cut-off level on each axis creates a grid with four quadrants:

- Along the market growth axis, the cut-off point distinguishing high-growth from low-growth markets corresponds to the growth rate of the GNP in real terms, or to the (weighted) average of the predicted growth rates of the different markets in which the products compete. In practice, high-growth markets are often defined as those growing by more than 10 per cent per year. Markets growing by less than 10 per cent are deemed low growth.
- Similarly, on the relative market share axis the dividing line is usually put at 1 or 1.5. Beyond this level, relative market share is high; below, it is low.

Thus the matrix relies on the concept of relative market share to leading competitor (see Chapter 6), which calculates the ratio of unit sales for one firm to unit sales for the largest share firm.

> If company A, for example, has a 10 per cent share of the market and the largest share belongs to company B, with 20 per cent, then company A has a relative market share of 0.5 (10 per cent/20 per cent). It has a low market share since the ratio is less than one. Similarly, company B has a relative market share of 2 (20 per cent/ 10 per cent). It has a high share of the market.

The use of relative market share is based on the assumption that market share is positively correlated with experience and therefore with profitability (see Chapter 8). Therefore, the competitive implications of holding a 20 per cent market share are quite different if the largest competitor is holding 40 per cent or only 5 per cent.

Product portfolio	Brand Sales (in million of €)	Number of competing firms	Sales of three of the firm's largest competitors (in millions of €)			Market growth (%)
Brand A	0.5	8	0.7	0.7	0.5*	15
Brand B	1.6	22	1.6*	1.6	1.0	18
Brand C	1.8	14	1.8*	1.2	1.0	7
Brand D	3.2	5	3.2*	0.8	0.7	4
Brand E	0.5	10	2.5	1.8	1.7	4

The BCG growth-share matrix

Total brand sales (in millions): 0.5 + 1.6 + 1.8 + 3.2 + 0.5 = 7.6 €
Brand shares in total company sales:
A = 6.6% B = 21.0% C = 23.7% D = 42.1% E = 6.6%
Brand relative market share (firm's to largest competitor)
A = 0.5 / 0.7 = 0.71
B = 1.6 / 1.6 = 1.0
C = 1.8 / 1.2 = 1.5
D = 3.2 / 0.8 = 4.0
E = 0.5 / 2.5 = 0.2

Average market growth rate
(15% + 18% + 7% + 4% + 4%) / 5 = 9.6% (or 10%).

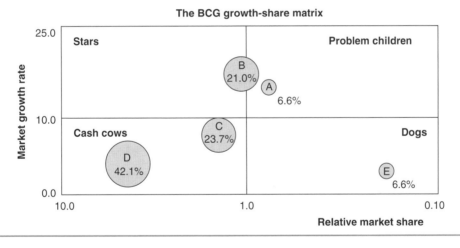

The BCG growth-share matrix

Figure 10.1   The BCG growth-share matrix
Source: Authors.

We thus obtain four different quadrants, each of which defines four fundamentally different competitive situations in terms of cash flow requirements and which need to be dealt with by specific objectives and marketing strategies.

Basic assumptions of the growth-share matrix

There are two basic assumptions underlying the BCG analysis: one concerns the existence of experience effects, and the other the product life cycle (PLC) model. These two assumptions can be summarised as follows:

1. Higher relative market share implies cost advantage over direct competitors because of experience effects; where the experience curve concept applies, the largest competitor will be the most profitable at the prevailing price level. Conversely, lower relative market share implies cost disadvantages. The implication of this first assumption is that the expected cash flow from products with high relative

market share will be higher than those with smaller market shares.

2. Being in a fast growing market implies greater need for cash to finance growth, added production capacity, advertising expenditures, and so on. Conversely, cash can be generated by a product operating in a mature market. Thus, the PLC model is employed because it highlights the desirability of a balanced mix of products situated in the different phases of the PLC.

The implication of this second assumption is that the cash needs for products in rapidly growing markets are expected to be greater than they are for those in slower growing ones. As discussed above, these assumptions are not always true. On this topic, see Abell and Hammond (1979, pp. 192–3).

Defining the type of business

Keeping in mind these two key assumptions, we can identify four groups of product markets having different characteristics in terms of their cash flow needs and/or contributions:

1. *Low growth/high share or cash cow products.* These products usually generate more cash than is required to sustain their market position. As such, they are a source of funds for the firm to support diversification efforts and growth in other markets. The priority strategy is to 'harvest'.

2. *Low growth/low share, dogs or lame ducks products.* Dogs have a low market share in a low-growth market, the least desirable market position. They generally have a cost

disadvantage and few opportunities to grow, since the war is over in the market. Maintaining these products generally turns into a financial drain without any hope of improvement. The priority strategy here is to 'divest' or in any case to adopt a low profile and to live modestly.

3. *High growth/low share or problem children products.* In this category, we find products with low relative market shares in a fast growing market. Despite their handicap vis-à-vis the leader, these products still have a chance of gaining market share, since the market has not yet settled down. However, supporting these products implies large financial means to finance share building strategies and to offset low profit margins. If the support is not given, these products will become dogs as market growth slows down. Thus, the alternatives here are to build market share or to divest.

4. *High growth/high share or stars products.* Here we have the market leaders in a rapidly growing market. These activities also require a lot of cash to finance growth; but because of their leading position they generate significant amounts of profits to reinvest in order to maintain their market position. As the market matures, they will progressively take over as cash cows.

Every activity can be placed in a matrix similar to Figure 10.1. The significance of an activity can be represented by a circle of size proportional to sales volume, sales revenue or profit contribution. This analysis should be made in a dynamic way, that is by tracking the progression or movements of each business unit over a period of time, as illustrated in Figure 10.2.

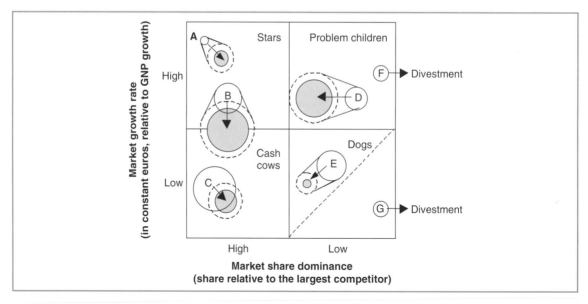

Figure 10.2   Dynamic analysis of the product portfolio
Source: Day (1977).

Diagnosing the product portfolio

In this approach, it is important to properly define the reference market in which the activity is competing. Relative market share compares the strength of a firm relative to its competitors. If the market is defined too narrowly the firm appears as the segment leader; if it is too wide, the firm appears too weak. The following points arise from the analysis:

- The position in the matrix indicates the credible strategy for each product: maintain leadership for stars; abandon or low profile for dogs; selective investment and growth for problem children; maximum profitability for cash cows.
- The position in the matrix helps evaluate cash requirements and profitability potential. Profits are usually a function of competitiveness; cash requirements generally depend on the phase of the product's life cycle, that is, on the reference market's degree of development.
- Allocation of the firm's total sales revenue or profit contribution according to each quadrant allows balancing of the product portfolio. The ideal situation is to have products that generate cash and products in their introductory or growing stage that will ensure the firm's long-term viability. The needs of the second category will be financed by the first.

Based on this type of diagnostic, the firm can envisage various strategies either to maintain or to restore the balance of its product portfolio. To be more specific, it allows the firm:

- To develop portfolio scenarios for future years on the basis of projected growth rates and tentative decisions regarding the market share strategies for the various activities, assuming different competitive reaction strategies.
- To analyse the potential of the existing product portfolio, and to put a figure on the total cash flow it can expect from each activity, every year, until the end of its planning horizon.
- To analyse the strategic gap, that is the observed difference between expected performance and desired performance.
- To identify the means to be employed to fill this gap, either by improving existing products' performance, or by abandoning products that absorb too much cash without any realistic hope of improvement, or finally by introducing new products that will rebalance the portfolio structure.

Too many ageing products indicate a danger of decline, even if current results appear very positive. Too many new products can lead to financial problems, even if activities are quite healthy, and this type of situation inevitably risks loss of independence.

Figure 10.3 describes two successful and two unsuccessful trajectories that can be observed for new or existing business units:

- The '*innovator*' *trajectory*, which uses the cash generated by the cash cows to invest in R&D and to enter the market with a product new to the world that will take over from existing stars.
- The '*follower*' *trajectory*, which uses the cash generated by the cash cows to enter as a problem child in a new market, dominated by a leader, with an aggressive market share build-up strategy.
- The '*disaster*' *trajectory*, whereby a star product evolves to the problem children quadrant as a consequence of insufficient investment in market share maintenance.
- The '*permanent mediocrity*' trajectory involves a problem child product evolving to the dogs' quadrant as a consequence of the failure to build market share for the product.

Let us remember that this type of diagnostic is only valid if the underlying assumptions mentioned earlier hold true. But, as already mentioned, the links between relative market share and profitability on the one hand and growth rate and financial requirements on the other are not always observed (see Abell and Hammond, 1979, pp. 192–3).

Limitations of the growth-share matrix

The most important merit of the BCG method is undoubtedly that it provides an appealing and elegant theoretical development which establishes a clear link between strategic positioning and financial performance. It is true that the initial assumptions are restrictive. But if they are true, they allow accurate analysis and valuable recommendations. General managers can thus concentrate on the major strategic problems and analyse the implications of alternative business strategies. Furthermore, the method is based on objective indicators of attractiveness and competitiveness, thus reducing the risk of subjectivity. Finally, it should also be added that the matrix provides a visual, vivid and easy to comprehend synthesis of the firm's activities, thus facilitating communication (see Figure 10.4).

There are, however, a number of limitations and difficulties which need to be emphasised because they reduce the generality of the approach:

- The implicit hypothesis about the relation between relative market share and cash flows means that this technique can only be used when there is an experience effect, that is in *volume industries*. Thus the experience effect might be observed in only some product markets

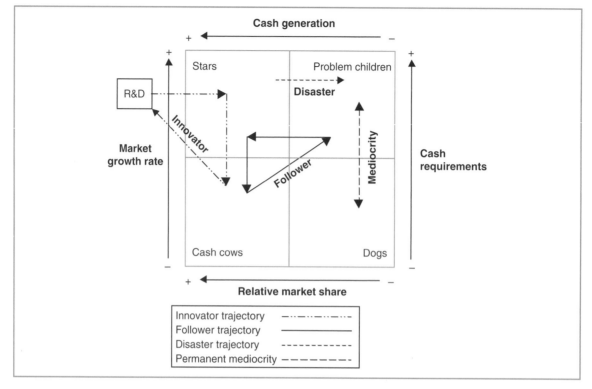

Figure 10.3   Portfolio scenario's alternatives
Source: Authors.

and not in all the product markets which are in the firm's portfolio.

- The method is based on the notion of *'internal' competitive advantage only* and does not take into account any 'external' competitive advantage enjoyed by the firm or the brand as a result of a successful differentiation strategy. Thus, a so-called dog could very well generate cash despite its cost disadvantage if the market accepts the paying of a premium price for the product, given its distinctive qualities.
- Despite its simple appearance, some *measurement problems* can arise. Should the definitions of the product market be broad or narrow? What share of what market? How do we determine market growth rate? Wind *et al.* (1983) have shown that the analysis is very sensitive to the measures used. For a discussion of these questions, see Day (1977, pp. 35–7).
- The recommendations of a portfolio analysis remain very vague and at most constitute *orientations* to be clarified. To say that in a given product market a strategy of 'harvest' or 'low profile' should be adopted is not very explicit. In any case, it is insufficient for an effective determination of policies regarding prices, distribution, communication, and so on. The main purpose of a portfolio analysis is to help guide, but not substitute for, strategic thinking.

These limitations are serious and restrict the scope of the growth-share matrix significantly, which is not equally useful in all corporate situations. Other methods based on less restrictive assumptions have been developed.

10.1.2. The multifactor portfolio matrix

The BCG matrix is based on two single indicators. But there are many situations where factors other than market growth and share determine the attractiveness of a market and the strength of a competitive position.

Clearly, a market's attractiveness can also depend on factors such as market accessibility, size, existing distribution network, structure of competition, favourable legislation, and so on.

> The market for portable computers is in principle highly attractive if we judge it by its high growth rate. There are, however, many other factors, such as rapid change in demand, expected price changes, products' fast rate of obsolescence, intensity of competition, and so on, which make this a risky and therefore relatively less attractive market.

Similarly, a firm's competitive advantage may be the result of strong brand image or commercial organisation,

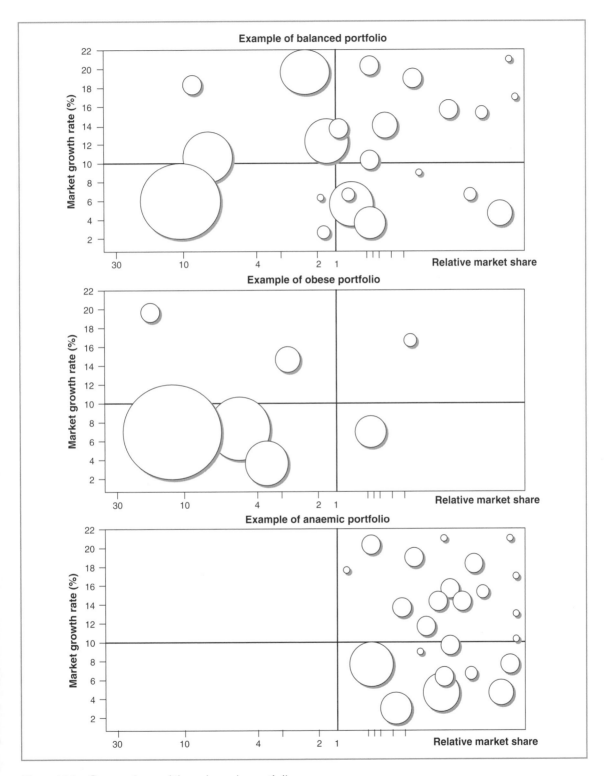

Figure 10.4   Comparison of three brands portfolios

Source: Authors.

technological leadership, distinctive product qualities, and so on, even if its market share is low relative to the major competitor.

When, in 1982, IBM introduced its personal computer, its competitiveness was very low according to the BCG matrix, since its market share was zero. Yet many analysts perceived IBM's competitive potential as very high because of its reputation in the computer market, its important technological know-how, its available resources and its will to succeed.

It is clear that several factors need to be taken into account to measure correctly the market's attractiveness and the firm's competitiveness potential. Instead of using a single indicator per dimension, multiple indicators can be used to assess attractiveness and competitiveness and to construct a composite index for each dimension. For an extensive list of possible factors, see Abell and Hammond (1979, p. 214). Thus, the BCG matrix described in the preceding section may be viewed as a special case of a more general theory relating market attractiveness and business competitiveness.

Development of a multifactor portfolio grid

To illustrate, Table 10.1 presents a battery of indicators selected to measure the attractiveness of five product markets from the textile industry, as well as a series of indicators evaluating the competitiveness of the company Tissex, which operates in these five product markets.

Since each situation is different, the relevant list of factors has to be identified and a multifactor portfolio grid is necessarily company-specific. The selection of the relevant factors is a delicate task and should involve several people from the strategic marketing group and from other departments as well. Precise definition of each indicator must be given and the nature of the relationship should be clearly determined. Once the grid is developed, each product market is evaluated against each indicator:

- A scale of 5 points is used, with 'low', 'average' and 'high' as reference points for scores equal to 1, 3 and 5, respectively.

Table 10.1   Multi-factor portfolio grid

	Weight (100)	Weak 1	2	Moderate 3	4	Strong 5
Indicators of attractiveness						
Market accessibility	—	Outside Europe and USA		Europe & USA		Europe
Market growth rate	—	≤5%		5–10%		≥10%
Length of the life cycle	—	≤2 years		2–5 years		≥5 years
Gross profit potential	—	≤15%		15–25%		≥25%
Strength of competition	—	Structured Oligopoly		Unstructured competition		Weak competition
Potential for differentiation	—	Very weak		Moderate		Strong
Concentration of customers	—	Very dispersed		Moderately dispersed		Concentrated
Indicators of competitiveness						
Relative market share	—	≤1/3 leader		≥1/3 leader		Leader
Unit cost	—	> direct competitors		= direct competitors		< direct competitors
Distinctive qualities	—	'Me too' product		Moderately differentiated		'Unique selling proposition'
Technological know-how	—	Weak control		Moderate control		Strong control
Sales organisation	—	Independent distributors		Selective distribution		Direct sales
Image	—	Very weak		Fuzzy		Strong

Source: Authors.

- As far as indicators of competitiveness are concerned, ratings are not attributed 'in abstract', but relative to the most dangerous competitor in each product market or segment.
- If some indicators appear to be more important than others, weighting can be introduced, but the weights must remain the same for every activity considered.
- The ratings should reflect, as much as possible, future or expected values of the indicators and not so much their present values.
- A summary score can then be calculated for each product market's global attractiveness and the firm's potential competitiveness.

Contrary to the BCG approach, subjective evaluations enter into these measures of attractiveness and competitiveness. But the process may nevertheless gain in interpersonal objectivity, to the extent that many judges operate independently. Their evaluations are then compared in order to reconcile or to explain observed differences and disagreements. This process of reconciliation is always useful in itself.

Interpretation of the multifactor grid

We then obtain a two-dimensional classification grid similar to the BCG matrix. It is current practice to subdivide each dimension into three levels (low, average, high), thus obtaining nine squares, each corresponding to a specific strategic position.

Each zone corresponds to a specific positioning. The firm's different activities can be represented by circles with an area proportional to their share in the total sales revenue

or profit contribution. The four most clearly defined positionings are those corresponding to the four corners of the matrix in Figure 10.5:

- In quadrant C, both the product market's attractiveness and the firm's competitive potential are high; the strategic orientation to follow is offensive growth. The characteristics are similar to those of 'stars' in the BCG matrix.
- In quadrant A, both attractiveness and competitiveness are low; strategic orientation is maintenance without investment or divestment. We have the case of 'dogs' as in Figure 10.1.
- Quadrant B depicts an intermediate situation: competitive advantage is low, but the reference market's attraction is high. This is typically the case of 'problem children'. The strategy to follow is selective growth.
- In quadrant D, we have the opposite situation. Competitive advantage is high but market attractiveness is low. A skimming and maintenance strategy without major new investment is called for. This is the equivalent of the 'cash cows' positioning in the BCG matrix.

The other intermediate zones correspond to strategic positions which are less clearly defined and often hard to interpret. The fuzzy value of the summary scores can reflect either very high marks on some indicators and very low marks on others, or simply an average evaluation on all the criteria. The latter case is often observed in practice and reflects imprecise information or simply lack of it.

Choice of future strategy

We thus have a visual representation of the firm's growth potential. By extrapolating each activity's expected growth under the assumption of 'no change' strategy, the firm is in

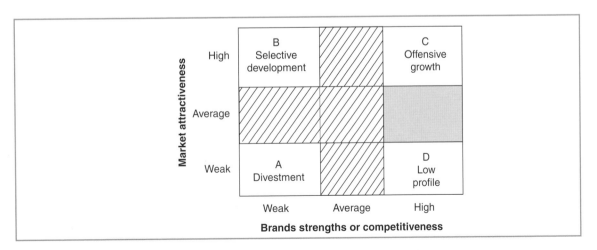

Figure 10.5 Multifactor portfolio grid
Source: Adapted from Abell and Hammond (1979).

a position to assess its future position. Alternative strategic options can also be explored, such as

- investing to hold aims at maintaining the current position and keeping up with expected changes in the market;
- investing to penetrate aims at improving the business position by moving the business unit to the right of the grid;
- investing to rebuild aims at restoring a position which has been lost – this revitalisation strategy will be more difficult to implement if the market attractiveness is already medium or low;
- low investment aims at harvesting the business, that is, the business position is exchanged for cash, for example, by selling the activity at the highest possible price;
- divestment aims at leaving markets or segments of low attractiveness or segments where the firm does not have the capacity to acquire or sustain a competitive advantage.

Figure 10.6 shows an example of multifactor portfolio analysis. It represents the portfolio of a firm from the food industry. Note that product markets' attractiveness is very average and the firm's competitiveness is evaluated as low for almost all the products considered. The future of this firm is clearly very bleak.

Evaluation of the multifactor portfolio grid

The multifactor portfolio model leads to the same kind of analyses as the BCG matrix, with one major difference: the link between competitive and financial performance (i.e. cash flow) is lost. However, since this model is not based on any particular assumption, it does overcome many of the shortcomings of the BCG method and it is more widely applicable. Furthermore, it is much more flexible because the indicators used are company-specific.

The use of these types of matrix suffers, nevertheless, from certain limitations:

- Measurement problems are more delicate and risk of subjectivity is much higher here. This shows up not only in the choice of indicators and their possible weighting, but especially when it comes to marking the criteria. The risk of subjectivity is greater for indicators of competitiveness, where there is necessarily self-evaluation.

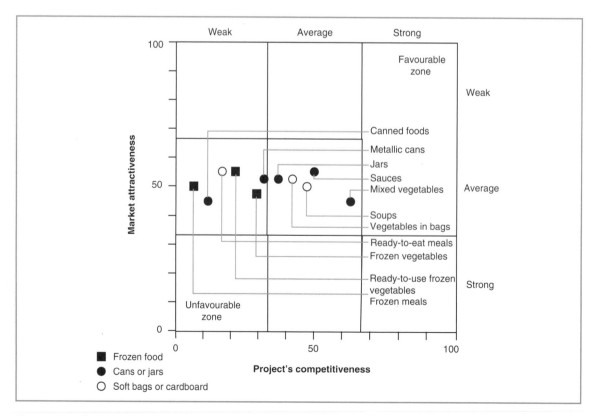

Figure 10.6   Example of a multifactor portfolio

Source: MDA Consulting Group, Brussels.

- When the number of indicators and the number of activities to evaluate are high, the procedure becomes heavy and demanding, especially when information is scarce or imprecise.
- The results are sensitive to the ratings and to the weighting systems adopted. Manipulation of weights can produce a desired position in the matrix. It is therefore important to test the sensitivity of results to the use of alternative weighting systems.
- As for the BCG matrix, recommendations remain very general and need to be clarified. Furthermore, the link with financial performance is less clearly established.

The two approaches will very likely yield different insights. But as the main purpose of a product portfolio analysis is to help guide, but not substitute for, strategic thinking, the process of reconciliation will be useful. Thus it is desirable to employ both approaches and compare results (Day 1977, p. 38).

10.1.3. The SWOT analysis

A widely used framework for organising the bits and pieces of information gained from the company internal information system and from the macro-marketing environment is a SWOT analysis, an acronym for Strengths, Weaknesses, Opportunities and Threats. Developed at Harvard by Andrews (1971), it is in fact a multifactor analysis similar to the two preceding methods with these two differences:

- the analysis is purely qualitative and is not based on objective measures or hard data;
- it gives a different definition of the two concepts of market attractiveness (external factors) and company competitiveness (internal factors).

SWOT analysis is a simple, straightforward model that provides direction and serves as a catalyst for the development of a viable marketing plan. It fulfils this role by structuring the *assessment of the fit* between what an organisation can (strengths) and cannot (weaknesses) presently do, and the environmental conditions working for (opportunities) and against (threats) the firm. Alternative strategies for the firm are developed through an appraisal of the opportunities and threats it faces in various markets, and an evaluation of its strengths and weaknesses. If done correctly a firm can highlight its strengths and minimises its weaknesses to pursue opportunities and avoid threats. The elements of a SWOT analysis are presented in Chapter 10.

The issues that can be considered in a SWOT analysis are numerous and will vary depending on the particular firm and industry being analysed. A list of potential issues is proposed in Box 10.1. The simplicity of the method and the lack of conceptual framework to guide the analysis often leads to difficulties of interpretation.

The SWOT analysis is more qualitative and general than the BCG or the multifactor portfolio methods. In addition to its apparent simplicity, its merit is to provide a more comprehensive view of the firm's strategic potential. In that sense, the SWOT analysis method can be more proactive than the traditional product portfolio methods. An example of SWOT analysis is given in Table 10.2.

10.1.4. Portfolio models in practice

As evidenced by the multi-year international survey sponsored by the consultancy firm Bain & Company about management tools and techniques (Bain, 2005), it appears (see Table 10.3) that strategic planning and portfolio analyses are ranked among the most popular managerial tools used by companies.

A portfolio analysis leads to different strategic recommendations according to the positioning of activities in the portfolio. As we saw, such recommendations are mainly general guidelines, such as invest, maintain, harvest, abandon, and so on, which require clarification and need to be put in a more explicit operational perspective.

Benefits of product portfolio analyses

Portfolio analysis is the outcome of the whole strategic marketing process described in the last four chapters of this book. A portfolio analysis rests on the following principles, irrespective of the method used:

- An accurate division of the firm's activities into product markets or segments.
- Measures of competitiveness and attractiveness allowing evaluation and comparison of different activities' strategic values.
- Links between strategic position and economic and financial performance, mainly in the BCG method.

Matrix representations help to synthesise the results of this strategic thinking exercise and to visualise them in a clear and expressive manner. Contrary to appearances, they are not simple to elaborate. They require complete and reliable information about the way markets function, about the firm's and its rivals' strengths and weaknesses. More specifically, this analysis implies the following:

- Considerable effort to segment the reference market. This is particularly important, because the validity of the recommendations is conditioned by the initial choice of segmentation.

BOX 10.1

IMPLEMENTATION PROBLEM: WHICH POTENTIAL ISSUES TO CONSIDER IN A SWOT ANALYSIS?

Potential internal strengths
  Abundant financial resources
  Any distinctive core competence
  Well-known as the market leader
  Economies of scale
  Proprietary technology
  Patented process
  Lower costs
  Good market image
  Superior management talent
  Better marketing skills
  Outstanding product quality
  Partnership with other firms
  Good distribution skills
  Committed employees

Potential external opportunities
  Rapid market growth
  Rival firms are complacent
  Changing customer needs and tastes
  Opening of foreign markets
  Mishap of a rival firm
  New uses for product discovered
  Economic boom
  Deregulation
  New technology
  Demographic shifts
  Other firms seek alliances
  High brand switching
  Sales decline for a substitute
  New distribution method

Potential internal weaknesses
  Lack of strategic direction
  Weak spending on R&D
  Very narrow product line
  Limited distribution
  Higher costs
  Out-of-date products
  Internal operating problems
  Weak market image
  Poor marketing skills
  Limited management skills
  Under-trained employees

Potential external threats
  Entry of foreign competitors
  Introduction of new substitutes
  Product life cycle in decline
  Changing customer needs/tastes
  Rival firms adopt new strategies
  Increased regulation
  Recession
  New technology
  Demographic shifts
  Foreign trade barriers
  Poor performance of ally firms

Source: Ferrel *et al.* (1999, p. 62).

Table 10.2 An example of SWOT analysis: the hard discounter retailer Aldi

Strengths	Weaknesses
Simplicity of operations	Manual systems used
Cost efficient	Limited assortment, limited appeal
Powerful price points	Minimal perishables, marginal quality
Private labels sourcing	Dependent on well-trained cashier
Price edge over other retailers	Not a pleasant experience
Understand economics of business	
Deep pocket of parent company	
Low breakeven stores	
Opportunities	*Threats*
Expand in other markets	Other limited assortment retailers who
Increase market penetration	understand the business and can operate
Continue to improve quality	better
Tap into institutional markets	
Hold tight to lowest cost positioning	

Source: Coriiolis Research.

Table 10.3   Top ten tools usage over time and satisfaction

1993	1996	2000	2004	Satisfaction 2004
Mission statements (88%)	Strategic planning (83%)	Strategic planning (76%)	Strategic planning (79%)	4.14*
Customer satisfaction (86%)	Mission statements (82%)	Mission statements (70%)	CRM (75%)	3.91
TQM (72%)	Benchmarking (79%)	Benchmarking (69%)	Benchmarking (73%)	3.98*
Competitor profiling (71%)	Customer satisfaction (79%)	Outsourcing (69%)	Outsourcing (73%)	3.89
Benchmarking (70%)	Core competencies (69%)	Customer satisfaction (60%)	Customer segmentation (72%)	3.97*
Pay-for-performance (70%)	TQM (66%)	Growth strategies (55%)	Mission statements (72%)	3.87
Re-engineering (67%)	Re-engineering (65%)	Strategic alliances (53%)	Core competencies (65%)	3.97*
Strategic alliances (62%)	Pay-for-performance (63%)	Pay-for-performance (52%)	Strategic alliances (63%)	3.95
Cycle time reduction (55%)	Strategic alliances (61%)	Customer segmentation (51%)	Growth strategies (62%)	3.91
Self-directed teams (55%)	Growth strategies (55%)	Core competencies (48%)	Business process re-engineering/TQM (61%)	3.90

Note: * Significantly above the overall mean. Scale: 1–5

Source: Bain and Company (2005).

- Systematic and careful collection of detailed information, which does not normally exist as such and needs to be reconstituted by cross-checking and probing; quality of results also depends on the reliability of this information.

This kind of analysis cannot be improved and it relies particularly on top management's complete support. Such a tool is obviously not a panacea, but it has the merit of emphasising some important aspects of management:

- It moderates excessively short-term vision by insisting on keeping a balance between immediately profitable activities and those that prepare the future.
- It encourages the firm to keep both market attractiveness and competitive potential in mind.
- It establishes priorities in allocation of human as well as financial resources.
- It suggests differentiated development strategies per type of activity on a more data-oriented basis.
- It creates a common language throughout the organisation and fixes clear objectives to reinforce motivation and facilitate control.

The main weakness of methods of portfolio analysis is that they can give an image of the present, or indeed of the recent past, and devote too little time to assessing future changes and strategic options for dealing with these changes. There is also a risk of too mechanistic application

of these methods. As already underlined, different methods could lead to very different classifications. The tools described here must be viewed more as guides to informed reasoning than as prescriptive tools.

These matrices can also be used in a dynamic perspective, for instance in comparing the present market positions held within each product market with the targeted positions for the next period. The matrix presented in Figure 10.6 is useful with this respect because it permits us to analyse the changing competitive positions of each business unit over time (Hussey, 1978).

10.2. The choice of a generic strategy

The first step in elaborating a development strategy is to clarify the nature of the sustainable competitive advantage which will serve as the basis for later strategic actions and tactics. We saw in the previous chapter that competitive advantage can be described by reference to two aspects (see Figure 10.1): productivity (cost advantage) and market power (advantage in terms of maximum acceptable price). The question is to know which of these two aspects should be given priority, given the firm's characteristics, its strengths and weaknesses and those of its rivals. In other words, which advantage is 'sustainable' in a given product market? This question can be examined in two perspectives: within the framework of existing markets and of future markets.

10.2.1. Two ways to approach strategy

What is strategy? Two different views of strategy can be adopted, which are more complementary than opposed. The first view of strategy, promoted by M. Porter (1985, 1996), is mostly relevant when the objective is to target existing or articulated needs in existing markets, while the second, promoted by G. Hamel and C.K. Prahalad (1994), is oriented more towards latent needs and future markets.

Competing for existing markets

A first view consists in selecting a market or a product market where the firm wants to be active and in which the firm will try to differentiate itself vis-à-vis direct competition, either by performing different activities from rivals or by performing similar activities in different ways (Porter, 1996). Identifying a strategic sustainable competitive advantage then requires an analysis of the competitive structure, and more specifically, answers to the following questions:

- What are the key success factors in a given product market or segment?
- What are the firm's strengths and weaknesses with regard to these factors?
- What are the strengths and weaknesses of the firm's direct rival(s) with regard to the same key success factors?

This systematic search for a sustainable competitive advantage is at the core of a differentiation strategy.

Competing for future markets

A second view of strategy is more proactive. The goal here is, 'to build the best possible assumption base about the future (through foresight) and thereby develop the prescience needed to proactively shape industry evolution' (Hamel and Prahalad, 1994, p. 73). Industry foresight helps managers answer three critical questions:

- First, what new types of customer benefit should we seek to provide in 5, 10 or 15 years?
- Second, what new competencies will we need to build or acquire to offer these benefits to customers?
- Third, how will we need to reconfigure the customer interface over the next few years?

This view of strategy is more proactive, since the objective here is to identify, understand and influence forces shaping the future of industry. As illustrated by Hamel and Prahalad, the US firm Motorola has such a point of view (Exhibit 10.1). More than a differentiation

---

EXHIBIT 10.1

THE VALUE STRATEGY OF MOTOROLA

Motorola dreams of a world in which telephone numbers will be assigned to people, rather than places; where small hand-held devices will allow people to stay in touch no matter where they are; and where the new communicators can deliver video images and data as well as voice signals. For this world to become reality, Motorola knows that it will have to strengthen its competencies in digital compression, flat screen displays, and battery technology. Motorola also knows that to capture a significant share of a burgeoning consumer market, it will have to substantially increase the familiarity of its brand with customers around the world.

Source: Hamel and Prahalad (1994, p. 74).

---

strategy of being better, faster, simpler, cheaper, and so on, the objective here is more fundamental and is to regenerate the core strategy of the firm and to reinvent the industry.

Kim and Mauborgne (1997) have proposed five recommendations in what they call a value strategy development:

- Challenge the inevitableness of industry conditions.
- Competition is not the benchmark.
- Focus on what most customers' value.
- Ask what we would do if we were starting anew.
- Think in terms of the total solution buyers seek.

To adopt value or discontinuous innovation strategy, it is necessary to create solutions to problems customers do not even know they have. Discovering new solutions means going beyond the old ones by challenging the fundamental rules of business and redrawing the boundaries to create new markets and industries.

10.2.2. Generic strategies in existing markets

Generic strategies will be different according to the type of competitive advantage sought, that is, whether they are based on productivity and therefore cost advantage, or whether they rest on an element of differentiation and are therefore based on a price premium. Porter (1980, p. 35) suggests that there exist four generic competitive strategies to outperforming other firms in an industry: overall cost leadership, differentiation, focused differentiation or cost focus (Figure 10.7).

Overall cost leadership

This first generic strategy is based on productivity and is generally related to the existence of an experience effect.

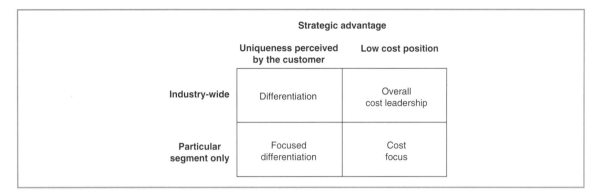

	Strategic advantage	
	Uniqueness perceived by the customer	Low cost position
Industry-wide	Differentiation	Overall cost leadership
Particular segment only	Focused differentiation	Cost focus

Figure 10.7   Four generic strategies
Source: Porter (1980).

This strategy implies close scrutiny (a) of overhead costs, (b) of productivity investments intended to enhance the value of experience effects, (c) of product design costs and (d) on cost minimisation in service, selling, advertising, and so on. Low cost relative to competitors is the major preoccupation of the entire strategy.

Having a cost advantage constitutes an effective protection against the five competitive forces (see Figure 10.2):

- Relative to its direct competitors, the firm is in a better position to resist a possible price war and still make a profit at its rivals' minimum price level.
- Powerful buyers can only drive down prices to the level of the most efficient competitor.
- Low cost provides a defence against powerful suppliers by providing more flexibility to cope with input cost increases.
- A low-cost position provides substantial entry barriers in terms of scale economies or cost advantage.
- A low-cost position usually places the firm in a favourable position vis-à-vis substitutes relative to competitors in the industry (Porter, 1980, p. 36).

Thus, cost leadership protects the firm against all five competitive forces, because the least efficient firms are the first to feel the effects of the competitive struggle.

Differentiation

The objective here is to give distinctive qualities to the product that are significant to the buyer and which create something that is perceived as being unique. What the firm tends to do is to create a situation of monopolistic competition in which it holds some market power because of the distinctive element (Chamberlin, 1933).

We saw before that differentiation can take many forms: design or brand image, technology, features,

customer service, dealer network, and so on. Differentiation, like cost domination, protects the firm from the five competitive forces, but in a very different way:

- Relative to its direct rivals, differentiation provides the firm with insulation against competitive rivalry because of brand loyalty and resulting lower price sensitivity. It also increases margins, which avoids the need for a low-cost position.
- The resulting customer loyalty, and the need for a competitor to overcome uniqueness, provides entry barriers.
- Higher profitability increases the firm's ability to resist cost increases imposed by powerful suppliers.
- Finally, the firm that has differentiated itself to achieve customer loyalty should be better positioned vis-à-vis substitutes than its competitors (Porter, 1980, p. 37).

Successful differentiation enables the firm to realise higher profits than its rivals because of the higher price the market is willing to accept despite the fact that costs are generally higher. This type of strategy is not always compatible with high market share, since most buyers are not necessarily prepared to pay a higher price, even though they recognise product superiority.

Differentiation strategies generally imply large investments in operational marketing, particularly in advertising expenditures to inform the market about the product's distinctive qualities.

Focus

A third generic strategy is focusing on the needs of a particular segment, group of buyers or geographic market, without claiming to address the whole market. The objective is to take a restricted target and to serve its narrow strategic target more effectively than competitors who are serving the whole market. It implies either differentiation or cost domination, or both, but only vis-à-vis the particular target.

For example, a paint manufacturer can decide to address professional painters only, excluding the public at large, car manufacturers and the naval industry. In the car industry, Mercedes only addresses the high end of the market, but it covers that segment more effectively than other car manufacturers having a full line of models.

The focus strategy always implies some limitations on the overall market share achievable. A focus strategy can give the firm a large share of the market in the targeted segment, but it may be low relative to the whole market.

10.2.3. Risks associated with generic strategies

The choice of one strategy against another is not a neutral decision, in the sense that they involve differing types of risks and also different priority preoccupations in the organisation. Exhibit 10.2 summarises the risks inherent in each generic strategy. The implementation of these strategies implies different resources and different know-how, which are given below:

- A cost domination strategy assumes sustained investment, a high degree of technological competence, close control of manufacturing and distribution costs and standardised products to facilitate production.
- A differentiation strategy assumes significant marketing know-how as well as technological advance. The ability to analyse and anticipate trends in market needs plays a fundamental role here. Interfunctional co-ordination among R&D, production and marketing is vital.
- Finally, a concentration strategy also assumes the previous characteristics vis-à-vis the targeted segment.

10.3. Assessing growth opportunities

There are growth objectives in most strategies considered by firms, whether they are of sales growth, market share, profits or size. Growth is a factor that influences firm vitality, stimulates initiatives and increases motivation of personnel and management. Independent of this element of dynamism, growth is necessary in order to survive assaults from competitors, thanks to the economies of scale and experience effects it generates.

A firm can envisage growth objectives at three different levels:

1. A growth objective within the reference market it operates; we shall refer to this as intensive growth.
2. A growth objective within the industrial chain, lateral expansion of its generic activity, backwards or forwards; this is integrative growth.

EXHIBIT 10.2

RISKS ASSOCIATED WITH GENERIC STRATEGIES

Risks of overall cost leadership

- Technological changes that nullify past investments or learning.
- Low-cost learning by industry newcomers or followers, through imitation or through their ability to invest in state-of-the-art facilities.
- Inability to see required product or marketing change because of the attention placed on costs.
- Inflation in costs that narrows the firm's ability to maintain enough of a price differential to offset competitors' brand images or other approaches to differentiation.

Risks of differentiation

- The cost differential between low-cost competitors and the differentiated firm becomes too great for differentiation to hold brand loyalty. Buyers sacrifice some of the features, services or image possessed by the differentiated firm for large cost savings.

- Buyers' needs for the differentiating factor fall. This can occur as buyers become more sophisticated.
- Imitations narrows perceived differentiation, a common occurrence as industries mature.

Risks of focus

- The cost differential between broad range competitors and the focused firm widens to eliminate the cost advantages of serving a narrow target or to offset the differentiation achieved by focus.
- The differences in desired products or services between the strategic target and the market as a whole narrows.
- Competitors find submarkets within the strategic target and out-focus the focused.

Source: Adapted from Porter (1980, pp. 45–6).

3. A growth objective based on opportunities outside its normal field of activity; this is growth by diversification.

To each of these growth objectives correspond a number of possible strategies. It is interesting to examine them briefly.

10.3.1. Intensive growth

A strategy of intensive growth is called for when a firm has not yet fully exploited the opportunities offered by its products within its 'natural' reference market (see Exhibit 10.3). Various strategies may be envisaged: market penetration, market development strategies and product development strategies.

Market penetration strategies

A market penetration strategy, also called organic growth, consists of trying to increase or maintain sales of current products in existing markets. Several options are open.

1. *Primary demand development*: to increase size of total market by expanding primary demand, for example,

- broadening the customer base by converting non-users into users (see Exhibit 10.4);
- increasing the frequency of purchase among present users;
- increasing the average quantity purchased per use occasion;
- identifying and promoting new uses.

Note that this strategy can benefit all competitors since it influences primary demand more than selective demand.

2. *Market share increase strategy*: to increase sales by attracting buyers from rival brands, through significant spending on marketing mix variables, for example,

- improved product or service offering;
- positioning the brands;
- aggressive pricing;
- significant reinforcement of the distribution and service network;
- major promotional efforts.

This more aggressive strategy will be mainly observed in market situations where primary demand is non-expansible, having reached the maturity phase of the PLC.

3. *Market acquisition*: to increase market share substantially by acquisition or joint venture, for example,

- acquisition of competitor to obtain its market share;
- joint venture to achieve control of a significant market share.

4. *Market position defence*: to defend current market position (i.e. customer relationships, network, share, image, and so on) by adjusting the marketing mix, for example,

- product or service minor modifications or repositioning,
- defensive pricing,
- sales and distribution network reinforcement;
- stepped-up or redirected promotional activities.

5. *Market rationalisation*: to modify significantly the markets served to reduce costs and/or increase marketing effectiveness, for example,

- concentration on most profitable segments;
- use of the most effective distributors;
- limiting individual customers served via minimum volume requirements;
- selective abandonment of market segments.

EXHIBIT 10.3

CAMPBELL SOUP COMPANY STIMULATES SOUP CONSUMPTION

Campbell Soup noted that US soup consumption is growing again, up 3 per cent so far this fiscal year (1999). That's good news for Campbell, which has a US market share of about 80 per cent despite some inroads by generic supermarket brands in recent years. Soup accounts for nearly half of the Campbell's revenue. [...]. In a remarkable about-face for Campbell, it has been investing heavily to develop new products that will make it easier for consumers to eat soup. Among the new products that the company expects to roll out nationally in the fall: tomato soup in resealable plastic bottle and single serving, microwaveable soups. Other products are also in the pipeline, including a refrigerated gourmet soup in-a-pouch. [...]. The Company is also trying to sell more soup through restaurants, convenience stores, cafeterias and college dining halls. Campbell is testing a soup-dispensing machine that works like a soda fountain in 7–11 stores, and is trying out other soup products with McDonald's and Subway. Some at the company even talk about one day selling soup from Campbell kiosks.

Source: Adapted from Wall Street Journal Europe, 20 May 1991.

EXHIBIT 10.4

SONY'S NEW STRATEGY: FROM A BOX COMPANY TO BECOMING A INFORMATION TECHNOLOGY COMPANY

Sony Corp. announced a sweeping corporate overhaul on Tuesday aimed at decisively changing the company's identity from a manufacturer of consumer electronics to a provider of digital network services. Sony's President, Mr Idei, says Sony's new focus would be the network business: essentially the business of linking consumers to a variety of services either through their computers or their televisions. We have to make it possible for Sony's customers to directly link themselves with our products and services and for Sony to distribute its movies, music, games and personal finance tools and services directly to its customers. In other words, the company intends to supply not only the computers and television sets through which people will gain access to its movies and music but also the pipeline. In the past three years, we have made a lot of efforts to move from being a 'box' company to becoming an information technology company, Mr. Idei said in an interview.

Source: Strom (1999).

---

6. *Market organisation*: to influence, using legally accepted practices, the level of competition within one's industry to enhance economic viability, for example,

- establishment of industry-wide competitive rules or guidelines, usually under government supervision;
- creation of joint marketing research organisations to improve information systems;
- agreement on capacity stabilisation or reduction.

These last three strategies are more defensive, aiming at maintaining the level of market penetration.

Market development strategies

A market development strategy refers to a firm's attempt to increase the sales of its present products by tapping new or future markets. This objective can be achieved using four alternative approaches.

1. *Unarticulated or latent needs among served customers*: to propose solutions to customers' needs not yet perceived or expressed. The objective here is to lead customers with new products (like digital photography), to educate them and to create a new market through a proactive marketing strategy.

2. *New market segments*: to reach new (un-served) groups of customers within the same geographic market, for example,

- introducing an industrial product to the consumer market or vice versa;
- selling the product to another customer age group (sweets to adults);
- selling the product to another industrial sector.

3. *New distribution channels*: to distribute the product through another channel of distribution, complementary to the current ones, for example,

- adopting a direct marketing system for specific groups of customers;
- distributing the products through vending machines;
- developing a franchise system parallel to the existing network.

4. *Geographic expansion*: towards other parts of the country or to other countries, for example,

- shipping existing products to foreign markets relying on local agents or on an independent worldwide trading company;
- creating an exclusive network of distributors to handle foreign business;
- Acquiring a foreign company in the same sector.

Market development strategies rely mainly on the distribution and marketing know-how of the firm.

Product development strategies

A product development strategy consists of increasing sales by developing improved or new products aimed at current markets. Several different possibilities exist.

1. *Discontinuous innovations*: to launch a new product or service that represents a major change in the benefits offered to customers and in the behaviour necessary for them to use the product. Customers must in some way discontinue their past patterns to fit the new product into their lives (mobile telephone and self-banking are good examples).

2. *Features addition strategy*: to add functions or features to existing products in order to expand the market, for example,

- increasing the versatility of a product by adding functions;
- adding an emotional or social value to a utilitarian product;
- improving the safety or convenience of the product.

3. *Product line extensions strategy*: to increase the breadth of the product line by introducing new varieties to increase or maintain market share, for example,

- launching different packages of different sizes;
- launching different product categories under the same umbrella brand name;
- increasing the number of flavours, scents, colours or composition;
- offering the same product in different forms or shapes.

The strategy of line extension can lead to product proliferation and the question of cannibalisation and synergistic effects should be addressed explicitly.

4. *Product line rejuvenation strategy*: to restore the overall competitiveness of obsolete or inadequate products by replacing them with technologically or functionally superior products, for example,

- developing a new generation of more powerful products;
- launching environmentally friendly new models of existing products;
- improving the aesthetic aspects of the product.

5. *Product quality improvement strategy*: to improve the way a product performs its functions as a package of benefits, for example,

- determining the package of benefits sought by each customer group;
- establishing quality standards on each dimension of the package of benefits;
- establishing a programme of total quality control.

6. *Product line acquisition*: to complete, improve or broaden the range of products through external means, for example,

- acquisition of a company with a complementary product line;
- contracting for the supply of a complementary product line to be sold under the company's name;
- joint venture for the development and production of a new product.

7. *Product line rationalisation*: to modify the product line to reduce production or distribution costs, for example,

- product line and packaging standardisation;
- selective abandonment of unprofitable or marginal products;
- minor product redesign.

The lever used in product development strategies is essentially R&D. These strategies are generally more costly and risky than market development strategies.

10.3.2. Integrative growth

An integrative growth strategy is justified when a firm can improve profitability by controlling different activities of strategic importance within the industrial chain. It describes a variety of make-or-buy arrangements firms use to obtain a ready supply of strategic raw materials and a ready market for their outputs. Examples include ensuring stability of supplies, controlling a distribution network, or having access to information in a downstream activity to secure captive markets. There is a distinction between backward integration, forward integration and horizontal integration.

Backward integration

A backward integration strategy is driven by the concern to maintain or to protect a strategically important source of supplies, be it raw or semi-processed materials, components or services. In some cases, backward integration is necessary because suppliers do not have the resources or technological know-how to make components or materials which are indispensable to the firm.

Another objective may be to have access to a key technology which might be essential to the success of the activity. For example, many computer manufacturers have integrated backwards in the design and production of semiconductors in order to control this fundamental activity.

Forward integration

The basic motivation for a forward integration strategy is to control outlets without which the firm will choke. For a firm producing consumer goods, this involves controlling distribution through franchises or exclusive contracts, or even by creating its own chain stores, such as Yves Rocher or Bata. In industrial markets, the aim is mainly to ensure the development of downstream industries of transformation and incorporation that constitute natural outlets. This is how some basic industries actively participate in creating intermediary transformation activity.

In some cases, forward integration is done simply to have a better understanding of the needs of buyers of manufactured products. The firm creates in this case a subsidiary playing the role of a pilot unit: to understand problems of users in order to meet their needs more effectively. The adoption of solution-to-a-problem strategy generally implies some form of forward integration. The new development strategy adopted by Xerox provides a good example of a forward integration strategy.

EXHIBIT 10.5

FUJITSU AND SIEMENS TO LINK EUROPE OPERATIONS

Fujitsu Ltd., the Japanese computer giant, and Siemens AG, the German electronic conglomerate, announced plans to create the world's fifth-biggest computer maker by merging their European operations. On the strength of ultra-light notebooks, Internet server and mainframes, the Japanese–German venture ambitiously aim to break into a global industry dominated by US technology manufacturers such as Compaq Computer Corp. 'We want to end the domination of U.S. PC vendors', said Judith Grindal, spokeswoman for Fujitsu Computers (Europe) Ltd. [...] With users now treating many personal computers as 'commodity boxes', keeping prices under perpetual pressure, Siemens and Fujitsu need a critical mass of purchasing power, sales volume and marketing channels to compete. 'The main goal is really economies of scale, although Siemens won some market share in recent years, on a world-wide basis, their PC business is clearly too small.'

Source: International Herald Tribune (1999).

Horizontal integration

A horizontal integration strategy has a totally different perspective. The objective is to reinforce competitive position by absorbing or controlling some competitors. There can be various arguments for this: neutralising a dangerous rival, reaching the critical volume so as to benefit from scale effects, benefiting from complementarity of product lines and having access to distribution networks or to restricted market segments (see Exhibit 10.5).

Growth by diversification

A strategy of growth by diversification is justified if the firm's industrial chain presents little or no prospect of growth or profitability. This may happen either because competitors occupy a powerful position, or because the reference market is in decline. Diversification implies entry into new product markets. This kind of growth strategy is as such more risky, since the jump into the unknown is more significant. It is usual to establish a distinction between concentric diversification and pure diversification.

Concentric diversification

In a concentric diversification strategy, the firm goes out of its industrial and commercial network and tries to add new activities, which are related to its current activities technologically and/or commercially. The objective is therefore to benefit from synergy effects due to complementarity of activities, and thus to expand the firm's reference market.

A concentric diversification strategy (see Exhibit 10.6) usually has the objectives of attracting new groups of buyers and expanding the reference market of the firm.

Pure diversification

In a pure diversification strategy, the firm enters into new activities which are unrelated to its traditional activities, either technologically or commercially. The aim is to turn towards entirely new fields so as to rejuvenate the product portfolio. At the end of 1978, for example, Volkswagen bought Triumph-Adler, which specialises in informatics and office equipment, for this very reason.

Diversification strategies are undoubtedly the most risky and complex strategies, because they lead the firm into unknown territory. To be successful, diversification requires important human as well as financial resources. Drucker (1981, p. 16) considers that a successful diversification requires a common core or unity represented by common markets, technology or production processes. He states that without such a unity core, diversification never works; financial ties alone are insufficient. Other organisational management specialists believe in the importance of a corporate culture or a management style which characterises every organisation and which may be effective in some fields and not others.

10.3.3. The rationale of diversification

Calori and Harvatopoulos (1988) studied the rationales of diversification in French industry. They identified two dimensions. The first relates to the nature of the strategic objective: diversification may be defensive (replacing a loss-making activity) or offensive (conquering new positions). The second dimension involves the expected outcomes of diversification: management may expect great economic value (growth, profitability) or first and foremost great coherence and complementarity with their current activities (exploitation of know-how).

EXHIBIT 10.6

THE DIVERSIFICATION STRATEGY OF BIC

For an outside observer, the entry of Bic in the disposable lighters and razors markets could be viewed as a double diversification strategy. In reality, it is not true for Bic which defines its core business as the distribution of moulded plastic disposable mass consumer products. For disposable pens, lighters or razors, the required core competencies are the same. The key success factors for those products rely essentially on technology (plastic injection), advertising, point of sales promotion and penetration in a large diversity of distribution channels. From a strategy point of view, all those products belong to the same domain of activity, and Bic means: 'cheap, relax life, a product simple and convenient'.

Source: Strategor (1997, p. 154).

Cross-classifying these two dimensions gives rise to four logics of diversification, as shown in Table 10.4.

1. *Expansion*, whereby the firm tries to reinforce its activity (offensive aim) while taking full advantage of its know-how (coherence). This kind of diversification strategy has been followed by Salomon, for example, world leader in ski bindings, which has gone into the market for ski boots, then the market for cross-country skiing and more recently into manufacturing golf clubs and ski poles.

2. *Relay*, which seeks to replace a declining activity (defensive objective), while using high quality staff (coherence). Framatome followed this strategy at the end of the 1970s, when the market for nuclear plants started to shrink.

3. *Deployment* is an offensive strategy seeking high economic value. This was the case for Taittinger diversifying into the deluxe hotel business.

4. *Redeployment* which is defensive in nature but seeks a new channel for growth. This strategy was followed by Lafarge which merged with Coppée and entered into biotechnology when faced with decline in the building industry.

Two more particular logics must be added to these basic ones: diversification driven by image improvement (*the logic of image*), and diversification driven by the will to watch the growth of a new promising technology (*the logic of window*).

Table 10.4   The rationales of diversification

Type of objective	Expected outcome	
	Coherence	Economic value
Offensive	Expansion (Salomon)	Deployment (Taittinger)
Defensive	Relay (Framatome)	Redeployment (Lafarge)

Source: Calori and Harvatopoulos (1988).

As a general rule, any successful diversification strategy is more or less based on synergies coming from the main activity of the firm. The provisional assessment of core competencies, talents or knowledge synergies between the present and the contemplated domain of activity constitutes a critical challenge in the design of a diversification strategy. The main risk is the over-evaluation of competencies' synergy between the two fields of activity, as in the FN case described above and the Bic case, with the failed launching of cheap perfume bottles targeted to the youth market.

It is important that management define the logic of diversification from the outset and as clearly as possible. Upon this logic, will depend the criteria for assessing and selecting potential activities. The alternative growth strategies reviewed in this chapter are summarised in Exhibit 10.7.

Diversification strategy based on core competencies

A particular form of diversification is based on the resources or the competencies that a firm considers as fundamental and intrinsically part of its core business. These core competencies can be used in different domains of activities as long as the objective of coherence is met.

10.3.4. The impact of disruptive technological innovations

On the technology front, and in parallel with globalisation, one observes a convergence of markets triggered by disruptive technological innovations, which upset

EXHIBIT 10.7

ALTERNATIVE GROWTH STRATEGIES

Intensive growth: to grow within the reference market

1. Penetration strategy: increase sales of existing products in existing markets:

   - Primary demand development.
   - Market share increase.
   - Market acquisition.
   - Market position defence.
   - Market rationalisation.
   - Market organisation.

2. Market development strategy: increase sales of existing products in new markets:

   - Target new market segments.
   - Adopt new distribution channels.
   - Penetrate new geographic markets.

3. Product development strategy: increase sales in existing markets with new or modified products:

   - Features addition strategy.
   - Product line extensions strategy.

   - Product line rejuvenation strategy.
   - Product quality improvement strategy.
   - Product line acquisition.
   - Product line rationalisation.
   - New product development strategy.

Integrative growth: to grow within the industrial chain

1. Backward integration.
2. Forward integration.
3. Horizontal integration.

Growth by diversification: to grow outside the industrial chain

1. Concentric diversification.
2. Pure diversification.

---

traditional market boundaries and change the traditional definition of an industry (Exhibit 10.8).

Digitalisation, for example, eliminates boundaries between printing, photography, television and image processing systems. Convergence is also observed in information technology, telecommunication, banking and insurance, office automation, etc.

By disruptive innovations, we mean a new way of playing the competitive game that is *both different and in conflict with the traditional way* adopted by established leaders (Charitou and Markidès, 2003). Examples include Internet banking, direct insurance, low-cost airlines, home book retailing, etc. As a result, established leaders in a variety of industries were asking the same question: Should we respond to these disruptive innovations, with the risk of damaging our core business?

Convergence leads companies to define their reference market in terms of generic needs instead of technologies and products, since technologies are fast changing while generic needs are stable. As a result, many firms tend to view themselves as a service firm, where the physical product is secondary but where the company mission is to propose to the client a *solution-to-a-problem* and not simply a product.

It is the case, for instance, of the company Automatic Systems, initially a manufacturer of metallic gates and doors, selling now 'access control systems'; of Nestlé who in addition to selling the Nescafé brand, is selling the Nespresso system; of IBM who is selling

'computerised solutions to managerial problems'; of Microsoft selling the Office system; of Starbucks who organises the distribution of its products in a franchised network of coffee shops, etc.

The fast development of technology also has a strong impact on innovation strategies. A distinction is often made between a *market-pull innovation*, that is, one that directly meet observed articulated needs, and a *technology or company-push innovation*, that is, one that results from research, creativity and technological opportunities and target latent needs.

1. In the first case of *market-pull innovation*, needs are expressed and articulated. The objective is to find wants and to fill them. Primary demand is latent and the task is to develop and stimulate this latent demand through operational marketing. This is *response strategic marketing (see Figure 1.2 above)*, the traditional role of strategic marketing, which still prevails in developing and growing economies.

2. In the second situation of *company-push innovations*, the products or services proposed are often ahead of expressed market needs. With so-called *discontinuous or disruptive innovations*, the market boundaries are not well defined, needs are not articulated, the competitive environment is blurred and often the innovation upsets the existing market practices and habits. Thus the key question is to know whether there is a need in the market for the company-push innovation.

EXHIBIT 10.8

HOW THE INTERNET KILLED THE PHONE BUSINESS

The term 'disruptive technology' is popular, but is widely misused. It refers not simply to a clever new technology, but to one that undermines an existing technology – and which therefore makes life very difficult for many businesses which depend on the existing way of doing things. [...]. This week has been a coming out party of sorts for another disruptive technology, 'voice over internet protocol' (VOIP), which promises to be even more disruptive, and of even greater benefit to consumers, than personal computers. VOIP's proponent is Skype, a small firm whose software allows people to make free calls to other Skype users over the internet, and very cheap calls to traditional telephones – all of which spell trouble for incumbent telecom operators. On 12 September 2005, eBay, the leading online auction-house, announced that it was buying Skype for $2.6 billion, plus an additional $1.6 billion if Skype hits certain performance targets in coming years. [...] The fuss over Skype in recent weeks has highlighted the significance of VOIP, and the enormous threat it poses to incumbent telecom operators. For the rise of Skype means nothing less than the death of the traditional telephone business, established over a century ago.[...] 'We believe that you should not have to pay for making phone calls in future, just as you don't pay to send e-mail.' says Skype co-founder, Niklas Zennstrom. [...] As is always the case with a disruptive technology, the incumbents it threatens are dividing into those who are trying to block the new technology in the hope that it will simply go away, and those who are moving to embrace it even though it undermines their existing businesses.

Source: Economist (2005).

In highly industrialised countries, it is the second situation – leading to proactive *strategic marketing (see Figure 1.2 above)* – which tends to prevail and to generate most growth opportunities. The role of operational marketing is more complex and risky here, since primary demand must be created.

The characteristics of high-technology industries have implications for the new product development process, namely speed and flexibility in product development, close co-operation with customers and systematic monitoring of the technological environment. Thus, in high-technology markets, strategic marketing has a crucial role to play, particularly in organising *cross-functional structure*, namely the 'R&D–Production–Marketing' interface to disseminate the market orientation culture throughout the entire organisation.

10.4. Choosing a competitive strategy

An important element of a growth strategy is taking explicit account of competitors' positions and behaviour. Measuring business competitiveness (Chapter 8) helps to evaluate the importance of the firm's competitive advantage compared with its most dangerous rivals, and to identify their competitive behaviour. The next task is to set out a strategy based on a realistic assessment of the forces at work, and to determine the means to achieve defined objectives.

Kotler establishes a distinction between four types of competitive strategy; his typology is based on the level of market share held and comprises four different strategies: market leader, market challenger, market follower and market nicher (Kotler, 1967/2006, p. 319).

10.4.1. Market leader strategies

In a product market, the market leader is the firm that holds a dominant position and is acknowledged as such by its rivals. The leader is often an orientation point for competitors, a reference that rival firms try to attack, to imitate or to avoid. The best-known market leaders are IBM, Procter & Gamble, Kodak, Benetton, Nestlé, L'Oréal, and so on. A market leader can envisage different strategies.

Primary demand development

The market leader is usually the firm that contributes most to the growth of the reference market. The most natural strategy that flows from the leader's responsibility is to expand total demand by looking for new users, new uses and more usage of its products. Acting in this way, the market leader contributes to expanding the total market size which, in the end, is beneficial to all competitors. This type of strategy is normally observed in the first stages of the product's life cycle, when total demand is expansible and tension between rivals is low due to high potential for growth of total demand.

Defensive strategies

A second strategy open to a firm with large market share is a defensive strategy: protecting market share by countering the actions of the most dangerous rivals. This kind of strategy is often adopted by the innovating firm which finds itself attacked by imitating firms once the market has been opened. This was the case for IBM in the mainframe computer market, for Danone in the fresh products market, for Coca-Cola in the soft drink market, and so on. Many defensive strategies can be adopted:

- Innovation and technological advance which discourages competitors.
- Market consolidation through intensive distribution and a full line policy to cover all market segments.
- Direct confrontation that is direct showdown through price wars or advertising campaigns.

We have seen this type of strategy between firms such as Hertz and Avis, Coca-Cola and Pepsi-Cola, and Kodak and Polaroid.

Aggressive strategies

A third possibility available to a dominant firm is an offensive strategy. The objective here is to reap the benefits of experience effects to the maximum and thus improve profitability. This strategy is based on the assumption that market share and profitability are related. In the previous chapter, we saw that this relationship was mainly observed in volume industries, where competitive advantage is cost-based. Its existence has also been empirically established by works of PIMS (Buzzell *et al.*, 1975) and confirmed by Galbraith and Schendel (1983). Although increasing market share is beneficial to a firm, there exists a limit beyond which the cost of any further increase becomes prohibitive. Furthermore, an excessively dominant position also has the inconvenience that it attracts the attention of public authorities who are in charge of maintaining balanced competitive market conditions. This, for instance, is the task of the Competition Commission within the European Union, and of anti-trust laws in the United States. Dominant firms are also more vulnerable to attacks by consumer organisations, which tend to choose the most visible targets, such as Nestlé in Switzerland and Fiat and Montedison in Italy.

De-marketing strategy

A strategy open to a dominant firm: reduce its market share to avoid accusations of monopoly or quasi-monopoly. Various possibilities exist. First, it can use de-marketing to reduce the demand level in some segments by price increases, or reduce services as well as advertising and promotion campaigns. Another strategy is diversification towards product markets different from those where the firm has a dominant position. Finally, and in a very different perspective, a last strategy could be a communication or public relations strategy with the objective to promote the social role of the firm vis-à-vis its different publics.

For example, mass food distributors having a dominant position in some markets, like to enhance their role in the fight against inflation through their pricing policy and namely through the launching on a large scale of 'no frills-low price' private labels which are 30–40 per cent less expensive than national brands.

In some cases, anti-trust laws may force companies to downsize.

10.4.2. Market challenger strategies

A firm that does not dominate a product market can choose either to attack the market leader and be its challenger, or to become a follower by falling into line with the leader's decisions. Market challenger strategies are therefore aggressive strategies with a declared objective of taking the leader's position.

The challenger faces two key questions: (a) the choice of the battleground from which to attack the market leader and (b) evaluation of the latter's reactive and defensive ability.

In the choice of the battleground, the challenger has two possibilities: frontal attack or lateral attack. A frontal attack consists of opposing the competitor directly by using its own weapons, and without trying to use its weak points. To be successful, a frontal attack demands a balance of power heavily in favour of the attacker. In military strategy, this balance is normally put at 3 to 1.

For example, when in 1981 IBM attacked the microcomputer market with its PC, its marketing tools, advertising in particular, were very clearly superior to those of Apple, Commodore and Tandy, which dominated the market (*Business Week*, 25 March 1985). Two years later IBM had become the leader.

Lateral attacks aim to confront the leader over one or another strategic dimension for which it is weak or ill-prepared. A lateral attack may, for example, address a region or a distribution network where the leader is not well represented, or a market segment where his or her product is not well adapted. A classic market challenger strategy is to launch a price attack on the leader: offer the same product at a much lower price. Many Japanese firms adopt this strategy in electronics or cars (Kotler *et al.*, 1981).

This strategy becomes even more effective when the leader holds a large market share. If the latter were to take up the lower price, it would have to bear large costs, whereas the challenger, especially if it is small, only loses over a low volume (Exhibit 10.9).

EXHIBIT 10.9

HP INVADES KODAK'S KINGDOM

For years, Hewlett-Packard considered itself the seller of printers and ink, not printing services. No longer, said Vyomesh Joshi, Executive Vice-President of HP's imaging and printing group. 'We are in the printing business', he said. US consumers, going again on industry expectations, have increasingly been printing their digital photos in stores rather than on home machines. The trend has forced HP to scramble to catch up to Kodak, which has some 60,000 photo kiosks in stores across America, like Walgreens, Wal-Mart and Rite-Aid. [...]. Without having its own printer kiosks in stores, the company (HP) has missed out on a slice of a $35 billion retail finishing business. [...]. Starting this month, HP is moving into that business, having signed up one US drugstore chain, Long Drugs, to install kiosks that will print albums, posters and calendars. [...].

Plain and simple, says an analyst of Citigroup Investment Research, 'HP is trying to be the next Kodak'. The competition is certain to be fierce. Kodak's Easy-Share online photo service, formerly known as Ofoto, is a leader in that field. But Kodak is not known for its printer technology, which gives HP an advantage[...]. Fuji with about 30,000 Aladdin Kiosks in US stores, just announced it was introducing new in-stores models called GetPix [...]. But will HP's low maintenance machines with faster printing speeds be enough to overcome Kodak's brand, which has meant preserving memories for several generations?

Source: Darlin (2006).

The major European steel producers severely suffered from price cuts offered by the Italian Bresciani mini-steelworks. The same phenomenon is observed in the oil market with 'cut-price firms' such as Seca in Belgium, Uno-X in Denmark and Conoco in Great Britain; dominant firms (BP, Exxon, Shell, and so on) had more to lose in a price war.

Lateral or indirect attacks can take various forms. There is direct analogy with military strategy and one can define strategies of outflanking, encircling, guerrilla tactics, mobile defence, and so on. See on this topic Kotler and Singh (1981) and Ries and Trout (1986).

Before starting an offensive move, it is essential to assess correctly a dominant firm's ability to react and defend. Porter (1980, p. 68) suggests using the three following criteria:

Vulnerability: to what strategic moves and governmental, macro-economic or industry events would the competitor be most vulnerable?

Provocation: what moves or events are such that they will provoke retaliation from competitors, even though retaliation may be costly and lead to marginal financial performance?

Effectiveness of retaliation: what moves or events is the competitor impeded from reacting to quickly and/or effectively given its goals, strategy, existing capabilities and assumptions?

The ideal is to adopt a strategy against which the competitor cannot react because of its current situation or priority objectives.

As was underlined earlier, in saturated or stagnant markets the aggressiveness of the competitive struggle

tends to intensify as the main objective becomes how to counter rivals' actions. The risk of a strategy based only on marketing warfare is that too much energy is devoted to driving rivals away at the risk of losing sight of the objective of satisfying buyers' needs. A firm which is focusing entirely on its rivals tends to adopt a reactive behaviour which is more dependent on rivals' actions than the developments in market needs. A proper balance between the two orientations is therefore essential (Oxenfeld and Moore, 1978).

10.4.3. Market follower strategies

As we saw before, a follower is a competitor with modest market share who adopts an adaptive behaviour by falling into line with competitors' decisions. Instead of attacking the leader, these firms pursue a policy of 'peaceful coexistence' by adopting the same attitude as the market leader. This type of behaviour is mainly observed in oligopolistic markets where differentiation possibilities are minimal and cross-price elasticities are very high, so that it is in no one's interest to start a competitive war that risks being harmful to all.

Adoption of a follower's behaviour does not permit the firm to have no competitive strategy, quite the contrary. The fact that the firm holds a modest market share reinforces the importance of having clearly defined strategic objectives which are adapted to its size and its strategic ambition. Hamermesch *et al.* (1978) analyse strategies of small firms and show that these firms can overcome the size handicap and achieve performance sometimes superior to dominant rivals. In other words, not all firms with low market share in low-growth markets are necessarily 'dogs' or 'lame ducks'.

Hamermesch *et al.* (1978, pp. 98–100) have uncovered four main features in the strategies implemented by companies with high performance and low market share:

Creative market segmentation. To be successful, a low market share company must compete in a limited number of segments where its own strengths will be most highly valued and where large competitors will be most unlikely to compete.

Efficient use of R&D. Small firms cannot compete with large companies in fundamental research; R&D should be concentrated mainly on process improvements aimed at lowering costs.

Think small. Successful low market share companies are content to remain small. Most of them emphasise profits rather than sales growth or market share, and specialisation rather than diversification.

Ubiquitous chief executive. The final characteristic of these companies is the pervasive influence of the chief executive.

A market follower strategy therefore does not imply passivity on the part of the chief executive of the firm, rather the concern to have a growth strategy which will not entail reprisals from the market leader.

10.4.4. Market niche strategies

A nicher is interested in one or few market segments, but not in the whole market. The objective is to be a large fish in a small pond rather than being a small fish in a large pond. This competitive strategy is one of the generic strategies we discussed earlier, namely focus. The key to a focus strategy is specialisation in a niche. For a niche to be profitable and sustainable, five characteristics are necessary (Kotler, 1997, p. 395), namely

- sufficient profit potential;
- growth potential;
- unattractive to rivals;
- market corresponding to the firm's distinctive competence;
- sustainable entry barrier.

A firm seeking a niche must face the problem of finding the feature or criterion upon which to build its specialisation. This criterion may relate to a technical aspect of the product, to a particular distinctive quality or to any element of the marketing mix.

From that point of view, it is interesting to refer once more to Simon (1996a, b) – already quoted in the preceding chapter – who has analysed the strategies adopted by a sample of 122 firms (a majority of German firms) which are (a) world or European leaders in their reference market, (b) of small or medium size and (c) unfamiliar to the general public. The nine main lessons are summarised in Exhibit 10.10.

EXHIBIT 10.10

THE NINE LESSONS FROM THE HIDDEN CHAMPIONS

1. Set a clear and ambitious goal. Ideally a company should strive to be the best and to become the leader in its market.
2. Define the market narrowly and in so doing include both customer needs and technology. Do not accept given market definition but consider the market definition itself as part of strategy. Stay focused and concentrated. Avoid distractions.
3. Combine a narrow market focus with a global orientation, involving worldwide sales and marketing. Deal as directly as possible with customers around the globe.
4. Be close to customers in both performance and interaction. Make sure that all functions have direct customer contacts. Adopt a value-driven strategy. Pay close attention to the most demanding customers.
5. Strive for continuous innovation in both product and process. Innovation should be both technology- and customer-driven. Pay equal attention to internal resources and competencies and external opportunities.
6. Create clear-cut competitive advantage in both product and service. Defend the company's competitive position ferociously.
7. Rely on your own strengths. Keep core competencies in the company, but outsource non-core activities. Consider co-operation as last resort rather than a first choice.
8. Try always to have more work than heads. Select employees rigorously in the first phase, and then retain them for the long term. Communicate directly to motivate people and use employee creativity to its full potential.
9. Practice leadership that is both authoritarian in the fundamental and participative in the details. Pay utmost attention to the selection of leaders. Observing their unity of person and purpose, energy and perseverance, and the ability to inspire others.

Source: Adapted from Simon (1996).

10.5. International development strategies

We emphasised in the second chapter that internationalisation of the economy means that a growing number of firms operate in markets where competition is global. As a result, international development strategies concern all firms, irrespective of whether they actively participate in foreign markets or not. We will examine here the stages of international development as well as the strategic reasoning of a firm that pursues an international marketing development strategy.

10.5.1. Steps in the internationalisation of markets

The period now referred to as the 'Golden Sixties' (years 1960–2000) corresponds to the beginning of the internationalisation of markets, a process that has continued up to the 1990s. At the European level, internationalisation took the form of the creation of the Common Market; at the world level it took the form of GATT (General Agreement on Tariffs and Trade) and the resulting progressive liberalisation of trade, the end of the Cold War and the expansion of East–West trade. All these factors contributed to the widening markets, and, in general, to the intensification of competition and the reappraisal of established competitive positions.

To the various stages of international development there often correspond specific forms of organisation at the international level, which reflect different views of international marketing. Keegan (1989/2004) suggests the following typology:

1. *Domestic organisation.* The firm is focused on its domestic market, and exporting is viewed as an opportunistic activity. This type of organisation is frequently in the 'passive marketing' stage as described above.

2. *International organisation.* Internationalisation takes place more actively, but at this stage the firm's orientation is still focused on the home market, which is considered as the primary area of opportunity. The *ethnocentric* company, unconsciously, if not explicitly and consciously, operates on the assumption that home country methods, approaches, people, practices and values are superior to those found elsewhere in the world. Attention is mostly centred on similarities with the home country market. The product strategy at this stage is a 'market extension' strategy that is products that have been designed for the home country market are 'extended' into markets around the world.

3. *Multidomestic organisation.* After a certain period of time, the company discovers that the difference in markets demands adaptation of its marketing in order to succeed. The focus of the firm is now multinational

(as opposed to home country) and its orientation is *polycentric*. The polycentric orientation is based on the assumption that markets around the world are so different and unique that the only way to succeed is to adapt to the unique and different aspect of each national market. The product strategy is adaptation, which is to change or adapt products to meet local differences and practices. Each country is managed as if it were an independent entity.

4. *Global or transnational organisation.* A global market is one that can be reached with the same basic appeal and message and with the same basic product. Both the product and the advertising and promotion may require adaptation to local customs and practices. The *geocentric* (or *regiocentric*) orientation of the global corporation is based on the assumption that markets around the world are both similar and different, and that it is possible to develop a global strategy that recognises similarities, which transcend national differences while adapting to local differences as well. This last stage is, at the moment, taking shape in the world and in particular in the European economy. It implies important changes in the logic of strategic marketing.

In the European and in the world economies, this internationalisation process took place during the years 1960–2000. This process also required a reinforcement of the analytical capabilities of the firm to successfully enter foreign markets.

10.5.2. Objectives of international development

International development is no longer limited to large enterprises. Many small firms are forced to become international in order to grow, or simply, to survive. Objectives in an international development strategy may be varied:

- To enlarge the potential market, thus being able to produce more and achieve better results thanks to economies of scale. For many activities, the critical volume is at such a level that it demands a large potential market.
- To extend the product's life cycle by entering markets which are not at the same development stage and still have expandable total demand, whereas in the domestic market of the exporting firm demand has reached the maturity phase.
- To diversify commercial risk by addressing buyers in different economic environments and enjoying more favourable competitive conditions.
- To control competition through diversification of positions on the one hand and surveillance of competitors' activities in other markets on the other.

- To reduce costs of supplies and production by exploiting different countries' comparative advantages.
- To exploit excess production capacity by exporting goods at low (marginal cost) prices.
- To achieve geographic diversification by entering new markets with existing products.
- To follow key customers abroad to supply or to service them in their foreign locations.

The phenomenon of globalisation of markets, already mentioned in Chapter 2, must also be added to these basic objectives: take advantage of the progressive liberalisation of world trade.

10.5.3. Forms of international development

A firm's internationalisation does not happen overnight, but results from a process that can be subdivided into six levels of growing internationalisation (Leroy *et al.*, 1978).

1. Exporting is the most frequent form. Often, the first attempts to export result from a necessity to clear surplus production. Later, exports can become a regular activity, but one which is reconstituted every year without there being any kind of medium- or long-term commitment to foreign countries. Relations are purely commercial.
2. The second stage is the contractual stage. Here the firm seeks more long-term agreements so as to stabilise its outlets, especially if its production capacity has been adjusted in terms of the potential to export. It will then sign long-term contracts, either with an importer or with a franchised distributor, or with a licensed manufacturer if it is an industrial firm.
3. In order to control the foreign partner or to finance its expansion, the firm may directly invest its own capital; this is the participatory stage which leads to commercial companies or co-ownership production.
4. After a few years, involvement can become absolute, with the firm owning 100 per cent of the capital of the foreign subsidiary; this stage is direct investment in a subsidiary with controlled management.
5. Gradually, the foreign subsidiary looks for ways of autonomous development, using local finance, national managers and its own programme of R&D which is distinct from the parent company. This is the autonomous subsidiary stage. If the parent company has many subsidiaries of this kind, this subsidiary becomes a multinational company. It would probably be more appropriate to use the term 'multidomestic', because it emphasises the point that each of these companies is more concerned about its own internal market, and the group's various companies coexist independently of each other.
6. The final stage of development is the one which is taking shape at the moment. It is the stage of the global enterprise that addresses the international market as if it were a single market. This kind of firm bases itself on interdependence of markets, and the latter are therefore no longer administered autonomously.

CHAPTER SUMMARY

Product portfolio analyses are designed to help guide a multi-product firm's strategic thinking by evaluating each activity with reference to indicators of attractiveness and of competitiveness. The growth-share matrix has the merit of simplicity and objectivity, but its underlying assumptions are restrictive and limit its scope of application. The multifactor matrix is more widely applicable and more flexible because the indicators used are company-specific, but the risk of subjectivity is higher and the procedure is more demanding in terms of available information. In elaborating a development strategy, the firm should clarify the nature of the sustainable competitive advantage which will serve as the basis for later strategic actions and tactics. Two views of strategy exist, one which is more relevant in existing markets, the other being better adapted for strategy development in future markets. Three generic options can be adopted in existing markets: overall cost leadership, differentiation or focus. The choice of one generic strategy is not neutral, but implies different resources, know-how and risks. In assessing growth opportunities, growth objectives can be considered at different levels: within the reference market (intensive growth), within the supply chain (integrative growth) or outside the current field of activity (diversification). For each of these three development strategies, several options are open which should be systematically explored in a strategic thinking exercise. A development strategy should explicitly take into account competitors' positions and behaviour on the basis of a realistic assessment of the forces at work. One can distinguish four types of competitive strategies: market leader, market challenger, market follower or market nicher. As a consequence of the globalisation of the world economy, international development is no longer limited to large enterprises and is motivated by a variety of strategic objectives. A firm's internationalisation does not happen overnight but results from a process which can be subdivided into different stages of international involvement and also in various organisational forms.

Review and Application Questions

1. A manufacturer of electronic components for industrial applications has five business units shown in the table below.

Strategic business units (SBU)	Sales in units (million)	Number of competitors	Sales of top 3 competitors	Market growth rate %
A	1.0	7	1.4/1.4/1.0	15
B	3.2	18	3.2/3.2/2.0	20
C	3.8	12	3.8/3.0/2.5	7
D	6.5	5	6.5/1.6/1.4	4
E	0.7	9	3.0/2.5/2.0	4

Using the BCG growth-share matrix evaluate the strength of the company's current and future position. What development strategies should it consider to improve the position of each business unit? Define clearly the conditions of application of this portfolio analysis method.

2. What are the shortcomings of the BCG growth-share matrix?

3. Design a multifactor portfolio grid for one of the following companies: Godiva International (chocolate pralines), Haagen-Dazs (ice-cream), Perrier (mineral water).

4. Which development strategy would you recommend for a small business firm having a very specialised and recognised know-how in a worldwide market, but which has very limited financial means?

5. In France and Belgium, the level of ice-cream consumption is much lower than in other European markets as well as in North America. You are responsible for a worldwide known brand of ice-cream; which development strategy (ies) would you consider in these two markets?

6. You are responsible for preparing a diversification programme for a company having a very strong know-how in the field of fruit purchase and transformation and which owns a well-known brand of jam and fruit preserves. Propose different avenues for diversification and assess their risks and opportunities.

Bibliography

Abell, D.E. and Hammond, J.S. (1979), *Strategic Market Planning*, Englewood Cliffs, NJ, Prentice-Hall.

Andrews, K.R. (1971/1980/1987), *The Concept of Corporate Srategy*, Homewood, IL, R.D. Irwin.

Boston Consulting Group (1972), *Perspectives on Experience*, Boston, MA, The Boston Consulting Group.

Boston Consulting Group (1998), *Perspectives on Strategy*, New York, John Wiley & Sons.

Buzzell, R.D., Gale, B.T. and Sultan, G.M. (1975), Market Share, a Key to Profitability, *Harvard Business Review*, 53, 1, pp. 97–106.

Calori, R. and Harvatopoulos, Y. (1988), Diversification: les règles de conduite, *Harvard-L'Expansion*, 48, Spring, pp. 48–510.

Chamberlin, E.H. (1933), *The Theory of Monopolistic Competition*, Cambridge, MA, Harvard University Press.

Charitou, D. and Markidès, C. (2003), Responses to Disruptive Strategic Innovation, *MIT Sloan Management Review*, 54, 2, pp. 55–63.

Damon, D. (2006), HP Invades Kodak's Kingdom, *International Herald Tribune*, February 24.

Day, G.S. (1977), Diagnosing the Product Portfolio, *Journal of Marketing*, 41, 2, pp. 29–38.

Drucker, P.F. (1981), The Five Rules of Successful Acquisition, *The Wall Street Journal*, 15, October, p. 16.

Economist (2005), How the Internet Killed the Phone Business, 17 September, p. 11

Ferrel, O.C., Hartline, M.D., Lucas, G.H. and Luck, D. (1999), *Marketing Strategy*, Fort Worth, TX, The Dryden Press.

Galbraith, C. and Schendel, D. (1983), An Empirical Analysis of Strategy Types, *Strategic Management Journal*, 4, 2, pp. 153–73.

Hamel, G. and Prahalad, C.K. (1994), *Competing For the Future*, Boston, MA, Harvard Business School Press.

Hamermesch, R.G. (1986), Making Planning Strategic, *Harvard Business Review*, 64, 4, pp. 115–20.

Hamermesch, R.G., Anderson, M.J. and Harris, J.E. (1978), Strategies for Low Market Share Businesses, *Harvard Business Review*, 56, 3, pp. 95–102.

Henderson, B.B. (1970), *The Product Portfolio*, Boston, MA, The Boston Consulting Group.

Hussey, D.E. (1978), Portfolio Analysis: Practical Experience with the Directional Policy Matrix, *Long Range Planning*, 11, 4, pp. 2–8.

International Herald Tribune (1999), Fujitsu and Siemens to Link Europe Operations, 18 June.

Keegan, W.J. (1989/2004), *Global Marketing Management*, Englewood cliffs, NJ, Prentice-Hall, 4th edition.

Kerin, R.A., Mahajan, V. and Varadarajan, P.R. (1990), *Comtemporary Perspectives on Strategic Market Planning*, Boston, MA, Allyn and Bacon.

Kim, W.C. and Mauborgne, R. (1997), Value Innovation: The Strategic Logic of High Growth, *Harvard Business Review*, 75, 1, pp. 102–12.

Kotler, P. (1967 / 2006), *Marketing Management*, Englewood Cliffs, NJ, Prentice-Hall, 12th edition.

Kotler, P. and Singh, R. (1981), Marketing Warfare in the 1980s, *Journal of Business Strategy*, 1, 3, pp. 30–41.

Leroy, G., Richard, G. and Sallenave, J.P. (1978), *La conquête des marchés extérieurs*, Paris, Les Editions d'Organisation.

Oxenfeld, A.R. and Moore, W.L. (1978), Customer or Competitor: Which Guide Lines for Marketing? *Management Review*, 67, 8, pp. 43–48.

Porter, M.E. (1980), *Competitive Strategy*, New York, The Free Press.

Porter, M.E. (1985), *Competitive Advantage*, New York, The Free Press.

Porter, M.E. (1996), What is Strategy?, *Harvard Business Review*, 74, 6, November–December, pp. 61–710.

Ries, A. and Trout, J. (1986), *Warfare Marketing*, New York, McGraw-Hill.

Rigby, D. (1998/2005), *Management Tool Mania*, The Newsletter of Bain & Company, Benelux, October.

Siddle, R. and Rigby, D. (2001), Which Management Tools are Most Popular? *European Business Forum*, 7, Autumn.

Simon, H. (1996a), *Hidden Champions*, Boston, MA, Harvard Business School Press.

Simon, H. (1996b), You Don't Have to be German to be a 'Hidden Champion', *Business Strategy Review*, 7, 2, pp. 1–13.

Strategor (1997), *Stratégie, structure, décision, identité*, Paris, InterEditions, 3rd edition.

Strom, S. (1999), Sony, in a Giant Overhaul, Sets Sights on Networking, *International Herald Tribune*, 9 March.

Wind, Y., Mahajan, V. and Swire, D.S. (1983), An Empirical Comparison of Standardized Portfolio Models, *Journal of Marketing*, 47, 2, pp. 89–99.

 COMPANION WEBSITE FOR CHAPTER 10

Visit the *Market-driven Management* companion website at www.palgrave.com/business/lambin to find information on:

Entry Strategies in Foreign Markets

International Pricing

Part 4

implementing operational marketing

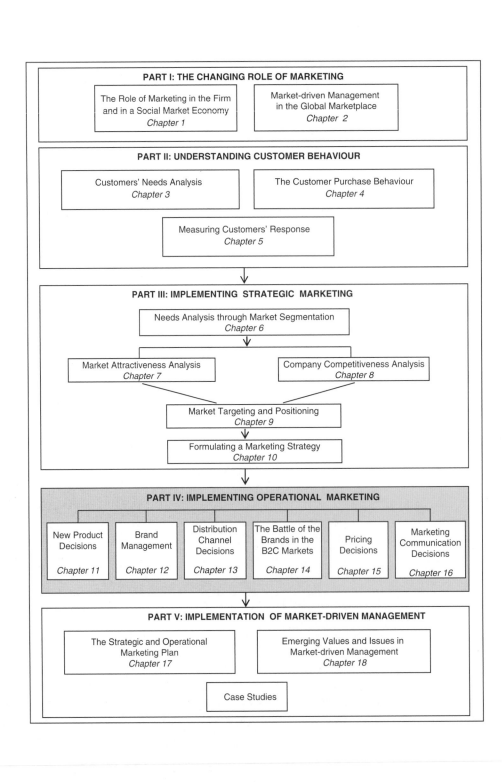

PART I: THE CHANGING ROLE OF MARKETING

The Role of Marketing in the Firm
and in a Social Market Economy
Chapter 1

Market-driven Management
in the Global Marketplace
Chapter 2

PART II: UNDERSTANDING CUSTOMER BEHAVIOUR

Customers' Needs Analysis
Chapter 3

The Customer Purchase Behaviour
Chapter 4

Measuring Customers' Response
Chapter 5

PART III: IMPLEMENTING STRATEGIC MARKETING

Needs Analysis through Market Segmentation
Chapter 6

Market Attractiveness Analysis
Chapter 7

Company Competitiveness Analysis
Chapter 8

Market Targeting and Positioning
Chapter 9

Formulating a Marketing Strategy
Chapter 10

PART IV: IMPLEMENTING OPERATIONAL MARKETING

New Product
Decisions

Chapter 11

Brand
Management

Chapter 12

Distribution
Channel
Decisions

Chapter 13

The Battle of the
Brands in the
B2C Markets

Chapter 14

Pricing
Decisions

Chapter 15

Marketing
Communication
Decisions

Chapter 16

PART V: IMPLEMENTATION OF MARKET-DRIVEN MANAGEMENT

The Strategic and Operational
Marketing Plan
Chapter 17

Emerging Values and Issues in
Market-driven Management
Chapter 18

Case Studies

new product decisions 11

Chapter contents

Chapter learning objectives

When you have read this chapter, you should be able to know and understand

- the components of innovation;
- the distinction between market-pull and technology-push innovation;
- the organisational procedures of the new product development process;
- the methods of idea generation;
- the methods of idea screening;
- the analysis of the customer's adoption process;
- the concept of portfolio of projects.

Chapter introduction

The objective of this chapter is to analyse the concepts and procedures that allow a firm to implement new product development strategies. Redeployment, diversification and innovation are at the heart of all development strategies. In a constantly changing environment, a company must continuously re-evaluate the structure of its portfolio of activities, meaning the decisions to abandon products, modify existing ones or launch new products. These decisions are of the utmost importance to the survival of the company and involve not only the marketing department, but all of the other functional areas as well. In this chapter, we shall examine the ways of establishing a dialogue between the various functional areas that play a role in the development of a new product. We do this in such a way as to minimise the risks in the strategy during the innovation process.

11.1. The strategic role of innovations

New product decisions are complex and risky decisions, but they are of vital importance for the development and the survival of the firm. The acceleration of technological change has reinforced this importance. In 1995, the share of sales derived from new or improved products commercialised within the previous five years was 45 per cent in average (Page, 1993). This percentage is even higher for high-tech products and tends to increase with time

> 1976–1981: 33 per cent
> 1981–1986: 40 per cent
> 1986–1990: 42 per cent
> 1990–1995: 45 per cent

New products also have a decisive impact on corporate profits. A study made by the Product Development and Management Association (PDMA), indicated that

On average 23.2% of 1990 profits came from internally developed new products introduced during the previous five years. Furthermore, this percentage is expected to increase to 45.6% for new products introduced during the 1990–1994 period. (Page, 1993, p. 285)

One American study (1999) found that the overall rate of return for some 17 successful innovations made in the 1970s averaged 56 per cent. Compare that with the 16 per cent average return on investment for all-American business over the past 30 years (*Economist*, 1999).

The data presented in Table 11.1 are interesting to assess the share of turnover generated by innovations. Examining first the bottom line, we observe that in the EU15, 10 per cent of companies can be considered to be 'highly innovative', with over half of their turnover generated by new or renewed products or services, and 20 per cent to be 'non-innovator' companies, with 0 per cent coming from innovations. Country by country comparison shows that this proportion differs considerably between EU Member States. Portugal, United Kingdom and Spain have the highest proportion of highly innovative companies. Belgium, Greece and France the highest proportion of non-innovator companies.

11.1.1. Components of an innovation

According to Barreyre (1980), an innovation may be subdivided into three elements (see Exhibit 11.1):

- A *need* to be satisfied or a function to be fulfilled.
- The *concept* of an object or entity to satisfy the need.
- The *inputs* comprised of a body of existing knowledge as well as materials and available technology, which allow the concept to become operational.

If we consider the need for music listening, the vinyl technology (long playing records) was replaced successively by the tape (minicassette), the laser (compact disc) and by the digital technology (Ipod). Both the concept and the technology were innovative.

The degree of risk associated with an innovation will thus depend on two factors: (a) the degree of originality and complexity of the concept, which will determine the receptivity of the market and transfer costs for the user (*market risk*); (b) the degree of technological innovation pertaining to the concept, which will determine the technical feasibility of the innovation (*technology risk*). Added to these two intrinsic risks is the degree of familiarity that the firm itself has with the market and the technology (*strategy risk*).

A true innovation is a product, a service or a concept which brings a new solution to consumers' problems, either by providing a better solution than the existing ones proposed by competition, or by offering a new or an additional function.

Table 11.1   Innovation in Europe: percentage of turnover coming from new products or services introduced during the last two years

	Sample size	0%	1–5%	6–10%	11–20%	21–50%	51% or more
Deutschland	286	14	25	17	16	16	11
Denmark	185	15	17	24	16	22	6
Ireland	95	19	14	19	17	19	12
Italy	294	21	22	22	16	13	7
Sweden	172	21	24	21	13	10	11
Portugal	87	22	14	15	17	17	15
Osterreich	172	22	23	21	14	11	9
Finland	90	23	34	17	10	12	5
UK	282	23	13	20	14	16	14
Spain	287	23	15	11	19	19	13
Nederland	198	23	34	19	12	9	3
Luxemburg	92	24	32	16	18	8	2
France	286	27	26	17	12	11	7
Ellas	94	32	21	15	12	13	8
Belgium	188	34	20	20	11	8	7
EU15	2849	20	22	18	15	14	10

Source: Innobarometer (2004, p. 7).

11.1.2. Market-pull versus technology-push innovations

As discussed in Chapter 1, a distinction can be made between a *market-pull innovation*, that is, one that directly answers observed needs, or a *technology-push* innovation, that is, one that results from R&D efforts and meets latent needs. This distinction is important because these innovations imply different marketing strategies: *response strategic marketing* for innovation coming from the market (*Is it doable?*) and *supply-driven or proactive strategic marketing* for technology-led innovations (*Is there a need?*).

Technology push innovations are often disruptive innovations, fulfilling needs not explicitly articulated by potential customers, and anticipating market demand to be created by operational marketing. For these reasons, these innovations are generally more risky. Having a strong market orientation very early in the development process is vital.

> R&D isn't worth anything alone; it has to be coupled with the market. The innovative firms are not necessarily the ones that produce the best technological output, but the ones that know what is marketable. (Mansfield and Wagner, 1975)

Thus, while a proactive innovation strategy must include R&D, it must also have a strong market orientation that is critical to the successful development of new products. So there is no opposition between market-pull and technology-push strategies; *both have to be market-driven*.

11.2. Organisation of the new product development process

The data presented in the previous section illustrate the high risk involved in launching a new activity. This risk may be reduced, however, by implementing a systematic evaluation and development procedure for new products. The key success factors are those that are controllable by the company. The purpose of this section is to examine the procedures and organisational methods that reduce the risk of failure throughout the innovation process. The objective is to organise a systematic and continuous dialogue between the relevant functions within an organisation, which is R&D, marketing, operations and finance. In a market-driven company, developing a new product is a cross-functional effort, which involves the entire organisation.

If it is true that top management has the final say in decisions concerning new product launches, it remains the case that an organisational structure with specific responsibilities is essential in managing and co-ordinating the entire innovation process. Different organisational structures are possible. Large companies have created new product management functions or new product departments, as Nestlé, Colgate Palmolive, Johnson & Johnson and General Foods have done.

11.2.1. Cross-functional organisational structures

A more flexible solution, which is available to all companies regardless of their size, is the new products committee or venture team in charge of a specific project.

1. *New products committee*. It is a permanent group of persons, which meets periodically, say, once a month. It is composed of individuals from different functions (i.e. R&D, operations, marketing, finance and human resources). Ideally, it is presided over by the managing director, whose responsibility is to organise and manage the development process of a new product from its conception to its launching.

2. *Self-organising project teams or 'venture teams'*. These are groups formed for the development of a specific project (task force). This group is composed of people from various departments, from which they are temporarily separated, either completely or partially. This allows better concentration on the creation of a new activity.

The Page study (1993) is instructive on the evolution observed on the organisational structures used for new product development. The respondents were asked to indicate which of the six forms of new product organisation structure best described the ones used by their firm (see Table 11.2). The multidisciplinary team was by far the most widely used organisation with a score of 76 per cent of the sample businesses while the new product department had a score of only 30 per cent (Page, 1993, p. 276).

No matter which organisational structure is adopted, the most important thing is a structure open to the ideas of new activities. The objective is to institutionalise preoccupation

Table 11.2   Organisational structures used for new product development

Organisational structures	Per cent
Multidisciplinary team	76.2
New product department	30.2
Product manager	30.2
New product manager	25.9
New product committee	16.9
Venture team	6.9

Source: Page (1993, p. 277).

with new products within the company and to do so in a way that is flexible and favours an entrepreneurial approach to problems.

Two processes are currently adopted by innovative companies, the sequential or the parallel development process.

11.2.2. Sequential development process

The *sequential development process*, evidenced by the Booz *et al.* study (1982), is where the project moves step by step from one phase to the next: concept development and testing, feasibility analysis, prototype development, market test and production. The whole process is described in Figure 11.1.

The merits of the sequential approach have already been discussed. But although it contributes to reducing the new product failure rate, it also has some shortcomings:

- First, the sequential process in itself leaves little room for integration since each functional specialist passes the project to the next one.
- The move to the next phase is done only after all the requirements of the preceding phase are satisfied. A bottleneck in one phase can slow or even block the entire process.
- Moreover, this product planning process is slow and requires long lead times. It avoids errors, but at large cost in terms of time.
- Changes in the market, entry of new competitors and risk of copying often result in a product arriving too late in the market.

Thus long lead times can very well increase rather than reduce the risk of failure. This will be particularly important for high-technology products, where speed is a key success factor.

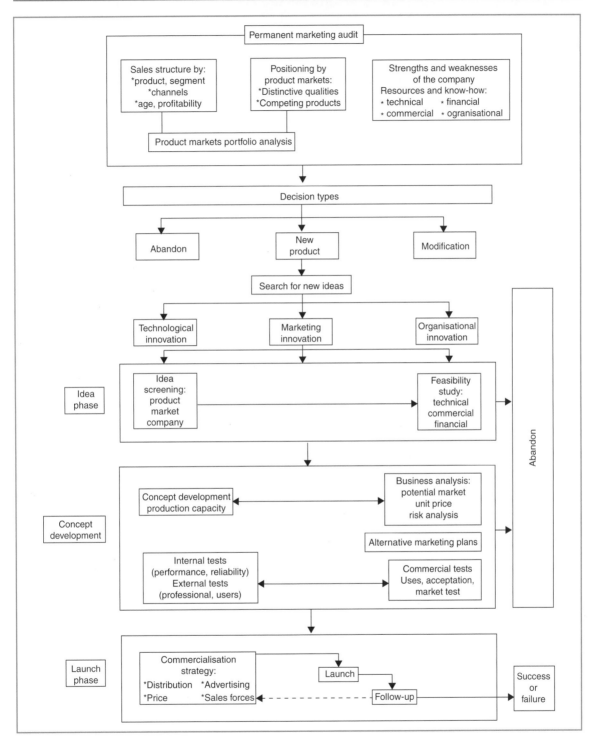

Figure 11.1   The sequential development process of new products

11.2.3. Speed as a strategy

The basic philosophy of the sequential development process is to go slowly, to avoid product failure and postpone heavy spending until it is clear that the product concept under study will be a winner. Schnaars (1998, pp. 168–70) mentions nine reasons to support the view that speed is a source of competitive advantage.

1. *Competitive advantage is not sustainable.* A truly sustainable competitive advantage has proved to be an elusive goal for companies. Speed as strategy sidesteps this problem by replacing it with quick response.
2. *Avoiding the need to predict the future.* Firms end up preparing a future that never comes. Moving quickly with markets, rather than trying to guess in which direction they will move, substitutes flexibility for forecasting.
3. *The law of large numbers.* A key benefit of speeding many new products to market without a great deal of formal market research is that the market decides which product will be successful and which will fail.
4. *Profits from new products.* Firms without a steady flow of new products ultimately face decline. The evidence shows that profit come mainly from new products.
5. *Shorter product life cycles.* Long-term growth has been replaced by a series of short-lived fads. That means that firms must get to the market before the peak of popularity passes.
6. *More competition in growth markets.* In the past, profits were supposed to be highest in the growth stage of the PLC. Today, most growth markets are crowded with competitors and are intensely competitive.
7. *Rampant copying.* Competitors routinely steal new product ideas in test markets. Today extensive testing is all but impossible. It would invite too many copycats.
8. *Gaining shelf space early.* A growing number of new products must compete for limited retail shelf space. That means that firms must get to the market quickly or risk being closed out of the best distribution outlets.
9. *Fostering a sense of creativity and experimentation.* A fast moving strategy promotes a culture of doing and trying rather than a culture of bureaucrats and paperwork.

The parallel development process tries to take the best of the two worlds by combining systematic analysis with speed (Stalk, 1988).

11.2.4. Parallel development process

The *parallel development process* advocated by Takeuchi and Nonaka (1986) speeds the process by relying on self-organising project teams whose members work together from start to finish. Under this organisational scheme, the process development process emerges from the constant interaction of a multidisciplinary team. Rather than moving in defined, highly structured stages, the process is born out of the team members' interplay. One of the potential benefits of the parallel development process is the overlapping of the tasks assumed by the different departments.

> While design engineers are still designing the product, production people can intervene to make sure that the design is compatible with production scale economies and marketing people can work on the positioning platform to communicate to the market.

The parallel development process is described in Figure 11.2. The merits of this organisational structure are important:

- The system facilitates better cross-functional co-ordination since each function is associated in the entire development process.
- Several activities can be organised simultaneously, which accelerates the process because the amount of recycle and rework – going back and doing it again – is greatly reduced.
- Each activity is better controlled since it directly determines the subsequent activities.
- Substantial time saving is achieved due to more intensive work and improved spontaneous co-ordination.

This type of organisational structure, because it stresses multifunctional activities, promotes improved teamwork. To go further on this topic see Larson and Gobeli (1988).

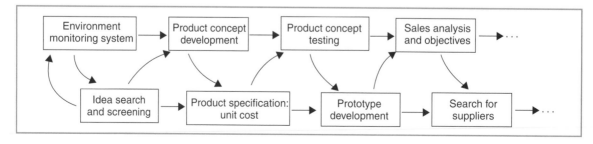

Figure 11.2   Parallel development of new products

11.3. New product idea generation

Naturally, the development process for innovation begins with researching new product ideas, which are in line with the chosen development strategy. Some companies adopt an empirical approach to this problem, relying on a spontaneous stream of ideas originating from external and internal sources. However, the mortality rate of these ideas is very high; therefore, it is essential to feed on new ideas regularly. Generally, ideas, especially good ones, do not happen by themselves; organisation and stimulation are needed to generate them. A company may use different methods for collecting ideas. These methods try to anticipate the change in needs and not simply respond to the demands expressed by the market. This is a 'proactive' versus a 'reactive' approach. A creative idea is nothing but an unexpected combination of two or more concepts. Creativity can therefore be defined as,

> The intellectual exercise of linking information in an unpredictable way so as to produce a new arrangement.

Idea generation methods can be grouped into two broad categories: (a) functional analysis methods which analyse products in order to identify possible improvements, and (b) methods which interview customers directly or indirectly to detect unsatisfied needs or ill-resolved problems with the existing products.

11.3.1. Methods of functional analysis

The rationale behind functional analysis methods is that a product's users can provide useful information on how the product could be modified and improved.

1. *Problem/opportunity analysis*: It starts with the customer. It is linked to the study of user behaviour in order to identify the kinds of problems a user may encounter during use of the product. Every problem or difficulty brought up could give rise to a new idea for improvement or modification. This modification is frequently used in industrial market studies with a panel of user clients.

2. *The attribute listing method*: This method has the same objectives as problem analysis, but instead of examining how the customer uses the product, it examines the characteristics of the product itself. The method consists of establishing a list of the principal characteristics and then recombining them in such a way as to create some improvement. Osborn (1963) defined a list of questions intended to stimulate ideas for new products.

> Can the product be used in any new way? What else is like the product and what can be learned from this comparison? How can the product be changed in meaning, function, structure, and use pattern? What can

be added to the product? To make it stronger, longer, thicker, and so on? What to delete? What to subtract, how to make it smaller, condensed, lower, shorter, lighter, and so on? (Osborn, 1963, pp. 286–7)

3. *Morphological analysis*: It consists of identifying the most important structural dimensions of a product and then examining the relationship between these dimensions in order to discover new and interesting combinations.

> Suppose we are studying a cleaning product. The six key structural dimensions are as follows: product support (brush, rag, sponge, and so on), ingredients (alcohol, ammonia, disinfectant, and so on), things to be cleaned (glass, carpet, sinks, walls, cars, and so on), substance to be got rid of (grease, dust, blood, paint, and so on), product texture (cream, powder, salt, liquid, and so on), and packaging (box, bottle, aerosol, bag, and so on).

Paired combinations of these dimensions are evaluated and considered in terms of their potential value as new products.

A last method for idea generation must be added, one that is old but very effective: *the suggestion box*. This can prove to be very helpful if certain rules are followed. Two rules are particularly important: follow up promptly on the proposed ideas and provide a complete recognition system to motivate employees.

There are other and varied methods for idea generation. Systematic analysis of competitive products through reverse engineering is also widely used. The most important objective for a firm is to keep a permanent portfolio of new product ideas, which is sizeable enough to allow the firm to face the competition in an environment where innovation is omnipresent.

11.3.2. Creativity groups and brainstorming

Methods, which are likely to stimulate creativity, can be grouped into two categories: unstructured and structured methods. *Unstructured methods* are essentially based on imagination and intuition. These methods are usually implemented in the form of *creativity groups*, relying on the hypothesis that a group of individuals is usually more creative than a person working alone. This assumption is based on the synergy effect or the interaction between group members.

Brainstorming is probably the most popular method, mostly because it is easy to organise. The only goal of a brainstorming session is to produce as many ideas as possible. Six to ten participants with diverse backgrounds and experience, from both within and outside the company, are gathered together and are given the objective of generating the greatest possible number of ideas on a particular theme in a spontaneous manner. The major rules governing a brainstorming session, according to Osborn (1963, p. 156), are the following:

- No evaluation of any kind is permitted, since criticism and judgement may cause people to defend their ideas rather than generate new and creative ones.
- Participants should be encouraged to think of the wildest ideas possible.
- Encourage a large number of ideas.
- Encourage participants to build upon or modify the ideas of others, as combinations or modifications of previously suggested ideas often lead to new ideas that are superior to those that sparked them.

This type of exercise is usually very effective; it is not out of the ordinary for a group to generate more than 100 ideas during a brainstorming session. Another somewhat more structured method is synectics (Gordon, 1965).

Synectics is another creativity method also developed by Gordon, which tackles the problem indirectly. The assumption is that habits prevent the development of a really new vision of a too familiar problem (see Exhibit 11.2).

> For a professional whose reflexes and perceptions of the environment have been moulded by a growing market and confirmed by success, it is very difficult to see the opportunity of doing the same thing differently. The acquired professionalism hides the perception of new way of operating. The adoption of a discontinuous strategy requires new reflexes and a distance from traditional activities. (Bijon, 1984, p. 104)

To become creative, it is sometimes necessary to take some distant view and to make a 'creative detour', before coming back to the problem under study. Once the problem is formulated in different, but related contexts, one is led to discover analogies and to propose more relevant and creative ideas.

11.3.3. New product generation from customer ideas

The idea generation methods presented so far are usually manufacturer-active, that is, the manufacturer plays the active role (see Table 11.3). In industrial markets, von Hippel (1978) has shown that often a customer request for a new product can generate a new product idea, at least in situations where the industrial customer is overtly aware of his new product need.

In the B2C sector, the role of the consumer is essentially that of a respondent, 'speaking only when spoken to'. It is the role of the manufacturer to obtain information on articulated or latent needs for new products and to develop a responsive product idea. In the B2B sector, it is often the role of the would-be customer to develop the idea for a new product and to select a supplier capable of making the product. We have here a *customer-active paradigm*.

Any statement of need made by a professional customer contains information about what a responsive solution should be. Consider the following statement of need of manufacturing firm X:

> (a) we need higher profits in our semi-conductor plant; (b) which we can get by raising output (c) which we can best do by getting rid of the bottleneck in process step D (d) which can best be done by designing and installing new equipment (e) which has the following functional specifications (f) and should be built according to these blueprints. (von Hippel, 1978, p. 41)

This need statement already contains the key elements of the solution to a problem sought by the would-be customer. The firm needs only to instruct its R&D and manufacturing people to manufacture the product according to the customer specifications spontaneously provided. This example underlines the importance of a systematic dialogue with customers to generate new product ideas.

In the field of industrial goods there are also several markets in which everyone knows what the customer wants, but progress in technology is required before the desired product can be realised.

> In the computer, plastics and semi-conductor industries, every one knows that the customer wants more calculation per second and per dollar in the computer business; every one knows that the customer wants plastics which degrade less quickly in sunlight; and

---

EXHIBIT 11.2

SELECTED EXAMPLES OF PREDICTION ERRORS

1895: Lord Kelvin, President of the Royal Society (UK):
'It is impossible to design flying machines heavier than air.'

1899 : Charles Duell, Director of the Patent Office (USA):
'Everything has already been invented.'

1905: Grover Cleveland, President of United States:
'Reasonable women will never ask for the right of vote.'

1920: Robert Millikan, Nobel price for physics:
'Man will never be able to exploit atomic power.'

1947: Thomas J. Watson Sr., President of IBM Corp.:
'I believe that there is a total market for approximately five computers.'

1977: Ken Olsen, CEO Digital Equipment Corp.:
'Why people would like to have a computer at home?'

Source: Quoted by de Branbandère (1998, pp. 99–107).

Table 11.3   Search for ideas of new industrial products

| Nature of customer need | Accessibility of new product opportunity to manufacturer-managed action | |
	Low	High
Overt	Customer active only	Customer and/or manufacturer active
Latent	Neither	Manufacturer active 1 only

Source: von Hippel (1978).

everyone knows that the semi-conductor customer wants more memory capacity on a single chip of silicon.

In these sectors, a customer request is not required to trigger a new product, only an advance in technology.

Idea generation methods are numerous and varied. Cooper (1993, p. 133) proposes a list of 25 different methods. What is important for the firm is to have permanently a *portfolio of new product ideas* sufficiently diversified to enable the firm to meet the challenge of competition in an environment where innovation is permanent and a key success factor for survival and development.

11.4. New product idea screening

The objective of the second stage in the development process is to screen the ideas generated in order to eliminate the ones that are incompatible with the company's resources or objectives or simply unattractive to the firm. The purpose is to spot and drop unfeasible ideas as soon as possible. This is therefore an evaluation phase, which presupposes the existence of criteria for choice. The goal of this screening is not to do an in-depth analysis, but rather to make a quick, inexpensive, internal evaluation about which projects merit further study and which should be abandoned. Therefore, this is not yet a feasibility study, but simply a preliminary evaluation.

Typically, the new product committee is in the best position to do the screening. A single and effective method is the *evaluation grid*, which has the following basic principles:

- An exhaustive inventory of all the key success factors (KSFs) in each functional area: marketing, finance, operations and R&D.
- Each factor or group of factors is weighted to reflect its relative importance.

- Each new product idea is scored against each KSF by the judges of the new product committee.
- A desirability or performance index is calculated.

This procedure ensures that all the important factors have been systematically and equally considered and that the objectives and constraints of the company have been attended to.

When computing the performance index, it is preferable to adopt a conjunctive method and not a simple weighted average procedure (compensatory approach). The conjunctive method does not result in a global score, but aids in identifying ideas, which are or are not compatible with the company's objectives or resources. The conjunctive approach presupposes that a maximum and minimum level of performance for each project has been specified. Only those ideas, which satisfy each specified threshold, are retained.

Several standard evaluation grids exist in the marketing literature, the best known being that of O'Meara (1961) and of Steele (1988). Such checklists provide a useful guideline for ideas evaluation. Ideally, an evaluation grid should be tailor-made and be adapted to the company's own needs. It is up to the new product committee to establish an appropriate structure, which reflects the corporate objectives and the unique situational factors of the firm. Figure 11.3 shows an evaluation grid used in a consumer goods company to evaluate the marketing feasibility of new product ideas. Similar grids have been developed for the other functions: R&D, operations and finance.

Cooper (1993, see Appendix C, p. 335) has also developed a diagnostic and screening grid. The questionnaire comprises 30 questions to be answered by several judges who evaluate the project on each criterion on a 10-point scale and who express their degree of confidence on their own evaluation, also on a 10-point scale. The profile of the project is then evaluated and compared with the observed profiles of hundreds of projects, which belong to the *NewProd* data bank.

New product idea: _____   Score: ___

	Scores				Not relevant
	Very good	*Good*	*Weak*	*Very weak*	
1. Market trend	Emerging	Growing	Stable	Declining	
2. Product life	10 years plus	5–10 years	3–5 years	2–3 years	
3. Spread of diffusion	Very fast	Fast	Slow	Very slow	
4. Market size (volume)	>10,000 T	5,000–10,000 T	1,000–5,000 T	1,000 T	
5. Market size (value)	1 billion	0.5–1billion	100–500 million	>100 million	
6. Buyer's needs	Not met	Poorly met	Well met	Very well met	
7. Receptivity of distribution	Enthusiastic	Positive	Reserved	Reluctant	
8. Advertising support required	Weak support	Moderate support	Important support	Strong support	
9. Market accessibility	Very easy	Easy	Difficult	Very difficult	

Indicators of competitiveness	Scores				Not relevant
	Very good	*Good*	*Weak*	*Very weak*	
1. Product's appeal	Very high	High	Moderate	Weak	
2. Distinctive qualities	Exclusivity	Major distinctive quality	Weak distinctive quality	'Me too' product	
3. Strength of competition	Very weak	Weak	High	Very high	
4. Duration of exclusivity	>3 years	1–3 years	–1 year	–6 months	
5. Compatibility with current products	Very good	Good	Weak	Very weak	
6. Level of price	Lower price	Slightly lower	Equal price	Higher price	
7. Compatibility with existing distribution network	Fully compatible	Easily compatible	Compatible but difficult	New network	
8. Capacity of the sales force	Very good	Good	Weak	Very weak	
9. Level of product quality	Clearly superior	Superior	Same	Inferior	

Figure 11.3   Example of a new product screening grid
Source: Authors.

The simulation model provides a probability of success and also analyses the strong and the weak points of the project.

11.5. New product concept development

At this phase of the development process, we move from 'product ideas' to 'product concepts'. The ideas having survived to the screening phase are now defined in more elaborate terms.

11.5.1. Product concept definition

A product concept can thus be defined as:

A written description of the physical and perceptual characteristics of the product and of the 'package of benefits' (the promise) it represents for an identified target group(s) of potential customers.

This is more than a simple technological description of the product, since the product's benefits to the potential user

are emphasised. The product concept definition highlights the notion of a product as a package of benefits. In defining the concept, a company is forced to be explicit in its strategic options and market objective. A clear and precise definition of the product concept is important in many respects:

- The concept definition describes the *positioning sought* for the product and therefore defines the means required to achieve the expected positioning.
- The product concept is a kind of *specification manual for R&D*, whose job it is to examine the technical feasibility of the concept.
- The description of the product's promise serves as a *briefing* for the advertising agency that is in charge of communicating the new product's identity and claims to the marketplace.

Thus, the product concept defines the reference product market or segment in which the future product should be positioned. Four questions come to mind:

1. Which attributes or product characteristics do potential customers react favourably to?
2. How are competitive branded products perceived with regard to these attributes?

3. What niche could the new product occupy, considering the expectations of the target segment and the positions held by competition?
4. What is the most effective operational marketing programme that will achieve the desired positioning?

The answers to these questions presuppose the existence of a fine-tuned market segmentation analysis, which is able to quantify the size of the potential market.

11.5.2. Designing a green product concept

Sensitivity towards the environment is today a must for business success and the accountable firm should assess the environmental implication of a new product not only at the concept development phase, but also at each phase of the product life cycle 'from cradle to grave' as explained in Chapter 2 of this book. Numerous opportunities exist for refining existing products or developing new ones that meet environmental imperatives and satisfy customers' expectations. These opportunities must be considered in a proactive way very early in the development process. Ideas for action are presented in Exhibit 11.3 (Ottman, 1993).

While adopting the green product concept, the firm has to be careful and must prove its environmental credentials in scientific terms and by reference to the entire life cycle of the product. This is not always easy, because 'green' is *relative* and also because large uncertainties remain on the ecological impact of products and raw materials.

11.5.3. Testing the new product concept

Concept testing represents the first investment (other than managerial time) a firm has to make in the development process. It consists of submitting a description of the new product concept to an appropriate group of target users to measure the degree of acceptance.

The product concept description may be done in one of two ways: neutral, that is, with no 'sell', or by a mock advertisement, which presents the concept as if it were an existing branded product. The former is easier to do and avoids the pitfalls of the inevitable and uncontrollable creative element inherent in an advertisement. The advantage of the advertisement, however, is that it more accurately reproduces the buying atmosphere of a future branded product and is therefore more realistic. The following descriptions illustrate 'neutral' and 'advertising' forms of concept testing, respectively, for a new dessert topping.

> Here is a new dessert topping made of fruit and packaged in a spray can. It comes in four flavours: strawberry, cherry, apricot and redcurrant. It can be used in cakes, puddings and frozen desserts.

> Here is a new delicious fruit topping for desserts conveniently packaged in a spray can. These new toppings will enhance the desserts you serve your family. Your choice among four flavours: strawberry, cherry, apricot and redcurrant will certainly embellish all your desserts including cakes, puddings, frozen desserts and more.

Twenty to fifty people with varying socio-demographic profiles are gathered to assess the degree of concept acceptance. They are shown slides or videos on the new concept and asked to react to it with questions similar to those presented in Box 11.1.

Obviously, the key questions in Box 11.1 are the ones dealing with intentions to buy (question 5). A score of positive intentions (i.e. 'would definitely buy' and 'would probably buy' responses grouped together) that adds up to less than 60 per cent is generally considered insufficient, at least in the field of consumer goods.

EXHIBIT 11.3

THE GREEN PRODUCT CONCEPT: IDEAS FOR ACTION

- Source reduce products and packaging.
- Eliminate or lightweight packaging.
- Concentrate on products.
- Use bulk packaging or large sizes.
- Develop multipurpose products.
- Use recycled content.
- Conserve natural resources, habitats and endangered species.
- Make products more energy efficient.
- Maximise consumer and environmental safety.

- Make products more durable.
- Make products and packaging reusable or refillable.
- Design products for remanufacturing, recycling and repair.
- Take products back for recycling.
- Make products and packaging safe to landfill or incinerate.
- Make products compostable.

Source: Ottman, (1993).

BOX 11.1

IMPLEMENTATION PROBLEM: HOW TO TEST A NEW PRODUCT CONCEPT?

1. Are the benefits clear to you and believable?
2. Do you see this product as solving a problem or filling a need for you?
3. Do other products currently meet this need and satisfy you?
4. Is the price reasonable in relation to the value?
5. Would you (definitely, probably, probably not, definitely not) buy the product?
6. Who would use this product, and how often would it be used?

Source: Kotler (1967 / 2006).

11.5.4. Predictive value of buying intentions

Results from concept testing should be interpreted with care, especially when the concept is very new. Consumers are asked to express their interest in a product, which they have never seen or used. They are therefore often unable to judge whether or not they would like the new product. Numerous products, which received mediocre scores during the concept-testing phase, actually turned out to be brilliant successes. Inversely, expensive failures were avoided using concept testing.

Measuring intentions to buy is not always the best indication of the respondents' degree of conviction regarding a new product's ability to solve problems or to satisfy unmet needs. Yet, this is clearly a KSF. In a test situation, respondents may express a willingness to purchase a new product out of simple curiosity or concern for keeping up with the latest innovation, or a need for variety. In light of this, scores for intention tend to overestimate the true rate of acceptance.

In order to deal with this problem, Tauber (1973) suggests using concept-testing results based on measurements of perceived needs as well as of purchase interest. In an experiment on eight new product concepts, Tauber observed that virtually all the respondents who claimed that a product solved a problem or filled an unmet need had a positive intention to purchase the new product, while a considerable number of respondents who expressed purchase interest did not believe the product solved a problem or filled an unmet need. This observation suggests that overstatement of purchase intent may be simply those with curiosity to try but with little expectation of adopting. Thus, basing new product decisions on purchase intent data could be misleading in predicting the true rate of product adoption for regular use.

A more reliable way to estimate the adoption rate of a new product for regular use would be to base the decision on the percentage of people giving an affirmative answer to both questions, that is, *they do intend to buy and they are convinced that the new product solves a problem or fills an unmet need*. The adjusted purchase intent rates of Table 11.4 illustrate the argument. The ranking of the eight product concepts is significantly different from the ranking observed for the positive purchase intention.

11.5.5. The use of conjoint analysis

More elaborate approaches to concept testing may be used, including the conjoint analysis, which has been successfully used over the last few years (Green and Srinivasan, 1978). The distinctive value of conjoint analysis is to allow the impact of the product concept's key characteristics on product preferences, information which is not revealed by an overall reaction to the concept. The basic principles of this method were described in Chapter 5 and an example was presented in Chapter 6.

In concept testing, conjoint analysis helps in answering the following questions:

■ What is the *partial utility or value* that a target group attaches to different characteristics of the product concept?
■ What is the *relative importance* of each product characteristic?
■ What kind of *trade-offs* are potential buyers ready to make between two or more product characteristics?
■ What will be the *share of preferences* with regard to different product concepts each representing a different bundle of characteristics?

The collected data are simple rankings of preference for the various concept combinations. Each concept constitutes a different assortment of characteristics. These preference data are submitted to one of the conjoint analysis algorithms and the output is partial utilities for each component of the product concept and for each individual respondent.

Conjoint analysis results provide the market analyst with four useful results:

■ The identification of the *best concept*, that is, the combination of concept components with the highest utilities, among all possible combinations.
■ Information on what will be *the utility or disutility* of any change in the concept characteristics. This enables a selection of the most attractive trade-offs among concept components.

New product concepts	A	B	C	D	E	F	G	H
Gross intentions Percentage of respondents with positive buying intention.	71	62	60	60	51	46	44	22
Adjusted intentions Percentage of respondents with positive intentions and convinced of the novelty of the product.	45	37	18	19	27	37	10	19
Rate of conviction Percentage of respondents convinced within the group with positive intentions.	63	59	30	31	53	79	26	86

Table 11.4   Interpretation of intention-to-buy scores

Source: Tauber (1973).

- Information on the *relative importance* of each component.
- Possibility of constructing *segments* based on the similarity of the respondents' reactions to the tested concepts.

On the basis of these results, alternative scenarios can be developed and the expected share of preferences estimated in each case.

The problems raised by concept testing are usually less subtle in B2B markets, since industrial clients' needs are generally more clearly specified. Moreover, the respondent is a professional, and trade-off analysis is a more natural way of thinking. Conjoint analysis has many applications within industrial markets.

11.5.6. Example of a concept test

To illustrate the contribution of conjoint analysis, let us examine the following example. The product studied is a hairspray, targeted at the Belgian market and defined in terms of the following five characteristics:

- Design: two designs are considered: the existing one and a new one.
- Product's claim: 'styling spray', 'extra strong hairspray' or 'fixing spray'.
- Price: three price levels are considered; 109, 129 and 149 Belgian francs.
- Product range: the product may be offered singly or included in a range comprising a gel, a mousse and a styling cream.
- Brand: the brand may be A, B or C.

These variables give a total of 108 possible combinations for new product concept ($2 \times 3 \times 3 \times 2 \times 3$). Using a fractional factorial design we can reduce the number of concepts to be tested to 18. All pertinent information on each of the characteristics is retained, but information on interactions of orders greater than 2 are lost. In order to estimate partial utilities, regression analysis is conducted, using binary variables (0, 1) to describe the presence or absence of the product characteristics at each level. Figure 11.4 shows the average utility curves obtained from the sample examined.

The results show that consumers are very sensitive to the brand name and that they noticeably prefer brand B to the other brands. They also show the price elasticity to be -0.81. The new design is also clearly preferred over the old one. With regard to the product's claim, there appears to be very little sensitivity on the part of the respondents, who probably understand the claim poorly (Rochet, 1987). These results are useful to develop alternative launching scenarios and to obtain estimates of the likely rate of adoption of the new product concept.

11.6. Business analysis and marketing programming

Once the product concept has been developed and accepted by top management, it is up to the marketing department to quantify the market opportunity and to develop alternative marketing programmes. This implies sales forecasting and market penetration objectives under different marketing budgets. The economic viability of the new product within the chosen time horizon must be assessed and the risk of the new venture evaluated.

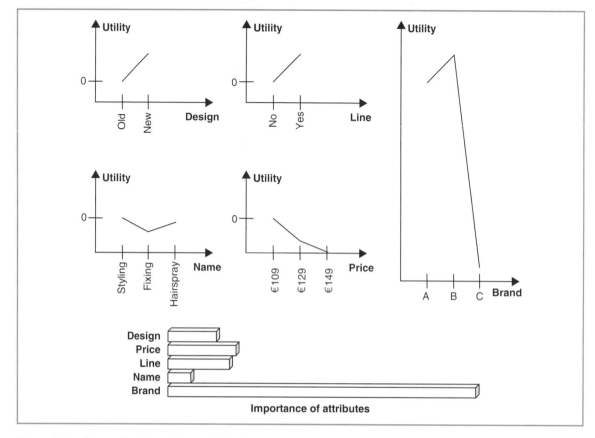

Figure 11.4   Example of conjoint analysis: hairspray products
Source: Rochet (1987).

11.6.1. Estimating sales volume

Estimating the sales projection for the first 3 years is the first problem to examine, which will condition the rest of the analysis. Given the estimates of total potential sales in the target segment, what will be the expected sales volume or market share of the new product under different assumptions regarding the size of the marketing efforts? Different methods to approach this question can be used: subjective methods, feasibility studies and methods based on a test market.

Subjective methods: rely on the marketing information system of the firm, but also on experience, judgement and on information accumulated more or less informally within the firm. This accumulated knowledge is based on sales history of similar products, on information from distributors, on the sales force, on comparison with competing products, and so on.

Feasibility studies: aim to gather the missing information in the field by interviewing directly potential customers, distributors, retailers, and so on. Purchasing intention scores are collected and used to estimate sales volume.

Market tests: allow for observation of customer behaviour in the real world. Trial and repeat purchase rates can be estimated and used for early projection of sales. Alternatives to market tests are in-home use tests, mini-test panels, laboratory experiments and regional introduction.

These three groups of methods are not exclusive and may be used jointly where uncertainty and the degree of newness for the company are high. Regardless of the approach adopted, the marketing department needs to set a sales revenue objective and to estimate whether sales will be high enough to generate an acceptable profit.

11.6.2. Typical sales patterns

The new product sales pattern over time will differ according to whether it is a one-time purchase product, a durable good or a frequently purchased product.

■ For *one-time purchased products*, the expected sales curve increases steadily, peaks and then decreases progressively as the number of potential buyers diminishes. Thus, in this case, the occupation rate of the market is the key variable.

- For *durable goods*, total demand can be subdivided into two parts: first equipment and replacement demand. First equipment demand is time dependent and determined by income variables, while replacement demand is determined by the product's obsolescence, be it technical, economic or style.
- Purchases of *frequently purchased products* can be divided into two categories: first-time and repeat purchases. The number of first-time purchasers initially increases and then diminishes as the majority of potential buyers have tried the product. Repeat purchases will occur if the product meets the requirements of a group of buyers, who eventually will become loyal customers, and the total sales curve will eventually reach a plateau. In this product category, repeat purchases are the best indicator of market satisfaction.

The typical sales patterns for trial, repeat and total sales of a frequently purchased product are presented in Figure 11.5.

11.6.3. Panel data projection methods

In the case of frequently purchased products, the Parfitt and Collins theorem (1968) can be used to decompose market share and to generate market share projections. These measures are normally obtained from a consumer's panel. Market share can be divided into three distinct components:

1. The *penetration rate* of a brand is defined as the cumulative trial, that is, the percentage of buyers having made a trial purchase at time *t*; this rate first increases after launching and then tends to stabilise fairly rapidly as the stock of potential first-time buyers diminishes.

2. Those buyers having tried the product express the *repeat purchasing rate* as the proportion of total purchases in the product field. After a certain number of purchases, the repeat purchase rate will level off to some equilibrium state.

3. The *intensity rate*, or buying level index, compares the rate of quantities purchased of the studied brand to the average quantities purchased within the product category. A distinction can be made here between heavy, light or average buyers (by volume) in the product field.

The expected market share is estimated by multiplying these three values.

Suppose that the estimated rate for trial purchase is 34 per cent and that the repeat purchase rate is around 25 per cent. If the average quantities purchased are the same for the brand and the product category, the expected market share will be:

34 per cent × 25 per cent × 1.00 = 8.5 per cent

In cases of segmented markets, the expected market shares are calculated for each group. For example, the buying level index may vary according to the type of buyer. It may reach 1.20 for heavy buyers and 0.80 for light buyers. The expected market share in each of these cases will be around 10.2 and 6.8 per cent, respectively.

This kind of market share projection can be quickly formulated after the first few months of launching a new product. This method also allows for measurement of the impact that advertising and promotional activities have on market share. For more on this topic, see Parfitt and Collins' seminal article (1968).

No method can estimate future sales with certainty. Therefore, it is useful to give a range of estimations, with minimum and maximum sales, in order to assess the extent of risk implied by the new product launch.

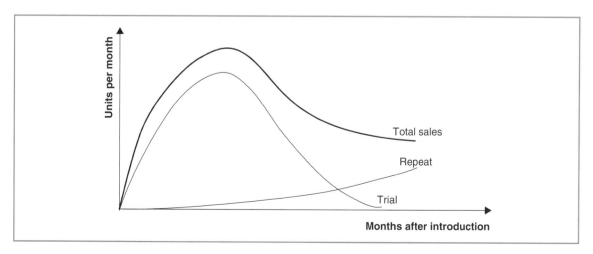

Figure 11.5   Typical sales pattern for trial and repeat sales

11.7. The customer adoption process

The design of a new product-launching plan, to be effective, must be based on a good understanding of the adoption process of the innovation followed by the target group of customers. In the general case, the adoption process can be described as a sequence of steps (see Table 11.5) followed by the prospect, from the stage of innovation discovery to its possible adoption or rejection.

This adoption process described by Rogers (1962/1995) and by Robertson (1971) is very similar to the learning process described in Chapter 4 and also to the Lavidge and Steiner (1961) model which is commonly used in the analysis of advertising effectiveness. As shown in Table 11.5, this adoption process can be subdivided into six phases.

1. *Knowledge*: the potential customer knows of the branded product's existence; informative advertising and word-of-mouth communication play an important role at this stage.
2. *Comprehension*: it is based on knowledge and represents the customer's conception of what the branded product is and what functions it can perform.
3. *Attitude*: as explained in Chapter 5, attitude is thought of as the predisposition of the individual to evaluate an object of his environment in a favourable or unfavourable manner. Concept advertising, distributors and prescribers are the main sources of influence.
4. *Conviction*: the individual develops a favourable attitude, is convinced of the product's superiority and that purchase is the appropriate course of action.
5. *Trial*: the individual uses the branded product on a limited scale, stimulated by a promotion or by sampling.

6. *Adoption*: the customer accepts the branded product and continues to purchase and/or use it. The adoption process is now complete and it is the intrinsic product quality that will determine the level of satisfaction.

In the design of a launching plan, it is therefore important to select the types of marketing instrument better adapted to each stage and to monitor the progress made by the target group along the adoption process.

11.7.1. Duration of the diffusion process

The speed of diffusion will be a function of the type of innovation. Five characteristics have been found to affect diffusion speed (Rogers, 1962/1995, p. 208):

Relative advantage: the degree of improvement that the innovation represents over existing alternatives (fax machines' superiority over telex).

Complexity: the inherent difficulty associated with the new idea or product. High levels of complexity can make it more expensive for a customer in terms of learning costs (personal computers).

Compatibility: how well the innovation fits with the existing practices of potential adopters. If customers have to modify their prior use patterns, changeover or adoption costs exist and the speed of diffusion will be slower. Conversely, if the product is fully compatible with prior use, the adoption can be very rapid (fluoridated toothpaste versus the electric toothbrush).

Communicability: the ease with which the essence of the innovation can be conveyed to potential adopters. Some benefits have a high degree of visibility and some products lend themselves well to usage demonstration, such as

---

Table 11.5   The adoption process of an innovation

Stages of the process	Hierarchy of effects (Lavidge and Steiner, 1961)	Adoption process (Robertson, 1971)
Cognitive level	Awareness	Knowledge
	↓	↓
	Knowledge	Comprehension
	↓	↓
Affective level	Liking	Attitude
	↓	↓
	Preference	Conviction
	↓	↓
Behavioural level	Conviction	Trial
	↓	↓
	Purchase	Adoption
	↓	
	Loyalty/Forgetting	

Sources: Lavidge and Steiner (1961), Robertson (1971).

cars, telephones, VCRs, and so on. Conversely, innovations with long-term benefits (like health protection) are more difficult to promote and therefore are susceptible to diffuse more slowly.

Trialability: the innovation's capability of being tried out on a smaller scale prior to purchase, thereby reducing the adoption costs.

Other factors can also determine the speed of diffusion like the degree of uncertainty of the innovation itself, particularly in the case of discontinuous innovations (Frambach, 1995). Three sources of uncertainty may exist:

- Uncertainty concerning the reality of the benefits claimed, particularly when those benefits are expected in the long term.
- Uncertainty concerning the adoption costs (resistance to change) associated with the implementation of the innovation in the customer's life or organisation.
- Uncertainty concerning the pace of innovation itself and the length of its product life cycle.

The analysis of these factors prior to the launching of the innovation is useful to evaluate correctly the duration of the introductory phase and also to design the most appropriate communication programme.

11.7.2. Categories of adopters

Rogers (1962/1995, p. 5) defines the diffusion process as the manner in which new ideas, products, or practices spread through a culture, or (in marketing terms) through a target market. Rogers proposed classifying adopters, by reference to the timing of adoption, into five types, ranked from those who first adopt the innovation to those who come last to the adoption phase (see Figure 11.6).

The basic assumption is that the numbers of people falling into each category will approximate a normal distribution.

Innovators (2.5 per cent): the very early purchasers of the innovation; they are independent, venturesome and willing to try new ideas at some risk. They represent a very small proportion of the market.

Early adopters (13.5 per cent): a larger group composed of opinion leaders in their social group. They adopt new ideas early, but with prudence.

Early majority (34 per cent): they adopt new ideas before the average person but they need information and they are not leaders.

Late majority (34 per cent): they are sceptical; they adopt an innovation only after a majority of people has tried it. They follow the majority rule.

Laggards (16 per cent): they are tradition bound; they are suspicious and resistant to changes.

This categorisation approximately follows a normal distribution, its cumulative distribution taking the form of an S-shaped diffusion curve.

11.8. Pricing new products

The more a new product is distinct and brings an innovative solution to the satisfaction of a need, the more sensitive it is to price. This price is a fundamental choice upon which depends the commercial and financial success of the operation. Once the firm has analysed costs, demand and competition, it must then choose between two very contradictory strategies: (a) a high initial price strategy to skim the high end of the market, and (b) a strategy of low price from the beginning in order to achieve fast and powerful market penetration.

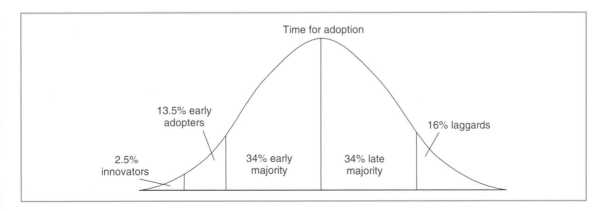

Figure 11.6   Adopters categorisation – based on relative time of adoption
Source: Rogers (1962/1995).

11.8.1. Skimming pricing strategy

This strategy consists of selling the new product at a high price and thus limiting oneself to the upper end of the demand curve. This would ensure significant financial returns soon after the launch. Many considerations support this strategy; furthermore, a number of conditions need to be met for this strategy to prove successful (Dean, 1950):

- When there are reasons to believe that the new product life cycle will be short, or when competition is expected to copy and to market a similar product in the near future, a skimming price strategy may be recommended because a low price strategy would make the innovation unprofitable.
- When a product is so innovative that the market is expected to mature slowly and the buyer has no elements on which to compare it with other products, demand is inelastic. It is tempting to exploit this situation by setting a high price and then readjusting it progressively as the market matures.
- Launching a new product at a high price is one way of segmenting the market. The segments have different price elasticities. The launching price skims the customers who are insensitive to price. Later price cuts then allow the firm to reach successively more elastic segments. This is a form of time discriminatory pricing.
- When demand is hard to evaluate, it is risky to anticipate what kind of demand growth or cost reduction can result from a low price. This is particularly true when the manufacturing process is not yet stabilised and costs are likely to be underestimated.

To be effective, the introduction of a new product requires heavy expenditure on advertising and promotion. When the firm does not have the financial means necessary for a successful introduction, charging high prices is one way of generating the resources.

Price skimming strategy is definitely a cautious strategy, which is more financial than commercial. Its main advantage is that it leaves the door open for a progressive price adjustment, depending on how the market and competition develop. From a commercial point of view, it is always easier to cut a price than to increase it. The importance of the strategy lies mainly in its financial aspect: the fact that some capital, which can be used for alternative activity, is freed early on.

11.8.2. Penetration price strategy

Penetration strategy, on the other hand, consists of setting low prices in order to capture a larger share of the market right from the start. It assumes the adoption of an intensive distribution system, the use of mass advertising to develop market receptivity, and especially an adequate production capacity from the beginning. In this case, the outlook is more commercial than financial. The following general conditions must prevail to justify its use:

- Demand must be price elastic over the entire demand curve; there are no upper segments to be given priority and the only strategy is to address the whole market at a price low enough to satisfy the greatest number.
- It is possible to achieve lower unit costs by increasing volumes significantly, either because of economies of scale or because of potential experience effects.
- Soon after its introduction, the new product is threatened by strong competition. This threat of new entrants is a powerful reason for adopting low prices. The penetration strategy is used here to discourage competitors from entering the market. Low prices act as very efficient barriers to entry, as discussed in Chapter 8.
- The top range of the market is already satisfied; in this case, penetration policy is the only valid policy to develop the market.
- Potential buyers can easily integrate the new product in their consumption or production; the transfer costs of adopting the product other than its price are relatively low and, therefore, a mass market can be developed rapidly.

A penetration price strategy is therefore more risky than a skimming price strategy. If the firm plans to make the new product profitable over a long period, it may face the situation that new entrants might later use new production techniques, which will give them a cost advantage over the innovating firm.

11.9. Assessing the financial risk

The launch of a new product is a strategic decision process, which concerns every function within the firm and not just the marketing function. The success of this process largely depends on a sound co-ordination of each function involved. Moreover, the time factor is important and may modify the profitability of the new product. To ensure a good co-ordination, the firm must have at its disposal analytical tools to monitor the development process step by step and to assess its conformance with the profitability and timing objectives.

For each product launch, it is important to determine as precisely as possible when the elimination of risk is supposed to occur. There are three levels of risk, identified in Figure 11.7.

1. The *simple break-even point*, the moment where the new activity leaves the zone of losses and enters into the zone of profits.

2. The *equilibrium break-even point*, when the present value of total receipts covers the present value of total expenses. The company has recouped its capital layout.

3. The *capital acquisition point*, the point where the new activity generates a financial surplus allowing for reinvestments to prolong the economic life of the activity or for supporting the development of other businesses within the firm.

Ideally, the capital acquisition point should be reached before the maturity phase of the product's life cycle in order to allow the company timely redeployment, which is before competitive pressure begins to erode profit margins. These three criteria will eventually determine the economic viability of the project. To be operational these criteria must be viewed in a dynamic perspective.

How do we proceed to select priority projects when financial resources are limited, opportunities too many and the risks very different from one project to the other? There is a vast literature in the field of capital budgeting on this topic, but the methods proposed are strictly financial, quantitatively oriented and do not consider qualitative criteria, which are often very important to assess the attractiveness of a particular project. Moreover, they require precise financial data, which are not often available at the evaluation phase of a project.

A crude but useful financial indicator is the payback period index (in years) which answers the question when shall I get all my money back? This index is calculated as follows:

$$\text{Payback} = \frac{\text{Development and commercial costs}}{(\text{Annual sales (\$/year)}) . (\text{Profit margin as a percentage of sales})}$$

This criterion is simple, easily understood and is based on data usually available at the evaluation phase. The reciprocal of this index gives a very crude estimate of the return as a percentage. Alternative and more rigorous methods are net present value (NPV) or discounted cash flow (DCF) as well as internal rate of return (IRR).

It is often useful to add explicitly a risk factor and qualitative indicators similar to those used in the screening grid (see Figure 11.3). We would then have a new project evaluation matrix similar to that presented in Figure 11.8. In this matrix the projects are evaluated along two dimensions:

- The first horizontal dimension measures *the value to the firm* of each project, using a multi-attribute composite index based on quantitative and qualitative indicators reflecting the value of the project to the firm.
- A second vertical dimension measuring *the probability of technological and/or commercial success* of each project as evaluated by management after the investigation or development phase.

We thus have a two-dimensional grid composed of four quadrants, where each project is represented by a bubble

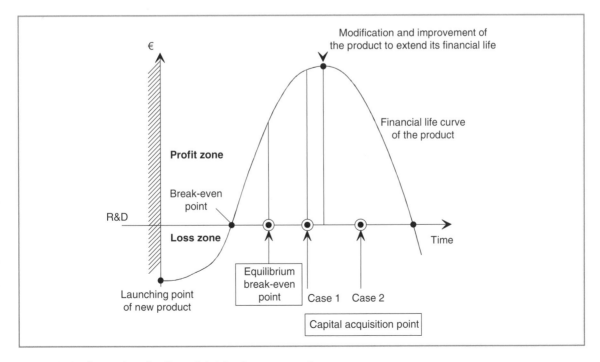

Figure 11.7   Assessing the financial risk of a new product
Source: Daudé (1980).

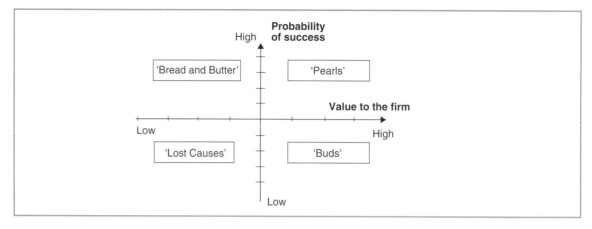

Figure 11.8   Portfolio analysis of new product concepts
Source: Cooper (1993).

denoting the size of the resources to be devoted to each project:

- In the *upper-right quadrant* are *the Pearls*, that is projects having a high value to the firm and a high probability of success.
- In the lower-right quadrant, are *the Buds*, very desirable projects for the firm but still having a low probability of success.
- In the upper-left quadrant, are *the Bread and Butter* projects, with a good probability of success (and a low risk) but ordinary or low value to the firm.
- In the lower-right quadrant are *the Lost Causes*, the bad projects, a low commercial payoff and a low probability of success.

This project portfolio grid is used during the annual budgeting exercise to identify the priority projects.

Decision rules might be

- allocate resources by priority to the development and the launching of Pearls projects;
- invest in some Buds projects to reinforce their competitiveness by gathering additional market information or by redesigning the product concept;
- cut back on Bread and Butter projects which often absorb too much time and resources;
- delete from the portfolio the Lost Causes projects.

This type of portfolio analysis is also useful to help the firm to allocate R&D efforts towards new projects.

CHAPTER SUMMARY

The new product development process consists of three phases: (a) idea phase (idea generation and screening), (b) concept phase (concept development, concept testing, business analysis) and (c) launching phase. In market-driven companies this process tends to be more a parallel than a sequential development process in order to ensure better interfunctional co-ordination. The concept development phase is crucial for incorporating the market orientation upfront and also for adopting a thorough approach to product greening. In the business analysis, the economic viability of the new product must be assessed in a dynamic perspective under alternative marketing programmes and the risk of the new venture evaluated. The market-oriented firm tries to have a permanently balanced portfolio of projects, a useful tool for identifying priority projects.

Review and Application Questions

1. Proceed to the morphological analysis of one of the following three products: office chair, an electric fryer, and a document binding system.
2. You are responsible for the launching of a new electronic device for automatic video recording of TV programmes through a system of code numbers (type Show-View). Prepare a written description of the product concept (a) to be communicated as a brief to the advertising agency and (b) to be used in a product concept test within a sample of housewives owning a video and belonging to the 40 years and over age group.
3. There is a general agreement that the strategy of joint development between R&D and strategic marketing is likely to improve the productivity of R&D investment? How would you promote these joint efforts?
4. Give three examples of products new to the world. Show the key components of these innovations and the type of risk the innovating firm will be confronted with.
5. In your opinion, what are the merits and demerits of the parallel and sequential approaches in the organisation of the new product development process?
6. The travel agency Frontiers has developed different tourist concepts using three characteristics – activity, site and price – each at three levels. These service concepts have been tested within three segments of potential customers: juniors, families and seniors. Through conjoint analysis, the following utilities were identified:

Characteristics		Segment		
		Juniors	Families	Seniors
Activity	Culture	+0.10	−0.20	+0.20
	Sport	+0.30	−0.10	−0.20
	Leisure	−0.40	+0.30	0
Prices	20,000 F/S	+0.50	+0.40	+0.30
	40,000 F/S	−0.10	−0.10	−0.10
	50,000 F/S	−0.40	−0.30	−0.20
Sites	Sea	+0.10	+0.50	−0.30
	Mountain	+0.10	+0.10	−0.10
	Cities	−0.20	−0.60	+0.40

Analyse the sensitivity of each segment to the different service characteristics. Which tourist service would you propose by priority to each segment? Would it be possible to develop a service concept that would suit the three segments?

Bibliography

Barreyre, P.Y. (1980), Typologie des innovations, *Revue Française de Gestion*, January–February, pp. 9–15.

Bijon, C. (1984), La stratégie de rupture, *Harvard-L'expansion*, Autumn, pp. 98–104.

Booz, Allen, and Hamilton (1982), *New Product Management for the 1980s*, New York.

Cooper, R.G. (1993), *Winning at New Products*, Reading, MA, Addison-Wesley, 2nd edition.

Daudé, B. (1980), Analyse de la maîtrise des risques, *Revue Française de Gestion*, January–February, pp. 38–48.

De Brabandère, L. (1998), *Le management des idées*, Paris, Dunod.

Dean, J. (1950), Pricing Policies for New Products, *Harvard Business Review*, 28, 6, pp. 28–36.

Economist (1999), 20 February.

European Commission (2004), *Flash Innobarometer*, Brussels, September.

Frambach, R.T. (1995), Diffusion of Innovations in Business-to-Business Markets, in *Product Development*, Bruce, M. and Biemans, W.G. (eds), New York, John Wiley & Sons.

Gordon, J.J. (1965), *Stimulation des facultés créatrices dans les groupes de recherche synectique*, Paris, Hommes et Techniques.

Green, P.E. and Srinivasan, V. (1978), Conjoint Analysis in Consumer Research: Issues and Outlook, *Journal of Consumer Research*, 5, 2, pp. 103–23.

Flash Eurobarometer 144, (2004), *Innobarometer: A Survey Organised in 2003 by the Directorate General Enterprise*, Brussels, European Commision.

Kotler, P. (1997/2005) *Marketing Management*, Englewood Cliffs, NJ, Prentice-Hall International, 9th edition.

Larson, E.W. and Gobeli, D.H. (1988), Organizing for Product Development Projects, *Journal of Product Innovation Management*, 5, 3, pp. 180–90.

Lavidge, R.J. and Steiner, G.A. (1961), A Model of Predictive Measurement of Advertising Effectiveness, *Journal of Marketing*, 25, October, pp. 59–62.

Mansfield, E. and Wagner, S. (1975), Organizational and Strategic Factors Associated with Probabilities of Success in Industrial R&D, *Journal of Business*, 48, 2, pp. 179–98.

O'Meara, J.T. (1961), Selecting Profitable Products, *Harvard Business Review*, 39, 1, pp. 110–18.

Osborn, A.F. (1963), *Applied Imagination*, New York, Charles Scribner's Sons, 3rd edition.

Ottman, J.A. (1993), *Green Marketing*, Lincolnwood, IL, NTC Business Books.

Page, A.L. (1993), Assessing New Product Development Practices and Performance: Establishing Crucial Norms, *Journal of Product Innovation Management*, 10, 4, pp. 273–90.

Parfitt, J.M. and Collins, J.K. (1968), Use of Consumer Panels for Brand Share Prediction, *Journal of Marketing Research*, 5, 2, pp. 131–45.

Steele, L.W. (1988), Selecting R&D Programs and Objectives, *Research & Technology Management*, March–April, pp. 17–36.

Robertson, T.S. (1971), *Innovative Behavior and Communication*, New York, Holt, Rinehart and Winston.

Rochet, L. (1987), *Diagnostic stratégique du potentiel d'extension d'une marque de laque*, Louvain-la-Neuve, Institut d'Administration et de Gestion.

Rogers, E.M. (1962/1995), *Diffusion of Innovations*, New York, The Free Press, 4th edition.

Schnaars, S.P. (1998), *Marketing Strategy: Customers and Competition*, New York, The Free Press, 2nd edition.

Stalk, G. (1988), Time – The Next Source of Competitive Advantage, *Harvard Business Review*, 66, 4, pp. 41–51.

Steele, L.W. (1988), Selecting R&D Programs and Objectives, *Research & Technology Management*, March–April, pp. 17–36.

Takeuchi, H. and Nonaka, I. (1986), The New Product Development Game, *Harvard Business Review*, 64, 1, pp. 137–46.

Tauber, E.M. (1973), Reduce New Product Failures: Measure Needs as well as Purchase Interest, *Journal of Marketing*, 37, 3, pp. 61–70.

Von Hippel, E. (1978), Successful Industrial Products from Customer Ideas, *Journal of Marketing*, 42, 1, pp. 39–49.

brand management 12

Chapter contents

Chapter learning objectives

When you have read this chapter, you should be able to understand

- the growing importance of brands for consumers and companies;
- the functions of brands for both the customer and the manufacturer;
- the concepts of brand identity, brand image and brand equity;
- the advantages and risks of brand extension and of co-branding;
- the usefulness of brand portfolio management;
- the methods of brand evaluation.

Chapter introduction

Brand management has become an important topic for both academics and marketers. The objective of this chapter is first to describe the reasons for the growing importance of brands for customers and for firms. We will define what the concept of brand covers and examine the brand functions from the manufacturer's and the customers' point of view. Three key concepts will be reviewed: brand identity, brand image and brand equity. In the second part of this chapter, we will focus on brand strategies. We will first identify how to create a brand, going form the brand identity creation to the selection of name and logo. We will also examine what are the key strategies available to develop a branding strategy covering, in particular, brand extension strategies and brand internationalisation. We will end this chapter with a review of brand portfolio management and the tools to evaluate brand value.

12.1. Strategic role of branding

Brands have been considered as key strategic assets since many years in the fast moving consumer goods (FMCG) industry. Companies such as Procter & Gamble, Unilever, l'Oréal or Nestlé were among the first to focus on brands management. After an intensive phase of mergers and acquisitions, a very limited number of FMCG multinationals now own the majority of well-known brands in the world. Services companies have also developed strong brands in banking (UBS, HSBC), airlines (British Airways, Singapore Airlines), express mail (DHL, Federal Express), credit cards (Visa, Master Card) or Internet (Yahoo, Google, Amazon).

Even B2B companies have started to successfully use branding strategies. A case in point is the Intel brand, which was created before the end of patent expiration, a very successful example of 'component branding'. The Intel brand is now ranked among the top five brands worldwide in terms of value. Other examples of successful component brands are Goretex and Lycra. B2B companies such as Arcelor or Total are also deploying branding strategies to improve the perception of their corporate image by end-users. Last but not least, the development of private labels in the food sector that has been a great success in Europe over the past few years (see Chapter 13).

12.1.1. What is a brand?

According to the definition given by the American Marketing Association,

A brand is a name, term, sign, symbol, or design or a combination of them intended to identify the goods and services of one seller or group of sellers and to differentiate them from those of competition.

As illustrated in Figure 4.5 (see Chapter 4), a branded product is formed by a set of tangible and intangible attributes, the core service plus peripheral services, necessary or added and by a set of mental associations. By mental associations, we mean intangible benefits such as personality, emotional or symbolic attributes that are recorded in the customers' minds and which form what Kapferer (2004) calls the brand identity.

The strength of a brand like Mercedes cannot be understood by referring only to its tangible benefits of quality and solidity. It covers also elements such as brand personality (serious, sober, cold), country of origin (German) or emotional benefit (social achievement).

Some brands are differentiated mainly by reference to tangible benefits: Volvo (safety), Mr Proper (grease removal), Bang and Olufsen (design), while other brands base their differences more on intangible benefits (Lancôme, Chanel or Gucci). All strong brands are, however, recorded in the mind of consumers as *a set of strong rational and emotional associations*. In this chapter, we place more emphasis on the role and importance of those mental associations or intangibles attributes.

Brands are now present everywhere. They exist because they generate trust. This trust is based on a close relationship that brands have built over the years with consumers. We find brands mainly in product categories where perceived risks are high. The higher the perceived risk in a product category, the more significant will be the role of a brand to minimise perceived risks. As discussed in Chapter 4, there are many types of risks, not only functional risks – such as performance or safety – but also social or psychological risks.

In view of the importance of brands for the customers, for the firms and for the financial markets, brands have to be managed carefully, developed and even nurtured to ensure the their long-term development and, therefore, the firm's long-term performance. Procter & Gamble was the first company to create the concept of 'brand management' as early as the 1930s. As discussed in Chapter 1 of this book, it has one manager responsible for developing a brand as a mini-CEO. Since then, most firms having strong brands have adopted the brand management system.

12.1.2. Importance of brands

By the end of the 1980s, companies realised that acquisitions of brands were becoming more important than the acquisitions of plants, workers or other tangible assets. Brands started to be viewed as real asset that was providing a strong competitive advantage for firms owning them. They were not only strong barriers to entry for competition, but also a source of increased profit performance. They were generating steady revenues thanks to the high rate of customer loyalty. For the financial markets, this was the best guarantee of increased value for shareholders. This explained the wave of mergers and acquisitions that started in the mid-1980s and that were exclusively driven by the motivation of acquiring strong brands. It was key for multinational companies to acquire powerful brands, possibly international brands to become a global leader. Many brands were purchased at very high prices. Perrier, for example, was bought by Nestlé for €2.4 billions. The trend is still the same as indicated by the recent purchase of Rolls Royce by BMW.

> In 2003, BMW acquired the Rolls Royce name for more than £40 millions. Interestingly, BMW could only acquire the right to use the name and exploit the famous 'spirit of ecstasy' logo but could not buy the plants and the know-how of Rolls Royce's skilled workers. They felt that the brand was so strong that they had no problem investing another £65 millions to build a plant and hire new workers.

Coca-Cola has also been trying during several years to buy the well-known French Orangina softdrink brand that was finally purchased by its rival Cadbury Schweppes. They were ready to pay more that €800 million. This also explained the recent acquisition of Gillette by P&G in 2005 to add two global brands – Gillette and Duracell – to their existing brand portfolio.

Some brands are still very attractive potential purchase for some companies:

> The well-known European cosmetic leader Nivéa (Beiersdorf from Germany) is viewed as such a valuable asset that two multinational companies (P&G and l'Oréal) have been fighting for some years to acquire this company, so far without success.

Brands are also important for consumers. Today it is difficult to find product categories where products are not branded. Brands are everywhere, not only for fashion, clothes or perfumes but also in services, Hi-Fi or Internet, despite some negative reactions raised against the pre-eminence of brands in the lives of consumers.

12.2. The branded product, as a bundle of attributes

A brand is perceived by a potential customer as a bundle of attributes and of mental associations which, taken together, will form the distinctive elements of the brand's identity. The composition of the bundle, the relative importance and the perceived presence of the attributes will contribute to influence potential customers 'purchasing decision'.

The different elements of the conceptual brand model are presented in Table 12.1. The integration of these elements leads to a measure of the brand perceived value

---

Table 12.1   Modelling the branded product as a bundle of attributes

Objective characteristics	Tangible and intangible attributes	Evaluation of attributes		Partial utilities	Total utility
		Importance	Performance		
C_1	A_1	W_1	X_1	u_1	U
C_2	A_2	W_2	X_2	u_2	
...	....	....	....	...	
C_n	A_n	W_n	X_n	u_n	
Reality	Bundle of attributes	Priorities	Perceptions	Values	
Technical description	Qualitative research	Proportion scale	Interval scale	Integration model	

Source: Lambin (1989).

for a specific potential client, which can be interpreted as an indicator of his/her brand purchase probability.

12.2.1. Objective characteristics

They are the antecedents of the tangible and intangible attributes, that is, the technical characteristics generating the attributes or the benefits sought. They constitute the technical profile of the brand. In general, several characteristics are required to produce the benefit sought. Potential customers rarely give much attention to the objective characteristics, being more interested by the benefits generated, except when those characteristics reinforce the prestige or the credibility of the brand.

12.2.2. Attributes

By 'attribute', one designates the advantage or the benefit sought by the customer and which is used as a selection criterion. Customers generally consider several attributes in evaluating a brand. These attributes can be functional and tangible (power, comfort, etc.), but also intangible (trust, reliability, etc.). The global evaluation of the brand requires a process integrating the specific evaluations made on each attribute.

An attribute is a variable susceptible to have different values or levels (discrete or continuous) measuring the degree of presence of the attribute in the focal brand. Each brand constitutes a specific bundle of attributes, given that the attributes are present at different levels in each bundle.

Attributes can be classified by focusing on their impact on customer's satisfaction. Using the Kano diagram presented in Figure 12.1 one can distinguish three types of attributes.

1. *Basic attributes* are the 'must haves' factors that a product must deliver to be acceptable by customers. Customers barely notice them, but poor delivery leads to complaints (a TV set in a hotel room). These basic attributes are also called threshold factors (see curve #1 in Figure 12.1) because at higher levels they provide diminishing returns in terms of customer satisfaction (i.e. increasing the number of ashtrays in a car).
2. *Performance attributes* keep adding to customer satisfaction when more of them are provided. Continuing improvements in fuel economy fall in this category. Similarly, in the microprocessor industry more calculation per second, in the plastic industry less degradation in sunlight, etc. As far as the customer is concerned there is no saturation effect. These attributes provide ample opportunities for valuable differentiation. Typically, customers shop around to get the best deal on performance attributes.
3. *Excitements attributes* are unexpected and highly appreciated benefits. If not delivered, they do not increase dissatisfaction; but if delivered, they inspire a more than proportional increase in satisfaction (see curve #3 in Figure 12.1). They are the 'nice-to-have' attributes.

If these excitements attributes are tangible they tend to be short-lived because they are rapidly matched by competition, thereby destroying the excitement effect. If they are mental associations generated by the prestige of the brand or by its positioning, they are part of the brand identity. These mental associations are particularly important in B2C markets.

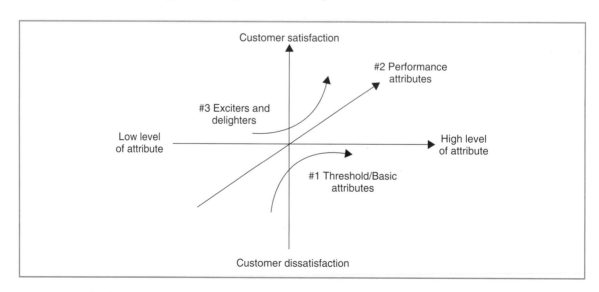

Figure 12.1   The Kano diagram
Source: Walden (1993).

12.2.3. Importance of attributes

The attributes considered do not have the same importance for the potential customer. The attribute's importance for a particular individual reveals his or her value system and the priorities given to each benefit sought, given the potential customer will have to make trade-off or compromise between the different benefits.

Every reasonable individual wishes to obtain the most for the least: not only the best service and performance but also the lowest possible price, fast delivery, etc. Given that these expectations are generally incompatible, potential customers are induced to search for compromises and to decide what are finally the most important benefits.

Knowing what are the priorities for different segments of the market enables the firm to design different brand concepts targeting specific segment(s) and to respect the diversity of customers needs.

Market research studies have demonstrated that individuals (at least when confronted with articulated needs), and of course organisations, are perfectly able to conceptualise and communicate their preferences in a survey.

12.2.4. Performance: the attribute's perceived degree of presence

A particular attribute can be perceived as very important for an individual but not perceived by this individual as very present in a particular brand. The importance scores must therefore by complemented by scores revealing the perceived degree of presence in each attribute.

Consumers have preconceived ideas and perceptions regarding brand performance attributes. These perceptions are based on past experience, word-of-mouth communication, objective information or simply advertising. These perceptions which do not necessarily correspond to the reality of the brand, are nevertheless components of the brand image and therefore a reality for the firm. These perceptions can be measured by qualitative and quantitative market research.

To identify a brand, consumers use not only the brand name but also other observable characteristics like the packaging, the design, the logo, the colours, etc. These external characteristics are part of the brand equity since they are used by potential customers to assess the presence of performace and excitements attributes, and to classify brands according to the type of promise they represent.

12.2.5. The value of a particular attribute

The value of a specific attribute is determined by the conjunction of two factors: its importance score and its perceived degree of presence score. This value is called the attribute partial utility, that is, the subjective values associated at each attribute level. The total utility of brand for a specific individual is given by the sum (or the product) of all partial utilities. This supposes the use of an integration model. The most frequently used model is the compensatory and additive model (Fishbein, 1967):

- Compensatory, because a weak score on a particular attribute can be compensated by a high score on another attribute.
- Additive, because it is assumed that mentally individuals evaluate the total utility by simply making the sum of the partial utilities. This implies the lack of interaction among attributes.

Other integration models can be used. In particular, non-compensatory models that should be used when consumers tend to privilege some attributes over others (disjunctive model) – like safety for instance – or when minimal values are expected on the degree of presence of some attributes (conjunctive model).

The total utility measured reveals the attitude of a particular individual vis-à-vis a brand and is therefore a good leading indicator of his or her purchase probability. This information is of great value to design a branding strategy. Several options can be considered, such as

- adding important performance or excitement attributes currently not present in the brand;
- augmenting the degree of presence of key attributes;
- communicating better about the key attributes present in the brand, but ignored by the market.

12.3. Functions of the brand

The brand plays an important role in a market economy, not only for the customer but for the producer as well. We will examine separately the brand functions in the B2C and in the B2B markets.

12.3.1. Functions of the brand for the customer in B2C markets

Five distinct functions of direct use to the customer can be identified, and four brand functions of strategic importance to the firm.

1. *A landmarking function.* A brand name is perceived by the potential buyer as a message proposing a specific package of attributes both tangible and intangible, and the buyer uses this information to guide his (or her) choice given the needs or the consumption situation confronted.

In this sense, the brand is a *signal* to potential buyers who can identify, at a low personal cost, the set of existing solutions to their problems. By structuring supply, this brand's landmarking function contributes to the market transparency, a service particularly useful in industrialised economies where brands proliferate.

2. *A decision simplification function.* The brand is a simple and practical way to memorise the brand characteristics and to put a name to a specific assortment of benefits. Easy to memorise and to recognise, the brand makes possible a *routine purchase behaviour*, thereby reducing the time spent for shopping, a task more and more perceived as a bore by buyers attracted by more stimulating activities. Similarly, the advertiser having promoted a promise to the market can simply re-advertise the brand name or its logo. Thus, from a semiotics perspective, all the importance for the brand, logo, colour, sign.

3. *A guarantee function.* A brand is a signature, which identifies the producer and creates a long-term responsibility, since the brand owner commits himself to give a specific and constant level of quality. A brand represents a pact between brand owner and consumer. The more a brand is known, the more this pact is binding, since the producer cannot afford to deceive his customer base and to undermine the brand's accumulated capital of goodwill. The fiction of 'generic products' without brand names, popular few years ago, has triggered strong negative reactions from the consumerists who rightly want that the product's origin be clearly identified.

4. *A personalisation function.* The diversity of taste and preferences is central in a market economy. To meet this diversity, firms market differentiated products, not only on tangible attributes, but on the intangibles as well, such as emotion, aesthetics, social image, etc. Brands give consumers the opportunity to claim their difference, to demonstrate their originality and to express their personality through their brand choices. Viewed in this perspective, the brand is a social communication tool giving to consumers the possibility to privilege certain attributes in their choices, thereby communicating their value system.

5. *A pleasure-giving function.* In affluent societies, consumers' primary or basic needs are largely met, and the needs for novelty, change, surprise, and stimulation become vital necessities. As seen in Chapter 6, the need to try varied experiences, to live different lifestyles, the possibility to try new products and to have new sources of satisfaction form an important subject matter in this type of societies. Brands such as Swatch, Club Med, McDonald, Cartier, Coca-Cola, contribute to the fulfilment of those needs through their branding policies.

In the Internet, the landmarking function of the brand is particularly important.

12.3.2. Functions of the brand for the producer in B2C markets

To the above five functions mainly useful to the customer, other brand's roles must be added which are critical for the firm's long-term and competitive strategy.

1. *A positioning tool.* It is the same landmarking function described above but viewed from the brand owner's side. A brand gives to the firm the opportunity to position its offering vis-à-vis competition, to express its difference and to claim its distinctive characteristics. This positioning function is very important for the advertising communication, particularly in markets where comparative advertising is authorised. Viewed in this perspective, the brand is a competitive weapon, which contributes to increase in the market transparency. Is it necessary to repeat that this process of competitive emulation remains the best protection for consumers against abuse of power?

2. *A communication function.* The brand is of strategic importance to manufacturers because it enables the firm to communicate directly with end-consumers regardless of the actions of the middlemen. This communication link is vital to the survival of many of the world's leading grocery companies. Without brands, such manufacturers would be at the mercy of large retail chains whose influence and power over the last 10 years have grown dramatically.

3. *A protection function.* Property rights (trade marks, patent, copyrights) protect the brand name against imitations or counterfeiting. The firm can take action for infringement of patent or trademarks in order to establish its intellectual property rights. A brand owner can register the brand in several product categories according to an international classification. He thereby has a clear legal title, which enables him to oppose any fraudulent imitation, forgery or counterfeit. A centralisation procedure (convention of Madrid) facilitates the registration at the international level, but it is only in 1993 that the concept of European Community brand has been established along with common rules of property rights (de Maricourt, 1997, p. 693). This manufacturer's brands' protection function is particularly important today in view of the 'copycat' own label strategy adopted by some large retail chains in France and in the United Kingdom (see Kapferer, 1995), and also by manufacturers based in Latin America or in Asia.

4. *A capitalisation function.* The brand, and in particular the brand image, serves to capture not only the past advertising investments put into it, but also the capital of satisfaction generated by the brand. Many brands are more than 100 years old (see Exhibit 12.1). To the firm, they constitute a valuable asset, an intangible capital, resulting from several years of past advertising investments. Brands therefore introduce stability into businesses; they allow planning and investment in a long-term perspective.

EXHIBIT 12.1

THE HISTORY OF SELECTED BRANDS

The need to associate a new product with a brand name has first implied the use of the company name or his founder's name. Cinzano is one of the oldest names in business. As long ago as 1757, Carlo Stefano Cinzano and Giovanni Giacomo Cinzano were distilling the beverage that bears their name in a factory near Turin. Among the brands born during the last century, some of them are still alive and well: Nestlé (the milky flour from Henri Nestlé, 1867), Maggi (soups from Jules Maggi,

1883), Levi's (from Levi Strauss & Co., 1856), the biscuits of Mr. Lefèvre and Miss Utile (1856) will become the brand Lu, similarly the aperitif anise from Pernod (1850). Today, the brand is a part of our daily environment.

Source: de Maricourt (1997, p. 687).

---

5. *A loyalty function.* The existence of the brand permits to create a relationship with customers as they will be willing to repurchase the same brand. Having a group of loyal customers is vital for the long-term development of the brand.

6. *A barrier of entry function.* As a result of the previous functions, brands create a real *barrier to entry* for competitors. They not only benefit from a group of loyal customers, but also enjoy a high awareness and strong image. It would be extremely costly for any new competitor to invest in order to reach similar awareness and image levels. These entry barriers are in fact financial and linked to the economies of scale that strong brands can benefit from. Brands such as Coca-Cola and Pepsi-Cola have created real entry barriers. It is nearly impossible for any brand to launch a Cola drink and compete with them. It would cost fortunes to reach same levels of awareness and it might even be impossible, what ever the investments, to build such strong images.

12.3.3. The functions of the brand in B2B markets

Globally the functions performed by the B2B brands are similar to the ones described for the B2C brands with the exception of the pleasure-giving function. As shown by Malaval (1998/2001) differences exist, however, as the result of two characteristics specific to B2B brands, such as brand purchasability and brand visibility. B2B brands sold to the industrial firm are neither always visible nor purchasable by the end-user.

■ The brand *purchasability* can be defined as the possibility for the general public to buy, or not to buy, the industrial good as a separate product and not only as incorporated part in the finished product. The individual consumer, for example, cannot purchase an Intel microprocessor or an Air-bag cushion. Other industrial goods, however, like spare parts or office equipment, can be purchased by visiting specialised distributors. Depending on the situation, the role of the brand will be different and sometimes confined to the sole customer incorporating firm.

■ The brand *visibility* by the general public is determined by the possibility for the consumer to know the B2B brand, either through direct physical contact with the brand or through communication. Different levels of visibility exist: at the purchasing time, during utilisation, during disassembling or without any visibility. Depending on the situation, the B2B functions and communication mode and target will have to be adapted accordingly.

For the direct customer two functions of the B2B brands are particularly relevant. The first is linked to the safety and guarantee functions and the second to the role of the supplier brands for the incorporating customer.

The traceability function

A brand has a landmarking function, a signal, a signature and a guarantee providing to the customer a double safety: first a certainty regarding the product sourcing and authenticity and second the certainty that, in case of product deficiency, recourse can be made to the supplier.

The function of traceability refers to the possibility to track the incorporated product and to identify the components of the finished product. In case of quality problems, the customer-manufacturing firm has the possibility to reassure itself – and also to reassure its own customers – that the responsibility of the upstream supplier is engaged and will be easily demonstrated, in order to obtain repair or compensation. Thus, traceability is the response provided by the supplier to the customer's expectation of guarantee for itself and its own customers. For the decision centre and for the purchaser, the supplier's brand contributes to reduce the perceived risk, in particular when the brand is strong and well known in the market.

The facilitation functions

Beyond the traditional functions of a brand, B2B firms have specific expectations regarding their suppliers. Malaval (1998 and 2001) has analysed the expectations and fears of a large sample of industrial firms.

The positive expectations can be regrouped into four categories presented here in an order of decreasing importance.

1. Performance facilitation in the *production* process, that is, the capacity of the supplier brand to improve the manufacturing process of the client, through better quality control or through better maintenance.
2. Performance facilitation in *innovation*, that is, the capacity of the supplier's brand to improve the design of the customer's end-product.
3. Performance facilitation in *operational marketing*, that is, the capacity of the supplier's brand to give a commercial argument or distinctive profile, thanks to the reputation of the supplier's brand.
4. Performance facilitation in the *decision-making process*, that is, the capacity to facilitate the acceptance of change and of new materials and to obtain rapidly a consensus within the firm's decision centre.

The most important expectation is on the technical partnership. Purchasers are in general more sensitive to the performance facilitation in the decision process, while marketing people have greater expectations regarding the commercial impact of the component brand.

Fears vis-à-vis strong suppliers' brands

Malaval (1998/2001) has also studied the main perceived risks associated with the adoption of strong suppliers' brands. By decreasing order of importance, the main fears are the following:

1. The risk of a *too high price* justified by the communication investments made on the brand.
2. The *risk of dependence* vis-à-vis the supplier's brand, that is, the difficulty of changing of suppliers given the technical choices made and given the possible impact of the supplier's brand on the end-customer.
3. The risk of *too strong influence* and impact of the brand's supplier on the internal organisation of the firm.
4. The risk of *arrogance* from the staff of the supplier's brand reflecting an unfavourable balance of power.

Logically, it is the risk of excessive price that is perceived as the most important.

The challenge of invisible suppliers' brands

The specific functions of the suppliers' brands described so far are mainly instrumental vis-à-vis direct customers, that is, the professional purchasers and not so much vis-à-vis end-customers, that is, the general public at large. Since a large number of suppliers' brands cannot be purchased and are not visible by the general public, these brands are generally unknown with some exceptions such as Gore-Tex, Lycra, Rhodyl or Tetra Pak.

> ## EXHIBIT 12.2
>
> ### EXAMPLES OF STRONG B2B BRANDS
>
> *Construction industry*: Acova, Grohe, Isover, Lafarge, Llegrand, Somfy, Technal, Villeroy & Boch.
>
> *Packaging industry*: Ato, BSN, Combibloc, Elopak, Mead Emballages, PLM, Saint Gobain Emballages, Tetra Pak.
>
> *Automotive equipment industry*: Bertand Faure, Bosch, Michelin, Sommer Allibert, Valeo.
>
> *Textile Industry*: DMC, Dorlastan, GoreTex, Lycra, Rhovyl, Tactel, Tergal, Woolmark.
>
> *Source*: Malaval (1998/2000).

During the last years, one has observed a growing number of B2B firms adopting communication strategies targeting the general market, and not just specialised professionals. This evolution can be explained by the following considerations:

- The willingness of the B2B firms to differentiate their offerings, too often perceived as commodities or as raw materials with no added value.
- The necessity to explain the 'how and the why', of sophisticated products, in particular, in the high-tech sectors.
- The concern to communicate the identity of the supplier in order to increase its awareness and reputation among professionals and the general public.
- The objective of leapfrogging direct customers by inciting end-customers to demand the supplier's brand in the finished product, thereby reducing the pressure on prices.
- The concern to certify a product during and after utilisation, based on the guarantee and given the commitments taken regarding the after sales services.
- The objective to meet the expectations of end-consumers who, better informed and more professional, want more detailed information and a guarantee.

Successful examples of such communication strategy are given by suppliers' brands such as Intel and Gore-Tex, among many others (see Exhibit 12.2).We would not be complete without mentioning here the fast development of private labels in FMCG markets. This point will be covered in more detail in the next chapter.

12.4. Key brand management concepts

Branding is not only about image or about communication. Strong brands are not artificial build-up. They are based on outstanding product or service and strive to remain at the top. If physical product concepts follow a certain life cycle and die one day, if well managed, a brand can live forever.

The CEO of Procter and Gamble cites as an example the brand Tide, launched in 1947 and still in a growth phase in 1976. In reality, the product was modified 55 times in its 29 year existence to adapt to market changes including consumption habits, characteristics of washing machines, new fabrics, etc. (quoted by Day, 1981, p. 61). This brand is still alive and well in 2005.

12.4.1. Brand positioning

Having segmented the reference market, the firm decides to cover by priority one or several segments and to 'position' its offering (brand) in a way which is both consistent with potential customers' expectations and different from competitors' offerings. It consists in giving a 'raison d'être' to a product.

As discussed in Chapter 9 (see Section 9.2.1), the firm at the very start of the brand development process makes the positioning decision. It is based on an in-depth analysis of the market, consumers and competitors that can be summed by the four following questions.

- A brand for what? This refers to the brand promise and the customer benefit.
- A brand for whom? This refers to the target segment.
- A brand for when? This refers to the use or consumption situation.
- A brand against whom? This question refers to the direct competitor.

It is the platform of the brand success. In the FMCG sector, when competition was less intense than today, it was common practice to base the brand positioning on the brand's unique selling proposition (USP), that is, on the uniqueness or the exclusive benefit offered by the brand. It is not always easy to find today a sustainable USP in the light of the high number of 'me-too' brands existing in the market. Moreover, the traditional USP brand positioning tends to focus only on the brands tangible attributes but do not give enough information on the brand personality or country of origin. (Some authors translate USP as: unique selling personality.) This is also why the concept of brand identity was created in the late 1980s (Kapferer, 1991, 2004).

12.4.2. Brand identity

Brand identity is close to the concept of brand positioning but it is more complete, because it communicates other elements about the brand that are strategically important for its development.

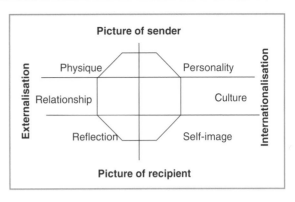

Figure 12.2   The brand identity prism
Source: Kapferer (2004, p. 107).

How to distinguish between Coca-Cola and Pespi-Cola, between Hertz and Avis, between Google and Yahoo? The positioning of these brands is largely similar but their personalities can be very different.

Kapferer (1991/2004) has developed the 'brand identity prism' (Figure 12.2) that defines the brand identity in terms of six facets.

1. Physique: the brand's tangible attributes.
2. Personality: the brand has also a certain personality that can be described and measured by human personality traits.
3. Culture: set of values that the brand is built on, influenced by the country-of-origin image.
4. Relationship: style of the relationship created with consumers.
5. Reflection: the way consumers using the brand would like to be seen.
6. Self-image: the image that people have of themselves when using the brand.

For example, the identity of the sport car Porsche in France (Variot, 1985) can be described as follows

1. Physical: performance.
2. Personality: perfectionist.
3. Relationship: personal rather than family-oriented.
4. Cultural: German technology.
5. Buyer's image: winners' car.
6. Self-image: surpassing oneself.

The brand identity concept is used in designing advertising messages. This advertising approach is very demanding because it requires great coherence of expression. The reason is that form, style and tone are more important than substance in constructing the image. Good examples of this creative approach are the different advertising campaigns launched by Perrier in Western Europe.

12.4.3. Brand image

Brand positioning and brand identity are manufacturer's concepts. They have been created by the seller and should not be confused with the brand image. (Table 12.2 gives an example of brand identity.) The brand image is the perception of the brand identity in the minds of consumers. Large differences can exist between the brand identity and the brand image. The brand or corporate image can define in the following terms.

> The set of mental representations, both cognitive and affective, that a person or a group of persons holds vis-à-vis a brand or a company.

A good understanding of the brand image and of its perceived strengths and weaknesses is an indispensable prerequisite to any strategy and communication platform definition. With this respect, it is useful to make a distinction between three levels of brand image analysis.

1. The *perceived image* or how the people see and perceive the brand: an *outside-in perspective*, based on field interviews within the reference market or segment.
2. The *actual image* or the reality of the brand, an *inside-in perspective* based on the brand's strengths and weaknesses identified by the firm through an internal audit.
3. The *desired image* (its identity) or the way brand management wishes the brand to be perceived by the target segment as a result of a positioning or brand identity decision.

Clearly, important differences can exist between these three levels of image measurement and reconciliation may be necessary.

- A gap may exist between the actual image and the perceived image, in a positive or negative sense.

- If the gap is in favour of the brand, communication has an important role to play in the reconciliation process; in the opposite case, the brand concept must be revised.
- A gap may also occur between the desired image and the reality of the brand, that is, its know-how, its quality, or its communication; it is the credibility of the positioning strategy which is at stake here.

This last problem is particularly acute in service firms where the contact personnel directly contribute to the perceived image of the firm. Internal marketing has an important role to play here.

To measure the perceived image, the analysis will be based on the three levels of market response discussed briefly in Chapter 9 (see Table 9.1), using successively indicators of the cognitive, affective and behavioural response.

12.4.4. Brand equity concept

The last few years have seen brand equity become one of the hottest topics in business among professionals and academic researchers as well (Aaker, 1991, 1996; Kapferer, 1992), although the economists have adopted the concept since many years (Nerlove and Arrow, 1962). Two definitions are currently used.

> Broadly stated, brand equity refers to the 'capital of goodwill' accumulated by a brand and resulting from past marketing activities. (Nerlove and Arrow, 1960)

Alternatively,

> A consumer perceives a brand's equity as the 'value added' to the functional product or service by associating it with the brand name. (Aaker, 1991)

In both definitions the concept refers to the brand's strength which can vary largely among brands and which is

---

Table 12.2   The identity of Levi's brands of jeans

Attributes and benefits	Associations
Product-related attributes	Blue denim, shrink-to-fit cotton fabric, button-fly, two horse patch, and small red pocket tag.
User imagery	Western, American, blue collar, hard working, traditional, strong, rugged, and masculine.
Usage imagery	Appropriate for outdoor work and casual social situations.
Brand personality	Honest, classic, contemporary, approachable, independent and universal.
Experiential benefits	Feeling of self-confidence and self-assurance.
Symbolic benefits	Comfortable fitting and relaxing to wear.
Functional benefits	High quality, long lasting and durable.

Source: Quoted by Keller (1998/2004).

EXHIBIT 12.3

PRICE ADVANTAGES OF THE STRONGEST BRANDS

To gauge how important brands are to customers during the purchase process, McKinsey (1996) examined 27 case studies, based on over 5,000 customer interviews in the United States, Europe and Asia. On average, prices of the strongest brands (in terms of the brand's importance behind the decision to buy) were 19 per cent higher than those of the weakest brands. Relative to second tier brands, the leading brands commanded an average price premium of 5 per cent.

Source: Court *et al.* (1996, p. 178).

Figure 12.3   Brand equity sequence
Source: Feldwick (1996).

determined by its awareness, personality perceived quality, leadership or stock value.

The idea was to find a concept summarising the strengths of a brand. The brand equity concept was crated because traditional data such as market share or volume sold were not satisfactory to reflect the value of a brand, and because they are not taking into account the associations that existed in the consumers' mind (Exhibit 12.3).

The concept has two faces. On the one hand, it gives a financial definition of the brand equity to evaluate the brand's 'financial' value (*financial brand equity*). It is especially important for financial analysts and companies to evaluate this strategic company asset. On the other hand, it covers the value of the brand from the customer viewpoint, the *customer-based brand equity*, as a set of associations made by the customers and generating the brand's strengths (Figure 12.3).

Feldwick (1996) suggests referring to three, distinct but complementary, meanings.

1. The set of perceptions, associations or beliefs, both cognitive and affective, the customer has about a brand, which is traditionally called the *brand image*.
2. The strength of customers' *attachment to a brand* revealed namely by the price premium customers are ready to pay.
3. The total value of a brand as a *separable asset*, when it is sold or included in a balance sheet.

These three different meanings are linked and the causal chain would be 1: brand attributes; 2: brand strengths; 3: brand value. The attributes of the brand influence what we can call the strengths of the brand that lead to the financial value of the brand on the market. Table 12.3 gives the financial value of selective brands.

12.5. Building a successful brand

The branding decision is at the interface of strategic and operational marketing. Branding is about de-commoditising products. Brand development can be viewed as an iceberg. The visible part of the iceberg shows the brand name, its advertising and its logo. But the brand can only be successful if the foundations of the brand are well built. In the hidden part of the iceberg, one must have effective R&D, reliable manufacturing and logistics, appropriate selection of a target segment and a creative brand positioning/identity decision. These elements are essential to brand success.

12.5.1. Brand architecture

Brand architecture is the way in which the brands within a company's portfolio are related to, and differentiated from, one another (see Figure 12.4). The architecture should specify brand roles and the nature of relationships between brands. Following Aaker and Joachimsthaller (2000), we identify three generic brand naming strategies.

1. *A branded house strategy*. Companies such as Nivéa, Virgin, Sony, Adidas and Mercedes-Benz choose to use a single name (a company name or a master brand) across all the activities and this name is how all their stakeholders know them. The advantage is to minimise communication and support costs as all products carry the same name and benefit from the master brand's awareness and image, which is used as an umbrella brand. A single brand communicated across products and over time is much easier to recall. A functional descriptor accompanies the master brand to describe the offering (GE Capital, Nivéa Deodorant, Virgin Music, and so on). The risk of this strategy is the brand diluting effect if the products are too different or not performing equally. Also it does not allow too different identities when targeting different product markets.

2. *House of brands strategy*. At the other extreme, companies such as Unilever and Procter & Gamble have focused on individual subbrands. Unilever used to operate

Table 12.3   Evaluation of selective European brands

Brands	Countries	Value ($ b)	Brands	Countries	Value ($ b)
Nokia (5)	Finland	35.04	BP (74)	United Kingdom	3.25
Mercédès (12)	Germany	21.73	Shell (77)	UK/Holland	2.84
BMW (22)	Germany	13.86	Moët & Chandon (79)	France	2.43
Nescafé (23)	Switzerland	13.25	Heineken (82)	The Netherlands	2.27
Volkswagen (35)	Germany	7.34	Nivéa (87)	Germany	1.78
Louis Vuitton (38)	France	7.05	Johnnie Walker (89)	United Kingdom	1.65
SAP (43)	Germany	6.31	Armani (91)	Italy	1.49
Ikéa (46)	Sweden	6.01	Absolut (93)	Sweden	1.38
Gucci (50)	Italy	5.36	Guinness (94)	United Kingdom	1.36
Reuters (52)	United Kingdom	5.24	Financial Times (95)	United Kingdom	1.31
Philips (55)	The Netherlands	4.90	Carlsberg (96)	Denmark	1.08
Chanel (61)	France	4.27	Siemens (98)	Germany	1.03
Rolex (69)	Switzerland	3.70	Swatch (99)	Switzerland	1.00
Adidas (70)	Germany	3.65	Benetton (100)	Italy	1.00

Legend: (n) = Place in the 100 global brands.

Source: Business Week (2001), 6 August.

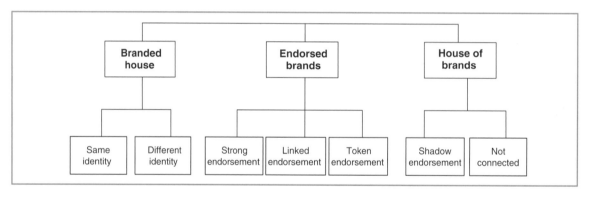

Figure 12.4   The brand architecture

Source: Adapted from Aaker and Joachimsthaller (2000).

with 1,400 brands with little connections to each other and still operates today with 400 brands. It gives the possibility to the firm to cover the same market with different brands or to target specific segment. Each brand is independent and there is no link to the company. If there is a problem of quality with one particular brand, it will not affect other products or the company reputation. Another advantage is to avoid a brand association that would be incompatible with an offering. For example, Volkswagen would adversely affect the images of Porsche and of Audi if the brands were linked. It is however a costly strategy because each brand has to be supported individually.

3.   *The endorsed brands strategy.* The brands are still independent but they are endorsed by the corporate brand or by the company name. Examples of *strong endorsements* are: Kit-Kat by Nestlé, Polo by Ralph Lauren or Lycra by DuPont. Another type of endorsement is a *linked name*, like Nesttea, Nescafé and Nesquick from the Nestlé company or like the HP Jet series: Laserjet, DeskJet, OfficeJet, Inkjet. A linked name provides the benefit of a separate name without having to establish a second name from scratch. A weaker endorsement type is the *token endorsement* taking the form of a logo or of a seal of guarantee. It is a way to support brands not yet well established by providing reassurance and credibility. Finally, in a *shadow endorsement* the brand is not connected visibly to the endorser but many consumers know about the link. Two examples are Lexus from Toyota and Dockers from Levi Strauss. Endorsements reduce marketing support costs.

Subbrands are brands connected to a master (or umbrella brand) brand that augment or modify the associations of the master brand. For example, Sony Walkman. A common role of a subbrand is to extend a master brand into a new segment. It is more than a functional descriptor; it has a co-driver role, like Gillette Sensor, for instance, or Porsche Carrera.

12.5.2. Brand name and logo selection

Finding the right name is important because it will help communicate the benefits of the brand and its personality. This name has to fit to the brand identity. If the brand is supposed to have a dynamic or fun personality, the brand name has to be selected accordingly.

Certain criteria have to be taken into account in the name selection. The name should be simple and easy to memorise to facilitate brand recall and recognition in the consumers' minds. It has to be international to meet the challenge of globalisation. The brand name should not be too descriptive or too generic to avoid the risk of being easily copied by competition, especially by private labels.

It is only recently that pharmaceutical companies have realised that they did not sell products but brands and that they should not necessarily name their products by reference to the generic molecule name. Strong brands such as Viagra and xxxx have succeeded to create their own personality.

The logo is the flag of the brand. Certain brands are so strong that they are recognised by their logo only. Good examples are: Nike, Mercedes, Ferrari, Lacoste. Some symbolic persons or animals can also serve as identifier of the brand such as the Bibendum of Michelin, Mr Proper, the horse of Ferrari, the elephant of Cote-d'Or. Firms are inclined to give more importance to their brand symbols as a way to cultivate the brand cultural identity.

12.5.3. Characteristics of successful brands

Peter Doyle has identified five major characteristics of successful brands that can be summarised as follows (Doyle, 1994/ 2003).

A quality product. Satisfactory experience in use is the major determinant of a brand success. Quality or sustained quality is the number one requirement. If the brand quality deteriorates, customers will switch to competing brands and the brand positioning will be undermined.

Being the first in the market. The innovator is not necessarily successful but being the first facilitates market penetration. It is easier to take a position in the customers' mind when the brand has no competitors and comes with an innovative proposal.

Unique positioning. If the brand is not the innovator, it must have a unique positioning concept that will differentiate the brand from competing brands: the case of Swatch in the traditional watch market is a good example.

Strong communication programme. To be successful the brand requires a strong advertising, selling and promotional support to communicate the brand's proposition and to create the brand identity.

Time and consistency. Building a successful brand takes time and requires investment to maintain, to rejuvenate and/or to reposition the brand in a changing environment.

Table 12.4 gives the top ten traits of successful brands.

12.5.4. Brand life cycles

The typical brand life cycle profile is described in Figure 12.5. Caron (1996) studied the historical evolution

---

Table 12.4   The top ten traits of successful brands

1. The brand excels at delivering the benefits customers truly desire.
2. The brand stays relevant.
3. The pricing strategy is based on consumers' perceptions of value.
4. The brand is properly positioned.
5. The brand is consistent.
6. The brand portfolio and hierarchy make sense.
7. The brand makes use of and co-ordinates a full repertoire of marketing activities to build equity.
8. The brand's manager understands what the brand means to consumers.
9. The brand is given proper support, and that support is sustained over the long run.
10. The company monitors sources of brand equity.

Source: Keller (2000).

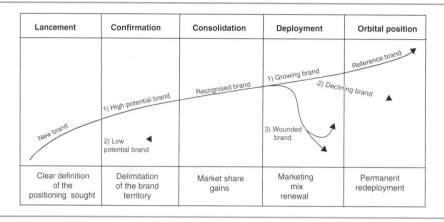

Figure 12.5 Typical brand life cycle
Source: Caron (1996).

EXHIBIT 12.4

THE BRAND LIFE CYCLE

Caron (1996) reports that Carré Noir has studied the strategy of a sample of 1,000 brands and has observed that the typical brand life cycle comprises in total five phases. In about 85 per cent of the studied cases, the BLC was limited to two or four.

1. *Launching*. More than one million of brands are registered every year in the world, of which 61,583 in France in 1995. During this phase, the new brand concentrates its marketing efforts to claim its identity.

2. *Confirmation*. Once the fashion effect is gone, sales of the low potential brands fall and these brands are de-listed from the distributors purchasing centres. The surviving brands delimit their brand territory.

3. *Consolidation*. The recognised brands have to reaffirm their national and/or international strategic ambition, claim their difference, improve their distribution rate, etc. The objective is to 'hold' and to increase their market share.

4. *Deployment*. Thanks to a constant renewal of their marketing mix to meet the market changes, the expanding brands redeploy and conquer new breed of consumers. Some do not find rejuvenating ideas to reinvent themselves and decline. Others have accidents.

5. *Orbital position*. The brand is fully in charge. Rich from its accumulated experience, consolidated by its success, by its reputation and its status among its customer base, the brand has reached the high orbit. To keep that position, the brand will have to continuously create its own style and language that will be assimilated by its customers.

Even in this final phase, the brand remains threatened. The difficult trajectory of development for the five phases (see Figure 12.5) looks like a real combat track.

Source: Adapted from Caron Gérard (1996).

---

of more than one thousand brands and has identified five phases in the typical brand life cycle (see Exhibit 12.4). The profile of the cycle is very similar to the one observed by Hinkle (1966) in the US food and cosmetic sectors.

It is clear that the life cycle of a brand is essentially determined by factors under the control of the company: the marketing strategy adopted and the amount of effort dedicated to it.

12.5.5. Brand extension and stretching strategies

In targeting different customer segments, the firm can use the same or different brand names.

1. A *brand extension strategy* means using a brand name that is successfully established for one segment to enter another one within the same market. For example, the brand name of the facial cream Nivèa has been used by Beiersdorf to cover other needs in the cosmetic market.

2. A *brand stretching strategy* means transferring the successful brand name to quite different markets. This is the strategy adopted by Canon to move from cameras to copiers, printers, and so on.

Companies have used the brand extension/stretching strategies frequently in the last few years. The idea is to benefit directly from the awareness and image of a strong existing brand by using the same brand name for launching new products in different categories. It is the idea of umbrella branding, discussed in the previous section. If it was traditional for luxury goods companies to extend their name to different product categories, it is now used in many different business sectors.

The rapid development of brand extension is explained by the high cost of introducing new brands in the markets and also of supporting them by advertising. The key question is to evaluate how far the brand can be stretched without risks. The risks are first to dilute the brand image of the mother brand, second to reduce the chances of success of the new product if the brand image does not fit the new brand concept.

> For example Levi, which has built a brilliant brand in jeans, attempted to market a range of high quality formal suits to middle-class males under the Levi name. The brand extension failed because the new target market did not see the informal, denim association of the Levi name as adding value in this sector. (quoted by Doyle, 1996, p. 176)

The decision between brand extension and individual brand names should be guided by the similarity of the competitive advantage and of the target market segment, as illustrated in Figure 12.6.

- If the brands appeal to the same target segment and have the same competitive advantage, then a pure brand extension strategy is safe and consistent. This would be the case of Nivéa in the cosmetic market.
- If the competitive advantage is the same but the target markets are different, the brand can be extended but qualified to give a signal to the target segment. For example, both the Mercedes-200 and -500 base their competitive advantage on quality but the more expensive Mercedes-500 targets the prestige-conscious segment.

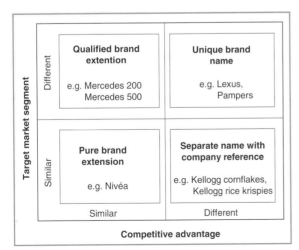

Figure 12.6   Brand extension strategies
Source: Adapted from Doyle (1994/2003).

- If the company has different competitive advantages but target the same segment it could use both company and brand names.
- Finally, if both the target and the competitive advantages are different, using unique brand names is the more appropriate strategy (Doyle, 1996/2000).

12.5.6. Co-branding strategies

Co-branding consists of making an alliance between two brands to launch a new product or promotion (see Exhibit 12.5). It can constitute a way to grow the business. The value of co-branding can be first to benefit from the awareness of both brands and to broaden the consumer target by benefiting from the consumers of the other brand. Co-branding also permits in some cases to access more rapidly to new markets via the network of the co-brand. When two leading brands are partners, it can reinforce the brand loyalty because both brands are very trusted brands. Co-branding permits also to leverage the technological advantage or other know-how of one of the partner. It reduces also the cost of development of the new initiative as costs are shared between both firms.

Co-branding also has limits. Long lead times are often needed to develop and finalise such deals. There is the risk that the new product may cannibalise one of the existing product (Yolka). It is also important to ensure that both brands are equally strong so that each brand benefit from the deal. It would not make sense that a strong brand get associated with a less known brand. The partners also need to take into account the difficulty to evaluate the benefits that will need to be shared by both partners after the launch. There are two types of co-branding:

1. *Strategic co-branding* represents long-term associations and relatively large investments from both partners: Swatch and Mercedes (Smart), Douwe Egberts and Philips (Senseo), Nestlé and Krupps (Nespresso).
2. *Tactical co-branding* represents short-term alliances that usually cover promotional deals. They imply relatively low investments from both partners. It focuses more on communication activities than product initiatives, for example, Procter & Gamble and Fisher Price.

Nestlé and Coca-Cola created together the 'Beverage Partners Worldwide' firm to market drinks based on teas. It would exploit the know-how of Nestlé in that type of product and the commercial network of Coca-Cola.

12.6. International branding strategies

As seen in Chapter 2, in the current context of globalisation, firms have concentrated their efforts in developing international brands. As a result, international

---

EXHIBIT 12.5

EXAMPLE: CO-BRANDING PHILIPS – NIVÉA

Philips is a strong proponent of co-branding to improve its brand image to end-consumers. It has made several partnerships these last few years with Beiersdorf (Nivéa), Douwe Egberts (Senseo), Procter & Gamble and Inbev. Concerning the co-branding with Nivéa, they decided to create together the Philishave Cool Skin. This was a new electric shaver with Nivéa dispensing. This co-branding was making sense as both brands were leaders in their respective markets. Many advantages were identified in this partnership: possibility to attract new users and to enter new channels of distribution that they had no access so far; reinforcement of their respective brand image and combined advertising support; shared development launch costs of this new initiative.

---

brand portfolios have been restructured and many successful local brands have been eliminated.

Unilever, for example, is at the end of the process of eliminating 1,200 brands from its brand portfolio to concentrate on just 400 brands. P&G has kept 300, after selling many local brands. L'Oréal has built its success on 16 worldwide brands. Nestlé has been giving priority to their six strategic worldwide brands including Nescafe and Buitoni, and Mars has been investing since many years mainly in global brand names.

Strong local brands have essentially been eliminated from multinational brand portfolios, not because they do not represent strong brand franchises locally, but rather because their relative sales volumes do not permit economies of scale.

In Europe, at the end of the 1990s, Procter & Gamble were seriously thinking about eliminating the leading detergent in Italy – known as Dash – despite the fact that the brand was a national institution and extremely profitable in Italy. The company's motivation at the time was that the Dash brand was creating cost complexities, where Ariel was the European leader.

12.6.1. Advantages of international and global brands

It is clear that international and global brands present many important advantages to the firm. They permit to generate strong economies of scale. It is well known that a globalised brand can generate significant cost reductions in all areas of the business system, including R&D, manufacturing and logistics. The move to a single global brand name also provides substantial economies in packaging and communication costs. Another advantage is the development of a unique brand image across countries. The speed to market for new product initiatives that international brands offer is also very important for international companies. They can now launch new product initiatives in the fast

moving goods industry on a regional or global scale within 12–18 months. Another advantage is the possibility of supporting any global brand with very large budgets in the communication area. This is especially important today in the context of very high advertising and media costs.

12.6.2. Advantages of local brands

Local brands also present some interesting advantages that are not often highlighted. Local brands represent many years of marketing investment. They are well known in their markets, and often create strong relationships with local consumers over the years. In Europe, there are still many more local than international brands, even if the trend is for the proportion of local brands to diminish. Although industries such as the car industry, computers and high-tech businesses are well known for their strong international brands, many sectors are still characterised by having many local brands.

In the oil industry in Germany, British Petroleum (BP) acquired the local leader Aral and decided, in view of its strong brand equity, to keep the local brand name. In France, the leading whisky brands are not the well-known J&B or Johnny Walker but the local Label 5, Clan Campbell and William Peel. In the Czech republic, Danone did not succeed in imposing its 'Lu' brand on that market, and has had to use the local brand franchise 'Opavia' to develop its business. In Belgium, the leader in the mineral water market is the local leader Spa, with shares well ahead of the international leader Evian. (Schuiling and Kapferer, 2004)

The advantages of local brands are the following:

Local brands offer a better response to local needs. A local brand can be designed to respond to the specific needs of the local market. The local brand product has the flexibility to be developed so that it genuinely provides an answer to a particular need of local consumers. Such local branding can not only provide a unique product, but also select its positioning and generate an advertising campaign that reflects local insights.

Local brands can be also more flexible on pricing. They can offer the price that is in line with the strength of the brand. Such flexibility can lead to increased profits when prices can be fixed at a higher level.

A local brand can also be used to respond to local or international competition, or even fight against retailer brands. A local brand can be repositioned and the marketing mix adapted accordingly. In contrast, the marketing strategy for an international brand has to follow predefined regional or global marketing strategy.

Local brands also offer the possibility of better balancing a portfolio of brands and therefore better balancing the risk on a worldwide basis. An international portfolio that mostly comprises international and global brands can be very powerful, but also presents risks. A problem arising with one of these mega brands in one particular country can have a negative impact on a worldwide basis.

12.6.3. Impact on international positioning strategies

Too often the globalisation versus customisation debate is presented in terms of a 'all or nothing' question. In reality, intermediate solutions exist and the real question is to know how to reconcile the two approaches. We support the view that branding and positioning are two independent decisions, which can occur in varying combinations as shown in Table 12.5.

Brand and position globally

In *Strategy #1*, brand names and positioning are globalised. This situation will tend to prevail in a global environment where the global forces are strong and the local forces weak.

Classical examples of this strategy are Marlboro, Coca-Cola, Gillette Sensor, Sony Walkman, McDonald, Levi, Gucci, Pampers, etc.

These genuinely global brands deliver the same benefits (tangible and intangible) to consumers who value them in all countries: Coke for the convenience and the appeal of American young imagery; Sony for the attraction of 'music on the move'; Hermes for fashion and romance. These benefits can be hard-to-copy innovations such as Pampers or (Ipod) Sony digital cameras, or emotional benefits such as Dunhill or Cartier.

An especially strong kind of positioning to be exploited globally involves national stereotypes: German quality in cars, for example, or French style and romance in perfume, or English conservatism in men's tailoring, or American youth and fun in fast food.

Procter & Gamble seems to have adopted this policy regarding brand names since 70 per cent of its turnover is made by brands sold all over the world, such as Oil of Olaz, Ariel, Pampers, Clearasil and Vicks. One exception: the P&G shampoo Wash & Go is launched in 60 different countries, but under six different brand names. The concept 'two in one' is the same in each market, however. Slight variations in the advertising expressions also exist. This last example illustrates the fact that a complete globalisation will probably never be possible.

Brand globally but adopt a local positioning

Strategy #2 globalises brand names but localises the strategic positioning. This situation will probably prevail in transnational environments where both global and local forces are strong.

Examples of this strategy are given namely by Bacardi and Volvo-truck and also to a lesser degree by P&G with the shampoo Wash & Go. These firms use the same brand name worldwide but the positioning themes and/or expressions are adjusted in each country.

Table 12.5   Alternative international branding and positioning strategies

Brand name	International positioning	
	Global	Local
Same brand name	Strategy #1: Brand and position globally	Strategy #2: Brand globally and position locally
Different brand names	Strategy #3: Brand locally and harmonise positioning	Strategy #4: Brand and position locally

Source: Adapted from Sandler and Shani (1992).

In instances where brand standardisation tends to be high, localised advertising gives the firm the possibility to take into account local culture and sensitivity and to position the brand in the local market.

Brand locally and harmonise positioning globally

Strategy #3 harmonises the brand positioning but keeps local brand names. This is a strategy adopted by European firms, such as Unilever and Kraft, having developed their portfolio of brands through acquisitions. Unilever management, for example, seems to believe (Fraser, 1990) that as long as core brand values can be harmonised, the name does not really matter. Unilever tends to draw the line in its harmonising policy at changing names.

> Unless the original name is meaningless, it would be very dangerous to drop it. Names that have been built up over years and years are an essential part of brand's franchise or equity. (Fraser, 1990)

This is the justification of the approach taken with a Unilever fabric softener called Cajoline in France, Coccolino in Italy, Kuschelweich in Germany, Mimosin in Spain and Snuggle in the United States. Although the name is different in every country, it suggests cuddly softness everywhere. And the product benefits are always presented by a talking teddy bear, a universally understood symbol of softness. Far from being a disadvantage, the different names actually bring the brand closer to the hearts of local consumers.

> The 'same positioning-different name' approach has also been used for the fish fingers of Unilever. The well-known salty sea captain has appeared in commercials throughout Europe even though he is variously known as Birds Eye, Findus or Iglo. All he has to do is change his cap and speak a different language in each country, which leads to significant cost savings in the production of television commercials.

Kraft General Food also manages to combine centralised European marketing with local brand sensitivity. It does not, for example, market a multinational ground coffee brand, but it does own over a dozen such brands in various European countries where it is the uncontested number one.

> Because of the way the company grew, mainly via acquisitions, we control many local brands. There was a tentative effort by Klaus Jacobs (the former proprietor of Jacobs Suchard which was bought by General Foods) to internationalise them. But it has been abandoned. Discouraged by the costs of such an alignment, management also recognised the gigantic waste that killing of the local brands, rich in capital and heritage, would represent.(Subramanian, 1993)

This attitude is very different from the one adopted by Mars. Has Mars carried things too far by investing major sums in the name changes of successful brands: Raider to Twix, Marathon to Snickers, Kal-Kan to Whiskas? Too much centralisation leads naturally to excessive standardisation.

In Europe, the dominant concept seems to be 'brand locally, harmonise positioning globally', taken as a way to manage European diversity. For the Americans, on the contrary, the natural concept seems to be 'brand and position globally'.

Brand and position locally

Strategy #4 will be adopted in environments where the local forces are strong and the global forces weak. In general, it is considered that this situation prevails in the food sector where tastes, flavours and colours are important factors.

This strategy of complete decentralisation seems more and more difficult to maintain for an international firm, because *speed and scale* are, and will be, more and more crucial success factors in the newly integrated European market.

> We were at trouble competing well with companies like P&G because we needed speed and scale – and we didn't have that when we had to go through 16 or 17 countries, explains Alfred Jung, one of Lever's first Euromanagers. (Dalgic, 1992)

At Unilever, two types of difference can exist: (a) same product but different brand names or (b) same brand name but different products.

> Iced sparkling tea is sold under the brand name Liptonic in France, Lipton Ice Tea in Belgium and Lipton Ice in the United Kingdom. On the other hand, under the same brand name Lipton Ice Tea, the drink is sparkling and non-sparkling in France. Similarly, Calvé is a salty mayonnaise in Belgium and a sweet one in Holland.

It is clear that with the development of cross-border purchases, this diversity of brand names and content is very confusing for the consumer and that some degree of standardisation is required. In the European context, the word *harmonisation* of branding policies rather than 'standardisation' is probably more appropriate.

12.6.4. Brand portfolio management

It is not only necessary to create and manage a brand; it is also essential for the company to manage successfully a *portfolio of brands*. Many companies own many brands and the relationships between these brands have to be managed in a logic way in the brand portfolio (see Table 12.7 for examples). Acquisitions often leave companies with far more brands than they can profitably handle. Taking a stricter look at marketing resources forces companies to look more critically at their brand portfolio composition. There are a number of issues to address:

- How do brands relate to the corporate brand?
- What do the brands derive from the parent brand? And what do they give back?
- What role does each brand have in the portfolio?
- Are the different brands and subbrands sufficiently differentiated?
- Does the customer understand the differentiation?
- Is the whole architecture of the brand portfolio greater than the sum of its parts?

This is a complex matter and currently a very hot topic for marketers. In order to properly manage a brand portfolio, it is essential to follow the following steps

Each brand should have a clear role to play within the portfolio

For example, in Europe Ariel is targeted to the demanding housewives who are looking for a superior cleaning performance, Bonux is targeted to housewives looking for a value for money proposition, Dreft is targeted to housewives who want to treat their garments carefully, and Vizir is targeted to housewives searching simplicity and rapidity. Each brand is positioned on a distinctive benefit.

Each brand should be ensured to receive the right level of resources from the company (financial, sales, R&D)

For example, L'Oreal has made clear decisions in the way they manage their innovations and give priority to their brands. At first, they will give the best innovations to the premium brands distributed in the selective distribution channel such as Lancôme and will then be given to the l'Oréal brand in supermarkets at a later stage.

The firm should clearly know which brand to build, which brand to eliminate, which brand to extend or even to acquire

For this, the firm must know which segments of the market the firm want to cover by priority. A manager having portfolio responsibilities can only do this at the highest level of the organisation. The ideal brand portfolio will have the following characteristics:

- Fits the company future vision and destination.
- Prioritises markets and key segments.
- Efficiently covers the priority segments.
- Ruthlessly prunes out those that do not fit.
- Fills gaps through new or extended brands and acquisitions.

To achieve these objectives the techniques of portfolio analyses reviewed in Chapter 10, and in particular the multifactor portfolio matrix, are useful. An example of a brand portfolio in the food sector is presented in Figure 12.7.

Examples of indicators of market attractiveness and of competitiveness (brand's strengths) are presented in Table 12.6 with a set of scores for each indicator proposed by Davidson (1997). As already underlined in Chapter 10, this type of quantified analysis is a useful graphic device for comparing the competitive positions of brands on common

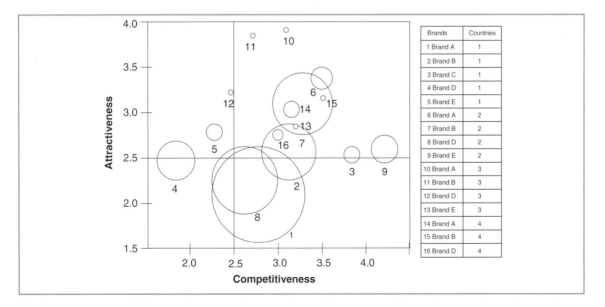

Figure 12.7 A multifactor brand portfolio
Source: Industry.

Table 12.6   Example of brand portfolio score sheet

Market attractiveness		Brand's strengths	
Score sheet	Maximum score	Score sheet	Maximum score
Market size	8	Brand profitability	12
Market growth rate	15	Relative consumer value	15
Profitability	20	Relative brand share	9
Pricing trends	10	Market sector position	7
Competitive intensity	10	Sales level and trend	7
Failure risk	6	Differentiation	12
Opportunity to differentiate	10	Distribution strength	7
Segmentation	9	Innovation record	6
Retail structure	12	Extendability	10
		Awareness and loyalty	7
		Investment support (adv. and R&D)	8
Total	100	Total	100

Source: Davidson (1997).

Table 12.7   Examples of brand proliferation

Colgate Palmolive	Crest
Colgate	Crest
Colgate 2 in 1	Crest Dual Action Whitening
Colgate Baking Soda and Peroxide	Crest Multi-care
Colgate Fresh Confidence	Crest Neat Squeeze
Colgate Max fresh	Crest Sensitive
Colgate Sensitive	Crest Tartar Protection
Colgate Simply White	Crest Vivid White
Colgate Sparkling White	Crest Whitening
Colgate Total Whitening	Crest Whitening Expression
Colgate Cavity Protection	Crest Extra Whitening
Colgate Tartar Control	Crest Rejuvenating Effects
Colgate Total	Crest Cavity Protection
Colgate Children's	Crest Kids
(2 in 1 Kids, Colgate Barbie, Blue's Clues, Fairly Odd Parents)	

Source: Published sources.

criteria and for guiding strategic investment priorities. Answers to the following questions can be obtained.

- On what basis should brands be invested in for future growth?
- Which should be maintained as local players, which should enter the global arena? And, if they should, how?
- What can be extended?
- What should be sold off or killed?

Portfolio analysis also permits to avoid major mistakes in portfolio management, the major mistake being to allow each brand to be managed in isolation because what is right for an individual brand may be wrong for the portfolio. Here are the major mistakes:

- Too many brands in too many segments; there may be too many brands in relation to consumer needs, retailer space and company ability to promote.
- Duplication and overlap.
- Gaps in priority market segments.
- Inefficiencies in operation and the supply chain.
- Diffused and therefore ineffective resource allocation.

The use of a family tree can also be useful (Aaker, 2004) to evaluate the portfolio structure.

CHAPTER SUMMARY

A brand is perceived by a potential customer as a bundle of attributes and of mental associations which, taken together, will form the distinctive elements of the brandís identity. The composition of the bundle, the relative importance and the perceived presence of the attributes will contribute to influence potential customers' purchasing decision. Brands are now present everywhere. They exist because they generate trust. This trust is based on a close relationship that brands have built over the years with consumers. The brand plays an important role in a market economy, not only for the customer, but for the producer as well. In this chapter, the brand functions in the B2C and in the B2B markets are examined. Having decided to cover by priority one or several segments, the firm has to 'position' its offering (brand) in a way which is both consistent with potential customers' expectations and different from competitors' offerings. It consists in giving a 'raison d'être' to a product. Kapferer (1991/2004) has developed the 'brand identity prism' that defines the brand identity in terms of six facets. Brand positioning and brand identity are manufacturer's concepts. They have been created by the seller and should not be confused with the brand image. The brand image is the perception of the brand identity in the minds of consumers. In both definitions the concept refers to the brand's strength which can vary largely among brands and which is determined by its awareness, personality perceived quality, leadership or stock value. The brand equity concept was created, to summarise the strengths of a brand because traditional data such as market share or volume sold were not satisfactory to reflect the value of a brand, and because they are not taking into account the associations that existed in the consumers' mind. Brand architecture is the way in which the brands within a company's portfolio are related to, and differentiated from, one another. The architecture should specify brand roles and the nature of relationships between brands. Companies have used the brand extension/stretching strategies frequently in the last few years. The idea is to benefit directly from the awareness and image of a strong existing brand by using the same brand name for launching new products in different categories. It is clear that international and global brands present many important advantages to the firm. They permit to generate strong economies of scale. It is well known that a globalised brand can generate significant cost reductions in all areas of the business system, including R&D, manufacturing and logistics.

Review and Application Questions

1. Select a well-known consumer brand and give examples of basic, performance and excitement attributes.
2. What is brand loyalty? Contrast behavioural brand loyalty and attitudinal brand loyalty. How are these concepts related?
3. Compare the functions of a brand in a B2C and in a B2B markets. What are the main similarities and the differences?
4. What are the differences between brand identity, brand positioning and the brand image?
5. Nestlé decided to co-brand with Krupp to develop the Nespresso system. What are the advantages and risks of this strategy? Which criteria should be used to select the partner?
6. Two brands are competing in the same reference market. Brand A has a loyalty rate of 80 per cent and an attraction rate of 30 per cent. The market shares are respectively 30 per cent for brand A and 70 per cent for brand B. What are the expected equilibrium market shares of these two brands if the loyalty and attraction rates remain unchanged? What would you do if you were the brand manager of brand B?
7. Compare four makes of microcomputers using four attributes (A, B, C and D) having the following determinance rates: 0.40/0.30/0.20/0.10. The score obtained (on a 10-point rating scale) by the brands on the four attributes are: A = 10/8/6/4; B = 8/9/8/3; C = 6/8/10/5; D = 4/3/7/8. Compute a total utility score for each brand using these data. Compare and interpret the results.

Bibliography

Aaker, D.A. (1991), *Managing Brand Equity*, New York, The Free Press.

Aaker, D.A. (1996), *Managing Strong Brands*, New York, The Free Press.

Aaker, D.A. (2004), *Brand Portfolio Strategy*, New York, Free Press.

Aaker, D.A. and Joachimsthaller, E. (2000), *Brand Leadership*, New York, The Free Press.

Business Week (*online*)(2005) Top 100 Global Brand Scoreboard.

Caron, G. (1996), Le devenir des marques, *Futuribles*, Févier, pp. 27–42.

Court, D., Freeling, A., Leiter, M. and Parsons, A.J. (1996), Uncovering the Value of Brands, *The McKinsey Quarterly*, 4, pp. 176–8.

Dalgic, T. (1992), Euromarketing: Charting the Map for Globalization, *International Marketing Review*, 9, 5, pp. 31–42.

Davidson, H. (1997), *Even More Offensive Marketing*, London, Penguin Books.

Day, G.S. (1981), Product Life Cycle's Analysis and Applications, *Journal of Marketing*, 45, 4, pp. 60–7.

de Maricourt, R. (ed.) (1997), *Marketing Européen: Stratégies et Actions*, Paris, Publi-Union.

Doyle, P. (1994/2003), *Marketing Management and Strategy*, New York, Prentice-Hall, 1st and 2nd editions.

Feldwick, P. (1996), What is Brand Equity Anyway, and How do You Measure It? *Journal of Market Research Society*, 38, 2, April, pp. 85–104.

Fishbein, M. (1967), Attitudes and Prediction of Behaviour, in *Readings in Attitude Theory and Measurement*, Fishbein, M. (ed.), New York, John Wiley and Sons, pp. 477–92.

Fraser, I. (1990), Now Only the Name's Not the Same, *Eurobusiness*, April, pp. 22–25.

Hinkle, J. (1966), *Life Cycles*, New York, Nielsen Cy.

Kapferer, J.N. (1991), *Les Marques Capital de l'entreprise*, Paris, Editions d'Organisation.

Kapferer, J.N. (1992/2004), *La marque capital de l'entreprise*, Paris, Editions d'Organisation.

Kapferer, J.N. (2004), *The New Strategic Brand Management*, London, Kogan Page.

Kapferer, J.N. and Thoenig, J.C. (1989), *La marque*, Paris, Ediscience International.

Keller, K.L. (1998/2004), *Strategic Brand Management*, Upper Saddle River, NJ, Prentice-Hall, 1st and 2nd editions.

Keller, K.L. (2000), The Brand Report Card, *Harvard Business Review*, 78, 1, pp. 147–57.

Lambin, J.J. (1989), La marque et le comportement de choix de l'acheteur, in *La marque*, Kapferer, J.N. and Thoenig, J.C. (eds), Paris, Ediscience International.

Macrae, C. (1996), *The Brand Chartering Handbook*, Addison-Wesley Publishing Company.

Malaval, P.H. (1998/2001), *Strategy and Management of Industrial Brands, Business to Business, Products & Services*, Kluwer Academic Publishers.

Nerlove, M. and Arrow, K. (1962), Optimal Advertising Policy under Dynamic Conditions, *Economica*, 29, pp. 131–45.

Sandler, D.M. and Shani, D. (1992), Brand Globally but Advertise Locally, an Empirical Investigation, *International Marketing Review*, 9, 4, pp. 18–31.

Schuiling, I. and Kapferer, J.N. (2004), Real Differences between Local and International Brands: Strategic Implications for International Marketers, *Journal of Internatinal Marketing*, 12, 4, pp. 97–112.

Sheppard, A. (1995), Adding Brand Value, in *Brand Power*, Stobart, P. (ed.), London, The MacMillan Press Ltd., pp. 85–110.

Stobart, P. (ed.) (1995), *Brand Power*, London, The MacMillan Press Ltd.

Subramanian, D. (1993), In Search of Eurobrands, *Media & Marketing*, pp. 22–3.

Variot, J.F. (1985), *L'identité de marque*, Paris, Institut de recherches et d'études publicitaires, Journées d'études de l'IREP, Juin.

Walden, D. (1993), Kano's Methods for Understanding Customer-defined Quality: Introduction to Kano's Methods, *Center for Quality Management Journal, 2, 4, Fall.*

distribution channel decisions 13

Chapter contents

Chapter learning objectives

When you have read this chapter, you should be able to

- understand the role and the functions performed by distribution channels in a market economy;
- understand why companies use distribution channels and the tasks performed by the different actors in these channels;
- identify the main configurations of a distribution channel and analyse the distribution cost structure of each possible channel;
- explain the different market coverage and communication strategies open to the manufacturer;
- understand the emerging role of private labels in B2C markets;
- describe the alternative entry strategies in foreign markets open to the international firm.

Chapter introduction

In most markets, the physical and psychological distance between producers and end-users is such that intermediaries are necessary to ensure an efficient matching between segments of demand and supply. Distributors and facilitating agencies are required because manufacturers are unable to assume by themselves, at a reasonable cost, all the tasks and activities implied by a free and competitive exchange process. The use of intermediaries means a loss of manufacturer control of certain distributive functions, since the firm subcontracts activities that could, in principle, be assumed by marketing management. Thus, from the firm's point of view, channel decisions are critical ones, which involve developing a channel structure that fits the firm's strategy and the needs of the target segment. The design of a channel structure is a major strategic decision, neither frequently made nor easily changed. In this chapter, we shall first examine the channel design decisions from the manufacturer's point of view (see Figure 13.1) and then analyse the type of positioning strategies available to retailers in consumer markets.

13.1. The economic role of distribution channels

A distribution channel is the structure formed by the interdependent partners participating in the process of making goods or services available for consumption or use by consumers or industrial users. These partners are the producers, intermediaries and end-users. Distribution channels are organised structures performing the tasks necessary to facilitate exchange transactions (Figure 13.1). Their role in a market economy is to bridge the gap between manufacturers and end-users by making goods available where and when they are needed and under the appropriate terms of trade. The functions of distribution channels are to create time, space and state utilities that constitute the added value of distribution.

13.1.1. The tasks of distribution

Channels of distribution provide many functions. These occur for the benefit of the producer or consumer or both. For producers, distribution channels perform seven different functions:

1. *Transporting*: to make the goods available in places close to consumers or industrial users.
2. *Breaking of bulk*: to make the goods available in quantity or volume adapted to consumers' purchasing habits.
3. *Storing*: to make the goods available at the time of consumption, thereby reducing the manufacturer's need to store its own products in company-owned warehouses.
4. *Sorting*: to constitute a selection of goods for use in association with each other and adapted to the buyer's use.

5. *Contacting*: to establish personalised relationships with customers who are numerous and remote.
6. *Informing*: to collect and disseminate information about market needs and about products and terms of trade.
7. *Promoting*: to promote the products through advertising and promotions organised at the point of sales.

In addition to these basic functions, intermediaries also provide services such as financial credit, guarantees, delivery, repairs, maintenance, atmosphere, and so on. The main economic role of distribution channels is to overcome the existing disparities between demand and supply.

13.1.2. The distribution flows

These functions give rise to distribution flows between partners in the exchange process. Some of these flows are forward flows (ownership, physical and promotion), others are backward flows (ordering and payment), and still others move in both directions (information). The five main flows are the following:

1. *Ownership flow*: the actual transfer of legal ownership from one organisation to another.
2. *Physical flow*: the successive movements of the physical product from the producer to the end-user.
3. *Ordering flow*: the orders placed by intermediaries in the channel and forwarded to the manufacturer.
4. *Payment flow*: successive buyers paying their bills through financial institutions to sellers.
5. *Information flow*: the dissemination of information to the market and/or to the producer at the initiative of the producer and/or the intermediaries.

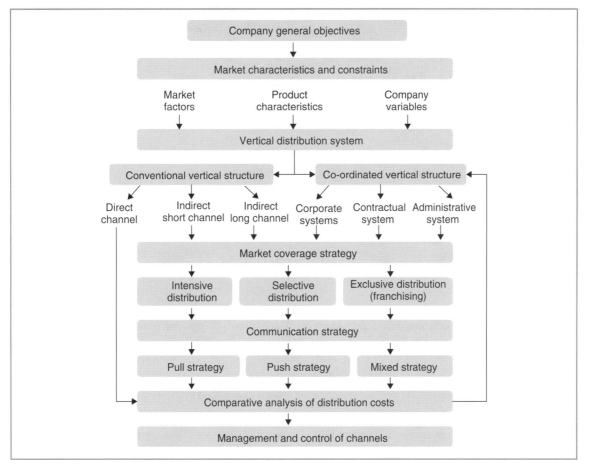

Figure 13.1 Overview of distribution channel's decisions
Source: Authors.

The key question in designing a channel of distribution is not whether these functions and flows need to be performed, but rather who is to perform them. These functions and the management of these distribution flows can be shifted between channel's partners. The problem is to decide who could perform these economic functions most efficiently: the producer, the intermediary or the consumer.

13.1.3. Rationale for marketing channels

The distribution functions cannot be eliminated, but rather simply assumed by other more efficient channel members. Innovations in distribution channels largely reflect the discovery of more efficient ways to manage these economic functions or flows. Various sources of efficiency enable intermediaries to perform distribution functions at a lower cost than either the customer or the manufacturer could by himself or herself. This is particularly true for

consumer goods, which are distributed to a large number of geographically dispersed customers.

Contactual efficiency

The complexity of the exchange process increases as the number of partners increases. As shown in Figure 13.2, the number of contacts required to maintain mutual interactions between all partners in the exchange process is much higher in a decentralised exchange system than in a centralised one. Figure 13.2 shows that, given three manufacturers and five retailers who buy goods from each other, the number of contacts required amounts to 15. If the manufacturer sells to these retailers through one wholesaler, the number of necessary contacts is reduced to eight. Thus, a centralised system employing intermediaries is more efficient than a decentralised system of exchange, by reducing the number of transactions required for matching segments of demand and supply.

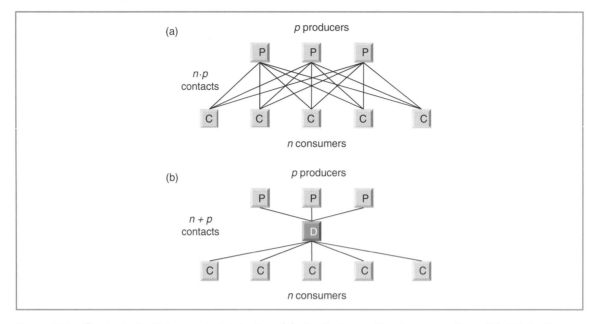

Figure 13.2   Contactual efficiency of distribution: (a) distribution without intermediary; (b) distribution with intermediary
Source: Authors.

Economies of scale

By grouping the products of several manufacturers, intermediaries can perform one or more distribution tasks more efficiently than manufacturers. For example, a wholesaler's sales representative can spread costs over several manufacturers and perform the selling function at a lower cost per manufacturer than if each firm paid its own company sales representative.

Reduction of functional discrepancies

By purchasing large volumes of goods from manufacturers, storing them and breaking them down into the volume customers prefer to purchase, wholesalers and retailers enable manufacturers and their customers to operate at a more efficient scale. Rather than having to make small production runs to fill the orders of individual customers, manufacturers can achieve economies of scale. Similarly, their customers can buy small quantities without having their capital tied up in large inventories.

   If a particular organisation is responsible for two separate functions (for instance, manufacturing and distribution) that have different optimum levels of operations, there is a risk for one of the two functions, or even for each of them, to operate at a suboptimum level. Costs go up and prices have to be higher. When some functions are subcontracted to middlemen the producer's costs and prices are lower.

Better assortment

At the manufacturer's level, the assortment of goods produced is largely dictated by technological considerations, whereas the assortment of goods consumers usually desire is dictated by the use situation. Typically, consumers desire a limited quantity of a wide variety of goods. The role of intermediaries is to create wide assortments and to make it possible for consumers to acquire a large variety of products from a single source with one transaction. This reduces the time and effort that consumers must expend in finding the goods they need. The same economy of effort also exists on the manufacturer's side. For example, a manufacturer of a limited line of hardware items could open its own retail outlets only if it were willing to accumulate a large variety of items generally sold at this type of outlet. In general, hardware wholesalers can perform this assortment function more efficiently than individual manufacturers.

Better services

The intermediary is close to the end-users and therefore can have a better understanding of their needs and desires and adapts the assortment to local situations. The superior efficiency of intermediaries in a market system is not absolute, however. A particular middleman will survive in the channel structure as long as the other channel partners in the exchange process consider that there is no other more efficient way to perform the function. Thus, the issue of who should perform various distribution tasks is one of relative efficiency.

13.2. Channel design alternatives

The design of a channel structure implies decisions regarding the responsibilities to be assumed by the different participants in the exchange process. From the manufacturer's point of view, the first decision is whether or not to subcontract certain distribution tasks and, if so, to what extent to subcontract and under which trade conditions.

13.2.1. Types of intermediary

There are four broad categories of intermediaries that a firm might include in the distributive network of its product: wholesalers, retailers, agents and facilitating agencies.

Wholesalers

These intermediaries sell primarily to other resellers, such as retailers or institutional or industrial customers, rather than to individual consumers. They take title of the goods they store and can provide quick delivery when the goods are ordered because they are usually located closer to customers than manufacturers. The case of wholesalers in the pharmaceutical industry described in Exhibit 13.1 is illustrative in this respect.

They purchase in large lots from manufacturers and resell in smaller lots to retailers. Wholesalers generally bring together an assortment of goods, usually of related items, by dealing with several sources of supply. In the food industry, full-service wholesalers have been confronted with the competition of mass retail distributors who have assumed by themselves the wholesaling function. Wholesalers have reacted by creating voluntary chains that consist of a wholesaler-sponsored group of independent retailers engaged in bulk buying and in common merchandising.

There are two types of wholesalers: Cash-and-carry ones operate stores, similar to warehouses, where they sell food and drink, mostly to traditional retailers and small HORECA. Customers select and take away their purchases themselves. Delivery wholesalers, by contrast, deliver goods from their warehouses directly to their customers, mostly mid-size of large service operators. Delivery wholesalers are particularly numerous; generally small, local family businesses, they supply 50–60 per cent of the market in all countries. Cash-and-carry outlets serve 10–20 per cent of it and other intermediaries, such as retail hypermarkets and a few food manufacturers supply the rest. Wholesalers play an important role in European markets as illustrated by the data of Table 13.1.

Retailers

Retailers sell goods and services directly to consumers for their personal, non-business use. Retailers take the ownership of the goods they carry, and their compensation is the margin between what they pay for the goods and the price they charge their customers. There are several schemes for classifying retailers. A traditional classification makes a distinction between three types of independent retailers: food retailers, specialty retailers and artisan retailers (bakers and butchers).

They can also be classified according to the level of service they provide (self-service versus full-service retailing) or according to their method of operation (low margin/high turnover or high margin/low turnover). Low margin/high turnover retailers compete primarily on a price basis, while high margin/low turnover retailers focus on unique assortment, specialty goods, services and prestigious

EXHIBIT 13.1

WHOLESALERS IN THE PHARMACEUTICAL INDUSTRY

- How 350 pharmaceutical laboratories and 250 suppliers of para-pharmaceutical products can respond as rapidly as possible to the needs of 22,000 French pharmacies, knowing that 12 million health products are sold every day?
- To do the job specialty wholesalers have netted the French territory with warehouses to meet this demand. As a result, today these wholesalers distribute 81 per cent of health products. The remaining 19 per cent are delivered directly to hospitals (12 per cent) or to pharmacies (7 per cent).

- Twice a day, pharmacists place their orders through tele-transmission, to be served early afternoon before the end of the schools' closing hour, or the following day morning before the store's opening hour. The staff has less than two hours to handle the orders.

Source: Le Monde, 16 March 1993.

Table 13.1 Wholesale fragmentation in Europe

Type of goods	France	Germany	Italy	Spain
Meat	700	2,000	3,645	5,229
Fish	900	130	2,451	8,161
Fruits and vegetables	1,250	2,000	11,913	9,622
Frozen foods	420	800	783	na
Beverages	4,500	3,600	6,019	6,276
Dry food	1,100	2,800	16,059	12,213

Source: Castrillo *et al.* (2003).

store image. The number of independent retailers has drastically decreased in most European countries, mainly due to the competition of mass merchandisers.

Integrated distribution

Since the beginning of the century, profound changes have taken place in the distribution sector and it is useful to briefly summarise this evolution:

- The first revolution goes back to 1852 with the establishment in Paris of the first department store. The innovating principles were broad assortment, low mark-ups and rapid turnover, marking and displaying the prices, free entry without pressure or obligation to purchase. The best-known department stores today are Harrods in London, Galeries Lafayettes in Paris, Macy's in New York, La Renascente in Milan, and so on.
- The next generation of stores was the specialty-stores chain located in suburban shopping centres closer to consumers. A store concept based on a limited assortment and economies of scale due to large purchased quantities.
- The next generation was the popular store, which sells goods at low prices by accepting lower margins, working on higher volume and providing minimum service (typically Prisunic in France and Belgium).
- The fourth revolution is the supermarket revolution; a store concept based on self-service operations and designed to serve the consumer's total needs for food, laundry and household maintenance products. The one-stop shopping concept. Supermarkets have moved towards larger stores, the superstore or the hypermarché as Carrefour in France.

The supermarket concept has been extremely successful in Europe, in particular in the fast moving consumer goods sector. Six managerial rules characterised this selling formula:

1. A broad assortment and wide variety of popular merchandise to facilitate multiple-item purchases and fast stock rotation.

2. A low purchase price thanks to the high volume purchased and strong bargaining power vis-à-vis suppliers.
3. Low margins and low sales prices.
4. Dynamic promotional activities in order to stimulate store traffic.
5. Economies of scale on physical distribution (in transportation, handling and packaging).
6. Long credit terms (typically 90 days) for products usually sold within 15 days in order to generate substantial financial by-products.

This selling formula has given a substantial competitive advantage to integrated distributors over independent retailers. The situation is changing today as new expectations emerge among consumers and as independent distributors propose new store concepts.

The new food discounters

The fifth revolution in mass merchandising is currently taking place with a new breed of retailers called the hard discounters, led mainly in Western Europe by the German distributors Aldi and Lidl. It is a retailing system characterised by the permanent and generalised adoption of low prices, thanks to a systematic cost control and limited service policies.

The main features of discount retailing, sometimes called minimum marketing, as observed in a typical Aldi store, are the following:

- a limited store size: between 3,000 and 7,000 square feet in the United Kingdom, the average size in France being 662 square metres (LSA, 1998);
- a small product range, approximately 600 lines, with a single offer per product category, mainly set out in full boxes on pallets;
- approximately 70 per cent of the range is own brand or at least a brand name with a 'packed exclusively for Aldi' qualification;
- prices aim to be 20–25 per cent lower than average major multiples;

- limited number (four or five) of multifunctional sales attendants;
- prices are memorised by checkout operators and there is no EpoS;
- only cash payments, credit cards are not accepted;
- plastic bags are charged for and the stores are often renovated warehouses or cinemas.

According to a survey published by the LSA (1998), hard discounting is in good shape in France with more than 2,000 units in 1998 and a growing market share of 6–7 per cent, with the German retail giants Lidl and Aldi leading, followed by Leader Price and ED Le Marché Discount. The growth of hard discounters is also significant in the United Kingdom with Aldi and Rewe (Penny) from Germany and Netto from Denmark. The two UK discount chains, Kwik Save and Lo Cost, dominate the discounting market.

Agents

These are functional intermediaries who do not take title of the goods with which they deal but who negotiate sales or purchases for clients or principals. They are compensated in the form of a commission on sales or purchases. They are independent business persons or freelance sales people who represent client organisations. Common types of agent include import or export agents, traders, brokers and manufacturers' representatives. Manufacturers' representatives usually work for several firms and carry non-competitive, complementary goods in an exclusive territory or foreign country.

Facilitating agencies

Facilitating agencies are business firms that assist in the performance of distribution tasks other than buying, selling and transferring title. From the firm's standpoint, they are subcontractors carrying out certain distribution tasks because of their specialisation or special expertise. Common types of facilitating agencies are: transportation agencies, storage agencies, advertising agencies, market research firms, financial agencies, insurance companies, and so on. These agencies are involved in a marketing channel on an as-needed basis and they are compensated by commissions or fees paid for their services.

Many different types of institutions participate in a distribution channel. The channel structure will be determined by the manner in which the different distribution tasks have been allocated among the channel participants.

Cybermediaries

With the development of e-commerce, new types of intermediaries have emerged performing key functions that make exchanges easier, cut the costs of carrying out the sales transaction and improve the responsiveness to customers' needs. These functions are the following:

Aggregation. The aggregated demand of buyers by a single intermediary, or the aggregation of several suppliers by a distributor, are alternatives to the situation where each buyer must find a direct source of good and each producer must sell products directly to individual customers. This aggregation process cuts transaction costs and favours economies of scale.

Trust. Intermediaries can also provide a guarantee and protect buyers (or sellers) against opportunistic or manipulative actions. This function is particularly important in the anonymous world of e-commerce, where mechanisms assuring confidence in the retailer, confidentiality and security are not yet fully established.

Facilitation. Transferring information to a decentralised market can be costly because each participant must seek out and exchange information with other economic players. A broker can speed up this process. Intermediaries can also speed up exchanges by offering associated services, such as managing financial and administrative arrangements.

Matching. Intermediaries have several ways to find buyers and vice versa. They can be database administrators, focusing efforts on customer about suppliers' preferences and sending selective information.

As e-commerce continues to develop, these new intermediary functions will grow more important and sophisticated (Jallat and Capek, 2001).

13.2.2. Configurations of a distribution channel

Distribution channels can be characterised by the number of intermediary levels that separate the manufacturer from the end-user. Figure 13.3 shows the different channel designs commonly used to distribute industrial or consumer goods. A distinction can be made between direct and indirect distribution systems:

- In a *direct distribution system*, the manufacturer sells directly to the end-user and there is no intermediary in the channel. This structure is also called a direct marketing system.
- In an *indirect distribution system*, one or several intermediaries participate and bring the product closer to the final buyer. An indirect system is said to be 'short' or 'long' depending on the number of intermediary levels.

In the field of consumer goods, distribution channels tend to be long and involve several intermediaries, typically wholesalers and retailers. In industrial markets, channels are generally shorter, particularly when buyers

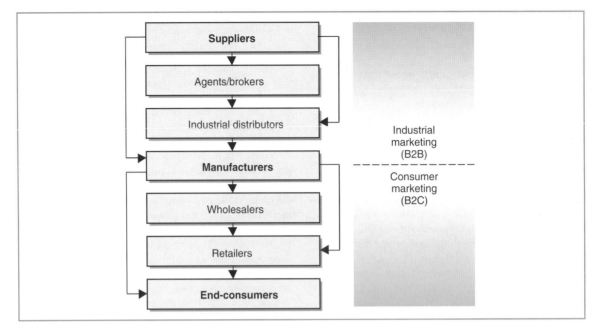

Figure 13.3   Structure of a conventional vertical marketing system
Source: Authors.

are large and well identified. From the producer's point of view, the longer the channel, the more difficult the problem of control.

In most market situations, companies use multiple channels to reach their target segments, either to create emulation among distributors or to reach separate target segments having different purchasing habits. For example, many industrial companies use distributors to sell and service small accounts and their own sales force to handle large accounts.

13.2.3. Types of competition among distributors

In a distributive network several types of competition may exist among distributors as shown in Figure 13.4.

Horizontal competition. The same type of intermediaries at the same channel level competing with each other.

Intertype competition. Different types of intermediaries at the same channel level competing with each other (self-service versus full service).

Vertical competition. Channel members at different levels in the channel competing with each other, such as retailers integrating the wholesaling function or vice versa.

Channel system competition. Complete channel systems competing with each other as units. For instance, the competition between indirect distribution through

wholesalers and retailers and direct marketing through direct mail.

Distribution has experienced large changes over the last 30 years, which have contributed to reinforcing the competitive struggle among intermediaries. The growth of vertical marketing systems illustrates this evolution.

13.3. Factors affecting the channel structure

The selection of a particular channel design is largely determined by a set of constraints related to market and buyer behaviour factors and to product and company characteristics. These factors and their implications for the channel configuration are described in Table 13.2.

The number of potential buyers determines the size of the market. A very general heuristic rule about market size relative to channel structure is: if the market is large, the use of intermediaries is more likely to be needed. Conversely, if the market is small, a firm is more likely to avoid the use of intermediaries and to assume most of the distribution tasks. Also, the more geographically dispersed the market, the more difficult and expensive is the distribution. The more geographically dispersed the market, the more likely it is that intermediaries will be used because of the high costs involved in providing adequate services to many dispersed customers.

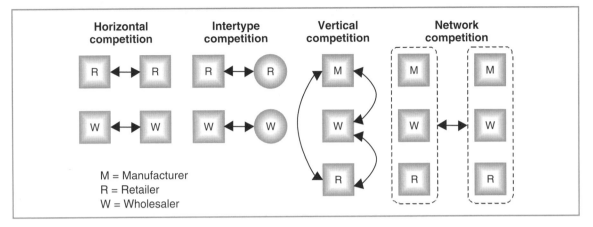

Figure 13.4   Types of competition among distributors

Source: Palamountain (1955).

Table 13.2   Factors affecting channel structure

Influencing factors	Direct	Indirect short	Indirect long	Comments
Market factors				
Large number of buyers		**	***	
High geographical dispersion		**	***	
Purchases in large quantity	***			
Buying highly seasonal		**	***	
Product characteristics				
Perishable products	***			
Complex products	***			
Newness of the product	***	**		
Heavy and bulky products	***			
Standardised products		**	***	
Low unit value		**	***	
Company variables				
Large financial capacity	***	**		
Complete assortment	***	**		
High control sought	***	**		

Patterns of buying behaviour also influence the channel structure. If customers typically buy in very small quantities and if demand is highly seasonal a long distribution channel involving several intermediaries will be more appropriate.

13.3.1. Product variables

Characteristics of the product also determine the channel structure. Channels should be as short as possible for highly perishable products. Heavy and bulky products have very high handling and shipping costs and the firm should try to minimise these by shipping the goods only in truckload quantities to a limited number of places; the channel structure should also be short.

Short structures are also desirable for complex and technical products requiring extensive after-sales service and assistance in use. Similarly, for innovative products requiring aggressive promotion in the introductory stage of the product life cycle (PLC), a shorter channel will facilitate the development and control of promotion activities aiming at creating product acceptance by the market. Long channel structures will be more adequate, on the other hand, when products are highly standardised and when they have low unit value. In this latter case, many other products handled by the intermediaries can share the costs of distribution.

> For example, it would be difficult to imagine the sales of packages of crisps by the Smiths Company to the consumer. Only by spreading the costs of distribution over the wide variety of products handled by wholesale and retail intermediaries is it possible to buy a packet of crisps at retail for €1.20.

A manufacturer's channel choice is also influenced by the extent of its product line. The manufacturer with only one item may have to use wholesaling intermediaries, whereas it could go directly to retailers if it made several products that could be combined on a large scale. A retailer ordinarily cannot buy a truckload of washing machines alone, but it might buy a truckload of mixed appliances.

13.3.2. Company variables

The key variables here are the size and the financial capability of the producer. Large firms in general have large financial resources and therefore the capacity to assume several distribution tasks directly, thereby reducing their dependence on intermediaries. Several distribution activities, such as transportation and storage,

imply fixed costs. Large companies are better able to bear these costs. On the other hand, the use of intermediaries implies a cost, which is proportional to the volume of activity, since their compensation takes the form of commissions on actual sales revenue. Therefore, small firms will be inclined to have extensive recourse to intermediaries. In some cases, the entire output is sold under the retailer's brand. The disadvantage of this arrangement is that the producer is completely at the mercy of its one large retailer.

Other considerations are also important. For example, the lack of marketing expertise necessary to perform the distribution tasks may force the firm to use the services of intermediaries. This happens frequently when the firm is penetrating new or foreign markets. Also, high-technology companies built upon the engineering abilities of management often rely heavily on distributors to do the marketing job. A manufacturer may establish as short a channel as possible simply because it wants to control the distribution of its product, even though the cost of a more direct channel is higher.

13.4. Vertical marketing systems

If the adopted channel structure is indirect, some degree of co-operation and co-ordination must be achieved among the participants in the channel (see Exhibit 13.2). Two forms of vertical organisation can exist: conventional

---

EXHIBIT 13.2

FORMS OF CO-OPERATION BETWEEN RESELLERS

Retailer co-operatives. Groups of independent retailers forming their own co-operative chain organisation. Typically, they agree to concentrate their purchases by forming their own wholesale operations. In many cases, they also engage in joint advertising, promotion and merchandising programmes.

Wholesalers-sponsored voluntary chains. Wholesalers organise voluntary chains by getting independent retailers to sign contracts in which they agree to standardise their selling practices and to purchase a certain proportion of their inventories from the wholesaler. This gives the wholesaler greater buying power in its dealings with manufacturers. Some voluntary chains also have a common brand store.

Franchise systems. Franchising is in the form of co-operation between the distinct enterprises in which a supplier (franchiser) grants a dealer (franchisee) the right to sell products in exchange for some type of consideration, such as some percentage of total sales. The franchiser helps to furnish equipment, buildings, management know-how and marketing assistance. The franchisee must agree to operate according to the rules of the franchiser.

Rack jobbing. Rack jobbers perform purchasing and stocking function for retailers. Impulse products that have short life cycles (such as toys, books, records) may be supplied by rack jobbers to avoid the inconvenience to retailers of having to deal with unfamiliar products. They physically maintain the goods by refilling shelves, fixing displays and maintaining inventory records. Retailers have only to furnish space. Thus, a limited-service wholesaler usually operates on a consignment basis. The retailer is remunerated by some percentage of sales.

Cash-and-carry wholesalers. Cash-and-carry wholesalers are limited-service wholesalers who sell to customers who pay cash and furnish transportation or pay extra to have products delivered. The middlemen usually handle a limited line of products such as groceries, construction materials, electrical supplies or office supplies.

Source: Authors.

vertical structures and co-ordinated vertical structures, called vertical marketing systems:

- In a *conventional vertical structure* each level of the channel behaves independently as a separate business entity seeking to maximise its own profit, even if it is at the expense of the overall performance of the distribution channel. This is the traditional way in which a distribution network works, where no channel member has control over the others.
- In a *co-ordinated vertical structure*, the participants in the exchange process behave like partners and co-ordinate their activities in order to increase their bargaining power and to achieve operating economies and maximum market impact. In this type of vertical organisation, a channel member takes the initiative of co-ordination, be it the manufacturer, the wholesaler or the retailer.

Several forms of vertical marketing system have emerged. A distinction is usually made between corporate, contractual and administered vertical marketing systems.

13.4.1. Corporate vertical marketing systems

In corporate vertically integrated marketing systems, a particular firm achieves co-ordination and control through corporate ownership. The firm owning and operating the other units of the channel may be a manufacturer, wholesaler or retailer. Firms such as Bata in shoes and Rodier in clothing own their own retail outlets. However, it is not always the manufacturer that controls the channel system through forward integration. Backward integration occurs when a retailer or a wholesaler assumes ownership of institutions that normally precede them in the channel. Sears in the United States, for example, and Marks & Spencer in the United Kingdom have ownership interest in several manufacturing firms that are important suppliers of their private brands.

13.4.2. Contractual vertical marketing systems

In a contractual vertical marketing system, independent firms operating at different levels of the channel co-ordinate their activities through legal contracts that spell out the rights and duties of each partner. The three basic types of contractual system are: retail co-operatives, wholesale-sponsored voluntary chains and franchise systems. Franchise systems have expanded the most in recent years. Their organisation is discussed in more detail in the next section.

13.4.3. Administered vertical marketing systems

In this third system, firms participating in the channel co-ordinate their activities through the informal guidance or influence of one of the channel members (and not through ownership or contractual agreements). The leading firm, usually the manufacturer, bases its influence on the brand or company reputation or managerial expertise. Companies such as L'Oréal in cosmetics and Procter & Gamble in detergents are examples of firms having successfully achieved this form of co-operation.

Vertical marketing systems have become the dominant mode of distribution in the field of consumer marketing over the past 20 years. They can be viewed as a new form of competition (channel system competition, setting complete channels against other complete channels) as opposed to traditional vertical competition (opposing channel members at different levels of the same channel, that is, retailers versus wholesalers, manufacturer versus wholesaler, and so on). Vertical marketing systems help eliminate the sources of conflict that exist in conventional vertical structures, and increase the market impact of their activities.

13.5. Market coverage strategies

If the decision made by the producer is to use intermediaries to organise the distribution of its products, the firm must then decide on the number of intermediaries to use at each channel level to achieve the market penetration objective. Three basic market coverage strategies are possible:

- Hollywood distributes its chewing gums wherever possible: in food stores, tobacconists, drug stores, through vending machines, and so on.
- Pierre Cardin distributes his dresses and women' in carefully selected clothing stores and tries to present in the most elegant shops.
- VAG (Volkswagen Audi Group) distributes its through exclusive dealerships; each dealer ha exclusive territory and no other dealer is au carry the VAG makes.

Hollywood is adopting an *intensive* distribu Cardin a *selective* strategy and VAG an *exclus.* The best strategy for a given product depends on the n of the product itself, on the objective being pursued and on the competitive situation.

13.5.1. Consumer goods classifications

In the field of consumer goods, the choice of a particular market coverage strategy is largely determined by the shopping habits associated with the consumers of the distributed product. Consumer goods fall into four subgroups: convenience goods, shopping goods, specialty goods and unsought goods. The purchasing behaviour associated with these products varies primarily in the amount and type of effort consumers exert in buying these products.

Convenience goods

Convenience products are purchased with as little effort as possible, frequently and in small quantities. We have here a routine buying behaviour. Convenience goods can be further subdivided into staple goods, impulse goods and emergency goods:

- *Staple goods* are purchased on a regular basis and include most food items. Brand loyalty facilitates routine purchase and the goods must be pre-sold, namely through repetitive advertising.
- *Impulse goods* are purchased without any planning (crisps, magazines, sweets, and so on). These goods must be available in many places; the packaging and the in-store displays in supermarkets are important in the sale of these products.
- *Emergency goods* are those needed to fill an unexpected and urgent need. These goods are purchased immediately as the need emerges and therefore they must be available in many outlets.

For these three product categories, the firm has practically no alternative. These products require intensive market coverage. If the brand is not found at the point of sale, consumers will buy another brand and the sales occasion will be lost.

Shopping goods

Shopping goods are high perceived risk products. For these products, consumers are willing to spend time and effort to shop around and to compare product alternatives on criteria such as quality, price, style, features, and so on. Examples include major appliances, furniture and clothing, which are expensive and infrequently bought products. Prospective buyers visit several stores before making a decision and sales personnel have an important role to play by providing information and advice.

For shopping goods, maximal market coverage is not required and a selective distribution system will be more appropriate, more especially as the co-operation of the retailer is necessary.

Specialty goods

Specialty goods are products with unique characteristics and sufficiently important to consumers that they make a special effort to discover them. Examples would include specific brands, fancy goods, exotic foods, deluxe clothing,

sophisticated photographic equipment, and so on. For these products, prospective buyers do not proceed to comparisons; they search for the outlet carrying the wanted product. Brand loyalty or the distinctive features of the product are the determining factors. For specialty goods, retailers are especially important; thus the firms of such goods will tend to limit their distribution to obtain strong support from the retailers. A selective or exclusive distribution system is the best option for the producer.

Unsought goods

Unsought goods are products that consumers do not know about or know about but do not consider buying. Examples are heat pumps, smoke detectors, encyclopaedias and life insurance. Substantial selling efforts are required for those products. The co-operation of the intermediaries is indispensable, or the firm must adopt a direct marketing system.

Other factors must be taken into consideration in the choice of a market coverage strategy. As a general rule, selective and exclusive distribution systems imply a higher level of co-operation among distributors, a reduction of distribution costs for the supplier and a better control over sales operations. On the other hand, in both cases, there is a voluntary limitation of the product retail availability. Thus potential buyers will have to actively search for the product. The firm must therefore maintain a good balance between the benefits and the demerits of each distribution system.

13.5.2. Intensive distribution

In an intensive distribution system, the firm seeks the maximum possible number of retailers to distribute its product, the largest number of storage points to ensure maximum market coverage and the highest brand exposure. This strategy is appropriate for convenience goods, common raw materials and low-involvement services. The advantages of intensive distribution are to maximise product availability and to generate a large market share due to the brand's broad exposure to potential buyers. There are, however, significant disadvantages or risks associated with this strategy:

- The sales revenue generated by the different retailers varies greatly, while the contact cost is the same for each intermediary. If the firm receives many small orders from an intensive network of small retailers, distribution costs (order processing and shipping) can become extremely high and undermine the overall profitability.
- When the product has an intensive distribution in multiple and very diversified sales points, it becomes difficult for the firm to control its marketing

strategy: discount pricing, poor customer service and lack of co-operation from retailers are practices difficult to prevent.

■ Intensive distribution is hard to reconcile with a brand image building strategy and with a specific product positioning strategy due to the lack of control of the distributive network.

For these reasons, market-driven companies are induced to adopt a more selective distributive system once the brand awareness objectives have been achieved.

13.5.3. Selective distribution

In a selective distribution system, the producer uses fewer distributors than the total number of available distributors in a specific geographic area. It is an appropriate strategy for shopping goods that customers buy infrequently and compare for differences in price and product features.

A selective distribution may also be the result of the refusal from distributors to carry the product in their assortment. To have a selective distribution, the firm must decide the criteria upon which to select its intermediaries. Several criteria are commonly used:

■ The *size of the distributor*, measured by its sales revenue, is the most popular criterion. In the majority of markets, a small number of distributors achieve a significant share of total sales revenue. In the food sector, for instance, the concentration ratio is very high in Switzerland, the United Kingdom and Belgium, where the first five distributors in the food sectors account for 82, 53 and 52 per cent, respectively of the total turnover (Nielsen, 2006). In these conditions, it is obviously unprofitable to contact all distributors.
■ The *quality of the service* provided is also an important criterion. Intermediaries are paid to perform a certain number of well-defined functions and some dealers or retailers are more efficient than others.
■ The *technical competence* of the dealer and the availability of up-to-date facilities, mainly for complex products where after-sales service is important, is a third important criterion.

In adopting a selective distribution system, the firm voluntarily agrees to limit the availability of its product in order to reduce its distribution costs and to gain better co-operation from the intermediaries. This co-operation can take various forms, such as

■ participating in the advertising and promotion budget;
■ accepting new products or unsought products requiring more selling effort;
■ maintaining a minimum level of inventory;
■ transferring information to the producer;
■ providing better services to customers.

The main risk of a selective distribution system is to have insufficient market coverage. The producer must verify whether the market knows the distributors handling the brand or the product. If not, the reduced availability of the product could generate significant losses of sales opportunities. It may happen that the firm has in fact no alternative and is forced to maintain a certain degree of selectivity in its distributive network, for example

■ a retailer will accept a new product, which is not yet a proven success, only if it receives an exclusive right to carry the product in its territory;
■ if the assortment is large because the consumer must be able to choose among several product forms (design, colour, size), selectivity will be necessary, otherwise the expected sales revenue will be too low to motivate the retailer;
■ if the after-sales service implies long and costly training of the dealers, selectivity will be necessary to reduce the costs.

If the firm decides to adopt a selective distribution system, it is important to realise that this decision implies the adoption of a 'short' indirect distribution channel. It is very unlikely indeed that wholesalers will agree to voluntarily limit their field of operation simply to meet the strategic objectives of the producer.

13.5.4. Exclusive distribution and franchise systems

In an exclusive distribution system, the manufacturer relies on only one retailer or dealer to distribute its product in a given geographic territory. In turn, the exclusive dealer agrees not to sell any competing brand within the same product category.

Exclusive distribution is useful when a company wants to differentiate its product on the basis of high quality, prestige or excellent customer service. The close co-operation with exclusive dealers facilitates the implementation of the producer's customer service programmes. The advantages and disadvantages of exclusive distribution are the same as in selective distribution, but amplified. A particular form of exclusive distribution is franchising.

Franchising is a contractual, vertically integrated marketing system, which refers to a comprehensive method of distributing goods and services. It involves a continuous and contractual relationship in which a franchiser provides a licensed privilege to do business and assistance in organising, training, merchandising, management and other areas in return for a specific consideration from the franchisee. Thus, the franchisee agrees to pay an initial fee plus royalties calculated on the sales revenue for the right to use a well-known trademarked product or service, and to receive continual assistance and services from the franchiser. In fact, the franchisee is buying a proven success from the franchiser.

Types of franchise systems

The franchiser may occupy any position within the channel; therefore there are four basic types of franchise system:

1. The *manufacturer–retailer franchise* is exemplified by franchised automobile dealers and franchised service stations. Singer in the United States, Pingouin and Yves Rocher in France are good examples.
2. The *manufacturer–wholesaler* franchise is exemplified by the soft drink companies such as Coca-Cola and 7-Up who sell the soft drink syrups they manufacture to franchised wholesalers who, in turn, carbonate, bottle, sell and distribute to retailers.
3. The *wholesaler–retailer* franchise is exemplified by Rexall Drug Stores, by Christianssens in toys and Unic and Disco in food.
4. The *service sponsor–retailer* franchise is exemplified by Avis, Hertz, McDonald's, Midas and Holiday Inn.

The faster growing franchises include business and professional services, fast food, restaurants, car and truck rentals, and home and cleaning maintenance.

Characteristics of a good franchise

A good franchise must be above all a transferable proven success, which can be replicated in another territory or environment. According to Sallenave (1979, p. 11), a good franchise must

- be related to the distribution of a high quality product or service;
- meet a universal need or want which is not country- or region-specific;
- be a proven success in franchiser-owned and -operated pilot units which serve as models for other franchisees;
- ensure the full transfer of know-how and to provide the training of the franchisee in the methods of doing business and modes of operation;
- offer to the franchisees initial and continuing service to gain immediate market acceptance and to improve modes of operation;
- have a regular reporting and information system which permits effective monitoring of the performance and collection of market information;
- specify initial franchise fees and the royalty fees based on the gross value of a franchisee's sales volume (generally 5 per cent);

- involve the franchisee in the management and development of the franchise system;
- specify legal provisions for termination, cancellation and renewal of the franchise agreement, as well as for the repurchase of the franchise.

Franchise systems constitute a viable alternative to completely integrate corporate vertical marketing systems. In a franchise system, funds are provided by the franchisees, who invest in the stores and in the facilities. From the franchiser's point of view, the establishment of franchised dealers is an ideal means to achieve rapid national or international distribution for its products or services without committing large funds and while keeping the control of the system through contractual agreements.

> John Y. Brown, President of Kentucky Fried Chicken Corporation, has stated that it would have required $450 million for his firm to have established its first 2700 stores if they would have been company-owned. This sum was simply not available to his firm during the initial stages of its proposed expansion. The use of capital made available from franchisees, however, made the proposed expansion possible. (McGuire, 1971, p. 7)

Thus a franchise system is an integrated marketing system controlled by the franchiser but financed by the franchisees. A successful franchise is a partnership in which the mutual interests of both franchiser and franchisees are closely interdependent.

Benefits to the franchiser

The motivations to the franchiser for creating and developing a franchise system are the following:

- To acquire funds without diluting control of the marketing system.
- To keep high flexibility in the use of the capital collected for developing the system.
- To avoid the fixed overhead expenses associated with distribution through company-owned branch units or stores.
- To co-operate with independent business people, the franchisees, who are more likely to work hard at developing their markets than salaried employees.
- To co-operate with local business people well accepted and integrated in the local community or in the foreign country.
- To develop new sources of income based on existing know-how and marketing expertise.
- To achieve faster sales development thanks to the snowball effect generated by the franchising of a successful idea.
- To benefit from economies of scale with the development of the franchise system.

Franchisers provide both initial and continuous services to their franchisees (McGuire, 1971). Initial services include: market survey and site selection; facility design and layout; lease negotiation advice; financing advice; operating manuals; management training programmes and franchisee employee training. Continuous services include field supervision; merchandising and promotional materials; management and employee re-training; quality inspection; national advertising; centralised purchasing; market data and guidance; auditing and record keeping; management reports and group insurance plans.

The franchise system is present in almost all business fields, and total franchise system sales have grown dramatically during the last decade.

Benefits to franchisees

From the perspective of the potential franchisee, the most important appeal is to benefit from the franchiser's reputation of quality and corporate image. Franchising has several other strong appeals that explain the success of this distribution arrangement:

■ Franchising enables an individual to enter a business that would be prohibitively expensive if the individual tried to go it alone.
■ The amount of uncertainty is reduced, since the business idea has been successfully tested.
■ The extensive services provided by the franchiser, both initial and continuous, reduce the risks of the operation.
■ Franchising offers better purchasing power, access to better sites and the support of national advertising.
■ The introduction of new products and the constant rejuvenation of the product portfolio are made possible.
■ Managerial assistance in marketing and finance is provided.
■ The opportunity is provided for individuals to operate as independent business people within a large organisation.

Franchising is a very flexible organisation and many variants exist. Three basic rules must be met to have a successful arrangement:

■ The will to work as partners.
■ The right to mutual control.
■ The value of the business idea.

This last condition is crucial. Franchising will work only if the business idea is a proven success. It is not a solution for a firm to declare itself a franchiser if there is no proven success.

13.6. Communication strategies in the channel

Gaining support and co-operation from independent intermediaries is a key success factor for the implementation of the firm's marketing objectives. To obtain this co-operation, the firm can adopt two very distinct communication strategies: a *push* strategy or a *pull* strategy. A third alternative is a combination of the two.

13.6.1. Push strategies

In a push communication strategy, the bulk of the marketing effort is devoted to incentives directed to wholesalers and retailers to induce them to co-operate with the firm, to carry the brands in their range, to keep a minimum level of inventory, to display the products and to give them enough visibility on their shelf spaces. The objective is to win voluntary co-operation by offering attractive terms of trade, that is, larger margins, quantity discounts, local or in-store advertising, promotional allowances, in-store sampling, and so on. Personal selling and personal communication are the key marketing instruments here. The role of the sales representatives and of the merchandisers will be particularly important. Table 13.3 lists a variety of incentives the firm can use to increase the motivation of channel members.

A programme of incentives is indispensable to get the support of intermediaries. The larger their negotiation power, the more difficult it will be for the firm to obtain the support of distributors. In markets where distribution is highly concentrated, it is the intermediary who specifies the conditions for carrying the brand. The risk of an exclusive push strategy is the absence of countervailing power and the dependence of the firm on the intermediary who controls the access to the market.

The only alternative for the firm is the adoption of a direct marketing system which completely bypasses intermediaries. This is a costly operation, however, since all distribution tasks must then be assumed by the firm. Recent developments in communication technologies present new opportunities, however.

13.6.2. Pull strategies

When adopting a pull strategy, the manufacturer focuses its communication efforts on the end-user, bypassing intermediaries and trying to build company demand directly among potential customers in the target segment. The communication objective is to create strong customer demand and brand loyalty among consumers in order to pull the brand through the distribution channel, forcing the intermediaries to carry the brand to meet consumers' demand.

To achieve these objectives, the manufacturer will spend the largest proportion of its communication budget on media advertising, consumer promotions and direct

---

Table 13.3   Incentives for motivating channel members

Functional performance	Examples of channel incentives
Increased purchases or carry large inventories	Large margins, exclusive territories, buy-in promotions, quantity discounts, buy-back allowances, free goods, shelf-stocking programmes.
Increased personal selling effort	Sales training, instructional materials, incentive programmes for channel members' salespeople.
Increased local promotional effort	
Local advertising	Co-operative advertising, advertising allowance, print, radio, TV ads for use by local retailers.
Increased display space	Promotion allowances tied to shelf space.
In-store promotions	Display racks and signs, in-store demonstrations, in-store sampling.
Improved customer service	Service training programmes, instructional materials, high margins on replacement parts, liberal labour cost allowances for warranty service.

Source: Boyd and Walker (1990).

---

marketing efforts aimed at winning end-customer preferences. If this branding policy is successful, the manufacturer has the power to influence channel participants and to induce them to carry the brand, since a substantial sales volume will be achieved. The strategic objective is to neutralise the bargaining power of the intermediary who could block access to the market.

Procter & Gamble generally adopts a pull strategy in its new product launching strategies. However, the consumer advertising campaign starts only when the new brand has achieved almost 100 per cent distribution at retail. It goes without saying that such a result can be achieved only because P&G's sales reps are in position to demonstrate to retailers the advertising that will be organised to support the new product market introduction. Thus, retailers are willing to co-operate with the company.

Pull strategies imply in general large financial resources to cover the costs of brand image advertising campaigns. These costs are fixed overhead expenses, while the costs of a push strategy are proportional to volume and therefore easier to bear, particularly for a small firm.

In fact, a pull strategy must be viewed as a *long-term investment*. The goal of the firm is to create a capital of goodwill, brand equity, around the company name or around the brand. A strong brand image is an asset for the firm and is the best argument for obtaining support and co-operation from intermediaries.

In practice, these two communication strategies are used in combination, and it is hard to imagine a market situation where no incentives would be used to motivate

intermediaries. With the development of marketing expertise and the increased cost of personal selling, the trend among market-driven companies is to reinforce branding policies and pull communication strategies. As the average cost of a call to a customer made by a salesperson keeps on increasing, the selectivity of mass media tends to improve and therefore to lower the unit cost of a contact through advertising.

13.7. Distribution cost analysis

The distribution cost is measured by the difference between the unit sales price paid by the end-user and the unit cost paid to the producer by the first buyer. Thus, the distribution margin measures the added value brought by the distribution channel. If several intermediaries participate in the distribution process, the distribution margin is equal to the sum of the different distributors' margins. The margin of a particular distributor is equal to the difference between its selling price and its purchase cost. The two definitions coincide when there is only one intermediary in the channel.

13.7.1. Trade margins

A trade margin is often expressed as a percentage. This is sometimes confusing, since the margin percentage can be computed on the basis of purchase cost (C) or on the basis of selling price (P). The trade margin (D) is then referred

---

Table 13.4 Definitions of trade margins

- Distributor margin

    Distributor margin = sales price − purchase cost

$$D = P - C.$$

- Distributor margin in per cent

    'Discount' 'Mark-up'

$$D^* = \frac{P-C}{P} \qquad D^0 = \frac{P-C}{C}.$$

- Transformation rules

$$D^* = \frac{D^0}{1 + D^0} \qquad D^0 = \frac{D^*}{1 - D^*}.$$

- Examples of 'discount' versus 'mark-up'

Discount (%)	Mark-up (%)
50	100
33	50
30	42.86
25	33.33
20	25

- Retail price determination

    If the purchase cost is €90 and the discount 25%,
    the retail price will be: €90 /(1 − 25%) = €90/75% = €120

    Since a 25% discount is the equivalent of a 33.33% mark-up, we also
    have €90 × (1+33.33%) = €90 × 1.3333 = €120

- Purchase cost determination

    If the retail price is €120 and the discount 25%, the purchase cost is,
    €120 × (1 − 25%) = €120 × 75% = €90.

    Since a 25% discount is the equivalent of a 33.33% mark-up, we also
    have, €120 / (1 + 33.33%) = €120/1.3333 = €90.

Source: Authors.

---

to as a 'mark-up' or as a 'discount'. The conversion rules are presented in Table 13.4.

Suppose a retailer purchases an item for £10 and sells it at a price of £20, that is, at a £10 margin. What is the retailer's margin percentage? As a percentage of the selling price, it is

£10/£20 × 100 = 50 per cent

As a percentage of cost, it is

£10/£10 × 100 = 100 per cent

Trade margins are usually determined on the basis of selling price, but practices do vary between firms and industries.

Trade margins are based on a distributor's place in the channel and represent payment for performing certain distribution tasks. In some cases, several margins are quoted to distributors, as illustrated in Table 13.5. The manufacturer's problem of suggesting a list price, that is the final suggested price of the product, is more complex, as the number of intermediaries between the producer and the final consumer increases.

13.7.2. List price versus invoice and pocket prices

Distribution margins are generally only a part of the total trade margin, and managers who oversee pricing often focus on prices of the invoices, which are readily available, but the real story goes much further. A distinction must be made among *list price, invoice price, pocket price and pocket margin.*

- The *list price* is the standard price published in the firm's tariff or price list.
- The *invoice price* is the list price after deduction of 'on-invoice' leakages that should be considered in

addition to the standard distributor discount, like special distributor discount, end-customer discount and on-invoice promotion.

■ The *pocket price* is the invoice price after deduction of *off-invoice leakages* like cash discount for prompt payment, the cost of carrying accounts receivables, co-operative advertising allowances, rebates based on distributor total annual volume, off-invoice promotional programmes and freight expenses.

In a case reported by McKinsey (Marn *et al.*, 2003), the *invoice price* and the *pocket price* were respectively at 67.2 per cent and 50.9 per cent of the list price, including a 16.3 per cent in revenue reductions that did not appear on invoices (Figure 13.5).

For companies offering customised products, unique solutions packages or unique forms of logistical or technical support, the cost of these services should be subtracted from the pocket price to identify the *pocket*

Table 13.5   Developing a price structure

■ Trade margins are based on a distributor's place in the channel and represent payment for performing certain distribution tasks.

■ Prices are usually quoted to distributors as a series of numbers depending on the number of functions performed.

■ In the case of large retail chains, we would have the following quotation:

'30, 10, 5, and 2/10, net 30'

The first three numbers represent successive discounts from the list price:

■ 30% as functional discount for the position the retailer occupies in the channel;

■ 10% as compensation for performing the storage function, usually performed by the wholesaler;

■ 5% as an allowance for the retailer's efforts to promote the product through local advertising;

■ 2/10: as cash discount, 2%, as reward for payment of an invoice within 10 days;

■ Net 30: the length of the credit period; if the payment is not made within 10 days, the entire invoice must be paid in full within 30 days.

Source: Adapted from Monroe (1979, p. 169).

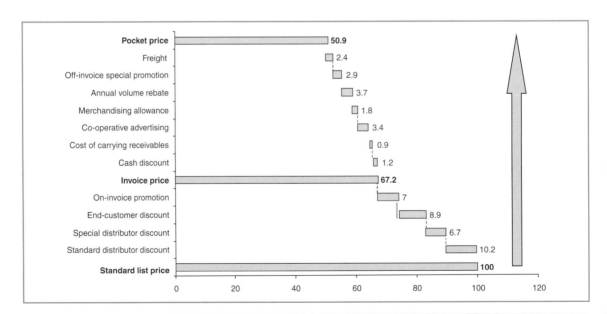

Figure 13.5   From list price to pocket price
Source: Marn *et al.* (2003).

Table 13.6 Distribution cost analysis of two distribution channels

| Distribution task | Indirect long channel | | Indirect short channel | |
	Cost	Comments	Cost	Comments
Transport		M → W: in charge of M – more expensive	—	M → warehouses: in charge of M – cheaper
		W → R: in charge of R – cheaper		Warehouses → R: in charge of R – more expensive
Assortment	Covered by the wholesaler margin 16% of the manufacturer's SR	In charge of W and R: better assortment	—	In charge of R: risk of incomplete assortment
Storage		Warehouses: in charge of W	€750,000	7 warehouse (fewer)
		Stocks: in charge of W	2.5% of SR	4 rotations/an (rate 10%)
		Clients: in charge of W	1.25% of SR	Payment at 45 day (rate 10%)
Contacts		In charge of W, risk of inertia	€500,000	25 sales people at €20,000. More dynamic (push strategy)
Information	2.5% of SR	Push strategy on W and R	1.5% of SR	Pull strategy
Sales administration	€30,000	Mainly in charge of W, small team	€200,000	Mainly in charge of M; large team
Total cost	€30,000 + 18.5% of SR	Cost proportional to the level of activity	€1,450,000 + 5.25% of SR	Largest part of cost is fixed

Note: M = manufacturer; R = retailer; W = wholesaler; SR = sales revenue.
Source: Authors.

margin, the true measure of the profitability. In another case also reported by McKinsey, the costs of customer-specific services averaged 17 per cent of the list price, leaving a pocket margin of 28 per cent, to be compared with the standard gross margin of 45 per cent.

13.7.3. Comparison of distribution costs

The distribution margin compensates the distribution functions and tasks assumed by the intermediaries in the channel. If some of these distribution tasks are assumed directly by the producer, it will have to support the organisation and the costs implied. By way of illustration, Table 13.6 shows a cost comparison of two indirect distribution channels: a 'long' indirect channel involving two intermediaries, wholesalers and retailers, and a 'short' indirect channel involving only retailers, the wholesaling function being assumed by the manufacturer.

In the *indirect long channel*, most of the physical distribution tasks (storage and transportation) are taken on by wholesalers and the distribution costs are largely proportional to the rate of activity and covered by the wholesalers' and distributors' margin. The manufacturer has to maintain a minimum sales administration unit and the overhead costs are minimised. In this type of conventional vertical marketing organisation, however, the producer is dependent on the goodwill of the distributors and has only limited control on the sales organisation. To offset this handicap, the producer can create its own sales force (merchandisers) to stimulate sales at the retailers' level and also to use mass media advertising to create brand awareness and brand preference among end-users through a 'pull communication' strategy.

Examining now the cost structure of the *indirect short channel*, one observes that overheads or fixed costs represent the largest share of total distribution costs. It means that the manufacturer has to support the costs of the physical distribution functions and organise a network of

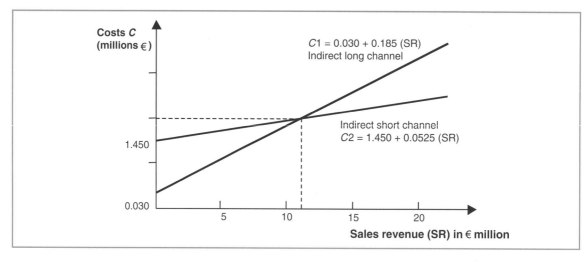

Figure 13.6   Comparing the cost structures of two distribution channels

Source: Authors.

warehouses plus a much more extensive sales administration unit. The financial costs involved in inventory management and the customers' accounts receivable are also completely assumed by the producer, as well as the selling function.

By adopting a selective distribution strategy, the firm has to contact 2,500 retailers at least once a month. One sales representative can perform on average 4.8 calls per day during 250 working days per year. The required sales force is therefore 25 sales representatives to achieve the market coverage objective.

Thus, adopting an indirect short distribution channel implies a major financial risk for the producer. The benefits of this strategy, however, are better control of the commercial organisation and a closer contact with the end-users. The two cost equations are compared in Figure 13.6.

In general, the sales revenue expectations are not the same for each distribution channel. The profitability rate of each channel will be determined as follows:

$$R = \frac{\text{Sales revenue} - \text{distribution costs}}{\text{distribution costs}},$$

where R is an estimate of the expected rate of return when all the costs are taken into account for each channel. This quantitative indicator must of course be interpreted with care and with due consideration of the more 'qualitative' factors discussed above.

CHAPTER SUMMARY

Distribution channels are organised structures performing the tasks necessary to facilitate exchange transactions. The functions of distribution channels are to create time, space and state utilities which constitute the added value of distribution. Distributors (wholesalers, retailers, agents, brokers) are required because manufacturers are unable to assume by themselves, at a reasonable cost, all the tasks implied by a free and competitive exchange process. Distribution channels can be characterised by the number of intermediary levels that separate the supplier from the end-user. The selection of a particular channel design is determined by factors related to market, buyer behaviour and company characteristics. When the channel structure is indirect, some degree of co-operation and co-ordination must be achieved among the participants in the vertical marketing system. Regarding the number of intermediaries necessary, three market coverage strategies are possible: intensive, selective or exclusive distribution. Exclusive distribution through franchising is a popular system present in almost all business fields. The distribution margins, or trade margins, compensate the distribution functions and tasks assumed by the intermediaries in the channel.

Review and Application Questions

1. You are responsible for the organisation of the distribution of a new chemical compound to be used for the maintenance of water in swimming pools. Suggest alternative distribution channels to be considered to reach the different potential customer groups and describe the functions to be performed by the producer and distributor(s) for each alternative.

2. 'Middlemen are parasites'. This charge has been made by many and in particular by Marxists. Referring to a market economy system, how would you react to this charge?

3. Godiva chocolates are sold exclusively through company-owned or franchised boutiques. The company wishes to maintain the positioning of Godiva chocolates as a luxury item. What changes in distribution strategy could be contemplated by management in order to increase Godiva's market share?

4. A supplier gives a 5 per cent promotional discount to a distributor who already receives a 7 per cent quantity discount. The list price is €4. Calculate the distributor's purchase price with the 7 per cent quantity discount and then with the 5 per cent promotional discount.

5. A distributor's purchase price before taxes is €120. For this product category, VAT is 20.5 per cent and the distribution margin before taxes is 30 per cent. What will the retail price of this product be?

Bibliography

Boyd, H.W. and Walker, O.C. Jr (1990), *Marketing Management: A Strategic Approach*, Homewood, IL, R.D. Irwin.

Business Week (1998), E-Shop Till You Drop, 9 February, pp. 14–15.

Castrillo, J., Martinez, J.M. and Messner, D. (2003), A Wholesale Shift in European Groceries, *The McKinsey Quarterly*, 1, pp. 67–77.

Cespedes, F.V. and Smith, H.F. (1993), Database Marketing: New Rules for Policy and Practice, *Sloan Management Review*, 34, 4, pp. 7–22.

Glémet, F. and Mira, R. (1993a) The Brand Leader's Dilemma, *The McKinsey Quarterly*, 2, pp. 3–15.

Glémet, F. and Mira, R. (1993b) Solving The Brand Dilemma, *The McKinsey Quarterly*, 4, pp. 87–98.

Jallat, F. and Capek, M.J. (2001), Disintermediation in Question: New Economy, New Networks, New Middlemen, *Business Horizons*, 44, 2, pp. 55–60.

Kotler, P. (1997/2005), *Marketing Management*, Englewood Cliifs, NJ, Prentice-Hall.

Kuttner, R. (1998), The Net: A Market Too Perfect for Profits, *Business Week*, 11 May, p. 13.

Libre Service Actualités (LSA) (1996), L'Europe des achats: le nouveau pactole, 29 February, pp. 26–30.

LSA (1998), Le hard discount en Pleine for me, 1571, 12 Février, pp. 28–31.

Marn, M.V., Roegner, E.V. and Zawada, C.C. (2003), The Power of Pricing, *The McKinsey Quarterly*, 1, pp. 27–39.

McGuire, E.P. (1971), *Franchised Distribution*, New York, The Conference Board, Report 523.

Monroe, K.B. (1979), *Pricing: Making Profitable Decisions*, New York, McGraw-Hill.

Nielsen (2006), L'univers alimentaire en Belgique, Belgium, A.C. Nielsen.

Palamountain, J.C. (1955), *The Politics of Distribution*, Cambridge, MA, Harvard University Press.

Quelch, J.A. and Takeuchi, H. (1981), Non-store Marketing: Fast Track or Slow?, *Harvard Business Review*, 59, 4, pp. 75–84.

Sallenave, J.P. (1979), *Expansion de votre commerce par le franchisage*, Montréal, Gouvernement du Québec, Ministère du Commerce et du Tourisme.

Sheth, J.N., Banwari, M. and Newman, B.I. (1999), *Customer Behavior and Beyond*, Fort Worth, Tx, The Dryden Press.

Vandaele, M. (1998), *Commerce et industrie: le nouveau partenariat*, Paris, Librairie Vuibert.

COMPANION WEBSITE FOR CHAPTER 13

Visit the *Market-driven Management* companion website at www.palgrave.com/business/lambin to find information on:

Direct Marketing
Entry Strategies in Foreign Markets

the battle of the brands in B2C markets 14

Chapter contents

Chapter learning objectives

When you have read this chapter, you should be able to understand

- the emerging power of distributors;
- the behaviour of the consumer as a smart shopper;
- the concept of s store as a multi-attribute concept;
- the branding strategies of the distributor in B2C markets;
- the alternative retail positioning to be adopted by retailers;
- the defensive options susceptible to be adopted by the brand manufacturer.

Chapter introduction

A significant change of the last 10 years, in Europe and in the United States as well, is the growing power of the retailers. From passive intermediaries in the channel, retailers are now active marketers developing new store concepts and own-label brands designed for well-targeted segments. They are now directly competing with manufacturers' brands; they have the power to dictate terms to their suppliers and to push their brands off the shelves if they are not leaders in their product category. In this chapter, after an overview of the changes in the retailing sector, we shall review the differentiation strategies susceptible to be adopted by retailers, and in particular, their private brand strategies. Taking then the point of view of manufacturers, we shall analyse the strategic options, defensive and offensive, susceptible to be adopted by brand manufacturers.

14.1. The changing retailing sector

In consumer markets, retailers are today irreplaceable actors actively and constructively participating in the globalisation process. In these markets, being consumer-driven is not enough. The firm must become *distributor-driven* to avoid the risk of being de-listed and should design retailer-driven *B2B* marketing programme based on in-depth understanding of their generic needs, such as a desired store image, efficient order fulfilment, protection from undue competition, etc.

14.1.1. The power of the retailers

Several factors (given below) explain this shift of power from manufacturers to retailers.

1. The high *concentration rate* of retailers, specifically in the fast moving consumer goods (FMCG) sector. In 12 European countries, the top three retailers account for 50 per cent of the market.
2. The adoption by retailers of sophisticated *store brand policies* targeted to segments often neglected by manufacturers (the low end of the market) and the growth of private labels, with market share as high as 42 per cent in Switzerland, 30 per cent in Great Britain and higher than 15 per cent in six other European countries.
3. Several retailers are adopting rapid internationalisation strategies, such as Wal-Mart in the United Kingdom, Carrefour in Latin America and Japan, Delhaize in Eastern Europe, United States and Asia, Ikea in the world and most recently in Russia and Malaysia, the Dutch Ahold, the German Aldi, the British Tesco, etc. (see Table 14.1).

4. The emergence of new breed of retailers, the *hard discounters*, who in warehouse stores, charge very low prices on their own private brands while excluding suppliers' brands from their shelves.

The result has been to deeply transform consumer markets and to modify the balance of power between manufacturers and retailers. Today powerful brands such as Coca-Cola and Nestlé need large retailers more than retailers need them, even if the development of e-commerce creates new opportunities for manufacturers who could strike back and bypass traditional intermediaries.

Vertical competition reduces the market power of large international brands, facilitates adaptation to local needs and stimulates price competition, as evidenced by the success of private labels.

Significant changes have occurred during the 1990s in the way retailers, and in particular large retailers, perceive their roles in the exchange process. Traditionally, retailers have limited their role to intermediaries, acting rather passively between the producer and the consumer by simply performing the physical tasks of distribution and by making the goods available to consumers in the condition, place and time required by them. From this rather passive role, intermediaries are increasingly adopting an innovative and active role, thereby modifying the balance of power between manufacturers and retailers.

This evolution has coincided with significant socio-cultural changes in affluent economies, which have induced retailers to redefine their roles as economic agents and to adopt a more market-driven perspective. From a traditional 'shop' or 'in-house' orientation, retailers are now discovering strategic marketing and are moving away from a business philosophy where the marketing function is confined to the physical distribution tasks and to the purchasing function.

Table 14.1   The top 15 global retailers in 2006

Rank	Country of origin	Company name	2003 retail sales (US$ million)	Number countries of operation
1	US	Wal-Mart	256,329	10
2	France	Carrefour	79,796	30
3	US	Home Depot	64,816	4
4	Germany	Metro	60,503	28
5	US	Kroger	53,791	1
6	UK	Tesco	51,535	12
7	US	Target	46,781	1
8	Netherlands	Ahold	44,584	21
9	US	Costco	41,693	8
10	Germany	Aldi Einkauf	40,060	12
11	Germany	Rewe	38,931	13
12	France	Intermarché	37,472	7
13	US	Sears	36,372	3
14	US	Safeway, Inc.	35,553	3
15	US	Albertsons	35,436	1

Source: Deloitte (2006).

14.1.2. Major changes in the retailing sector

The major changes of the macro-environment have been described in Chapter 2. In many West European countries, retailing has become a mature industry, and several indicators confirm this observation:

- Keeping pace with the growth of the economy, the retailing industry has experienced zero or minimal growth for several years, particularly in the food sector. The share of large retail chains has reached a plateau and is even declining in some markets.
- The proliferation of retailers has created over-capacity, and today a retailer must compete against a crowd of competitors, not only in the food sector, but also in sectors such as clothing, household appliances and even in the newest product categories such as home computers.
- Competition is intensive and based almost exclusively on price for all the branded products. In most product categories, consumers can buy exactly the same product or brand at a discount store at bargain prices as they could at a department store at its full price.
- In several European countries, a high level of concentration is observed among large distributors. Figure 14.1 displays the concentration ratios of the top three distributors in the food sector. These distributors have substantial purchasing power (and bargaining power), reinforced recently by the creation of joint purchasing units at the European level.

All these characteristics – maturity, over-capacity, concentration and price competition – which are typical of commodity markets suggest that the retailing industry has become *commoditised*. This conclusion must be qualified, however, by country and by product category. Several factors explain this evolution.

- During the 1960s, manufacturers' brand names became prominent in a broadening range of product categories, and more and more retailers began featuring these brands. Thus, the presence of the brand in the retailer's assortment became the determining choice criterion in choosing a particular store. In the process, retailers abdicated much of their stores' marketing and positioning responsibilities to the manufacturers.
- This situation has stimulated the development of discount stores, who sell well-known brands exclusively on bargain pricing with minimum services. In 2004, the discounters had a 16.6 per cent market share in Western Europe coming from 9.4 per cent in 1991 (A.C. Nielsen, 2006b) – see Figure 14.2.
- The proliferation of slightly differentiated brands and the adoption of intensive distribution strategies by manufacturers have also contributed to reducing store differentiation, most stores carrying the same assortments of brands.
- Retailers once had the major responsibility for after-sales service, and choosing a retailer was important when one bought products such as appliances and consumer electronics. Now consumers can get

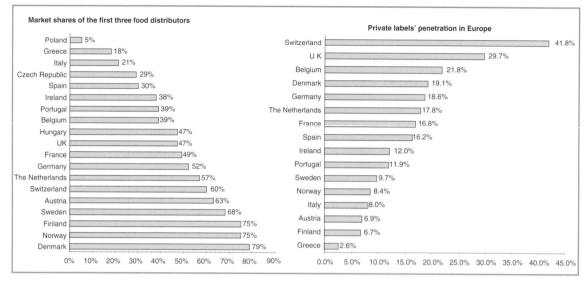

Figure 14.1   The growing power of large food distributors

Source: IHT, 23–24 August 2003, and Ernst and Young and A.C. Nielsen 1999, p. 32.

after-sales service for most products independently of the retailer, and this type of store differentiation is also waning.

- The lack of customer services at retail to improve productivity has generated an important self-production of services by consumers which contribute to increase in the 'total price' of mass distribution.
- Finally, the tremendous growth in bank credit cards also contributes to undermine store loyalty. Consumers no longer choose a store because they have established credit there: bankcards entitle customers to buy items almost anywhere they please.

These factors have all contributed to reducing store differentiation and loyalty, to killing the concept of shopping for enjoyment and to modifying consumer's buying behaviour, particularly for working housewives attracted by other more rewarding and stimulating activities.

14.1.3. Changes in consumers' retail buying behaviour

Retail consumers today behave differently, not only because of the social and demographic changes described above, but also because they are more educated and professional in their purchase decisions. As already discussed in Chapter 2, one of the biggest changes is the

rise of the *smart shopper*. Being a smart shopper implies several capabilities:

- Being informed about the products one wants to buy and being able to compare and choose independently of brand, advertising, store and salesperson's recommendations. It means finding the best value for money.
- Being able to separate the product features and the benefits and services provided by a store to augment the product value. Smart shoppers distinguish between what is inherent in the product and can therefore be obtained anywhere they buy it, and what a specific store adds to the purchase. They routinely compare stores as well as brands on this basis.
- Being able to recognise that brands have become increasingly similar. They will not necessarily choose a well-known brand over a less well-known one simply because it is familiar or because of its image. The product must also be viewed as offering superior value.
- In addition, for many consumers, and for a broadening range of goods, shopping is no longer viewed as fun or recreational, but rather as a tedious task to be performed as economically and efficiently as possible. In their search for value, an expanding group of consumers seek not only good merchandise but savings of time and effort as well.

According to A.C. Nielsen's latest Global Online Consumer Opinion Survey (A.C. Nielsen, 2006a), half of

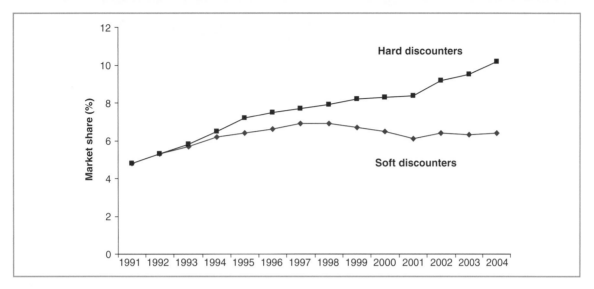

Figure 14.2   Evolution of discounters in Western Europe
Source: A.C. Nielsen (2006).

the world's online consumers agree that globalisation has improved their lives considerably, from gaining access to international news and entertainment, to enabling ownership of goods and services, the same as anywhere in the world, to breaking down cultural differences and creating more job opportunities.

14.2. Differentiation strategies of the retailer

Confronted with these changes, the retailer has to review his traditional strategic positioning by redefining his store concept and by adopting a positioning which provides unique value to consumers. The adoption of a store differentiation strategy becomes a necessity in a market place where retailing has become commoditised. Thus the concepts of strategic marketing developed for product marketing can be directly applied to retail marketing.

14.2.1. The multi-attribute concept of a store

From the consumer standpoint, the store concept can be viewed as a package of benefits, and the multi-attribute product concept described in Chapter 3 is useful here to help design the store concept. Six different characteristics

or attributes can be identified in a store, which constitute as many action variables for the retailer:

Location. This defines the territorial coverage or trading area within which to develop business relations. The alternatives are downtown location, community, suburban or regional shopping centres.

Assortment. The number of product lines that will be sold, which implies decisions on the product assortment breadth (narrow or wide) and product assortment depth (shallow or deep) for each product line.

Pricing. The general level of prices (high or low gross margins) and the use of loss-leaders, discount pricing and price promotions.

Services. The extent of the service mix. A distinction can be made between pre-purchase services (telephone orders, shopping hours, fitting rooms, and so on), post-purchase services (delivery, alterations, wrapping, and so on) and ancillary services (credit, restaurants, baby sitting, travel agencies, and so on). On this topic see de Maricourt (1988).

Time. The time required for a shopping trip. Proximity is the key factor, but also opening and closing hours, accessibility, ease of selection, fast completion of transaction and queuing time at checkout counters.

Atmosphere. The layout of the store, and also the light, the space the musical ambience, the look and the interior decoration, and so on.

These store attributes are used by consumers when they compare retail stores. It is up to the retailer to define a

EXHIBIT 14.1

THE TESCO MARKET SEGMENTATION STRATEGY

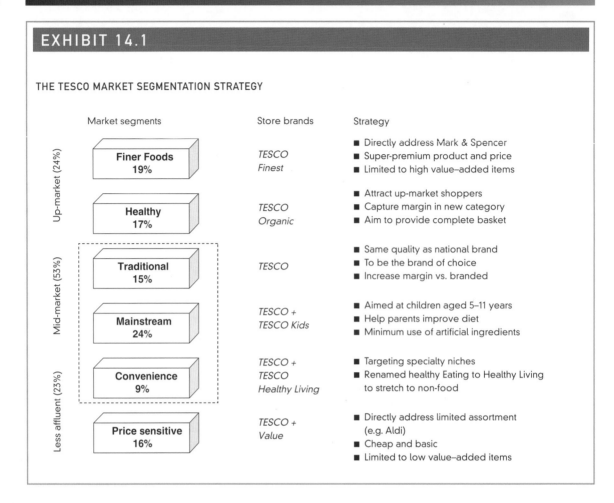

Market segments	Store brands	Strategy
Finer Foods 19% (Up-market 24%)	*TESCO Finest*	■ Directly address Mark & Spencer ■ Super-premium product and price ■ Limited to high value–added items
Healthy 17%	*TESCO Organic*	■ Attract up-market shoppers ■ Capture margin in new category ■ Aim to provide complete basket
Traditional 15% (Mid-market 53%)	*TESCO*	■ Same quality as national brand ■ To be the brand of choice ■ Increase margin vs. branded
Mainstream 24%	*TESCO + TESCO Kids*	■ Aimed at children aged 5–11 years ■ Help parents improve diet ■ Minimum use of artificial ingredients
Convenience 9% (Less affluent 23%)	*TESCO + TESCO Healthy Living*	■ Targeting specialty niches ■ Renamed healthy Eating to Healthy Living to stretch to non-food
Price sensitive 16%	*TESCO + Value*	■ Directly address limited assortment (e.g. Aldi) ■ Cheap and basic ■ Limited to low value–added items

store concept based on some innovative combination of these attributes, which constitutes a package of benefits differentiated from the competition. A good example of a store segmentation strategy is given by the British retailer Tesco as shown in Exhibit 14.1.

14.2.2. Alternative store positioning strategies

The positioning strategies to be adopted by the retailer vary with sectors. Retail outlets can be classified according to two dimensions: the level of the gross margin (high or low) and the type of benefit sought by the consumer, that is, symbolic or functional. We thus have a two-dimensional map as shown in Figure 14.3, which describes four distinct positioning strategies.

1. Among the functional products sold with a high gross margin (upper-left quadrant), we will have the *specialty stores* having selected or specialised assortments in food or in audio-visuals, computers, tools, and so on.

2. Among the functional products with low margins are the 'everyday' food products sold in supermarkets and superstores, low-price furniture (Ikea), do-it-yourself centres, cheap audio-visual goods, and so on.

3. The symbolic products with high margins are sold through prestige specialty stores, such as fashion stores (Benetton, Rodier), and also include jewellery, watches, and so on.

4. Symbolic products sold at low prices, these are distributed through discount stores selling national brands at prices lower than those prevailing in conventional stores.

Three basic store positioning strategies can be adopted by the retailer: product differentiation, service and personality augmentation, and price leadership.

1. A *product differentiation strategy* is based on offering products that are intrinsically different, for example, different brands or different styles from those in the same product category offered by other stores.

2. In a *service and personality augmentation strategy*, a retailer offers products that are intrinsically similar to those offered by competitors, but adds specific services and personality to differentiate the store.

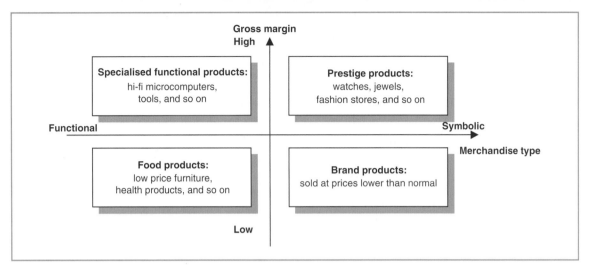

Figure 14.3   Retail positioning strategies
Source: Wortzel (1987).

3. A *price leadership strategy* means offering the same products as the competition at lower prices.

Several alternative positioning strategies can be contemplated by the retailer who has under his control several action variables. Thus, a strategic marketing plan can be elaborated and implemented through an action programme consistent with the chosen objectives to gain a sustainable competitive advantage over competition.

14.2.3. Private label development

Large retailers have successfully implemented differentiation strategies based on private brand development during the last decade. In Belgium, for instance, private labels' market shares increased from 11.4 per cent in 1983 to 19.8 per cent in 1992 (Nielsen, 1997). Private labels' market shares in other European countries are presented in Figure 14.1. This development coincides with the growth of the market power held by large retailers due to three groups of factors, namely

■ the creation of powerful purchasing centres at the European level, which has contributed to a substantial increase in the bargaining power of large retailers;

■ the development of centralised warehousing and delivery systems which has created a physical barrier between the supplier and the local supermarket;

■ The generalisation of electronic point of sales (EPOS), a computerised system for recording sales at retail checkouts which give the retailer instant information on each product sold at the retail outlet.

As the result of these technological changes, one observes a shift in the balance of power between suppliers and retailers.

This increased market power has induced retailers to develop their own branding policies in order to improve their profitability. This private label strategy goes back more than 20 years in Western Europe, but it has been gaining a new dimension recently. Several types of private labels exist in the European market:

Store brand names. The proposition here is to provide the same performance as national brands, but at more moderate prices. Typical examples are Delhaize, St Michael from Marks & Spencer, and Casino. The brand name is that of the chain and is used as a way of furthering the store's image.

Generic brands. The products are unsophisticated, presented in simple package at lowest prices and without brand name. Typically the white products from GB in Belgium.

Invented brand names. The retailer presents them as regular brands but they are distributed exclusively in the stores of the chain. Many retail chains sell invented brands such as Beaumont at Monoprix, O'Lacy at Asko and Saint Goustain and Chabrior at Intermarché.

First price. Their role is to stave off the invasion of the hard discounters, namely Aldi. The name of the store is not mentioned.

It is worth noting that the development of private labels (see Figure 14.1) has been stimulated by the growth of the 'first price' brands and by the dynamism of hard discounters such as Aldi and Lidl (Germany) and Kwik-Save (United Kingdom) which operate through warehouse retail stores.

This offensive of private labels has been fruitful and, as a consequence, loyalty towards national brands is decreasing and suppliers are forced to reduce their price differentials.

It seems, however, that, in France and in the United Kingdom, private labels are stagnating at the current level reached. In a survey carried out in France by *LSA* (May, 1997), only 24 per cent of the consumers interviewed were in favour of an extension of the range of private brands in their usual store and 70 per cent were opposed, a result similar to that observed in 1995.

14.2.4. Strategic objectives of distributors

Retailers' marketing strategies tend to become more sophisticated. They do not simply imitate existing products but develop new product concepts targeted at well-defined market segments which are then produced by international manufacturers specialising in private labels. For retailers, three objectives can be pursued with private labels, namely

- to reduce power of manufacturers by reducing their volume and their brand franchise and to eliminate small competitors;
- to enhance category margins since private labels can deliver 5–10 margin points more than national brands;
- to provide a differentiated product to build the retailer's image.

This last objective is now gaining in importance among the most sophisticated and dynamic retailers.

As illustrated by Figure 14.4, the distributor can adopt different price/quality positioning strategies:

Same quality, cheaper. It is the most frequent strategy adopted for store brands: to propose a level of quality similar to that offered by the leading national brand but at a price 15–20 per cent lower.

Lower quality, cheaper. This strategy is based on the invented brand names and on the generic brands: to propose a lower level of quality in simplified packages at a price 30–40 per cent lower than the prices charged by national brands.

Better quality, same price. To propose a level of quality higher than national brands at the same price. Sainsbury in the United Kingdom adopts this positioning strategy for a certain number of product categories, using invented brand names exclusively found in Sainsbury stores.

Better quality, higher price. A less frequent strategy, adopted by distributors targeting the high end of the market with homemade or handicraft products.

As a result of these aggressive price label strategies, there is general pressure on prices. Within large supermarket chains, three types of brands are observed within the same product category:

- *National brands* and preferably the brand leader in the product category (the A brands) which are supported by heavy advertising and promotional activities.
- *Own labels, store or umbrella brands* (the B brands) created by the retailer to improve profitability and to build the store image.
- *First prices* (the C brands) which are used as price-fighters to stop the hard-discounters by offering an alternative to customers.

In this competitive struggle, the weakest manufacturers' brands are the first to be eliminated from the supermarkets.

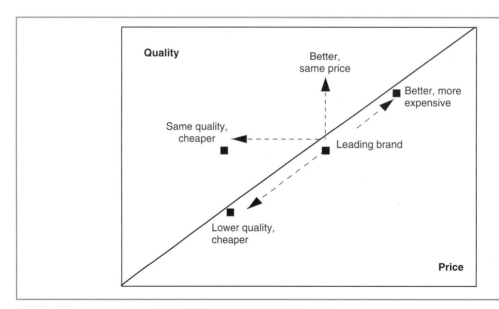

Figure 14.4 Price quality ratios for private labels
Source: Authors.

14.3. Strategic options for manufacturers' brands

As discussed in Chapter 1 (see Section 1.3.3), in the global economy, the balance of power evolves continuously between the two key market actors, manufacturers and distributors, changing the nature of their relationships, moving from a manufacturer-dominated business model (see Figure 1.6) to a retailer-dominated model (see Figure 1.7). In this new context, the brand manufacturer has to decide which defence strategy to adopt.

14.3.1. Four basic options

Confronted with the growing power of large supermarket retailers, what are the defence strategies for consumer brand manufacturers? Four basic strategic options exist:

Pull strategy. To promote an innovative (unique) product or well-differentiated brand through creative segmentation and media advertising targeted to the end-consumer, in order to induce the distributor to list the brand in his assortment.
Direct marketing. To bypass the retailers by adopting a non-store marketing strategy where purchases are made from the home and delivered to the home.
Subcontracting operational marketing. To concentrate on R&D and manufacturing and to leave the operational marketing function to a well-diversified group of retailers.

Trade marketing. To view distributors as intermediate customers and to design a retailer-driven marketing programme.

In what follows, we shall review the strategic options available to a national brand through a pull strategy and through trade marketing.

14.3.2. Alternative options in a pull strategy

From the manufacturer's point of view, the ideal situation is to have a well-differentiated brand, strongly supported by advertising and demanded by consumers. In this situation of manufacturer's domination, the distributor is captive and is forced to list the brand in his assortment. Such a situation is not likely to prevail indefinitely, however, and even big-name manufacturers can be threatened by private labels as illustrated by the success story of Classic Cola of Sainsbury against the mighty Coca-Cola.

> Classic Cola, a private label made by the Cott Corporation for J. Sainsbury in the United Kingdom, was launched at a price 28 per cent lower than Coca-Cola. Today the private label accounts for 65 per cent of total cola sales through Sainsbury and for 15 per cent of the UK cola market.

Once confronted with the private label challenge, how should national brands react? Hoch (1996) suggests four basic strategic moves that a national brand can make to improve its competitive position (see Figure 14.5). These

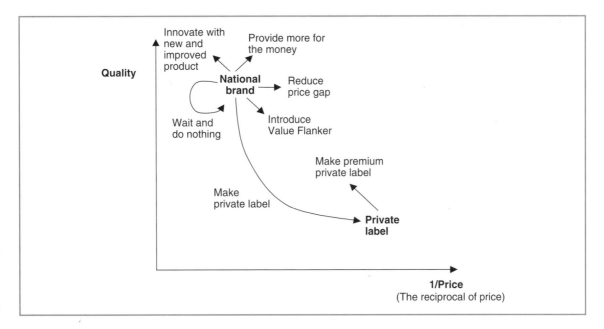

Figure 14.5 Strategic options for national brands
Source: Hoch (1996).

options are meant to be neither mutually exclusive nor exhaustive.

1. *Wait and do nothing.* In markets characterised by high volatility and fluctuation, it may be imprudent for a national manufacturer to react quickly and aggressively.

2. *Increase distance from private labels.* Distancing moves could be to 'provide more for money' or 'new and improved' products. It does necessarily imply line extensions, which too often tend to dilute rather than enhance the core brand.

3. *Reduce the price gap.* Empirical evidence shows that small price gaps increased unit sales of national brands relative to the private label. Because consumers appear more willing to trade up quality rather down, price changes by national brands affect private labels more than corresponding changes by private labels affect national brand sales.

4. *Formulate a 'me too' strategy.* Two options are possible here. To introduce a 'value flanker' by offering a lower-priced, possibly lower-quality item to crowd out the private label. The risk here is to cannibalise sales currently accruing to the premium national brand. In another strategy, the national brand can elect to manufacture private labels directly for the retailer.

Regarding this last strategy, Quelch and Harding (1996, p. 103) suggest that private label manufacturing opportunities often appear profitable to manufacturers, because they are evaluated on an incremental marginal cost basis. If private label manufacturing were evaluated on a full cost rather than on an incremental basis, it would, in many cases, appear much less profitable. Every company considering producing private label goods should answer three questions:

(a) What is the true contribution from private label products?
(b) What fixed costs are attributable to private label production?
(c) How much will the private label goods cannibalise the company's national brands?

14.3.3. Trade marketing

Trade marketing is simply the application of the marketing concept to distributors who are no longer viewed as 'intermediaries' in the channel but as partners or customers in their own right. The marketing process targeted to resellers or distributors can be subdivided into four phases:

■ Segmentation of the reseller population, or the identification of groups of distributors having the same expectations from suppliers.
■ Selection of one or several segment(s) to be targeted by priority.
■ Analysis of their needs, that is, understand factors that shape resellers decisions, their functioning mode, their objectives and expectations.
■ Design of an adapted marketing programme.

EXHIBIT 14.2

EDI AND EWR: TWO IMPORTANT TOOLS OF TRADE MARKETING

EDI: Electronic Data Interchange

This system of data interchange between suppliers and resellers is more and more popular in the United States and in Europe. Its principle is simple: to establish a direct connection which hooks together computers of the commercial partners via telephone lines to swap information. Once established, this connection facilitates and accelerates communication within the chain and generates substantial cost savings. One of the benefits of EDI is the time reduction for order taking. If order taking for 500 stores generally requires 12 hours, 10 minutes are sufficient with EDI. This operation is followed up by a control which takes 2 hours for validating the orders. EDI also contributes to the reduction of the execution costs of an order, from its initiation to its transmission: it is 3 FF with EDI against 17 FF with a magnetic support and 54 FF for a paper document. EDI creates a new management mode: the one of real-time commerce.

EWR: Efficient Warehouse Response

L'EWR can be defined as a logistic partnership proposing an exchange of information through EDI. This communication between manufacturers and resellers is mainly concerned by inventory flows with the objective to achieve productivity gains at each level of the logistic chain. These cost savings are then shared between the channel partners. The main benefits expected are

■ produce and sell as much as possible in real time;
■ reduce the number of stock outs;
■ gain a better understanding of stocks movements and of demand to reduce real inventory;
■ rationalise the flow of merchandise to make economies of scale.

The most important field of application of EWR is the optimisation of the flow of goods; the other domains are organisation of sales promotions and new products development.

Source: Adapted from Vandaele (1998, chapter 2).

Efficient order fulfilment is one domain of application of trade marketing where the benefits for the two parties are directly observable. In this partnership approach, the goal is to maximise the profits for the entire supply chain (Exhibit 14.2). This requires that, (a) the supplier is linked with store-shelf inventory data, which is updated as soon as customers buy products from the store, (b) production is based on real-time store sales forecast, (c) warehouse facilities are relocated closer to the stores by the supplier.

These actions together minimise the inventory costs throughout the system, and the supplier is able to pass on the savings to resellers, and through them, to consumers. Both consumers and resellers get better value in terms of lower prices and merchandise availability due to reduced stock outs.

In order to manage this business-to-business relationship with resellers, suppliers will have to develop an in-depth understanding of their logistic problems, their desired store image and the perceived importance of a particular product category for the chain store's positioning. The most fundamental change is the shift from an adversarial practice to one of partnership. A good understanding of the objectives and constraints of the intermediate customer is a prerequisite for the development of a successful relationship marketing strategy. To go further on the subject of trade marketing see Vandaele (1998), Corstjens and Corstjens (1996) and Buzzell and Ortmeyer (1995).

CHAPTER SUMMARY

Distributors are increasingly adopting an innovative and active role, thereby modifying the balance of power between manufacturers and retailers. Maturity, over-capacity, concentration and price competition are typical characteristics suggesting that the retailing industry has become *commoditised*. Retail consumers today behave differently, not only because of the social and demographic changes described above, but also because they are more educated and professional in their purchase decisions. From the consumer standpoint, the store concept can be viewed as a package of benefits and the multi-attribute product concept described in Chapter 3 is useful here to help design a store concept. Retail outlets can be classified according to two dimensions: the level of the gross margin (high or low) and the type of benefit sought by the consumer, that is, symbolic or functional. Retailers' marketing strategies tend to become more sophisticated. They do not simply imitate existing products but develop new product concepts targeted at well-defined market segments which are then produced by international manufacturers specialising in private labels. Four basic strategic options exist for the brand manufacturer: a pull strategy, direct marketing, subcontracting operational marketing and trade marketing.

Review and Application Questions

1. In view of the dynamism and of the growing power of mass merchandisers in the fast moving consumer goods (FMCG) sector, what type of defence or redeployment strategies can be adopted by brand manufacturers? Analyse the merits and the difficulties of each strategic option.
2. Describe the different types of store brands available in the FMCG markets.
3. What motivates FMCG distributors to launch their own store brands? What are the limitations of this strategy?
4. What are the differences between the retailer's brands and the hard discounter's brands?
5. Private brands are produced by manufacturers having themselves national brands sold by large retailers. What can motivate these manufactures to produce those private brands for large retailers and what are the risks?
6. Could you explain why store brands are less successful in the following product categories: razors, cereals, cosmetics and diapers?
7. How can you explain the price differentials as high as 30 per cent observed between a distributor's own brand and a manufacturer's brand of the same quality level?

Bibliography

A.C. Nielsen (1997), *L'univers alimentaire en Belgique*, Brussels, A.C. Nielsen Belgium.

A.C. Nielsen (2006a), *Consumer Insights into Globalisation. A.C. Nielsen Worldwide, August*.

A.C. Nielsen (2006b), *Univers alimentaire 2005*, Brussels, A.C. Nielsen.

Business Week (1998), E-Shop Till You Drop, 9 February, pp. 14–15.

Buzzell, R.D. and Ortmeyer, G. (1995), Channel Partnerships Streamline Distribution, *Sloan Management Review*, 36, 3, pp. 85–9.

Corstjens, J. and Corstjens, M. (1996), *Store Wars*, New York, John Wiley.

Deloitte (2006), *2005 Global Powers in Retailing*, Deloitte & Touche USA LLP.

de Maricourt, R. (1988), Vers une nouvelle révolution de la distribution: de l'hypermarché à l'hyperservice, *Revue Française du Marketing*, 118.

Glémet, F. and Mira, R. (1993a), The Brand Leader's Dilemma, *The McKinsey Quarterly*, 2, pp. 3–15.

Glémet, F. and Mira, R. (1993b), Solving the Brand Dilemma, *The McKinsey Quarterly*, 4, pp. 87–98.

Hoch, S.J. (1996), How Should National Brands Think about Private Labels? *Sloan Management Review*, 37, 2, pp. 89–102.

Hogarth-Scott, S. and Rice, S.P. (1994), The New Food Discounters: Are They a Threat to the Major Multiples? *International Journal of Retail & Distribution Management*, 22, 1, pp. 20–8.

Jallat, F. and Capek, M.J. (2001), Disintermediation in Question: New Economy, New Networks, New Middlemen, *Business Horizons*, 44, 2, pp. 55–60.

Kotler, P. (1997/2005), *Marketing Management*, Englewood Cliffs, NJ, Prentice-Hall.

Libre Service Actualités (*LSA*) (1996), L'Europe des achats: le nouveau pactole, 1481, 29, pp. 26–30.

LSA (1997), Marque de distributeurs: les clients les perçoivent mal, 1540, 22, pp. 30–4.

LSA (1998), Le hard discount en pleine forme, 1571, 12, pp. 28–31.

Quelch, J.A. and Harding, D. (1996), Brand versus Private Labels: Fighting to Win, *Harvard Business Review*, 74, 1, pp. 99–109.

Santi, M. (1997), Marques de distributeurs: six idées fausses, *L'Expansion Management Review*, March, pp. 64–78.

Vandaele, M. (1998), *Commerce et industrie: le nouveau partenariat*, Paris, Librairie Vuibert.

Wortzel, L.H. (1987), Retailing Strategies for Today's Mature Market-place, *Journal of Business Strategy*, 7, 4, pp. 45–56.

pricing decisions 15

Chapter contents

Chapter learning objectives

When you have read this chapter, you should be able to

- understand the buyer's perception of price and its significance for the firm;
- analyse the cost and profit implications of different pricing alternatives;
- list and explain the factors affecting the customer's price sensitivity;
- describe and compare different methods of pricing in a market-oriented perspective;
- discuss the impact of the competitive structure on the firm's pricing strategy;
- describe the way to approach the problem of setting the price for a set of related products;
- explain the pricing issues facing a firm operating in foreign markets.

Chapter introduction

Each product has a price, but each firm is not necessarily in a position to determine the price at which it sells its product. But when the firm has developed strategic marketing and thus has gained some degree of market power, setting the price is a key decision, which conditions the success of its strategy to a large extent. From the firm's point of view, the question of price has two aspects: the price is an instrument to stimulate demand, much like advertising, for example, and at the same time price is a determinant factor of the firm's long-term profitability. Therefore the choice of a pricing strategy must respect two types of coherence: an internal coherence that is setting a product price, respecting constraints of costs and profitability, and an external coherence that is setting the price level keeping in mind the market's purchasing power and the price of competing goods. After describing the strategic role of price in marketing, we will analyse pricing decisions that emphasise costs, competition and demand successively. Figure 15.1 describes the general problem of price setting in a competitive environment.

15.1. The customer's perception of price

Price is the monetary expression of value and as such occupies a central role in competitive exchange. From the customer's point of view, the price he or she is willing to pay measures the intensity of the need and the quantity and nature of satisfaction that is expected. From the seller's point of view, the price at which he or she is willing to sell measures the value of inputs incorporated in the product, to which the seller adds the profit that is hoped to be achieved. Purchasing behaviour can be seen as a system of exchange in which searching for satisfaction and monetary sacrifices compensate each other. See Figure 15.1.

15.1.1. Market definition of price

Formally, monetary price can be defined as a ratio indicating the amount of money necessary for acquiring a given quantity of a good or service:

$$\text{Price} = \frac{\text{Amount of money provided by the customer}}{\text{Quantity of goods provided by the seller}}$$

In fact, the notion of price is wider and goes beyond the simple coincidence of purely objective and quantitative factors. The amount of money paid incompletely measures the sacrifices made, and, in the same way, the quantity of good obtained measures actual satisfaction imperfectly.

The price as a measure of value

We saw in Chapter 4 that, as far as the customer is concerned, a product is a bundle of benefits and the services that are derived from the product are many, not only the product's core service, but also the other peripheral services – both objective and perceptual – that characterise the product or the brand. Therefore, the price must reflect the value of all such satisfactions to the buyer.

> Let us compare two watches having the same objective technical quality. Brand A is a prestigious one, with an elegant design, sold exclusively by watchmakers; it carries a five-year guarantee and is advertised using sport and theatre personalities. Brand B is little known, soberly designed, sold in department stores with a 6-month guarantee and advertised as being reliable. Although these two watches provide the same core or functional service (time measurement), we can see that they are two distinct products and their value as perceived by potential buyers will be very different.

Therefore, from the customer's point of view, price must be conceived as the compensation for all services rendered and set according to the total value or total utility perceived by the buyer. Hence the importance of a well-defined positioning before setting the selling price.

The total cost of acquiring a product

Just as the obtained quantity of goods measures actual satisfaction imperfectly, the amount of money paid measures the importance of actual sacrifice imperfectly. In fact, the price is the money received by the seller as the result of a transaction. It does not reflect all the costs supported by the customer. These costs borne by the customer not only covers the price paid, but also the terms of exchange, that is, all the concrete practical procedures that lead to transfer of ownership, such as conditions of

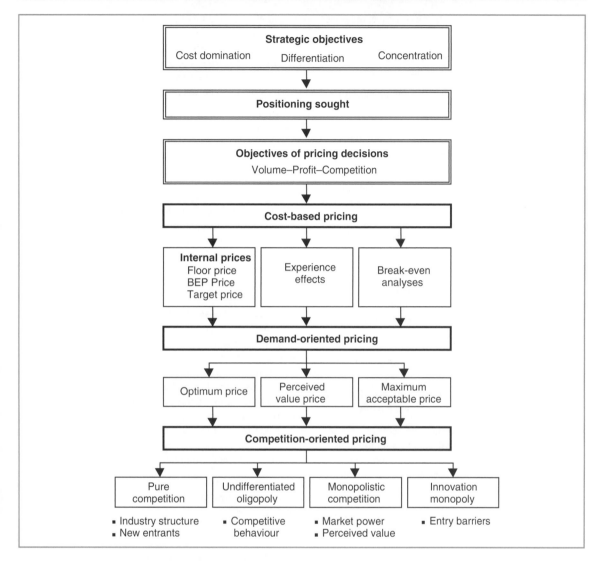

Figure 15.1   An overview of pricing decisions

Source: Authors.

payment, delivery terms and times, after-sales service, and so on. In some cases, the buyer may have to bear important costs to compare prices, transact and negotiate. This can happen if, for example, the buyer is located in isolated regions. Similarly, the customer may face high transfer costs, if he or she changes suppliers after having set the product specifications in relation to a given supplier. The main sources of transfer costs are as follows:

- Costs of modifying products so as to fit a new supplier's product.
- Changes in habits of consuming or using the product.
- Expenditures on training and reorientation of users.

- Investments to acquire new equipment necessary for the use of the new products.
- Psychological costs related to change.

All these costs may be higher for some clients than others. When transfer costs exist, the real cost to the buyer is much higher than the product's monetary price.

Therefore, from the customer's point of view, the notion of price goes well beyond that of monetary price. It involves *all the benefits provided by the product and all the monetary and non-monetary costs borne by the customer*. Hence, measures of price sensitivity must take into account all these benefits and costs as well as the product's nominal price. Viewed from the customer's perspective, the price can be redefined as follows:

$$\text{Price} = \frac{\text{Total cost (monetary and non-monetary)}}{\text{Total benefits (tangible and intangible)}} .$$

$$\text{Price} = \frac{\text{supported by the customer}}{\text{provided by the product}} .$$

To illustrate the complexity of price viewed in the customer perspective, one can identify eight different ways of changing the above price ratio (Monroe, 1979):

- Change the quantity of money given up by the buyer.
- Change the quantity of goods and services provided by the seller.
- Change the quality of goods or services provided.
- Change the premiums or discounts to be applied for quantity variations.
- Change the time and place of transfer of ownership.
- Change the place and time of payment.
- Change the acceptable forms of payment.
- Change the name or the brand of the product.

15.1.2. Importance of pricing decisions

The following points highlight the importance of pricing strategies in the current macro-marketing environment:

- The chosen price directly influences demand level and determines the level of activity. A price set too high or too low can endanger the product's development. Therefore, measuring price sensitivity is of crucial importance.
- The selling price directly determines the profitability of the operation, not only by the profit margin allowed, but also through quantities sold by fixing the conditions under which fixed costs can be recovered over the appropriate time horizon. Thus, a small price difference may have a major impact on profitability.
- The price set by the firm influences the product or the brand's general perception and contributes to the brand's positioning within potential buyers' evoked set. Customers perceive the price as a signal, especially in consumer goods markets. The price quoted invariably creates a notion of quality, and therefore is a component of the brand image.
- More than any other marketing variable, the price is a direct means for comparison between competing products or brands. The slightest change in price is quickly perceived by the market, and because of its visibility it can suddenly overturn the balance of forces. The price is a forced point of contact between competitors.
- Pricing strategy must be compatible with the other components of operational marketing. The price must

allow for financing of promotional and advertising strategy. Product packaging must reinforce high quality and high price positioning; pricing strategy must respect distribution strategy and allow the granting of necessary distribution margins to ensure that the market coverage objectives can be achieved.

Recent developments in the economic and competitive environment, which were discussed in Chapter 2, have played their part in increasing the importance and complexity of pricing strategies significantly:

- Acceleration of technological progress and shortening of product life cycles means that a new activity must be made to pay over a much shorter time span than previously. Given that correction is so much more difficult, a mistake in setting the initial price is that much more serious.
- Proliferation of brands or products that are weakly differentiated, the regular appearance of new products and the range of products all reinforce the importance of correct price positioning; yet small differences can sometimes modify the market's perception of a brand quite significantly.
- Legal constraints, as well as regulatory and social constraints, such as price controls, setting maximum margins, authorisation for price increases, and so on, limit the firm's autonomy in determining prices.
- Reduced purchasing power in most Western economies makes buyers more aware of price differences, and this increased price sensitivity reinforces the role of price as an instrument of stimulating sales and market share.

Given the importance and complexity of these decisions, pricing strategies are often elaborated by the firm's general management.

15.1.3. Alternative pricing objectives

All firms aim to make their activities profitable and to generate the greatest possible economic surplus. This broad objective can in practice take different forms and it is in the firm's interest to clarify from the outset its strategic priorities in setting prices. Generally speaking, possible objectives can be classified in three categories, according to whether they are centred on profits, volumes or competition.

Profit-oriented objectives

Profit-oriented objectives are either profit maximisation or achievement of a sufficient return on invested capital. Profit maximisation is the model put forward by economists. In practice, it is difficult to apply this model. Not only does it assume precise knowledge of cost and demand functions for each product; it also assumes a stability that is seldom enjoyed by environmental and competitive factors. The objective of target return rate on investment (ROI) is widespread. In practice it takes the form of calculating a target price, or a sufficient price; that is, a price, which, for a given level of activity, ensures a fair return on invested capital. This approach, often adopted by large enterprises, has the merit of simplicity, but is incorrect, because it ignores the fact that it is the price level that ultimately determines the demand level.

Volume-oriented objectives

Volume-oriented objectives aim to maximise current revenue or market share, or simply to ensure sufficient sales growth. Maximising market share implies adopting a penetration price that is a relatively low price, which is lower than competitors' prices, in order to increase volume and consequently market share as fast as possible. Once a dominant position is reached, the objective changes to one of sufficient or 'satisfactory' rate of return. As we saw in Chapter 8, this is a strategy often used by firms having accumulated a high production volume and who expect reduced costs due to learning effects. A totally different strategy is that of skimming pricing. The goal here is to achieve high sales revenue, given that some buyers or market segments are prepared to pay a high price because of the product's distinctive (real or perceived) qualities. The objective here is to achieve the highest possible turnover with a high price rather than high volume.

Competition-oriented objectives

Competition-oriented objectives either aim for price stability or to be in line with competitors. In a number of industries dominated by a leading firm, the objective is to establish a stable relationship between prices of various competing products and to avoid wide fluctuations in prices that would undermine customers' confidence. The objective of keeping in line with other firms reveals that the firm is aware of its inability to exercise any influence on the market, especially when there is one dominant firm and products are standardised, as in undifferentiated oligopolies. In this case, the firm prefers to concentrate its efforts on competing on features other than price. Forms of non-price competition will often prevail in this type of market.

To elaborate a pricing strategy, three groups of factors must be taken into consideration: costs, demand and competition. We will now examine successively each of these factors and their implications for price determination.

15.2. Cost-based pricing procedures

Starting with cost analysis is certainly the most natural way to approach the pricing problem, and it is also the one most familiar to firms. Given that the manufacturer has undergone costs in order to produce and commercialise a product, it is natural that its main preoccupation would be to determine various price levels compatible with constraints such as covering direct and fixed costs and generating a fair profit. Figure 15.2 shows a typical cost

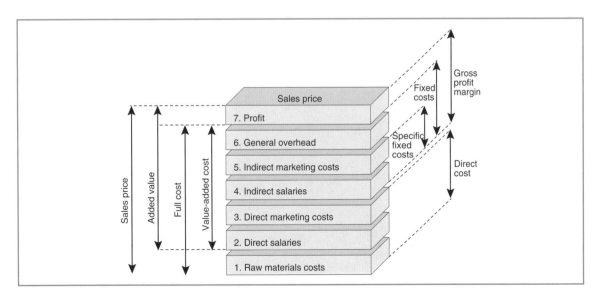

Figure 15.2 The elements of price

Source: Monroe (1979).

structure in which the definitions of the main cost concepts are given.

15.2.1. Cost-based price concepts

Prices, which are based on costs and make no explicit reference to market factors, are called cost-based prices. Cost analysis identifies four types of cost-based prices, each responding to specific cost and profit requirements.

The 'floor price'

The floor price, or the minimum price, corresponds to direct variable costs (C), also known as 'out-of-pocket costs'. It is the price that only covers the product's replacement value, and therefore implies zero gross profit margins.

$$\text{Floor price} = \text{Direct variable cost.}$$

This price concept is useful for negotiating exceptional orders or for second market discounting, when the firm has unused capacity and has the possibility to sell in a new market such

that there will be a negligible loss of sales in its main market. Floor prices, also called marginal price, are the absolute minimum selling price the firm should accept. Any price above the floor price can allow a firm to use its production capacity to a maximum and still generate extra funds to cover overheads or improve profits. Exceptional orders, generics for large retail chain and foreign markets, provide opportunities for this form of discriminatory pricing strategy.

The 'break-even price'

The break-even price (BEP) corresponds to the price where fixed and direct costs are recovered, given the sales volume assumed. It ensures that both the product's replacement value as well as fixed costs (F) are recovered.

$$\text{BEP} = C + F / E(Q),$$

where $E(Q)$ denotes expected sales volume. The BEP corresponds to the full cost concept, where the level of activity is used as a criterion for allocating the fixed costs.

Break-even prices are usually calculated for different volume levels, as shown in the example of Exhibit 15.1.

EXHIBIT 15.1

EXAMPLE OF COST-BASED PRICE DETERMINATION

Basic data
  Production capacity: 180,000 units.
  Capital invested (K): €24,000,000.
  Expected rate of return (r): 10 per cent.
  Direct cost (C): €105/unit.
  Fixed cost (F): €9,000,000/year.
  Expected sales = $E(Q) = Q_2$ = 120,000 units.
  Pessimistic estimate = Q_1 = 90,000 units.
  Optimistic estimate = Q_3 = 150,000 units.

Floor Prix (P_L):

$$P_L = C = €105/\text{unit.}$$

Break-even price (P_t):

$$P = C + \frac{F}{E(Q)} = 105 + \frac{9,000,000}{E(Q)},$$

$$P_{t_1} = €205 \qquad P_{t_2} = €180 \qquad P_{t_3} = €165.$$

Target price (P_c):

$$P = C + \frac{F}{E(Q)} + \frac{r \cdot K}{E(Q)},$$

$$P = 105 + \frac{9,000,000}{E(Q)} + \frac{(0.10) \times (24,000,000)}{E(Q)},$$

$$P_{c_1} = €231.7 \qquad P_{c_2} = €200 \qquad P_{c_3} = €181.$$

Contemplated sale price (P_V):

$$P_V = €195/\text{unit.}$$

Break-even volume:

$$Q_n = \frac{F}{P - C} = \frac{9,000,000}{195 - 105} = 100,000 \text{ units.}$$

Break-even in sales revenue:

$$SR_n = \frac{F}{(P - C)/P} = \frac{9,000,000}{0.46} = €19,565,217.$$

Source: Authors.

This defines a range of minimum prices. Note that the BEP depends on the volume of activity and only coincides with the full cost at that level.

The 'target price'

The target price, or sufficient price, includes, apart from direct and fixed costs, a profit constraint, which is normally determined by reference to a 'normal' rate of return (r) on invested capital (K). This cost-based price is also calculated with reference to an assumed level of activity.

$$\text{Target price} = C + \frac{F}{E(Q)} + \frac{r \cdot K}{E(Q)}$$

where K denotes invested capital and r the rate of return considered as sufficient or normal. Like the BEP, target price depends on the activity volume being considered.

The 'mark-up price'

The mark-up price is set by adding a standard mark-up to the BEP. Assuming that the firm wants to earn a 20 per cent mark-up on sales, the mark-up price is given by,

$$\text{Target price} = \frac{\text{Break-even price}}{(1 - \text{desired margin})}$$

This pricing method, popular for its simplicity, ignores demand and competition. It will work only if the expected sales level is achieved.

15.2.2. The risk of circular logic

Target and mark-up prices are used widely, because of their simplicity and the apparent security arising from the illusory certainty of a margin, since mark-up and target pricing procedures promise to ensure a given return on cost. Their most important shortcoming is the lack of any relationship between price and volume. In fact, they implicitly contain a built-in circular logic: volume determines costs, which determine price, which in turn determines the level of demand.

Indeed, there is no guarantee that the adopted target price or mark-up will generate the activity volume on the basis of which it was calculated. Exhibit 15.1 shows what happens to the target price if the firm's sales volume is below the assumed level.

> In the example, of Exhibit 15.1, the expected activity level is 120,000 units and the corresponding target price is £2,000. If demand is only 90,000 units, to maintain the desired profitability level the price would have to be increased and the product sold at £2,317.

Is raising price the appropriate response in the face of declining demand? Similarly, if the firm's sales exceed expectations, fixed costs are spread over a larger volume and the target price declines. Should management respond to excess demand by cutting prices?

This pricing behaviour runs counter to economic logic and leads to inappropriate recommendations. The firm that sets price from the sole perspective of its own internal needs generally forgoes the profit it seeks. If all firms within a given industry adopt the same mark-up or target rate of return, prices tend to be similar and price competition is minimised.

BOX 15.1

IMPLEMENTATION PROBLEM: HOW MUCH POCKET MONEY ARE WE MAKING ON THIS PRODUCT?

As already discussed in Section 13.7.2, managers who oversee pricing often focus on invoices' prices, which are readily available, but the real story goes much further. A distinction must be made among *list price, invoice price, pocket price and pocket margin*.

From the standard list price, there are several 'on-invoice' and 'off-invoice' leakages that should be considered. In a case reported by McKinsey (Marn *et al.*, 2003), the *on-invoice leakages* included standard distributor discount, special distributor discount, end-customer discount and on-invoice promotion. *Off-invoice leakages* included cash discount for prompt payment, the cost of carrying accounts receivables, cooperative advertising allowances, rebates based on distributor total annual volume, off-invoice promotional programmes and freight expenses. In the end, the *invoice price* and the *pocket price*

were respectively at 67.2 and 50.9 per cent of the list price, including a 16.3 per cent in revenue reductions that did not appear on invoices.

For companies offering customised products, unique solutions packages or unique forms of logistical or technical support, the cost of these services should be subtracted from the pocket price to identify the *pocket margin*, the true measure of the profitability. In another case also reported by McKinsey, the costs of customer-specific services averaged 17 per cent of the list price, leaving a pocket margin of 28 per cent, to be compared with the standard gross margin of 45 per cent.

Source: Marn *et al.* (2003).

In practice, cost-based prices are used only as a convenient starting point, because, in general, firms have more reliable information about costs than about demand factors. The concept of pocket price is defined in Box 15.1.

15.2.3. Usefulness of cost-based pricing

Cost-orientated prices constitute a starting point for setting a market price. They cannot be the only basis for determining prices because these pricing procedures ignore demand, product perceived value and competition. However, they do have a real usefulness, because they provide answers to the following types of questions:

- What are the sales volume or sales revenue required to cover all costs?
- How does the target price or the mark-up price compare with prices of direct competition?
- To what level of market share does the level of sales at the break-even point correspond?
- What is the expected sales increase required to cover a fixed cost increase, such as an advertising campaign, assuming constant price?
- If prices go down, what is the minimum volume increase required to offset the price decrease?
- If prices go up, what is the permissible volume decrease to offset the price increase?
- What is the implied price elasticity necessary to enhance or maintain profitability?
- What is the rate of return on invested capital for different price levels?

Cost analysis is the first necessary step, which helps to identify the problem by focusing attention on the financial implications of various pricing strategies. Armed with this information, the firm is better placed to approach the more qualitative aspects of the problem, namely market sensitivity to prices and competitive reactions.

Initiating price cuts

Initiating a price cut with a view to stimulate demand is relevant only when total demand for the product can grow. Otherwise, if the firm reduces its price and if all the competitors react immediately and follow suit, the profits of each will drop and their respective market shares will remain exactly as before in a market that remains the same size, although average price has decreased. There are, however, some situations, which might be favourable to a price cut in a non-expansible market, without entailing rapid reactions from competitors:

- When competitors' costs are higher and they cannot lower their prices without endangering profitability; not following the price cut implies a loss of market share unless factors of differentiation neutralise the price difference.

- Smaller firms can use a price cut more easily. This represents a lighter investment for them as opposed to larger enterprises, which hold a higher market share, because the cost of promoting a product via price is proportional to sales volume. Larger competitors may indeed prefer to maintain their prices and react on a different front, for example by increasing advertising, which represents a fixed cost.

A firm may therefore choose not to follow a price cut, particularly when its product's perceived value is above that of its immediate competitors. It will then be protected from the effects of a price cut by differentiation factors, such as brand image, range of services or customer relations. Changing suppliers implies transfer costs, which are not always compensated by the price difference. In industrial markets, for example, it is frequently observed that customers accept price differentials of up to 10 per cent without much difficulty if relationships with the usual supplier are well established.

Determining the cost of a price cut

It is important to realise that the cost of a price cut is often very high, especially for a firm with a high proportion of variable costs. The data in Table 15.1 define the necessary increases in sales revenue and in volume required to retain the same gross margin (25 per cent in this case) at different levels of price cut.

In this particular case, where the gross margin of 25 per cent is to be held before the price cut, the number of units sold must more than double to compensate for a price cut of 15 per cent. One can imagine that the necessary increase in sales can rapidly be above the impact that can reasonably be expected from a price cut.

Furthermore, it can be shown that a price cut is less favourable to a firm with high variable costs, because the necessary increase in sales to keep the same margin will be higher, the higher the proportion of variable costs (Monroe, 1979, p. 73). In general, for a price decrease, the necessary volume increase to maintain the same level of profitability is given by

$$\text{Volume increase } (\%) \ = \left(\frac{x}{M^* - x}\right) \times 100$$

where x is the percentage price decrease expressed as a decimal and M^* is the gross profit margin as a percentage of selling price before the price cut.

To illustrate, if a price cut of 9 per cent is envisaged and the gross profit margin is 30 per cent, the required sales volume increase is

$$\text{Volume increase } (\%) \ = \left(\frac{0.09}{0.30 - 0.09}\right) \times 100$$

$$= 42.86 \text{ per cent}$$

> **Table 15.1**   Minimum volume and sales revenue increase required for offsetting a price decrease
>
> | Price decrease (%) | Percentage of minimum sales revenue increase required | Percentage of minimum volume increase required |
> | --- | --- | --- |
> | 5 | 18 | 25 |
> | 10 | 50 | 66 |
> | 15 | 112 | 150 |
> | 20 | 300 | 400 |
>
> *Note*: Assuming a gross profit margin of 25 per cent.
>
> *Source*: Monroe (1979, pp. 70–3).

If the gross profit margin were to decrease to 25 per cent or 20 per cent the same price cut of 9 per cent would require sales increases of 56.25 per cent and 81.82 per cent, respectively. For the derivation of the break-even formula, see Nagle (1987/1994, pp. 44–6). Therefore, the firm having the lowest variable costs will be induced to initiate a significant price cut, in the knowledge that other firms could not follow suit.

Computing implied price elasticity

It is also possible to derive implied price elasticity from these figures. This is the price elasticity that should prevail within the targeted group of buyers before profits could be increased.

In the previous example, the price cut of 9 per cent ought to give rise to a 42.86 per cent increase in sales volume in order to retain the gross profit margin at 30 per cent. Therefore, the implied price elasticity is

$$\varepsilon = \frac{+42.86\%}{-9\%} = -4.76$$

A price elasticity of −4.8 per cent is very high and assumes a very price sensitive demand. If it is considered that the product market's demand is less elastic, and if profit is the only choice criterion, then the price cut is not economically justified.

The risk of a price war is always present in an oligopolistic market, which explains why firms are reluctant to initiate price cuts. There are, however, situations where a price cut can improve the competitive position of the firm. As discussed in Chapter 8, reducing the profit margin with price cuts may be compensated for by market share gains, which in the long run mean higher profitability because of cost reductions due to experience effects. Another reason for a price war might be to eliminate a potentially dangerous competitor.

Experience curve pricing

As discussed in Chapter 9, in sectors where the cost of value added represents a large proportion of total unit cost,

substantial cost reductions can be obtained as accumulated production increases. If consumers in this market are price sensitive, a good strategy for the firm having the largest experience is to price aggressively, even below current cost, as illustrated in Figure 15.3(a). This strategy presents several advantages. First, competing firms will have to leave the market and the leading company will be confronted with fewer rivals. Second, the firm can benefit from the sales of the other firms and gain experience more rapidly. Also, because of the lower prevailing market price, new buyers will be encouraged to enter the market.

However, pricing below cost cannot be maintained for extended periods of time. A less aggressive pricing strategy is the one depicted in Figure 15.3(b) where a parallel is maintained between cost and price reductions.

Initiating price increases

Initiating a price increase is also a difficult decision. The firm initiating the increase must be certain that competitors are willing to follow suit. Generally speaking, this willingness depends on the prevailing market conditions at the time, and in particular when production capacity is fully used and demand is growing. As in the case of a price cut, before starting any initiative, it is in the firm's interest to evaluate its margin for manoeuvre.

If price is increased, the permissible volume decrease (i.e. leaving the previous level of profit unchanged) is determined as follows:

$$\text{Permissible volume decrease } (\%) = \left(\frac{x}{M^* + x}\right) \times 100$$

where x is the percentage price increase expressed as a decimal. If a 9 per cent price increase is contemplated and if the gross profit margin is 30 per cent, the percentage sales volume decrease is

$$\text{Volume decrease } (\%) = \left(\frac{0.09}{0.30 + 0.09}\right) \times 100$$

$$= 23.08 \text{ per cent,}$$

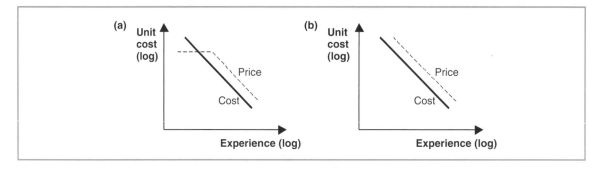

Figure 15.3   Experience curve pricing strategies – (a) an aggressive and (b) a less aggressive pricing strategy
Source: Authors.

and the implied price elasticity is −2.56. For the price increase to enhance profit, market demand must have a price elasticity below the implied price elasticity of −2.6.

15.3. Demand-oriented pricing procedures

Pricing based exclusively on the firm's own financial needs is inappropriate. In a market economy, it is the buyer who ultimately decides which products will sell. Consequently, in a market-driven organisation an effective pricing procedure starts with the price the market is most likely to accept, which in turn determines the target cost. As illustrated in Figure 15.4, it is the market acceptable price that constitutes the constraint for R&D, engineering and purchasing. Thus, price determination in a demand-oriented procedure puts customer sensitivity as the starting point.

15.3.1. The price elasticity concept

An important concept in demand analysis is the notion of elasticity. Elasticity directly measures customers' price sensitivity and ideally allows the calculation of quantities demanded at various price levels. Recall the definition of price elasticity: it is the percentage change in a product's unit sales resulting from a 1 per cent change in its price.

$$\varepsilon = \frac{\% \text{ of variation of unit sales}}{\% \text{ of variation of price}}$$

Price elasticity is negative, since a price increase generally produces a decline in sales while a price cut generally produces an increase in sales. As an illustration, Table 15.2 compares the impact of price elasticity on quantities and on sales revenue for an elastic (−3.7) and an inelastic (−0.19) demand.

We first examine the main factors affecting price sensitivity, and then describe various approaches that can be adopted to measure it.

Factors affecting price sensitivity

Every buyer is sensitive to prices, but this sensitivity can vary tremendously from one situation to another, according to the importance of the satisfaction provided by the product, or conversely depending on the sacrifices, other than price, imposed by obtaining the product. Nagle and Holden (1994) have identified nine factors affecting buyers' price sensitivity:

1. *Unique-value effect*: buyers are less price sensitive when the product is unique.
2. *Substitute awareness effect*: buyers are less price sensitive when they are less aware of substitutes.
3. *Difficult comparison effect*: buyers are less price sensitive when they cannot easily compare the quality of substitutes.
4. *Total expenditure effect*: buyers are less price sensitive the lower the expenditure is to a ratio of their income.
5. *End benefit effect*: buyers are less price sensitive the lower the expenditure is compared with the total cost of the end product.
6. *Shared cost effect*: buyers are less price sensitive when part of the cost is borne by another party.
7. *Sunk investment effect*: buyers are less price sensitive when the product is used in conjunction with assets previously bought.
8. *Price-quality effect*: buyers are less price sensitive when the product is assumed to have more quality, prestige or exclusiveness.
9. *Inventory effect*: buyers are less price sensitive when they cannot store the product.

The questions to examine for assessing customers' price sensitivity are presented in Box 15.2.

Note that these determinants of price sensitivity apply equally to the decision of buying a particular product category (primary demand price sensitivity) and that of buying a particular brand within a product category (interbrand price sensitivity). In the first case, the question

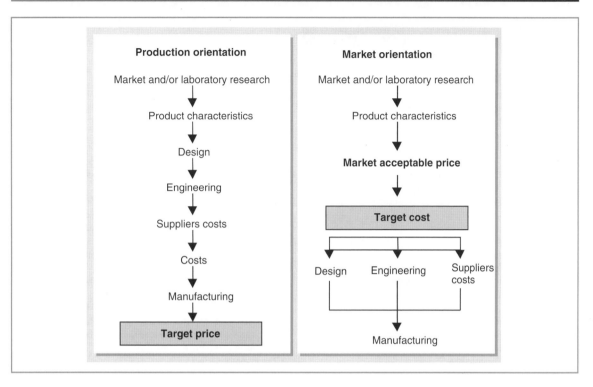

Figure 15.4   Price determination in a market-oriented perspective
Source: Authors.

Table 15.2 Impact of price elasticity on quantity and on sales revenue					
Elastic demand curve: $\varepsilon = -3.7$			Inelastic demand curve: $\varepsilon = -0.19$		
Price	Quantity (in 000)	Sales revenue (in 000 €)	Price	Quantity (in 000)	Sales revenue (in 000 €)
12,000	80	960	8.00	300	2,400
9,000	400	3,600	6.00	320	1,920
7,000	1,200	8,400	4.00	340	1,360

Source: Authors.

would, for example, be to choose between a laptop computer and a hi-fi; in the second case, the alternatives would be, for example, to buy an Asus or an HP laptop computer. The price level of the alternatives affects both kinds of decision.

Price sensitivity of the B2B customer

We saw in Chapter 3 that in B2B markets, customers' needs are generally well defined and the functions performed by products clearly specified. In these conditions, it is sometimes easier to determine the importance of price to the B2B customer. Porter (1980, pp. 115–18) observed that customers who are not price sensitive tend to have the following behavioural characteristics or motivations:

- The cost of the product is a small part of the customer's product cost and/or purchasing budget.
- The penalty for product failure is high relative to its cost.
- Effectiveness of the product (or service) can yield major savings or improvement in performance.
- The customer competes with a high quality strategy to which the purchased product is perceived to contribute.

BOX 15.2

IMPLEMENTATION PROBLEM: HOW TO IDENTIFY FACTORS AFFECTING PRICE SENSITIVITY?

1. The unique value effect
   - Does the product have any (tangible or intangible) attributes that differentiate it from competing products?
   - How much do buyers value those unique, differentiating attributes?
2. The substitute awareness effect
   - What alternatives do buyers have (considering both competing brands and competing products)?
   - Are buyers aware of alternative suppliers or substitute products?
3. The difficult comparison effect
   - How difficult is it for buyers to compare the offers of different suppliers? Can the attributes of a product be determined by observation, or must the product be purchased and consumed to learn what it offers?
   - Is the product highly complex, requiring costly specialist to evaluate its differentiating attributes?
   - Are the prices of different suppliers easily comparable, or are they stated for different sizes and combinations that make comparisons difficult?
4. The total expenditure effect
   - How significant are buyers' expenditures of the product in cash terms and (for a consumer product) as a portion of their incomes?
5. The end benefit effect
   - What benefit do buyers seek from the product?

- How price sensitive are buyers to the cost of the end benefit?
- What portion of the benefit does the product's price account for?

6. The shared cost effect
   - Do the buyers pay the full cost of the product?
   - If not, what portion of the cost do they pay?
7. The sunk investment effect
   - Must buyers of the product make complementary expenditures in anticipation of its continued use?
   - For how long are buyers locked in by those expenditures?
8. The price–quality effect
   - Is a prestige image an important attribute for the product?
   - Is the product enhanced in value when its price excludes some consumers?
   - Is the product of unknown quality, and are there few reliable cues for ascertaining quality before purchase? If so, how great would the loss to buyers be of low quality relative to the price of the product?
9. The inventory effect
   - Do buyers hold inventories of the product?
   - Do they expect the current price to be temporary?

Source: Nagle and Holden (1994).

- The customer seeks a custom-designed or differentiated variety.
- The customer is very profitable and/or can readily pass on the cost of inputs.
- The customer is poorly informed about the product and/or does not purchase from well-defined specifications.
- The motivation of the actual decision-maker is not narrowly defined as minimising the cost of inputs.

Industrial market research studies can help in identifying these behavioural characteristics or requirements. These are useful to know in order to direct pricing policy.

15.3.2. Optimum price based on elasticity

The economic and marketing literature contains many econometric studies on measuring price elasticity, as shown in Table 15.3. For a summary of elasticity studies, see Hanssens *et al.* (1990). Tellis (1988) found a mean price elasticity of −2.5. Broadbent (1980) reported an average price elasticity of −1.6 for major British brands. Lambin, covering a sample of 137 brands, reported an average price elasticity of −1.74 (Lambin, 1976, 1988),

Bijmolt *et al.* (2005) observed an overall mean price elasticity of −2.62.

Economic theory shows that the less elastic (in absolute terms) the demand for a product, the higher the optimal price, that is the price that maximises profit; if we know the elasticity, the optimal price can be calculated as follows:

$$P_{opt} = C \times \frac{\varepsilon}{\varepsilon + 1}$$

or in words,

optimal price = unit direct cost × cost mark-up

where

$$\text{cost mark-up} = \frac{\text{price elasticity}}{\text{price elasticity} + 1}.$$

Thus, the optimal price is obtained by multiplying the unit variable cost (or marginal cost) by a percentage, which depends on the price elasticity and is independent of cost. The derivation of this optimisation rule is presented in Lambin (1994, p. 301).

Table 15.4 shows that the optimal mark-up is higher when price elasticity is lower in absolute value, that is closer to unity and gives some comparisons of mark-up coefficients for a range of elasticity.

Table 15.3   Optimal cost mark-up as a function of price elasticity

Price elasticity $\varepsilon_{q.p}$	Optimal cost mark-up $\varepsilon_{q.p}/\varepsilon_{q.p+1}$	Price elasticity $\varepsilon_{q.p}$	Optimal cost mark-up $\varepsilon_{q.p}/\varepsilon_{q.p+1}$
−1.0	—	2.4	1.71
−1.2	6.00	2.6	1.00
−1.4	3.50	—	—
−1.6	2.67	3.0	1.50
−1.8	2.22	4.0	1.33
−2.0	2.00	5.0	1.25
−2.2	1.83	—	—
—	—	15.0	1.07

Source: Authors.

Table 15.4   Evaluation of methods of collecting price response data

Methods/ criteria	Expert judgements	Customer surveys		Price experiments	Historical market data
		Direct	Conjoint analysis		
Validity	Medium	Low	Medium-high	Medium-low	High
Reliability	Medium-high	Uncertain	Medium-high	High	Low
Costs	Very low	Medium-low	Medium	Medium-high	Depends on availability and accessibility
Applicability to new products	Yes	Questionable	Yes	Yes	No
Applicability to established products	Yes	Yes	Yes	Yes	Yes
Overall evaluation	Useful for new products, new situations	Questionable	Very useful	Useful	Useful for established products

Source: Dolan and Simon (1996, p. 75).

One observes that, when price elasticity is high, which is the case in highly competitive markets of undifferentiated products, mark-up is close to unity; the firm's market power is weak and the price accepted by the market is close to unit costs. Conversely, the closer elasticity is to unity, the higher is the price acceptable by the market (see Box 15.3).

Optimisation rules proposed by economic theory, initially developed in the monopoly case (Dorfman and Steiner, 1954), have been extended to the oligopoly case (Lambin *et al.*, 1975) and also to the dynamic case when market response is distributed over time (Nerlove and Arrow, 1962; Jacquemin, 1973).

15.3.3. Methods of price sensitivity measurement

Several methods exist to estimate customers' price sensitivity. These methods can be grouped into four main categories:

1. The *expert judgement* method consists in asking market experts to provide three estimates or points of the price response curve, successively the lowest realistic, the highest realistic prices and the associated sales volume, plus the expected sales at the medium price.
2. *Customer surveys*, directs or indirects. The most popular is the indirect method through conjoint

BOX 15.3

IMPLEMENTATION PROBLEM: HOW TO CALCULATE THE OPTIMAL PRICE (ELASTICITY BETWEEN −1.7 AND −2.1)

By way of illustration, if $\varepsilon = -2.1$ and $C = €105$, the optimal price is equal to,

$$P_{opt} = (105) \cdot \left(\frac{-2.1}{(-2.1) + 1} \right) = (105) \cdot (1.9) = €205$$

The optimal mark-up is here equal to 1.9.

Source: Authors.

Table 15.5   Price elasticity estimates: two examples from the US market

Demand for automobiles		Demand for air transport	
Sub-compact	−0.83	First class	−0.75
Compact	−1.20	Economy	−1.40
Intermediate	−1.30	Discount	−2.10
Full-size	−1.54		
Luxury	−2.07		

Source: Automobile data from Carlson (1978); air transport data from Oum and Gillen (1981).

analysis, illustrated with examples of application in Chapter 11.

3. Price experimentations, *field or laboratory experiments*. We are here in the domain of causal research as discussed in Chapter 4.

4. *Econometric studies* based on time series data or on panel data. As underlined above, the availability of scanner data greatly facilitates this type of analysis, particularly in the food sector.

Each of these methods has its own advantages and disadvantages; they are summarised in Table 15.4.

Usefulness of elasticity measures

Knowledge of the order of magnitude of an elasticity is on the whole useful in many ways:

- Elasticity provides information about the direction in which prices should change in order to stimulate demand and increase turnover.
- Comparing elasticity of competing brands identifies those that can withstand a price increase better, thus revealing their market power.
- Comparing elasticity of products in the same category helps to adjust prices within the category.
- Cross-elasticity helps to predict demand shifts from one brand to another.

To illustrate, Table 15.5 shows estimated price elasticity in the car market and in the market for air transport in the United States. Although the estimates have insufficient precision for the exact calculation of prices, the results are nevertheless very enlightening as far as pricing policy orientation for each product category is concerned.

By way of illustration, the results of a consumer survey organised by Kodak are presented in Table 15.6. Respondents were provided with a description of a new generation of instant cameras and then asked several questions to stimulate considerations of the pros and cons of these cameras in order to stimulate an actual purchase intention. Respondents were then presented prices of €150, €80 and €40 and asked to indicate their purchase intention on a 7-point scale, from 'Definitely not buy' to 'Definitely would buy'. When Kodak finally introduced a camera at a suggested retail price of €39.95, its president cited these data in his report to shareholder.

Limitations of price elasticity measures

Despite the relevance of these works, there have been very few practical applications of this highly quantitative approach to the problem of pricing, except maybe in some large enterprises. The reason is that the notion of elasticity presents a number of conceptual and operational difficulties, which reduce its practical usefulness:

- Elasticity measures a relationship based on buying behaviour and is therefore only observable (after the fact); its predictive value depends on the stability of the conditions that gave rise to the observation; it cannot, for example, be used to determine the price of new products.
- In many situations, the problem is not so much as to know how to adapt prices to present market sensitivities, but to know how to change and act upon this sensitivity in the direction sought by the firm. From this viewpoint, it is more interesting to know the product's perceived value by the targeted group of buyers.

- Elasticity measures the impact of price on quantity bought, but does not measure the effect of price on the propensity to try the product, on repeat purchases, exclusivity rate, and so on. But these are all important notions for understanding consumers' response mechanisms with respect to prices. Therefore, other measures, which are less aggregate, need to be developed for marketing management.

Furthermore, in practice it is often very hard to get sufficiently stable and reliable estimates of price elasticity, which could be used to calculate an optimal selling price. A summary of econometric work on marketing variables elasticity is presented in Table 15.7.

In a recent meta-analysis of price elasticity based on 81 publications and 1,860 price elasticity estimates, the overall mean price elasticity was -2.62 (median $= -2.22$, standard deviation $= 2.21$). The frequency distribution of the observed price elasticities is strongly peaked; 50 per cent of the observations are between -3 and -1, and 80 per cent between -4 and 0 (Bijmolt *et al.*, 2005). This average price elasticity of -2.62 is substantially larger in magnitude than the average price elasticities reported in Table 15.7.

15.3.4. Value pricing

Value pricing is a customer-based pricing procedure, which is an outgrowth of the multi-attribute product concept. From the customer's viewpoint, a product is the bundle of benefits that is received when using the product. Therefore, the customer-oriented company should set its price according to customers' perceptions of product benefits and costs. To determine the price, the marketer needs to understand the customers' perceptions of benefits as well as their perceptions of the costs other than price (Box 15.4). Customers balance the benefits of a purchase against its costs. When the product under consideration has the best relationship of benefit to cost, the customer is inclined to buy the product. This customer-based pricing procedure can be implemented in different ways.

The product's perceived value

The basic idea behind this method is the same: it is the product or the brand's perceived value, which should determine the price level. By analysing and measuring the buyers' perception and its determinants

---

Table 15.6 Purchase intention for instant camera

7-point scale	Stated prices €150	€80	€40
1. Definitely would buy	4%	5%	15%
2.	—	—	2%
3. Probably would buy	7%	14%	30%
4.	1%	2%	4%
5. Probably would not buy	22%	24%	18%
6.	2%	2%	1%
7. Definitely would not buy	65%	54%	30%

Source: Simom (1999).

Table 15.7 Comparing average elasticity of marketing variables

Published sources	Number of observations	Average value of estimated elasticity Advertising	Price	Quality	Distribution
Lambin (1976, 1988)	127	0.081	−1.735	0.521	1.395
Shultz (1980)	25	0.003–0.230	—	—	—
Assmus *et al.* (1984)	22	0.221 (0.264)	—	—	—
Hagerty *et al.* (1988)	203	0.003 (0.105)	−0.985 (1.969)	0.344 (0.528)	0.304 (0.255)
Neslin and Shoemaker (1983)	25	—	−1.800	—	—
Tellis (1988)	220	—	−1.760	—	—

BOX 15.4

IMPLEMENTATION PROBLEM: HOW TO EVALUATE CUSTOMER PERCEIVED VALUE OF MY PRODUCT?

- If I bought this desktop computer at this store, I feel I would be getting my money's worth.
- If I acquired this desktop computer at this store, I think I would be getting good value for the money I spend.
- The desktop would be a worthwhile acquisition because it is reasonably priced.
- Buying this desktop computer from this store makes me feel good.

- I would get a lot of pleasure knowing that I got this desktop at this price from this store.
- Taking advantage of this price gives me a sense of joy.

Source: Xia and Monroe (2004).

Table 15.8 Perceived value analysis: an example

Attributes other than price (1)	Importance of attributes (2)	Absolute performance (scale from 1 to 10)		Relative performance Brand A (5 = 3 ÷ 4)
		Brand A (3)	Direct competitor (4)	
Tangibles				
A_1	10	8.1	7.2	1.13
A_2	20	9.0	7.3	1.23
A_3	20	9.2	6.5	1.42
A_4	15	8.0	8.0	1.00
Intangibles				
A_5	10	8.0	8.0	1.00
A_6	25	9.4	6.4	1.47
Total	100	—	—	—
Absolute performance	—	8.8	7.1	—
Relative performance	—	1.24	0.81	—

Source: Authors.

---

using the compositional method, a score of total perceived value can be derived and used to set the price. The notion of perceived value is a direct extension of the multi-attribute attitude model described in Chapter 4.

By way of illustration, let us examine the data of Table 15.8 and the scores given by a sample of potential buyers to brand A and to its direct competitor brand B over six tangible and intangible attributes. In the example presented, respondents have first evaluated on a 10-point scale the importance of each attribute and then on a 10-point scale the performance of each brand on each attribute.

The total perceived value of each brand is obtained by multiplying the scores given to each attribute by their respective degree of importance and by summing the weighted scores. The totals obtained are then expressed in index form by reference to the direct competitor. One obtains respectively,

brand A = 1.24 and brand B = 0.81.

Thus, one observes that brand A has higher perceived value than brand B, its direct competitor, because brand A performs better on the most important attributes (A_6, A_2 and A_3). If these results can be considered as representative of the target segment perceptions, and assuming that the other marketing factors are equal, the maximum acceptable price (MAP) for brand A could be determined by reference to the average perceived value (here 7.95), with brand A's MAP 10.7 per cent higher and for brand B a price 11 per cent lower.

If the average market price is equal to €5,000, brand A could charge a maximum price as high as €5,535 while brand B, to be accepted by the market, should charge a price as low as €4,450.

If brand A charges a price lower than its MAP, it will have an operational competitive advantage over brand B (better at the same price), which sooner or later will translate into a market share gain. This pricing procedure, based on a compositional approach, is particularly useful when price sensitivity is strongly influenced by qualitative attributes like brand image effect.

The maximum acceptable price

This second pricing procedure is particularly useful for setting the price of industrial products, whose core benefit to the buyer is a cost reduction. To evaluate what the customer is prepared to pay, the procedure followed is to identify and evaluate the different satisfactions or services provided by the product as well as all the costs (other than price) it implies. Thus the procedure is the following (see also Box 15.5):

- Understand the total use of the product from the buyer's point of view.
- Analyse the benefits generated by the product.
- Analyse the costs implied by the acquisition and the use of the product.
- Make cost–benefit trade-offs and determine the MAP.

The highest price that the customer will be willing to pay for the product is given by

$$Benefits - costs\ other\ than\ price = MAP$$

The benefits to consider can be functional (the core service), operational, financial or personal. Similarly, the costs implied other than price are just as diverse: acquisition costs, installation, risk of failure, habit modification, and so on.

If the target market is segmented, this analysis should be done for different groups of customers with non-identical behaviour. Comparing the MAP with competitors' prices helps evaluate the firm's margin for manoeuvre. Box 15.6 presents an example of the application of this method.

Contributions of conjoint analysis

The same kind of result can be obtained with a decompositional approach, or the conjoint analysis method described in Chapter 4. To illustrate, we refer to a conjoint analysis based on a sample of 200 individuals and made in the blended cigarettes market, in order to compare the price sensitivity of four leading brands: Marlboro, Barclay, Camel and Gauloises Blondes (see Lambin 1994, pp. 150–2). Let us examine here the results obtained for two respondents (no. 17 and no. 86, respectively). the utilities are expressed here in terms of preference ranks lost when

---

BOX 15.5

IMPLEMENTATION PROBLEM: HOW TO CALCULATE A MAXIMUM ACCEPTABLE PRICE (MAP)?

1. Product description
   - A chemical compound to be used in conjunction with the regular water-softening chemicals.
2. Uses of the product
   - To disperse the water softening compounds, thus lengthening their economic life.
   - To reduce rust formation in the boiler system.
3. Benefits of the product
   - Core benefit: reduce the amount of softening chemicals by 35 per cent.
   - Prevent rust formation.
   - Reduction in time and effort required for regenerating the softeners.
4. Costs other than price
   - Installation of a dispenser and of a storage tank in the plant.
   - Service of the installation and technical assistance.
   - Risk of breakdown.
   - Lack of reference of the supplier.
   - Custom modification.

5. Costs–benefit trade-off analysis
   - Average use: 40,000 gallons of softening per year.
   - Cost per gallon: 50 cents.
   - Average cost saving: 14,000 gallons (35 per cent) or €7,000.
   - Volume of Aqua-Pur: ratio: 1/7, or 3,715 gallons (26,000/7).
   - Cost of installation: €450, or €90 per year over 5 years.
   - Cost of maintenance: €320 per year.
   - Total maximum acceptable cost: €7,000 – (€90 + €320) = €6,590.
   - Maximum acceptable unit price: €6,590/3,715 gallons = €1.77 per gallon.
   - Price of direct competitor: €1.36.

Source: Authors.

BOX 15.6

IMPLEMENTATION PROBLEM: HOW TO CREATE ECONOMIC VALUE FOR BOTH THE CUSTOMER AND THE SELLER?

An example of value pricing taken from the telecommunication switch market is presented here. The customer's current telecommunication switch had a total cost of purchase of €1,000. The purchase price was only €300, but an additional €200 was spent for installation and start-up, as well as €500 in usage and other post-purchase costs. The business's new product offered customers a solution that could cut the start-up costs in half and reduce the usage cost by €100. At which price to sell the product? To the customer, the MAP is €500 corresponding to the parity price with the competitor's product. But the product has to be priced in a way that creates economic value for both customers and the seller. By setting its price at €375 (€75 more than the existing product) the seller created a solution that added €125 per switch to the customer's bottom line, while keeping a competitive advantage over its direct rival.

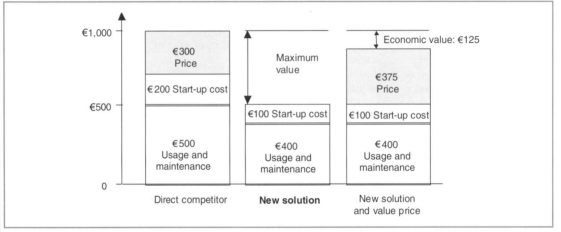

Source: Best (2000/2003).

the price increases from its lowest level (F57) to a higher one. For respondent no. 17, the following utilities were obtained:

(F62: U = −2.5),   (F67: U = −3.5),
(F72: U = −5.0).

We thus have three observations and using ordinary least squares (OLS) average price elasticity was calculated as: $\varepsilon = -3.59$ ($R^2 = 0.958$). For respondent no. 86, we obtained the following pairs of values:

(F62: U = −0.25),   (F67: U = −1.25),
(F72: U = 1.50)

The calculated elasticity here is: $\varepsilon = -1.11$ ($R^2 = 0.914$).

Note that the difference in price sensitivity between the two respondents is quite high. Now suppose that we have similar information for a representative sample of 200 buyers. Average price elasticity could be estimated for the whole sample as well as for subgroups of buyers of high or low price sensitivity.

This kind of elasticity coefficient measures price sensitivity in terms of utility rather than in terms of quantity. Although more vague, it is nevertheless useful for comparison of different buyers' relative price sensitivities and to determine the best price level.

15.3.5. Flexible pricing strategies

Firms do not have a single price, but a variety of prices adapted to different market situations. Flexible pricing strategies occur in market situations where the same product is sold to different customers at different prices. Flexible pricing strategies arise primarily because of customers' heterogeneity, showing different price sensitivities, but also because of cost differences or promotional objectives. Price flexibility can be achieved in different ways: by region, period, product form or from one segment to another. We shall examine five different ways of achieving price flexibility (Table 15.9). In the economic literature, the term price discrimination has been used to designate pricing variations not justified by cost differences.

Second market discounting

This situation occurs when a firm has excess production capacity and has the opportunity to sell in a new market such that there will be a negligible increase in fixed or variable costs and no loss of sales in its first market. The minimum acceptable selling price the firm should accept is the floor price, that is, the unit direct cost. Opportunities

Table 15.9 Flexibility in the prices of services

Single price	Personalised price	Price implying customer participation	Price change over time
1. A flat rate for an unlimited usage (amusement parks, ski pass). 2. A single price for a well-defined need (postal rate, subway ticket, etc.).	3. A reduced price linked to a status (student or senior rates). 4. A reduced price linked to a specific characteristic (handicapped, birthday, etc.).	5. Price reduction for self-service (cafeteria, self-banking, etc.). 6. Price reduction for customer participation in the 'servuction' process. 7. Price reduction for participation in the selling process.	8. Price reduction in low season (low traffic). 9. Price reduction for early or late booking (yield management). 10. Price reduction for early reservation (yield management). 11. High price for fast service (express or rush service).

Source: Adapted from Durrande-Moreau (2002).

for this pricing strategy exist in foreign trade, private label brands or special demographic groups, like students, children or senior citizens. The essential requirement for this strategy is that customers of the lower price market cannot resell the product in the higher price market because of the high transaction costs implied.

Periodic discounting

The pricing problem is different here. How to price a product confronted with different price sensitivity among potential buyers at the beginning and at the end of the seasonal period? Some buyers want to buy only at the beginning of the period and are not very price sensitive, while others want to buy the product at any time, but are price sensitive. To exploit the consumers' heterogeneity of demand, the firm will sell at the high price at the beginning of the period and systematically discount the product at the end of the period. This is the principle often involved in the temporal markdowns and periodic discounting of off-season fashion goods, off-season travel fares, matinee tickets and happy hour drinks.

An essential principle underlying this strategy of periodic discounting is the manner of discounting, which is predictable over time and generally known to consumers, who will, therefore, behave accordingly (Tellis, 1986, p. 150).

Random discounting

Which pricing strategy should be adopted in a market where the same product is sold at a low price by some firms and at a high price by others, knowing that some buyers are ready to spend time searching for the low price while others are not ready to do so? In this case, we have heterogeneity of demand with respect to perceived search costs among consumers. The objective of the firm is twofold here: (a) to sell at a high price to the maximum number of 'uninformed' consumers and at the same time (b) to prevent 'informed' consumers from buying at the low price of the competition.

The recommended strategy here is random discounting, which involves maintaining a high price and discounting the product periodically 'at random'. The manner of discounting is crucial: it should be indiscernible or random so that the uninformed buyers will buy randomly, usually at the high price and the 'informed' will look around or wait until they can buy at the low price (Tellis, 1986, p. 150).

Promotional prices

Companies are often led to temporarily reduce their prices in order to stimulate sales. Promotional prices can take various forms: loss leader pricing as frequently adopted by department stores or supermarkets, special events pricing, low interest financing as often proposed by car dealers, cash rebates, warranties and service contracts, and so on. Every promotion is in fact a disguised price reduction having the merit of being temporary and therefore enabling the seller to go back easily to the initial price.

During the past 10 years, promotions of all kinds have proliferated with, as the main result, a loss of credibility of the pricing policies adopted by manufacturers and resellers as well. To regain this credibility, two pricing policies are today of current application by resellers in the food sector namely: either *every day fair pricing*, or *every day low pricing* (EDLP), that is, slightly reduced price available on a permanent basis. This last pricing policy is the one adopted by the supermarket chain Colruyt in Belgium, which has developed a very sophisticated system of price monitoring, and commits itself to the lowest price charged in the market.

One form of promotional pricing regaining popularity among manufacturers is cash rebates, which can be used to stimulate sales without actually cutting prices. Cash rebates are coupons offered to encourage purchase, which have to be mailed back to the manufacturer after the purchase. The rebate may be as high as €75 for a Nikon camera or €50 for an image scanner. By comparison with a price cut, this promotional practice has certain number of advantages for the manufacturer:

■ The basic price is not modified and therefore the promotion has no negative effect on the brand image.
■ Manufacturers can offer price cuts directly to customers, independently of the retailer who could keep the same price on the shelf and pocket the difference.
■ Rebates can be rolled out and shut off quickly, leaving manufacturers to fine tune inventories or respond quickly to competitors without actually cutting the price.
■ Cash rebates are inexpensive to the extent that many customers never bother to redeem them, allowing manufacturers to offer phantom discounts.
■ Because customers fill out forms with names and addresses and other data, rebates also set off a gusher of information about customers useful in direct marketing.

According to a study published by the *Wall Street Journal* (11 February 1998), only 5–10 per cent of customers redeem cash rebates.

Price administration

Price administration deals with price adjustments for sales made under different conditions, in different quantities, to different types of intermediary in different geographic locations, with different conditions of payment, and so on. These price adjustments or discounts are designed to reward customers whose buying behaviour contributes to cost reductions for the firm. This is the case for quantity discounts, cash payment discounts, seasonal discounts, functional discounts, and so on. For more on this topic, see Monroe (1979, chapter 11).

15.3.6. Pricing of services and 'yield management'

Differential pricing is of common application in the service sector, and more particularly in sectors with limited and fixed production capacity, like hotels, airlines, media, and so on who have to yield income from perishable assets (see Exhibit 15.2). These sectors have in common the following characteristics:

■ the proposed service cannot be stocked;
■ the service can be booked in advance;
■ the production capacity is fixed and its increase would be very costly;
■ the market can be segmented on the basis of price and service flexibility criteria.

EXHIBIT 15.2

YIELD MANAGEMENT: BASIC PRINCIPLES

For the majority of seasonal products, the initial launching price is high and then progressively mark down to move the stock. Mark down will continue until the last product is sold. A similar system can be used by services to reach optimal capacity but it will not optimise revenues. Yield management works just the opposite. The lowest discount items are sold first and the highest priced sold last.

If all the seats on a 200-seat aircraft were priced at a discount fare of €125, the plane would fill quickly with leisure travellers. However, many individuals would be willing to pay more than €125 for a seat. These individuals tend to be business travellers who may not know their schedule until a day or two prior to departure or want more comfort than is offered in the coach section. In fact, these individuals may be willing to pay €300, €400 or more for the seat. Based on historical data and analysis of when passengers made reservations, yield

management will build a price schedule and reserve some of the seats for business travellers who are less price sensitive. They will price these seats at €350. Working backward, the airline may price the next 30 at €275, etc; and the last 60 at €125. To get the €125 price, the airline may have restrictions such as at least 30-day advance reservations, no refunds or exchange without a penalty, and a Saturday night Stayfree. Instead of the €25,000 sales revenue earned at the €125 price, €40,500 would be generated. When sales lag behind the schedule, the price is lowered to fill the seats that were allocated. As soon as all seats are sold at one price range, the price is increased to the next level. This increase in price will slow demand.

Source: Adapted from Kurtz and Clow (1998, pp. 254–5).

In the airline market, typically the market can be subdivided into two distinct segments:

- Business travellers who are not price sensitive, but are very sensitive to schedule flexibility and to comfort, they make their reservations at short notice.
- Vacationers who are very price sensitive, organise their holidays several weeks or months ahead and are ready to accept restrictions reducing their flexibility like advance booking, penalty for change, minimal comfort, and so on.

Using this heterogeneity of demand, airline companies sell their regular tickets at a high price and give high discounts to travellers purchasing their ticket well before their departure date. The problem for these companies is to allocate the production capacity in a dynamic way among different price categories in order to optimise sales revenue. By combining low tariffs and rigid schedules, airline companies can charge a sufficiently low price to attract vacationers without making price concessions to non-price sensitive travellers. This pricing method initially developed by American Airlines is now in application in numerous service sectors (Smith *et al.*, 1992).

15.3.7. Customising prices in online markets

Online commerce greatly facilitates one-to-one relationships and therefore should also facilitate price customisation, that is, the charging of different prices to end-customers on the basis of what they are willing to pay. In the real world, implementation is difficult and Reinartz (2001) has identified five conditions to be held, regardless of whether the context is online or offline.

1. Customers must be heterogeneous in their willingness to pay. Some are prepared to pay a high price, others will only be willing to buy at the lower price available.
2. The market must be *segmentable*. The web has significantly improved a firm's ability to segment a market in terms of willingness to pay by tracking individual purchase through the Internet.
3. Limited arbitrage – a person having purchased a product at lower price should not be able to resell it for a profit to customers having a higher willingness to pay.
4. The costs of segmenting must not exceed the revenue due to customisation. The Internet technology has contributed to reducing these costs substantially.
5. Notions of perceived fairness must not be violated. Perceived fairness is when the buyer feels that both parties in a transaction have gained.

This last condition is crucial. Nobody likes to learn that the very same product has been sold under the same trade terms but at a lower price.

In September 2000, Amazon.com charged consumers different prices for exactly the same DVD with price differentials as high as €15. The knowledge that Amazon sells at different prices provoked resentment and a feeling that the company is profiteering at the consumer's expenses.

Price customisation is a very challenging strategy and should be adopted with care, even if from a technological point of view such an implementation is indeed possible.

15.4. Competition-oriented pricing procedures

As far as competition is concerned, two kinds of factors greatly influence the firm's autonomy in its pricing strategy: the sector's competitive structure, characterised by the number of competing firms, and the importance of the product's perceived value:

- Competitive structures were described in Chapter 9. Clearly, when the firm is a monopoly, autonomy is great in setting its price; it tends to diminish as the number of competitors increases; we have monopoly and perfect competition at the extremes, and differentiated oligopoly and monopolistic situations as the intermediate positions.
- The product's perceived value results from the firm's efforts to differentiate in order to achieve an external competitive advantage. Where an element of differentiation exists and is perceived by the buyer as of value, the buyer is usually prepared to pay a price above that of competing products. In this case, the firm has some degree of autonomy over prices.

Table 15.10 presents these two factors, each at two levels of intensity (low or high). We can thus identify four distinct situations, in each of which the question of price determination takes on a different form.

Reality is, of course, more complex and there is a continuum of situations. Nevertheless, it is helpful to place a product in one of these quadrants to understand the problem of price determination:

- When the number of competitors is low and the product's perceived value is high, we are in structures close to *monopoly or differentiated oligopoly*. Price is a tool for the firm, which has a margin for manoeuvre varying with the buyer's perceived value of the differentiating attribute.
- At the other extreme, where there are many competitors and products are perceived as a commodity, we are close to the *perfect competition* structure where prices are largely determined by the interplay of supply and demand. The firm has practically no autonomy in its pricing strategy.
- The lower-left quadrant, with a low number of competitors and low perceived value, corresponds to an

Table 15.10	Competitive environments of pricing decisions	

| Perceived value of the product | Number of competitors | |
	Low	High
High	Monopoly or differentiated oligopoly	Monopolistic competition
Weak	Undifferentiated oligopoly	Pure or perfect competition

Source: Authors.

undifferentiated oligopolistic structure in which interdependence between competitors is often high, thus limiting their autonomy. Here prices will tend to be aligned with those of the market leader.

■ Finally, in the upper-right quadrant we have highly differentiated products offered by a large number of competitors; this corresponds to *imperfect or monopolistic competition* where there is some degree of autonomy, this being limited by the intensity of competition.

These market structures are very different and they can be observed at various stages of a product market's life cycle.

15.4.1. Anticipating competitors' behaviour

In many market situations, competitors' interdependence is high and there is a 'market price', which serves as reference to all. This is usually the case when there is undifferentiated oligopoly, where total demand is no longer expanding and the offerings of existing competitors are hardly differentiated. This type of competitive structure tends to prevail during the maturity stage of products' life cycle.

In these markets, the firm can align itself with competitors' prices or those of the industry leader. It can fix its price at a higher level, thus taking the risk of losing some market share. Alternatively, it can fix its price below the market level, thus seeking a competitive advantage that it cannot find from other sources, but also taking the risk of launching a price war. The problem therefore is to determine relative price. The outcome of these strategies largely depends on the reactions of competitors.

The objective of analysing competition in pricing strategies is to evaluate *competitors' capabilities to act and react*. In particular, one needs to estimate the reaction elasticity of the most dangerous competitor(s) if prices were to go up or down. We discussed the notion of reaction elasticity in Chapter 8.

The direction and intensity of competitors' reactions vary when prices move upwards or downwards. Elasticity is different on either side of the market price because of different competitive reactions. Some conditions are more favourable to price decreases and some to price increases. These are the conditions that need to be identified.

The risk of a price war is always present in oligopolistic markets and this is why firms are reluctant to start reducing prices. In few cases, however, a price war can help companies to improve their competitive positions. The Boston Consulting Group's contributions on the experience curve (see Chapter 10) have shown that reduced profit margins due to price reductions can be offset by market share gains which in the long term generate improved profitability thanks to cost reductions. Another objective of a price war can be the elimination of a potentially dangerous competitor.

15.4.2. Pricing in an inflationary economy

During inflation, all costs tend to go up, and to maintain profits at an acceptable level, price increases are very often a necessity. The general objective is that price should be increased to such a level that the profits before and after inflation are approximately equal. Decline in sales revenue caused by the price increase should be explicitly taken into account and the market reaction evaluated.

It should be noted that it is not always necessary for a company to increase prices to offset inflationary effects. Non-price measures can be taken as well to reduce the impact of inflationary pressures, namely by improving productivity to offset the rise in costs. Also price increases well above inflationary pressures can be justified to the market if the brand has a competitive advantage over competing brands.

15.4.3. Price leadership

Price leadership strategy prevails in oligopolistic markets. One member of the industry, because of its size or command over the market, emerges as the leader of the industry. The leading company then makes pricing moves, which are duly acknowledged by other members of the reference market.

Initiating a price increase is typically the role of the industry leader. The presence of a leader helps to regulate the market and avoid too many price changes. Oligopolistic markets, in which the number of competitors is relatively low, favour the presence of a market leader who adopts an anticipative behaviour and periodically determines prices. Other firms then recognise the leader's role and become followers by accepting prices. The leadership strategy is designed to stave off price wars and 'predatory' competition, which tends to force down prices and hurt all competing firms. There are different types of leadership:

1. *Leadership of the dominant firm*: that is, the firm with the highest market share. The dominant firm establishes a price and the other producers sell their products at this price. The leader must be powerful and undisputed and must accept maintaining a high price.

2. *Barometric leadership*: consists of initiating desirable price cuts or price increases, taking into account changes in production costs or demand growth. In this case, the leader must have access to an effective information system providing him or her with reliable information on supply and demand, competition and technological change.

3. *Leadership by common accord*: one firm is tacitly recognised as leader, without there being a formal understanding or accord. The latter would in fact be illegal. Such a leader could be the most visible firm in the sector, for example, the firm that leads in technology. It should also have a sensitivity to the price and profit needs of the rest of the industry.

According to Corey (1976, p. 177), the effective exercise of leadership depends on several factors:

- The leader must have a superior market information system for understanding what is going on in the market and reacting in a timely way.
- It should have a clear sense of strategy.
- It should have a broad concern for the health of the industry.
- The price leader should use long-term measures to assess managerial performance.
- It should want to lead and to act responsibly.
- It will tend to behave in a way that preserves short-run market share stability.

On the whole, the presence of a leader acts as a market stabiliser and reduces the risk of a price war.

15.5. Product line pricing

Strategic marketing has led firms to adopt segmentation and diversification strategies that have resulted in the multiplication of the number of products sold by the same firm or under the same brand. Generally a firm has several product lines, and within each product line there are usually some products that are functional substitutes for each other and some that are functionally complementary. This strategy of product development brings about interdependency between products, which is reflected either by *a substitution effect (or cannibalism) or by a complementarity effect*. Since the objective of the firm is to optimise the overall outcome of its activities, it is clearly necessary to take this interdependence into account when determining prices (Oxenfeldt, 1966).

15.5.1. The risk of a cannibalism effect

Figure 15.5 illustrates the possible scenarios of 'cannibalisation' between two brands of the same firm, the old and the new. The circles represent buyers, with the intersections representing switchers. The total market is defined by the outer boundaries of all circles combined. Brand X denotes the competing brands (Traylor, 1986):

- The first case is the worst; the new brand brings no advantage whatsoever and simply shares sales with the firm's current brand. This situation might still be tolerated if the new brand's gross margin is well above that of the old brand.
- The second case is better, because the new brand has increased the size of the market and also its market share, but without going over the competitor's position. The operation will be globally profitable if the margin obtained on sales to new buyers is greater than that lost on sales of the old brand.
- In the third scenario, the new brand overlaps with the old brand's market as well as with the competing brand's, while extending the size of the market by attracting new customers. As in the previous case, one needs to compare the margins lost and gained to evaluate whether there is a net positive gain.
- The fourth case is the ideal situation, with no cannibalisation. The new brand cuts into competitors' sales and reaches new buyers. Total market share increases and the new brand is bringing in a net cash flow increment (Traylor, 1986, p. 72).

How can a multibrand firm eliminate cannibalism? As firms look for finer and subtler definitions of new market segments, the risk of cannibalism goes up. The main objective to pursue is to position the firm's brands against each other as well as against competitors' brands. In addition, some form of cannibalism should be tolerated if

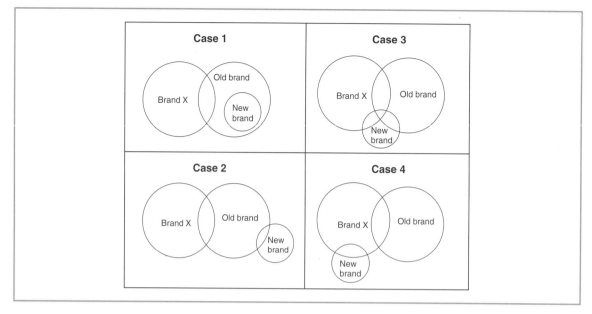

Figure 15.5   Cannibalism in multibrand firms
Source: Traylor (1986).

the net effect of the multibrand strategy is in the best strategic interest of the firm as a whole.

> Coca-Cola is a good example of a company that has flipped from a very conservative protectionism to an almost reckless use of the Coke name. The intended (Diet Coke, Cherry Coke) and unintended (Coke Classic) brand extensions represent radical departures from the company's traditional reluctance to extend the Coke name. (Traylor, 1986, p. 73)

A firm concerned about market power may accept short-term profit losses resulting from cannibalism if it stands to increase its market power overall.

15.5.2. Concept of cross-elasticity

Cross-elasticity measures the degree of interdependence between products sold by the same firm or under the same brand, and identifies the nature of this dependence when it exists: complementarity or substitution.

In the case of two products A and B, their cross-elasticity is defined as follows:

$$\text{Cross-elasticity} = \frac{\text{Percentage change of product A's sales}}{\text{Percentage change of product B's price}}.$$

If cross-elasticity is positive, the products are substitutes; if elasticity is negative, then they are complementary.
If elasticity is zero or very close to it, then the products are independent.

15.5.3. Contribution analysis in product line pricing

The complexity of product mix pricing is due to the fact that, apart from demand interaction, there is often cost interaction as well. For example, this is true when a change in the manufacturing process of one product affects the cost of other products. In this case, to study the implications of changing the price of one product in a range of products, it is important to take into account the effect of such a change on the overall result.

To illustrate, let us examine the data of an example presented in Table 15.11. A firm is selling three interdependent products and has a marketing programme, which it is planning to modify as follows.

> By increasing advertising by £50,000, it is expected that sales of product B will increase by 6,000 units at a price increased by £20, and increased packaging cost by £5. Sales of product A are expected to decrease by 1,000 units because of product interdependence, and sales of product C are expected to decrease by 3,000 units because of production capacity constraint. Should this change in the marketing programme for product B be adopted? (Blondé, 1964)

What would be the impact of such a change on the overall result? A convenient way to proceed is to reason in terms of variations (Δ). The variation in the gross margin (M) of product B is

$$\Delta(M) = \Delta(P) - \Delta(C),$$

Table 15.11 Product line pricing: an example

	Product A	Product B	Product C
Selling price (£)	200	220	100
Direct cost (£)	150	180	80
Unit profit margin (£)	50	40	20
Volume (units)	20,000	15,000	10,000
Total profit margin (£)	1,000,000	600,000	200,000
Fixed costs (£)	700,000	500,000	100,000
Net profit (£)	300,000	100,000	100,000
Total net profit (£)		500,000	

Source: Authors.

which in this case gives,

$$\Delta(M) = (+20) - (+5) = +15.$$

To determine the effect on the overall result, let us use the following expression, where F denotes fixed costs:

$$\Delta(R) = \Sigma_n [\Delta(Q) \cdot M + Q \cdot \Delta(M) + \Delta(Q) \cdot \Delta(M) - \Delta F].$$

The summation is over the n products made. In the case of this example, for the three products A, B and C we have

$$
\begin{aligned}
R = & (-1000) \cdot (50) + (20,000) \cdot (0) + (-1000) \cdot (0) \\
& - 0 + (+6000) \cdot (40) + (15,000) \cdot (15) \\
& + (+6000) \cdot (15) - 350,000 + (-3000) \cdot (20) \\
& + (10,000) \cdot (0) + (-3000) \cdot (0) - 0 \\
\Delta R = & -50,000 + 205,000 - 60,000 \\
\Delta R = & +\text{£}95,000, \text{ that is an increased profit} \\
& \text{of } 19 \text{ per cent.}
\end{aligned}
$$

The new marketing programme is therefore profitable. Total gross margin obtained from the new sales volume for product B with its new unit gross margin is higher than the loss of gross margins on products A and C, due to their lower sales volume and increased fixed costs.

15.5.4. Product line pricing strategies

When a firm is selling a set of related products, the price of each product must be set in such a way as to maximise the profit of the entire product line rather than the profit of a single product. The pricing strategy adopted will be different according to whether the related products are complementary to, or competitive with, each other.

Price bundling

When the products are related but are non-substitutes, that is, complementary or independent, one strategic option for the firm is optional price bundling, where the products can be bought separately, but also as a package offered at a much lower price than the sum of the parts. Because the products are not substitutes, it is possible to get consumers to buy the package instead of only one product of the line. This pricing strategy is common practice, for instance, in the automobile and audio-visual markets, where packages of options are offered with the purchase of a car or of stereo equipment. A simple example will illustrate the profit implication of this pricing strategy (Tellis, 1986, p. 155).

Assume a market situation where two related products are offered to two customers, who could buy one product or both. The maximum prices they are ready to pay are presented in Table 15.12.

What is the best pricing strategy to adopt if tying contracts are excluded?

■ Charging each customer the maximum price would yield a total revenue of €76. But this strategy, if not illegal, is difficult to implement if the buyers are sufficiently informed.

■ Adopting the lowest price for each product would mean selling product A at €12 and product B at €24 and could induce buyers to buy the two products, since the total cost (€36) for them would be compatible with their budget constraints, but the total sales revenue would be only €72.

■ Adopting the highest price for each product, that is, selling product A at €15 and product B at €25, will generate an even lower total revenue of maximum €49 (if they both buy product B), since the customers will not be able to buy the two products (at a total cost of €40) given their budget constraints.

The best solution is to price product A at €15 and product B at €25 and offer both at €37 for a total revenue of €74. Both customers will accept the package for €37 since this total cost is compatible with their budget constraints (adapted from Tellis, 1986).

This strategy of 'optional bundling', in contrast with 'indivisible bundling', leaves the option to the customer to buy only one product or the total package.

Several computer companies have adopted the indivisible bundling strategy. Under this pricing system, not only are the costs of hardware and profits covered, but also included are the anticipated expenses for extra

Table 15.12   Bundling pricing: an example

Products	Customer 1	Customer 2	Total
Product A	€12	€15	€27
Product B	€25	€24	€49
Budgets	€37	€39	€76

Source: Tellis (1986).

technical assistance, design and engineering of the system concept, software and applications to be used on the system, training of personnel and maintenance.

For the customer, this strategy is very attractive because the manufacturing firm is selling a 'solution' and not simply a product. To be able to sell a solution, however, the manufacturer has to cover the anticipated expenses for providing services and assistance in use and for keeping the system in working condition.

Bundling is a different strategy than the solution approach: bundling leads to a lower price while the solution approach implies the capacity to charge a premium price.

Such a bundling strategy also permits an ongoing relationship with the customer and first-hand knowledge of the customer's needs.

Premium pricing

This pricing strategy applies to different versions of the same product, a superior version and a basic or standard model. Potential buyers for the standard model are very price sensitive, while buyers of the superior model are not. If economies of scale exist, it is unprofitable for the firm to limit its activity to one of the two market segments. The best solution is to exploit jointly economies of scale and heterogeneity of demand by covering the two segments, the low end of the market with a low price and the high end with a premium price. The following example illustrates this.

Consider a firm having the following target prices: $50 at 20 units and $35 at 40 units. The cost of producing a superior version of the same product is $10. Forty consumers per period are on the market for the product. Half of them are price-insensitive and are ready to pay $50 for the superior version. The other half is price-sensitive and will not pay more than $30. In what version and at what price should the firm sell the product? (Tellis, 1986, p. 156)

This pricing strategy is common practice in many markets, typically durable goods for which several versions differing in price and features cater to different consumer segments (see Exhibit 15.2 on yield management).

Image pricing

A variant of premium pricing is image pricing. The objective is the same: to signal quality to uninformed buyers and use the profit made on the higher priced version to subsidise the price on the lower priced version. The difference is that there is no real difference between products or brands, it is only in image or perceptual positioning. This is common practice in markets like cosmetics, dresses, snacks, and so on, where the emotional and/or social value of a product or a brand is important for the consumer.

Complementary pricing

The problem here is to determine the prices of complementary products, such as durable goods and accessories or supplies necessary for the use of the basic product. Examples of complementary products are razors and blades, cars and spare parts, computers and software, and so on. To the extent that buyers are source loyal and want to buy supplies or accessories from the original manufacturer, low prices can be charged for the main product and high prices for the supplies.

For example, Kodak prices its cameras low because it used to make its money on selling film. Those camera makers who do not sell film have to price their cameras higher in order to make the same overall profit.

In evaluating the effect of a price change of complementary products, management must examine the changes in sales revenue and costs not only for the product being priced, but also for the other products affected by the price change. By way of illustration, let us examine the pricing problem of a company selling personal computers and software.

In this company, the typical buyer of a personal computer also purchases on average three software packages. The gross profit margin on a computer is €1,000 or 40 per cent on selling price, while the profit margin on software is €250. If management treated sales of computers and software as independent, the break-even sales quantity for a 10 per cent price cut would be 33.3 per cent (−10 per cent / 40 per cent − 10 per cent = 0.333). Thus sales should increase by 33.3 per cent to justify the 10 per cent price cut.

How likely is this sales increase? In fact, the profit contribution for a computer sale is much higher than 40 per cent, since each buyer of a computer also purchases on average three software packages. Thus, the relevant gross profit margin here is €1,750 (€1,000 + (3 × €250)), or 70 per cent of the selling price. The adjusted break-even sales change is 16.7 per cent

(−10 per cent / 70 per cent − 10 per cent = 0.167 per cent). Thus, the company could cut its price even if it expects a percentage increase in sales much less than 33.3 per cent.

In retailing, the corresponding strategy is called loss leadership. It involves dropping the price on a well-known brand to generate store traffic.

CHAPTER SUMMARY

The choice of a pricing strategy must respect two types of coherence: an internal coherence, that is, setting a price respecting constraints of costs and profitability, and an external coherence, that is, setting a price compatible with the buyer's price sensitivity with the price of competing goods. Cost-based pricing (break-even, target and mark-up pricing) is a first and necessary step, which helps to identify the financial implications of various pricing strategies. Pricing based exclusively on the firm's own financial needs is inappropriate, however, since in a market economy it is the buyer who ultimately decides which product will sell. In demand-oriented pricing, the notion of price elasticity is central although difficult to estimate empirically with sufficient precision. The factors affecting buyers' price sensitivity are

useful to help estimate price elasticity in qualitative terms. Value pricing is a customer-based pricing procedure, which is an outgrowth of the multi-attribute product concept. Flexible pricing strategies (second market, periodic or random discounting) arise primarily because buyers' heterogeneity shows different price sensitivities. Two kinds of factors influence competition-oriented pricing: the competitive structure of the market and the product's perceived value. One objective of analysing competition in pricing is to evaluate competitors' capacity to act and react. Special issues in pricing are pricing new products (skimming versus penetration pricing), product line pricing (price bundling, premium pricing, image and complementary pricing) and international pricing (transfer price and export costs).

Review and Application Questions

1. A distributor sells an average of 300 units per week of a particular product whose purchase cost is €2.50 and sales price €3. If the distributor gives a 10 per cent price reduction during 1 week, how many units should the firm sell in order to keep its gross profit margin unchanged?

2. Company Alpha distributes a product in a market, which is price inelastic. Sales are 30,000 units per year. The operating data of the product are as follows:

   (i) Direct unit cost   €9.90
   (ii) Fixed unit cost   €3.30
   (iii) Total   €13.20
   (iv) Sales price   €19.80
   (v) Net profit per unit   €6.60

   The firm wants to increase its sales volume by 3000 units and, for that purpose, has adopted a €39,600 advertising budget per year. What minimum price increase the firm should adopt in order to leave its profit unchanged?

3. The Elix Company produces and distributes a product, which is differentiated from competing products by a better design. The average market price is €50 and the total market amounts to 1,000,000 units; Elix market share is 10 per cent. The price elasticity for this product category is in the range −1.7 to −2.0. The operating data for Elix are as follows:

   (i) Direct unit cost   €20
   (ii) Fixed costs   €2,000,000

   (iii) Expected rate of return   10 per cent
   (iv) Invested capital   €10,000,000

   The market research department has conducted a brand image study for Elix and for its priority competitor, the brand Lumina. The attributes' importance scores for the product category are respectively: 0.50/0.25/0.25; and the performance scores are: 10/6/9 for Elix; 8/7/9 for Lumina. Calculate the target price, the value price and the optimum price. What pricing strategy do you recommend?

4. Division X and Division Y are two divisions of the New Style Company. Division X manufactures the product Alpha. The operating data are:

Direct costs raw materials	€6
Labour	€4
Fixed costs	€2
Total	€12

   The Alpha market is a perfect competition market and the market price is €16. Alpha is also sold to Division Y. Market sales imply a selling cost of €2 per unit. Given that demand for Alpha is sufficiently large in order to permit Division X to work at full capacity, at what transfer price should Division X sell the Alpha product to Division Y?

Bibliography

Assmus, G., Farley, J.V. and Lehmann, D.R. (1984), How Advertising Affects Sales Meta-Analysis of Econometric Results, *Journal of Marketing Research*, 21, 1, pp. 65–74.

Best, R.J. (2000/2003), *Market-based Management*, Upper Saddle River, NL, Prentice Hall, 2nd and 3rd editions.

Bijmolt Tammo, H.A., Van Heerde, H.J. and Pieters Rik, G.M. (2005), New Empirical Generalizations on the Determinants of Price Elasticity, *Journal of Marketing Research*, 42, 2, pp. 141–56.

Blondé, D. (1964), *La gestion programmée*, Paris, Dunod.

Broadbent, S. (1980), Price and Advertising: Volume and Profits, *Admap*, 16, pp. 532–40.

Business Week (1975), Detroit Dilemma on Prices, 20 January, pp. 82–3.

Business Week (1977), Flexible Pricing, 12 December, pp. 78–88.

Business Week (1998), Let the Shopping Spree Begin, 3575, 27 April, pp. 44–5.

Carlson, R.L. (1978), Seemingly Unrelated Regression and the Demand for Automobiles of Different Sizes: A Disaggregate Approach, *The Journal of Business*, 51, 2, pp. 243–62.

Corey, E.R. (1976), *Industrial Marketing: Cases and Concepts*, Englewood Cliffs, NJ, Prentice-Hall.

Dean, J. (1950), Pricing Policies for New Products, *Harvard Business Review*, 28, 6, pp. 28–36.

Dolan, R.J. and Simon, H. (1996), *Power Pricing*, New York, The Free Press.

Dorfman, R. and Steiner, P.O. (1954), Optimal Advertising and Optimal Quality, *American Economic Review*, 44, 5, pp. 826–33.

Durrande-Moreau, A. (2002), Service et tactiques de prix: Quelles spécificités? *Décisions Marketing*, 25, January–March.

Hagerty, M.R., Carman, J.M. and Russel, G.J. (1988), Estimating Elasticities with PIMS Data: Methodological Issues and Substantive Implications, *Journal of Marketing Research*, 25, 1, pp. 1–9.

Hanssens, D.M., Parsons, L.L., and Schultz, R.L. (1990), *Market Response Models: Econometric and Time Series Analysis*, Boston, MA, Kluwer.

Jacquemin, A. (1973), Optimal Control and Advertising Policy, *Metroeconomica*, 25, May, pp. 200–7.

Kotler, P. (1997), *Marketing Management*, Englewood Cliffs, NJ, Prentice-Hall.

Kurtz, D.L. and Clow, K.E. (1998), *Services Marketing*, New York, John Wiley & Sons.

Lambin, J.J. (1976), *Advertising, Competition and Market Conduct in Oligopoly over Time*, Amsterdam, North-Holland.

Lambin, J.J. (1988), Synthèse des études récentes sur l'efficacité économique de la publicité, CESAM, Unpublished Working Paper, Louvain-la-Neuve, Belgium.

Lambin, J.J. (1998), *Le marketing stratégique*, Paris, Ediscience International, 4th edition.

Lambin, J.J., Naert, P.A. and Bultez, A. (1975), Optimal Marketing Behavior in Oligopoly, *European Economic Review*, 6, 2, pp. 105–28.

Leone, R.P. and Schultz, R. (1980), A Study in Marketing Generalisations, *Journal of Marketing*, 44, 1, pp. 10–18.

Leroy, G., Richard, G. and Sallenave, J.P. (1991), *La conquête des marchés extérieurs*, Paris, Les Editions d'Organisation.

Marn, M.V., Roegner, E.V. and Zawada, C.C. (2003), The Power of Pricing, *McKinsey Quarterly*, 1, pp. 26–39.

Monroe, K.B. (1979), *Pricing: Making Profitable Decisions*, New York, McGraw-Hill.

Nagle, T.T. and Holden, R.K. (1987/1994), *The Strategy and Tactics of Pricing*, Englewood Cliffs, NJ, Prentice Hall, 2nd edition.

Nerlove, M. and Arrow, K.J. (1962), Optimal Advertising Policy under Dynamic Conditions, *Economica*, 29, pp. 129–42.

Neslin, S.A. and Shoemaker, R.W. (1983), Using a Natural Experiment to Estimate Price Elasticity, *Journal of Marketing*, 47, 1, pp. 44–57.

Oum, T.H. and Gillen, D.W. (1981), *Demand for Fareclasses and Pricing in Airline Markets*, Queen's University School of Business, Working Paper No. 80–12.

Oxenfeldt, A.R. (1966), Product Line Pricing, *Harvard Business Review*, 44, 4, pp. 137–44.

Porter, M.E. (1980), *Competitive Strategy*, New York, The Free Press.

Reinartz, W. (2001), Customising Prices Online, *European Business Forum*, 6, Summer.

Ross, E.B. (1984), Making Money with Proactive Pricing, *Harvard Business Review*, 62, 6, pp. 145–55.

Shapiro, B.P. and Jackson, B.B. (1978), Industrial Pricing to Meet Customers 'Needs', *Harvard Business Review*, 56, 6, pp. 119–27.

Simon, H. and Kucher, E. (1993), The European Pricing Time Bomb and How to Cope with It, *Marketing and Research Today*, February, pp. 25–36.

Smith, B.C., Leimkuhler, J.F. and Darrow, R.M. (1992), Yield Management at American Airlines, *Interfaces*, 22, 1, pp. 8–31.

Tan, S.J., Lim, G.H. and Lee, K.S. (1997), Strategic Responses to Parallel Importing, *Journal of Global Marketing*, 10, 4, pp. 45–66.

Tellis, G.J. (1986), Beyond the Many Faces of Price: An Integration of Pricing Strategies, *Journal of Marketing*, 50, 4, pp. 146–60.

Tellis, G.J. (1988), The Price Elasticity of Selective Demand: a Meta-Analysis of Econometric Models of Sales, *Journal of Marketing Research*, 25, 4, pp. 331–41.

Terpstra, V. and Sarathy, R. (2000), *International Marketing*, Chicago, IL, Dryden Press, 8th edition.

Traylor, M.B. (1986), Cannibalism in Multibrand Firms, *The Journal of Consumer Marketing*, 3, 2, pp. 69–75.

Wall Street Journal (1998), Manufacturer's Boon: Few Consumers Redeem Rebates, 11 February.

Xia, L. and Monroe, K.B. (2004), Price Partitioning on the Internet, *Journal of Interactive Marketing*, 18, 4, pp. 63–74.

COMPANION WEBSITE FOR CHAPTER 15

Visit the *Market-driven Management* companion website at www.palgrave.com/business/lambin to find information on:

International Pricing

marketing communication decisions 16

Chapter contents

Chapter learning objectives

When you have read this chapter, you should be able to know and/or understand

- the nature of the different modes of marketing communication;
- the steps in designing an effective communication programme;
- the tasks and objectives of relationship selling;
- the different objectives of advertising communication;
- the roles and impact of sales promotions;
- the objectives of public relations and of sponsoring.

Chapter introduction

We saw in Chapter 1 that market-driven management is an action-oriented process as well as a business philosophy. To be effectively implemented, the firm's strategic choices must be supported by dynamic action programmes, without which there is very little hope for commercial success. To sell, it is not enough to have a competitively priced product made available to target potential customers through a well-structured distribution network. It is also necessary to advertise the product's distinctive features to the target segment, and to stimulate the demand through selling and promotional activities. An effective marketing strategy requires the development of a communication programme having the two interrelated objectives of informing potential customers about products and services and persuading them to buy. Such a programme is based on various means of communication; the most important of which are personal selling, advertising, promotion and public relations. The objective of this chapter is to examine the major decisions facing a firm when developing its communication programme (see Figure 16.1).

16.1. The role and nature of marketing communication

To ensure an efficient matching of segments of demand and supply, communication flows must be organised between the trading partners to facilitate the exchange process. It is therefore up to the producer to initiate and control these communication flows to create a brand or a corporate image consistent with the firm's strategic objectives (Figure 16.1).

16.1.1. The marketing communication mix

Marketing communication refers to all the signals or messages made by the firm to its various publics, that is, customers, distributors, suppliers, shareholders and public authorities, and also its own personnel. The four major communication tools, called the communication mix, are advertising, personal selling, promotion and public relations. Each of these communication tools has its own characteristics:

- *Advertising* is a unilateral and paid form of non-personal mass communication, designed to create a favourable attitude towards the advertised product and coming from a clearly identified sponsor.
- *Personal selling* has the objective of organising a verbal dialogue with potential and current customers and to deliver a tailor-made message with the short-term objective of making a sale. Its role is also to gather information for the firm.

- *Promotion* includes all short-term incentives, generally organised on a temporary and/or local basis, and designed to stimulate immediate purchase and to move sales forward more rapidly than would otherwise occur.
- *Public relations* involve a variety of actions aimed at establishing a positive corporate image and a climate of understanding and mutual trust between a firm and its various publics. Here, the communication objective is less to sell and more to gain moral support from public opinion for the firm's economic activities.
- *Direct advertising* – in addition to these traditional communication tools, one must also add direct mail, catalogue selling, fairs and exhibitions, telemarketing, and so on.

Although these means of communication are very different, they are also highly complementary. The problem is therefore not whether advertising and promotion are necessary, but rather how to allocate the total communication budget to these various communication tools, given the product's characteristics and the chosen communication objectives.

16.1.2. The communication process

Any communication involves an exchange of signals between a sender and a receiver, and the use of a system of

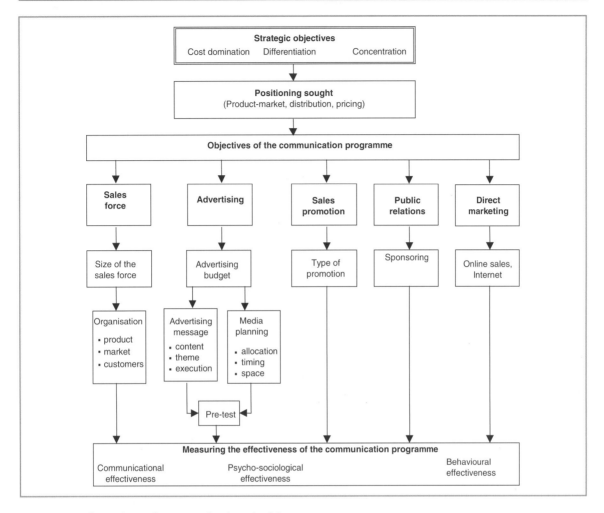

Figure 16.1   Overview of communication decisions
Source: Authors.

encoding and decoding which allows the creation and the interpretation of the message. Figure 16.2 describes the communication process in terms of nine elements (Kotler, 1997, p. 568).

1. Sender: the party sending the message to another party.
2. Encoding: the process of transforming the intended message into images, language, signs, symbols, and so on.
3. Message: the information or the claim to be communicated to the receiver by the sender.
4. Media: the communication channel through which the message moves from the sender to the receiver.
5. Decoding: the process through which the receiver assigns meaning to the symbols transmitted.
6. Receiver: the target audience.
7. Response: the set of reactions that the receiver has after exposure to the message.

8. Feedback: the part of the target audience's response that the receiver communicates to the sender.
9. Noise: the distortions that occur during the communication process.

Figure 16.2 describes the relationship between these nine factors and helps to determine the conditions for effective communication.

Four conditions can be identified:

Communication objectives. Senders must know what audiences they want to reach and what type of response they want. This implies the choice of a target audience and the determination of specific communication objectives. These tasks are typically the responsibilities of strategic marketing people.

Message execution. Communicators must be skilful in encoding messages and be able to understand how the

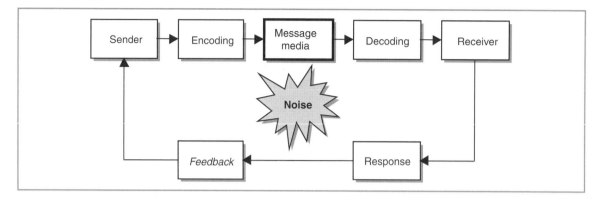

Figure 16.2   The communication process
Source: Kotler (1967/2005).

target audience tends to process messages. This involves designing advertisements and ensuring, through testing, that the target group processes them in the intended manner to produce the desired communication effect.

Media planning. Two decisions are involved here. First, media selection, that is, 'where' to reach the target audience most efficiently; second, media scheduling, that is, 'how often' the target audience needs to be reached to produce the intended communication objective.

These last two tasks are in general assumed by advertising agencies and/or by agencies specialising in media planning.

Communication effectiveness. The advertiser must identify the audience's response to the message and verify to what extent the communication objectives have been achieved. This is again the task of marketing management.

Applying the concept of market orientation to advertising implies developing messages that relate to buyers' experiences, namely by adopting a language they can decode. These four conditions for efficient communication determine the various decisions to be taken in any marketing communication programme.

16.1.3. Personal versus impersonal communication

The two most important tools of marketing communication are personal communication, assumed by the sales force, and impersonal communication, achieved through media advertising. The problem is to know when direct intervention by a sales representative is more effective than advertising. A comparison of the main features of each of these two means of communication is shown in Table 16.1.

This comparison suggests the following:

■ Personal selling is by far the most efficient and powerful communication tool. But it costs almost a hundred times more to contact a prospect with a salesperson's visit than with an advertising message.
■ Media advertising, however, has the advantage over personal selling in that it can reach a large number of people in a short period of time, while a sales representative can only visit a limited number of customers within a day.
■ When a product is complex and difficult to use and is targeted to a limited number of people, a sales representative is clearly much more effective than an advertising message, which is necessarily too general and too simplistic.
■ A salesperson acts directly and can obtain an immediate order from the customer, whereas advertising works through brand awareness and through attitude formation. These are often long-term effects.

Consequently, whenever the personal factor is not essential to communication, advertising is more economical both in terms of costs and of time. Recent developments in the field of advertising tend to reconcile the advantages of these two communication means, which is indeed the objective of interactive or response advertising.

It is therefore not surprising to observe that firms selling industrial goods devote a larger proportion of their communication budget to personal selling than firms operating in the field of consumer goods.

16.1.4. Costs of communication activities

It is difficult to evaluate the costs of communication activities because available information is sketchy.

Table 16.1   Comparing personal and impersonal communication

Elements of the communication process	Personal communication	Impersonal communication
Target	■ Very well-identified target	■ Average profile of the target
Message	■ Tailor-made message ■ Many arguments ■ Weak control of form and content	■ Standard message ■ Few arguments ■ Strong control of form and content
Media	■ Personalised and human contact ■ Few contacts	■ Impersonalised contact ■ Several contacts
Receiver	■ Continued attention ■ Weak consequence of encoding error	■ Volatile attention ■ Strong effect of encoding error
Response	■ Immediate behavioural response possible	■ Immediate behavioural response difficult

Source: Adapted from Darmon et al. (1982, p. 398).

Table 16.2   Advertising expenditures in Europe and in the United States (2004)

	Germany	Spain	France	Italy	UK	Europe	USA
Investments (M€)	15,752	6,376	10,696	9,102	17,700	59,536	122,057
Investment/PIB (%)	0.73	0.80	0.66	0.67	0.95	0.76	1.24
Investment/habitant (€)	191	161	177	155	271	193	399
Press (%)	53.4	32.4	38.2	28.2	38.7	40.2	32.3
– daily	17.5	18.6	9.8	13.4	15.5	15.0	21.0
– free	12.4	—	8.3	—	4.5	6.1	—
– magazine	16.3	8.7	15.3	12.7	12.1	13.5	8.4
– professional	7.2	5.1	4.8	2.1	6.6	5.6	2.9
Radio (%)	4.5	9.2	9.0	5.7	5.5	6.3	13.6
Television (%)	32.8	48.2	37.0	56.5	41.5	41.4	45.4
Cinema (%)	1.4	0.7	1.0	0.8	1.6	1.2	—
Publicity outside (%)	5.9	8.0	13.2	7.7	8.5	8.5	9.9
Internet (%)	2.0	1.5	1.6	1.1	4.2	2.4	4.8

Source: AdBarometer.

Furthermore, orders of magnitude vary tremendously with the field of activity. It is nevertheless generally accepted that personal communication expenses devoted to the sales force are greater by far than advertising expenditure; they are also more significant in industrial markets as compared to consumer goods markets.

Data from Table 16.2 provide evaluation of the relative importance of advertising expenditures in eight European countries and also compare the relative weight of above and below the line advertising outlays. Inspection of this data suggests the following comments: Below the line communication expenditures account for 60 per cent of total advertising communication expenditures. Direct marketing (20.6 per cent) is the most important medium

followed by press advertising (19.2 per cent), sales promotions (18.1 per cent) and television (16.3 per cent). The strongest growth is observed for direct marketing (after cinema advertising, which remains marginal).

Total advertising communication expenditures are growing at an average 5 per cent rate during recent years. The cost of personal selling keeps on increasing, mainly in the industrial markets, while the cost per advertising contact is decreasing as the result of better media selectivity.

McGraw-Hill annually reported the cost of sales call, but discontinued the preactice in the late 1980s. In 1987, the last year of the survey, the average sales call

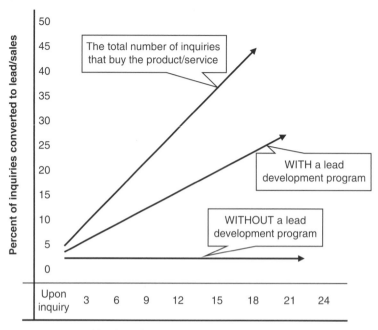

Number of months between inquiry and sales

Figure 16.3   Percent of inquiries converted to leads and purchase vs. time
Source: Coe (2004).

cost was $254. Most recent surveys have placed the average now at between $350 to $500. (Coe, 2004)

This cost comparison has generated a general reassessment of the respective roles of advertising and of personal selling, in view of the development of new media such as on-line communication (see Figure 16.3). As observed in various survey researches (Coe, 2004) on the cost of the sales force observed in selected industrial sectors, it has been verified – as expected – that the share of the sales force is higher in business-to-business than in consumer markets.

16.2. Selling or personal communication

Personal selling is the most effective means of communication at certain stages of the buying process, especially when preferences need to be developed and the decision to buy spurred on (see Figure 16.4). Due to the developments in communication technology, the role of salespersons is now undergoing a major transformation. Their role in strategic marketing is on the increase and the more routine tasks are increasingly being assumed by cheaper impersonal means of communication.

16.2.1. Sales force tasks and objectives

The first step in developing a personal communication strategy is to define the role of the sales force in the overall marketing strategy. This can only be

done by clearly defining the kind of relationship the firm wants to establish with its customers in each product market.

As illustrated in Figure 16.5, one can identify three types of activity that any sales force exercises:

- *Selling*, which implies prospecting and approaching potential buyers, negotiating sales conditions and closing sales.
- *Servicing*, which implies delivery, technical assistance, after-sales service, merchandising, and so on.
- *Information gathering*, which involves market research, business intelligence, monitoring of competitors' activities, needs analysis, and so on.

Thus, the salesperson is not only the firm's commercial arm, but also an important element in its marketing information system.

In practice, the terms 'salesperson' and 'sales representative' can cover very different missions, depending on the emphasis placed on one or other of the three functions above. The following categories of salesperson can be identified:

- *The delivery person's* function is to ensure the physical delivery of the product.
- *The sales clerk's* role is to assist customers in their choice and to take orders. Sales clerks operate at the point of sale or stand behind the counter.

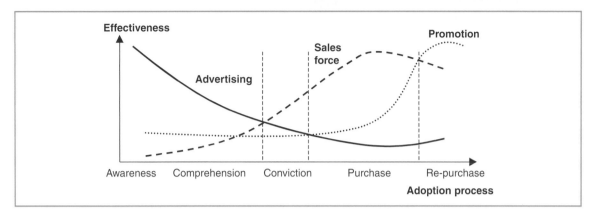

Figure 16.4 Marketing communication effectiveness at different stages of the adoption process
Source: Adapted from Kotler (1967/2006).

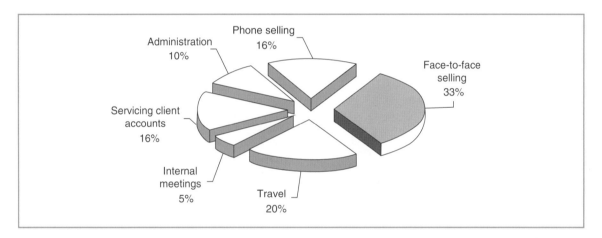

Figure 16.5 The tasks of the sales force
Source: O'Connell and Keenan (1990).

- *The travelling salesperson* visits the retailers or the distributors, takes their orders and performs non-selling activities such as checking inventory, handling retailers' complaints, and so on.
- *The merchandiser's* role is not to sell but rather to organise promotional activities at the sales point and to arrange point-of-purchase displays.
- *The missionary delegate* is not permitted to take an order, but has a role to inform and educate potential users. This is typically the role played by the medical representatives in the pharmaceutical industry.
- *The sales engineer* has a technical competence and operates as a consultant vis-à-vis the customer, providing assistance and advice. It is the role played by IBM sales engineers.
- *The sales representative* is an independent salesperson selling durable goods like cars and vacuum cleaners, or services like insurance, where creative selling is very important.

- *The negotiator* is in charge of the financial engineering of vast industrial projects and responsible for negotiations with government authorities and industrial partners.

Once the type of mission assigned to the salesperson is defined, the problem is to know how to organise commercial relations and which tasks to assign to the sales force, to the distribution network and to advertising.

16.2.2. The new role of the sales force

Generally speaking, the true role of a salesperson remains first and foremost tied to satisfying the need for two-way communication felt by well-informed customers who have demands about how the product can be adapted to their own needs. From the firm's viewpoint, the sales force's new effectiveness is mainly linked to their ability in collecting and transmitting information so as to increase the speed of adjustment to market changes. This is how a Japanese firm conceives the role of the sales force.

> Salesmen are irreplaceable canvassers of information; they must be trained: (a) to listen to the customer, much more than to know seductive sales speech of the kind: 'the ten secrets of selling'; (b) to be humble when criticised, much more than display militant pride of the kind: 'the products of firm X are the best'; (c) to be in solidarity with other salesmen and with his firm to facilitate cross-checking and return of information, much more than pursue the superficial solitude of the sales person who only tries to reach his quota in order to improve his own performance. (Xardel, 1982)

This evolution in the notion of the role of the sales force therefore tends to increase its direct participation in strategic marketing. In addition to operational marketing functions, the sales force now exercises various strategic functions. The typical functions of the sales force are

- winning acceptance for new products;
- developing new customers;
- maintaining customer loyalty;
- providing technical service to facilitate sales;
- communicating product information;
- gathering information.

Several of these selling objectives, such as winning acceptance for new products, developing new customers and gathering information, are typically related to strategic marketing. The salesperson can therefore play an important role in strategic marketing, in so far as he or she participates in elaborating product policy through the information they supply regarding buyers' needs.

16.2.3. Opposition between transactional and relationship selling

Commercial negotiation and selling techniques are often thought to be the same. These are, however, two completely different procedures.

> Selling is convincing someone – the customer – that a proposed product or service best answers his or her needs; 'negotiating' is jointly analysing a situation where there is some common interest, even though diverging interests are apparent and each party has something to sell or conditions to impose, so as to come to a mutually satisfying agreement. (Guérin *et al.*, 1979, quoted by Dupont, 1994, p. 247)

Selling techniques are indubitably efficient to close the sale and are often associated with various aggressive selling methods: hard sell or manipulative marketing. These techniques were popular in the 1960s in operational

marketing when the sales orientation was predominant (see Chapter 1). They have been challenged over the past 10 years, under the influence of all the changes in customer behaviour and in the competitive environment, as mentioned previously.

The differences between single transaction and relationship selling are many. Transaction selling focuses on a discrete, individual sale. The relationships end once the sale is consummated.

- Relationship selling is oriented towards a strong and *lasting relationship*. Maintaining and cultivating the customer base is the key objective, in order to create a mutually profitable relationship.
- Relationship selling presupposes the opportunity for *shared benefits*, while transaction marketing works on a model of contradictory needs: the buyer wants a good price; the seller wants a high profit.
- Single transaction sellers are sometimes part of the seedier side of marketing.

> New York City electronic retailers, for example, often run afoul of the authorities for advertising unrealistically low prices, then once the consumer is in the store, engaging in 'bait-and-switch' and other less savoury sales tactics. They can get away with it because of the steady flow of tourists and the almost complete lack of repeat business. Their goal is not to build lasting relationships with customers but to make a continuous series of first-time purchases. Other merchants, with a greater incidence of repeat business, would not last long with such practices. (Schnaars, 1998, p. 190)

Relationship selling differs from transactional selling in other respects as well. While the latter focuses almost solely on price, the former shifts the *emphasis to non-economic benefits*, such as services, delivery time and the certainty of continued supply. Traditional selling techniques had to evolve towards relationship selling for three reasons.

1. In traditional selling (based on the systematic application of selling techniques), it is rarely understood that selling is above all an *act of communication*, a mutual discovery of questions and answers and not a unilateral act of manipulation.
2. If traditional selling techniques seem less efficient today and often come up against resistance and scepticism from well-informed prospects (partially due to consumerism), this is because the decision to buy depends more upon *complex mechanisms of social influence* and less upon elementary psychological mechanisms.
3. Third, traditional selling techniques do not consider the fact that the practice of relationship selling, that is helping a customer find the solution to a problem, has become the core principle of a market-oriented strategy,

where selling is *customer problem solving*, not merely selling available products.

As many markets reached maturity in highly industrialised economies, it became increasingly obvious that keeping existing customers happy was less costly than recruiting new customers, a difficult and risky strategy implying increased price competition (Reichheld and Teal, 2001). Progressively, in non-expansible markets, the objective of 'customer retention' over customer attraction has gained acceptance.

This new paradigm implies that the objective becomes more to maximise customers' share than market share. In practice, it means that once a customer is gained, to try and cover the largest share of his or her purchases within the product category. Instead of trying to close a transaction, it is preferable to build a long lasting and mutually profitable relationship with the customer. The main differences between the two approaches are summarised in Table 16.3.

This new selling orientation have several impacts on the marketing process.

- It creates a new culture where the relationship is more important than the transaction itself. Success is measured by reference to the number of lasting relationships generated.
- It creates a change in the analysis tools used. Personal data banks are key. All the information concerning the customer are recorded and everybody within the firm has a free access to the bank.
- It creates a change in the selling and communication instruments used. The tools of direct marketing, *mailing, call centre*, and so on, are the more popular instruments.
- A new managerial tool emerges *Consumer Relationship Management (CRM)* which, as *Market-Driven Management*, is a new corporate philosophy requiring a deep reorganisation of the firm's management, not only within the marketing department, but also within the other functions.
- CRM constites the natural continuation of the movement triggered by *Market-Driven Management*, with a stronger emphasis on the relationship.

The practice of relationship or counselling selling – as opposed to the 'impose–convince–suggest–please' system – is characterised by the importance given (a) to true and non-manipulative exploration of the customer's motivations and motives and (b) to the search for a long-lasting mutually satisfactory relationship between buyers and sellers. Relationship selling has shifted attention from 'closing' a singular sale to creating the necessary conditions for a long-term relationship between the firm and its customers that in the long run breeds successful sales encounters.

> Relationship selling is customer-oriented, as opposed to traditional selling which is product-oriented. Selling is customer problem-solving, not merely selling available products. (Donaldson, 1998, p. 79)

In market-oriented firms, there is a tendency to change the vocabulary from sales force to *sales counsellors*, professional representatives or sales consultants.

In a company having chosen to develop a market-oriented strategy, commercial negotiation has received a mission, which is capital for the firm's survival: to build a sustainable relationship with customers. This means a relationship which is profitable for both parties. In relationship selling, *the profit centre is the customer* and not the product or the brand. Attracting new customers is viewed as an intermediate objective; maintaining the existing customer base is a major objective for a long-term mutually profitable relationship. In this context, the monitoring of the customer's portfolio composition and of the quality of the market share are of primary importance. Read Slymotsky and Shapiro (1993) on this subject.

Pitfalls of relationship selling

As pointed out by Schnaars (1998, p. 190), sometimes relationships are forced, namely when the sellers engineer switching costs into their transactions that tie the customer in a way that denies the buyer a real choice and makes him a *captive customer*. Firms that rely on proprietary technologies and patented parts also forced lasting

---

Table 16.3 The opposition between transactional and relationship selling

Criteria	Transactional selling	Relationship selling
Mission	Conquest	Loyalty building
Objective	Transactions, market share	Relationships, customer share
Organisation	Brand (product) management	Customer management
Information	Market research	Dialogue, data bases
Environment	Non-saturated markets	Saturated markets
Types of markets	B2C and B2B	B2B

Source: Adapted from Donaldson (1998).

relationships. Long-term contracts do the same. In each of these cases the seller may bolt given the opportunity to do so. There are other limitations to relationship marketing:

- The firm that builds a relationship usually charges a *premium price* and is therefore vulnerable to price competition from low price sellers.
- Some customers may refuse to become dependent on a *single supplier*, a very sensitive issue in B2B markets.
- Customers may place their *easy-to-fill orders* to lower-price competitors and leave the more difficult or less profitable orders to the high service firm.
- In other cases, there may be simply *no mutual benefit* for the buyer and seller (see Table 16.4).

Relationship selling is particularly useful in B2B marketing where this supplier–customer link is especially close, lasting and important for both parties. This is also the philosophy underlying trade marketing, in the relationship binding manufacturers and distributors. In general, relationship selling is the irreplaceable complement to a strategy based on the *solution-to-a-problem approach* as described earlier.

Setting up a relationship selling process

Approaching customers in relationship selling is different from traditional selling because of the emphasis on pre-sales and post-sales activities. There are five different phases in relationship selling:

1. *Systematic search for information.* This means identifying prospects, potential customers who might need the product and who might buy it. This is a permanent activity.
2. *Selecting a target.* Here the purpose is to analyse the objective reasons why a prospect could become a prospective customer and have reasons for becoming a buyer. The real question is to find out to what extent our firm can be useful to this customer.
3. *Convincing good customers.* It is essential that the salesperson attract customers whose value and potential

justify the time and effort which will be devoted to them. This is the beginning of the selling phase itself, which includes the sales presentation, negotiation, answers to objections and the conclusion of the agreement.

4. *Building the relationship.* A relationship of trust must be built up and, once the relationship is established, the follow-up must be organised. The salesperson is the problem-solver, who sells, not a product, but the service (or the solution) provided by the product.

5. *Maintaining and reinforcing the relationship.* Maintaining a relationship is particularly based on personalised service achieved through better understanding of customers' needs. The objective is to maintain close contact with the customer and to build up customer loyalty. The firm can thus construct a barrier to competition, as changing suppliers would imply switching costs.

Relationship selling implies giving the role of advisor to the salesperson, as *a seller of solutions*. In a company which has opted for market orientation, a salesperson is a partner working towards the customer's long-term performance, even if he or she cannot see the possibility of an immediate sale. Relationship selling has developed substantially in the B2B context and is progressively gaining a foothold in B2C markets through the possibilities offered by direct and interactive marketing.

16.2.4. Organisation of the sales force

A firm can organise its sales force in different ways. The organisation can be by territory, by product, by customer or even a combination of these.

Territory-based organisation. This is the most common structure and also the simplest organisation. The salesperson is the firm's exclusive representative for its full product line for all current and potential customers. This structure has several advantages: first, it defines clearly the sales representative's responsibilities; second, it motivates the salesperson, who has the full exclusivity on the

---

Table 16.4   Typology of sales calls

- *Cold calling* – also called blind call.
- *Lead qualification* – determining if the firm or individual qualifies.
- *Lead development* – keeping the sales opportunities alive.
- *Proposal or closing* – going for the sale.
- *Up-sell and cross-sell* – finding other opportunities within the customer.
- *Relationship building* – creating more in-depth relationship with key people.
- *Routine servicing* – sometimes referred to as 'go see' call.
- *Problem resolution* – handling some type of problem.
- Most B2B sales managers feel that between 8 and 10 calls are required to close a complex sale.

Source: Coe (2004).

territory; and finally, it minimises costs and travel expenses. This structure is only appropriate when products are few in number or similar and when customers have the same kind of needs. A firm producing paints and varnishes, whose customers are wholesalers, retailers and industrial users (building painters, car bodies, and so on) clearly cannot use the same salesperson to cultivate these different customer groups.

Product-based organisation. This second structure is preferable when products are very different, technically complex and require appropriate technical competence. In this case, the salesperson is more specialised and better equipped to meet clients' needs and also to counter rivals. The problem with this structure is that costs may increase manifold, since several salespersons from the same firm may visit the same customer. For example, Rank Xerox uses different salespersons for photocopying machines and for word-processing units.

Customer-based organisation. Organisation by customer categories is adopted when clients' needs are very different and require specific abilities. Customers may be classified by industrial sector, by size or by their method of buying. We find here the same criteria as those of segmentation presented in Chapter 6.

The advantage of a customer-based structure is that each sales force is specialised and becomes very knowledgeable about specific customer needs. But if customers are dispersed geographically, this organisation can be very costly. Most computer firms organise their sales force by customer groups: banks and insurance, industrial customers, retailers, and so on.

Other more complex forms of organisation combining pairs of criteria also exist. Salespersons can be specialised by product–territory, customer–territory or even by territory–customer–product. This normally happens in very large enterprises with many products and varied clients.

16.2.5. Deciding on the size of the sales force

Determining the number of salespeople is a problem logically similar to the advertising budget (see Box 16.1). In practice, however, it can be resolved more simply because market response is easier to measure. Different approaches are possible. The simplest no doubt is the one based on the salesperson's work load. The procedure is as follows:

The underlying philosophy in *the call-load approach* is that large customers should be serviced differently from medium-sized customers, and medium-sized customers differently from small customers.

- *The first step* is to have a breakdown of customer by class, size, sector or geographic location.
- *The next step* is to develop a theoretical call frequency for each class. Experience shows that as customer grows larger, the number of sales calls does not grow in direct proportion to the increase in sales. Churchill *et al.* (1997) suggested that the relationship between customer size and sales calls can be clearly seen when these two factors are plotted on semi-log paper, which reflects the presence of diminishing returns. For every customer class, multiplying the call frequency times the number of account in any class provides a specific call frequency.
- *In the third step*, the number of calls made by an average salesperson during 1 year must be determined.

The factors to consider here are: number of working days after deducting holidays, weekends, vacations, and so on; percentage of non-selling time devoted to sales meetings, sick leave, laboratory training, and so on; number of calls made per day by salesperson and by territory; and variation in call capacity between urban and rural territories.

Given the number of visits that a salesperson can make in a given customer class, it is then possible to determine

---

BOX 16.1

IMPLEMENTATION PROBLEM: HOW TO CALCULATE THE COST OF SALES CALL?

Number of calls per year
5 weeks/year (i.e. 2 weeks for holiday; 3 weeks for vacation/time off/sick time) and 2 weeks for meetings trade shows, etc.

Therefore, 45 selling weeks:
5 days/week − 1 day for calls/paper work = 4 days/week selling time
2–3 face-to-face calls per day = *360–540 calls per year*

Yearly cost of a salesperson
$75K average compensation (salary, commission, bonus, etc.)
+$15K in benefits @ 20% salary

+$45K in travel costs $1K/week average
+$40K allocated for sales management cost @20% of $200K
= *$175 total cost of field person*

Cost per call
$175/ 540 calls/year = $324 per call
$175/ 360 calls/year = $486 per call

Source: Coe (2004).

Average cost per call using these totals is $405

the size of the necessary sales force from the following expression:

$$FDV = \frac{(\text{Number of potential customers}) \cdot (\text{Frequencies of visits})}{(\text{Average number of visits per salesmen})}$$

The calculation is repeated for each customer class. This approach is valid for current customers and must be extended to prospective customers as well. For other methods of setting the size of the sales force, see Semlow (1959) and Lambert (1968).

Other methods are based on direct or indirect measures of market response to an increase of the frequency of calls through the sales force. The method developed by Semlow is based on several indicators of buying power within each sales territory. A successful application of this method to the insurance sector is presented by Lambin (1965).

In business-to-business markets, direct sales measures of visit frequency are more easily obtainable. An econometric study conducted by Lambert (1968) in the hospitals market has contributed to improve in a significant way the overall allocation of selling efforts among sales territories.

16.3. Advertising communication decisions

Advertising is a means of communication by which a firm can deliver a message to potential buyers with whom it is not in direct contact. When a firm resorts to advertising, it is effectively following a pull communication strategy. Its main objective is to create brand image and brand equity, and to ensure co-operation from distributors. Just as the

sales force is the best tool for a push strategy, advertising is the best means for a pull strategy.

In Chapter 4 (see Section 4.2.5), we described what advertising represents for the advertiser and its utility to the customer. Recall briefly that

- for the firm, the function of advertising is to produce knowledge for consumers and to generate interest among them in order to create demand for its product;
- for consumers, advertising allows them to learn about the distinctive characteristics claimed by the manufacturer. Advertising also helps them to save personal time, since the information reaches them directly without their having to collect it.

16.3.1. The value of advertising information

The amount of information contained in advertising is an important societal issue and advertising's informational function lends some legitimacy to advertising in a market economy. The information categories or 'cues' present in advertisements are listed in Table 16.5.

In a meta-analysis conducted by Abernethy and Frank (1996) across 118 data sets (for a total of 91,438 ads), the mean number of cues was 2.04. More than 84 per cent of the ads had at least one cue, 58 per cent had two or more cues and 33 per cent had three or more cues. The type of information most commonly presented is performance, which appeared in 43 per cent of the ads studied. Other common types of information are availability (37 per cent), components (33 per cent), price (25 per cent), quality

---

Table 16.5   Advertising information content categories

1. *Price*: What does the product cost? What is the value retention capability?

2. *Quality*: What are the product's characteristics that distinguish it from competing products?

3. *Performance*: What does the product do and how well it does what it is designed to do in comparison to alternative purchases?

4. *Components*: What is the product comprised of? What ingredients does it contain?

5. *Availability*: Where can the product be purchased? When, will the product be available for purchase?

6. *Special offers*: What limited-time non-price deals are available with a particular purchase?

7. *Taste*: Is evidence presented that taste is perceived as superior by a sample of potential customers?

8. *Nutrition*: Are specific data given concerning the nutritional content of the product or is a direct comparison made with other products?

9. *Packaging*: What package is the product available in which makes it more desirable alternatives?

10. *Warranties*: What post-purchase assurances accompany the product?

11. *Safety*: What safety features are available on a particular product compared to alternatives?

12. *Independent research*: Are results of research gathered by an independent research firm presented?

13. *Company research*: e-data gathered by a company to compare its product with a competitor's presented?

14. *New ideas*: Is a totally new concept introduced during the commercial? Are its advantages presented?

Source: Adapted from Resnik and Stern (1977).

(19 per cent) and special offers (13 per cent). It is interesting to note that ads from developed and developing countries had relatively similar number of cues: on average, 2.08 and 1.92 respectively.

Given that advertising information is an information source dominated by the producer, it does not have the same value as other sources of information in the eyes of the consumer. It is indeed a sales appeal, which generates information designed to emphasise the positive aspects of the product. However, as far as the consumer is concerned, the utility of this type of information is twofold:

- on the one hand, the consumer can get to know the distinctive qualities claimed by the producer and to see whether what the product 'promises' corresponds to what the consumer is seeking;
- on the other hand, it helps him save personal time, since the information reaches him or her without the consumer having to collect it.

Lepage (1982, p. 53), underlines the fact that the important point for the consumers is that the efficiency of the advertising message intended to reach them should be higher than it would have cost them to collect the same information by other means, for example, by displacing themselves. These two services performed by advertising have the effect of helping the consumer to perceive opportunities of choice and of new potential forms of satisfaction at a minimum cost (Kirzner, 1973).

16.3.2. The different forms of advertising communication

Since the advent of the early form of advertising, advertising communication objectives have diversified considerably, and different forms of advertising can be identified while using the same media.

Concept advertising

This is a media-advertising message with a mainly 'attitudinal' communication objective: to influence the buyer's attitude towards the brand. Its role can be defined as follows,

> The creative efforts of many national advertisers are designed, not to induce immediate action, but to build favourable attitudes that will lead to eventual purchase. (Dhalla, 1978)

This definition implies that the effectiveness of this type of advertising can only be viewed from a long-term perspective. The notion of attitude holds a central position here. The objective is mainly to create an image based on communicating a concept.

Promotional advertising

This is a media-advertising message with a mainly 'behavioural' communication objective: to influence the buyers' purchasing behaviour rather than their attitudes. The objective is to trigger the act of purchase. Its effectiveness is evaluated directly in terms of actual sales. This is the most aggressive type of communication, although it is not incompatible with image creation. However, its immediate purpose is to achieve short-term results.

Response advertising

This is a personalised message of an offer, having the objective of generating a 'relationship' with the prospect by encouraging a response from the latter on the basis of which a commercial relation can be built.

This type of advertising tries to reconcile the characteristics of the two previous ones: building an image, but also encouraging a measurable response allowing an immediate appraisal of the effectiveness of the communication. This type of media advertising is expanding rapidly now, and is directly linked to interactive marketing, discussed in Chapter 12.

16.3.3. Prerequisites of concept advertising

There are still too many firms that tend to assimilate advertising with marketing and to approach marketing by advertising. In fact, advertising is only a complement, which is sometimes, but not always, indispensable to a more fundamental process of strategic marketing. For advertising to be effective, a number of prerequisites should ideally prevail:

- Advertising is one element of the marketing mix and its role cannot be separated from the roles of the other marketing instruments. As a general rule, advertising will be effective only when the other marketing factors have been chosen: a differentiated and clearly positioned product sold at a competitive price through a well-adapted distribution network.
- Advertising is useful to the consumer mainly for complex products having *internal qualities* that cannot be discovered by inspection. For experience goods (such as food products or shampoos) and for credence goods (such as motor oil and medical services) consumers have lots to gain from truthful advertising.
- To be effective, advertising should promote a *distinctive characteristic* to clearly position the brand in the minds of consumers as being different from competing brands. The distinctive characteristic can be the promise of the brand, but also its personality, its look or its symbolic value.

- Advertising is particularly effective in markets or segments where *primary demand is expansible*. Its role is then to stimulate the need for the product category as a whole. In non-expansible markets, the main role of advertising is to stimulate selective demand and to create communication effects at the brand level.
- The size of the reference market must be large enough to absorb the cost of an advertising campaign, and the firm must have enough financial resources to reach the threshold levels of the advertising response function.

Thus, the advertising communication platform is the complement of a strategic marketing programme. The advertising positioning sought must be in line with the marketing positioning adopted and based on a sound strategic thinking, without which advertising cannot be effective.

16.3.4. Alternative advertising objectives

To determine the objectives of advertising communication, it is useful to refer back to the three levels of market response analysed in Chapter 9 (see Table 9.1):

- *Cognitive response,* which relates to awareness and to knowledge of the product characteristics. At this level, the advertiser can set objectives of information, recall, recognition or familiarity.
- *Affective response*, which relates to the overall evaluation of the brand in terms of feelings, favourable or unfavourable judgements and preferences. The objectives will be to influence attitude and to create purchase intention.
- *Behavioural response*, which refers to buying behaviour and to post-purchase behaviour, but also to all other forms of behavioural response observed as the result of a communication, such as visiting a showroom, requesting a catalogue, sending a reply coupon.

It is common practice to consider these three levels as a sequence, as potential buyers pass successively through the three stages: cognitive, affective and behavioural (Lavidge and Steiner, 1961). This sequence of reactions is known as the learning model. As noted in Chapter 9, this model needs to be adjusted in terms of the buyer's degree of involvement (see Figure 9.1). Although not generally applicable, the learning response model nevertheless remains a useful tool for defining the priority objectives of communication.

Keeping this hierarchy of objectives in mind, Rossiter and Percy (1987) have identified five different communication effects that can be caused, in whole or in part, by advertising. These effects reconstitute the process followed by the buyer when confronted with a purchasing decision; there can therefore be as many possible objectives for communication.

Development of primary demand

Existence of need is a prerequisite that determines the effectiveness of any act of communication. Every product satisfies a product category need. Perception of this need by potential buyers can be stimulated by advertising. Advertising thus helps develop total demand in the market. Three distinct situations can exist:

- The category need is *present and well perceived* by potential customers. In this case, generic advertising is not justified. This is the case for many low-involvement, frequently purchased products, where purchasing is done on a routine basis.
- The category need is *perceived but neglected or forgotten* and the role of generic advertising is to remind the prospective customer of previously established need. This is the case for infrequently purchased or infrequently used products like pain remedies.
- The perception of the *category need is weak or not established* in the target group of potential users. In this case, generic advertising can sell the benefits of the product category. The typical example is the campaign in favour of the use of condoms to fight against the spread of AIDS. Selling category need is a communication objective for all new products, and in particular for new-to-the-world products.

In generic advertising campaigns, the advertising content places the emphasis on the core service of the product and/or on the product benefits (see Exhibit 16.1). This type of communication message will not only benefit the advertiser but also the competing firms.

Creating brand awareness

This is the first level of cognitive response. In Chapter 6, we defined brand awareness as the buyer's ability to identify a brand in sufficient detail to propose, choose or use a brand. Three kinds of advertising objectives, based on awareness, can be identified:

- To create or maintain *brand recognition* so the buyers identify the brand at the point of sale and are induced to check the existence of a category need.
- To create or maintain *brand recall* to induce buyers to select the brand once the category need has been experienced.
- To emphasise *both brand recognition and brand recall*.

These communication objectives imply different advertising contents. For brand recognition, the advertising content will emphasise the visual elements (logo, colours and packaging), while for brand recall the advertising will seek to repeat the brand name in audio and visual media and in headlines, to associate the brand name with the core service.

EXHIBIT 16.1

IS ADVERTISING OF PRESCRIPTION DRUGS DIFFERENT?

In the United States, since the Food and Drug Administration (FDA) relaxed its guidelines on television advertising in August 1997, spending on direct-to-consumer advertising has taken off. Spending in America on ads for prescription drugs, estimated at more than $1 billion in 1998, now exceeds that on beer advertising. A study published in 1998 by *Prevention* magazine and supported by the FDA found that 90 per cent of the 1,200 people questioned had seen a drug advertisement and a third had visited their doctors as a result. Remarkably, 80 per cent of doctors agreed to prescribe the drug.

In Europe, a 1992 ruling from the European Commission prohibits prescription-drug companies from selling their wares directly to Europe's consumers. This means that they cannot advertise their products in the popular press or on television. They can pitch them to doctors and pharmacists only in medical journals and other professional publication. At the same time the European Commission and many European governments talk loftily of the need for 'patient empowerment'; greater public awareness and understanding about diseases and their therapies. Many advocates for patients' rights raise the following question: can patients simultaneously be asked to take more responsibility for their health and denied access to some of the information that may help them to do so?

It remains that it is right to treat advertising of prescription drugs differently from advertising of baked beans. Drugs have side effects and patients may ignore them more readily than their doctor would. Drug firms are also tempted to make misleading claims. In addition, in Europe, patients pay far less of the drugs bill than those in the United States. So advertising may encourage patients to put pressure on their doctors to dispense something that appears almost free to them, but raises the bill to the taxpayer.

However, consumer advertising is also a powerful way to stimulate public interest in health. It need not become a tough sell. Indeed in Europe, people still think of themselves as patients rather than health-care consumers. As a first step, it would be reasonable to insist that advertising gives information about diseases and alternative treatments rather than merely pushing a single product. For, if patients are to take more responsibility for their health, they do deserve reliable information on available treatments.

Source: Adapted from *The Economist* (1998, pp. 57–8).

Creating a favourable brand attitude

The objective is to create, improve, maintain and modify buyers' attitudes towards the brand. It is therefore affective response which intervenes here (see Exhibit 16.2). Chapter 9 describes the components of attitude. The following communication strategies are open to the advertiser:

- To convince the target audience to give more *importance* to a particular product attribute on which the brand is well placed in comparison to rival brands.
- To convince the target audience of the firm's *technological superiority* in the product category.
- To *reinforce beliefs* and the conviction of the target audience on the presence of a determining attribute in the brand.
- To *reposition the brand* by associating its use with another set of needs or purchase motivations.
- To *eliminate a negative attitude* by associating the brand with a set of positive values.
- To call attention to *neglected attributes* by consumers in their decision-making process.
- To alter the beliefs of the target audience about *competing brands*.

The last strategy can only be adopted in countries where comparative advertising is authorised, as in the United Kingdom. The European Commission has recently published a directive for comparative advertising in the European Union.

It is important to identify clearly the implicit assumptions of a communication strategy based on brand attitude. They can be summarised as follows:

- The advertiser must emphasise the features or characteristics in which it has the strongest competitive advantage.
- It is useless to try to modify buyers' perceptions when the brand does not really have the claimed characteristic.
- The major criticism directed against advertising is the adoption of arguments or themes, which are totally unrelated to product attributes important to the buyer.

In other words, a market-driven communication strategy is based on the idea that advertising is mainly designed to help the buyer buy and not simply to praise the advertiser. This vision of a communication strategy falls well in line with the market orientation concept.

Stimulate brand purchase intention

Purchase intention is halfway between the affective and the behavioural response. Two kinds of situations may arise:

- The buyer is weakly or not at all involved in the purchasing decision and there is no conscious, prior

EXHIBIT 16.2

KODAK FOCUSES ON TEEN-GIRLS CONSUMERS

Eastman Kodak Co. has seen the future: it is female and barely adolescent. In an attempt to boost sales in what it regards as a lucrative demographic group, the US Company is launching its first youth marketing campaign, one that targets so-called tween girls – generally defined as those from 9 to 15 years old. Kodak's internal marketing presentations proclaim that this is an era of 'girl power' in which females, 13–15 years olds, are 'hyper consumers' and the 'key drivers' of today's trends and pop culture. Kodak says it will spend $75 million over 5 years to reach tweens through television, radio, print and Internet banner ads created by the ad agency Saatchi & Saatchi PLC. [...] A company study

shows that tween girls are more likely than boys to own a camera , 75 per cent to 49 per cent. An independent study used by Kodak shows that teen girls consider taking pictures as popular as dating. And pictures, they say, are more important possessions than their own pets. [...] In its print ads, Kodak beckons to tween girls by saying that its disposable cameras 'get guys to smile at you with the touch of a button' and that the camera 'attracts a crowd like flies to the school cafeteria.'

Source: The Wall Street Journal Europe, 17 June 1999.

intention to buy until the last minute at the point of purchase. This is the case for low perceived-risk products and also for routinely purchased products. In this type of situation, to stimulate brand purchase intention is not an advertising objective.

- The buyer has a conscious purchase intention during advertising exposure. In the latter case, promotional advertising can play a role by using incentives (price reductions, special offers, and so on) that precipitate the buying decision or encourage repurchase.

Recall that the intention to buy is only expressed when there is also a *state of shortage*, that is, when the category need is felt. Thus, the two states, need and intention, are closely associated. Yet intention to buy is not a frequently recurring event in any particular consumer.

Markets that are huge in their annual volume are made up of buying decisions made by very small numbers of people in a given period of time. For example, in a typical week in 1982, American retailers sold over $365 million worth of shoes. But during that week (as shown in our study that year) only six persons in 100 bought shoes for themselves or their children. Similarly, only 28 adults in 1000 bought any kinds of women's slacks, jeans, or shorts in the course of a week, and only 21 bought a dress. Fourteen in 1000 bought a small appliance; 18 in 1000 bought furniture; 3 in 1000 bought an article of luggage. (Bogart, 1986, p. 267)

Hence, many markets with very high turnovers, such as those mentioned in the examples above depend each week on the buying decisions of a small number of people. It is not surprising to find that advertising messages give rise to relatively few immediate purchase intentions, since in most cases the prerequisite is not there: namely the existence of a state of need.

Purchase facilitation

This last objective of advertising communication deals with the other marketing factors (the four Ps), without which there can be no purchase: a product that keeps its promise, retail availability of the product, acceptable price, and competence and availability of the sales force. When these conditions are not all met, advertising can sometimes help to reduce or minimise problems by, for example, defending the market price, or by working as a substitute to distribution through direct marketing.

Advertising objectives are numerous and very diversified and it is important to define them clearly before the organisation of an advertising campaign. As already indicated above, it is up to strategic marketing people, generally brand managers, to propose the advertising communication objective.

16.4. Sales promotion decisions

Sales promotion includes all the incentive tools which, often locally and in a non-permanent way, are used by the firm to complement and reinforce advertising and the sales force action, and to stimulate quicker and/or larger purchase of a good or service. Sales promotion is part of the overall marketing strategy as suggested by the following definition

Sales promotion is a process combining a set of communication tools and techniques, implemented within the framework of the marketing plan designed by the firm, in order to induce among the target groups, in the short or in the long term, the adoption or the modification of a consuming or purchase behaviour. (Ingold, 1995, p. 25)

During the last decade, promotion has gained in importance and sales promotion expenditures have been increasing annually as a percentage of the total communication budget.

According to the Havas study (1998), promotion expenditures in the UK amounted to 17,210 Mln GBP in 1997, against 15,917 Mln in 1996, or a 8.1 per cent increase. Direct marketing expenditures amounted to 2890 Mln GBP in 1997. In percent of total marketing communication expenditures, promotion amounted to 17.2 per cent and direct marketing to 16.8 per cent. (Havas 1998, p. 26)

The share of promotion expenditures in the total marketing communication budget observed in each European country is shown in Table 16.6.

Several factors, both internal and external, have contributed to the rapid growth of sales promotion:

- Consumers, confronted with a decline of their purchasing power, are more price sensitive and react positively to promotional activities.
- Distributors, more concentrated and powerful, demand from manufacturers more promotions to help them build store traffic.
- Competition intensifies and competitors use consumer and trade promotions more frequently.
- Effectiveness of mass media advertising has declined because of rising costs, media clutter and similarity among competing brands.
- Companies confronted with a slowing down of sales are more concerned by short-term results.
- Any promotion is in fact a disguised price reduction, but which is limited in time and scope. This flexibility is highly praised by marketing people.

To these factors, one must also add the development of direct marketing, which by nature often has a promotional content.

16.4.1. Objectives of sales promotion

The objectives of sales promotion vary with the type of promotions; it is common practice to make a distinction according to the sender of the promotion (manufacturer or distributor) and according to the target (consumer, distributor, sales force). Following Ingold's classification (1995, p. 26), we will make a distinction between four types of promotions:

1. *In consumer promotions* a direct, indirect or hypothetical benefit (samples, coupons, rebates, cash refund offer, and so on) is proposed to consumers to stimulate the purchase of a product. Manufacturers generally offer consumer promotions through the distribution channel.
2. *Trade promotions* are proposed to retailers or wholesalers, generally taking the form of money allowances, to persuade them (a) to carry the brand, (b) to carry more units than the normal amount, (c) to promote the brand by featuring display or price reductions or (d) to push the products in their stores.
3. *Commercial promotions* are promotional activities organised by distributors and targeting their own customers' base, generally using the financial support given by manufacturers.
4. *Sales force or network promotion*, where the objective is to stimulate all the partners involved in the selling activities (sales force, wholesalers, retailers) through individual incentives.

Table 16.6   Share of sales promotion expenditures in the total marketing communication budget

Countries	Share of promotion expenditures in the communication budget in 1997 (%)	Expenditures in local currencies
Germany	15.7	22,054 million DM
United Kingdom	17.2	2,965 million GBP
France	15.9	25,109 million FRF
Italy	22.2	7,735 billion ITL
Spain	16.6	212,217 million ESP
The Netherlands	19.7	3,096 million NLG
Belgium	35.2	60,694 million BEF
Switzerland	19.5	1,664 million CHF

Source: Havas Europub (1998).

Table 16.7   Objectives by types of promotions

Consumer promotions	Commercial promotions
Trial	Visit to new outlets
First purchase	Customer retention
Repurchase	Visit frequency increase
Loyalty	First purchase
Retention	Purchase in new store facings
Reduced prices	Increase of the average basket
Increase of quantity purchased	
Increase of quantity consumed	
Purchase frequency increase	
Trial of a new variety	
Distributor promotions	**Network promotion**
List of new products	Increase of quantity sold
Stock	Gain in distribution presence
Facing increase	Introduction of new products
Point of purchase display	Increase in size or range
Participation to advertising	Reselling actions

Source: Ingold (1995, p. 63).

These distinctions are sometimes artificial to the extent where a specific promotion can take simultaneously one of these forms. The distinction remains useful, however, to define as clearly as possible the promotion objective. Examples of promotion objectives are presented in Table 16.7. For a more detailed description of these objectives, see Ingold (1995, pp. 63–70).

16.4.2. The different promotion tools

There are many different sales-promotion tools which can be divided, as proposed by *LSA* (1982), into four main groups:

1. *Price reductions.* Essentially this is selling something for less money; several methods exist.
2. *Selling with premiums or gifts.* Small items are given to buyers either at the time of purchase or afterwards.
3. *Samples and trials.* Free distribution, trials or tasting allow consumers to test the product.
4. *Games and contests.* These games give buyers a chance to win a big prize.

There are many ways of applying each group as shown in Table 16.8.

New sales-promotion tools have appeared over the last few years based upon information obtained from bar codes, via, for instance, customer loyalty cards and coupons (see Exhibit 16.3). Electronic coupons are immediately distributed to customers targeted through their purchases electronically recorded when they pay.

The system developed by Catalina Marketing is based on reading bar codes by an intelligent scanner and thus avoids giving out coupons to customers who would not be interested in the product. The scanner instructs the computer to print out a coupon for Fanta for someone who had just bought Orangina. Or a customer who had just bought baby products receives a coupon for Pampers.

This has just been brought before the courts in France by Orangina as unfair competition. A decision has not yet been made (*LSA*, 1997, pp. 18–19). It is the misappropriation of clientele which is at stake here.

In other words, Orangina would accept that customers buying Coca-Cola get a coupon for Fanta (which belongs to the same group) or that those buying Mars get a Coca-Cola coupon (complementary product) but not a coupon from a competitor for the same product category.

The issue at stake is important: do distributors have the right to orient customers to any products they choose? May a distributor dispose of his clientele as he wishes?

This explosion of sales-promotion tools and actions has of course a negative side in that they present a high cost both for the manufacturer and for the distributor. At the same time the positive effect of promotions is assailed by competitors who counterattack a successful sales-promotion action with a 'reaction' sales promotion. While such an escalation of promotions benefits the consumer, it ends up by providing never-ending promotions, weakening their effect and provoking speculation and a state of expectancy from consumers.

This explains the *Every Day Low Price* strategy that Procter & Gamble launched with Wal-Mart in the

---

Table 16.8   Description of promotion tools

1. Premiums

With-pack premium: an extra product
  accompanies the product inside (in-pack) or on
  pack (outside).
Recipe: recipe files offered with purchased product
Differed premium: an advantage, which is offered
  at a later date.
Sample: a sample is included.
Package: a reusable container, which can be used
  after consuming the product
Premium (gifts): merchandise offered at a
  relatively low cost or free.
Self-liquidating premium: item sold below its
  normal retail price at no cost for the brand.

2. Games and contests

Contests: possibility of winning a big prize in a
  contest based on consumer's observation,
  knowledge or suggestion.
Sweepstakes: diverse forms of games based on
  chance with a lottery draw.
Winner per store: (or patronage award): a lottery
  where a client may win even without
  purchasing.

3. Price reductions

Coupons: certificates entitling the bearer to a
  stated saving on the purchase of a specific product
Special offer: a reduced price for a limited period
  of time.
Extra-pack: three products for the price of two, four
  products for the price of three, etc.
Banded pack: two related products banded
  together.
Cash refund: provide a price reduction after the
  purchase with proof of full payment.
Buy back: the manufacturer buys back obsolete
  model of the brand.

4. Trials and samples

Free sample: offer on a limited base of a free
  amount of product or service.
Gifts: merchandise offered as an incentive to
  purchase a product, to visit a store, etc.
Free trials: invite prospective buyers to try the
  product without cost and without obligation to buy.
Demonstrations: point of purchases (POPs)
  displays and commercial presentations,
  sometimes with trials or tastiness.

Source: Adapted from *LSA* (1982).

United States where P&G promises to deliver its products without sales promotion but at the lowest possible cost.

16.4.3. Impact of promotions on sales

The effects of sales promotion are complex and go beyond just affecting sales even if that is the main objective. We can distinguish between effects on consumers and effects on distributors. Along with such immediate effects there are long-term consequences which can sometimes be negative for a brand. A distinction must be made between the impact on consumers and on distributors.

Impact of promotions on consumers

These effects are many and varied as illustrated in Figure 16.6. They can be felt before, during and after the promotion action itself:

Internal transfer effect. Loyal buyers take advantage of an offer but would have bought the brand in any case.

Anticipation effect. Sales go down just before a promotion comes into effect because consumers wait for the promotion to buy. This is particularly true when the periodicity for sales promotions is regular.

Decay effect. Sales go down after a special promotion because consumers have stocked up on the product.

Cannibalisation effect. There are purchasing transfers among different sizes and varieties within a range of products during sales promotions.

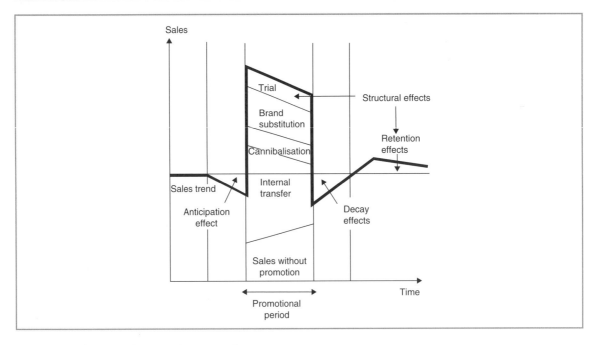

Figure 16.6 Impact of promotions on sales
Source: Ingold (1995).

Brand switching effect. This is what was intended. Additional sales through a switch from some other brand to the brand under promotion.

Trial effect. Whatever the tool, it induces consumers to use the product. This is especially important for new products.

Retention effect. Here we have the positive effects that survive the period of promotion and can keep the product at a superior level of sales after the promotion.

These promotion effects vary according to the phase of product life cycle (PLC) reached by the reference market. During the introduction and growth phases, sales promotion has an accelerator effect in the development of primary demand, by inducing consumers to try out the product. In contrast, during the maturity phase of the PLC, the benefits obtained through promotion are made at the expense of competition, and this can trigger a chain reaction of sales promotion.

Impact of promotions on distributors

Sales promotions organised at the point of sales always have an impact on distributor behaviour. Three major effects can be identified:

Postponement effect. Distributors know, and demand to know, the operational marketing programme of their suppliers and tend to defer purchases in order to stock up for sales promotions.

Overstocking effect. When ordering at times of sales promotions, distributors tend to order as a function of their storage space, which decreases post-promotion orders.

Deviant ordering. Some distributors only order when the products are on promotions and refuse to purchase the product at full price. This is the attitude adopted systematically by hard discounters who can then charge very competitive prices.

Promotions have an important role to play in creating traffic flow in the store and in stimulating shelf rotation. As mentioned earlier, sales promotions also add to logistic and administrative costs for distributors. This means that it is important to check that the proposed promotions are compatible with the distributors' operating mode.

Negative side-effects of promotions

Overly frequent sales promotions can produce a certain number of negative side-effects on buying behaviour and brand image. There are four types of negative effects:

Escalation of promotions. As already mentioned, because of the very success of a first sales promotion, promotion after promotion may be launched. This is desirable neither for the manufacturer nor for the distributor.

Brand confusion. If there are too many promotions the brand image is weakened and promotions can conflict with the brand positioning strategy.

Table 16.9   Cost and profit impact of promotions

Distributors	Cost of promotions in % of turnover	Increase of turnover (in %)	Net income per franc spent
GB	5	13	1.79 F
Delhaize	4	9	1.26 F
Cora	9	19	2.73 F
Match	7	6	0.68 B
Mestdagh	8	11	1.46 F

Source: Van Poppel (1998).

Speculation. If a growing number of purchases are made during sales promotions, consumers may change their buying behaviour by postponing their purchases. This of course is counterproductive, as the purpose of promotions is to increase sales in normal periods. The anticipation effect is then prevalent. It is however important to distinguish between consumers who wait for sales-promotion periods and the very particular group that waits for sales-promotion actions.

Difficulty in price comparison. The multiplication of sales promotions increases the difficulty of evaluating a 'fair price' and of comparing prices. This can reduce a consumer's sensitivity to prices, as Chapter 15 showed (see Box 15.2).

Several authors, one of whom is Froloff (1992), can be consulted on the sensitivity of consumers to sales promotions.

Profitability of sales promotions

Measuring the effectiveness and profitability of sales promotions can often be done by direct observation when detailed sales figures are available, as is usually the case for consumer goods. The development of new measuring techniques based on scanning panels, mentioned earlier in Chapter 5, has revolutionised this. The Nielsen Company, in particular, has developed several tools, among which are Sabine and Scanpro, for directly measuring the impact of sales promotions.

The Accuris group in Belgium has developed a measuring system helping companies to optimise expenditures in sales promotions. Table 16.9 gives some of the results published recently which can explain why sales promotions are so popular.

16.4.4. Pan-European promotions

With the globalisation of markets, and particularly of the European economy, marketers are striving for a consistent and international message. Apart from the economies of scale to be gained, a consistent pan-European promotion message can help strengthen a brand. But setting up an effective pan-European promotion to run in 12 languages across a dozen countries sounds like the ultimate marketing nightmare. For companies having global brands – like Kodak, Mars, Swatch, British Airways, American Express, and so on – the tools at their disposal for promoting them through retail channels around Europe are far from harmonious. Table 16.10 summarises some of the tactics allowed in a few key European markets.

The European Commission is working to find agreement between Member States on all forms of cross-border communications. They even form an expert group to advise and recommend on the issues. What is likely to emerge is a system of 'mutual recognition', in which companies can carry out sales-promotion activities in the target country as long as they are legal in the company's country of origin. The fact that on-pack, in-pack, vouchers and prize giveaways can be run in many European countries simultaneouly will mean economies of scale in managing such campaigns. It also means that brand owners can print the same message – granted a multilanguage one – on all European products rather than distinguishing which will be on some and not on others, as is required today. The issue of local adaptation will remain however.

> A sales promotion is trying to prompt changes in consumer behaviour, not attitudes, and people's behaviour differs from one market to another. You are never going to succeed if you try to homogenise the mechanics of a pan-European promotion. Even if the laws regarding sales promotion were the same in different countries, you probably wouldn't want to do it. (Kiernan, 1992)

For example, recently Pepsi ran an on-pack promotion across nine countries that offered exclusive Spice Girls prizes, with a menu of different tactics available in each of the countries where the promotion ran to ensure that the campaign was tailored to each market's needs and legal environment (Stewart-Allen, 1999, p. 10).

Table 16.10	Cross-border conflicts of European sales promotions				
Tactic	Germany	France	UK	Netherlands	Belgium
Onpack price reductions	Yes	Yes	Yes	Yes	Yes
In-pack gifts	??	??	Yes	??	??
Extra product	??	Yes	Yes	??	??
Money-off vouchers	No	Yes	Yes	Yes	Yes
Free prize contest	No	Yes	Yes	No	No

Note: Yes: legally allowed; ??: under review; No: not legally allowed.

Source: U.K. Institute of Sales Promotion, in, *Marketing News,* 26 April 1999, p. 10.

16.5. Public relations decisions and non-media decisions

In the first three styles of communication, the product or brand is at the heart of the advertising message. Institutional advertising does not talk about the product, but aims to create or reinforce a positive attitude towards the firm. The objective is therefore to create an image, but that of the firm: to describe the firm's profile and stress its personality in order to create a climate of confidence and understanding. The purpose is to communicate differently in a saturated advertising world and to fight against the fatigue of product advertising with a softer approach, by drawing attention to the firm itself, its merits, its values and talents. Clearly, the effectiveness of this kind of communication can only be evaluated in the long term and can essentially work on attitudes.

16.5.1. Objectives of public relations

Public relations group the communications tools developed by the firm to promote the corporate activities, goals and value, and create a positive corporate image in the general public and more particularly among the key market actors, distributors, prescribers, and institutional, financial and commercial partners. Public relations differ from other forms of marketing communication in three ways.

Objectives are different. It is not a matter of selling but rather of gaining moral support from public opinion to pursue its economic activity.

Targets are more diversified. The target is broader than just customers, covering all market stakeholders who, directly or indirectly, are active players in the market, including public opinion.

Tools are varied. Along with the house journal and press releases, they include sponsoring and patronage.

The objective is to use an intermediary (a journalist, an event) to convey the information with greater credibility.

In a research conducted by des Thwaites *et al.* (1998) in Canada to identify the objectives of sponsoring sports, events, the following objectives emerge as presented in Table 16.11.

16.5.2. The tools of public relations

There are many tools in public relations, which can be grouped under four headings:

- *Information on the company*, such as launching of new products, signing a major contract, R&D results, a merger or an acquisition, and so on. Once the information is chosen, PR specialists organise press releases or press conference.
- *Publications*, such as annual reports, house journals, catalogues, and so on, which now are often directly available on CD-ROM or on the Internet.
- *Events or special occasions* or communication through events such as sports competitions, concerts, exhibitions sponsored by the company or through events specially organised by the company, such as open house days, factory visits, training sessions for dealers combined with leisure activities, and so on.
- *Patronage*, where the company supports a particular cause of general interest, humanitarian, scientific or cultural.

The last two PR tools belong to what is called institutional advertising where the company tries to position itself in public opinion as a good corporate citizen. This type of communication can be very effective as illustrated by the data of Table 16.12 where the attitude scores of companies' users and non-users of institutional advertising are presented (de Jaham, 1979).

Table 16.11   Sports sponsorship objectives

Objectives	Number	Mean	Std. Dev.
Community involvement	43	5.60	1.55
Enhance company image	44	5.32	1.39
Increase public awareness of the company	44	5.18	1.24
Corporate hospitality	41	4.88	1.40
Build business/trade relations and goodwill	40	4.82	1.55
Increase media attention	42	4.79	1.57
Reinforce market perception of product	41	4.56	1.90
Increase sales	40	4.55	1.69
Increase current product awareness	40	4.48	1.87
Identify product with a particular market segment	40	4.40	2.02
Enhance staff/employee's relations and motivation	41	4.37	1.88
Alter public perception of the company	41	4.07	1.77
Increase new product awareness	40	3.97	2.02
Alter market perception of product	39	3.90	1.90
Block competition	41	3.68	2.11
Personal objectives of senior managers	41	2.95	1.83
Counter adverse publicity	41	2.66	1.77

Note: Mean scores based on a 7-point scale: 1 = not important; 7 = very important.

Source: Des Thwaites *et al.* (1998, p. 41).

Table 16.12   Measuring the effectiveness of institutional advertising

Indicators of attitude	Types of advertisers	
	Non-users of institutional advertising (%)	Users of institutional advertising (%)
Awareness of company name and activities	82	93
Familiarity with company name and activities	63	77
Overall positive image of company	38	51

Source: de Jaham (1979).

16.5.3. Sponsoring and patronage

These are two specific ways of institutional advertising. The latter runs the risk of tiring the public, which can become irritated and view these campaigns as attempts at self-satisfaction. Hence new forms of communication have developed, based on the idea that 'there is more splendour in being virtuous than taking credit for it' (Van Hecke, 1988).

A typical example of one of these media stunts is the financing by American Express of the restoration of Van Eyck's masterpiece L'agneau mystique, which considerably increased its prestige in a way that no other campaign could have done.

The objective is to increase awareness of the firm's brand and to improve its image by association with positive values. The event being supported, which often unfolds in an unpredictable manner, thus reinforcing the credibility of the message, must have a testimony value, in the sense that a link should exist between the sponsored event and the sponsoring organisation, even if the link is indirect.

Whether the firm is sponsoring an expedition in the Himalayas or a transatlantic race, it is emphasising its adherence to moral values such as team spirit and courage. On the one hand it proves its open-mindedness and its harmonious integration in society, and on the other hand, with regards to internal communication, it increases support from its personnel and develops a favourable climate within the firm. (Van Hecke, 1988)

It should be noted that sponsorship is a commercial operation, implying a two-way relation of rights and obligations: on the one hand material or financial support for the sponsored event, and on the other direct and methodical exploitation of the event by the firm. Thus sponsorship is distinct from patronage, in which generosity and lack of interest in profit are dominant.

It is clear that forms of advertising, pursued objectives and the means used to achieve them are very different. Before launching the advertising, it is therefore important to have a clear view of the role that advertising is to play in the marketing programme.

16.5.4. Worldwide sponsorships expenditures

The figures of Table 16.13 give an idea of the importance of sponsorship in the world as marketing communication tool. There are several interesting observations that can be drawn from this table:

■ First of all, the table clearly shows that sponsorship is indeed a worldwide phenomenon in terms of the number of countries reporting substantial sponsorship activity.

A closer examination of these figures indicates that six countries (Germany, Italy, UK, US, Japan and Australia)

account for 70 per cent of total global expenditures, a fact which clearly associates large-scale sponsorship activity with mature consumer economies.

However, it is also important to note that even where sponsorship expenditure is miniscule in world terms, this medium still accounts for 5 or 6 per cent of advertising expenditures in the local domestic market, a share very close to that observed at world market level.

A special form of sponsorship, which is growing in popularity, is *cause-related marketing* which is gradually replacing philanthropy or charity. In this type of promotion, the firm commits itself to donate a part of the sales revenue generated to a cause or to a non-profit organisation. The promotion organised by American Express to help finance the restoration of the Statue of Liberty in New York is an excellent example.

There were three goals in the promotion: (1) increase the use of the Amex card by current holders; (2) encourage distributors to accept payment with the card; and (3) improve company image and profile. American Express promised to give 1 cent for every transaction in the US and 1 dollar for every new card issued during the last quarter of the year. The campaign was a success both for the sponsor and the cause. Close to 1.7 million dollars went to the renovation project and the rate of use of the Amex card increased by 2.8 per cent over the preceding year and

---

Table 16.13   Worldwide Sponsorship Activities

Sponsorship spending worldwide (in US$ billions)	2003	2004	2005
Worldwide	25.9	27.9	30.4
North America	10.2	11.1	12.1
Europe	7.4	7.8	8.4
Pacific Rim	4.7	5.2	5.8
Central, South America	2.2	2.3	2.5
Other	1.4	1.5	1.6

Active sponsor categories (%)	2003	2004
Nonalcoholic beverage	44	44
Banks	30	37
Automotive	35	30
Beer	29	27
Telecommunications	26	26
Specialty retail (clothing, toys, etc.)	19	22
Food	18	18
Supermarket	11	15
Airlines	13	14
Insurance	11	14

Source: Marketing News, July 2005.

was accepted more readily by distributors. (Meenaghan, 1998, p. 14)

Except for promotion activities directly linked to such a cause, it is difficult to measure the real impact of sponsoring and patronage activities (see Exhibit 16.4). Analysis of this kind of action for the Olympic Games shows that there are positive results for the companies involved. On this topic, see Stipp (1998).

EXHIBIT 16.4

AMBUSH MARKETING

In a survey conducted a month after the 1996 Olympics in Atlanta, consumers were asked to name the official sponsors of the Summer Games. For credit cards, 72 per cent named Visa whereas only 54 per cent named American Express. Those results were almost identical to a similar survey conducted after 1994 Winter Olympics, in which 68 per cent named Visa and 52 per cent named American Express. One might conclude from these surveys that Visa does a better job than American Express in promoting its association with the Olympics Games – except Visa paid $40 million for the exclusive rights to be an official sponsor in the credit card category, while American Express was not an official sponsor of the Olympics Games. How did American Express achieve such a high level of recognition as an official sponsor without being one? It engaged in what is known as 'ambush marketing', a strategy aimed at creating the false impression of being associated with an event to gain some of the benefits and recognition of official sponsors.

Source: Shani and Sandler (1999).

CHAPTER SUMMARY

Marketing communication refers to all the signals and messages made by the firm to its various publics. The four major communication tools, called the communication mix, are personal selling, advertising, sales promotion and public relations. The four tasks in designing a communication programme are communication objective, message execution, media planning and communication effectiveness. Due to developments in communication technology, the role of the sales force is undergoing a major transformation and relationship selling and commercial negotiation are tending to replace traditional selling techniques. This evolution gives salespeople an important new role to play in strategic marketing. When a firm resorts to advertising, it is effectively following a pull communication strategy. Its main objective is to create a brand image and brand equity and to ensure co-operation from distributors. Advertising objectives can be defined by reference to the three levels of market response: cognitive, affective and behavioural. The share of sales promotion expenditure is growing in the total marketing communication budget as a result of the development of direct marketing. There are a large variety of promotion tools whose effects are complex and which can sometimes have a negative impact on the brand image. Public relations is a form of softer communication, which is gaining in popularity as one observes a decrease in the communication effectiveness of media advertising. Sponsorship and patronage are two special forms of institutional advertising, which are more frequently observed in industrialised economies.

Review and Application Questions

1. Compare traditional selling techniques with relationship selling. Show how and why relationship selling is well in line with the market orientation business philosophy and with the problem-solution approach?

2. Sales representatives of a fast moving consumer goods (FMCG) company visit hypermarkets once every fortnight and supermarkets once a month. The company is rethinking the organisation of its sales force for an area with 200 supermarkets and 30 hypermarkets. Knowing that a visit to a hypermarket takes an average of one and a half hours for a sales rep and a visit to a supermarket takes one hour, how many sales reps will the company need for this area? (A representative works 8 hours a day and 5 days a week.)

3. Compare the objectives of product advertising, institutional advertising, response advertising and publicity.

4. Can one expect some long-term sales or market share effects of a sales promotion?

5. How can we evaluate today the effectiveness of Internet advertising? What are the merits of this form of advertising?

6. Why are sponsorship and patronage as communication forms gaining in popularity in industrialised economies?

7. Under which conditions can a firm contemplate basing a communication campaign on a cause of general interest?

8. Is ambush marketing unethical?

Bibliography

Abernathy, A.M. and Frank, G.R. (1996), The Information Content of Advertising: A Meta-analysis, *Journal of Advertising*, 25, 2, pp. 1–17.

Bogart, L. (1986), *Strategy in Advertising*, Lincolnwood Hill, NTC Business Book.

Churchill, G.A., Ford, N.M. and Walker, O.C. (1997), *Sales Force Management*, Chicago, IL, Irwin, 5th edition.

Coe, J.M. (2004), The Integration of Direct marketing and Field Sales to Forma New B2B Sales Coverage Model, *Journal of Interactive Marketing*, 18, 2, pp. 62–74.

Darmon, R.Y., Laroche, M. and Petrov, J.V. (1982), *Le Marketing, Fondements et Applications*, Montreal, McGraw-Hill, 2nd edition.

Dartnell Corporation (1994), *28th Survey of Sales Force Compensation*, Chicago, IL, Dartnell Corporation.

De Jaham, M.R. (1979), Le défi de la publicité institutionnelle, *Revue Française du Marketing*, 77, pp. 33–41.

de Maricourt, R., Andréani, J.C., Bloch, A. (1997), *Marketing Européen, Stratégies et Actions*, Paris, Publi-Union.

des Thwaites, D., Anguilar-Manjarrez, R. and Kidd, C. (1998), Sports Sponsorship Development in Leading Canadian Companies: Issues and Trends, *International Journal of Advertising*, 17, 1, pp. 29–49.

Dhalla, N.K. (1978), Assessing the Long Term Value of Advertising, *Harvard Business Review*, 56, 1, pp. 87–95.

Dupont, C. (1994), *La négociation: conduite, théorie et applications*, Paris, Editions Dalloz.

Donaldson, B. (1998), *Sales Management: Theory and Practice*, London, Macmillan, 2nd edition.

Dwyer, F.R., Schurr, P.H. and Sejo, O.H. (1987), Developing Buyer–Seller Relationships, *Journal of Marketing*, 51, 2, pp. 11–27.

Economist, The (1998), Go On, Its Good for You, 8 August, pp. 57–8.

Forsyth, D.P. (1987), *Cost of a Business-to-Business Sales Call*, McGraw-Hill Research, Laboratory of Advertising Performance, LAP Report 8013.9.

Fournier, S., Dobscha, S. and Mick, D.G. (1998), Preventing the Premature Death of Relationship Marketing, *Harvard Business Review*, 76, 1, pp. 43–51.

Froloff, L. (1992), La sensibilité du consommateur à la promotion des ventes: de la naissance à la maturité, *Recherche et Applications en Marketing*, 7, 3, pp. 69–88.

Havas (1998), *Europub; le marché publicitaire Européen*, Paris, Havas.

Ingold, P. (1995), *Promotion des ventes et action commerciale*, Paris, Vuibert.

Jackson, B.B. (1985), *Winning and Keeping Industrial Customers*, Lexington, MA, Lexington Books.

Kiernan, P. (1992), The Euro Promo Comes of Age, *Marketing Week Sales Promotion*, 18 September.

Kirzner L.M. (1973), *Competition and Entrepreneurship*, Chicago, IL, Chicago University Press.

Kotler, P. (1997), *Marketing Management*, Englewood Cliffs, NJ, Prentice-Hall, 9th edition.

Lambert, Z.V. (1968), *Setting the Size of the Sales Force*, Philadelphia, PA, University Press.

Lambin, J.-J. (1965), *La décision commerciale face à l'incertain*, Paris, Dunod.

Lavidge, R.J. and Steiner, G.A. (1961), A Model of Predictive Measurement of Advertising Effectiveness, *Journal of Marketing* 25, 6, pp. 59–62.

Lepage, H. (1982), *Vive le commerce*, Paris, Donod Collection L'oeil économique.

Libre Service Actualité (*LSA*), (1982), Les techniques promotionnelles, 19 December, pp. 869–70.

LSA (1997), La justice veut moraliser le couponing électronique, 27 November, pp. 18–19.

Meenaghan, T. (1998), Current Developments and Future Directions in Sponsorship, *International Journal of Advertising*, 17, 1, pp. 3–28.

O'Connell, W.A. and Keenan, W. (1990), The Shape of Things to Come, *Sales & Marketing Management*, January, pp. 36–41.

Payne, A. (ed.) (1995), *Advances in Relationship Marketing*, London, Kogan Page.

Reichheld, F.F. and Teal, T. (2001), *The Loyalty Effect: The Hidden Force Behind: Growth Profit and Lasting Value*, Boston, MA, Harvard Business School Press.

Resnik, A. and Stern, B.L. (1977), An Analysis of Information Content in Television Advertising, *Journal of Marketing*, 41, 1, pp. 50–3.

Rossiter, J.R. and Percy, L. (1997), *Advertising and Promotion Management*, New York, McGraw-Hill, 2nd edition.

Schnaars, S.P. (1998), *Marketing Strategy*, New York, The Free Press.

Semlow, W.J. (1969), How Many Salesmen Do You Need?, *Harvard Business Review*, 37, 3, pp. 126–32.

Shani, D. and Sandler, D. (1999), Counter-attack: Heading off Ambush Marketing, *Marketing News*, 18 January, p. 10.

Slymotsky, A. and Shapiro, B.P. (1993), Leveraging to Beat the Odds: The New Marketing Mind Set, *Harvard Business Review*, 71, 5, pp. 97–107.

Stipp, H. (1998), The Impact of Olympic Sponsorship on Corporate Image, *International Journal of Advertising*, 17, 1, pp. 75–87.

Stewart-Allen, A.L. (1999), Cross-border Conflicts of European Sales Promotions, *Marketing News*, 26 April.

Van Hecke, T. (1988), Avis aux mécènes: la brique est porteuse, *La Libre Belgique*, 11 June.

Van Poppel, Ad. (1998), Promotion 10%, et puis?, *Tendances Trends*, 19 February, p. 59.

Xardel, D. (1982), Vendeurs: nouveaux rôles, nouveaux comportements, *Harvard-l'Expansion*, 25, Summer, pp. 59–75.

COMPANION WEBSITE FOR CHAPTER 16

Visit the *Market-driven Management* companion website at www.palgrave.com/business/lambin to find information on:

Measuring the Cognitive Response

Measuring the Affective Response

Direct Marketing

Advertising Budget Decisions

Part 5

implementation of market-driven management

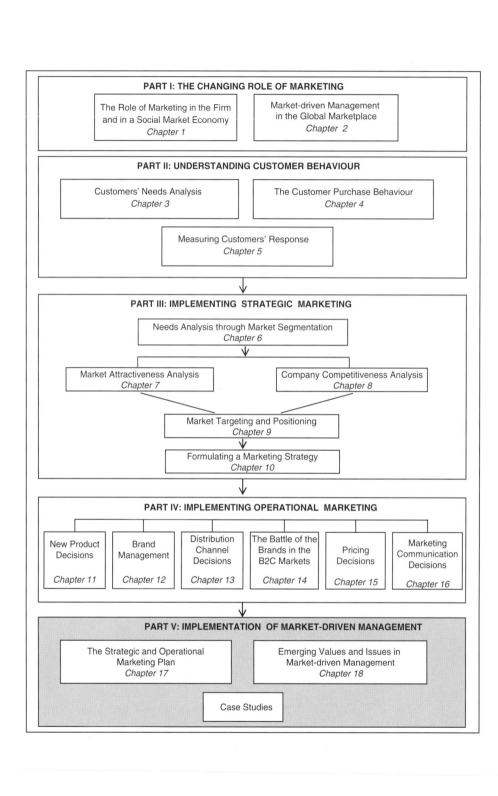

the strategic and operational marketing plan

17

Chapter contents

Chapter learning objectives

When you have read this chapter, you should be able to

- understand the usefulness of formal strategic planning;
- define the structure and content of a strategic plan;
- conduct an external and internal audit (SWOT analysis);
- define operational objectives and action programmes;
- prepare a projected profit and loss statement;
- test the robustness of a strategic plan.

Chapter introduction

Sound strategic thinking about the future must be spelled out in a written document, which describes the ends and means required to implement the chosen development strategy. In the short term, the firm's success is directly dependent on the financial performance of its ongoing activities. In the longer run, however, its survival and growth imply the ability to anticipate market changes and to adapt the structure of its product portfolio accordingly. To be effective, this strategic and proactive thinking must be organised in a systematic and formal way. The role of strategic marketing planning is the design of a desired future and of effective ways of making things happen. Its role is also to communicate these choices to those responsible for their implementation. This planning task is of course particularly hard when great uncertainties prevail in the firm's environment. Anticipating the unexpected is also part of the strategic planning process. In this chapter, we shall build on the concepts and procedures described in previous chapters and examine the steps needed to make strategic marketing happen in the firm..

17.1. Overview of marketing planning

The raison d'être of a strategic plan is to formulate the main strategic options taken by the firm, in a clear and concise way, in order to ensure its long-term development. These strategic options must be translated into decisions and action programmes. We shall briefly examine the overall structure of a plan and the benefits expected from strategic planning.

17.1.1. Overall structure of the strategic marketing plan

As shown in this book, the strategic marketing process can be summarised around six key questions. The answers provided to these questions constitute the backbone of the plan and also the objectives for the firm.

1. What business are we in and what is the firm's mission in the chosen reference market?
2. Within the defined reference market, what are the targeted product markets or segments and what is the positioning strategy likely to be adopted within each segment?
3. What are the key business attractiveness factors in each segment and what are the opportunities and threats presented by the environment?
4. Within each segment, what are the firm's distinctive qualities, strengths and weaknesses and competitive advantages?
5. Which development strategy and strategic ambition should be adopted for each activity in the firm's product portfolio?

6. How do these strategic options translate into operational marketing programmes defined in terms of product, distribution, pricing and communications decisions?

Once the answers to these questions are obtained as the result of a strategic marketing audit, the task remains to summarise the options taken, to define the means required to achieve the stated objectives, to design the specific action programmes and, last but not least, to prepare projected profit and loss statements for each activity and for the company as a whole.

In fact, a strategic marketing plan is nothing more than a financial plan, but with much more information on the origins and destinations of the financial flows. As illustrated by Figure 17.1, the strategic marketing plan has direct implications on all the other functions of the firm and vice versa:

■ Research and development: market needs must be met through new, improved or adapted products and services.
■ Finance: the marketing programme is subject to financial constraints and to availability of resources.
■ Operations: sales objectives are subject to production capacity and to physical delivery constraints.
■ Human resources: the implementation of the plan implies the availability of qualified and well-trained personnel.

Thus strategic planning will result in a better integration of all the company's functions and contribute to maximisation of efforts in reaching corporate goals. In a market-driven organisation, the mission of strategic marketing is to identify prospects for growth and profit given the company

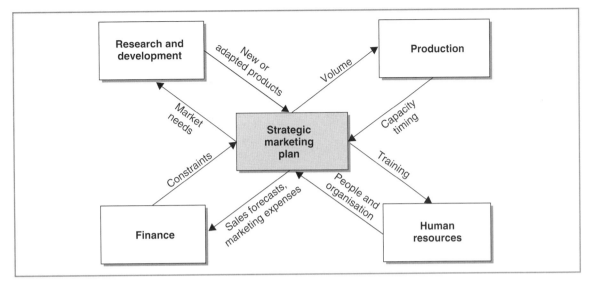

Figure 17.1   The strategic plan of a cross-functional responsibility
Source: Authors.

resources and savoir faire. As already emphasised in this book, this role is much broader than the traditional domain of marketing management, and implies interfunctional co-ordination.

17.1.2. Importance of strategic planning

Every company, even those reluctant to engage in the idea of formal planning, has to formulate forecasts in a minimum of three areas:

- The calibration of the investment programme required to meet the level of market demand or to penetrate a new product market.
- The production programme organisation needed, given the seasonality of sales and the periodicity of orders.
- The financial liquidity, based on income and expense forecasts, which is required to meet the financial liabilities.

These managerial problems are common to all companies and they imply that reliable sales forecasts should be handled properly.
    In addition to this argument of necessity, other arguments in favour of formal strategic planning exist:

- The plan expresses the value system, philosophies and views of top management. This information gives people a sense of direction and a sense of how to behave.
- The plan presents the facts on 'where the business has come from and where it stands'. The situation analysis helps to understand the reasons for the strategic options taken by top management.

- The plan facilitates co-ordination among the different functions, maintains consistency in the objectives, and facilitates trade-offs among conflicting goals.
- The plan is a monitoring instrument which provides the opportunity to review the progress made in implementing the plan and to redirect parts of the action programme that are off target.
- The plan minimises the degree to which the company is taken by surprise to the extent that 'best case–worst case' scenarios have been explored.
- The plan encourages a more rigorous management of scarce resources by using standards, budgets, schedules, and so on, thereby reducing the risk of improvisation.

Most strategic plans are complemented by some form of contingency plan to be activated if certain events occur. Contingency plans are developed for factors which are key to the survival of the company.

17.1.3. Objections to formal planning

Although strategic planning is a widely adopted practice, a certain number of firms avoid using formal written strategic plans. Three types of objections to formal planning are usually given: the lack of relevant information, the futility of forecasting in a fast-changing environment and the rigidity of planning.

Lack of needed information

Ideally, the planner would have at hand all the pertinent information required on industry and market trends, competitive intentions, market share, technological innovations and so forth. The most common complaint concerns lack of adequate information for the purpose of planning. On deeper investigation, however, it nearly always turns out to be a case of too much information rather than too little. The real problem is (much more) than the lack of in-depth analysis.

The existence of a market information system, similar to the one described in Chapter 5 (see Figure 5.1), is today a vital necessity to maintain the firm's competitiveness. Thus, market information and business intelligence systems must exist in any case, and this is a costly operation with or without formal planning.

Futility of forecasting

In a turbulent environment, what good are strategic plans which will be contradicted by future events? This attitude results from a misunderstanding as to the nature of forecasting, which is erroneously likened to a crystal ball. A forecast is a quantitative or qualitative estimate of what one expects, given a set of assumptions on the environment. A forecast is not an end in itself, but a forward thinking exercise, a tool used to increase the company's responsiveness and adaptability to the unexpected. This objective can be achieved even if the predicted outcome is not attained.

Bureaucratic rigidity

Formal planning would commit the firm to a given direction, whereas adaptability and flexible response are required in a fast-changing environment. This objection questions more the authoritarian planning style than planning itself. A plan should be designed to enhance creativity and quick reaction to changes. The mere fact of having analysed possible changes in the market in advance will help to revise programmes and objectives faster, whenever it is desirable to do so.

In practice, strategic planning is widely used, as evidenced by the Bain survey (2005) conducted every year.

17.2. Content of a strategic marketing plan

A strategic marketing plan typically sets out to answer the six key questions presented at the beginning of this chapter. In this section, we shall describe the basic elements of a strategic marketing plan and the type of information required on which to base recommendations.

17.2.1. The mission statement

Sometimes called a creed statement or a statement of business principles, a mission statement reveals the company's long-term vision in terms of what it wants to be and who it wants to serve. It defines the organisation's value system and its economic and non-economic objectives. The mission statement is important from both an internal and external point of view:

■ Inside the company, it serves as a focal point for individuals to identify with the organisation's direction and to ensure unanimity of purpose within the firm, thereby facilitating the emergence of a corporate culture.
■ From an external point of view, the mission statement contributes to the creation of corporate identity, that is, how the company wants to be perceived in the marketplace by its customers, competitors, employees, owners and shareholders, and by the general public.

A mission statement should include at least the four following components.

History of the company

Knowledge of the past history of the company, its origin and successive transformations is always useful to understand its present situation and the weight given to some economic or non-economic goals and objectives.

Materne-Confilux celebrated its 100th anniversary in 1987. This company has accumulated a broad experience in the field of purchase and transformation of fruits and has succeeded in maintaining a family managerial structure. This strong foothold in the fruit sector is a key factor to consider when exploring alternative diversification strategies.

In searching for a new purpose, a company must remain consistent with its past achievements and fields of competence.

Business definition

This is a key component in the mission statement. As emphasised in Chapter 3, what customers buy and consider valuable is never the product, but rather its utility, that is, what a product or a service does for them (Drucker, 1973, p. 61). Thus, the market definition should be written in terms of the benefit provided to the buyer. As discussed in Chapter 5, the three relevant questions to examine here are

■ what business(es) are we in?
■ what business(es) should we be in?
■ what business(es) should we not be in?

These are not easy questions to answer, particularly when the environment is changing very quickly. Ideally, the mission statement should be stated in terms narrow enough to provide practical guidance, yet broad enough to stimulate imaginative thinking, such as openings for product line extensions, or for diversification into adjacent product areas. At the Grumman Corporation, the guidelines for the mission statement advise:

> We should be careful not to confine the market boundaries by our existing or traditional product participation. The market definition analysis is purposely meant to create an outward awareness of the total surrounding market, and of its needs and trends that may offer opportunity for, or on the other hand challenges to, our current or contemplated position. (Hopkins, 1981, p. 119)

Every organisation has a unique purpose and reason for being. This uniqueness should be reflected in the market definition. In a market-driven organisation, the market definition will reflect the degree of customer orientation of the firm. By adopting a business definition formulated in terms of generic need or in terms of 'solution to a problem', the firm emphasises its market orientation and limits the risk of market myopia.

Corporate goals and restraints

Goals set the direction for both long- and short-term development and therefore determine limitations and priorities to comply with. These general goals, usually defined at the corporate level, are constraints within which the strategic plan must be developed. They should be clearly defined in advance to avoid proposals that contradict objectives of general management or corporate shareholders.

These goals may be economic but also non-economic. Examples are: a minimum rate of return on investment, a growth objective, the conservation of the family ownership of the company, the refusal to enter particular fields of activity, or a minimum level of employment, and so on.

The description of available company resources (capacity, equipment, human resources, capital, and so on), also forms part of the restraints and should be made explicit

in order to avoid the adoption of a 'mission impossible' given the resources needed. Codes of conduct and corporate ethics for dealing with others (customers, distributors, competitors, suppliers, and so on) should also be formulated.

Basic strategic choices

Independent of the general goals imposed at the corporate level by general management, basic strategic options can be defined for each strategic business unit. For example, the extent of the strategic ambition and the role played by the firm in the target segment, that is, leader, follower, challenger or nicher, may be defined. The strategic ambition must of course be compatible with the available resources of the firm.

Reference could be made here also to the three basic positioning strategies suggested by Porter (1980) and discussed in Chapter 8: cost advantage, differentiation and focus. The type of competitive advantage sought should also be defined. At this stage of the strategic plan, only broad orientations are given. They will be redefined in quantitative terms in the action programmes developed for each business unit.

In a survey conducted in the United States by David (1989), out of a total of 181 responses received, 75 organisations provided a formal description of their mission statements. The main components included are summarised in Table 17.1.

17.2.2. External audit – market attractiveness analysis

This external audit – also called opportunities and threats analysis – is the first part of the situation analysis. As explained in Chapter 7, an attractiveness analysis examines

---

Table 17.1 What components are included in a mission statement? (a survey: $N = 75$)

■ Customer	Who are the company's customers?
■ Products and services	What are the firm's products or services?
■ Location	Where does the firm compete?
■ Technology	What is the firm's core technology?
■ Concern for survival	What are the commitments to economic objectives?
■ Philosophy	What are the basic beliefs, values, aspirations and philosophical priorities?
■ Self-concept	What are the firm's major strengths and competitive advantages?
■ Public image	What are the firm's public responsibilities and what image is desired?
■ Concern for employees	What is the firm's attitude towards its employees?

Source: David (1989).

the major external factors, that is, factors which are out of the control of the firm, but which may have an impact on the marketing plan. The following areas should be reviewed:

- Market trends.
- Buyer behaviour.
- Distribution structure.
- Competitive environment.
- Macro-environmental trends.
- International environment.

These external factors may constitute opportunities or threats that the firm must try to anticipate and monitor through its marketing information system and through business intelligence. In what follows, we shall simply list the critical questions to address in each of these areas. The precise type of information required will of course differ by product category: consumer, durable or non-durable goods, services or industrial goods.

Market trends analysis

The objective is to describe, segment by segment, the total demand's general trends within a 3–5-year horizon. The task is to position each product market in its life cycle and to quantify the market size. Both unit volume and monetary values should be identified.

Questionnaire 1: Reference market trends

- What is the size of the total market, in volume and in value?
- What are the trends: growth, stagnation, decline?
- What is the average per capita consumption?
- How far are we from the saturation level?
- What is the rate of equipment per household or per company?
- What is the average lifetime of the product?
- What is the share of replacement demand of total demand?
- What is the seasonal pattern of total sales?
- What are the main substitute products performing the same service?
- What are the major innovations in the sector?
- What are the costs per distribution channel?
- What is the structure of the distributive system?
- How will supply–demand relationships affect price levels?
- What is the level of total advertising intensity?
- What are the most popular advertising media?

This list is certainly incomplete. It simply illustrates the type of information required. If the product studied is an industrial good, several information items should pertain not only to the direct customers' demand, but also to the demand expressed further down the line in the industrial chain by the customers of the direct customers.

Customer behaviour analysis

The task here is to analyse customer behaviour in terms of purchasing, use and possession. In addition to a description of buyers' purchasing habits, it is also useful to know the buying process and to identify the influencing factors.

Questionnaire 2: Customer behaviour analysis

- Per segment, what is the customer's socio-demographic profile?
- What is the composition of the buying centre?
- Who is the buyer, the user, the payer?
- What is the decision process adopted by the customer?
- What is the level of involvement of the buyer, the user, the payer?
- What are the main motivations of the buying decision?
- What is the package of benefits sought by the buyer, the user, the payer?
- What are the different uses of the product?
- What changing customer demands and needs do we anticipate?
- What are the purchasing frequency and periodicity?
- To which marketing factors are customers most responsive?
- What is the rate of customer satisfaction or dissatisfaction?

These descriptive data must be complemented with measures of the cognitive and affective response (recall, attitudes, preferences, intentions, and so on), as well as with brand or company image analyses.

Distribution structure analysis

This part of the external audit is probably more relevant in the field of consumer goods than in the sector of industrial goods, where direct distribution is common practice. The objective is to assess the future development of distribution channels and to understand the motivations and expectations of the company's trading partners.

Questionnaire 3: Structure and motivation of distribution

- What are industry sales by type of outlet?
- What are product type sales by type of outlet?
- What are product type sales by method of distribution?
- What is the concentration ratio of distribution?
- Is distribution intensive, selective or exclusive?
- What is the share of advertising assumed by distributors?

- What change does one observe in the assortments?
- What is the market share held by private brands?
- Which market segments do the different channels cover?
- What are the total distribution costs?
- What is the distribution margin for each channel of distribution?
- What kind of distributor support is currently provided?
- What is the potential of direct distribution?

The distributor, as a business partner, has strong negotiation powers vis-à-vis the firm. One of the roles of a distribution analysis is to assess the degree of autonomy or dependence of the firm in the distributive system.

Competitive environment analysis

The competitive structure of a market sets the framework within which the firm will operate. As put by Porter (1980), 'The essence of strategy formulation is coping with competition'. The basic attractiveness of a market segment is largely determined by the strength of competitors' capabilities. Assessment of what is driving competition is of vital importance to the firm.

Questionnaire 4: Competition analysis

- What is the market's competitive structure?
- What is the market share held by the top three rivals?
- What type of competitive behaviour is dominant?
- What is the strength of competing brands' images?
- What is the nature of the competitive advantage of direct competitors?
- To what extent are these competitive advantages well protected?
- What are the competitors' major objectives?
- What is the current strategy being used to achieve the objectives?
- What are the strengths and weaknesses of competitors?
- What are their likely future strategies?
- Are there entry barriers in this market?
- Which are the main substitute products?
- What is the bargaining power of customers and suppliers?

The gathering of this type of information implies the development of a competitor intelligence system. For a more detailed framework of competitor analysis, see Porter (1980, chapter 3).

Macro-environmental trends

This section describes the macro-environmental trends – demographic, economic, political/legal and socio-cultural – that bear on the studied market's future development. These external factors can provide productive opportunities or severe limitations for the company's products.

Questionnaire 5a: Economic macro-environment

- What is the expected GNP rate of growth?
- What major economic changes could affect our business?
- What is the expected level of employment?
- What is the expected rate of inflation?
- Do these trends affect our business and how?

Questionnaire 5b: Technological environment

- What major changes are occurring in product technology?
- How can we adjust our activities to cope with these changes?
- What major generic substitutes might replace our product?
- Do we have the required R&D capabilities?
- Do we need to update our equipment and at what cost?

Questionnaire 5c: Socio-demographic and cultural macro-environment

- What are the major demographic trends that affect our business?
- What is the cultural climate within which our business operates?
- Are present and future lifestyles favourable to our business?
- Is society's attitude towards our business changing?
- Are there changes in society's values that could affect our business?

Questionnaire 5d: Political and legal macro-environment

- Are there any specific changes in the law that affects our company?
- Are there legal or political areas that affect our customers?
- Which regulations could affect our advertising or selling strategy?
- Is our industry subject to criticisms from consumer organisations?
- Are there political or legal trends that could be used to our advantage?

Questionnaire 5e: International environment

- To what extent are we dependent on imports for key components?
- What is the economic and political stability of the supplier country?
- What alternatives do we have should our imports be interrupted?
- What is the economic and political stability of the customer countries?

- What opportunities do the European single market represent?
- Are there emerging global segments in our business?
- Is our business affected by changing world trade patterns?

Questionnaire 5f: Ecological environment

- Are our products environmentally friendly?
- Do we use processes or raw materials that threaten the environment?
- Is green marketing a potential strategy for our company?
- Is our industry a potential target for environmentalists?
- How can we improve the ecological quality of our products?

Questionnaire 5g: Industry and corporate ethics

- Does our company or industry have a stated code of ethics?
- What is the ethical level of our industry?
- Are industry values in alignment with those expected by society?
- How could our industry improve its ethical practice?

This information, dealing with the macro-environment of the firm, is indispensable for exploring alternative scenarios of market development. Generally, at least two scenarios will be explored: a base scenario, but also one or several alternative scenarios based on vulnerability factors.

The sources of information are numerous and varied, but often very scattered. Professional organisations and local chambers of commerce have economic data available for their members to use in planning. In addition to national statistics and foreign trade institutes, international financial institutions like the Bank for International Settlements (BIS), the International Monetary Fund (IMF), the World Bank (WB), the Office for Economic Co-operation and Development (OECD), the United Nations (UN), and so on, are the major public sources, with periodic publications readily available. University research centres and large international consulting firms, like Business International, McKinsey, the Economist Intelligence Unit, and so on, also publish newsletters, articles and monographs which are very useful for planning purposes.

17.2.3. Internal audit – company competitiveness analysis

The objective of the internal audit, also called the company strengths and weaknesses analysis, is to assess company resources and to identify the type of sustainable competitive advantage on which to base the development

strategy. Strengths and weaknesses are internal factors, in contrast with opportunities and threats, which are external factors. Company strengths (or distinctive qualities), point to certain strategies the company might be successful in adopting, while company weaknesses point to certain things the company needs to correct. A competitiveness analysis should not be abstract. Reference to competition in general is too vague. Therefore, competition should be referred to in terms of the most dangerous competitors, called priority competitors.

To illustrate, distinctive qualities for a brand of laptop computer, as compared to those of the priority competitor, might be

- excellent brand awareness and an image of high quality;
- dealers who are knowledgeable and well trained in selling;
- an excellent service network and customers who know they will get quick repair service.

The *weaknesses* of the same brand could be

- the screen quality of the brand is not demonstrably better than the quality of competing machines, yet screen quality can make a big difference in brand choice;
- the brand is budgeting only 5 per cent of its sales revenue for advertising and promotion while major competitors are spending twice that level;
- the brand is priced higher relative to other brands without being supported by a real perceived difference in quality.

The strengths of the company or of the brand constitute potential *competitive advantages* on which to base the positioning and the communication strategy. The weaknesses determine the vulnerability of the brand and require remedial action. Some weaknesses may be structural that is linked to the size of the firm and therefore difficult to correct. Examples of structural weaknesses are given below.

- National market share leadership, if not accompanied by international distribution, creates home country vulnerability to the extent that the local company has little freedom for retaliation in the country of foreign competitors.
- If a single powerful distributor generates total sales volume, the company has weak bargaining power.
- A small- or medium-sized company does not have the financial capability to use the most powerful media, like television advertising.

So a distinction must be made between the weaknesses that the company can correct and therefore which become priority issues that must be addressed in the plan, and the high-risk structural weaknesses which are beyond the control of the firm and which require a high degree of surveillance.

Competitiveness analysis is organised much like attractiveness analysis. The major difference comes from the fact that the company, and not the market, is the central subject of the analysis.

Company's current marketing situation

Data on the served markets for each of the products of the company's portfolio, in volume and market shares for several years and by geographical areas, are presented, as well as data on the current marketing mix.

Questionnaire 6: Product portfolio analysis

- What is the rate of current sales per product, segment, distributive channel, region and country, and so on, in volume and value?
- What is the current market share per product category, segment, distributive channel, region, country, and so on?
- How does the quality of our products compare with that of competition?
- How strong is the company's product brand image?
- Does the firm have a complete product line?
- What is the structure of our portfolio of customers?
- How concentrated is our total turnover?
- What is the age profile of our product portfolio?
- What is the contribution margin per product, segment, channel, and so on?
- What is the current level of nominal and relative prices?

This analysis is to be repeated for each product of the company's portfolio. Profit and loss statements for the last 3-years should be presented along with the current budget. A typical profit and loss statement is shown below in Table 17.6.

Priority competitor analysis

Priority competitor(s) should be identified for each product market. For each of these competitors, the same data collected for the company products will be gathered and compared as shown in Table 17.2 (see also Appendix). Other information is required to assess the strength of priority competition.

Questionnaire 7: Priority competition analysis

- What is the relative market share?
- Does competition have a cost advantage?
- What is the relative price?
- What is the competitive behaviour of rivals?
- How strong is the image of competing products?
- On what basis are competing products differentiated?
- How large are their financial resources?

- What is their retaliation capacity in case of frontal attack?
- Which are their major sources of vulnerability?
- What type of aggressive actions could they take?
- What kind of retaliatory or protective actions could we adopt?
- What changes could modify the present balance of power?
- Is competition able to destroy our competitive advantage?

With the information provided by questionnaires 6 and 7, a product portfolio analysis can be conducted using one of the procedures described in Chapter 10.

Distribution penetration analysis

Distributors, a company's partners in the marketing process, control the access to the end-users' market and play an important role in ensuring the success of the contemplated marketing programme. In addition, if they are powerful buyers they have a strong bargaining power vis-à-vis their suppliers. In fact, distributors must be viewed as intermediate customers just like end-user customers. The role of trade marketing is to analyse the needs and requirements of these intermediate customers in order to develop a mutually satisfactory exchange relationship.

Questionnaire 8: Distribution analysis

- How many distributors do we have in each channel?
- What is our penetration rate in number and value in each channel?
- What is the sales volume by type of distributor?
- What are the growth potentials of the different channels?
- What are the efficiency levels of the different distributors?
- Are the present trade terms motivating for distributors?
- What changes could modify relationships with our dealer network?
- Should the firm consider changing its distribution channels?
- What is the potential of direct marketing in our business?
- Are there new forms of distribution emerging in the market?

The objectives pursued by the firm and by its distributors are not exactly the same and conflicts can arise in the channels. Distributors are no longer passive intermediaries in most markets. The role of 'trade marketing' is to ensure that the firm views distributors as partners and as intermediate customers.

Table 17.2 Priority competitors analysis form (each factor must be evaluated on a 10-point scale)

Marketing variables	Our product	Competitor 1	Competitor 2	Competitor 3
Product				
Quality:	_____	_____	_____	_____
Company price:	_____	_____	_____	_____
Product line:	_____	_____	_____	_____
Packaging:	_____	_____	_____	_____
Evaluation on				
Attribute 1:	_____	_____	_____	_____
Attribute 2:	_____	_____	_____	_____
Attribute 3:	_____	_____	_____	_____
Distribution				
Dist. number:	_____	_____	_____	_____
Dist. value				
Channel 1:	_____	_____	_____	_____
Channel 2:	_____	_____	_____	_____
Channel 3:	_____	_____	_____	_____
Facing:	_____	_____	_____	_____
Margin:	_____	_____	_____	_____
Discounts:	_____	_____	_____	_____
Promotion:	_____	_____	_____	_____
Sales force				
Size of sales force:	_____	_____	_____	_____
Quality:	_____	_____	_____	_____
Call frequency:	_____	_____	_____	_____
Training:	_____	_____	_____	_____
Advertising				
Size of budget:	_____	_____	_____	_____
Media mix				
Medium 1:	_____	_____	_____	_____
Medium 2:	_____	_____	_____	_____
Medium 3:	_____	_____	_____	_____
Advertising copy:	_____	_____	_____	_____
Advertisement quality:	_____	_____	_____	_____
Promotion				
Size of budget:	_____	_____	_____	_____
Type of promotion				
Consumer price:	_____	_____	_____	_____
Distribution margin:	_____	_____	_____	_____
Other promotions:	_____	_____	_____	_____
Services				
Range of services:	_____	_____	_____	_____
Delivery terms:	_____	_____	_____	_____
After-sales service:	_____	_____	_____	_____
Research and development				
Size of budget:	_____	_____	_____	_____
Staff:	_____	_____	_____	_____
Performance in R&D:	_____	_____	_____	_____
Marketing research				
Quality of MIS:	_____	_____	_____	_____
Data banks:	_____	_____	_____	_____
Performance:	_____	_____	_____	_____

Communication programme analysis

Mass media advertising, interactive advertising, personal selling, publicity, and so on are powerful competitive weapons if properly used, that is, when the target markets are well chosen and when the content of the communication programme is well in line with the product positioning, pricing and distribution strategies.

Questionnaire 9: Communication programme analysis

- What is the advertising intensity compared to direct competition?
- What is the advertising cost per thousand target buyers per medium?
- What is the communication effectiveness of media advertising?
- What are the consumers' opinions on the advertisement content?
- What is the number of reply coupons stimulated by direct advertising?
- How well are the advertising objectives defined?
- What is the sales or market share effectiveness of advertising?
- What is the impact of advertising on awareness, attitude, and intentions?
- What is the average number of sales calls per sales representative per week?
- What is the number of new customers per period?
- What are the sales force costs as a percentage of total sales?

These questionnaires should be used as guidelines for periodically reviewing the company's marketing situation within the framework of a marketing audit.

Pricing policy analysis

Price is the only component of the marketing mix generating income, by contrast with the other marketing instruments. Price also has the highest visibility in the marketplace and can be easily compared with rivals.

Questionnaire 10: Pricing policy analysis

- What is the price elasticity of primary demand?
- What is the price elasticity of our own demand or market share?
- What are the market 'maximum acceptable' prices of our brands?
- At what level are the perceived value prices of our brands?
- How do our prices compare with direct competitors' prices?
- Is price sensitivity very different from one segment to another?

- What is our policy in terms of price discounting?
- Are our prices stated in euros competitive in the European market?
- What type of price adjustment do we have to consider in the European market?

It is important to keep in mind that price is a determining factor in the brand positioning strategy and that it must be compatible with the other elements of the marketing mix.

17.3. Objectives and programmes

At this point, management knows the major issues and has to make some basic decisions about the objectives. Using the information provided by the strategic marketing audit and by the positioning statement, the firm's identified priority objectives must then be translated into operational action programmes.

17.3.1. Definition of objectives

Every firm has several objectives that can be grouped into two broad categories: marketing and non-marketing objectives:

- Non-marketing objectives have been described in the firm's mission statement. They describe the overall value system of the company and as such they apply for all market targets.
- Marketing objectives are of three types: sales, profit and customers. They should be defined for each product market or segment.

Sales objectives

It is a quantitative measure of the impact the firm 'wants' to achieve in the future within a particular product market. It is not simply a forecast of what one 'expects' may occur in the future. It is an active, not a passive, statement about the future. Sales objectives can be stated in currency, in volume or in market share. Examples of sales-oriented objectives are presented in Table 17.3.

Table 17.3   Examples of sales-oriented objectives

- Achieve total sales revenue of €2,150,000 by the end of 1992.
- Attain a 20 per cent market share of the management distance learning market.
- Reach a sales volume of 150,000 units per year.

Source: Authors.

- *Sales revenue objectives* are the most convenient way to express a sales objective because they are easily integrated in the accounting and financial system. Sales revenue may be misleading, however, if not adjusted for inflation and also for modifications in the sales mix if, for example, the share of high-priced products has changed from one period to another.
- *Unit sales* represent the best indicator, provided there is no change in the volume definition. In the soft drink sector, for example, it is current practice to think in terms of case sales. What about cases of 12 or 18 bottles? Conversion to 'litre equivalent cases' must be made. In many markets a meaningful unit definition simply does not exist. For example, in life insurance the number of policies taken out is not a good indicator of sales performance.
- *Market share* is the best indicator of competitive performance. Also, in volume industries where experience effects occur, high market share implies a cost competitive advantage over direct competition.

Sales data are a key element in the projected income statement. They must be translated into financial terms.

Profit objectives

Marketing, as for all other functions within the firm, must be accountable for profits. The inclusion of formal profit objectives forces marketing people to estimate the cost implications of the stated sales objectives. Examples of profit objectives are presented in Table 17.4.

The definition of profit objectives implies a close interfunctional co-ordination within the firm. A statement of profitability cannot be made without a close look at the cost–volume relationship and capacity constraints. For new products, the investment in fixed costs and working capital, in addition to manufacturing and marketing costs, should be analysed before launching. Similarly, the marketing expenses involved in implementing the proposed marketing strategy must be carefully evaluated and their expected contribution to sales and/or market share development assessed. Go back to Figure 1.2 for a description of the interrelationships between the key managerial functions.

Customer objectives

Customer objectives are deduced from the positioning statement. They describe the type of behaviour or attitude the firm would want customers to have towards its brands or services. Examples of customer objectives are presented in Table 17.5.

These customer objectives are important because they provide directions to advertising people for the development of communication strategies and for supporting the positioning theme adopted.

Market share objectives

Market share is the best indicator of the brand's competitive performance based either on the product intrinsic superiority or on a more attractive price.

As suggested by Best (2004, p. 74), an index of market share can be created from a combination of market share effects. The share development tree of Figure 17.2 traces a hierarchy of market share effects that leads to a particular level of indexed market penetration. Interestingly, it appears that the overall market share index is the interaction between effects. Should one perform poorly, the overall index will perform poorly. Each share effect is derived from a particular component of what is the 'marketing mix'. It includes,

$$\text{Market share} = \text{communication} \times \text{product} \times \text{price} \times \text{distribution} \times \text{service}.$$

Because there are many other factors that can affect actual market share, the market share index – 7.6 per cent in the example of Figure 17.2 – is simply an indicator of what market share should be, given certain expected levels of market performance. The market share development tree provides three important benefits:

- It helps in identifying important sources of lost market share opportunity.
- It provides a mechanism to assess the market share change when a certain level of improvements is directed in a key area of poor performance.
- It enables the brand manager to estimate what might be a reasonable market share potential given reasonable levels of performance in each area along the purchase path.

In the example of Figure 17.2, if a business could succeed in building its brand availability to customers intending to buy from 57 to 70 per cent, it could increase its overall market share index from 7.6 to 9.3 per cent. This hierarchy of market share effects is based on a learning model that is observed mainly in markets where the degree of customers' involvement is high.

Table 17.4   Examples of profit objectives

- Produce net profits of €150,000 before tax by December 2007.
- Earn an average 15% return on investment during the next 5 years.
- Produce a dollar contribution of €350,000 at the end of the fiscal year.

Source: Authors.

Table 17.5 Examples of customer objectives

- Create at least 60% awareness for brand A within the 15–25 age group by the end of 2007.
- To increase by 20% the repeat purchase rate of brand A within the 15–25 age group by the end of 2007.
- To position brand at the high end of the market in the minds of consumers belonging to the upper income bracket.

Source: Authors.

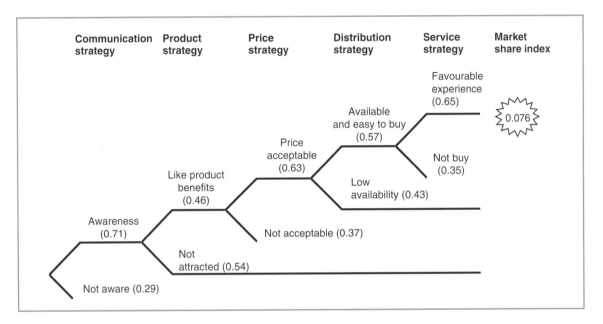

Figure 17.2 Market share development tree
Source: Best (2004, p. 73).

Integration of objectives

Kotler (1997, p. 99) suggests starting with the profit objectives and deducing the required sales and customer objectives.

For example, if a company wants to earn €1,800,000 profit, and its target profit margin is 10 per cent on sales, then it must set a goal of €18 million in sales revenue. If the company sets an average price of €260, it must sell 69,230 units. If total industry sales will reach 2.3 million units, this implies a 3 per cent market share. To maintain this market share, the company will have to set certain goals for consumer awareness, distribution coverage, and so on.

Thus, the line of reasoning is the following:

- to define the expected net profit;
- to identify the turnover required to achieve this result;

- given the current average company price, to determine the required sales volume (in units);
- given the expected level of primary demand in the reference segment, to calculate the corresponding required market share;
- given this target market share, to determine the target objectives in terms of distribution and communication.

The corresponding marketing objectives should therefore be

- to achieve a given turnover, which represents an increase over previous year of *x* per cent;
- this would imply a sales volume of *x* units, corresponding to a *y* per cent market share;
- to determine the level of brand awareness required to achieve this market share objective and also the required proportion of purchase intentions within the target segment;
- to determine the increase of distribution rate;
- to maintain the average company price.

This logical and apparently simple procedure is difficult to implement in the real world because it implies complete knowledge of the functional relationships between market share and price, market share and distribution, market share and awareness, and so on. The merit of this approach is to identify clearly the required information for sound marketing planning.

17.3.2. Characteristics of good objectives

Sound marketing objectives should have the following characteristics. They must be (a) clear and concise, avoiding long statements and phrases; (b) presented in a written form to facilitate communication and to avoid altering objectives over time; (c) stated within a specific time period and (d) in measurable terms; (e) consistent with overall company objectives and purpose; (f) attainable but of sufficient challenge to stimulate effort and (g) name specific results in key areas, such as sales, profits and consumer behaviour or attitudes (Stevens, 1982). In addition, individual responsibilities should be clearly defined as well as the calendar and the deadlines to be met.

17.4. Selection of the strategic path

To define an objective is one thing. To know how to reach that objective is another story, since the very same objective can be achieved in different ways.

A 10 per cent revenue increase can be obtained, for instance, by increasing the average selling price, or by expanding total demand through a price decrease, or by increasing market share without price change but through intensive advertising or promotional actions.

Clearly these alternative actions are not substitutes and their efficiency will vary according to market and competitive situations. Thus, beyond the general directions given by the basic strategic options discussed in Chapter 10, it is necessary to specify the action programme segment by segment.

17.4.1. Alternative action programmes

A defence strategy

If the strategic option is *to defend current market* position with existing products in an existing segment, the alternative actions to consider in a market position defence strategy could be

■ product or service modifications, for example, new features or packaging, or product repositioning through concept advertising;

■ sales, distribution and service network reinforcement;
■ stepped-up or redirected promotional activities;
■ defensive pricing through bundling or premium pricing.

A market penetration strategy

If the objective is *to increase the turnover by 10 per cent* in a specific segment or product-market by adopting a market penetration strategy without modifying the composition of the product portfolio, the brand manager could adopt one the following alternative strategic paths:

■ to target the non-users of the brand through promotional actions to induce a trial purchase;
■ to stimulate irregular users to become regular users by proposing special deals at a reduced price;
■ to increase consumption per usage occasion by offering larger packaging.

A market development strategy

If the objective were *to increase sales revenue* through a market development strategy without modifying the composition of the product portfolio, the strategic paths to consider would be the following:

■ to extend the geographic distribution by creating a commercial network in a neighbouring country, where the per capita consumption of the product is much lower;
■ to reinforce the distribution coverage by increasing the number of companies regularly visited by the sales force;
■ to augment the number of facings in the supermarket chains.

A brand extension strategy

If the objective is *to complete, improve or broaden the range of products*, the alternative of a product line extension strategy could be

■ filling gaps in the existing product line;
■ introduction of new products to serve untapped segments in related business areas;
■ systematic brand proliferation to blanket the market;
■ acquisition of a company with a complementary product line;
■ contracting for the supply of a complementary product line to be sold under the company's name;
■ joint venture for the development and production of a new product line.

An international development strategy

If the objective is *international development* by shipping existing products to foreign markets, the alternatives could be

- use of an independent, worldwide trading company;
- use of a network of export agents to handle all foreign business;
- setting up of a network of distributors or import agents in target markets;
- acquisition of a foreign company in the same industrial sector;
- a joint venture to enter a restricted foreign market.

These alternative strategy paths may have very different implications in terms of resources, both financial and human, and their feasibility must be carefully assessed.

17.4.2. The strategy statement

The strategy statement requires making basic choices among the strategy alternatives. It is a summary overview designed to state 'how' the objectives for the business unit will be met. The strategy statement will govern not only marketing planning, but the manufacturing, financial and R&D functions. It is the mainstream guidance from which all subsequent planning functions flow. The strategy statement should address the following:

- Market segments selected and targeted.
- Positioning relative to direct competition.
- Product line requirements, mix, extensions, and so on.
- Channels of distribution, direct, indirect, and so on.
- Pricing and price structure.
- Personal selling.
- Advertising and promotion.
- After-sales, warranty, services, and so on.
- Marketing research.

The strategy statement should not exceed two or three pages of text. At this point, general management should review and approve the objectives.

17.4.3. Criteria for selecting a strategic option

A certain number of simple rules, inspired by military strategy, should be followed in selecting a strategy:

- Feasibility: assess skills and resources constraints.
- Strength: always try to have a strength advantage.
- Concentration: avoid scattering of efforts.
- Synergy: ensure co-ordination and consistency in efforts.

- Adaptability: be ready to respond to the unexpected.
- Parsimony: avoid waste of scarce resources.

In the 2000s environment, forward thinking is a dynamic exercise which requires adaptability and flexibility.

17.5. Design of the marketing programme

Once the course of action is identified, a detailed description of the means required will be made for each component of the marketing mix. The strategy statement allows the product manager to prepare a supporting budget, which is basically a projected profit and loss statement.

The strategy statement gives a general direction that must then be translated into specific actions for each component of the marketing mix with a description of the resources available to implement those actions. These resources include human and financial resources; they are described in the action programme and in the budget.

The action programme includes a detailed description of the actions to be undertaken. In addition to financial considerations, the budget should also specify the timing of the action programmes and the responsibilities, that is, who is in charge of what. An example of budget structure is presented in Table 17.6.

The expected level of sales of a given brand is a function of the intensity and continuity of operational marketing efforts. The support given to each product of the firm's portfolio must be described with precision and summarised in financial terms in a projected profit and loss statement.

17.5.1. Negotiation of the marketing budget

Different budgeting modes can be adopted to design a strategic marketing plan. The ideal procedure should be as simple as possible and involve the whole organisation and in particular the functions responsible for the plan implementation. The most popular budgeting process observed in a survey of 141 companies (Piercy, 1987, p. 49), is the bottom-up/top-down process:

> Managers of the subunits in marketing submit budget requests, which are co-ordinated by the chief marketing executive and presented to top management, who adjust the total budget size to conform with overall goals and strategies.

A good strategic marketing plan should be a written document: it takes the form of a contract. To be effective the plan should have the following characteristics:

- Be sufficiently standardised as to permit fast discussion and approval.
- Consider alternative solutions to be adopted if environmental conditions change or if corrective actions have to be taken.

- Be regularly re-examined or updated.
- Be viewed as a managerial aid, which implies being (a) strict on the applications of corporate goal and on long-term strategic options, and (b) flexible on short-term forecasts.

The planning horizon is in general a 3-year moving horizon.

Usually, every month there is a comparison between current and expected results in order to monitor closely the implementation of the plan and to facilitate the adoption of fast remedial actions.

17.5.2. Alternative marketing programmes

In the design of the marketing programme, the product or brand manager has to decide on the level of each of the key marketing mix instruments, that is, price, advertising, visit frequency of the sales force to distributors, promotional activities to organise to support the brand in the distributive network, and so on (see Figure 17.3). Since these marketing instruments are partly substitutable, the brand manager can explore the sensitivity of the break-even volume to different combinations of the marketing mix variables. It is common practice to establish a base programme and then to analyse the implications of alternative scenarios. By way of illustration, let us consider the following (fictitious) case.

The direct cost of a new product is £10 (C); the annual depreciation cost plus the share of general overhead (F) add up to £38,000. Executive opinion held that £16 is a price (P) on the low side while £24 is a price on the high side; and that £10,000 is a low budget for advertising (S) and personal selling (V), respectively, and £50,000 is a high budget. This yields eight strategy combinations.

The break-even volume can be estimated as a function of the elements of the marketing mix as follows,

$$Q_n = \frac{F + S + V}{P - C}.$$

The break-even volume will vary with the product price and the amount of marketing effort devoted to the new product,

$$Q_n = \frac{38,000 + S + V}{P - 10}.$$

In Figure 17.3, eight alternative marketing programmes are listed for this product along with the implied break-even volume. For example, in the case of Mix #1, one has,

$$Q_1 = \frac{38,000 + 10,000 + 10,000}{16 - 10} = 9,667 \text{ units.}$$

Each mix is a polar case. They imply not only different break-even volumes, but also differences in the target market sensitivity to each element of the marketing mix.

- For example, Mix #1 represents the common strategy of setting a low price and spending very little for promotion. This works well when the market is highly price conscious, possesses good information about available brands, and is not easily swayed by psychological appeals.
- Mix #4 represents a strategy of low price and heavy promotions. The same low price policy as in Mix #1 is supported by heavy promotion and advertising. Thus, we have here the maximum marketing pressure that should produce a high sales volume but also that requires a high sales volume to break even. In this launching strategy, the firm creates high barriers to entry.
- Mix #5 consists of a high price and low promotion and is used typically in a seller's market where the firm wants to maximise short run profits, since the break-even volume is very low (4,143 units). In this programme, it is implied that the market is not price sensitive and that the reputation of the brand is sufficiently high and speaks by itself. This entry strategy does not create barriers of entry to competition attracted by the high market prices and by the absence of high communication costs.
- Mix #8 consists of a high price supported by high communication; this strategy is often used in a market where customers are sensitive to psychological appeals and to quality. It is interesting to note that the break-even volume is approximately the same for Mix #1 and Mix #8. Yet, the high price, high promotion character of Mix #8 promises greater losses or greater profits for deviations from the break-even volume.

The other Mixes (#2, 3, 6, 7) are variations on the same themes, with the additional feature that different assessments are made of the comparative effectiveness of advertising and personal selling. The alternatives presented here opposed a push versus a pull communication strategy. But it should be noted that while the division of a given budget between advertising and personal selling affects the actual sales volume, it does not affect the break-even volume.

17.5.3. Sales multiplier concept

In the field of fast moving consumer goods (FMCG), sales evolution beyond the first year is mainly determined by the repeat purchase rate. This rate is often difficult to estimate with precision. If the firm has information on the sales patterns of similar products, the product's penetration curve can be estimated on this basis. For example, the observation made by the firm could be the following:

Brand sales in this type of product category have a short life cycle; they reach their maximum level after 12 months, stay on this plateau during the second year and then decay during the third year at a rate that varies with the size of marketing efforts.

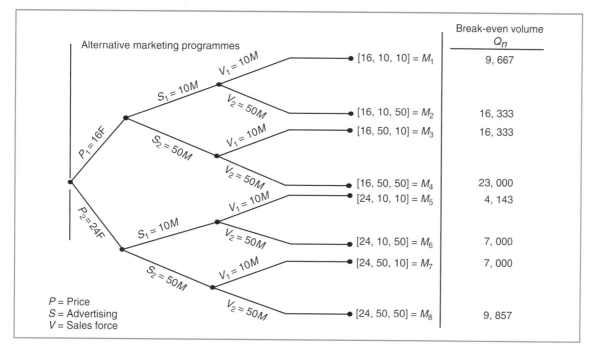

	Break-even volume Q_n
[16, 10, 10] = M_1	9, 667
[16, 10, 50] = M_2	16, 333
[16, 50, 10] = M_3	16, 333
[16, 50, 50] = M_4	23, 000
[24, 10, 10] = M_5	4, 143
[24, 10, 50] = M_6	7, 000
[24, 50, 10] = M_7	7, 000
[24, 50, 50] = M_8	9, 857

Figure 17.3   Minimum volume requirements as a function of marketing mix
Source: Adapted from an example presented by Kotler (1964, p. 44).

If the average decay rate observed for similar products is 20 per cent, third-year sales would then be 80 per cent of second-year sales. The sales multiplier of first-year sales over three years would then be 2.80 (1 + 1 + 0.80). This number (2.80) is called the sales multiplier or 'blow-up factor'. With this information, it is possible to develop a projected profit and loss statement over 3 years.

17.5.4. Risk or sensitivity analysis

A projected profit and loss statement, such as presented in Table 17.6, is based on assumptions about the sales growth rate and the size of the marketing budget. Management knows that this information is imperfect and risk analysis consists in testing the sensitivity of these assumptions on expected sales and profit.

Given the absence of reliable information on the trial and repeat purchase rates of the product, first year and subsequent years' sales cannot be determined with precision, and it is therefore useful to have a range of likely sales, and not just a point estimate, to assess the risk implications of the project. Suppose that the brand manager's opinion is summarised in the following terms:

The product manager is satisfied with the sales estimate of 2 million cases for the first year, although admitting that it contains some uncertainty. When pressed,

however, the product manager will admit that sales could be as low as 1 million cases in the first year, but points out that sales might also exceed the estimate by as much as 1 million cases. The operational definition of these extremes is that each has no more than 1 in 10 chance of occurring.

Using these estimates, one can derive a probability distribution for first-year sales and calculate the expected value of sales. The objective is to assess the risk of having a sales volume inferior to the break-even volume during the first year. The probability distribution is presented in Table 17.7.

The expected value of sales is 1,925,000 cases, which is very close to the deterministic estimation. There is, however, a three in ten chance that the sales volume in the first year will fall below the break-even volume. This is a significant risk.

Risk can also be measured in financial terms by computing the value of perfect information or the cost of uncertainty. The expected value of the choice given perfect information (VPI) is obtained by computing the expected value of the best conditional payoffs of Table 17.7.

$$E(\text{VPI}) = 0.10(0) + 0.20(0) + 0.25(0.938) + 0.25(4.635) + 0.10(8.331) + 0.10(11.028),$$

that is,

$$E(\text{VPI}) = \text{€}3,430 \text{ million.}$$

Table 17.6   Projected profit and loss statements form

	Year −3 (200-)	Year −2 (200-)	Year −1 (200-)	Current year (200-) Budget	Current year (200-) Estimated	Year +1 (200-)	Year +2 (200-)
Total market							
Volume (units)	____	____	____	____	____	____	____
Dollar sales (€)	____	____	____	____	____	____	____
Company sales							
Volume (units)	____	____	____	____	____	____	____
Marker share	____	____	____	____	____	____	____
Sales revenue (€)	____	____	____	____	____	____	____
Direct cost	____	____	____	____	____	____	____
Gross profit margin							
Value	____	____	____	____	____	____	____
% of net turnover	____	____	____	____	____	____	____
Directs marketing costs							
Promotions	____	____	____	____	____	____	____
Discounts	____	____	____	____	____	____	____
Folders and mailing	____	____	____	____	____	____	____
Misc.	____	____	____	____	____	____	____
Total direct costs	____	____	____	____	____	____	____
Semi-Fixed marketing costs							
Media advertising	____	____	____	____	____	____	____
POS	____	____	____	____	____	____	____
Public relations	____	____	____	____	____	____	____
Total semi-fixed costs	____	____	____	____	____	____	____
Fixed marketing costs							
Marketing department	____	____	____	____	____	____	____
Sales force	____	____	____	____	____	____	____
Market research	____	____	____	____	____	____	____
Sampling	____	____	____	____	____	____	____
Misc.	____	____	____	____	____	____	____
Total fixed costs	____	____	____	____	____	____	____
Total costs							
In % of net turnover	____	____	____	____	____	____	____
Net contribution							
Value	____	____	____	____	____	____	____
In % of net turnover	____	____	____	____	____	____	____
Net cumulative contribution	____	____	____	____	____	____	____

Note: Segment:____; Product:____; Zone:____.

Without perfect information, the optimal action is to go ahead, with an expected payoff of €2,232 million. Thus the expected gain from perfect information (or the uncertainty cost) is:

€3,430 million − €2,232 million = €1,198 million.

One observes that the uncertainty cost is high compared to the expected gain. Another way to assess the risk is simply to observe, referring to column 5 in Table 17.7, that there are 30 chances out of 100 to have a loss of at least €2,759,000 on this project. The cost of uncertainty measures in a way the opportunity cost of a decision taken

Table 17.7   Expected value of sales and profit

Classes	Sales* Midpoint	Probability	Expected sales	Conditional payoffs	Expected profit
0.5–1.0	0.75	0.10	0.075	−6.455	−0.646
1.0–1.5	1.25	0.20	0.250	−2.759	−0.552
1.5–2.0	1.75	0.25	0.438	+0.938	+0.235
2.0–2.5	2.25	0.25	0.562	+4.635	+1.159
2.5–3.0	2.75	0.10	0.275	+8.331	+0.833
3.0–3.5	3.25	0.10	0.325	+11.028	+1.203
Total	—	1.00	$E(q) = 1.925$	—	$E(\pi) = 2.232$

*In million cases or dollars.

under imperfect information. This amount also measures the value of additional information.

17.5.5. Calculation of the net marketing contribution

The net contribution is the direct measure of the adopted strategy's performance. The different elements of the net marketing contribution (NMC) are presented in Figure 17.4. Each term of the equation lends itself to some strategic thinking in order to determine the best way to improve the overall profitability. Several questions can be raised.

- Do we have to enter this segment or if we are already in do we have to divest?
- Which primary demand development strategy to adopt?
- How to increase our market share in the target segment?
- How to improve the profitability per customer? To increase volume sold? To raise prices?
- How to decrease delivery and service costs to our customers?
- How to improve the effectiveness of our advertising, of our promotional activities, of our sales force?

This last question is particularly sensitive: how to reduce fixed marketing expenses, for instance, in using intermediaries.

17.5.6. Gap analysis

In summarising the objectives of each business unit, it is instructive to project the current performance trends to verify whether the projected performance is satisfactory. If gaps appear between the current and the desired performance, then strategic changes will need to be considered. The graph presented in Figure 17.5 illustrates the contribution of growth opportunities under two growth scenarios:

- An 'all things being equal performance', where growth is achieved through a penetration strategy based on

existing products and existing markets, assuming no change in the current strategy.
- A 'desired performance', where growth is the outcome of the proposed marketing programme and of different growth opportunities.

As shown in Figure 17.5, the gap between these two performance levels can be subdivided into two parts:

- An 'operational gap', which reveals the improvement potential of existing businesses that could be achieved through a market and product rationalisation strategy, that is, reducing costs and/or improving marketing effectiveness, while keeping the structure of the product portfolio unchanged.
- A 'strategic gap', which requires new growth opportunities, that is, new products, new markets, international development, diversification or integration.

These growth opportunities should be listed in order of priority and their potential financial contribution to the desired performance evaluated.

17.6. Vulnerability analysis and contingency planning

The value of strategic planning is a continuing topic for debate. Not long ago, planning departments enjoyed a high status within the corporate organisation. Today, most corporate planners downplay their formal planning roles. Experience with such largely unforeseen upheavals as the two oil crises of the 1970s, the stock market crash of 1987, the Gulf War, the East European revolutions, and so on has revealed the shortcomings and the limitations of rigid planning procedures. Under fairly static conditions, planning works well, but when faced with uncertainties, turbulence, unanticipated market and competitive changes, general management becomes suspicious of the forecasts of revenue and profit performance that come from the business units.

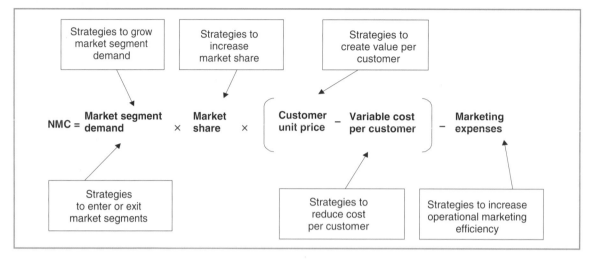

Figure 17.4 Computing the net marketing contribution
Source: Best (2004).

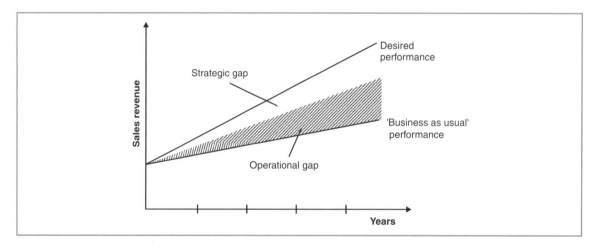

Figure 17.5 Gap analysis
Source: Thuillier (1987).

17.6.1. Testing the robustness of a strategic plan

Just because a strategy must be developed and implemented under turbulent and uncertain conditions is no reason to abandon the discipline of structured planning. Planning is necessary for the functioning of the firm. To improve strategic planning performance, it is therefore important to test the robustness of the proposed strategy. Gilbreath (1987) suggests applying a 'shake test' to the proposed strategy.

When structural or mechanical engineers wish to determine the reaction of a proposed design to mechanical vibrations, they either model it mathematically and calculate its response

to input vibrations or, if feasible, build a prototype, put it on a special 'shaking table' and actually witness the outcome. This is called a 'shake test'. It is proposed that a similar exercise be applied to strategic plans – giving them the shake test before the unforgiving test our markets and competitors will surely apply (Gilbreath, 1987, p. 47).

Day (1986) proposed testing the robustness of a proposed strategy through the following seven 'tough questions' to be examined by corporate management and operating managers.

Suitability. Is there a sustainable advantage given the potential threats to, and opportunities for, the business and in light of the capabilities of the firm?

Validity. Are the assumptions realistic? What is the quality of the information on which these assumptions rely?

Feasibility. Do we have the skills, resources and commitment?

Consistency. Does the strategy hang together? Are all elements of the strategy pointing in the same direction?

Vulnerability. What are the risks and contingencies?

Adaptability. Can we retain our flexibility? How could the strategy be reversed in the future?

Financial desirability. How much economic value is created? What is the attractiveness of the forecast performance relative to the probable risk?

Examples of vulnerability factors are presented in Table 17.8. Given the rapidity of environmental change, the test should be applied periodically to facilitate adaptability and revision. A good way to proceed is to apply this shake test with the assistance of outside persons to avoid the risk of myopia and wishful thinking.

17.6.2. Vulnerability analysis

The vulnerability of a strategic plan is determined by two factors: the strategic importance of risk and the degree of control the firm has over the risk factor. The risk factor is a combination of (a) the impact of extreme but plausible values on overall performance, and (b) the likelihood that these extreme values could occur during the planning period.

The vulnerability grid presented in Figure 17.6 can be used to position the different risk factors and to isolate those few that could cause the most damage. To each quadrant there corresponds a specific risk situation that requires appropriate action:

- In the *strategy quadrant*, that is, where both risk and degree of control are high, the risk factors are subject to company control, need to be understood very well, are the focus of major strategic actions and should be tightly monitored.
- In the *vulnerability quadrant*, the risks are high but the degree of control is weak. The factors positioned here

are critical and must be continuously monitored. Contingency plans should be developed.

- In the *fine-tuning quadrant*, the risks are low but the degree of control high. These factors are controlled and managed by operational management.
- In the *non-strategy quadrant*, both risk and degree of control are low and the factors positioned here will be included in the base scenario.

The vulnerability quadrant deserves particular attention, since major and unanticipated crises could come from these risk factors. Alternative strategies should be developed for these risk factors.

17.6.3. Strategic surprise management

In spite of the best planning efforts, some issues or unexpected changes will slip by the environmental monitoring system and become 'crises' or 'strategic surprises' in Ansoff's terminology (1984). A crisis is characterised by four elements:

- The issue arrives suddenly, unanticipated.
- It poses novel problems in which the firm has little prior experience.
- Failure to respond implies either a major financial reversal or loss of a major opportunity.
- The response is urgent and cannot be handled promptly enough by the normal systems and procedures (Ansoff, 1984, p. 24).

The combination of these four elements creates major problems for the firm. A crisis or disaster can be any emergency that happens suddenly, that disrupts the routine of the organisation and that demands immediate attention. Examples of crises are numerous.

The 'Nestlé kills babies' affair, the Tylenol incident, the Union Carbide disaster in Bhopal, the Société Générale of Belgium's take-over bid, the Pan Am Boeing 747 crash at Lockerbie, the Chernobyl and Three Mile Island nuclear accidents, the mad cow disease in the United Kingdom,

---

Table 17.8   Identifying vulnerability factors

Vulnerability factors	Stability factors
Reliance on fads	Projection of lasting symbols
Single use	Multiple use of products
Technology dependence	Technology transcendence
Single distribution network	Multiple distribution network
Heavy capital investment	Leasing, renting and joint ownership
Prescriptive identities	Non-restrictive identities
Building with products outside our control	Building with unchanging needs

Source: Adapted from Gilbreath (1987).

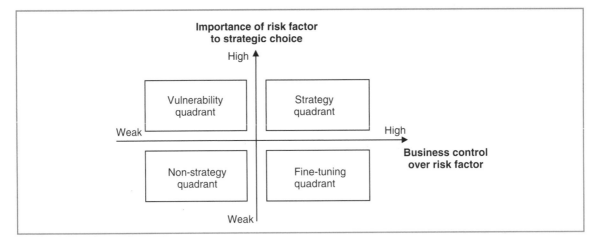

Figure 17.6 Vulnerability grid
Source: Day (1986).

the New York Madrid and London terrorist attacks, and so on.

The suddenness and the prospect of a major loss create a danger of widespread panic, and 'business as usual' managerial systems are inefficient to deal with a crisis. The firm needs to invest in a crisis recovery plan, because disaster recovery planning is more conducive to a rational perspective and more cost-effective if the process is begun before a crisis, rather than pulled together in the heat of battle (Phelps, 1986, p. 6).

To develop a contingency planning system the following steps must be taken:

- Identify the sensitive factors and the zones of danger through a vulnerability analysis.
- Establish a monitoring system with warning signals based on early-warning indicators.
- Prepare a crisis recovery plan based on a previously identified alternative strategy.
- Adopt this procedure for the major risks.

According to Ansoff (1984) and Lagadec (1991), a crisis recovery plan should have the following characteristics:

- A emergency communication network which crosses normal organisational boundaries, filters the information and rapidly communicates with the entire organisation.
- A repartition of top management responsibilities between three groups: one in charge of the organisation's morale control and maintenance; one in charge of 'business as usual'; and one in charge of the response to the surprise.

- A strategic task force to deal with the surprise whose members crosses normal organisational lines.
- The task force and communication networks are pre-designed and trained under non-crisis conditions before they are put to the actual test.

This procedure will not eliminate the occurrence of completely unexpected events but will contribute to reduce the consequences of major risks that can be identified. As put by Augustine (1995, p. 151), 'when preparing for crises, it is instructive to recall that Noah started building the ark before it began to rain'. To go further on the topic of crisis management, see the excellent book by Lagadec (1991).

17.6.4. New roles of global strategic planning

Business International (1991) has conducted a survey with 18 of the world's leading global companies on three continents to gain insights into their approaches to global planning. The ten most frequently mentioned functions of corporate planners are the following:

- Compiling of information for top management.
- Competitor research.
- Forecasting.
- Consulting services.
- Creating a common language.

- Communicating corporate culture.
- Establishing and communicating corporate objectives.
- Group facilitation and team leadership.
- Guardianship of the planning system.
- Developing planning methods.

Most corporate planners downplay their formal planning roles and instead emphasise their functions as 'facilitators', 'communicators' or 'consultants'. They see their role less as representatives of corporate authority than as consultants charged with assisting the divisions in developing their own plan and strategies.

Appendix

Table 17A.1   The search for a sustainable competitive advantage in the value chain

Managerial functions	Evaluation*				
	1	2	3	4	5
Marketing					
High relative market share	___	___	___	___	___
Brand reputation	___	___	___	___	___
High distribution coverage	___	___	___	___	___
Size of the sales force	___	___	___	___	___
Effective sales force	___	___	___	___	___
Level of sales training	___	___	___	___	___
Quality sales support	___	___	___	___	___
Low relative price	___	___	___	___	___
Balanced customer portfolio	___	___	___	___	___
Size of the advertising budget	___	___	___	___	___
Advertising quality (creativity)	___	___	___	___	___
Marketing data bank	___	___	___	___	___
Fast delivery	___	___	___	___	___
Training for dealers	___	___	___	___	___
Fine-tuned segmentation	___	___	___	___	___
Customers level of satisfaction	___	___	___	___	___
Extent of product line	___	___	___	___	___
/ ... /	___	___	___	___	___
Operations					
Large production capacity	___	___	___	___	___
Convenient location of production units	___	___	___	___	___
Extension potential	___	___	___	___	___
Advanced technology	___	___	___	___	___
Age of equipments	___	___	___	___	___
Total quality control	___	___	___	___	___
Equipment versatility	___	___	___	___	___
Availability of quality labour force	___	___	___	___	___
Fast manufacturing	___	___	___	___	___
Quality, reliability of components	___	___	___	___	___
Flexible manufacturing	___	___	___	___	___
Production to customer specifications	___	___	___	___	___
Defect-free manufacturing	___	___	___	___	___
Fast, reliable repairs	___	___	___	___	___
/ ... /	___	___	___	___	___
Finance					
High cash flow	___	___	___	___	___
Good profitability	___	___	___	___	___
Availability of credit	___	___	___	___	___
Availability of capital	___	___	___	___	___

Continued

Table 17A.1   Continued

Managerial functions	Evaluation*				
	1	2	3	4	5
Low debt ratio	___	___	___	___	___
High stock turnout	___	___	___	___	___
No long-term debt	___	___	___	___	___
Good return on equity	___	___	___	___	___
Efficient invoicing	___	___	___	___	___
Good customer credit	___	___	___	___	___
/ ... /	___	___	___	___	___
Administration					
Qualification of personnel	___	___	___	___	___
Sufficient inventory	___	___	___	___	___
Strategic, attractive location of office	___	___	___	___	___
Low operating costs	___	___	___	___	___
Good customer after-sales service	___	___	___	___	___
Good training programmes	___	___	___	___	___
Up-to-date office equipment	___	___	___	___	___
Office automation	___	___	___	___	___
Efficient order processing	___	___	___	___	___
/ ... /	___	___	___	___	___
Technology					
Fast new product development	___	___	___	___	___
Up-to-date technology	___	___	___	___	___
Engineering know-how	___	___	___	___	___
Product patents	___	___	___	___	___
Process patents	___	___	___	___	___
High creativity in R&D	___	___	___	___	___
Good management of R&D	___	___	___	___	___
High R&D budget	___	___	___	___	___
Performance of R&D	___	___	___	___	___
/ ... /	___	___	___	___	___

Note: *1 = not at all important; 5 = very important.

CHAPTER SUMMARY

This chapter has provided a scheme for developing a formal strategic marketing plan. The role of strategic planning is to design a desired future for the company and to define effective ways of making things happen. The plan summarises, in a formal way, the marketing strategy development phase. One of the key elements of the strategic plan is the mission statement which should reveal the company's long-term vision of what it wants to be and whom it wants to serve. The strategic plan is based on an external audit. The environment is ever-changing and complex and the firm must constantly scan and monitor the environment to identify the main threats and opportunities. The assessment of strengths and weaknesses is also an essential task in the strategic process. The objective is to evaluate company resources in order to identify a sustainable competitive advantage on which to base the development strategy. Using the information collected in the external and internal audits (SWOT analysis), the next task is to define priority objectives to be translated into operational action programmes and in a marketing budget. Testing the robustness of a strategic plan is useful to improve the strategic planning performance. Also, in the current turbulent environment, vulnerability and risk analysis is required to help the firm anticipate the unexpected through contingency planning and crisis management.

Review and Application Questions

1. What difference do you see between a marketing plan and a marketing strategy?
2. Pick a company whose activities and corporate goal you know well and prepare a mission statement.
3. How do you associate as closely as possible the different echelons within the firm with the preparation and the adoption of a strategic plan? Compare the merits and the weaknesses of the 'top-down' and the 'bottom-up' budgeting processes?
4. Referring to Table 17.8, give examples of three vulnerability factors and three stability factors to be used to test the robustness of a strategic plan.
5. What are the chances that strategic planning will succeed in a company whose chief executive is not interested in it and delegates the task to staff people?
6. List five variables on which success in the home construction industry depends.
7. Since it is natural for managers to want to justify their actions and decisions, is it possible for a company to make a truly objective appraisal of its strengths and weaknesses?
8. A financial executive questions the need for formal planning. Prepare a defence of strategic marketing planning.

Bibliography

Ansoff, H.I. (1984), *Implanting Strategic Management*, Englewood Cliffs, NJ, Prentice-Hall.

Augustine, N.R. (1995), Managing the Crisis you Tried to Prevent, *Harvard Business Review*, 73, 6, pp. 147–58.

Bain Survey (2001), Which Management Tools are Most Popular?, *European Business Forum*, 7, Fall.

Best, R.J. (2004), *Market-based Management*, Upper Saddle River, NJ, Prentice-Hall, 3rd edition.

Business International (1991), The Changing Face of Corporate Planning in the 1990's, Bimonthly Report, August 19.

David, F.R. (1989), How Companies Define Their Mission?, *Long Range Planning*, 22, 1, pp. 90–7.

Day, G.S. (1986), Tough Questions for Developing Strategies, *The Journal of Business Strategy*, 6, 3, pp. 67–75.

Drucker, P. (1973), *Management, Tasks, Responsibilities, Practices*, New York, Harper & Row.

Gilbreath, R.D. (1987), Planning for the Unexpected, *The Journal of Business Strategy*, 8, 2, pp. 44–9.

Greenley, G. (1987), An Exposition of Empirical Research into Marketing Planning, *Journal of Marketing Management*, 3, 1, pp. 83–102.

Hopkins, D.S. (1981), *The Marketing Plan*, New York, The Conference Board, Report No. 801.

Kotler, P. (1964), Marketing Mix Decision for New Products, *Journal of Marketing Research*, 1, 1, pp. 43–9.

Kotler, P. (2005), *Marketing Management*, Englewood Cliffs, NJ, Prentice-Hall, 11th edition.

Lagadec, P. (1991), *La gestion des crises*, Paris, Ediscience International.

Piercy, N.F. (1987), The Marketing Budgeting Process: Marketing Management Implications, *Journal of Marketing*, 51, 4, pp. 45–59.

Phelps, N.L. (1986), Setting Up a Crisis Recovery Plan, *The Journal of Business Strategy*, 6, 4, pp. 5–17.

Porter, M.E. (1980), *Competitive Strategy*, New York, The Free Press.

Stevens, R.E. (1982), *Strategic Marketing Plan Master Guide*, Englewood Cliffs, NJ, Prentice-Hall.

Thuillier, P. (1987), *De l'étude de marché au plan marketing*, Paris, Les Editions d'Organisation.

COMPANION WEBSITE FOR CHAPTER 17

Visit the *Market-driven Management* companion website at www.palgrave.com/business/lambin to find information on:

Market Share Movements Analysis

emerging values and issues in market-driven management

18

Chapter contents

Chapter learning objectives

When you have read this chapter, you should be able to understand

- the emerging power of the civil society;
- the impact on management of the new generation of electronic commerce;
- the implications of the shareholder versus stakeholder debate;
- the issues of corporate social responsibility;
- the challenge of poverty in the world.

Chapter introduction

In the twenty-first century, three major evolutionary changes have and will have a profound impact on the functioning of markets: (a) the globalisation of the world economy, (b) the integration of electronic commerce into our professional and private lives and (c) the emergence of new values promoting a market economy model aimed at sustainable development. These three evolutionary changes are not really new. But the disruptive events of 2000–2002 have dramatically highlighted their strategic impact.

18.1. Affirmation of civil society's power

In the industrialised world, being better educated and exposed to the consumerist culture, consumers represent a force of responsible citizen-consumers that firms and public authorities can no longer ignore. Six attitudes characterise the new consumer:

1. *A feeling of power*: Consumers behave in markets where supply is plentiful, brands proliferate, competition for consumer's loyalty is intense and information sources numerous.
2. *A professional purchasing behaviour*: Well-educated and experienced, consumers are smart shoppers, able to make trade-off among brands, stores, advertising and the recommendations of salespeople. They become increasingly discriminating in their demand for customised services and want complete information about their purchases. From passive consumers, they become more active or 'consumactors'.
3. *The satisfaction–delight–loyalty relationship*: The new consumer holds the firm responsible in case of dissatisfaction. Thus a dissatisfied customer is a lost customer, a damaging effect in zero-growth markets, where replacing a lost customer by a new one is particularly difficult and costly. Moreover, research results show that simply giving what is expected is not enough to keep a customer loyal. The objective should be to give more than expected, to have *delighted customers*.
4. *A search for new values*: In industrialised countries, economic prosperity and mass consumption have lifted the aspirations of consumers from materialistic needs to the search for new values. Initially looking mainly for comfort and safety, they are more and more looking for stimulation, pleasure, change, innovation, surprise.
5. *A need for a dialogue*: Consumers are represented by powerful and vocal consumerist and by non-governmental organisations (NGOs). Just as significant is the growing influence of environmental groups, human rights activists, labour and religious groups and a host of other organisations who collectively make up 'civil society'.

6. *Ethical consumption*: In addition, consumers want an *ethical consumption* and do not want to have guilty feelings from their purchases nor from the advertising associated with their brands. Shopping with attitude. Buying and using products and brands having acceptable price and quality ratios, but also brands meeting ethical criteria such as the product greenness, the social and human practice of the firm, its political and strategic commitments, etc.

This emerging trend toward ethical consumption is confirmed in the United Kingdom by the survey results conducted in 1994 and in 2004 by Co-op UK (see Exhibit 18.1). The key conclusion is that consumers today (2004) are more concerned with ethical issues (up 23 per cent compared to 1994) as shown by three key measurements:

- 64 per cent (up 12 per cent) say that they are more concerned about ethical issues.
- 84 per cent (up 35 per cent) say they are ready to pay a little extra for products that meet ethical standards, provided that quality is as good.
- 80 per cent (steady) say that are prepared to boycott a product on ethical ground.

A more recent evolution is the so-called *politically correct consumption* (or the committed consumption), which designates a purchasing behaviour in which the consumer is more involved by considering that a brand purchase is similar to a political act. To select a brand or a company is comparable to a political vote: one selects a candidate in whom we trust. Similarly, in the market place one can make politically correct purchase decisions.

A case in point is the Mecca-Cola brand recently launched in the French market and targeting the Muslim community. Its slogan is: 'Do not drink stupid, drink committed' (Ne buvez plus idiot, buvez engagé). The brand also promises to give 10 per cent of its net profit to Palestinian charities (info@mecca-cola.com).

Since the beginning of the Iraq war, boycott calls proliferate on the web, either from Arab countries

EXHIBIT 18.1

WHO CARES ABOUT ETHICS? (*A CO-OP UK CONSUMER SURVEY*)

Ethical issues	1994 n = 31,000 (%)	2004 n = 29,500 (%)	Change (%)
General concern about issues – Are you more concerned now than in the past?	57	64	+12
Support for Third World – Should retailers help growers in developing countries?	55	80	+45
Willingness to pay more – Are you willing to pay a little extra for ethical alternatives?	62	84	+35
Active boycotting – Have you boycotted a product on ethical grounds?	33	29	−12
Preparedness to boycott – Are you likely in the future?	60	60	Steady
Informative labelling – Would food labels give full information?	62	96	+54
Honest labelling – Should misleading labels be banned?	62	90	+56
Farm animal welfare – Very important that retailers buy humanely reared meat	66	71	+7
Wildlife welfare – very important to support products not harmful to wildlife	59	70	+18
Conserve natural resources – Very important to stop products from non-sustainable sources	55	64	+16
Pollution of environment – Very important that business minimises pollution	52	67	+29
Packaging – very important that retailers minimise packaging	52	58	+11
Average increase across all areas of study		Up 23	

Source: Croft (2004).

suggesting the boycott of American products or from American sites inviting in particular to the boycott of French products.

By way of an example, the American site www.howtobuyamerican.com published a list of 450 French (and other) brands, indicating the American substitute product or brand that should be preferred. Similarly, an Arab site gives a list of American products to boycott in quoting their prices in the number of war bullets that Israel could purchase (a Coca-Cola = 7 bullets, a pizza = 140, etc.).

It is hard to assess the real impact of systematic boycott targeting consumer products such as Coca-Cola, Pizza Hut, Pepsi, McDonald, Starbucks, Estée Lauder, all products having local equivalents. Since September 11, it is Saudi Arabia that has suffered most from the boycott with a drop of 43 per cent of American exports during the first quarter of 2002 (Reuters, June 2002). In France, wine exports to the United States have declined by 21 per cent during the first 4 months of 2003, a decline too high to be attributed to the sole rise of the euro to the dollar.

This growing power of citizens generates new expectations which directly contribute to improving the functioning and transparency of the market: liberty of choice, better information, pressure on prices, product safety, after-sales responsibility of the manufacturers and ecologically friendly products. It also constitutes a *strong countervailing power* to the power of companies and even to the power of public authorities. New and more responsible relationships between consumers and the industrial world are developing which challenge the stereotype of a manipulated and defenceless consumer.

In short, globalisation of the world economy increases the complexity of markets: competition intensifies, new actors become powerful players, consumers are more vocal and demanding and technological innovations are changing the configurations of traditional markets. Arguably this increased market complexity creates huge difficulties for the firm and requires a greater understanding of the global environment and a more finely tuned strategic analysis of market behaviour.

A recent study published by the American consultant Bain (Root and Smith, 2003) covering a sample of 729 international companies from seven countries (France, Germany, Italy, United Kingdom, Japan, Australia and the United States) having a sales revenue larger than $500 million, has shown that only 124 companies (or 1 out of 6) have succeeded during the years 1996–2000 to achieve a profitable growth strategy of at least 8 per cent (i.e. the GNP growth plus the inflation effect).

This observation illustrates the fact that to be an international successful player in a globalised market is far from being an easy game. For an interesting discussion over the merits and drawbacks of globalisation, see Laudicina (2005).

18.2. The integration of electronic commerce

The crisis in the New Economy and the collapse of the Internet start-ups in the NASDAQ are still present in everybody's memory. The causes of these failures are known today:

■ Too fast international development and under-estimation of the time required to reach the break-even point.
■ A lot of good ideas but rapidly imitated due to the lack of entry barriers and the absence of strong brands.
■ Absence of value proposals sufficiently differentiated from the bricks-and-mortars retailers.
■ Misunderstanding of the consumer behaviour on the web, more interested in browsing than in buying.
■ Priority given to sales and communication and not to delivery.

Despite its growth crisis, the New Information and Communication Technologies (NICT) have grown exponentially during the last 5 years, but the speed of change has often confused companies, provoking widespread questioning and reassessment of the way markets are likely to be organised and marketing strategy developed in the future.

18.2.1. A new generation of electronic commerce

In fact, we are entering in a second generation of electronic commerce: by electronic commerce (EC), we mean,

Any electronic exchange which contributes to the commercial and marketing activities of the firm and which facilitates relationships between customers, suppliers and/or any other partners.

Too often EC is merely perceived as a narrow selling instrument deployed through a website – little more than a banner presenting the company and a catalogue of products from which customers can directly order online. The reality is that very few firms (particularly SMEs) have so far been able to sell to their end-customers through the web. By contrast, however, many have adopted Electronic Data Interchange (EDI) systems, which hook together computers of commercial partners via telephone lines. Once established, this connection facilitates and accelerates communication within the supply chain for ordering between suppliers, distributors and customers, for disseminating information and thereby generating substantial cost savings.

In addition to selling online and to EDI, other EC applications include an extranet to reinforce links with traditional commercial partners (wholesalers, importers, retailers), multimedia kiosks at the points of sale to present a catalogue, or a system of personalised electronic messages to maintain continuous relationships.

The main characteristics of electronic commerce are well known.

Virtual ubiquity of demand and supply – easy access to quality information by a large public any where, any time – worldwide comparison of offerings and prices – absence of entry barriers – separation between production and selling – equal opportunities for each seller, etc.

These characteristics of EC are improving the efficiency of markets. We are close to a situation of pure (or perfect) competition, where the tools of strategic marketing (differentiation, innovation, loyalty,) are to some extent neutralised. In this context, the objective of value creation for the client becomes more difficult to achieve given the limited potential for differentiation and the absence of protection of new ideas.

In this new environment, the firm controlling the delivery to the market has a major competitive advantage. In traditional business structures, selling is seen and organised as a servant to production. In EC, instead of selling what it makes, *the virtual company will sell what it can deliver, no matter who makes the products*. The contact with the market and the *savoir-faire* in terms of physical distribution and logistics become the core competence (Drucker, 2000).

18.2.2. The concept of virtual market

One of the main causes of failure of the start-ups in the New Economy was the lack of sufficiently differentiated proposals by comparison with the proposals made by the physical stores. Online applications should not systematically replace traditional activities. The challenge is to redesign the traditional proposal by presenting a more global offering or a new combination of traditional offerings thereby giving more value to the client.

For example, a real-estate agency going online can provide information not only on available apartments or houses, but also on house renovation, home insurance, house equipment, or removal services, selecting the assortment of services by reference to the set of needs of the client in search of a shelter.

Added value analysis based on what is called *the meta-market concept* (Sawhney *et al.*, 2004) leads to an offering or to an assortment of offerings defined by reference to all the elements (activities and services), which comprise the cognitive space of the client. For more developments on this subject, go back to Chapter 7. While, in general, markets are organised around products and services, the consumer purchasing process is structured by references to activities that are linked in cognitive space.

> For example, on the supply side the car market is organised around car manufacturers, car dealers, car insurance brokers, financing services, garage and maintenance services, mechanics, etc. By contrast, the cognitive space of a car purchaser is composed of information search, evaluation, price negotiation, purchasing decision, insurance, financing maintenance and eventually resale value.

The web firm has the possibility to match the supply market concept, which is based on the products with the meta-market concept, which is based on the logic and the perceptions of the consumer. Thus, the meta-market concept gives to the virtual firm the opportunity to fully implement the customer orientation concept. In this way the e-market places can position themselves as a new intermediary between the buyers and sellers, thereby upsetting traditional sectors and creating competition stretching across conventional market boundaries.

18.2.3. Reconfiguration of distribution networks

Once the potential EC applications are identified, it is useful to verify whether each online application 'complements' or 'replaces' off-line operations. Online applications do not systematically replace traditional activities. In many cases, the best solution is a combination of the two, thereby promoting complementarities (the '*click-&-mortar*' concept). A classic mistake is to do online only what is done manually off-line, simply to generate costs reductions. The firm's marketing strategy should dictate policy in this case.

> This mixed strategy is the one adopted by Barnes & Noble, Toy-R-Us, Virgin-Express, by contrast with Amazon.com, Dell-Computer and Ryan-air, which operate online only.

A second strategic issue raised by EC is the reconfiguration of the distributive network. A commonly held view is that EC will enable companies to deal directly with the end-customer, leapfrogging an existing distribution network and thereby reducing transaction costs. Why remunerate middlemen, the thinking goes, if one can communicate directly with the customer through an electronic link, giving her or him the possibility to place an order directly at lower cost? This is called *disintermediation*.

In reality, the challenge is far greater. Taken separately, the cost of the direct contact is indeed lower, but managers need to view the *total cost of the transaction*. In many situations, the reduced cost of the person-to-person relationship can be offset by substantially increased logistics costs. The issue is not one of sidelining distributors, rather of redistributing the tasks and functions among the existing actors in the chain. This redistribution (or re-allocation) of tasks is particularly relevant for product information, advice to customers, after-sales services, physical delivery, product and service bundling and product demonstrations or trials. Several options exist, which are given below:

- Place on the company's web site – little more than a banner presenting the company and a catalogue of products without the price list. The distributors then perceive the site as a promotional support.
- Charge on the website the same price as the market price but add delivery costs, which keeps the traditional distributor's offering attractive.
- Sell on the website but return a commission to the distributors located in the geographic zone where the product is sold.
- Adopt the same pricing strategy as the distributors, which is an aggressive strategy creating direct competition vis-à-vis the distributors.

Thus, the issue is more a question of re-allocation of the distribution tasks among the different actors. It would be possible therefore for a firm to deal directly with the end-customer where the provision of up-to-date information is at stake, while leaving to intermediaries those tasks requiring physical proximity (Dimitriadis *et al.*, 2003).

EXHIBIT 18.2

SMALL CAN ALSO BE BEAUTIFUL

- The roses purchased today in the streets of New York and of Saint Petersburg, in winter or in summer, are shipped every week by air cargo from family owned horticultural companies situated on the hills surrounding Quito (Ecuador), where conditions for roses cultivation are ideal with every day climatic conditions of the four seasons.
- The green and rosy paving stones found today in the European market – hand carved stones an activity traditionally done at Quenast (Belgium) – are now shipped directly by boat from India.
- In 1999, software development accounted for 10.5 per cent of total export in India and according to a McKinsey report will represent more than 30 per cent of total export in 2008.

18.2.4. The geographic market coverage

Adopting EC technology does not necessarily imply that companies should suddenly start operating on a global stage. If EC facilitates communication, international physical delivery and logistics still require specific competence and significant financial resources. Thus, decisions concerning market coverage should be taken only after considering the physical (delivery) and psychological (communication) implications.

The spectacular development of the NICTs and the resulting globalisation of the world market can give the illusion that distance does not matter anymore. In reality, distance is a multidimensional concept and a distinction must be made between the four dimensions of distance (Ghemawat, 2001): geographic (physical remoteness), administrative (preferential trading agreements), economic (wealth differences) and cultural (linguistic ties). The NICTs have eliminated only one component of geographic distance: the communication link.

As a result, an increasing number of companies are succeeding overseas without massive foreign investment by adopting a global business model called *netchising* (Morrison *et al.*, 2004). This new business model relies on the Internet for procurement, sales and maintaining customer relationships, and non-equity partnership arrangements to provide direct customer interfaces and local adaptation and delivery of products and services. Netchising offers potentially huge benefits over traditional exporting or foreign direct investment approaches to globalisation (see Exhibit 18.2).

18.2.5. Electronic communication

The development of electronic communication not only modifies the respective roles of personal selling and of advertising, but also changes the objectives and the content of advertising communication. The characteristics of electronic communication are well known.

> Interactive communication – advertising on demand – more informative and factual communication – a personalised electronic mail system – an egalitarian medium – a worldwide communication any where any time.

The most important impact of electronic communication has been to reduce dramatically interaction costs, that is, the administrative costs borne to get people to work together, to collect information, to co-ordinate activities and to exchange goods and services. According to a McKinsey report, these costs amount to 55 per cent of the total administrative costs of companies operating in advanced economies. The reduction of telecommunication and transport costs, with its massive diffusion of ever cheaper and more powerful information, progressively eliminates barriers between markets and gives access to the international market to any individual having talent or ideas.

18.2.6. Private life protection on the Internet

The individualisation of online communication creates the need for personalised data to customise the offering. Therefore, any element of information susceptible to differentiate the potential customer and to draw its detailed profile is gaining a commercial value. This explains the development of personal data banks and by way of consequence the highly sensitive issue of privacy and of private life protection on the Internet.

The objective of the European Data Privacy Directive issued by the EU in 1995 protects all personal data and allows its collection for specific, explicit and identifiable purposes, but does not allow any further processing. Data collectors must inform the individual of the specific purpose for the recorded information and must keep the information accurate and up to date. Data subjects are guaranteed access to review personal information and they must be given the right to refuse to have their personal data transferred to a third party. In addition, if data are collected for one purpose and is later used for another, the data subject must be notified and given an opportunity to opt out of the second use (Gladstone and Scheibal, 2001).

Thus, the days when companies could do pretty much as they pleased over privacy are disappearing. Pressure from governments and customers to comply with new rules is intensifying. This EU Data Privacy Directive is a first manifestation of a form of world governance.

In short, electronic commerce provides to the firm new opportunities for dealing with the market in a more efficient manner, not only in terms of costs savings but also in terms of greater customisation of the firm's offering and of its communication and selling strategy. EC has a strong impact on operational marketing and is also a major challenge for strategic marketing.

18.3. The emergence of new values

Our era is characterised by a number of paradoxes (de Woot, 2005).

> Our capacity to produce wealth has never been greater while the inequalities in the world have never been larger. The extraordinary dynamism of the market economy exists alongside the near total poverty of half of humanity. The economic tendency is towards

globalisation while politics have remained mainly national in character. It is as if the technical and economic system had been left to its own devices. The environment is deteriorating while scientific knowledge, technical know-how and accumulated wealth could safeguard the planet.

This situation that is the result of an extremely complex accumulation of factors affects companies and obliges them to rethink their responsibilities towards society and to consider the market economy in its environment together with its strengths but also its weaknesses and malfunctions. Today an increasing number of voices are being raised (European Commission, business leaders, NGOs, etc.) supporting the idea of sustainable development and what is called the stakeholders approach in management.

18.3.1. The 'shareholders' versus 'stakeholders' debate

Since the mid-1980s we have witnessed an increasing focus on shareholder value in particular in US and UK companies. The traditional *shareholder approach*, following the views of Nobel Prize winner Milton Friedman (1970), holds that the purpose of business is to increase profits or shareholder value. The main argument for supporting a shareholder value is quite straightforward: failure by managers to recognise the primacy of the shareholder value group will result in poorer returns to shareholder, reduced motivation for potential investors and eventually reduced activity and unemployment. An example of the mission statement of a shareholder-focused business is that of the Coca-Cola Company which states:

> We exist to create value for our share owners on a long term basis by building a business that enhances the Coca-Cola trademarks. This is also our ultimate commitment.

On the other hand, the *stakeholder approach* asserts that the firm is responsible to and should be run for the benefit of number constituencies, that is, its stakeholders. Who are these stakeholders? (see Figure 18.1). A popular definition is that stakeholders are any groups or individual who can affect or are be affected by the organisation's objectives: employees, customers, suppliers, local community and the environment. The stakeholder approach does not specify, however, which stakeholder group has priority over another. An example of a mission statement of a stakeholder business is that of Cadbury Schweppes which states:

> Our task is to build our tradition of quality and value and to provide brands, products, financial results and management performance that meet the interest of our shareholders, consumers, suppliers and the communities in which we operate.

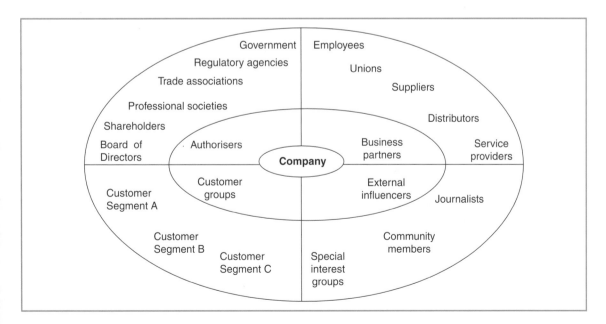

Figure 18.1   Corporate stakeholders
Source: Dowling (2001).

At the heart of the stakeholders model – a somewhat slippery concept – is the principle that all persons must be respected and that the firm exists to equally satisfy all stakeholders, a complex objective. Multiple stakeholders only compound the complexities.

This is highlighted when executives bestow upon themselves huge pay increases, with paltry rises to employees, when returns to shareholders have been modest, and prices to consumers have not dropped, nor service enhanced. A notorious case is Barclay bank in 1998, which awarded its CEO massive pay rises while reducing its workforce by 7,500 and closing down 172 branches.

At first sight, it seems that it is difficult for both approaches to coexist in harmony within a particular economy. The argument for supporting the stakeholders approach has its own merit, however. Unless the needs of stakeholders are properly addressed there will be an adverse effect on company performance and therefore on shareholders returns.

The idea that satisfying the needs of all those with a stake in the business can go hand in hand with superior returns to shareholders has obvious appeal. The emergence of new values described in this section suggests that substantial progress is made in that direction.

18.3.2. The adoption of the socio-ecological view of consumption

The environmental movement and the socio-ecological view of consumption (Figure 18.2) reflect a new awareness of the scarcity of natural resources, the uncontrolled growth of waste and the social cost of consumption.

Between 1890 and 1990, the world population has been multiplied by 4, while consumption in industrial products was multiplied by 40, energy use by 16, water consumption by 9, fish consumption by 35 and the total world production by 14. This discrepancy between population and consumption growth is even higher in highly industrialised countries.

This new awareness regarding the scarcity of resources reflects a changed attitude to consumption as something, which is no longer viewed as an end in itself but which must take into account its upstream (opportunity cost) and downstream (repair and prevention cost) implications. Globalisation is positively disseminating this new culture as markets become more interdependent and as procurement and production activities spread across the planet.

The basic argument of the ecologist is to set a price on the use of the environment which was until recently regarded as a 'free good'.

The economic instruments that used to set a price to the use of the environment generally take the form of a direct tax on the polluting activities, either in prevention (eco-taxes) or in a repairing perspective (eco-fees).

The life-cycle inventory (LCI) model is the basic tool used by the ecologist and through which a product's total environmental impact is evaluated from *'cradle to grave'*.

Life cycle inventory (LCI) is a process that quantifies the use of energy, resources and emission to the

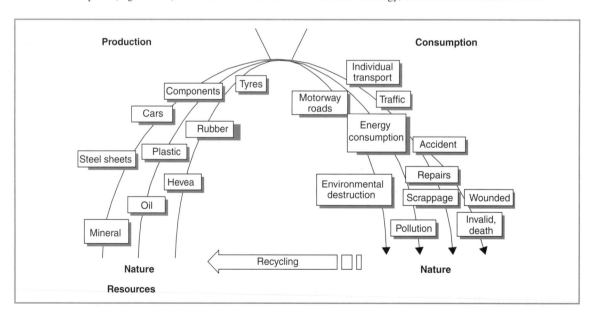

Figure 18.2   The socio-ecological view of consumption
Source: Authors.

environment associated with a product throughout its life cycle. It accounts for the environmental impact of raw material's procurement, manufacturing and production, packaging, distribution and in-use characteristics straight through to after-use and disposal.

Faced with this thinking, firms are being forced to review their underlying product concepts in the light of everything from raw material procurement to after-use and disposal. In future, the certification ISO-14001, which measures and certifies the degree of greenness, will probably become a pre-condition for being short-listed in international tenders, as it is already the case for the ISO-9000 norm.

A new EU directive currently under consideration by the European parliament is a good example of the practical implications of ecology.

Under its terms, vehicle makers will have to bear the expense of recycling their cars, buses and trucks. The directive encourages the use of recycled material. It requires 85 per cent of the weight of all vehicles sold in the European Union after 2007 to be made from reclaimed substances. This directive will be in application retroactively as soon as 2006, which means that the European automobile industry will have to recycle 170 million cars currently in use in Europe.

The environmental concern behind this directive comes from the market and is the expression of new needs within society. It is not a fad or a protest trend. It is a way of life, which has and will spread rapidly throughout all levels of society and throughout the world. This preponderance of collective over individual needs is a new economic phenomenon and represents a check to the wilder forms of capitalism.

Until recently, such environmental consciousness could be viewed as a preoccupation of industrialised economies, but the interdependence of markets that comes with globalisation has changed this. It also explains why new environmental norms are at the core of the ongoing international trade negotiations, although the European Union's attempts to impose higher standards are often seen by the United States as an obstacle to free trade and by developing countries as a form of disguised protectionism.

18.3.3. The objective of eco-efficiency

The socio-ecologic view of consumption induces firms to improve their 'eco-efficiency', that is, to increase the volume of production per unit of natural resource. This objective will be reached by applying to the use of natural resources the principle adopted by Henri Ford during in the years 1920 in the use of human resources: 'to do more with less'.

Historically, labour productivity has increased by a factor 200 in industry and by a factor 20 in agriculture.

This means that, in industry, one worker do the job where 200 workers were required three centuries ago. By comparison the productivity in the use of natural resources and energy per production unit has increased by a factor 10 only since the eighteenth century. Nevertheless, this productivity gain makes possible today to produce one ton of steel with 10 times less energy than before. (Lambin, 2004/2007)

All specialists agree: the potential for improving the eco-efficiency of most products is enormous (through de-carbonisation, de-materialisation, reduction of waste and pollution, etc.). Beneficial for the environment, improving the eco-efficiency also improves the firm's profitability thereby creating a *win-win situation*, where gains are achieved both on the environmental and economic sides. (See Exhibit 18.3.)

Last but not least, the image of the firm having a good ecological reputation is becoming a stronger argument for creating loyalty among customers, employees and shareholders. Today, more investors are expressing their preferences for ethical funds regrouping firms having good social and ecological credentials, as illustrated by the growth of sustainable investments funds (Louche, 2003).

18.3.4. Towards global governance

The globalisation of the world economy raises the issue of the role of the State and of global governance. It is an established fact that national States are deprived from their national prerogatives to the extent that they do not control transnational activities. The contrast between the means that the nations have at their disposal for national governance (between 30 and 50 per cent of GNP) and the weakness of resources at the global level is striking. It is recognised that a market economy needs a strong governance to define and enforce the rules of the competitive game. It is up to the State, for example, to balance the main macro-economic issues (such as price stability) and to ensure a minimum social cohesiveness and solidarity. A market economy, be it national of global, needs a strong governance to function smoothly. In a market that is hardly regulated or not regulated at all, the risk to see wild capitalism prevailing is high.

If the market economy system in Russia did not work well during the first years of its adoption it was largely due not to the market, but to a too weak government and to the absence of the market and economic regulations that are necessary to ensure a smooth functioning of a market economy. In this type of unregulated market, 'might is right' and the mafia or a bunch of corrupted individuals are running the show.

EXHIBIT 18.3

ECONOMIC ANALYSIS OF ENVIRONMENTALISM

- In 1972, the Meadow report of the Club de Rome called the attention of the economic and social world to the limits of economic growth, the risk of exhausting non-renewable resources, the destruction of the environment and the uncontrolled growth of waste. This new awareness led public authorities and political movements to listen to the recommendations made by economists.
- To the economist, the environment is part of the economy and the best way to protect the environment is to assign a price to its use instead of considering it as a free public good, in contrast with the other goods found in a market economy.
- If there is no market price, consumers and manufacturers are motivated to use the environment, as a 'free reservoir' even if the social costs generated by their polluting behaviour are high, since the market does not assess these costs. Thus, the ones generating these social costs do not pay them and

are not held responsible for the costs involved by their elimination.
- The solution proposed by the economists is to set a price to the use of the environment. This price should be equal to the sum of the total social costs generated by pollution as the polluted parties evaluate them. Given this price, polluters would use the environment only to the extent the expected benefits of this use are higher than the price they would have to pay. This way, the polluters would assume the social cost of pollution. This is the idea behind the principle 'who pollutes pays'.
- The economic instruments used to set a price to the use of the environment generally take the form of a direct tax on the polluting activities, either in prevention (eco-taxes) or in a repairing perspective (eco-fees).

Source : Authors.

But in an under-regulated global market, which international organisation will assume this global governance? In other words, if there is a *'global village'* which municipal board will be in charge?

In today's world, the urge to maintain and to claim one's own cultural identity is stronger than ever and, in the years to come, it will be the *'subsidiarity principle'* that will guide decision-making. *What can be best dealt with at a local level should be addressed locally.*

For transnational issues on the other hand, such as ecology, privacy on the web, safety, terrorism, health, etc., forms of world governance are necessary. A world government is hardly on the agenda but new forms of concerted global effort – similar to the Kyoto, Montreal and The Hague conferences in the field of ecology, and to the Davos and Porto Alegre forums in the socio-economic field – can contribute to solutions.

Global capitalism needs strong countervailing powers, which go beyond the power of national governments. Contrary to the demands of the anti-globalisation supporters, the powers of supranational organisations like the WTO, the IMF and the World Bank should be reinforced and new supranational organisations created to deal with these transnational issues. Without them, the risk is increased that we end up with a much wilder form of capitalism than we have at the moment, operating in a completely deregulated market.

18.3.5. Corporate societal responsibility

Firms everywhere are embracing the concept of corporate societal responsibility (CSR), and the financial corporate

scandals in the United States (Enron, Worldcom) have contributed to reinforce this evolution. The reasons for the adoption of this business philosophy at the corporate level can be summarised as follows:

- Any firm needs a healthy and prosperous environment to reach its own development objectives. Economic progress cannot be built on a social disaster.
- A global economic system under which half of the humanity finds itself excluded is obviously not viable politically nor acceptable morally.
- The welfare state and the social and fiscal solutions it implies have clearly reached its limits, both on qualitative and financial grounds.
- Rather than paying more taxes, civil society should wake up and commit itself, where it has the appropriate skills and resources.

The responsible corporation acknowledges that it has a responsibility towards society and not only to its shareholders. It is an organisation, large or small, which wishes to establish a long-term and sustainable relationship with the community where it lives and from which it gains its prosperity. Participating in social life, the responsible corporation commits its resources and competence to help combat social problems, often in co-operation with public authorities. The domains where the responsible corporation can contribute are several and varied.

To develop the economic fabric of a region; to maintain or develop employment; to participate in education programmes; to protect the environment; to dialogue with stakeholders; to promote urban development; to fight against social exclusion.

A key part of the vision is that corporations are the most powerful force for change in the modern world: state, church and university should not shy away but their actions, slower by nature, merely complement the more important role of companies.

In the new global economy, ethical behaviour which consists of 'doing well (financially) by doing good (socially)', is not only compatible with the objective of modern capitalism – as evidenced by the success of ethical funds – it represents a competitive advantage by meeting the market's demand (Exhibit 18.4). Again the interdependence of markets created by globalisation helps ensure that these new standards of behaviour become an imperative for any firm with the ambition to become a player in the global market.

This philosophy of responsible management is rapidly gaining acceptance in Europe in the business community, as evidenced by the proliferation of charters and codes of conduct, the growing adoption of the *Triple Bottom Line* (TBL) reporting systems, the charter of Human Responsibility suggested by the Alliance for a responsible world, the efforts of Transparency International, the anti-bribery convention of the OECD, etc. TBL is particularly important. The TBL represents the idea that businesses should account for their performance on economic, environmental and social criteria and attempt to satisfy their stakeholders on all three sets of criteria.

18.3.6. The potential impact of social accountability certification

As the world becomes more linked and interconnected by global media, alleged and actual corporate social misbehaviour is rapidly made public.

For example, Nike's labour and environmental practices in Vietnam during the 1990's quickly became a public scandal and a significant marketing problem for Nike, resulting in boycotts, loss of revenue and, most significantly, tremendous damage to Nike's corporate reputation.

A major social responsibility issue that corporations must address is the contextual nature of what constitutes a 'social good'. In Europe and in the United States, children are protected by society and are not considered a household economic asset. But this is simply not true in some cultures where the economic value of children is a significant contribution to household income.

These differences in what is considered the proper and responsible use of resources by businesses are motivation factors that are driving initiatives such as the United Nation's nine principles and the adoption of ISO-14000 (environment) and SA8000 (CSR) certification by global corporations.

SA8000 is a set of international workplace and human rights standards developed by Social Accountability International, with inputs from the United Nations and numerous NGOs. SA8000 is enjoying widespread adoption similar to that of ISO-9000, ISO-14000 as multinational corporations are encouraged by their stakeholders to become more socially accountable (Box 18.1).

This global and comprehensive set of CSR guidelines can be applied throughout a marketer's supply chain, and it is possible that SA8000 certification may eventually become an 'international passport' for registered firms or a barrier of entry for unregistered firms in international and domestic markets. The standards are also expected to eventually trickle down to the suppliers of the larger firms, that is, the small and medium-sized enterprises (Exhibit 18.5).

EXHIBIT 18.4

HOW TO IMPROVE ETHICAL REASONING?

1. *The legal test.* Does the contemplated action violate the law?

2. *The duties test.* Is this action contrary to widely accepted moral obligations such as: fidelity, gratitude, justice, non-malfeasance, and beneficence?

3. *The special obligation test.* Does the proposed action violate any other special obligation that stem from the type of marketing organisation at focus? (pharmaceutical firms, toy manufacturers, etc.).

4. *The motive test.* Is the intent of the contemplated action harmful?

5. *The utilitarian test.* Is there a satisfactory alternative action that produces equal or greater benefits to the parties affected than the proposed action?

6. *The rights test.* Does the contemplated action infringe upon property rights, privacy rights or the inalienable rights of the consumer (such as the right to information, the right to be heard, the right to choice and the right to remedy)?

7. *The justice test.* Does the proposed action leave another person or group less well-off?

Source: Laczniak and Murphy (1993, p. 49).

BOX 18.1

IMPLEMENTATION PROBLEM: HOW TO APPLY SOCIAL ACCOUNTABILITY STANDARDS – THE SA8000 STANDARDS?

1. *Child labour.* Prohibits the use of child labour (less than 15 years of age, unless local regulations are higher), require corporate support for the education of school-age workers; time spent daily on work and school cannot be more than 10 hours; that the corporation does not expose children inside or outside the work place to hazardous or healthy situations.

2. *Forced labour.* Prohibits the use of 'forced labour'.

3. *Health and safety.* Requires safe and healthy working conditions, health and safety training for all workers, clean and sanitary working and living conditions (if company provided).

4. *Freedom of association and the right to collective bargaining.* Requires the corporation to allow without discrimination, workers to form trade unions and engage in collective bargaining.

5. *Discrimination.* Prohibits discrimination based on gender, race, caste, etc, in hiring, compensation, training, promotion, or retirement.

6. *Disciplinary practices.* Prohibits use of coercion or corporal punishment.

7. *Working hours.* Prohibits required work in excess of 48 hours/week, and requires at least 1 day in 7 off. Allows up to 12-hours/week overtime at a wage premium.

8. *Compensation.* Requires that the corporation pay workers a legal minimum and locally derived 'living wage'.

9. *Management systems.* Requires a company policy for social accountability that includes social accountability audits for the corporation itself and its suppliers and subcontractors.

Source: SA8000 (2001).

What is the link, if any, between social responsibility and financial performance? In other words, does it pay to be good? The two stakeholder areas that seem to dominate the relationship are those of employees and customers. The data linking customer orientation and corporate financial performance is compelling. Companies that are more responsive to customers tend to generate greater profits. For a review of these studies see Gottleland (2005). Several studies (Kotter and Heskett, 1992) have also found that a variety of HR practices are positively correlated with financial performance. Beyond employees and customers, the evidence linking other stakeholder areas to financial performance is very weak. There is little evidence that a company's commitment to social activity in its various forms such as traditional philanthropy, cause-related marketing or events involving local communities etc. will increase profits, at least directly, even if many firms believe that such activity may improve their corporate image (Johnson, 2003).

18.3.7. Marketing and poverty

One of the big challenges of the twenty-first century will be to deal with the world poverty issue. Some 4 billion people – approximately two-thirds of the world population – live on less than 1,000 dollars a year. They outnumber the rich – or at least those earning $10,000 or more a year – by a factor of 8 to 1. It is today a well-established fact that economic growth of a country is closely correlated to the creation of new enterprises of this country. Thus, entrepreneurship

can be a powerful means to reduce poverty (Rahul, 2002).

As observed in the field of finance where the development of micro-credit have contributed in a significant way to facilitate entrepreneurship in poor countries, should not we – marketing scholars and marketing professionals – also develop forms of *low-cost or low-frills marketing* – both in strategic and operational marketing – to give poor countries' entrepreneurs appropriate marketing instruments? Some companies are now deliberately targeting the poor by adopting strategies like the following (Little, 2003):

- Reformulating consumer goods being sold in much smaller packages, thus making them affordable for the poor (selling jeans in ready-to-assemble packs).
- Trying to cut transaction costs by introducing more appropriate distribution systems that link old and new technologies (bicycles and mobile phones).
- Adopting technologies to make products more affordable and socially beneficial, like solar cells to generate electricity in low-income communities.
- Reducing prices of the good or waive any profits in order to help the poor and the disadvantaged. This issue is hotly debated today in the pharmaceutical sector.

Thus, it seems that Business, and in particular marketing, have a role to play in selling more to the poor. It can be profitable for the companies involved and it can help to improve the quality of life of the poor. If making profits from poverty may make good financial sense, is it ethically acceptable? The argument goes like this: if those who are currently excluded from consumer society are not brought

EXHIBIT 18.5

IS SELF-REGULATION EFFECTIVE?

To promote corporate social responsibility the importance of self-regulation and codes of conduct as main instrument of voluntary rule-setting has long been embraced (Arrow, 1973). Thirty years later, questions about effectiveness of self-regulation continue to be raised, in view of the growing number of companies spontaneously adopting corporate codes of conduct. The question is particularly relevant knowing that the American company Enron, one year before the financial scandal was made public, was congratulated for the quality of its corporate code of conduct. Kolk and van Tulder (2002) have closely examined the nature of child labour codes of six pioneering international garment companies (Levi Strauss, Nike, Gap, C&A, Hennes & Mauritz and WE) active in the textile and footwear sectors where child labour is a very sensitive issue. The authors clearly conclude that self-regulation, with codes of conduct as most common instruments, is considered effective in promoting corporate social responsibility, in particular when monitored systems exist such as the SA8000 international certification.

Source: Kolk and van Tulder (2002).

---

into the economy, the divide between rich and poor will widen further, creating more social tension and undermining future development.

In short, the emerging values in the corporate world place the shareholder versus stakeholder debate in a new perspective and suggest that there is an increasing convergence between the shareholder and the stakeholder models. Our views can be summarised as follows:

- The shareholder approach is the foundation stone of a market economy system and should be clearly reaffirmed: *the role of the firm is to create shareholder value*. To challenge this view is like shooting on his own foot and undermine the credibility of the capitalist system and the trust of investors, keeping in mind that those investors are increasingly institutional investors.
- In a competitive market economy, there is no other way for creating shareholder value than *by creating first customer value*. Compelling empirical evidence (see for instance Anderson *et al.*, 2004) supports the proposition that customer satisfaction generates shareholder value. Thus, the objective of customer satisfaction should be the central preoccupation of the firm by adopting the market-driven business philosophy described in this book.
- Today's customers are more demanding in their recognition of value. They do not want to have guilty feelings in their consumption. They expect from the firms or the brands they are dealing with to meet good behaviour criteria such as product greenness, social and human practice of the firm, its political and strategic commitments, ethical conduct, etc.

It is therefore the objective of customer satisfaction that will eventually induce (force) firms to adopt the stakeholder approach. The market-oriented firm will joyfully adopt this approach because it will contribute to increase shareholder value.

18.4. Implications for market-driven management

Within the globalised economy, strategic marketing has a more important social role than it ever had. It remains the best mechanism to adjust demand to supply, but it also triggers a virtuous circle of economic and social development, reinforced today by the social, cultural and technological changes observed in the market. These evolutions in the interconnected global economy create grounds for optimism in that they are contributing to a more democratic and transparent market economy, based on new values. In this new environment, national and supranational authorities have a key role to play: to monitor and to control the initiatives taken to meet emerging needs in order to reconcile market efficiency with the imperatives of a social vision.

What are the managerial implications of the three evolutionary changes reviewed in this chapter? As discussed in the previous chapter, the market orientation paradigm is complex and can be defined by reference to three dimensions: culture, analysis and action. To what extent do the market evolutionary changes described above impinge on these three dimensions?

1. *Culture.* The corporate philosophy is the one of a social market economy system. It is by creating value for the customer that the firm will achieve its own objectives of profit and growth, thereby creating shareholder value. More relevant than ever, this objective is also more challenging in a globalised and interconnected competitive economy. Moreover, to meet the expectations of the new consumers, companies will have to integrate the objectives of sustainable development and of social solidarity that differentiate a social market economy system, a model largely accepted within the European Union.

2. *Analysis.* The objective of strategic marketing is to propose to a well-defined market segment a value proposition both differentiated from competition and sustainable by the firm. In the new economy, this objective is more difficult given the complexity of world markets with the emergence of new powerful players such as the civil society voice, consumer power, vocal NGOs, mass merchandisers, etc. This new complexity of markets requires a reinforcement of the strategic brain of the firm.

3. *Action.* Stimulated and empowered by the development of the NICT, the firm's commercial arm has until today unthinkable capabilities: one-to-one segmentation, personalised communication, access to the world market any where, any time, low barriers of entry, customised pricing, relationship selling, etc. In short the capacity to move away from a 'strategy of product' towards a 'strategy of solution'. As a result of these changes, the mass market is turning into a "mass of niches" (The Economist, 2006).

Review and Application Questions

1. Does the growing environmental concern represent a threat or an opportunity for the firm? How would you proceed to answer this question in your own company?
2. Are you personally in favour of the legal application of the 'Who pollutes pays' principle? Compare the marketing and social impact of eco-taxes versus eco-fees.
3. Assuming that you are in favour of the accountable marketing concept, to what extent will this state of mind, new for your company, affect your marketing strategy and your practices regarding product, distribution, communication and pricing policies?
4. Is green marketing the right answer from the firm to meet society's environmental concern? Examine what green marketing means for each component of the marketing mix.
5. Is it the firm's responsibility to deal with the issue of poverty in the world?
6. Compare the shareholder and the stakeholder model. Is it possible to reconcile these two visions of the firm' s corporate social responsibility?
7. What are the main difficulties facing marketers in today's global market environment?

Bibliography

Anderson, E.W., Fornell, C. and Mazvanceryl, S.K. (2004), Customer Satisfaction and Shareholder Value, *Journal of Marketing*, 68, 4, pp. 172–85.

Arrow, K.J. (1973), Social Responsibility and Economic Efficiency, *Public Policy*, 21, pp. 303–17.

Begley, T. M. and Boyd, D.P. (2003), The Need for a Corporate Global Mind-set, *MIT Sloan Management Review*, 44; 2, pp. 25–32.

Charitou, C.D. and Markidès, C.C. (2003), Responses to Disruptive Strategic Innovations, *MIT Sloan Management Review*, 44, 2, pp. 55–63.

Croft, D. (2004), Shopping with Attitude: How Citizen-consumers are Behind a Radical Overhaul of the Co-op Brand, *European Retail Digest*, 42, pp. 38–41.

de Woot, P.H. (2005), *Responsabilité sociale de l'entreprise*, Paris, Economica.

Dimitriadis S., Chapelet B., Deglaine, J. and Matmati, M. (2003), Integrating Electronic Commerce in SMEs, *European Business Forum*, 12, Winter, pp. 54–7.

Dowling (2001), *Creating Corporate Reputation. Identity, Image Performance*, Oxford, Oxford University Press.

Drucker, P. (2000), Can e-Commerce Deliver? The World in 2000, *The Economist*, p. 122.

Economist, The (2006), Shopping and Philosophy: Post-modernism is the new black – How the shape of modern retailing was both predicted and influenced by some unlikely seers, 23 December.

Friedman, M. (1970), The Social Responsibility of Business is to Increase its Profits, *New York Time Magazine*, 13 September.

Ghemawat, P. (2001), Distance Still Matters: The Hard Reality of Global Expansion, *Harvard Business Review*, 79, 8, pp. 137–47.

Gladstone, J.A. and Scheibal, W.J. (2001), Privacy on the Internet: Europe and the US Converge, *European Business Forum*, 5, Spring, pp. 45–9.

Gotteland, D. (2005), *L'orientation marché: Nouvelle méthode, Nouveaux outils*, Paris, Editions d'Organisation.

James, R. and John, S. (2003), Matching Global Growth to Industry Structure, *European Business Forum*, 14, Summer, pp. 82–4.

Johnson, H.H. (2003), Does it Pay to be Good? Social Responsibility and Financial Performance, *Business Horizons*, 46, 6, pp. 34–40.

Keegan, W.J. (1989), *Global Marketing Management*, Englewood Cliffs, NJ, Prentice-Hall International, 4th edition.

Kolk, A. and van Tulder, R. (2002), The Effectiveness of Self-regulation: Corporate Codes of Conduct and Child Labour, *European Management Journal*, 20, 3, pp. 260–71.

Kotter, J.P. and Heskett, J.L. (1992), *Corporate Culture and performance*, New York, The Free Press.

Laczniak, G.R. and Murphy, P.E. (1993), *Ethical Marketing Decisions*, Boston, MA, Allyn and Bacon.

Lambin, E. (2003), *La terre sur un fil*, Paris, Le Pommier. [Translation (2006) Chicago, Chicago University Press.]

Lambin, E. (2004), *La terre sur un fil*, Paris, Edition Le Pommier. See also the English edition, Lambin, E. (2007), The Middle Path: Avoiding Environmental Catastrophe, Chicago, University of Chicago Press.

Laudicina, P.A. (2005), *World out of Balance: Navigating Global Risks to Seize Competitive Advantage*, New York, McGraw-Hill.

Little, A.D. (2003), *The Ethics of Making Money from the Poor*, Boston, MA, ADL Environment and Risk Discussion Forum.

Louche, C. (2003), Sustainable Investment, an Invitation to Dialogue, *European Business Forum*, 15, Autumn, pp. 52–5.

Morrison, A., Bouquet, C. and Beck, J. (2004), Netchising: The Next Global Wave?, *Long Range Planning*, 37, pp. 11–27.

Rahul, J. (2002), A No-frills Chain Sells to the Poor, *Financial Times*, March 25.

Sawhney, M. (1999), Making New Markets, *Business 18.0*, May, pp. 116–21.

Sawhney, M., Balasubramaniam, S. and Krishna, V.V. (2004), Creating Growth with Services, *MIT Sloan Management Review*, 45, 2, pp. 34–43.

Shuiling, I. (2002), *La force des marques locales et ses determinants par rapport aux marques internationales*, Louvain-la-Neuve, UCL, Presses Universitaires de Louvain.

COMPANION WEBSITE FOR CHAPTER 18

Visit the *Market-driven Management* companion website at www.palgrave.com/business/lambin to find:

A Questionnaire to Measure the Level of Market Orientation of a Firm

case studies

Chapter contents

COMPANION WEBSITE FOR CASE STUDIES

Visit the *Market-driven Management* companion website at www.palgrave.com/business/lambin to access additional case studies.

Case Study Guide

Case Studies	Chapters																	
	Strategic marketing										Operational marketing							
	1	2	3	4	5	6	7	8	9	10	11	12	13	14	15	16	17	18
1. The Ikea case	***					**			*									
2. GP textile Bulgaria	***	**																
3. The wonderful world of Mr. Zhi		***								**								
4. Procter & Gamble	***	***																
5. Raex Lazer Steel Finland			***	**														
6. Trenitalia						***			*									
7. Volvo Truck Belgium						***												
8. The PolyColor Company						***	**	**		**			*		*	*	*	
9. Levi Strauss (1)		*				**	**	***				**	*					
10. Levi Strauss (2)									***	*								
11. The Sound Company										***								
12. Geox			*						*		***	*				*		
13. The Foodsnack Company											***						*	
14. Tesco versus Aldi in the UK						**							*	***				
15. Universal Plastics Company								*							***			
16. The Tissex Company							*	*		***							*	
17. Club Med						*				***		*					*	

(***) = very good application for the indicated chapter; (**) or (*) also relevant for other chapters applications

The IKEA Case

IKEA IS A VERY SUCCESSFUL EXAMPLE OF A EUROPEAN company that has managed, over only a few decades, to become the worldwide leader in the furniture industry. It is today active in 44 countries all over the world and accounts for more than 90,000 employees. Sales reached €14.8 billion in 2005, and can be split into three regions: Europe (81 per cent), North America (16 per cent) and Asia/Australia (3 per cent).

Founder Ingmar Kamprad had the vision that people would buy more furniture if the price is low enough, the furniture is of decent quality and no delays exist in delivery. The IKEA business idea is therefore 'to offer a wide range of well designed, functional home furnishing products at prices so low that as many people as possible will be able to afford them'. This concept was totally innovative in the market after the Second World War when IKEA was created. At that time, furniture was expensive and mainly targeted to people with higher revenues. IKEA succeeded to identify a segment of the market where consumer needs were not yet satisfied. It was composed of young couples whose budget was low and needed to be totally furnished. This business concept required large volumes to be built in order to be profitable.

Kamprad always had one obsession: reduce costs in all areas of the business system. This led him to innovate and create new ways of developing and selling furniture. First, he outsourced manufacturing in countries where labour was less expensive. Poland was one of the first producing countries followed by other low-cost countries such as China. He also decided to select less expensive wood than what was traditionally used for furniture and acquired even forests to control the whole process. He was then a pioneer in what we can call now vertical integration. He also discovered that 'knocking down' furniture shipped in flat boxes would reduce transportation costs dramatically, by more than 80 per cent.

He also asked consumers to contribute to the development process. Consumers have to assemble themselves the knocked down furniture, get them in the stores and transport them home. This process was totally new and the only way to reduce costs to the maximum. Kamprad also built unique relationship with suppliers. His vision was to ensure fixed volume for a certain period of time to suppliers in exchange for lower costs. This was a 'win–win' strategy to benefit from efficiency and long productions runs.

Finally, stores were and are still located outside cities to take advantage of cheap land. This was quite different from competition that was usually located in the centre of cities. All these innovations have permitted IKEA to sustain a strategy of offering prices as low as possible. Interestingly, prices have even been lowered by 2 per cent in 2005 versus one year earlier.

The product range is developed to be extensive enough to have something that appeals to everyone and to cover all functions in the home. It counts over 10,000 articles. Design is functional and modern, in line with the unique Swedish style. Today, all products are still designed in Sweden in Almhult. The IKEA tradition is also to give names to all its products. Names are still given in Swedish (OCKERO, VALLO) and not translated in the different countries of the world as part of the IKEA Swedish image. Interestingly, unique additional services are provided to consumers to maximise the shopping experience such as a buffet style restaurant with food offered at a very good price and special children areas to keep children busy when their parents shop. IKEA has even recently created a teen area with videos games for the same reasons. IKEA also offers long opening hours.

Communication has always been focused primarily on the IKEA catalogue where a maximum of furniture can be visualised. Of the IKEA annual marketing budget, 70 per cent is being spent on this alone. This catalogue is published in 45 different editions and 23 different languages. In 2005, 160 millions catalogues were distributed all over the world. This is the most widely distributed commercial publication in the world. Other media now being used to an increasing degree include TV, radio and Internet-based communication.

Source: Author. (This case was written by Professor Jean-Jacques Lambin.)

Questions

1. What are the target segments of IKEA?
2. What is so unique with their positioning?
3. How can they manage to maintain low prices?
4. How coherent is the marketing mix with the marketing strategy?

Case study 2

GP Textile Bulgaria

IN THE FALL OF 2002, MR GEORGI PANAYOTOV, PRESIDENT AND majority stockholder of Panayotov Textile Ltd, returned from a business trip to Western Europe, initiated in view of the likely accession of Bulgaria into the European Union by 2007. While there, he had extensively visited a number of textile companies and former business associates, one of whom was the CEO of a large and very successful Belgian textile company. Mr Panayotov was particularly interested with this contact because of the very similar history of the two formerly family-owned companies. His discussions with this particular individual had raised some doubts in his mind as to whether or not his company was sufficiently conscious of the value of a strong market orientation.

Mr Panayotov, a former prominent member of the Bulgarian communist party, had founded the company to weave cotton cloth in 1990, when Bulgaria held its first multiparty election since the Second World War and began the contentious process of moving towards political democracy and a market social economy. The company remained a family-held enterprise until 2000, when the public was invited to subscribe to the new capital required for financing the company's expansion. In the textile and clothing sector, the industrial output had increased substantially in 2002 in comparison with 2001 and the sector had become one of the most attractive fields for investments from Italian, German and Greek companies.

Immediately following the public offering, the company experienced a remarkable growth. By 2001, the number of employees had risen to 4,000, the number of spindles to over 100,000, and the number of looms to over 4,200. Investment in plant and equipment increased substantially during this period.

In late 2002, Mr Panayotov widened the scope of the company's activities through both backward and forward integration and, also, by diversifying its product line. Backward integration was accomplished by Panayotov Textile's entry into the spinning business so as to supply its own yarn. Forward integration was undertaken through the introduction of printing, finishing, and dyeing processes, which enabled the company to control the entire production cycle of its products.

Panayotov Textile Ltd sold its products through a network of 46 independent distributors. Cloth was shipped to these distributors who held it on consignment until sold to retailers and to small manufacturers who produced limited lines of ready-to-wear apparel. Consigned goods were usually sold within 30 days of delivery to distributors. Another group of customers consisted of some 72 large garment manufacturers who were served directly from the company's plant.

Mr Panayotov's Belgian friend had surprised him considerably with his views on the market orientation concept. 'In essence', his friend told him,

> this concept holds that market-driven management is literally the most important part of a business. You're in business to make a sale, and you can best do this by understanding the wants and needs of the ultimate consumer of your products. Once this much is understood, all of your actions – and certainly all of your decisions – must be geared to finding ways to satisfy these wants. Everybody in the organisation must focus on the consumer and must strive constantly to find new and better ways of serving him or her.

While Mr Panayotov thought that he understood what his friend was saying, he was not too sure of how this concept should be implemented within his own organisation. His friend had pointed out that Panayotov Ltd really had no operational marketing organisation and that its product line was made up largely by designers and colour experts who had very little contact with the housewives or the male consumers who ultimately purchased the fabrics in one form or another produced by the company. It was also pointed out that Panayotov Ltd. had no market research department, no company-owned brands, did no consumer advertising, and did little or nothing to help its direct customers (integrators or distributors) to sell the merchandise in which their products were incorporated.

In attempting to apply the market orientation concept to his company, Mr Panayotov considered setting up a separate company, which could be likened to a sales agent. Essentially, this new company would serve solely as a marketing agency and would be responsible for 'ordering out' all production. It would be responsible for selling all company products, researching the market to determine what new patterns to produce and in what quantities, and advertising the various company products to the consumer – often in co-operation with the larger garment manufacturers and retailers. Under such an arrangement, the company's present sales force of five men and the entire staff of designers would be transferred to the new organisation. The present organisation – minus those personnel shifted – would literally function solely as a production unit.

The sales agency would be a wholly owned subsidiary. It would include the company's name in its title and would establish separate offices in the heart of Sofia, the capital city of Bulgaria. It would buy all merchandise from the plant at cost plus 10 per cent. Its responsibilities would include, however, the setting of all prices – including quantity discounts. It would be responsible for making profits – in fact, its profits would be an important part of the company's over-all profits.

Mr Panayotov recognised that this type of organisational change would meet considerable resistance within the company, and yet the more he thought about it, the more he was convinced that it was a good idea.

Source: Author. (This case was written by Professor Jean-Jacques Lambin.)

Questions

1. Do you believe that the Panayotov Ltd. Company has a problem?
2. What do you think of the new organisational structure proposed by Mr Panayotov? Analyse the merits and the disadvantages of the proposed structure.
3. Suggest other possible organisational structure(s) aiming at reinforcing the level of the market orientation of the firm?

The Wonderful e-World of Mr Zhi

By 2006, Ne Chi Zhi had the best of both worlds. He was a real entrepreneur, shaping his own destiny in a responsive, risky, innovative world. He was also part of Colourful Paints, a division of one of the world's largest and best-known companies. In some ways, the change he had seen over the past decade had been subtle. His job title was essentially the same, what he did at work had not changed much; his salary was not significantly higher. But in the ways that mattered, to him and to the business, the difference was dramatic. Not only was Chi Zhi a part owner of the company, but every day he could see that he had real choices – and that how he made those choices would have a measurable impact on the success or failure of the firm.

Ten years earlier, when he first joined Dallas-based Colorful Paints, Mr Zhi was excited to be part of the US company which boasted a dominant market share in paints and other chemical products around the world. While the company was a household name in China, sales in Mr Zhi's home country made up only 2 per cent of the corporation's worldwide revenues. It did not take long for him to learn what that meant – lots of control from the home office, and little opportunity to change the Colorful way. But then Colorful made a major decision. As it watched technology evolve – and faced up to the costs and limits of global operations – Colorful Paint Worldwide decided that it did not make sense to own operations around the world. Like many multinationals, Colorful found global operations less than reliably profitable. Cost was one issue, but so was the difficulty to truly understand and operate effectively in foreign markets – especially with a treasured, worldwide brand to protect. Time and time again Colorful recruited strong local talent, then saw those individuals learn the basics, perform well, but chafe under the restrictions from the home office. Many eventually joined or even founded local competitors that, being closer to the market, seemed better able to exploit local opportunities. The Colorful brand was still valuable worldwide. But with lacklustre market performance like this, worldwide operations weren't building the brand; instead, they were slowly diluting it. Meanwhile, the talent and resources needed to create and oversee a global empire – even a slow moving one – were badly needed in the United States, where competition was more intense than ever. Eventually Colorful decided that by focusing on its home market, it could increase performance in all key

dimensions: quality, market share, innovation, brand equity and profit.

So operations outside the United States had been spun off, with the exception of affiliates in Brazil and Mexico that were simply too profitable to disturb. Many of the rest had been bought by overseas employees and were now run in ways that resembled franchisees. The Colorful brand was still the crown jewel, so the headquarters in the United States directly monitored a small but critical set of metrics through effective electronic connections to sensors in manufacturing plants, at customer sites and even on their buyers' mobile phones around the world. The bottom line? Colorful was not only more profitable than ever, but was continuing to expand its reputation for high quality products, customer service and innovation. Global 'reach' had gone from a mandatory drain to a powerful resource.

As for the national companies, they were not only more profitable, but more fun as well. Ne Chi Zhi remembered his first years with the company before the change, when Colorful China was quite restricted in what it could do. To protect the brand, Colorful had adopted tough worldwide standards. That way, the headquarters could more easily manage quality and comparability of products around the world. But in order to conform these global standards, the same often-costly ingredients had to be used in every market. For Colorful China, this meant that the end products were extremely expensive – true luxury goods – even though their local reputation for performance was no better than less expensive Chinese paints.

But now, under the new ownership scheme, Colorful China was free to compete much more effectively, using locally accepted products in its paint manufacturing as long as the paint met durability, colourfastness and longevity tests, and adhere to Chinese safety standards. Mr Zhi could also see his company reaping the benefits of global scale more strongly than ever. In 2004, because of unusually wet weather in the South of China, Colorful China's executives decided to introduce a paint that had been reformulated in the Philippines for moist conditions. They were able to make the decision far more quickly than in the old days, negotiating directly with Colorful Philippines, without any need for approval from the headquarters. Even more important, under the old system the Philippines' paint was not available at all; it could not have been developed, because a global standard for tropical paint already existed.

The new structure made hiring good people easier too. The best chemical engineers, for example, liked the feeling that they would actually be creating solutions, not just working for the technologists back in Dallas. And the possibility of their solutions being used in other affiliates worldwide was icing on the cake. Executive recruitment had also grown easier. The old, centralised Colorful had had a global policy against first-class travel. But in China, it was tough to hire executives without providing that particular perk. Now Colorful China was able to make such tradeoffs for itself, weighing cost and appearance against local customs and needs. Add to that autonomy and ownership and the national company had a very powerful package to attract local executive talent.

The ability for the 'parent company' to spin off its national entities and still feel confident that they had control of their brand was made possible only by aggressive use of proven technologies. Internet cameras and low-cost sensors placed at random customer locations monitored the wear and tear of products. They were complemented by sensors at the factory that ensured Colorful China was consistently adhering to the quality standards it had set for itself. Colorful Paints in the United States also relied on sensors – not constant travel and expensive expatriates – to make sure that customer satisfaction was high and produce quality met certain standards around the globe. Furthermore, advances in automated trade exchange agents enhanced the ability of national companies to make very sophisticated and money-saving vendor choices – which only the headquarters thought itself capable of making in the past.

The bottom line of course was profit. And rather than seeing most of its profits repatriated to the United States, Colorful China now kept its cash at home. Fees were paid, of course, along with a percentage of profit, and the total outlay was significant. But with its newfound ability to control costs, to innovate and to operate as local conditions demanded, Colorful China could generate far more profit than before. And most of those profits were its own, to be parcelled out as they saw fit. Naturally, the government was delighted by these developments as it created opportunities for innovation and local content that had not been present in the past. But most importantly, at every step in the value chain (suppliers, buyers, national companies, the US office) companies were making more money and employees feeling more autonomy and creativity that they had ever before.

Source: Reprinted. Excerpt from: Morrison, A., Bouquet, C. and Beck, J. (2007), Netchising: the Next Global Wave? *Long Range Planning (LRP)*, 37, pp. 11–27. Reproduced with permission of the publisher.

Questions

The authors of the case use the neologism *netchising* to describe the model of a decentralised global strategy adopted by the Colorful Paints Company. Read the full article in *LRP* and prepare a presentation explaining the concept and covering the following questions:

1. What were the main difficulties confronted by the company in its original approach of globalisation?
2. What are the business trends that will impact globalisation?
3. Referring to the standardisation–adaptation dilemma, what are the main benefits of *netchising*.
4. Draw a parallel between *franchising* and *netchising*.

Procter & Gamble

GEORGE S. DAY (1994) HAS IDENTIFIED IN HIS RESEARCH work that successful market-driven organisations combine three key elements in the areas of culture, firm capabilities and firm configuration. A series of business examples in the Services and Industrial sectors illustrate these findings. We propose to evaluate how they apply to a key actor in the fast moving consumer goods sector – Procter & Gamble – by giving some insights on its market driven capabilities.

The first element identified by Day is the externally oriented culture. At P&G, the mission statement clearly indicates that delivering products that satisfy consumer needs in a superior way is a key objective credo. All departments try to contribute to this mission. The culture at P&G is also influenced by the Brand Management system, created by P&G in 1936 and used now throughout the consumer goods companies. It focuses the attention of the organisation on brands so that brand team responsibilities are to understand their consumers better than anybody else. P&G also has a culture of competitiveness. It wants to satisfy the consumer in a superior way that implies – *de facto* – the desire to beat competition and achieve leading positions in the market. This addresses the question raised by Day as to whether a firm can be both customer- and competitor-oriented. Market-driven firms such as P&G are often intensely competitive.

The second element is the *distinctive capabilities in market sensing*. Day considers that successful companies are better educated about their market than their rivals. By 'market', we mean consumers, competitors and distributors. To acquire knowledge about consumers and competitors, brand people at P&G conduct monthly analysis of Nielsen data, regularly check stores to 'feel the market' and to pick up any change in consumer attitude or in the competitive context, organise qualitative consumer testing, and run monthly evaluations of new product launches. To better meet the needs of distributors, P&G a few years ago adapted the sales function by moving from a geographic focus to a key account focus. A sales team is now fully dedicated to a key account (distributor) in order to better understand the needs of this 'intermediate' customer. P&G activities in Category management, ECR,

and EDI underline its interest in better fulfilling the needs of the distributors.

The third element is *firm configuration*. The brand management system, as already mentioned, gives a natural focus to the market. A couple of years ago, however, P&G felt that this system was no longer always ideal for an increasingly complex global market. The company has therefore reinforced the organisation by creating multidisciplinary teams for key projects like new brand launches or re-launches. The marketing person in most cases remains the leader but key individuals from other important functions – R&D, Manufacturing, Logistics, Finance and Sales – are involved at the beginning of a project to provide initial input. The result has been a reduction in unnecessary re-work and greater responsiveness.

Day also highlights the importance of a shared knowledge base and the ability to make fact-based decisions. At P&G, a brand person can only convince with facts. At every stage of a project like a brand launch, specific objectives are set and research is required to prove whether objectives are met and whether to proceed. Technical tests, blind tests, various concept tests, concept and use tests, advertising tests are just some of the more important and regular initiatives. The ensuing knowledge is then spread through the organisation via formalised written reporting – an exercise considered burdensome by some, essential for disseminating the relevant information. Managers, after all, often complain that knowledge does not circulate fast enough, or get to the right people.

A key question at P&G, however, is whether its strong globalisation drive is hampering its market-driven capabilities. Standardisation of brands is now the name of the game and the company's strategic objective is to get economies of scale in all areas of the business – R&D, manufacturing and marketing. One product, one brand name and one brand positioning worldwide is the desired scenario.

Standardising brands – a process driven by supply considerations – requires looking for the smallest common denominator between consumers in different countries to satisfy the largest number of people. Is there not a risk, though, of not being able to answer perfectly to the needs of the consumers? Another danger is that the centralised global strategy teams created by P&G in the 1990s to manage their 11 product categories worldwide may be too far from local markets' and local consumers' tastes.

An organisation looking for cost, as a key competitive advantage, becomes more focused on the bottom line than on the consumer. This might have an impact after a few years on the culture, the firm capabilities of market sensing and the firm configuration. It will be interesting to follow

P&G's future evolution in these three key areas identified by Day.

Source: I. Schuiling (2000) Commenting (see p. 38), the article of Day G., 'How to become successful market-driven organisation', *European Business Forum*, Issue 4, Winter 2000, pp. 35–41.

Question

1. Is P&G a market-driven company?

Raex Lazer Steel Finland

RAUTARUUKKI IS THE PRIMARY STEEL COMPANY IN FINLAND, with their main manufacturing operations located in Finland, Sweden and Norway with secondary manufacturing locations in parts of the former Soviet Union and Eastern Europe. Their products lines encompass those of many steel companies – hot- and cold-rolled plates and sheets, zinc- and colour-coated sheets, and building products, as well as one division that focuses on tubes and pipes. Rautaruukki was founded in 1960 and at its inception was owned entirely by the Finnish government. The company was listed on the Helsinki Stock Exchange in 1989 and is now owned approximately 60 per cent publicly and 40 per cent by the Finnish government. With annual steel production of just over 4 million tons Rautaruukki, is one of the smaller players in the European steel market.

Rautaruukki realised early on that given their size relative to other players in their market (they are roughly one-tenth the size of their largest competitor), a strategy of market specialisation, of carving out niches for themselves and serving the needs of those niches, would be the most preferred way to compete. Therefore, the driving force behind their marketing strategy in recent years has become one of what they have termed the 'Total Service Concept' – having an in-depth knowledge of their customer base and then using this knowledge to focus their product offerings around customer needs with fast, flexible and reliable deliveries to customers within a reasonably close geographical proximity to cut down on shipping costs and delivery time.

The emergence of a market opportunity

In the early 1990s, Rautaruukki's distributors in Germany began to notice an increasing dissatisfaction from many of their customers who were seeking steel to use in their laser cutting machines. Laser cutters had been around since the mid-1970s, but the cost of the early machines was beyond the reach of many job shops, which constituted a significant portion of the users of steel used for this purpose. However, as the cost of the machines began to decrease somewhat and the range of their applications began to expand during the late 1980s and early 1990s, more and more of these job shops began to acquire these cutters. Another change that was taking place was in the nature of the jobs for which the laser cutters were used.

When laser cutters were first introduced, laser cutting was a process used for special applications where the need for accuracy in the cutting process was not very precise. However, as these job shops began to test the abilities of these machines, it was soon noticed that laser cutting gave the advantages of good dimensional accuracy as well as a higher cutting speed that could be accomplished by more traditional cutting methods. Thus, the market for laser cutters began to expand, especially in the continent of Europe.

Even though the cost of laser cutters had decreased somewhat, they were still fairly expensive, often costing upward of US$200,000. Therefore, many manufacturers could not justify purchasing such an expensive machine to use on a part-time basis; so as a result, laser cutting was often outsourced to job shops specialising in this procedure. Orders to these shops could range anywhere from cutting a single plate to cutting several tons. Laser cutting had become especially popular in Germany and it was there that the Rautaruukki distributors first became aware of an opportunity to relieve the dissatisfaction customers were having with the current sources of steel supply.

When laser cutters first began to be used, steel was only available in a few thicknesses in one grade. There were a number of producers of this steel so there was a fairly wide variation in the properties of this steel from one producer to another. However, as the use and application of laser cutters expanded and the need for different thickness and grades of steel began to rise, these job shops became increasingly dissatisfied with the available product offerings. The German distributors noticed this dissatisfaction and reported back to Rautaruukki the need for a product customised to the specific needs of this market.

Rather than simply changing to the market with a predetermined idea of what their customers would want, Rautaruukki was careful to listen to the 'voice of the customer' to gain insight into what their customers' needs were and become 'hardwired' – having a direct permanent connection – into those customers. Rautaruukki conducted a series of discussions with distributors, current customers, and past customers to gain a better understanding of what each groups' dissatisfactions were. What they discovered was that customers were looking not only for a better grade of steel but a host of support services to go with the physical product. It was then that Rautaruukki began to give serious consideration so as to determine what their entire product offering might look like and how they might be able to meet all these customer needs in one package with a single identifiable brand.

As was mentioned above, the primary market for this steel was mainly job shops that not only needed to provide a good quality product but one that was delivered in relatively short time frame to allow them to meet the needs of their customers. The job shop business tends to be largely transactional in nature – a customer contacts a job shop with a need that usually must be handled quickly and expediently. If the job shop handles the transaction with minimal difficulty, the chance of receiving a repeat order is increased. As these job shops would purchase this steel from their distributors primarily on as-needed basis, it was critical for Rautaruukki to have the complete and total co-operation of their distributors to not only process and deliver orders quickly, but to share inventory when possible. These job shops also needed Rautaruukki to understand the nuances of the laser cutting process and offer technical support when needed, which was a bit unusual in the steel industry. Finally, they needed all of this done with a supplier with a recognised corporate name that could be relied upon for an extended period of time and who would also take the opportunity and initiative to build the trust necessary to consummate these transactions. To make this happen, all of Rautaruukki's employees had to be committed to a common operating standard and be willing to assist either the distributor or end-user with whatever needs they might have. In short, Rautaruukki's distributors were looking for a complete package – all of these features wrapped up in an identifiable branded product that could meet all these needs.

Source: Reprinted. Excerpt from: McQuiston, D.H., (2007), Successful branding of a commodity product: The case of Raex Lazer Steel, *Industrial Marketing Management*, 33, no. 4, pp. 345–54. Reproduced with permission from Elsevier.

Questions

1. Describe the role and the needs of the different market actors in this business.
2. How should Rautaruukki construct a total solution to the different customer groups' problems? What should be the components of the solution provided?
3. How to create a sufficiently differentiated solution to avoid being viewed as a commodity in the market?
4. What steps should Rautaruukki take internally to create a solution-ready environment within the company?

Trenitalia

THE PASSENGERS BUSINESS UNIT OF TRENITALIA HAS developed and implemented an interesting segmentation approach of the medium and long distance rail transportation market which is operated in Italy by different train services: Eurostar, Intercity and Treni Notte (night trains).

The segmentation is based on a combination of several segmentation criteria: requirements and expectations expressed by customers for each category of services provided by Trenitalia and characteristics of personal attitudes (such as family, social status, individual aspirations, etc.). The segmentation is based on a survey of 3,330 travellers and on the factorial analysis of the collected data. As a result of the analysis, eight benefit market segments were identified and described using travelling habits, socio-demographic and socio-cultural as indicators. We thus have here a case of benefit segmentation but complemented by descriptive and behavioural criteria. The eight identified segments are the following:

- Elaborate comfort
- Speed
- Transparency, cleanness, convenience   67 per cent
- Easy access, enrichment

- Social comfort
- Rapidity, technology, privacy   22 per cent

- Demanding but reserved,
- Base transportation service for   11 per cent
  long distance

The segmentation strategy adopted by the company is focused on the first four segments representing 67 per cent of the total demand. As a result, an improved rail service has been designed by reference to the requirements of this particular segment. The offer of Eurostar is targeted to the first two segments (elaborate comfort and speed). For example, the profile of 'elaborate comfort' segment is as follows.

Socio-demographic profile

Age over average; low proportion of women; average level of education; high income; conservative and sophisticated, relaxed and moderate.

Socio-cultural profile

Average ambition, having been confronted with interesting opportunities in their life and having reached a good socio-economic level. They know what kind of standards they can expect in travelling by train. They appreciate comfort and luxury and are ready to pay.

Travelling habits

Frequency in line with the average (2–8 trips per month); train travelling represents 75 per cent of the total of their travelling: business trips, but also holidays and shopping trips.

Within this framework an action programme has been developed in order to provide more value to the customers of this priority segment not only for the service itself (ambiance, comfort, cleanness, food service, punctuality, speed) but also for the distribution (ticketing, online booking) and for the communication (advertising, online information).

Source: Marco Raimondi, *Marketing del prodotto-servizio*, Milano, Hoepli, 2005.
The case is based on a presentation made by Paolo Ripa, Direttore Marketing Trenitalia, Divisione Passeggeri.

Questions

1. Evaluate this segmentation analysis using the five criteria of an effective segmentation: differential response, adequate size, measurability, accessibility and actionability.
2. What would you propose to improve the services provided to the priority segment?

Volvo Trucks Belgium

DURING THE LAST DECADE, THERE WAS A CONSIDERABLE increase in the quantities of goods transported by road and one result of this has been a significant growth in sales of trucks. This state of affairs must surely be due in part to the major improvement in the Western Europe road network, but was equally the result of the advantages that road transport has over other means of haulage (water, rail, air). These can be summed up as flexibility, cost saving, just-in-time delivery, product integrity. Since 1985, the total sales figure for trucks in Belgium has evened out with something of the order of 5,500 new truck registrations being recorded each year.

Current practice within the truck industry is to describe the truck market by referring to the figure of maximum permitted cargo weight (gross vehicle weight or GVW) and to make a distinction between light trucks (under 7 tons), medium weight trucks (from 7 to 16 tons) and heavy trucks (over 16 tons). The light and medium segment comprises 51 per cent of the whole market based on registrations and is contested by four main manufacturers: Mercedes, Daf, Scania and Renault. In the heavy truck category, which comprises 49 per cent of the total market, the main competitors are Volvo, Daf, Scania and Mercedes.

A second method of dividing up the market which is in current use is by the size of the fleets owned by truck customers: 57.3 per cent of all haulers have a fleet of three vehicles or less; 18.3 per cent own between four and ten vehicles and 24.4 per cent own more than ten trucks.

The advantage of these two segmentation criteria, GVW and fleet size, is that developments within the market place can be easily monitored as the registration statistics include this information and these are published at regular intervals.

An analysis of the truck buyer profile according to the use to which the vehicles are put suggests that they can be divided up into three types of business: leasing companies (of minor importance in Belgium), own-account carriers (65.6 per cent) and professional carriers (34.4 per cent). Own-account carriers consist of businesses which transport their own products as part of their manufacturing (e.g. a brewery) or commercial (e.g. a supermarket chain) activity, whereas, professional carriers perform transport of goods on behalf of others over regional, national or international distances. Some of these are specialists in transporting particular types of goods.

According to a recent survey among haulers, 11.5 per cent are own-account haulers having a fleet of ten trucks or more, while 14.7 per cent are professional transporters with a fleet of maximum three trucks. In each of these categories, there are three types of haulage based on distance: regional haulage (almost entirely composed of retail distributors and building materials transport), national haulage and international freight.

Source: Author. (This case was written by Professor Jean-Jacques Lambin.)

Question

1. How would you proceed to segment this market and to design a segmentation grid?

The PolyColor Company

THE MARKET FOR PAINT COATINGS CAN BE DIVIDED INTO trade sales and industrial sales. Trade sales include products sold primarily to households, professional painters and contractors. Industrial sales include sales of numerous products for original applications (cars, ships, trucks, construction components, etc.). Total sales of paint coating are divided equally between trade and industrial sales. Households account for approximately 45 per cent of trade sales. Contractors and professional painters account for 35 per cent. Government, exports and miscellaneous applications account for the remainder.

Approximately one in four households purchase interior house paint in any given year and about 15 per cent of households purchase exterior house paint. The popularity of do-it-yourself painting has necessitated an expanded product line of paint and sundry items carried by retail outlet. Many people view paint as a commodity. But, among household purchasers, there are a significant number of people who desire service in the form of information about application, surface preparation and durability. There is a difference between professional painters and contractors. Professional painters do seek quality products since their reputation is on the line. They want paint that is durable, washable and that will cover in a single coat. Contractors are involved in large-scale painting jobs and, in many instances, they want white wash and strive for the lowest price.

The PolyColor Company

PolyColor (or PCL) is a privately held regional corporation that is involved in trade paint sales under the brand name PolyColor. In addition to producing a full line of paints, the company sell paint sundries (brushes, rollers, thinners, etc.), even though the company does not manufacture these items. Company trade paint sales revenue (excluding allied products) in 2004 was K€84,700 and the net profit before taxes was K€8,215. Euro sales had increased at an average annual rate of 10 per cent per year over the past decade. Paint volume, however, had remained stable over the past 5 years. The company has been very aggressive in raising prices to cover increased material and labour costs, and as a result the PolyColor brand is the highest-priced paint in its reference market. In 2004, the cost of goods sold was 65 per cent of net sales.

The paint market

The PCL geographic reference market is subdivided in two service areas: the urban zone (UZ) and the residential zone (RZ). The estimated volume of paints sold to the market was 87.5 million litres (excluding contractors sales). The UZ (where total sales are flat) was estimated to account for 60 per cent of this figure, with remaining paint and allied products being sold in the RZ, where total sales are growing. Do-it-yourself households' buyers were believed to account for 70 per cent of non-contractor related volume in UZ and 90 per cent in RZ.

PolyColor sales

PolyColor sales are distributed evenly between UZ and RZ with an aggregate 8.8 per cent volume market share. The company distributes its product through 200 independent paint stores and hardware outlets. Forty per cent of its outlets are located in the UZ and the remaining ones in the RZ. Research indicates that 1,000 of these outlets operate in the total market with 300 of them located in the UZ. The PCL outlets of the RZ carry only PolyColor's product line, while outlets in the UZ carry two or three lines with PCL's line being premium priced. Mass merchandisers (hard discounters) control 50 per cent of the household paint segment in the UZ, where price seems to be the main attraction.

PolyColor employs eight sales representatives who are responsible for monitoring PCL inventories of paint and sundry items in each retail outlet as well as for order taking, assisting in store display and co-ordinating co-operative advertising programmes. Sales representatives are paid a salary and a 1 per cent commission on sales. The company spends 3 per cent of net sales on advertising and sales promotion efforts. About 55 per cent of advertising and sales promotions monies are allocated of co-operative programme with retail accounts. The co-operative programme applies to newspaper advertising and seasonal catalogue distributed door to door in a retailer's immediate trade area.

The management committee

The PolyColor's CEO assembles senior management executives to consider the various trade paint market segments served. The CEO insists, in his opening statement, on the necessity to come to a decision for the next marketing plan. Each senior manager is invited to express his or her views on the priority issue.

VP OF ADVERTISING: I believe that we must direct our efforts toward bolstering our presence in the urban zone (UZ) market that is the large segment. I have just received the results of our UZ consumers advertising awareness study. In this market, where consumers' involvement is low, awareness is directly related to purchase behaviour. Industry research on paint purchase behaviour indicates that the majority of consumers decide ahead of time what brand they will buy before shopping and think about paint they have seen advertised. It seems to me that we need an awareness level of at least 30% (against 22% right now) to materially affect our market share. Do not forget also that national paint firms and mass merchandisers outspend us tenfold. Preliminary talks with our ad agency indicate that an increase of €4 million in corporate brand advertising beyond what we are now spending, with an emphasis on television, will be necessary to achieve this awareness level. Furthermore, this television coverage will reach consumers in the residential zone as well.

VP OF OPERATIONS: I do not agree. Advertising is not the way to go and reference to the urban zone (UZ) market alone is too narrow a focus. We have to be competitive in the household paint market, period. Our shopper research program indicated that dealers would quickly back off from our brand when the customer appears price sensitive. We must cut our price by 20 per cent on all paint products to achieve parity with national paint brand. Look here in today's newspaper, we advertise a price-off special on our exterior paint, and our price is still noticeably higher than a mass merchandiser's everyday price. With both ads on the same page, a customer would have to be an idiot to patronize one of our dealers.

VP OF SALES: Forget the urban zone, where total sales are flat and where mass merchandisers are very powerful. Cutting the price is suicidal. We ought to be putting our effort into the residential zone, where half of our sales and most of our distributors exist right now. We have only added five new accounts in the last five years; our account penetration is the residential zone is only 17 per cent. There are 300 or so professional painters in the UZ and 100 in the RZ. Our survey on the retail account indicated that 70 per cent of unit sales through our UZ outlets went to the professional painters, while 70 per cent of unit sales through our RZ outlets went to households. We should add one additional sales representative whose sole responsibility is to develop new retail account leads and presentations or call on professional painters. I have figured the cost to keep one rep in the field at €50,000 per year.

VP OF FINANCE: Everyone is proposing a change in our orientation. Let me be the devil's advocate and favour pursuing our current strategy. We now sell to both the home-owner and the professional painter both in the UZ and in the RZ through our dealers. We have been and will continue to be profitable by guarding our margins and controlling costs. Our contribution margin is 35 per cent (see Table CS 8.1). Everyone suggests that increasing our costs will somehow result in greater sales volume. Let me remind you that we have said that it is our policy to recoup non-capital improvement expenditures within a one-year time horizon. If we increase our advertising by an incremental amount of €2.541 million, then we had better see the incremental sales volume as well. The same goes for additional sales representatives and, I might add, the across-the-board cut in price.

THE CEO OF POLYCOLOR: All of you have valid arguments, but we must prioritise. Let's quit pushing our pet projects and think about what is best for the company. Let us think about your proposals again.

Table CS 8.1	Current situation of PCL (in 000)
■ Cy Sales Revenue:	K€84,700
■ Direct costs:	K€55,055 (65%)
■ Fixed costs:	K€21,430
■ Profit:	K€8,215 (9.7% of SR)
■ Total market:	87.5 million litres
■ Market share:	8.8%
■ Cy sales in units:	7.7 million litres
■ Average Cy price:	€11.0 per litre
■ Unit cost:	K€55,055 / Klt 7,700 = €7.15 per litre
■ Gross margin:	€3.85 per litre (or 35%)
■ Advertising:	3.0% of SR (or €2.541 million)

Source: Author.

Adapted from Kerin R.A. and Peterson R.A. (1998) *Strategic Marketing Problems: Cases and Comments*, 8th Edition, Prentice-Hall.

Questions

1. Why is it so difficult to come to an agreement?
2. How would you segment this market? Prepare a segmentation grid.
3. Which market segment(s) should be targeted by priority?
4. Evaluate the pros and cons of each proposal (use implied elasticity).
5. Formulate a recommendation for the short and for the longer term.

Levi Strauss (1)

WHO DOESN'T KNOW LEVI'S, THE AMERICAN BLUE JEANS icon known all over the world? Today, Levi's is one of the world's largest brand-name companies in the blue jeans and casual pants markets. Its products are sold under the Levi's, Dockers and Levi Strauss Signature brands. While Levi's conveys an image of quality and innovation, the brand is mostly recognised for its status as the original pioneer brand among international customers. With sales in more than 100 countries, Levi's is a global company with three geographic divisions: the Americas, Europe Middle East and Africa and Asia Pacific.

In 1853, during the California gold rush, Levi Strauss set up his own business in San Francisco. He sold durable and tough pants that became a standard dress for miners, dockworkers, railroad workers and 'cow boys'. However, the first blue jeans were born in 1873. At that time, Jacob Davis, a Levi's customer, suggested Levi Strauss to patent the process of putting copper rivets in pants for strength. They went into business together and founded what would become the world's most popular clothes.

After the Second World War, American products met a great success in the world and enjoyed a strong popularity in Europe. Jeans symbolised American freedom and conveyed many of the core values of American democracy. Therefore, people wore Levi's jeans as a symbol of their freedom and individuality. Hollywood also had a huge impact on the popularity of blue jeans. By wearing blue jeans, James Dean, for example, in *The Rebel Without a Cause* brought fame to blue jeans and other popular actors did the same. With such images, blue jeans became synonymous with rebelliousness, danger, adventure, and most of all, a non-conformist youth culture.

Until late 1960s, there was no or minimal competition and the company decided to expand distribution internationally. In the early 1970s, the business environment quickly changed and Levi's faced its first real competitors. It was not prepared to compete in a fast-paced climate and the business became unprofitable. By early 1980s, the company recovered its initial position by focusing on its core competencies and by late 1980s, Levi's identified a new fashion trend, the casual dress, and established a leadership position in that segment with the introduction of the 'Docker' brand.

Levi's started to lose share in the 1990s

Despite the fact that Levi's created the market, was synonymous with the word blue jeans and led the category for decades, Levi's started in the 1990s to lose significant share of the blue jeans market. Levi's felt that it was benefiting from such a high brand awareness and brand leadership position that nothing could happen to itself.

New trends started to develop in the market, especially in the teenage market. In the 1990s, Levi's was such a hot and great brand that it thought it would be able to sell the same product to everyone. Though, it did not take into account that young people were more fashion-oriented

The identity of Levi's brands of jeans	
Attributes and benefits	Associations
Product-related attributes	Blue denim, shrink-to-fit cotton fabric, button-fly, two horse patch, and small red pocket tag.
User imagery	Western, American, blue collar, hard working, traditional, strong, rugged, and masculine.
Usage imagery	Appropriate for outdoor work and casual social situations.
Brand personality	Honest, classic, contemporary, approachable, independent, and universal.
Experiential benefits	Feeling of self-confidence and self-assurance.
Symbolic benefits	Comfortable fitting and relaxing to wear.
Functional benefits	High quality, long lasting and durable.

Source: Quoted by Keller (1998).

than before. Indeed, it neglected the teenagers' aspirations, which is a non-sense for a brand once synonymous with rebellious youth movement. The blue jeans were not cool anymore and became out of fashion. It was more suitable for parents than for fashion teens. US teens describe Levi' jeans as 'too straight', 'not baggy enough', 'too plain' and 'preppy'. (Preppy is a chiefly *American* adjective traditionally used to describe the characteristics of *White, Anglo-Saxon, Patrician Protestants* (usually with some personal or familial connection to *New England,* even if only historic, who attend or attended major private, secondary *university-preparatory schools.*) Young people were looking for a product allowing them to show their identity, to set their own style and trends. They could not show their individuality anymore by wearing pants of their parents. Then, a new fashion style emerged at the expense of the traditional blue jeans: the trend towards wide-leg, baggy jeans and combat pants. This new fashion was one of the answers to teenagers' needs. In fact, it reflected an underground style representing what young people were looking for: authenticity, functionality and non-conformity. It was first adopted by skateboarders and clubbers and after by the youth market as a whole.

The type of competition also changed. Competitive threats were not only coming from the classical competition such as Wrangler or Lee. Numerous new companies entered the jeans market. First of all, top-end designers such as Gucci or Armani launched their own high-fashion denim ranges. Companies such as Diesel or Miss Sixty also developed high-fashion jeans at high price. Other brands also entered the market such as Benetton, H&M, Zara in Europe while Tommy Hilfiger, CK Calvin Klein, Guess, Polo Jeans, Gap, Old Navy and Guess were expanding in the denim in the US. Finally, the discounters also began to sell private labels. 'Ignoring competitive threats is the beginning of the end. Success leads to arrogance and arrogance leads to failure.'

Additionally, Levi's restricted distribution policy further eliminated market share opportunities. The current distribution strategy focuses on seeking a more high profile presence in the form of boutiques located within department stores and an emphasis on the brand as the strongest element. 'To preserve and enhance consumers' impression of the brand, the majority of our products will be sold through dedicated distribution, such as Levi's Only Stores and in store chops.' Explosive growth of discount mass-merchants Wal-Mart and Target, as well as specialty retailers like The Gap, further eroded business opportunity and future profits.

As a result, Levi's started in 1996 a 6-year sales decline. Levi's had to close more than half its US plants due to the erosion of its dominant market share: the teen sales. Levi's had 30.9 per cent of the US blue jeans market in 1990 but had only 18.7 per cent market share in 1997 after the Levi's crisis. After having put new strategies in place, Levi's stabilised the business and the year 2002 was a turning point.

Source: Author. (This case was written by Professor Isabelle Schuiling and by Julie Lardinois, assistant in the Marketing unit at the IAG Louvain School of Management.)

Questions

1. What went wrong with Levi Strauss strategic marketing?
2. Use the Porter's matrix to analyse the competitive structure of the Levi Strauss' reference market?
3. Use the competitors identification matrix to assess the competitive threats confronted by Levi Strauss.

L EVI'S HAD BEEN SLOW TO REACT BUT IT FOUND DIFFERENT ways to overcome the problems encountered. First, it decided to reorganise and change its strategy. Levi's overall strategy was now to sell 'relevant products at the right price in the places where people shop'. Levi's expanded its distribution channels and product ranges in order to reach more consumer segments. Indeed, it added new retail shops in the United States, launched new products at a lower price in Europe and expanded its market penetration in China and Pakistan.

In the fall of 1996, Levi Strauss announced that it will launch a new line of men's dress slacks under the brand Slates. The pant will be marketed to men in their forties who had grown tired of the traditional look of dress pants. 'We found there was a void between Khakis and suits', says Westfall, the President of Slates. Levi's is launching a 22 million marketing campaign for Slates. It is building in-store displays at 240 department stores across the United States and launching an advertising campaign in the fall of 1996. Levi's hopes the new slacks will capitalise on the growing trend to corporate down-dressing. Westfall said, 'the slacks could be for dress-up occasions at super-casual companies, or for dress-down days at more formal firms'. Competitors say Levi's has no place in the dress pants world.

Second, it decided to revitalise Levi's image and brands by constantly innovating. Indeed, innovation was considered as the key way to differentiate the brand. In 2002, the company decided to launch new products more often to appeal to teenagers and young adults. In fact, new designs would appear every 6 weeks. This was essential in some markets where consumers expect new styles more frequently (i.e. the juniors' market).

Third, Levi's decided to launch a new brand, marketing a new value-priced blue jean called Levi's Signature. The new Levi's Signature would be introduced in Wal-Mart and would be available at other discount retailers within the first quarter of 2003. The goal of the value-priced Signature line was to use the equity of the Levi's brand to compete with national brands and private label pricing. The new brand was available in Wal-Mart stores in 2003 and in Europe in 2004. Experts wondered if Levi's would not dilute its brand image by implementing a mass market channel strategy. The Levi's answer was that the Levi Strauss Signature would be run as a separate brand. Indeed, jeans would be distinctive from the traditional line by having no red tab or leather patch.

Fourth, it resegmented the market by delivering a specific product for every consumer segment. The segments identified were trend initiators, trend influencers, early adopters, traditional and value-driven (see Figure CS 10.1 and Tables CS 10.1 and CS 10.2. Levi's teams were also looking at the different segments

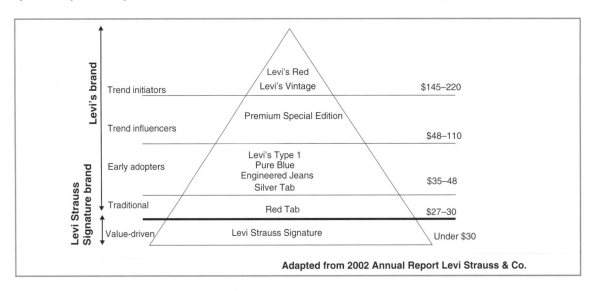

Figure CS 10.1   US segmentation model jeanswear

Table CS 10.1   Levi Strauss net sales in dollars per region and per brand in 2002–2003

Brands	Years	North America	Europe	Asia-Pacific	Total
Levi's brand	2002	1,596,575	954,553	401,445	2,952,573 (71.2%)
	2003	1,381,377	891,008	480,631	2,753,016 (67.3%)
Dockers	2002	908,887	94,664	20,689	1,024,240 (24.7%)
	2003	820,531	101,132	21,947	943,610 (23.0%)
Signature	2002	169,053	—	—	169,053 (4.0%)
	2003	388,460	—	5,644	394,104 (9.6%)
Total	2002	2,674,515	1,049,217	422,134	$4,145,866
	2003	2,590,368*	992,140	508,222	$4,090,730

Note: * Due to the elimination of Slates dress pants business which contributed to $24.2 million to the decline.

Source: Levi Strauss Annual Report, 2003.

Table CS 10.2   Levi Strauss consolidated operations in 2003

In 000 dollars	2003	2002	Changes
Net sales	4,090,730	4,145,866	−1.3% (−5.7% at constant currency)
Cost of goods sold	2,516,521	2,456,191	+2.5%
Gross profit	1,574,209 (38.5%)	1,689,675 (40.7%)	−6.8%
Selling and administration expenses	1,353,314	1,285,855	+5.2%
Other income or charge	(92,454)		
Operating income	313,349	254,145	+23.3%
Interest and other expenses	344,641	227,558	
Income before taxes	(31,292)	26,587	−217.7%
Income tax expense	318,025*	19,248	
Net income (loss)	(349,317)	7,339	

Note: *Due to a substantial increase in valuation of assets.

Source: Levi Strauss Annual Report, 2004.

within the youth market to find out their expectations from the brand. For example, Levi's decided to pump up the Silver Tab line because it was considered to be more stylish among young consumers and to expand the line with more tops, new khaki pants and more fashion styles.

Fifth, Levi's also decided to focus more significantly on the women market. It realised that its products were too masculine. In fact, Levi's created women's denim models from men's patterns. Consequently, pants did not quite fit the women's curves. Levi's had to overcome its bad habits by launching models with better fits and hipper fashion. Men also got more attention by getting sexier styles for jeans.

Sixth, Levi's also considered that it had to be more cost competitive. Therefore, it decided to close eight plants in 2002 and it moved also out of domestic manufacturing.

Seventh, Levi's revitalised its retail relationships. Indeed, the company turned its retail customers' relationships into strong and mutually beneficial ones. Actually, Levi's and the retail accounts have worked together in order to provide a better shopping experience for consumers.

Finally, it decided to change its advertising campaign by focusing more on the Levi's brand than on the different products. It designed a new high-fashion advertising campaign especially aimed at teenagers. The company wanted to reinforce its image and stress its brand values (rebellious mind, tough cow-boy, etc.).

After the different actions, the business started to stabilise but Levi's management realised it had to take additional actions to make the implemented strategies of 2002 work harder.

Source: This case was written by Professor Isabelle Schuiling and by Julie Lardinois, assistant in the marketing unit at the IAG Louvain School of Management. This case was compiled from published sources.

Questions

1. How would you segment the jeans market?
2. Do you think that the introduction of a Levi's brand in the mass retail distribution is a good idea?
3. What do you think about Levi's redeployment marketing strategy?

Case study 11

The Sound Company

WITH THE INVENTION OF THE TRANSISTOR IN THE BELL Telephone laboratories, the manufacturing of small-size electronic instruments became possible.

Rapidly, the Sound Company decided to enter into this growing market and developed black and white TV sets. Then capitalising on its technological know-how, the firm diversified its activities in to Hi-Fi market, while constantly improving the existing products. Confronted with a slowing down of its sales the firm launched DVDs and a Gamestation to compete directly with Segam and Nitindo, the two main market players in this market. It is a success and Sound has just launched a new model of its Gamestation.

The CEO of Sound is now considering to penetrate the digital photography and the microcomputer markets in order to improve the balance of its product portfolio.

Domains of activity	TV	
	2001	2002
Sound	580,000	702,000
Philipes	690,000	780,000
Sansoung	808,000	848,000
JDC	1,028,000	1,244,000
Thompson	810,000	835,000
Total	3,916,000	4,409,000

Domains of activity	Hi-Fi	
	2001	2002
Sound	120,800	150,000
Philipes	826,000	810,000
Sansoung	328,000	336,000
Pionire	172,000	80,000
Thompson	454,000	320,000
JDC	600,000	848,000
Yamama	114,000	116,000
Total	2,614,800	2,660,000

Domains of activity	Video games	
	2001	2002
Sound	1,706,000	1,792,000
Nitindo	952,400	1,000,000
Segam	1,190,800	1,250,000
Mixosoft	1,020,000	1,070,800
Total	4,869,200	5,112,800

Domains of activity	DVD	
	2001	2002
Sound	726,000	810,000
Philipes	142,800	160,000
Sansoung	308,000	336,000
Pionire	72,000	100,400
Thompson	464,000	520,000
JDC	545,000	565,000
Yamama	104,000	116,000
Total	2,361,800	2,607,400

Source: This case was written by Olivier Joffre and Loïc Plé, CREPA, IX-Dauphine University of Paris. The English translation was made by Professor Jean-Jacques Lambin.

Question

1. Use the information provided in the above tables to analyse the structure of the Sound Company product portfolio. Is it a good idea to further diversify the product portfolio?

Geox

The Geox case

What does it take to break into a mature business in a saturated market already awash with brands? For Mario Moretti Polegato, it was drive, determination and an infatuation with sweaty feet. The story of the Italian company Geox is the story of its system (patented less than 10 years ago), whereby rubber soles are perforated and contain a special micro-porous membrane that recreates an ideal micro-climate inside the shoe, keeping the feet dry and at the right temperature. The name Geox comes from a mixture between the Greek word 'geo' (hearth) and 'x' a letter-element symbolising technology. On this disruptive product technology, the company built its development in world business, with turnover growth rates of 40 per cent per year, reaching a 2004 production level of over 9 million pairs of shoes and operating in 68 countries.

Behind all the glamour, the force propelling the business remains Mr Polegato's obsession with the idea that sweaty feet can and should be avoided. Such conviction can come only from personal experience. Mr Polegato was out jogging in Reno, Nevada, during a hot summer 13 years ago and wanted to keep his feet cool. Cutting a number of holes in the soles of his trainers did the job, but it was clearly not a long-term solution, especially if he were to hit the street in a rainy city. Even worse, can you imagine using a public lavatory while wearing shoes with holes in them? So he came up with a membrane. In Mr Polegato words: 'I learnt of a special material called "membrane" which is used in the NASA space suits. *I got in touch with its American suppliers, I obtained the material and I brought it to Italy. Joining the membrane to a perforated device, I invented this new technology, which has been developed and improved with the help of some engineers and people from Italian university.*' With patents protecting his invention, and hoping to profit quickly from his idea, Mr Polegato knocked on the doors of some of the biggest names in the leisure-footwear business such as Fila, Adidas and Timberland. None was interested. Having failed to get a big producer to take up his idea, he decided to do it himself and this led to a company that now employs 2,800 people directly and several thousand indirectly through subcontractors.

Although Geox is marketed as an Italian brand, it is in fact manufactured in two main units: one in Romania (with 1,750 employees) and one in Slovakia (with 400 employees). In addition to this, the company owns two units in Italy where R&D, product design activities and prototyping are carried out.

The way production processes are delocalised and centrally managed is a key success factor. Delocalisation traditionally poses problems related to know-how transfer. Romania, and in particular Timisoara, where Geox has outsourced production, had a long standing tradition of footwear production. For this reason, the company could rely on skilled local staff. The integration with headquarters is very close and includes purchasing of raw material (both leather and rubber), accessories, as well as plant equipment, while technical specifications are managed centrally. The strict control of production has the twofold objective of monitoring quality and reducing the risk of counterfeit. The Geox research centre is located in the company headquarters in Montebelluna and employs 12 engineers. Geox collaborates with the University of Padua (Italy) and the University of Trondhein (Norway). Geox's activity has progressively been oriented towards technological solutions able to guarantee transpiration and impermeability. Mr Polegato plans to diversify into clothing by applying the technology to jackets by using strips of the fabric, which allows the rising warm air and humidity to escape through special aerating holes. All the innovative solutions developed by Geox have been patented.

Geox is a purely Italian idea but with a strong international appeal. It is sold in over 60 countries worldwide, through a widespread tailored distribution network of more than 230 single-brand Geox shop stores and about 8,000 multibrand points of sales. In the first half of 2004, approximately 46 per cent of sales revenue was realised on foreign markets, mainly in Germany, France, Spain and the United States. Geox allocates 10 per cent of its sales revenue to communication, in particular to press and outdoor advertising messages emphasising the main product benefit.

Source: Authors. (This case was written by Professor Jean-Jacques Lambin and Dr. E. Tesser.)

Question

1. How can you explain the success of Geox?

Case study 13

The FoodSnack Company

MR BROWN, NEWLY APPOINTED NEW PRODUCTS Marketing Director, is considering the possibility of marketing a new highly nutritional food product, having a large variety of use. This product can be consumed as a snack, a camping food or as a diet food. The product is to be generically labelled FoodSnack.

Because of this wide range of possible uses, the company has had great difficulty in defining the market. The product is viewed as having no direct competitors but a lot of substitute competitors. Early product and concept tests have been very encouraging. These tests have led Mr Brown to believe that the product could easily sell 2 million cases (24 packages in a case) under the proposed marketing programme involving a 24c retail price per package and an advertising programme involving €3 million per year. The projected P&L for the first year is shown in Table CS 13.1.

There will be no capital expenditures required to go national, since manufacturing is to be done on a contract pack basis. These costs have been included in the projected P&L. The company has an agreement with the contract packer requiring that once a decision to go national is made, the company is obligated to pay fixed production costs (€1 million per year) for 3 years even if the product is withdrawn from the market at a later time. Even though there are no capital requirements, it is the company's policy not to introduce new products with profit expectations of less than €0.5 million per year (a 3-year planning horizon is usually considered).

Mr Brown is quite confident of his sales estimates (and hence his profit estimate) although he does admit that they contain some uncertainty. When pressed, he will admit that

sales could be as low as 1 million cases in the first year, but points out that sales might also exceed his estimate by as much as 1 million cases. His operational definition of these extremes is that each has no more than a 1 in 10 chance of occurring. He is more concerned about sales after the first year. Historically, most new products with which he is familiar have had sales that decayed over time. After some effort, he summarised his feelings about the first sales for the new product and the decay rate in Table CS 13.2.

There are also other marketing programmes under consideration. A first alternative involves a 10c-price increase (34c retail price) to be used to finance higher advertising expenditures (€6 million) in the first year. The advantage of this second programme is that higher advertising intensity during the first year could bring as many people into the market as the 24c price and that, in subsequent years, advertising expenditures could then be cut back to the €4 million level. There is some concern that the higher price would affect repeat sales, hence sales might decay even faster over time under this plan. A casual estimate is that the decay rate might increase by 50 per cent due to the higher price. There is also some discussion of coupling the lower price with high advertising (€6 million) or using a middle price (29c) and a middle level of advertising expenditures (€4.5). These alternatives have not as yet been fully explored.

Mr Brown believes that the potential of the product is so high that national introduction should be started as soon as possible. His primary concern is the choice of the appropriate marketing programme.

Table CS 13.1   The initial marketing programme

Sales volume	2 million cases (24 units per case)
Company sales revenue	€8.064 million (70% of the retail price is revenue to the manufacturer)
Manufacturing costs	€3.00 million (€1 million fixed manufacturing costs plus €1 per case as variable cost)
Advertising	€3.00 million/year
Net margin	€2.064 million

Table CS 13.2   First year sales estimates

First year's sales	Probability	Decay rates per year	Probability
0.5–1.0	0.10	+10% to −10%	0.25
1.0–1.5	0.20	−10% to −30%	0.50
1.5–2.0	0.25	−30% to −50%	0.25
2.0–2.5	0.25		
2.5–3.0	0.10		
3.0–3.5	0.10		

Source: Authors. (Adapted from Day, G. (1983), *Cases in Computer and Model Assisted Marketing Planning*, The Scientific Press.)

Questions

1. If Mr Brown has to decide whether to introduce FoodSnack which marketing programme would you recommend?

2. Proceed to a break-even analysis and describe the strategic and financial implications of each contemplated marketing programme.

3. How would you use Mr Brown's probability estimates in the risk analysis?

Tesco versus Aldi in the UK Market

Tesco is proof of the good a little dressing-up can do. Tesco abandonned its discount format with its down-market image for a variety of dressier mid-market formats. The company runs 968 stores in the United Kingdom where it is the #1 food retailer. Its operations include 83 hypermarkets (Tesco Extra), 447 supermarkets (Tesco Superstore), 161 convenient high street stores (Tesco Metro), 277 petrol stations (Tesco Express) and financial services through Tesco Personal Finance.

Tesco is a global player. It is well established in Ireland, Central Europe (Poland, Slovakia and the Czech Republic) and Asia (Thailand and South Korea). In the United States, Tesco owns a 35 per cent stake in the grocery chain Safeway's Grocery Works. In 2004, through strong growth both in the United Kingdom and internationally, Tesco is the fourth largest supermarket retailer in the world with sales revenue of £46.2 billion after Wal-Mart (US$256.3), Carrefour (€70.5) and Ahold (€56.1).

Arrival of Euro-competition

In the early 1990s, Tesco faced in the United Kingdom a situation similar to that faced by many retailers in Europe – low population growth, economic recession, well-developed and relatively saturated supermarket market, increasing difficulty in getting planning permission for large green fields sites, several strong competitors (in the United Kingdom, Sainsbury, Safeway and Asda) and, last but not least, the arrival of two new store formats: warehouse clubs (Costco) and limited assortments stores with Aldi (1990), Netto (1990) and Lidl (1994). These hard discounters have a low-cost logistics and operational systems that work on a 12 per cent gross margin and a 2 per cent net margin. Their strategy is low-priced, high-quality private labels sold in no frills stores located in low-income neighbourhoods away from costly real estate such as strip malls. Aldi and Netto offer significant price savings against conventional supermarkets, their relative price index (average = 100) being as low as 71 for Netto and 77 for Aldi against 105 for Tesco and Sainsbury.

Strategic response

Aldi generated a lot of publicity when it entered the UK market and grew its UK stores numbers by 36 per cent per year for 10 years. In the year 2000, Aldi had 240 stores, Netto 119 and Lidl 118. By reintroducing the 'very low' price concept – personified until then by Kwik Save, Britain's leading discounter – to a market, which had been moving in the direction of one-stop quality superstores, Aldi and Netto have had a destabilising effect disproportionate to their numbers. Their advent coincides with an economic recession and gave the impression among consumers that they might be paying too much for their food.

Existing supermarket chains responded somewhat successfully to the hard discounters' invasion in a number of ways. High-end stores attempted to distance themselves from the price end of the market through larger selections and new products, like organic food. They have upgraded their services, improved the ancient facilities and launched new store formats. Supermarkets have also attempted to reduce the price differential by offering a limited range of low-price private label products under a second label, the Tesco Value range, Safeway's Savers and Sainsbury's Essentials. Major chains have also launched shopper loyalty club cards: Sainsbury Card, Clubcard for Tesco and ABC Club for Safeway.

A price war

To counter Aldi, supermarket chains also started a market-wide price war in a small range of basic grocery items. The price war (as low as to 1p-a-can) began with the legendary Baked Beans War – a key input in the British cuisine – and rapidly spread to other basic grocery lines like butter and bread. The overall effect was to lower consumers price expectations for a narrow range of core products. As noted by the *Daily Mail* (October 1994) 'Prices of basic groceries in some supermarkets have fallen by 17% over the last two years. The stores have slashed prices to compete with discount chains, resulting in a savings of £357 a year on a weekly basket of essentials.'

The shakeout that followed drove marginal players out of business. In 1995, Kwik Save was taken over by Somerfield and its stores sold or closed. Other poorly financed discount formats (LoCost, Penny Market, Ed and Shoprite) were also driven out of business.

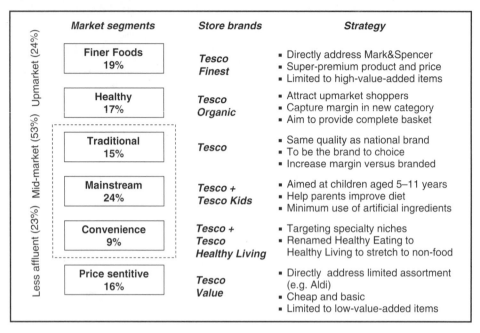

Figure CS 14.1   Tesco's private label architecture
Source: Coriolis Research, 2004.

Tesco's defence strategy

The defence strategy of Tesco was based on four pillars: Tesco Clubcard holders' segmentation combined with a strong private label programme, a change in store numbers and format, an expansion into financial services and the development of an online sales site through the Internet. Analysing data from 10 million Tesco Clubcard holders, the Tesco market has been subdivided into six segments: the finer foods segment (19 per cent); the healthy (17 per cent); the traditional (15 per cent) and the convenience (per cent) both located in the mid-market; the mainstream (24 per cent) and the price sensitive (23 per cent) segments. In designing its private labels portfolio, Tesco launched subbrands to target each identified segment, as shown in Figure CS 14.1. In 2004, private labels' sales represented 55 per cent of Tesco UK sales from 21 per cent in 1980, or £16.9 billion.

Tesco has adapted its stores to meet the needs of its customers. The different Tesco formats are designed to suit the varied shopping patterns of consumers. Tesco has four different formats.

- Tesco Extra (7,500m2), a destination very large store offering the maximum food and non-food range (the number of stores = 83).

- Tesco Superstore or Compact Superstore (1,900–3,600m2), one-stop weekly shop offering a full range and many non-food products (the number of stores = 447).
- Tesco Metro (1,000m2) a high street store in large city centre shopping areas aimed at workers, shoppers and local residents (the number of stores = 161).
- Tesco Express (200m2), petrol station forecourt shops selling a range of everyday products (the number of stores = 277).

where m2 = square meters

In 2004, Tesco had 968 stores compared to 412 in 1993.

Source: Author. (Adapted from Coriolis Research Report (2004).)

Questions

1. Evaluate the defence strategy adopted by Tesco to counter the hard discounters offensive strategy.

2. What are the risks of this strategy?

The Universal Plastics Company

OVER A PERIOD OF 2 YEARS, THE PRICE OF POLYETHYLENE pipe had dropped steadily and significantly. This fact, coupled with the recognition that his company was operating in an industry chronically faced with excess capacity, made Mr Walter Riley, the marketing manager of Universal Plastics Company, realised that his company might have to alter its pricing policy. Located in San Francisco, the Universal Plastics Company was a relatively small manufacturer of polyethylene and other plastic products. The company's main product, accounting for 60–70 per cent of annual sales, was polyethylene pipe, which was manufactured in a variety of sizes ranging from 1/2 inch to 6 inches in diameter. About 30–40 per cent of the company's sales came from a variety of plastic compounds intended for industrial uses such as wall panels, electrical installations and soundproofing. Polyethylene is also widely used by other manufacturers in the production of sheeting, bottles, toys, appliance components and automotive parts, but the Universal Plastics Company had not entered these markets.

Compared with metal pipe, the plastic product was lighter, easier to install, non-corrosive, and less expensive. Polyethylene pipe was an excellent product for farm irrigation, wells, lawn sprinklers and other uses where the liquid pressure requirements were relatively low – up to 100 pounds per square inch. For the transmission of potable water, the only polyethylene pipe used was made from virgin materials and carried the National Sanitation Foundation (NSF) seal. Pipe not made from virgin material was considered the 'second-grade line'. About 60–80 per cent of the polyethylene pipe produced were of the second-grade, non-NSF, lower-priced variety intended for consumer and industrial market uses other than transmitting drinking water.

Since the end of the Second World War, the growth of the plastic pipe industry had been phenomenal, as many new uses for the product were quickly developed. Because of the attractiveness of this market, many new firms entered the industry and generated a production capacity well in excess of the level, which even the expanding market could absorb. A major factor enabling this over-capacity to develop was the ease of entry into the industry. Initial investment requirements were low, and the basic technical knowledge could be acquired easily. The producers of the raw-materials and the manufacturers of the extrusion machines, used in making the pipe, eagerly supplied the engineering and production information. The extrusion rates on a mixed basis of pipe 1/2 to 6 inches in diameter were such that one machine operating 24 hours a day, 7 days a week, could produce in excess of 1 million pounds of finished pipe per year. Two major producers alone had more than 50 machines, each capable of producing 1 million pounds of finished polyethylene pipe per year.

There were about 60 manufacturers of polyethylene pipe located over the entire United States, but only a small number marketed their products nationally. Most of the manufacturers were regional extruders, making only a limited line of polyethylene pipe. The Universal Plastics Company fell in this category, operating 12 machines and marketing in California, Oregon and Arizona. The machine used by Universal Plastics Company for extruding polyethylene pipe could also be used for the production of other plastic products. By marketing in a limited geographic area, the Universal Company could fill orders faster and give better service generally than the large, national firms.

The company's financial position was strong. However, its profit margins, while adequate, were endangered by the price-cutting in the industry. Universal Plastics had a sales force of ten men. They reached the consumer market by selling to sprinkler installation firms, to lawn equipment dealers and distributors and to landscape contractor-gardeners. In the industrial market, the salesmen sold to agricultural co-operatives, agricultural equipment dealers and plumbing and heating wholesalers. In many cases, Universal sold directly to large farms, to businesses, which wanted to install a lawn sprinkling system, and to manufacturers with industrial watering systems.

The conditions of excess capacity in the plastic pipe industry had induced many firms to cut their prices in an attempt to broaden their market share and thus utilise some of the excess production capacity in their plants. Because it was difficult, if not impossible, to differentiate its products from those of its competitors, the Universal Plastics Company had been forced to cut its prices to meet the competition. Over the past 2 years Universal's price for non-virgin polyethylene pipe had dropped from 52 cents a pound to 38 cents a pound. During the most recent year, unit sales remained relatively constant, so the potentially depressing effect on profits was evident. Currently, the cost of raw materials was 40–50 per cent of the selling price. High-quality pipe meeting NSF standards sold for proportionately more than the second-grade product line.

Mr Riley was studying several alternative courses of action in an attempt to stimulate sales and to stem the profit decline. His first thought was to reduce prices further and try to do a better job of promoting the Universal brand. He hoped to bring the product into a price range, which would attract a new market, not heretofore users of polyethylene pipe. He believed that these actions would increase unit sales volume high enough to more than compensate for the unit price reductions. Mr Riley realised that competitors undoubtedly would retaliate if Universal's prices were reduced. The speed and effectiveness of this price retaliation would be a function of Universal's ability to differentiate its product, the ability of the customer to judge product quality, and the importance of price in the consumer's buying decisions. Another unknown factor was the extent to which prices, once cut, could ever be restored to their former levels. Mr Riley was also considering the alternative of reducing product quality and thus reducing costs enough so that unit prices could be cut without any loss of unit gross or net profit.

The Production Manager, Mr Pope, had recommended an almost polar-opposite plan. He suggested that Universal produce and market a new high-quality line made from superior resins. This new pipe would be sold at a price above even that of the premium pipe now produced to NSF standards. The intention would be to break away entirely from the 'price-football' image of the second-grade and the virgin product line. Mr Pope believed that the company's distributors and ultimate users could be convinced that this new product was truly of higher quality and thus warranted a higher price. To help convince both the distributors and the users, Mr Pope would institute a distinctive warranty programme. Under it, Universal Plastics would pay for all labour and materials charges incurred in replacing or repairing defective pipe.

Source: Authors. (Adapted from Stanton, W.J., (1964), *Fundamentals of Marketing*, New York, McGraw-Hill.)

Question

1. What course of action should the company follow to counter the problems of price reductions and excess capacity?

The Tissex Company

Tissex is a French company whose sole activity is the production and sales of fabrics composed of artificial and synthetic fibres. In spite of a turnover of FF536 million and a gross profit margin of 17 per cent obtained last year, the net result was not very high. Its know-how in production processes (gluing, weaving, dyeing, finishing) combined with advanced technical collaboration with manufacturers of fibres have so far been sufficient to maintain its position in comparison with both French, European or Japanese competitors. A turnover of FF220 million from exports, mainly to the Common Market but also to the United States, gives the group an international dimension.

Tissex offers a large range of products which includes fabrics for clothing (polyester silks), linings, sportswear (anoraks, clothes, etc.) and household linen (quilts, bedspreads, etc.) as well as safety fabrics (technical fabrics for the army, the police, the chemical and oil industries, etc.), printing ribbons (ready to be inked) for typewriters and computers. Over the past 3 years Tissex has invested in modern equipment and machinery. This policy should be sustained if Tissex wants to maintain its position in the international market.

Henry Bonnet, the new CEO, must evaluate the company's overall performance and develop a strategy for the next 3 years. This is what he says about the situation of his company:

We have five factories, mainly in the Lyon area. However, by acquiring St. Renard in 1980, we now have two other plants in Roubaix, in the North of France.

This acquisition brought us a turnover of FF123 million in 1983, mainly from linings, but we are, however, more interested in St. Renard's technical fabrics. Up until then our activity in this area has been secondary, let's say from FF4 million to FF5 million three years ago. We have concentrated all of this activity in Roubaix so that today we have 30% of the market with a turnover of 33 million FF. This is really good for a market with an average annual growth rate of 9%, especially as the gross margin for this activity is over twice that of the Group's average.

Competition rose quickly! Particularly textile companies of Northern France and among them Guillez with a turnover of FF20 million last year. They followed our example and started to export their goods. The other competitors are smaller, companies with a 5 to 10% market share each. Most of them are French. So far, however, we are well protected because of the highly specialised demands of our customers. Exporting is slow to get off the ground but we're not in a hurry; we are confident in our know-how. The Germans and English cannot catch up with us right away. Furthermore, each country still has its own standards. There are approximately 100 potential clients in all of Europe and what they are looking for is 'service'.

As for linings, the situation is completely different: this is a depressed market, as is the case for the traditional garment industry. It will decline from 2 to 3% next year, as it did in previous years. Womenswear was in a somewhat better position, but as a whole the sector is doing poorly. We have over 2,000 clients in this activity but every year there are several bankruptcies. Our sales representatives have standing orders not to deliver unless they have the go ahead from Sales Information Service. The price war is fierce and when you're the leader in the European market, with only 12% of the market, you have a hard time maintaining your position. Belgian companies are the toughest to compete with: they have invested a lot over the past few years. For example, Deckerman who has only 7% of the market earned more money than we did. Up until now we have tried to hold on even if the gross margin for linings is largely inferior to that of the Group average: 10%, this is worrying. Luckily the Japanese can't come in on this market, as the price per metre is too low.

Our objective is clear: slightly increase prices to maintain the same level of turnover (FF160 million) without affecting the volume of production and without losing our French clients who represent 45% of our turnover. We will also reach some new markets because our weaker competitors will have disappeared – in France, Germany, England and maybe outside the Common Market as well. We have 12 multicard agents in France and our headquarters are in charge of foreign markets. The Roubaix plant delivers to Paris, Northern France, the Benelux and Great Britain. Roanne sends goods out to Southern France and to all other countries. Germany receives special treatment because an own sales subsidiary was created five years ago for some obscure reasons. Results there are very poor and we now plan on dealing directly from France for large orders.

Roanne is a real headache. Last year we had to lay off 90 people, mostly working on polyester. Globally Roanne had a 1983 turnover of FF256 million with FF70 million for linings and the rest for clothing. Moreover, weaving of polyester fabric is divided between two workshops equipped with different weaving machinery. One third of production comes from very modern and rapid machines and two thirds are produced traditionally. With a gross margin of 7% the polyester activity is the worst of our Group and the market has not increased for the past few years.

The Japanese have hurt us in this area. They now have over 5% of the European market with good quality products they can sell at a higher price than we can. We are far behind with just 1% of the market. However we do export 40% of our production thanks to the quality of our sales network but at very low prices. And we can't ask our clients to pay more. However we can observe that this market is also being concentrated: many clients have disappeared. Five years ago we had 2,500 clients; today there are 800 in France and 600 in the other European countries. These numbers will still decrease until we will only have the most interesting companies as clients.

Luckily there is the Lyon factory: a FF157 million turnover last year and 6 to 7% of growth in value every year. The sportswear activity is advancing rapidly, 8% per year as compared to 6% for printing ribbons for computers and typewriters (but ribbons in the U.S. are increasing by 20% annually). As a matter of fact, the Lyon factory has two really distinct activities and I wonder if we shouldn't separate them completely. The factory manager has a real problem with his production planning.

We keep very little stock on hand for printing ribbons. Whatever is produced is delivered immediately and we have three eight-hour shifts. The looms are rapid, with air or water jets, and, most important, high quality is constant. Our clients know us very well; there are only 90 throughout the world including 10 in France. We export 60% of our production. Three years ago, the Japanese were the first to drastically reduce their prices by 30% but in this activity we were able to follow their lead and we invested in very modern Swiss equipment. We have 5% of the market, just a bit lower than the two world leaders who are Japanese and German. The Spaniards and English are now beginning to invest. This is going to be a running battle. We just hope that the market can be maintained long enough for us to write off our investments over the next 2 or 3 years. In 5 years the market will have changed and we'll have to readapt but a 30% gross margin is acceptable today.

The sportswear fabric is less risky. Profit is still to be made, mainly for the special quality features we propose, and our clients seem to maintain their positions. The FF67 million turnover is spread evenly over 30 customers and, even if we do have a low export profile here, our clients export their goods pretty well. The Sporting Company is the top competitor with 20% of the French market, but 2 or 3 of us are close behind. We must pass the others and I believe we can catch up with Sporting as they have had a problem with deliveries and quality when there was a strike at their fibre supplier's. We always have several supply sources so as to avoid this kind of problem. Thanks to Sporting's difficulties we have been able to reach customers who, up until now, were out of reach. If we can develop these contacts we'll go from 15% to 20% of the market next year or the following year.

The Italians of course have tried to compete with us but this market fluctuates too fast for them; you really have to be on the spot to anticipate demand and to manage your stock correctly. Most clients are located around Lyon or Paris and we know them very well. Our sales network is excellent and we work well with each of its members.

Our sales director will retire at the end of this year and I think that we will then no longer call upon the two multicard agents who now work for us. The gross margin is even higher than for technical fabrics (36%) and I am planning on maintaining the same level of sales.

Source: Authors. (Adapted from Gilles Marion, Ecole de Management (EM) de Lyon. Translated and used with the permission of "Centrale de cas et de medias pédagogiques" (Paris).)

Questions

1. Define the strategic segments that are relevant for Tissex's activities.

2. Make a strategic analysis of Tissex's portfolio of activities according to whatever method is, to your mind, the most appropriate (BCG matrix, multifactors portfolio matrix, etc.). According to this method, is there a problem facing Tissex? If so, what is this problem?

3. Identify the various strategies, which could be developed for each of Tissex's activities. Choose the one(s) you think are the most appropriate.

Case study 17

Club Med

CLUB MED IS ONE OF THE LEADERS IN THE TOURISM AND leisure industry. It owns about 100 villages in the most attractive locations all over the world. Club Med can be considered as the pioneer in all-inclusive prepaid vacation. Since mid-1990s, Club Med faced, however, financial problems linked to market shares decline. The Club Med concept was born in 1950 when Gerard Blitz, a Belgian sportsman, created a village camp where he invited about hundred friends to camp out in tents and practise sports on the exotic island of Majorca. From this idea was born a style of vacation.

Indeed, Club Med offers a certain way of life. In Club Med language, vacationers are named GMs (Gentils Membres) and organisers are called GOs (Gentils Organisateurs). Club Med promotes social interaction. Entertainment and activities are available the whole day long. Villages are dedicated also to sports from scuba diving to waterskiing, sailing, tennis, etc. Besides this, Club Med villages are usually located in unique and beautiful sites in the world. Big buffets 'à volonté' are also available. The ideas of freedom, pleasure, relaxation, fun and sports are associated with the Club Med concept. Target consumers were traditionally young people and families.

Club Med enjoyed a very strong leadership position during many decades. Its brand image was so powerful that it did not really need to invest in marketing campaigns because the product sold itself by word of mouth. It was a real innovator in the market. However, Club Med did not see the threat coming from outside. 'It's not that Club Med underestimated its competition – it didn't see the competition coming', said Philippe Bourguignon, ex-CEO of Club Med. Other all-inclusive resorts arrived on the market and imitated Club Med's concept largely during the 1980s.

Indeed, competitors analysed Club Med's weaknesses and provided customers with a better offer. For example, some Club Med's clients found the rooms too spartan, others thought activities were too regulated and mealtimes inflexible. Drinks were also not included in the price. Moreover, many villages' physical plants had deteriorated since the 1990s. Therefore, competitors took advantage of it and began to innovate. They provided customers with better rooms, included drinks in the price and offered more flexibility. 'When the competition gets stronger and stops

being a clone of what the founding company has done and starts innovating, it's a bit late to react', said Philippe Bourguignon. Nowadays, Club Med has to face competitors in Europe such as the giant TUI, Kuoni, Thomas Cook, Pierre et Vacances, FRAM, Look Voyages offering also all-inclusive formulas.

Club Med also failed to understand quickly enough changing lifestyles. Club Med advertising of tanned bodies and community life did not correspond to current values anymore that became more centred on the individual. Consumers' preferences also changed. People were less willing to pay a high price for vacation including activities they do not use and therefore, the product offering appeared overpriced and Club Med's formula was not suitable anymore. New tourism trends emerged such as low-cost tourist packages, cultural, adventure or discovery tourism, which made Club Med's concept outdated.

As a result, Club Med revenues and market shares declined as of mid-1990s. These problems were accelerated with the unfavourable and poor economic environment of the 1990s. Problems such as the Gulf War, September 11 and the recent tsunami, pushed the tourism industry in difficult situation. The company decided to undertake a whole recovery strategy and restructure each aspects of the business. The key challenge was to evolve while staying in line with the brand values.

In 1997, the first restructuration was conducted by a new CEO: Philippe Bourguignon. He decided to implement a mass market strategy to build volume. He first decided to recapture Club Med's original markets among the young and families. He launched 'Oyyo', an inexpensive all-inclusive formula for the 18–30 year old, offering pizza and pasta for dinner as well as basic hosting. Some villages were also upgraded from 2–3 Tridents and the product offering was improved with a greater variety of sports activities, a higher quality entertaining programme, better sports and dining facilities and additional equipment such as telephones and hair dryers.

Additionally, he decided to follow a massive diversification strategy by expanding the group into the broader leisure market. The idea was to offer leisure and holidays all over the year for individuals as well as for professionals. He developed the Club Med Gym, The Club Med World and Club Med Affairs. He also extended in other leisure-related activities. It developed its own product line that is sold by its partners under license such as Carrefour, Delsey and L'Oréal to name a few of them. At the end of 2000, Club Med had its brand on many different products from watches to volley balls, casual and sports shoes, beach towels, luggage, sun tan lotion and a sportswear line.

This strategy was not successful. Between 2001 and 2003, 35,000 loyal consumers left the brand to join competition. A new CEO, Henry Giscard d'Estaing, was appointed to turn around the business. He decided to fundamentally change the strategy. He shifted from a mass market strategy to an upmarket strategy and made customer satisfaction one of his first priorities. Therefore, it focused on the product instead of diversifying it and decided to move upmarket by targeting the leisure luxury hotel segment that offers prestigious vacation and the highest quality standards in terms of comfort and services. 'Now, it's no more about being the biggest ones but instead the best ones', said Henry Giscard d'Estaing. Club Med wants to develop a friendly and premium image.

An extensive marketing audit was conducted to better understand the brand perception among consumers

(Exhibit 1). Five handicaps were identified and programmes were developed to fix them. For example, they continued to renovate the villages and upgrade most of them to 3 and 4 Tridents. Today 91 per cent of the villages are 3 and 4 Trident categories and it will even go up to 95 per cent in 2008 (Exhibit 2). Besides that, Giscard's strategy is to refocus on clients and better differentiate Club Med villages by specialising them by types of activities. Villages are not presented anymore by geography but by affinities ('pashas', 'explorators', 'passionates' and 'clubbers'). The catalogue has been adapted accordingly. Hotel rooms are better decorated, linked to the local country, sports and entertainment are suggested, but not anymore imposed.

In 2005, for the first time in 4 years, Club Med has attracted new clients and financial results are positive. Are these changes going to lead to Club Med's real recovery?

Source: Authors. (This case was written by Professor Isabelle Schuiling and by Julie Lardinois, assistant in the Marketing unit at the IAG Louvain School of Management.)

EXHIBIT CS17.1

RESULTS OF THE MARKETING AUDIT

Five major handicaps are identified:

- Cost of Club Med vacation is viewed as to high versus what people get.
- Club Med is not synonymous of freedom but 'enbrigadement'?

- Club Med villages are viewed as ghettos far from the local life
- The 'see, sex and sun' image of Club Med provoked the departure of families
- The imposed familiarity was rejected.

Source: L'Expansion, June 29, 2005.

EXHIBIT CS17.2

SPLIT OF VILLAGES BY CATEGORY (%)

	1998	2005	2008 (forecast)
4 tridents	18	26	47
3 tridents	48	64	50
2 tridents	28	7	3
Bungalows	6	3	0

PROFITABILITY PER HOTEL DAY

	Profit (Euros)
4 tridents	47
3 tridents	47
2 tridents	27

Source: L'Expansion, June 29, 2005.

Questions

1. What are the key reasons for Club Med's loss of leadership?
2. What have been the changes to the key target segments over the years?
3. What are the strengths of the Club Med positioning? How unique is it?

4. What were the key issues coming from the first restructuration?
5. What do you think of the latest changes of the marketing strategy? Discuss pros and cons.

Name Index

Subject Index